STANFORD LEGAL ESSAYS

STANFORD
LEGAL ESSAYS

Edited by John Henry Merryman

——◆◉◆——

PRINTED AND DISTRIBUTED BY

Stanford University Press

Stanford, California

1975

Stanford University Press
Stanford, California
© 1975 by the Board of Trustees of the
Leland Stanford Junior University
Printed in the United States of America
ISBN 0-8047-0884-3   LC 75-182

Contents

Introduction   vii

Speedy Criminal Trial: Rights and Remedies   1
ANTHONY G. AMSTERDAM

Voir Dire: Preserving "Its Wonderful Power"   21
BARBARA ALLEN BABCOCK

Behind the Legal Explosion   43
JOHN H. BARTON

The Conscientious Legislator's Guide to Constitutional Interpretation   61
PAUL BREST

Congressional Power to Interpret Due Process and Equal Protection   79
WILLIAM COHEN

A Comment on the Jurisprudence of the Uniform Commercial Code   97
RICHARD DANZIG

The Legal Process in Foreign Affairs: Military Intervention—
a Testing Case   113
THOMAS EHRLICH

Personal Injury Accidents in New Zealand and the United States:
Some Striking Similarities   129
MARC A. FRANKLIN

The Rulemaking Power of the Supreme Court: A Contemporary Crisis   149
JACK H. FRIEDENTHAL

San Benito 1890: Legal Snapshot of a County   163
LAWRENCE M. FRIEDMAN

Do We Have an Unwritten Constitution?   179
THOMAS C. GREY

Learned Hand and the Origins of Modern First Amendment Doctrine:
Some Fragments of History   195
GERALD GUNTHER

Some Choice-of-Law Problems Posed by Antiguest Statutes:
Realism in Wisconsin and Rule-Fetishism in New York   251
MOFFATT HANCOCK

Some Reflections on the Control of the Publication of Appellate
   Court Opinions   267
   J. MYRON JACOBSTEIN

A Primer on Heroin   277
   JOHN KAPLAN

Politics and Health Care in China: The Barefoot Doctors   303
   VICTOR H. LI

Some Preliminary Notes on the American Antitrust Laws' Economic
   Tests of Legality   317
   RICHARD S. MARKOVITS

Legal Education There and Here: A Comparison   335
   JOHN HENRY MERRYMAN

The Covenant of Habitability and the American Law Institute   355
   CHARLES J. MEYERS

Preclusion of Judicial Review in the Processing of Claims for
   Veterans' Benefits: A Preliminary Analysis   381
   ROBERT L. RABIN

Moral Character   401
   D. L. ROSENHAN

Two Models of the Civil Process   413
   KENNETH E. SCOTT

Consumer Credit Law: Rates, Costs, and Benefits   427
   WILLIAM D. WARREN

Some Ingredients of a National Oil and Gas Policy   445
   HOWARD R. WILLIAMS

Index   463

Introduction

This collection of essays is in one sense a *mélange*. Each of the twenty-four authors was encouraged to write on a topic of his or her own choosing, and the result covers a wide diversity of subject matters. Many readers will find two or three essays that look particularly relevant to their interests and will turn directly to them. That is a reasonable procedure, but we hope that many readers will also browse; the essays are brief enough to encourage browsing and meaty enough to reward it. Indeed, we encourage readers to begin with Anthony Amsterdam's discussion of the right to a speedy trial and read their way through Howard Williams's argument for a coherent national policy for energy, and we believe that those who do so will be enlightened and entertained.

Since there is no common topic, one can reasonably ask what unifying principle is at work in this volume. One answer is that all of the authors presently teach at the Stanford Law School. Taken together, these essays accordingly give the reader a representative expression of the minds, styles, and interests of the faculty of the School.

Such a sample is of potential interest to a variety of audiences: to recent alumni, who knew many of us as their teachers; to older alumni, who we hope will find here reassurance that, although many of the familiar names and faces are gone from the School, institutional standards and qualities endure; to our colleagues at other law schools, who share with us a professional interest in each other's activities.

Potential law students, particularly those thinking of attending Stanford, are another audience for this volume. True, some of the essays will seem beyond the undergraduate untrained in law, but others are easily accessible to the educated general reader. Thus, one does not need a legal education to enjoy Lawrence Friedman's delightful stroll through San Benito County, California, in 1890; or to understand John Kaplan's illuminating "Primer on Heroin"; or to trace with Victor Li the complex relations between politics, health care, and law in contemporary China; or to be moved to a new level of understanding by David Rosenhan's discussion of moral behavior.

Much that is in this book should also prove interesting to our colleagues in other parts of Stanford University. The tendency for law teaching and scholarship to become ever more multidisciplinary has been nourished at Stanford by the extraordinary receptivity—often the positive interest, occasionally the initiative—of distinguished colleagues in other departments to joint teaching, joint appointments, and joint degree programs. Even more important, perhaps, is the responsiveness we in the Law School so frequently find to our informal requests for information, advice, and criticism from those elsewhere in the University. Our interest in them seems to be matched by their interest in us, and a number of the essays in this volume display the advantages of this easy and fruitful relationship.

Finally, this volume celebrates a major event in the life of the Stanford Law School: the completion and occupation of the Crown Quadrangle. For the first time in our eighty-two years we will be housed in buildings designed for the Law School. This means that the intimate, delicate, but profound interplay between the life of the School and the physical surroundings in which it operates will enter a new and, we believe, more productive and enriching phase for all concerned: most directly for the students, alumni, faculty, and staff of the Law School, but also for the rest of the University.

So great an occasion evokes the celebratory impulse in all who are associated with the School. As members of the faculty, we thought it appropriate that our contribution to the festivities take the traditional academic form of a *Festschrift*—literally "celebratory writing." We are deeply grateful to Richard E. Lang, who generously established a fund that helped support the preparation and publication of this book. We owe special thanks to the officers and staff of the *Stanford Law Review*, in which these essays were also printed, for uncounted hours of invaluable editorial assistance in preparing the essays for publication.

Congaudeamus.

J.H.M.

STANFORD LEGAL ESSAYS

Speedy Criminal Trial:
Rights and Remedies

Anthony G. Amsterdam*

In a quite literal sense, the sixth amendment right to speedy trial[1] has today become—to borrow the words of a celebrated procrastinator—more honored in the breach than the observance.[2] Various institutional arrangements and forces at work within the criminal process[3] have long tended to convert the right of every criminal defendant to have a speedy trial into a very different sort of right: the right of a few defendants, most egregiously denied a speedy trial, to have the criminal charges against them dismissed on that account. Recent decisions of the Supreme Court nurture the transformation.

I propose here to discuss those decisions after brief consideration of their doctrinal and practical setting. Before advancing to the work, let me say that I do not suppose for one moment that the law of the sixth amendment can significantly affect the speed with which most criminal cases are processed. Progress toward the difficult goal of providing expeditious handling for the large volume of the country's criminal business[4] cannot be achieved by the mere manipulation of legal doctrine. The ingredients of any prescription for the "national ill"[5] of lagging criminal justice must encompass far more basic institutional changes. Even a partial list would have to include improved deployment of the available resources of the courts, prosecutors' offices, public defenders' offices, police departments, and probation departments; considerable additions to all of these resources; considerable increases in the numbers of private practitioners willing and able to handle criminal cases, and of criminal-law paraprofessionals; and considerable diminution of the vast mass of largely wasteful intake that

* A.B. 1957, Haverford College; LL.B. 1960, University of Pennsylvania. Professor of Law, Stanford University.
1. U.S. CONST. amend. VI: "In all criminal prosecutions, the accused shall enjoy the right to a speedy . . . trial . . . ."
2. W. SHAKESPEARE, HAMLET act I, scene IV, line 16 (Hamlet, P., dubitante) [hereinafter cited as SLUGGISH PRINCE].
3. *See* text accompanying notes 96–100 *infra*.
4. *See* ABA PROJECT ON MINIMUM STANDARDS FOR CRIMINAL JUSTICE—STANDARDS RELATING TO SPEEDY TRIAL (Approved Draft 1968) [hereinafter cited as MINIMUM STANDARDS]; PRESIDENT'S COMMISSION ON LAW ENFORCEMENT AND ADMINISTRATION OF JUSTICE, REPORT: THE CHALLENGE OF CRIME IN A FREE SOCIETY 127, 154–56 (1967) [hereinafter cited as CRIME COMMISSION REPORT]; PRESIDENT'S COMMISSION ON LAW ENFORCEMENT AND ADMINISTRATION OF JUSTICE, TASK FORCE REPORT: THE COURTS 80–90 (1967) [hereinafter cited as TASK FORCE REPORT].
5. I refer to the title of Judge Godbold's article: Godbold, *Speedy Trial—Major Surgery for a National Ill*, 24 ALA. L. REV. 265 (1972).

now impedes the capacity of the system to function effectively.[6] Realistically considered, the content of sixth amendment law bears the same relationship toward an expeditious administration of the criminal justice machinery that man's aspiration to the stars bears toward efficient conduct of the space program. Assignment of a tolerably compassionate sentencing judge to the criminal calendar for a month will undoubtedly do more to clean up a year's backlog than could all the wisest sixth amendment decisions of the Supreme Court in a century. Nevertheless, it is the assumption of this Article that, if we are going to rely at all upon the sixth amendment to protect defendants' interests against undue delay in criminal prosecutions, we ought to have a sensible body of sixth amendment doctrines and enforcement procedures. The Article concludes that we do not now have them.

I. INTRODUCTION: THE PROCESS OF CRIMINAL PROSECUTION AND THE LEGAL CONTROLS UPON ITS TIMING

In order to develop my dissatisfactions with the present state of sixth amendment law and practice, it is necessary first to set the sixth amendment in the context of the process that it regulates.[7] For descriptive purposes, I shall distinguish two principal phases of a criminal prosecution, the *precourt phase* and the *court phase*. Under prevailing law, this distinction has limited doctrinal significance;[8] I make it because of its practical utility in differentiating a stage of proceedings over which the courts have merely post hoc corrective control from a stage in which the courts can, if they choose, exercise immediate directive control.

The precourt phase covers the period between commission of the alleged criminal offense and the first court appearance of the accused offender or the filing of the first charging paper (complaint, information

---

6. The diminution could best be effected by legislative pruning of the luxuriant growth of "trivial, imaginary [and] . . . otherwise dubious" crimes that now encumbers the agencies of law enforcement. H. PACKER, THE LIMITS OF THE CRIMINAL SANCTION 260 (1968). There are independent, sufficient reasons for this sort of pruning, as Professor Packer demonstrates. *See also* N. MORRIS & G. HAWKINS, THE HONEST POLITICIAN'S GUIDE TO CRIME CONTROL 1–28 (1970). Restriction of the intake processed by the criminal justice system can also be effected by the wise exercise of prosecutorial discretion, although reliance upon that approach involves dangers of irregularity and arbitrariness unless adequate controls are provided to assure the visibility and uniformity of prosecutorial decisionmaking. *See* K. DAVIS, DISCRETIONARY JUSTICE (1969); Wright, *Beyond Discretionary Justice*, 81 YALE L.J. 575 (1972).

7. My description of that process will be summary and general, leveling the differences that exist from jurisdiction to jurisdiction and omitting much technical detail.

8. In many jurisdictions, statutes or rules limiting the periods for taking designated prosecutive steps define the beginning of the first such period in terms of an event (first court appearance, or the filing of the first charging paper) that also marks the dividing line between the precourt and the court phases as I am using those rubrics. *See* note 42 *infra* and accompanying text. In other jurisdictions, the first period limited by law may begin earlier, for example at arrest, *see* note 19 *infra*, or later, for example at commitment following preliminary examination, *see* text accompanying note 45 *infra*. In the present state of the law, the sixth amendment right to speedy trial probably also "attaches" at arrest if arrest precedes the filing of court charges. *See* text accompanying notes 22–23 *infra*.

or indictment) against him, whichever occurs earlier. The duration of this phase is largely dictated by decisions of the prosecuting authorities, that is, the police and the prosecutor. It may be protracted for a number of reasons within their control. For example, proof of the offense may depend upon the testimony of an undercover informer who maintains his "cover" for a period of time before surfacing to file charges against one or more persons with whom he has dealt while disguised.[9] Other concerns against "blowing" an ongoing investigation may cause delay in the filing of charges against one suspect during the time necessary to investigate his suspected accomplices without forewarning them. Charging may be delayed beyond the time when there is sufficient evidence to support a criminal charge, in order to permit the gathering of additional evidence that will strengthen the prosecution's case;[10] or, if there is more than one possible charge against a suspect, some of them may be held back pending the disposition of others, in order to avoid the burden upon the prosecutor's office of handling charges that may turn out to be unnecessary to obtain the degree of punishment that the prosecutor seeks. There are many other motives for delay, of course, including some sinister ones, such as a desire to postpone the beginning of defense investigation, or the wish to hold a "club" over the defendant.

Additional reasons for delay may be partly or completely beyond the control of the prosecuting authorities. Offenses may not be immediately reported; investigation may not immediately identify the offender; an identified offender may not be immediately apprehendable.[11] When prosecution by indictment is required in a county that has only a few short criminal terms of court per year, an indictment may be delayed for weeks or even months until the impaneling of the next grand jury. It is customary to think of these delays as natural and inevitable; to some extent they are; but various prosecutorial decisions—such as the assignment of manpower

---

9. *See, e.g.,* Ross v. United States, 349 F.2d 210 (D.C. Cir. 1965). *Ross* and the tangled body of law spawned by *Ross* have received considerable comment in the reviews. *See* Widman, *The Right to a Speedy Trial: Pre-Indictment and Pre-Arrest Delay,* 7 AM. CRIM. L.Q. 248 (1969); Comment, *Pre-Arrest Delays and the Right to Speedy Arrest: Apologia Pro Vita Ross,* 11 ARIZ. L. REV. 770 (1969); Note, *Constitutional Limits on Pre-Arrest Delay,* 51 IOWA L. REV. 670 (1966); Note, *Pre-Arrest Delay: Evolving Due-Process Standards,* 43 N.Y.U.L. REV. 722 (1968).

10. *See, e.g.,* Cupp v. Murphy, 412 U.S. 291 (1973). Prosecutorial motivation to delay formal arrests and charges in order to gain further time for investigation is nothing new, *see, e.g.,* Ward v. Texas, 316 U.S. 547, 552–53 (1942); Haynes v. Washington, 373 U.S. 503 (1963); United States v. Vita, 294 F.2d 524 (2d Cir. 1961), but the motivation has been intensified in recent years by the development of increasingly stringent limitations upon police investigation following the commencement of "adversary judicial proceedings," Kirby v. Illinois, 406 U.S. 682, 688 (1972) (plurality opinion). *See, e.g.,* Massiah v. United States, 377 U.S. 201 (1964); United States v. Wade, 388 U.S. 218 (1967), *as construed in* Kirby v. Illinois, *supra;* Schneckloth v. Bustamonte, 412 U.S. 218, 240–41 n.29, 247 n.36 (1973) (dictum).

11. Obviously, my text here and in the preceding and following paragraphs is merely illustrative; it does not purport to set forth an exhaustive roster of the reasons for delay of the various stages of criminal prosecutions. Those reasons are manifold and often highly specific to particular cases: for example, the filing of homicide charges must necessarily be delayed until the fatally injured victim of a criminal assault expires, although assault or attempted murder charges may be filed earlier.

and priorities among investigations of known offenses—may also affect the length of such delays.

The principal legal control upon the duration of the precourt phase of a criminal prosecution is the applicable statute of limitations. In each jurisdiction, statutes of general[12] or specific [13] applicability bar prosecution unless the charging paper is filed within a stated time after the date of the offense charged.[14] If a defendant is not arrested prior to the filing of the first charging paper against him, these statutes are his only legal protection against undue delay in the precourt phase,[15] except the distant and currently undeveloped protection afforded by the due process guarantee of a fair trial;[16] the Supreme Court has rejected the notion that the sixth amendment limits the time within which an initial charging paper must be filed against an unarrested suspect.[17] After a defendant is arrested, prompt-arraignment statutes or rules in most jurisdictions require that he be taken before a magistrate without prolonged delay;[18] in a few jurisdictions, the arrest may also trigger a period limited by law for the conduct of other subsequent proceedings, such as trial;[19] and the sixth amendment right to speedy trial may attach at arrest.[20] But delay of the arrest itself is not presently regulated by law.[21]

---

12. *E.g.,* 18 U.S.C. §§ 3281–3282 (1970) (providing a 5-year statute of limitations for noncapital offenses).

13. *E.g.,* PA. STAT. ANN. tit. 18, § 4323(b) (Purdon 1973) (providing a 2-year limitation for bastardy nonsupport prosecutions); *id.* § 7362(b) (providing a 72-hour limitation for prosecutions for violation of the Sunday trading law).

14. Fugitivity or other circumstances may toll the period.

15. American courts have not followed the few 19th-century English decisions that apply a principle akin to laches to bar inordinately delayed criminal charges, *e.g.,* Regina v. Robins, 1 Cox Crim. Cas. 114 (Somerset Assizes 1844).

16. *See* United States v. Marion, 404 U.S. 307, 324–25 (1971) (dictum); *cf.* United States v. Chase, 135 F. Supp. 230 (N.D. Ill. 1955).

17. United States v. Marion, 404 U.S. 307 (1971).

18. *See* McNabb v. United States, 318 U.S. 332, 342–43 n.7 (1943); Culombe v. Connecticut, 367 U.S. 568, 584–85 n.26 (1961) (opinion of Frankfurter, J.). In actual practice, the prompt-arraignment statutes are frequently flouted, probably because no effective remedies for their violation are provided. *See id.* at 600–01 n.53.

19. *See* notes 43–44 *infra* and accompanying text. *See also* People v. Emblen, 362 Ill. 142, 199 N.E. 281 (1935), which, in construing a statute that required trial of an unbailed defendant within 4 months after "commitment," appears to hold that "commitment" refers to arrest rather than bind-over. *But see* People v. Rogers, 415 Ill. 343, 114 N.E.2d 398 (1953).

20. As indicated in the text accompanying note 17 *supra,* the 1971 *Marion* decision holds that an unarrested defendant's right to speedy trial does not attach prior to the time of filing of court charges against him. Considered dictum in the opinion asserts that the right does attach at the time of the first court filing, United States v. Marion, 404 U.S. 307, 325 (1971), and also recognizes that an "arrest" preceding "indictment, information, or other formal charge," *id.* at 321, would "engage the . . . protections of the . . . Amendment," *id.* at 320. Summarily, then, the teaching of *Marion* is that the sixth amendment right to speedy trial attaches at the time of arrest or of formal charge, whichever comes first. (However, I think it important to note that, because *Marion* involved a sixth amendment claim based *entirely* upon prearrest, precharge delay, it does not foreclose the possibility that prolonged delay prior to charging may be considered determinative of the speed with which postcharge stages of a prosecution must proceed in order to satisfy the sixth amendment in a case where a defendant complains of *both* precharge and postcharge delay. *Cf.* Taylor v. United States, 238 F.2d 259 (D.C. Cir. 1956).)

21. *See* Hoffa v. United States, 385 U.S. 293, 310 (1966), *quoted in* United States v. Marion, 404 U.S. 307, 325 n.18 (1971).

The institution of the court phase of a criminal prosecution gives judges at least theoretical control over the subsequent progress of the case. Some courts have customarily abnegated this control to the prosecutor, allowing him to determine the trial calendar[22] and intervening only upon motion by the defendant for expedition or delay of particular cases. This practice appears to be on the wane:[23] increasingly, trial assignments are being made by a calendar judge[24] or by a court clerk who, particularly in urban centers, may administer a complex, computer-assisted assignment program. However, calendar judges and clerks vary widely in the degree of strictness with which they insist that timetables be met;[25] some demand a concrete showing of good cause for delaying an initial trial assignment beyond the first available date,[26] while others routinely defer the assignment at the request of either party. Even where a judge or clerk attempts assiduously to enforce an expeditious timetable, problems of court structure or organization may cause delays. For example, individual trial judges frequently maintain separate calendars; once a case has been initially assigned for trial by Judge *A*, it may remain in Judge *A*'s court for all purposes; therefore, if a trial upon the initially scheduled date proves to be impossible, Judge *A* must reschedule the case for a date when he is available, even though Judge *B* or Judge *C* might have tried the case earlier.[27] And in the typical court system, responsibility for the conduct of felony proceedings is divided between two administratively unconnected courts: the preliminary examination is held before an inferior court or magistrate who binds the defendant over for trial in a superior court.[28] During the period

---

22. See Gleason v. Mullen, 204 Misc. 450, 121 N.Y.S.2d 605 (Special Term 1953); FED. R. CRIM. P. 50, Advisory Committee Notes.
23. See the description in King v. United States, 265 F.2d 567, 567–68 (D.C. Cir. 1959), of the system then used in the district. Coordinated judicial or administrative control of criminal calendars seems to be increasing in the wake of calls for such coordination by the National Crime Commission and the ABA Project on Minimum Standards for Criminal Justice. See note 4 supra.
24. I use the term generically. Various titles are employed: assignment judge, administrative judge, master-calendar judge, presiding judge, etc.
25. Until recent years, few courts have had formal timetables for the processing of criminal cases. In 1967 and 1968 respectively, the National Crime Commission and the ABA Project recommended the promulgation of such timetables, see CRIME COMMISSION REPORT, supra note 4, at 154–56; MINIMUM STANDARDS, supra note 4, at 14–16; and since 1972 the federal district courts have been required to maintain a local, written "plan for the prompt disposition of criminal cases which shall include rules relating to time limits within which procedures prior to trial, the trial itself, and sentencing must take place." FED. R. CRIM. P. 50(b), as amended (1972). I use the term "timetables" to include both formal rules of this sort and such informal standards as a calendar judge's or clerk's conventional notion of the speed with which criminal cases generally are, or should be, moved along.
26. See MINIMUM STANDARDS, supra note 4, at 13, 15.
27. I am not suggesting that a master calendar arrangement will necessarily expedite the processing of criminal cases. Under such an arrangement, forum shopping may multiply motions for continuances. See note 30, para. 2 infra.
28. For a summary description of the ordinary stages and processes of a criminal prosecution, see A. AMSTERDAM, B. SEGAL & M. MILLER, TRIAL MANUAL FOR THE DEFENSE OF CRIMINAL CASES 1-3 to 1-16 (3d ed. 1974). See also L. ORFIELD, CRIMINAL PROCEDURE FROM ARREST TO APPEAL (1947).

between bind-over and the time of filing of the ensuing information or indictment in the trial court, all judicial supervision over the progress of the case lapses, and control returns to the prosecutor.[29]

The occasions of delay during the court phase are innumerable and various. Cases (or "files," as they are too often considered by busy functionaries) may simply get lost in the shuffle between an inferior court and a superior court, or within the precincts of either. The making of an initial trial assignment may be deferred pending disposition of pretrial motions and then forgotten after the motions have been adjudicated. The initial trial date may be set at, or postponed to, a time long after arraignment in order to accommodate these same pretrial motions—motions to quash the charging paper, motions for the suppression of evidence, motions for discovery, and a host of others[30]—or in order to accommodate informal proceedings such as plea bargaining.[31] Continuances may be granted to the prosecution or the defense for numerous reasons[32]—in order to permit

---

29. There may be legal rules limiting the time within which various procedures (filing of the charging paper in the trial court, arraignment, trial) must occur following "commitment" or "bind-over," see note 41 infra, but these rules are judicially enforced only after the fact. One important consequence of the lapse of immediate judicial control over a case while it moves from court to court is that it is difficult or impossible as a practical matter for the defendant to obtain a judicial order requiring filing in the superior court prior to the maximum time prescribed by law, even in a case where particular circumstances render delay during the maximum period seriously prejudicial to the defendant's legitimate interests and where the prosecutor has no good reason for that delay.

30. A roster of common pretrial motions is found in A. AMSTERDAM, B. SEGAL & M. MILLER, supra note 28, at 1-205 to 1-206. See also id. at 1-133 to 1-134, 1-153 to 1-154. The roster has increased in recent years with the development of legal doctrines permitting criminal discovery, requiring the suppression of illegally obtained evidence, expanding the grounds for change of venue, and guaranteeing (at least in theory, and sometimes in fact) that criminal defendants will have lawyers to assist them in all of these and other pretrial matters. As a consequence, the impression appears to be prevalent that today's delays in criminal proceedings stem largely from the growth of procedures protective of the defendant, and that defendants have no just cause to complain of them. However, the new procedures would be less time consuming if they were more efficiently managed, see CRIME COMMISSION REPORT, supra note 4, at 154–55; commonly, it has not been the development of protective procedures, but rather their inadequate development, that causes delays. Criminal discovery provides one example of a supposedly protective device which has developed in forms that both insufficiently protect defendants and compel them to sacrifice their interest in a speedy trial in order to gain the scant benefits of the new "protection." While civil discovery in most states is now largely automatic (i.e., obtainable by discovery requests without court order), criminal discovery is almost universally required to be court-ordered upon motion; and trial judges are given exceedingly broad discretion to determine the scope of what the prosecutor must disclose. Defendants therefore frequently obtain less discovery than they should, and what they get is purchased at the cost of the delay entailed in noticing and hearing a discovery motion. Worse still, many states fail to provide for continuing discovery orders, and thereby require multiple motions.

I am quick to admit that a multiplication of pretrial motions is sometimes produced by defendants' strategic use of motions practice. But it is difficult to fault defense counsel for much of this, or to conclude that defendants should justly pay the piper in the currency of trial delay. Criminal procedures that do not provide for discovery depositions, for example, will inevitably encourage the use of suppression motions and other makeshift deposition-taking devices; and as long as the courts tolerate the present practice of extreme sentencing disparity from judge to judge, pretrial motions will continue to be used as a means of seeking out a lenient sentencer before whom a guilty plea may be safely entered.

31. For varieties of plea-bargaining practices, see D. NEWMAN, CONVICTION—THE DETERMINATION OF GUILT OR INNOCENCE WITHOUT TRIAL (1966). In some jurisdictions, trials may also be long delayed to accommodate interlocutory appeals.

32. See Kaplan, An Analysis and Survey of the Law of Continuances, 9 MIAMI L.Q. 385 (1955).

further time for trial preparation, to accommodate other obligations of counsel, to accommodate witnesses, etc. On the date of a trial listing, there may be no courtroom or no jurors available; the judge may be otherwise occupied; counsel may be tied up in another trial; the defendant or a witness may be ill; subpoenas may not have been served; a previously undetected defect in the pretrial proceedings may appear.[33] As a general matter, delays compound delays: the more frequently a trial has to be rescheduled, the more likely it is that one of the many accidents of life will occur on a second or successive trial date and require an additional postponement.[34]

A defendant aggrieved by these delays may invoke several distinct sources of law in support of his right to a speedy trial. Courts exercising their "inherent residual power" to control their own dockets[35] will customarily entertain motions to advance a trial date,[36] or to dismiss a case for nonprosecution.[37] In some jurisdictions, this authority is expressly conferred by statute or court rule,[38] which may also contain a more or less specific, albeit usually precatory, substantive directive—for example, that "[p]reference shall be given to criminal proceedings as far as practicable."[39] Statutes in many jurisdictions establish time limitations for various stages of some or all criminal cases:[40] they provide, for example, that an information or indictment must be filed within a specified time after bind-over;[41] that a defendant must be tried within a specified time after the filing of the information or indictment;[42] or that (irrespective of the time of filing of the information or indictment) a defendant must be tried

---

33. *See, e.g.,* Illinois v. Somerville, 410 U.S. 458 (1973) (involving previously undetected defect in original indictment).

34. For a glaring example, *see* King v. United States, 265 F.2d 567 (D.C. Cir. 1959).

35. MINIMUM STANDARDS, *supra* note 4, at 12, *quoting* FED. R. CRIM. P. 50, Advisory Committee Notes.

36. *See, e.g.,* Frankel v. Woodrough, 7 F.2d 796 (8th Cir. 1925); *cf.* United States v. Patrisso, 21 F.R.D. 363, 367 (S.D.N.Y. 1958).

37. *See* United States v. Hester, 325 F.2d 654 (9th Cir. 1963); *cf.* Mann v. United States, 304 F.2d 394 (D.C. Cir. 1962).

38. *See, e.g.,* PA. R. CRIM. P. 316, in PA. RULES OF THE COURT 614 (West Desk Copy 1974). FED. R. CRIM. P. 50(a) provides that: "The district courts may provide for placing criminal proceedings upon appropriate calendars," and FED. R. CRIM. P. 48(b) provides that: "If there is unnecessary delay in presenting the charge to a grand jury or in filing an information against a defendant who has been held to answer to the district court, or if there is unnecessary delay in bringing a defendant to trial, the court may dismiss the indictment, information or complaint."

39. FED. R. CRIM. P. 50(a), *as amended,* (1972). Note 25 *supra* discusses the recent trend toward development of more specific timetables.

40. The statutes and cases construing them are discussed in Note, *The Right to a Speedy Criminal Trial,* 57 COLUM. L. REV. 846 (1957); Note, *The Lagging Right to a Speedy Trial,* 51 VA. L. REV. 1587, 1590–91 (1965). *See also* MINIMUM STANDARDS, *supra* note 4, at 14–16. Some of the statutes (particularly those that continue the form of the English Habeas Corpus Act, *see* note 45 *infra*) apply only to jailed defendants.

41. *E.g.,* CAL. PENAL CODE § 1382(1) (West Cum. Pocket Part 1974); NEV. REV. STAT. ch. 178.556 (1973).

42. *E.g.,* ARK. STAT. ANN. § 43–1708 (Repl. Vol. 1964); N.Y. CRIM. P. LAW § 30.30(1) (McKinney Cum. Pocket Part 1974–1975); VA. CODE ANN. tits. 19.1–190, –191 (Cum. Supp. 1974).

within a specified time (expressed in days or terms of court) after the date when he was "taken into custody,"[43] or "imprisoned,"[44] or "committed."[45] Special state statutory provisions may apply to defendants who are imprisoned upon prior convictions within or without the state;[46] the latter situation is the subject of the elaborate Interstate Agreement on Detainers.[47] Most state constitutions contain a speedy trial guarantee in their respective Bills or Declarations of Rights.[48] Finally, there are the relevant guarantees of the federal Constitution: the due process clauses of the fifth and fourteenth amendments,[49] and the speedy trial clause of the sixth amendment, which the Supreme Court "incorporated" into the fourteenth amendment in 1967 and thereby made binding upon state as well as federal criminal prosecutions.[50]

II. *Strunk v. United States*: THE BASIC CONFUSION

As Judge Godbold has recently reminded us, at least three interests of the defendant may be protected by the right to a speedy criminal trial.[51] The first is his interest in physical freedom, his interest against unduly

43. ILL. ANN. STAT. ch. 38, § 103–5(a) (Smith-Hurd 1970).
44. MASS. ANN. LAWS ch. 277, § 72 (1968).
45. N.C. GEN. STAT. ANN. § 15–10 (Repl. Vol. 1965); PA. STAT. ANN. tit. 19, § 781 (Purdon 1964); S.C. CODE ANN. § 17–509 (1962). These are examples of the familiar form of "two-term" statute derived from the celebrated Habeas Corpus Act of 1679, 31 Car. 2, c. 2. "Commitment" is commonly read as signifying a bind-over, but has occasionally been construed to mean arrest. *See* note 19 *supra*. I have noted elsewhere that: "The statutes are generally very badly drafted and raise vexing problems of construction. Among the questions on which the jurisdictions split, for example, are: (a) under statutes requiring that a defendant 'committed' on a charge be indicted or tried within *x* period, (i) whether the statute applies only to jailed defendants, or to both jailed and bailed defendants; (ii) whether 'commitment' means arrest, or bind-over, or something else (such as receipt within the county of a defendant arrested elsewhere); (b) under statutes which require that a defendant not timely indicted or tried be 'discharged by the court,' (i) whether 'discharge' means release from custody or dismissal of the charges; (ii) if the former, release on what terms; (iii) if the latter, whether the dismissal is with or without prejudice; and (c) under statutes which excuse delay beyond the specified period if it happen 'upon the application of the defendant,' (i) whether defense application merely tolls the statutory period or entirely deprives the defendant of the statute's benefit after one 'application,' and (ii) whether 'application' means an express request for continuance, or may be made out if the defendant files a time-consuming motion of another sort (a motion to suppress, for example), or if he merely acquiesces in the delay." A. AMSTERDAM, B. SEGAL & M. MILLER, *supra* note 28, at 1-317 to 1-318.
46. *See* Virginia Note, *supra* note 40, at 1605–07, and authorities cited therein. For further discussion of the particular problems involved in providing a speedy trial for persons incarcerated under earlier sentences, *see* Schindler, *Interjurisdictional Conflict and the Right to a Speedy Trial*, 35 U. CIN. L. REV. 179 (1966); Tuttle, *Catch 2254: Federal Jurisdiction and Interstate Detainers*, 32 U. PITT. L. REV. 489 (1971); Walther, *Detainer Warrants and the Speedy Trial Provision*, 46 MARQ. L. REV. 423 (1963); Comment, *The Convict's Right to a Speedy Trial*, 61 J. CRIM. L.C. & P.S. 352 (1970); Note, *Convicts—The Right to a Speedy Trial and the New Detainer Statutes*, 18 RUTGERS L. REV. 828 (1964); Note, *Effective Guaranty of a Speedy Trial for Convicts in Other Jurisdictions*, 77 YALE L.J. 767 (1968).
47. The interstate compact is set out in MINIMUM STANDARDS, *supra* note 4, at 50–56. It is discussed in the writings cited in note 46 *supra*, and in Legislation, *Interstate Agreement on Detainers*, 32 ST. JOHN'S L. REV. 141 (1957).
48. *See* Columbia Note, *supra* note 40, at 847 n.7; Comment, *supra* note 46, at 356 n.54.
49. *See* note 16 *supra*.
50. Klopfer v. North Carolina, 386 U.S. 213 (1967); *see, e.g.*, Dickey v. Florida, 398 U.S. 30 (1970); Smith v. Hooey, 393 U.S. 374 (1969).
51. Godbold, *supra* note 5, at 268–72.

prolonged pretrial detention. "It is clearly unfair to a defendant to jail him for months without trial";[52] it is doubly unfair when "a substantial proportion of these jailed . . . defendants would never suffer any imprisonment because . . . they are either not convicted or the disposition of their cases does not include imprisonment";[53] and it is trebly unfair because jail conditions today are frequently so atrocious that a jailed defendant who *is* sentenced to prison after conviction experiences the modest but unmistakable delights of an ascent from hell to purgatory.[54] The second interest of the defendant is his interest against overlong subjection to the vexations and vicissitudes of a pending criminal accusation: anxiety, heightened vulnerability to the displeasure of public officials and private blackmailers, restrictions upon freedom of movement, upon employment and educational opportunities, upon "associations and participation in unpopular causes,"[55] upon the liberty to go one's own way owing nobody nothing. The third interest is the defendant's interest in a fair trial, his interest against delays that may entail the loss of defensive evidence or render the memory of witnesses to events at the time of the alleged offense "a dream, a kind of phantasmagoria, rather than an independent recollection."[56]

Although these three interests are not entirely unconnected,[57] they are separable in the sense that an infringement of one may occur without infringement of another. Among the various state-law guarantees of speedy trial described above,[58] some are designed to protect fewer than all of the defendant's interests in expedition. The common form of "two-term" statute modeled on the English Habeas Corpus Act of 1679,[59] for example, is often construed as directed only against the evil of protracted pretrial confinement; accordingly, its provision that an unbailed defendant who is not timely tried shall be "discharged from imprisonment" is commonly interpreted to mean "nothing more than that"[60]—release from custody, but

---

52. CRIME COMMISSION REPORT, *supra* note 4, at 154.

53. Foote, *The Coming Constitutional Crisis in Bail*, 113 U. PA. L. REV. 959, 960 (1965). *See also id.* at 1137.

54. *See id.* at 1143–46; Shelton v. United States, 242 F.2d 101, 103 (5th Cir.), *rev'd en banc*, 246 F.2d 571 (5th Cir. 1957), *rev'd*, 356 U.S. 26 (1958) (per curiam).

55. Klopfer v. North Carolina, 386 U.S. 213, 222 (1967).

56. United States v. Chase, 135 F. Supp. 230, 233 (N.D. Ill. 1955). For an early expression of the theme, *see* Regina v. Robins, 1 Cox Crim. Cas. 114 (Somerset Assizes 1844).

57. The oppressiveness of prolonged pretrial incarceration may, for example, exert strong pressures upon a defendant to enter an improvident guilty plea, or to forego time-consuming pretrial motions; or it may adversely affect the disposition of his case in other ways, *see* Foote, *supra* note 53, at 1146–51, that can fairly be described as impairing the "integrity of the criminal fact-determination process," Godbold, *supra* note 5, at 271, which underlies the adjudication of guilt and the selection of punishment.

58. *See* text accompanying notes 35–48 *supra*.

59. *See* note 45 *supra*.

60. Commonwealth v. Mitchell, 153 Pa. Super. 582, 586, 34 A.2d 905, 907 (1943), *aff'd per curiam on the opinion below*, 349 Pa. 559, 37 A.2d 443 (1944). *Accord*, State v. Walker, 48 Del. (9 Terry) 190, 100 A.2d 413 (Super Ct. 1953) (alternative ground).

neither expedition nor abatement of the criminal prosecution. The sixth amendment, on the other hand, has been consistently construed as protecting all three of the defendant's speedy trial interests: "This guarantee is an important safeguard to prevent undue and oppressive incarceration prior to trial, to minimize anxiety and concern accompanying public accusation and to limit the possibilities that long delay will impair the ability of an accused to defend himself."[61] Therein lies the great strength of the amendment, but also the source of confusion in its application.

The confusion is manifested in a recent opinion by Chief Justice Burger for a unanimous Court in *Strunk v. United States*.[62] Strunk's trial was delayed for 10 months following his indictment. Prior to trial, he moved to dismiss the indictment on the ground that his sixth amendment right to a speedy trial had thereby been violated. The district court denied the motion, and Strunk was convicted by a jury. On appeal, the Court of Appeals for the Seventh Circuit found that the 10-month delay did indeed violate the sixth amendment; but because Strunk neither claimed nor showed that the delay had prejudiced his ability to defend against the prosecution, the court also found that dismissal of the prosecution was an inappropriate remedy. It remanded the case with directions to reduce Strunk's sentence by the period of the unconstitutional delay.

The Supreme Court granted Strunk's petition for certiorari to decide whether, "once a judicial determination has been made that an accused has been denied a speedy trial, the only remedy available to the court is 'to reverse the conviction, vacate the sentence, and dismiss the indictment.' "[63] Since the Government did not cross-petition for "review [of] the determination of the Court of Appeals that the defendant had been denied a speedy trial,"[64] the Supreme Court—after expressing apparent doubt about the substance of that determination[65]—concluded to treat it as "unchallenged."[66] It then held that, when a defendant has been "denied a speedy trial,"[67] "dismissal must remain . . . 'the only possible remedy.' "[68]

On its face, this proposition is incredible. Anglo-American law has long provided remedies for denial of a speedy trial other than dismissal of the

---

61. United States v. Ewell, 383 U.S. 116, 120 (1966). *See also* Barker v. Wingo, 407 U.S. 514, 532 (1972); Smith v. Hooey, 393 U.S. 374, 378 (1969). The interest given sixth amendment protection in Klopfer v. North Carolina, 386 U.S. 213 (1967), was the interest against protracted pendency of criminal charges with their attendant "anxiety and concern," *id*. at 222; while in Dickey v. Florida, 398 U.S. 30 (1970), it was the interest against impairment of a fair opportunity to defend at trial.
62. 412 U.S. 434 (1973).
63. *Id*. at 435.
64. *Id*.
65. *See id*. at 436–37.
66. *Id*. at 440.
67. *Id*.
68. *Id*.

prosecution with prejudice.[69] State and lower federal courts enforcing sub-constitutional speedy-trial guarantees have frequently found other remedies appropriate;[70] and both lower courts[71] and the Supreme Court[72] have enforced the sixth amendment by other means. Surely, the primary form of judicial relief against denial of a speedy trial should be to expedite the trial, not to abort it.[73] Where expedition is impracticable for some reason, the Supreme Court's repeated recognition of the several distinct interests protected by a right to speedy trial suggests the propriety of fashioning various remedies responsive to the particular interest invaded in any particular case. If the sole wrong done by delay is "undue and oppressive incarceration prior to trial,"[74] the remedy ought to be release from pretrial confinement;[75] if prolongation of the "anxiety" and other vicissitudes "accompanying public accusation"[76] is sufficiently extensive, the remedy ought to be dismissal of the accusation without prejudice;[77] and it is only when delay gives rise to "possibilities [of impairment of] . . . the ability of an accused to defend himself,"[78] or when a powerful sanction is needed to compel prosecutorial obedience to norms of speedy trial which judges cannot otherwise enforce,[79] that dismissal of a prosecution with prejudice is warranted.[80]

Of course, *Strunk* came to the Supreme Court after conviction, and perhaps the Court is saying merely that dismissal with prejudice is the exclusive *posttrial* remedy for denial of a speedy trial. I could approve that limited proposition,[81] although it seems to me to highlight the importance (to

---

69. I have earlier mentioned the Habeas Corpus Act of 1679, which provided that persons not timely tried should be discharged from imprisonment. *See* note 45 *supra*; notes 59–60 *supra* and accompanying text. *See also* Godbold, *supra* note 5, at 267–68, 271–72.

70. *E.g.*, Mann v. United States, 304 F.2d 394 (D.C. Cir. 1962) (dismissal without prejudice); United States v. Patrisso, 21 F.R.D. 363 (S.D.N.Y. 1958) (expediting trial); Pelligrini v. Wolfe, 225 Ark. 459, 283 S.W.2d 162 (1955) (same); Commonwealth v. Mitchell, 153 Pa. Super. 582, 34 A.2d 905 (1943) (discharge from custody). *See also* Columbia Note, *supra* note 40, at 859–61. *Cf.* MINIMUM STANDARDS, *supra* note 4, at 40–42.

71. *E.g.*, Frankel v. Woodrough, 7 F.2d 796 (8th Cir. 1925). *See also* Note, *Dismissal of the Indictment as a Remedy for Denial of the Right to Speedy Trial*, 64 YALE L.J. 1208, 1208–09 (1955).

72. Braden v. 30th Judicial Circuit Court, 410 U.S. 484, 491 (1973); *cf.* Smith v. Hooey, 393 U.S. 374 (1969).

73. *See* Recent Case, 108 U. PA. L. REV. 414, 418, 421–23 (1960).

74. *See* text accompanying note 61 *supra*.

75. *See* text accompanying notes 59–60 *supra*.

76. *See* text accompanying note 61 *supra*.

77. *See* Mann v. United States, 304 F.2d 394 (D.C. Cir. 1962).

78. *See* text accompanying note 61 *supra*.

79. *See* text accompanying notes 89–90 *infra*.

80. *E.g.*, Dickey v. Florida, 398 U.S. 30, 38 (1970). I first suggested this approach to sixth amendment remedies in a casenote a dozen years ago. Recent Case, *supra* note 73. Perhaps it deserves the entire lack of notice that it has received. But in light of *Strunk* and the uncritical acceptance among latter-day commentators of the proposition that dismissal with prejudice is *the* remedy for speedy-trial denials, *see* notes 96 & 98 *infra*, it seems to me timely to try again.

81. The sentence-reduction remedy fashioned by the court of appeals in *Strunk* seems ineffective even to redress the evil of prolonged pretrial confinement to which it was immediately addressed. Trial judges have exceedingly broad sentencing discretion in most jurisdictions today; after conviction, they are likely to consider it more important to impose the sentence which they think that

which I shall shortly return) of developing far better pretrial remedies
against denial of a speedy trial than we now have—remedies that would
ordinarily avert occasions for resort to the drastic and unsatisfactory sanction of dismissal. Obviously, if a criminal prosecution is sufficiently well
founded to be instituted, it should usually proceed to disposition on the
merits[82] rather than abort through procedural deficiencies. There are certainly circumstances under which considerations of fairness or integrity
of the criminal justice system require that prosecutions be halted for reasons unrelated to the guilt or innocence of the defendant or to the appropriateness of subjecting him to criminal processes or sanctions. But those
circumstances should be prevented from arising insofar as possible. I cannot imagine that the Supreme Court would conclude otherwise; and its
unelaborated, carelessly stated acceptance of the dismissal sanction as the
" 'only possible remedy' "[83] for denial of a speedy trial is extremely puzzling—particularly in a unanimous opinion authored by the Chief Justice. Chief Justice Burger has recently called for the abrogation of the rule
excluding illegally obtained evidence in search-and-seizure cases,[84] and
there are some indications that he does not stand alone on the Court in
believing that the exclusionary rule unnecessarily impedes the pursuit of
public justice.[85] I myself emphatically disagree with that view,[86] but only
because I find the exclusionary rule an indispensable method of protecting
constitutional norms that the judiciary cannot otherwise enforce effectively.
Denials of the right to a speedy trial—or, at least those denials which occur
(as in *Strunk*) during the court phase of a criminal prosecution—are judicially controllable by other methods than dismissing the prosecution; and
it seems intolerable that "[t]he criminal is to go free because [a judge, or
the court system] . . . has blundered,"[87] if there are any other satisfactory
methods of controlling the blunderers.

I should add that Cardozo's term "blunder" is more apt in the speedy
trial context than in the search-and-seizure context where it was coined.
For, as I have indicated, undue trial delays often result from inadvertence

---

the offender needs or deserves than to give him rebates for unconstitutional pretrial confinement;
and they will usually be able to reduce those rebates to a fiction by inflating the initial sentence, in
any case in which a colorable speedy-trial claim is made, before "reducing" the sentence in supposed
vindication of the claim.

82. This does not necessarily mean a trial, or even a court disposition. It means a disposition of
the charges—whether determined by the court or in the exercise of the prosecutor's discretion—that
responds to the purposes of the criminal law as applied to the particular offense and offender.

83. *See* text accompanying note 68 *supra*.

84. Bivens v. Six Unknown Fed. Narcotics Agents, 403 U.S. 388, 411–27 (1971) (Burger, C. J.,
dissenting).

85. *See* United States v. Calandra, 414 U.S. 338, 348 n.5 (1974).

86. *See* Amsterdam, *Perspectives on the Fourth Amendment*, 58 MINN. L. REV. 349, 428–33
(1974).

87. I adapt Justice (then Judge) Cardozo's famous phrase from People v. Defore, 242 N.Y.
13, 21, 150 N.E. 585, 587, *cert. denied*, 270 U.S. 657 (1926).

or poor management rather than malevolence.[88] If such delays impair the defendant's ability to defend himself in any way, or even if that sort of impairment is a significant possibility,[89] I am quick to agree that the prosecution should be dismissed.[90] Moreover, I would not quarrel with the dismissal sanction as a remedy for undue delay in the precourt phase of a prosecution, where (like the exclusionary rule) it is the only effective means by which courts can make prosecuting officials obey the Constitution. But where undue delay occurs during the court phase and does not entail the likelihood of prejudicing the defendant in his defense, dismissal seems wholly inappropriate.

That observation brings me to the worst feature of the *Strunk* opinion. For, while the opinion need not and should not be read as holding that the posttrial dismissal sanction is exclusive of—or preferred over—more efficacious pretrial remedies against denial of the right to speedy trial,[91] *Strunk*'s approach to the substance of the speedy-trial right itself tends inevitably to eviscerate those remedies. Chief Justice Burger treats the sixth amendment right to speedy trial as though it were a single, indivisible right: a right that either is or is not violated, for all purposes, by a particular amount of delay under the circumstances of a particular case. It is that conception under which the Seventh Circuit's "unchallenged determination that [Strunk] . . . was denied a speedy trial"[92] leads to dismissal even though the Seventh Circuit also found no conceivable prejudice to Strunk's defense.

The conception is plainly unsound. If it is once admitted that the sixth amendment protects against at least three separate sorts of harm to the

---

88. *See* text accompanying notes 22–34 *supra.*

89. I agree with the well-reasoned arguments that a defendant need not demonstrate actual prejudice in order to secure dismissal of the prosecution for want of a speedy trial where undue delays have occurred which give rise to any nonspeculative possibility of impairment of the defense. *See* Columbia Note, *supra* note 40, at 864; Note, *The Right to a Speedy Trial,* 20 STAN. L. REV. 476, 493–97 (1968).

90. Strunk v. United States, 412 U.S. 434, 436–37 (1973); Barker v. Wingo, 407 U.S. 514, 531 (1972) (dictum). These decisions make plain that the Supreme Court has now thankfully abandoned the position that delays which may prejudice a defendant's ability to defend must also be "purposeful" or in any other sense "oppressive," Pollard v. United States, 352 U.S. 354, 361 (1957), in order to justify dismissal with prejudice. *See* Godbold, *supra* note 5, at 285–88.

91. I would think it unnecessary to belabor this obvious point so heavily but for two considerations. The first is that, even before *Strunk,* the lower federal courts were displaying a regrettable tendency to ignore speedy-trial concerns and remedies other than the concern against impairment of the defendant's ability to defend and the remedy of dismissal, *see* note 99 *infra;* and the badly crafted *Strunk* opinion will doubtless reinforce this tendency. Second, it is possible that the baneful implications of the *Strunk* opinion are not merely inadvertent, since its author (together with Justice Powell) joined Justice Rehnquist's dissent in Braden v. 30th Judicial Circuit Court, 410 U.S. 484, 502–11 (1973). That dissent forthrightly states the proposition that federal courts should not enforce the sixth amendment in state criminal trials by any other means than by permitting denial of a speedy trial and then invalidating the ensuing conviction; and it even goes so far as to characterize the sixth amendment right to speedy trial as nothing more than "a defense to a criminal charge." *Id.* at 505 (dissenting opinion). Hopefully, even in the wake of *Strunk,* lower federal courts will remember that the majority in *Braden* unequivocally rejected Justice Rehnquist's extreme position.

92. Strunk v. United States, 412 U.S. at 440.

criminal defendant when it guarantees him a speedy trial, then it seems apparent that a given delay, in the context of a particular prosecution, may infringe upon one of the defendant's interests but not the others, and may violate the sixth amendment for one purpose but not for all purposes. I have no doubt at all that Strunk was denied the speedy trial guaranteed by the sixth amendment, even though the Court appears to express misgivings on that score.[93] I have no doubt at all that Willie Barker's sixth amendment right to speedy trial was violated by delay of more than 5 years between his arrest and trial, even though the Supreme Court held in *Barker v. Wingo*[94] that it was not—where the question before the Court was dismissal of the prosecution with prejudice. To debate the question whether the sixth amendment has been violated in such egregious cases as these—and most of the other cases that now seem to be coming before the federal courts for decision[95]—is itself to make a feeble farce of the amendment. *Of course* the amendment has been violated in these cases. By that I mean that if the defendants had moved for expedition of their trials at a far earlier time than that at which they were actually tried, judges obedient to the sixth amendment would have had to order the trials expedited. I also mean that if they had moved for dismissal of the charges without prejudice at some far earlier time than the date of their motions for dismissal *with* prejudice, the sixth amendment would have required the motions to be granted. And if, being jailed without bail, or in default of bail, they had moved for discharge from custody at a still earlier time, the sixth amendment would have required that relief as well. It *is* debatable whether, in these cases, the sixth amendment ever came to require Strunk's or Barker's immunization from criminal liability. But surely constitutional doctrine cannot be so devoid of reason as to demand that, in order to invoke the sixth amendment as a ground of his request for the setting of an early trial date, a defendant must make the same showing necessary to obtain a sixth amendment dismissal of the prosecution with prejudice.

Even before *Strunk*, lower courts and commentators were coming increasingly to confuse the question whether the sixth amendment had been violated with the question whether it had been violated in the particular way that required dismissal as a remedy.[96] The cause of the confusion seems

93. *See* text accompanying note 65 *supra*.
94. 407 U.S. 514 (1972). The case is discussed in text accompanying notes 101–09 *infra*.
95. *See* Godbold, *supra* note 5, at 274–88.
96. It is instructive to compare the analysis (and the tenor of the case law discussed) in the relatively few writings published on the subject of speedy trial during the past two decades. An early Yale Note recognizes that dismissal is an unusual remedy for denial of a speedy trial. 1955 Yale Note, *supra* note 71. A slightly later Columbia Note, published in 1957, urges that dismissal should be the ordinary remedy. Columbia Note, *supra* note 40, at 847, 859–61, 866–67. A decade later, a Virginia Note admits the unsatisfactory nature of the dismissal remedy, but seems to accept the notion that courts enforcing the sixth amendment are powerless to fashion other remedies in the absence of

evident. For a variety of reasons, most reported judicial decisions applying the sixth amendment are handed down in posttrial appeals.[97] In this context, it has been natural to assume that dismissal is "the remedy for violation of the right to a speedy trial."[98] Given that assumption, it is not surprising that courts have focused on impairment of the defendant's ability to defend as the hallmark of denial of a speedy trial, and that his other speedy-trial interests have been treated as "generally unimportant."[99] Moreover, the specter of immunizing, of "turning loose," persons proved guilty of serious criminal offenses has been thoroughly repugnant to judges,[100] and they have accordingly held that shockingly long delays do not "violate" the sixth amendment. The amendment has thereby been twisted totally out of shape —distorted from a guarantee that all accuseds will receive a speedy trial into a windfall benefit of criminal immunity for a very few accuseds in whose cases the pandemic failure of our courts to provide speedy trials has attained peculiarly outrageous proportions. *Strunk* lends the comfort of uncritical Supreme Court acceptance to this development.

III. *Barker v. Wingo*: CONFUSION WORSE CONFOUNDED

Barker v. *Wingo*,[101] decided 1 year before *Strunk*, seems to me to compound the felony. The facts of the case are presently unimportant, since the Court took it as the occasion for a general pronouncement of "the criteria by which the speedy trial right is to be judged."[102] Probably the most significant issue resolved was the validity of the "demand rule," a doctrine previously espoused by the lower federal courts and most state courts.[103] Although the rule assumed varying forms, it is fair to describe it summarily as holding that a criminal defendant cannot obtain dismissal of his prosecution for want of a speedy trial unless he has previously demanded a

---

congressional implementing legislation patterned on the English Habeas Corpus Act. Virginia Note, *supra* note 40, at 1594–96. *Cf. id.* at 1619. Later writings simply assume that dismissal is *the* remedy for denial of a speedy trial. *See* note 98 *infra*.

97. Trial courts infrequently write opinions in ruling upon pretrial motions for expedited trial, for discharge from custody, or for dismissal without prejudice. In many jurisdictions, appellate courts have been largely unreceptive to pretrial prerogative writs challenging such rulings. (The writs frequently encounter jurisdictional and doctrinal problems, including the notion that mandamus will not lie to control "discretionary" acts, whereas the management of a trial court's calendar is within its discretion.) In other jurisdictions, appellate processes are even slower than trial processes, so that the use of pretrial writs is impracticable. And, where pretrial writs are used, they are commonly granted or denied in a terse, unpublished order.

98. Godbold, *supra* note 5, at 273. *See also id.* at 285, 288–89, 293, 294 n.7; Stanford Note, *supra* note 89, at 498; 1968 Yale Note, *supra* note 46, at 778 n.78.

99. Stanford Note, *supra* note 89, at 481. *See also id.* at 495; Godbold, *supra* note 5, at 284–85; Virginia Note, *supra* note 40, at 1594–95; 1968 Yale Note, *supra* note 46, at 769.

100. *See* Godbold, *supra* note 5, at 273–74, 288; Stanford Note, *supra* note 89, at 498 & cases cited nn.145–46.

101. 407 U.S. 514 (1972).

102. *Id.* at 516.

103. The rule is discussed in the writings collected in notes 96 & 98 *supra. See also* MINIMUM STANDARDS, *supra* note 4, at 17.

speedy trial and not received it—as holding, therefore, that the right to speedy trial is tolled (or, according to some courts, forfeited) by the defendant's failure to request an earlier trial than he gets. *Barker* rejects this form of the demand rule and announces that "the defendant's assertion of or failure to assert his right to a speedy trial is one of the factors to be considered [among an open-ended list of factors] in an inquiry into the deprivation of the right."[104]

But the demand rule was never designed to identify "one factor" pertinent to the timeliness of trial. Its purpose was to compel the defendant to go on record with a request for a speedy trial while it was still possible for the trial court to give him one.[105] It was, in other words, a device for insisting that the defendant resort to effective expedition remedies, so as to avoid all avoidable denials of a speedy trial and the consequent posttrial dismissal sanction. To convert a rule having this function into a factor for consideration among many factors in determining whether and when the right to speedy trial has been denied is equivalent to repealing the law requiring motorists to drive on the right-hand side of the road and decreeing instead that, in tort suits following motor vehicle accidents, it shall be a "factor" relevant to the defendant's liability whether he was driving on the right or the left.

I do not wish to be misunderstood as the proponent of an unqualified demand rule. If such a rule is recognized at all, it should be restricted by exceptions for situations in which the defendant is disabled or substantially impeded from making a demand for trial.[106] In cases where unwarranted delay gives rise to possibilities of impairment of a defendant's defense (that is, in most though not all cases where I think dismissal is ever appropriate[107]), I myself would abrogate the demand rule entirely because I find any doctrine of implied waiver of a fair trial altogether unacceptable. But to shut the demand rule out the door and let it in the window, as *Barker* does, is the worst of all possible resolutions. The "factor" approach simply further roils the turbid stew of substantive speedy-trial law[108] and thereby

---

104. 407 U.S. at 528.

105. *See* Columbia Note, *supra* note 40, at 853; Recent Case, *supra* note 73, at 418.

106. *See id.* at 417; MINIMUM STANDARDS, *supra* note 4, at 17.

107. *See* text accompanying notes 89–90 *supra*.

108. Contemporary judicial analysis of the constitutional right to speedy trial commonly begins and ends with the celebrated dictum of Beavers v. Haubert, 198 U.S. 77, 87 (1905), that the right "is necessarily relative . . . and depends upon circumstances." For discussion of the potpourri of "factors" commonly considered (or ignored without warning) by the courts, *see, e.g.,* Stanford Note, *supra* note 89, at 478–82; Virginia Note, *supra* note 40, at 1590–1610. Writing just prior to the *Barker* decision, Judge Godbold observed that "the ad hoc nature of the typical speedy trial decision and the sporadic acceptance and utilization of . . . four [commonly identified] factors suggest that the law of speedy trial is still in an immature state, and that these four indicia may not represent the ultimate conceptual approach." Godbold, *supra* note 5, at 275. *Cf.* Barker v. Wingo, 407 U.S. 514, 530 (1972): "A balancing test necessarily compels courts to approach speedy trial cases on an *ad hoc* basis. We can do little more than identify some of the factors which courts should assess . . . ." [There follow the usual four factors.]

licenses courts to find an additional reason for refusing to dismiss prosecutions when it seems obnoxious to them to do so.[109] It places defendants and defense counsel in the unconscionable position of having to choose between insisting on a speedy trial and gambling on the incalculable possibilities of speedy-trial dismissal. To the extent that they are willing to gamble and able to win, *Barker* finally reinforces the tendency of *Strunk* to promote dismissal at the expense of more satisfactory speedy-trial remedies.

IV. *Braden* and the Beginnings of an Effective Sixth Amendment

As I noted at the outset, no mere improvement of sixth amendment doctrine is likely to contribute much toward speeding up the generally laggard processing of criminal cases in this country. If, however, the sixth amendment is to serve the limited function that it can serve to protect defendants against the several evils of oppressive trial delay, what is needed is the development of doctrines and procedures that effectuate other speedy-trial remedies than the remote, over-costly and hence grudgingly administered dismissal remedy. This development must begin with judicial recognition that there is more than one sixth amendment right to a speedy trial, and that the rights guaranteed by the sixth amendment against various consequences of trial delay call for differing forms of redress and measures of the permissible duration of criminal proceedings. I do not suppose that the sixth amendment requires a dismissal with prejudice of the ordinary criminal prosecution if it is not tried within 4 weeks, or 4 months, after arrest. But I think that the sixth amendment is being flouted wholesale when hundreds of thousands of defendants who are (or could be) ready for trial are imprisoned in default of bail for more than 4 weeks, and when the typical criminal defendant who wants a trial cannot get either a trial or the dismissal of the charges against him (without prejudice) after more than 4 months. My choice of figures is approximative, of course, and I do not mean to imply that the sixth amendment requirements governing permissible periods of pretrial confinement or the pendency of criminal charges are determined solely by the clock without consideration of other circumstances. The important point is that courts must begin to work to define those requirements, after making plain that they are not measured by the present body of unendurable sixth amendment dismissal-remedy jurisprudence.

Procedural mechanisms to define and enforce the requirements are now available. *Braden v. 30th Judicial Circuit Court*[110] establishes that an im-

---

109. *See* text accompanying note 100 *supra*.
110. 410 U.S. 484 (1973).

prisoned state defendant may resort to federal habeas corpus, following
exhaustion of state remedies, in order to compel the state to try him or
release him. Since the Court has also recently recognized the obligations
of a bail bond or recognizance as sufficient "custody" to invoke the federal
habeas corpus jurisdiction,[111] the same relief should be available to most
unjailed state criminal defendants. Two important procedural propositions
remain to be settled, but I think that they flow logically from *Braden*. First,
since by definition the right to speedy trial is one for which "[r]elief . . .
must be speedy if it is to be effective,"[112] state remedies must be held exhausted for federal habeas corpus purposes[113] if they fail to provide prompt
consideration of a state defendant's sixth amendment claim.[114] Second,
the same denial or unavailability of prompt state-court relief that satisfies
the exhaustion requirement for federal habeas corpus should also satisfy
the comity requirement[115] for purposes of a federal injunctive action[116] to
secure any form of relief (such as dismissal of pending charges without
prejudice) that may be beyond the scope of habeas corpus.[117] The establishment of these propositions would enable federal district courts to furnish
effective pretrial sixth amendment remedies to state criminal defendants
wherever the state trial and appellate courts fail to provide them. Of course,
no one can relish the prospect of a multiplication of federal habeas corpus
and injunction actions, or ignore the impact of such a multiplication upon
federal criminal defendants' abilities to obtain speedy trials. But the multiplication is a greater danger in theory than it is likely to prove in fact.
More likely, the threat of federal intervention will cause state courts to
improve their own performance in the same way that the threat of federal

111. Hensley v. Municipal Court, 411 U.S. 345 (1973).
112. Stack v. Boyle, 342 U.S. 1, 4 (1951) (speaking of the right to bail).
113. Concerning the judicially developed doctrine of exhaustion of state remedies in *pretrial*
federal habeas corpus proceedings, *see* Amsterdam, *Criminal Prosecutions Affecting Federally Guaranteed Civil Rights: Federal Removal and Habeas Corpus Jurisdiction to Abort State Court Trial*, 113
U. PA. L. REV. 793, 882–96 (1965).
114. *Cf. In re* Shuttlesworth, 369 U.S. 35 (1962); St. Jules v. Beto, 462 F.2d 1365 (5th Cir.
1972); Dozie v. Cady, 430 F.2d 637 (7th Cir. 1970); Dixon v. Florida, 388 F.2d 424 (5th Cir. 1968);
United States *ex rel.* Goodman v. Kehl, 456 F.2d 863, 869 (2d Cir. 1972) (dictum).
115. I use the term "comity" to describe the complex of considerations that "counsels restraint
against the issuance of [federal] injunctions against state officers engaged in the administration of
the State's criminal laws in the absence of a showing of irreparable injury which is ' "both great
and immediate." ' " O'Shea v. Littleton, 414 U.S. 488, 499 (1974). None of the considerations that
impelled denial of relief in *O'Shea* or in the cases cited in *id.* at 499–501 seems to me to be applicable
when a federal injunctive suit makes "no effort to abort a state proceeding or to disrupt the orderly
functioning of state judicial processes," but is filed "not in an effort to forestall a state prosecution,
but to enforce the [state's] . . . obligation to provide . . . a state court forum." Braden v. 30th
Judicial Circuit Court, 410 U.S. 484, 491 (1973). And it is of course now settled that, if the requirements of comity are met in an injunctive action under the Civil Rights Acts, note 116 *infra*, the provisions of 28 U.S.C. § 2283 (1970) (prohibiting stay of state court proceedings) do not bar relief.
Mitchum v. Foster, 407 U.S. 225 (1972).
116. Such an action is authorized by Rev. Stat. § 1979 (1875), 42 U.S.C. § 1983 (1970), within
the jurisdiction conferred by 28 U.S.C. § 1343 (1970).
117. The inefficacy of habeas corpus would, in this situation, establish that there was no "adequate remedy at law." Younger v. Harris, 401 U.S. 37, 43 (1971).

postconviction habeas corpus has lately resulted in at least a modest improvement of state postconviction procedures. Some would no doubt argue
that the dismissal sanction upon which the Supreme Court has concentrated all of its attention is a more effective monitory device, because it
threatens what state courts and prosecutors fear most. I would perhaps
agree if there were any prospect that the dismissal sanction would be rigorously enforced to this end. But the lesson of the present sorry state of sixth
amendment law is precisely that dismissal as a remedy has the sole effect
of making judges almost universally prefer the disease.

Voir Dire: Preserving
"Its Wonderful Power"*

Barbara Allen Babcock†

In an Arkansas federal court more than 80 years ago, one Alexander Lewis was on trial for murder. The judge, with modern concern for efficiency, ordered that rather than wasting time asking prospective jurors questions in person, each party should be given a list of the names of those available for jury service and should simply strike those each did not want. Finding this procedure unfair, the Supreme Court of the United States reversed the subsequent conviction, holding that "[the accused] cannot be compelled to make a peremptory challenge until he has been brought face to face, in the presence of the court, with each proposed juror, and an opportunity given for such inspection and examination of him as is required for the due administration of justice."[1]

The "face-to-face examination in the presence of the court" is the voir dire: the questioning of prospective jurors in relation to their ability to decide a particular case. Voir dire provides litigants with information that enables them to select a jury either by arguing to excuse for cause or by challenging peremptorily. Currently, however, the voir dire procedure is being attacked as a cumbersome, time-consuming, meaningless part of the jury trial.[2] The Chief Justice has criticized it as "a major piece of litigation consuming days or weeks."[3] The California Supreme Court has recently spoken of the burden of "excess rococo examination," which can bring about a situation in which "the trial structure is endangered."[4] A number of devices for limiting the examination are in vogue; this Essay examines these devices and the role of voir dire generally in the trial system, conclud-

---

* For the full context in which this quotation appears, *see* text accompanying note 80 *infra*.

Jay Spears, Stanford 1976, deserves and has my gratitude for the fine research and substantive and editorial suggestions that contributed to this Essay. I wish also to thank my colleagues, Thomas Grey and Michael Wald, for their very helpful comments.

† A.B. 1960, University of Pennsylvania; L.L.B. 1963, Yale University. Associate Professor of Law, Stanford University.

1. Pointer v. United States, 151 U.S. 396, 408–09 (1894), *summarizing* Lewis v. United States, 146 U.S. 370 (1892).

2. *See* Craig, Erickson, Friesen & Maxwell, *Voir Dire: Criticism and Comment*, 47 Denver L.J. 465 (1970); Imlay, *Federal Jury Reformation: Saving a Democratic Institution*, 6 Loyola L. Rev. 247 (1973); Levit, Nelson, Ball & Chernick, *Expediting Voir Dire: An Empirical Study*, 44 S. Cal. L. Rev. 916 (1971); Note, *Judge Conducted Voir Dire as a Time-Saving Trial Technique*, 2 Rutgers Camden L.J. 161 (1970); 15 Vill. L. Rev. 214 (1969).

3. Address by Chief Justice Burger, National Conference on the Judiciary, Williamsburg, Va., Mar. 12, 1971, *reported in* Los Angeles Times, Mar. 13, 1971, at 17, col. 2.

4. People v. Crowe, 8 Cal. 3d 815, 819, 506 P.2d 193, 195, 106 Cal. Rptr. 369, 371 (1973).

ing that limited voir dire examination undercuts the ability of the litigant
to exercise his peremptory challenges, which are essential to the jury trial
right.[5] Also implicated is the equal protection clause, because of the relative
disadvantage of the poor litigant, deprived of a full voir dire, as compared
with the wealthy litigant, who has other resources for gathering information about the jury.

I. Limitations on Voir Dire Examination

Those who would limit the voir dire examination take three tacks. First,
in the name of efficiency, many courts curtail the number and kinds of
questions that can be asked. "It is not only the privilege but it is also the
duty of the court to restrict the examination of jurors within reasonable
bounds so as to expedite the trial."[6] The refusal by trial courts of proper
lines of inquiry is usually found to be errorless by appellate courts.[7] The
most egregious example of such an appellate reaction is the recent Supreme
Court case of *Ham v. South Carolina*,[8] upholding the failure to voir dire
a jury on the issue of their reactions to facial hair when the accused, a
bearded civil rights worker in a small town, defended a drug charge by
asserting that the police had framed him. Although the Court in *Ham*

---

5. This Essay deals only with the process of choosing jurors who are actually to hear a case;
it does not explore any of the issues involved in summoning and selecting prospective jurors from
whom panels are drawn to hear specific cases.

Also not a subject of this Essay is the procedure for exercising the challenges. ABA Project on
Minimum Standards for Criminal Justice—Standards Relating to Trial by Jury 77 (Approved
Draft 1968) [hereinafter cited as ABA Standards], notes the wide variety in methods for exercising
challenges: "The prevailing state practice with regard to exercise of peremptories is said to be the following: Twelve veniremen are called and examined, after which the prosecutor exercises such challenges
for cause as may appear and then exercises such peremptories as he then desires to use. Anyone
excused is immediately replaced in the box, so the prosecutor will tender 12 jurors to the defendant,
who likewise exercises challenges for cause and whatever peremptories he then desires to use. Again
those excused are immediately replaced, and when he is satisfied the defendant tenders the jury
to the prosecutor. This procedure continues until both parties have exhausted their challenges or
indicate their satisfaction with the jury. . . .

"Another fairly common practice is that which involves striking jurors. Under this practice, jurors
are first examined and challenged for cause by both sides. Excused jurors are replaced on the panel, and
the examination of replacements continues until a panel of qualified jurors is presented. The size of
the panel at this time is the sum of the number of jurors to hear the case plus the number of peremptories to be allowed all parties. The parties then proceed to exercise their peremptories, usually alter-
nately or in some similar way which will result in all parties' exhausting their challenges at approximately the same time. . . . This approach is not uncommon in the federal courts."

6. People v. Semone, 140 Cal. App. 318, 326, 35 P.2d 379, 383 (3d Dist. 1934), *quoted approv-
ingly in* People v. Crowe, 8 Cal. 3d 815, 828 n.22, 506 P.2d 193, 202 n.22, 106 Cal. Rptr. 369, 378
n. 22 (1973).

7. *See, e.g.,* United States v. Robinson, 475 F.2d 376 (D.C. Cir. 1973). The proposed questions
were: Do any members of the prospective jury panel feel that self-defense does not justify the will-
ful taking of a human life? Do any members of the prospective jury panel feel that they would be
unable to follow the court's instructions on self-defense because of their personal views on the subject?
(The form of the questions, which is probably improper, was not at issue in the case.) *See* United
States v. Cockerham, 476 F.2d 542 (D.C. Cir. 1973) (court refused to question on attitudes of
jurors toward insanity defense); United States v. Bowe, 360 F.2d 1 (2d Cir. 1966) (court, while
conducting voir dire on attitudes toward racial prejudice, refused to ask whether any veniremen
were members of organizations such as Ku Klux Klan, White Citizens Council, Minute Men).

8. 409 U.S. 524 (1973).

admitted that "we cannot say that prejudice against people with beards might not have been harbored by one or more of the potential jurors in this case,"[9] it added that it could not "distinguish possible prejudice against beards from a host of other possible similar prejudices."[10] Apparently the Court simply despaired of setting a standard for the propriety of particular lines of inquiry.[11]

In addition to limiting the questions that may be asked, another method of restricting the information-gathering function of voir dire is to address all questions to the jury panel at once, rather than as individuals. Such a procedure makes it difficult for people who are not accustomed to speaking in front of others to respond to the questions, and it also makes it easier for jurors who have an answer to some question to fail to respond. Experienced litigators know, and empirical studies have substantiated,[12] that it is part of the psychology of the venire for some people to decide that they want to be on the jury. To that end, such people will evade or misconstrue, unconsciously or deliberately, general voir dire questions in order to avoid answering and possibly being struck.[13] Such behavior is obviously more

---

9. *Id.* at 527.
10. *Id.* at 528.
11. The Court in *Ham* did reverse for failure to inquire on voir dire about racial bias, basing its decision on Aldridge v. United States, 283 U.S. 308 (1931), which held a black defendant entitled to such a question. *Aldridge* had not explicitly rested on a constitutional base, though it spoke of "essential demands of fairness" and the right to an "impartial" jury. *Id.* at 310, 314. The Court in *Ham*, however, stated that unlike the *Aldridge* Court, it was locating the right to ask about racial prejudice squarely in the history and purposes of the 14th amendment due process clause. There was no mention in the decision of the sixth amendment or consideration of any equal protection claim. *See* text accompanying notes 48–68 *infra*. Arguably, therefore, the case settles nothing about the types of voir dire questions that may be required by these latter provisions. Moreover, *Ham* involved issues of how far the federal Constitution is to be implicated in state voir dire procedure and may, as to the facial hair questions, indicate no more than an unwillingness to evolve a method of analysis for general constitutional supervision of voir dire in a case that could be reversed without such a discussion.
12. *See, e.g.,* Broeder, *Voir Dire Examinations: An Empirical Study,* 38 S. CAL. L. REV. 503, 511 (1965).
13. "[V]eniremen frequently deceive, many times consciously." *Id.* at 513. The lack of candor by the prospective jurors was one of the major findings in this study "based on the observation of a series of twenty-three consecutively tried jury trial cases held in a Federal District Court in the Midwest . . . over a one and one-half year period during the late 1950s." *Id.* at 503. Some of the examples of this are quite startling. "Compensated by defendant for personal injuries and property damage sustained in a collision with one of defendant's trains when no compensation was called for, [a juror named Powers] sat mute when plaintiff's counsel inquired whether anyone had ever had any business or other dealings with the defendant. While Powers was not questioned by the writer concerning his motives for remaining silent, it is known that he regarded his selection as an honor, had told many barroom friends that he had been summoned for jury duty, and wanted to (and did) use his experience as a barroom conversation piece, and as a way of getting recognition in the circle in which he moved.
"Jurors Summers, Woods and Ball, in *Grey,* a personal injury case, were similarly without excuses for silence. Summers knew the plaintiff's family very well and was familiar with the tragic details of plaintiff's marriage, yet said nothing when the panel was queried about possible connections with the parties. Mrs. Woods and Ball sat quietly when generally questioned as to possible friendships or connections with the lawyers. Mrs. Woods, private secretary to the president of a large bank represented by defense counsel, had frequently sat in on conferences between counsel and her employer. She had the highest regard for defense counsel's intellect and lawyer-like abilities. Ball knew the lawyers for both sides and had probably done considerable business

difficult when the questions are addressed to each juror individually.[14]

Increasingly, judges are conducting voir dire examinations rather than allowing counsel to propound questions. Expedience is the most important reason for favoring the judge-conducted voir dire, as exampled by a recent statement of the California Supreme Court: "We approve this method of curtailing the inordinate time consumed in the process of the selection of jurors."[15] The reason for the time saving is that judges are neither inclined nor as able to ask the appropriate next question when answers are evoked from the prospective jurors. Thus, for instance, when a potential juror responds that she has been the victim of a crime, the judge will typically ask whether this would tend to prejudice her in evaluating the testimony to be given in the case. An attorney conducting the voir dire would probe the nature of the crime, her evaluation of the police investigation and conduct toward her, whether she made an identification and testified in court.

with plaintiff's counsel who practiced in the small town where Ball's title and abstract business was located." *Id*. at 511 (footnote omitted).

While Broeder drew from these observations the conclusion that voir dire serves little useful purpose, it is important to note that the voir dires he observed were "more or less perfunctory, stilted affairs, quickly concluded," and normally "lasted approximately one-half hour," including "the time spent by the judge in welcoming the veniremen and by the clerk in drawing the names of the twelve veniremen." *Id*. at 503. Certainly, en masse questioning of this type would be "grossly ineffective, not only in weeding out 'unfavorable' jurors but even in eliciting the data which would have shown particular jurors as very likely to prove 'unfavorable.'" *Id*. at 505.

But Broeder's observations could lead to the opposite conclusion as well: voir dire can serve its very important role in the selection of an impartial jury only if there is more-than-perfunctory, individual questioning that probes at least the more apparent biases of jurors.

14. Another example from Broeder, *id*. at 510, illustrates this: "Mrs. Stoner . . . , who had only recently been disfigured in an auto accident, said nothing when a general inquiry as to involvement in accidents was propounded. Knowing that she had done wrong, Mrs. Stoner commented privately to several jurors that she was too nervous to speak out."

15. People v. Crowe, 8 Cal. 3d 815, 825, 506 P.2d 193, 199, 106 Cal. Rptr. 369, 375 (1973). The approval of a voir dire conducted entirely by the court came in the face of a statute that read: "It shall be the duty of the trial court to examine the prospective jurors to select a fair and impartial jury. He shall permit reasonable examination of prospective jurors by counsel for the people and for the defendant." *See* Tone, *Voir Dire, New Supreme Court Rule 24–1: How It Works*, 47 ILL. BAR J. 140, 143 (1958) (expressing support for judge-conducted voir dire). A court-conducted voir dire modeled on FED. R. CRIM. P. 24(a) is approved in ABA STANDARDS, *supra* note 5, at 9 (Standard 2.4): "The judge should initiate the voir dire examination by identifying the parties and their respective counsel and by briefly outlining the nature of the case. The judge should then put to the prospective jurors any questions which he thinks necessary, touching their qualifications to serve as jurors in the case on trial. The judge should also submit to the prospective jurors such additional questions by the defendant or his attorney and the prosecuting attorney as he deems proper." The Commentary to Standard 2.4 notes that this method of court-conducted voir dire is followed generally in the federal courts and in about 10 states; approximately the same number provide for examination only by the judge; in 22 states provision is made for examination by the judge and the attorneys, and in the other states examination is left to counsel.

Generally the federal method of court-conducted voir dire is urged as a reform which will cut down the time consumed in voir dire as well as curb other alleged abuses. *See* Tone, *supra* at 143; 15 VILL. L. REV. 214, 219 (1969).

In addition to the fact that it is time consuming, the other major criticism commonly leveled at attorney-conducted voir dire is that attorneys improperly use the procedure to influence the jurors, establish rapport, and indoctrinate them with their views of the law.

For a more thorough discussion of the pros and cons of attorney-conducted voir dire, *see* Gutman, *The Attorney-Conducted Voir Dire of Jurors: A Constitutional Right*, 39 B'KLYN L. REV. 290 (1972); McGuirk & Tober, *Attorney-Conducted Voir Dire: Securing an Impartial Jury*, 15 N.H. BAR J. 1 (1973); Note, *supra* note 2; Comment, *Voir Dire in California Criminal Trials: Where Is It Going? Where Should It Go?*, 10 SAN DIEGO L. REV. 395 (1973).

Such questions spring to the mind of the advocate, but would occur less often to the judge. This is true partly because the judge does not want to spend time asking the questions, partly because he does not have the advocate's awareness that soon he will be making peremptory challenges based on inferences from what prospective jurors have said, and partly because the judge does not know the case of either party in detail, so that he cannot realize when responses have opened areas for further inquiry.

In some jurisdictions an effort is made to remedy the defects of court-conducted voir dire by allowing counsel to suggest further lines of inquiry by the judge after the initial questions have been asked. But even if the judge is willing to probe deeply into some issue, he will seldom go as far as counsel would. The procedure, moreover, is unproductive, because the additional questions will not be asked until the judge has finished the initial query, whereas the pattern of effective questioning—that is, inquiry that elicits candid answers—is continuous and sequential. The flow cannot be maintained unless the lawyer can follow immediately with the question suggested by the previous answer.

In sum, the limited questions put by the judge to the panel as a group greatly reduce the information produced by the voir dire. In most cases, in most places, voir dire is a stark little exercise consuming minutes rather than hours and often eliciting no verbal responses at all. But without a reasonable amount of information about the prospective jurors, the litigant cannot realize his right to "select" the jury by challenges for cause and by peremptory strikes. In examining this consequence of the limited voir dire, we must first consider the dual nature of the challenge system and its relation to the guarantee of an impartial jury.

II. The Functions of Cause and Peremptory Challenges

Traditionally the cause challenge is allowed in narrow circumstances: when the juror is related to one of the parties, for instance, or has previously sat in the same case that ended in a mistrial.[16] Such challenges are often denied—even when common sense indicates that there *must* be bias—as

---

16. Hopt v. Utah, 120 U.S. 430, 433 (1887), detailed typical reasons for excuse for cause: "Consanguinity or affinity within the fourth degree to the person alleged to be injured by the offense charged, or on whose complaint the prosecution was instituted, or to the defendant; . . . Standing in the relation of guardian and ward, attorney and client, master and servant, or landlord and tenant, or being a member of the family of the defendant, or of the person alleged to be injured by the offense charged, or on whose complaint the prosecution was instituted, or in his employment on wages. . . . Having formed or expressed an unqualified opinion or belief that the prisoner is guilty or not guilty of the offense charged." ABA STANDARDS, *supra* note 5, at 69, lists the traditional grounds similar to those above and adds: "Some statutes also list additional grounds, such as: that he has served as a juror within the preceding year . . . ; that he is or has been engaged in carrying on a business in violation of the law, where the defendant is indicted for a like offense; that he has been indicted within 12 months for a felony or an offense of the same character as that with which the defendant is charged; that he is a party to a suit pending in that court at that term . . . ."

long as the potential juror says that she would decide the case "only on the evidence presented" and would not be influenced by any other factor.[17] A frequently occurring example is the refusal of a cause challenge when a prospective juror admits having formed an opinion about the merits of one side of a case but declares she will nevertheless be impartial. Courts, feeling helpless before questions of human psychology, are unable to decide whether a person can be fair in spite of having an opinion on the matter at issue— thus the technique of "just asking her." Once having asked, however, the court cannot easily impugn the credibility of a citizen who has professed her impartiality.[18] Peremptory challenges—totally unlike the narrowness of those for cause—are exercised "without a reason stated, without inquiry, and without being subject to the court's control."[19]

Both types of challenge are part of the civil and criminal procedure of

17. The idea that the prospective juror's own statement should be the basis for the judge's decision about removal for cause is embodied in statutes in many places. See, e.g., IND. ANN. STAT. § 1504 (Burns Repl. Vol. 1956), dealing with a disqualification for cause when a juror has formed or expressed an opinion as to the guilt or innocence of the defendant, and providing that if "the juror states on oath that he feels able, notwithstanding such opinion, to render an impartial verdict upon the law and evidence, the court, if satisfied that he is impartial and will render such verdict, may in its discretion, admit him as competent to serve in such case." See also CAL. PENAL CODE § 1076 (West 1970); ILL. ANN. STAT. ch. 78, § 14 (Smith-Hurd 1966); N.Y. CODE CRIM. PRO. § 376 (McKinney 1958). FED. R. CRIM. P. 24 and FED. R. CIV. P. 47(a) do not define challenges for cause or give similar provision for service by juror with prior opinion, but several Supreme Court cases have established the acceptability of this practice. See Irvin v. Dowd, 366 U.S. 717, 724 (1961); Holt v. United States, 218 U.S. 245, 248 (1910); Spies v. Illinois, 123 U.S. 131, 167–68 (1887); Hopt v. Utah, 120 U.S. 430, 432 (1887); Reynolds v. United States, 98 U.S. 145, 155–56 (1878).

18. The trial judge's discretion on the granting or refusal of challenge for cause is practically unreviewable: "It must be made clearly to appear that upon the evidence the court ought to have found the juror has formed such an opinion that he could not in law be deemed impartial. The case must be one in which it is manifest the law left nothing to the 'conscience or discretion' of the court." Reynolds v. United States, 98 U.S. 145, 156 (1878).

In extreme situations there are exceptions to the general rules that the judge has almost unlimited discretion in deciding upon challenges for cause and that the juror's sworn statement that she will not be biased is enough. Irwin v. Dowd, 366 U.S. 718 (1961), was such a case. It involved saturation pretrial publicity about a murder case, including press releases from the prosecutor and police stating that the defendant had confessed to six slayings. Some of the jurors finally selected had read the publicity and had formed an opinion thereon, but all stated under oath that they would nevertheless be able to judge the case only on the evidence that they heard in the courtroom. In this unusual situation, the Court held that in spite of the sworn statements, bias must be presumed if a person in a similar situation would feel prejudice.

In contexts other than that of pretrial publicity, but still rather unique, note the presumptions of bias made in spite of the jurors' statements of impartiality in Sims v. United States, 405 F.2d 1381 (D.C. Cir. 1968) (in case involving fatal shooting of taxi driver, presumption of bias by taxi drivers and those related to them); Jackson v. United States, 395 F.2d 615 (D.C. Cir. 1968) (presumption of bias from juror's involvement in love triangle strikingly similar to one leading to murder case on trial).

For an example of an "extreme" situation when bias was not implied, because of the juror's statement that he would decide the case only on the law as given, see State v. Square, 257 La. 743, 823, 244 So. 2d 200, 229 (1971), vacated on other grounds, 408 U.S. 938 (1972) (in case where black was on trial for crime against white person, juror indicated that his past association with Ku Klux Klan would not affect his ability to be impartial); Low v. State, 156 Tex. Crim. 34, 238 S.W.2d 769 (1951) (juror said he had fixed opinion which could be removed only by evidence; held qualified after saying that he could nevertheless "go in the jury box with an open mind").

19. Swain v. Alabama, 380 U.S. 202, 220 (1965).

every jurisdiction,[20] forming a system, participated in by the litigants and the judge, for meeting the constitutional requirement that juries be impartial.[21] If any prospective juror is felt by either party to be biased, that party either may argue to the court that the person should be struck for cause and, failing that, may strike him peremptorily, or may simply initially strike him without attempting elimination for cause. Of course, neither litigant is trying to choose "impartial" jurors, but rather to eliminate those who are sympathetic to the other side, hopefully leaving only those biased *for* him. But the interplay of the efforts of both sides to accomplish the same end should leave surviving jurors who are, as Lord Coke described them, "indifferent as they stand unsworn."[22]

Lord Coke's classic definition of impartiality as "indifference" is often cited, and must mean at least that the juror is not out to hang the litigant in a particular case. It cannot mean, however, that there is a possibility of drawing many jurors who have no opinions that they will bring to bear on the evidence or on what happens in the courtroom and jury room. All people have biases and opinions that will inevitably influence their decisions and perceptions, including those on jury duty. The Supreme Court has recognized this in cases in which it finds that jury selection procedures must assure a "fair possibility for obtaining a representative cross section of the community."[23] The reason for a cross section, stated explicitly in the opinions, is that it assures that a range of biases and experiences will bear on the facts of the case. Most recently in *Peters v. Kiff,*[24] the Court upheld

---

20. For an excellent history of the peremptory challenge, *see* Moore, *Voir Dire Examination of Jurors: 1. The English Practice*, 16 Geo. L.J. 438 (1927–8).

Of ancient lineage in felony prosecutions, peremptory challenges have no history in English civil procedure. *See* 3 W. Blackstone, Commentaries *353; 1 J. Stephen, History of Criminal Law 377 (1883). As stated in the text, however, they are part of the civil procedure in America, and although there may arguably be some difference in the basis or degree of the right in civil and criminal cases, *see* notes 21 & 37 *infra*, this Essay treats civil and criminal precedents interchangeably.

In England also, the peremptory was conceived as a defendant's right, *see* 3 W. Blackstone, *supra* at *359; 1 J. Stephen, *supra* at 301, while in America the Government's right to the challenge is well recognized. In fact, the major Supreme Court cases on the importance of the peremptory challenge are those that deal with challenges exercised by the prosecutor in criminal cases. *See* Swain v. Alabama, 380 U.S. 202 (1965); Hayes v. Missouri, 120 U.S. 68 (1887). In *Hayes, supra* at 70, the Court said: "It is to be remembered that such impartiality requires not only freedom from any bias against the accused, but also from any prejudice against his prosecution. Between him and the state the scales are to be evenly held.

"Experience has shown that one of the most effective means to free the jury box from men unfit to be there is the exercise of the peremptory challenge. The public prosecutor may have the strongest reasons to distrust the character of a juror offered, from his habits and associations, and yet find it difficult to formulate and sustain a legal objection to him. . . . In such cases the peremptory challenge is a protection against his being accepted."

21. The sixth amendment has an explicit impartiality requirement that is not replicated in the seventh. But any impartial jury is surely part of the basic right to a jury trial, and inheres in due process.

22. 1 Coke, Commentary upon Littleton *§ 155b.

23. Williams v. Florida, 399 U.S. 78, 100 (1970).

24. 407 U.S. 493 (1972).

the right of a white man to challenge a jury selection system that operated to exclude blacks: "When any large and identifiable segment of the community is excluded from jury service, the effect is to remove from the jury room qualities of human nature and varieties of human experience the range of which is unknown and perhaps unknowable. It is not necessary to assume that the excluded group will consistently vote as a class in order to conclude, as we do, that its exclusion deprives the jury of *a perspective on human events that may have unsuspected importance in any case that may be presented*."[25]

The ideal of an impartial jury as seen in the "cross section of the community" cases is much more that people should be different from each other than individually "indifferent." But if the "cross section" ideal presupposes that absolute indifference will not be achieved, then implicit in the goal of having a variety of people on the jury is the idea that "impartial" jurors are ones who would at least be willing to be persuaded and influenced by the life experiences of others.

For finding these "impartial" jurors, the peremptory challenge serves functions that the challenge for cause could never fill. The first of these is didactic; the peremptory challenge teaches the litigant, and through him the community, that the jury is a good and proper mode for deciding matters and that its decision should be followed because in a real sense the jury belongs to the litigant: he chooses it. Without giving any reason or meeting any legal test, he may dismiss from "his" jury those he fears or hates the most, so that he is left with "a good opinion of the jury, the want of which might totally disconcert him; the law wills not that he should be tried by any one man against whom he has conceived a prejudice even without being able to assign a reason for such dislike."[26] The ideal that the peremptory serves is that the jury not only should be fair and impartial, but should seem to be so to those whose fortunes are at issue. As Justice Frankfurter once wrote: "The appearance of impartiality is an essential manifestation of its reality."[27]

---

25. *Id.* at 503–04 (emphasis added).

26. 3 W. BLACKSTONE, COMMENTARIES *353. Blackstone wrote that the right to challenge peremptorily is "a provision full of that tenderness and humanity to prisoners for which our English laws are justly famous. . . . How necessary it is that a prisoner (when put to defend his life) should have a good opinion of the jury, the want of which might totally disconcert him." (The reference to being "put to defend his life" suggests that the peremptory challenge applied in virtually all felonies, since the death penalty was then common.)

27. Dennis v. United States, 339 U.S. 162, 182 (1950) (Frankfurter, J., dissenting). *See* Swain v. Alabama, 380 U.S. 202, 219 (1965), *quoting In re* Murchison, 349 U.S. 133, 136 (1955): "The function of the challenge is not only to eliminate extremes of partiality on both sides, but to assure the parties that the jurors before whom they try the case will decide on the basis of the evidence placed before them, and not otherwise. In this way the peremptory satisfies the rule that 'to perform its high function in the best way "justice must satisfy the appearance of justice." ' "

A second major function of the peremptory challenge, and perhaps its most important in the modern trial, is implicated in its didactic nature. The peremptory, made without giving any reason, avoids trafficking in the core of truth in most common stereotypes. It makes unneccessary explicit entertainment of the idea that there are cases that, for example, most middle-aged civil servants would be unable to decide on the evidence or that most blacks would not rule on impartially.[28] Common human experience, common sense, psychosociological studies, and public opinion polls tell us that it is likely that certain classes of people statistically have predispositions that would make them inappropriate jurors for particular kinds of cases.[29] But to allow this knowledge to be expressed in the evaluative terms necessary for challenges for cause would undercut our desire for a society in which all people are judged as individuals and in which each is held reasonable and open to compromise. Simply stated, we do not want the following colloquy to occur in court:

> Your honor, my client is a 20-year-old black "dude" who has never held a job and is wearing $100 shoes. I move to strike for cause all black men over 45 who hold jobs as porters, janitors, or grade-level fives or lower in the government, on the ground that they will be biased against my client.

Although experience reveals that black males as a class can be biased against young alienated blacks who have not tried to join the middle class,[30] to

---

28. In Dennis v. United States, 339 U.S. 162 (1950), a well-known Communist Party member being tried for contempt of Congress challenged the ability of any government employee to judge his case, because the "loyalty" of government employees was being subject to constant scrutiny and investigation and, to quote Justice Black's dissent, *id.* at 180, "[g]overnment employees have good reason to fear that an honest vote to acquit a Communist . . . might be considered a disloyal act." Justice Frankfurter sought from the Court a recognition that in some instances it was desirable to exercise "psychological judgments" about classes of people, and simply hold that they could not sit in a case; in *Dennis*, Frankfurter would have held that government employees as a class should be automatically disqualified, just as those related to either party are disqualified, or those who have a financial interest in the outcome. *Id.* at 181 (dissenting opinion). But a majority of the Court would not enlarge the situations "for disqualifying a whole class on the ground of bias." *Id.* at 181.

In the cases requiring that jury panels represent a cross section of the community, the Supreme Court has recognized, however, that there are group biases and that these may influence the functioning of the jury. Unless there are certain attitudes and mind-sets that can be associated with certain groups, there would be no need for a cross section. *See* Ballard v. United States, 329 U.S. 187 (1946) (women must be included in cross section); Thiel v. Southern Pacific Co., 328 U.S. 217 (1946) (economic and social classes); Glasser v. United States, 315 U.S. 60 (1942) (private organizations); Smith v. Texas, 311 U.S. 128 (1940) (racial groups).

29. *See, e.g.,* Simon, *The Influence of Social Status and Attitudes on the Jury's Decisions,* in THE JURY AND THE DEFENSE OF INSANITY 97 (1967); Robinson, *Bias, Probability and Trial by Jury,* 15 AM. SOCIOL. REV. 73 (1950).

30. An example of the use of the peremptory challenge by black defendants in a criminal case to eliminate most middle-class and older blacks occurred in the trial of 21 members of the Black Panther party for multiple charges of violent crimes in New York in 1969, State v. Shakur, No. 1848–69 (Super. Ct. N.Y., May 13, 1971). As described by Zimroth, *How They Picked the Panther 21 Jury,* JURIS DOCTOR, July–Aug. 1974, at 38, the defendants challenged about as many prospective black jurors as did the prosecution. Among those challenged was "a fifty-two-year-old black Post Office employee, who testified that he knew nothing about the Black Panther Party and almost nothing about Malcolm X or Marcus Garvey, never had any experience with police brutality, didn't read *The*

enunciate this in the concrete expression required of a challenge for cause
is societally divisive. Instead we have evolved in the peremptory challenge
a system that allows the covert expression of what we dare not say but know
is true more often that not.[31]

Challenges for cause, moreover, could not effectively screen those who
share biases and prejudices common to a racial or ethnic group, or an economic or social class. Such challenges depend on the juror's admitting actual bias or grounds for implied bias. Some jurors will intentionally deceive
the court, perhaps because they are ashamed to admit attitudes that are
socially unfashionable or even because they might welcome the chance to
seek retaliation against a litigant. Other jurors are simply not aware of
their prejudices or underestimate the impact of their biases on their ability
to weigh the evidence. This phenomenon is especially likely to occur in
cases of group bias where the individual juror may have no inkling that
his views are not shared by others outside his own group or that his attitudes so profoundly color his perceptions that he may be incapable of accepting testimony with an open mind.[32]

Another important function of the peremptory challenge is as a shield
for the exercise of the challenge for cause. Questioning in order to inves-

---

Amsterdam News (a major newspaper for the black community in New York), didn't 'think much
about [black power],' . . . accepted a segregated way of life, . . . thought that 'you've got to
have law and order around.' " *Id.* at 40.

Also challenged by the defense was a prospective juror "who worked for the New York State
Insurance Fund, said he hadn't been bothered by being in a segregated unit in the Army, . . .
thought that in general the police 'are a fine bunch of young men.' When asked about the difference
in living standards between whites and blacks he responded, 'People should try to better themselves.' " *Id.*

The account by Zimroth portrays the amazement of the defendants, their court followers, and
lawyers at such statements by blacks. But it is a common experience for criminal defense lawyers
who represent black clients to find many situations in which whites are less biased toward a black
defendant than a member of his own race.

Although the Panther trial is a good illustration for the textual statement that "black men as a
class can be biased against young alienated blacks," it is not a good example of the use of the peremptory challenge to prevent public dealing in the realities of class and group bias. In the Panther
trial, voir dire was greatly abused, and the prospective jurors were hostilely examined by attorneys
and by defendants who were representing themselves. Jeers and snide remarks were thrown at
jurors, and purely rhetorical voir dire questions were asked before jurors were struck peremptorily.
Id.

31. The idea that the peremptory challenge is the proper device for the litigant's expression of
his insights and feelings about the suitability for jury service of a member of a particular group led
the Court to observe in Swain v. Alabama, 380 U.S. 202, 218 (1965), that although peremptory
challenges are rarely made in England, "peremptories were and are freely used and relied upon in
this country, perhaps because juries here are drawn from a greater cross section of a heterogeneous
society." When there are a great many societal divisions, the numbers and kinds of biases held by
groups against each other are also great, so that in a heterogeneous society, any litigant has an increased chance of perceiving possible prejudice toward himself.

32. "It seems unlikely that a prejudiced juror would recognize his own personal prejudice—or
knowing it, would admit it. . . . What is more, the more prejudiced or bigoted the jurors, the less
can they be expected to confess forthrightly and candidly their state of mind in open court. The more
naive or sincere juror, who might be likely to discard prior knowledge for the purpose of his decision-making duty, would probably be more ready to acknowledge his state of mind and thus be
challenged." A. FRIENDLY & R. GOLDFARB, CRIME AND PUBLICITY 103 (1967).

tigate the appropriateness of a cause challenge may have so alienated a potential juror that, although the lawyer has not established any basis for removal, the process itself has made it necessary to strike the juror peremptorily. Without the insurance of the peremptory challenge, a party would be far less able to search for cause to eliminate jurors.

When the peremptory challenge is analyzed functionally, as above, it appears to be much more than mere custom or a supplement to challenges for cause.[33] Rather, as was stated in *Swain v. Alabama,* "[t]he persistence of peremptories and their extensive use demonstrate the long and widely held belief that peremptory challenge is a necessary part of trial by jury."[34] *Swain* is strong precedent because in the name of the sanctity of the peremptory challenge, the Court upheld the prosecutorial striking of all blacks from a jury that was to try a black man accused of the rape of a white woman. The basis for the Court's ruling on these highly charged facts was the critical importance of the peremptory challenge and the implicit finding that its essence would be lost were the motives for its exercise open for review.[35] The symbolic-educative, impartiality-promoting role of the peremptory challenge makes it central to the jury trial right.

Stilson v. United States,[36] is, however, often quoted for the proposition that the peremptory challenge is merely a statutory privilege which may be withheld altogether without impairing the constitutional guarantees of an impartial jury and a fair trial.[37] The statement in *Stilson,* however, is

---

33. In determining the incidents of jury trial, "the relevant inquiry . . . must be the function that the particular feature performs and its relation to the purpose of jury trial." Williams v. Florida, 399 U.S. 78, 99–100 (1970) (holding that a 12-person jury was not an incident of jury trial guarantee).

34. 390 U.S. 202, 219 (1965).

35. Mainly because of its abusive reading of the facts in the case, *Swain* prompted numerous critical commentaries. The criticisms were not, however, directed at the holding on the importance of the peremptory challenge. *See, e.g.,* Comment, Swain v. Alabama: *A Constitutional Blueprint for the Perpetuation of the All-White Jury,* 52 VA. L. REV. 1157 (1966); *The Supreme Court, 1964 Term,* 79 HARV. L. REV. 56, 135 (1965); Comment, *Fair Jury Selection Procedures,* 75 YALE L.J. 322 (1965).

36. 250 U.S. 584 (1919).

37. Swain v. Alabama, 380 U.S. at 219, *quoting* Stilson v. United States, 250 U.S. at 586. The sixth amendment in its original draft contained an explicit provision for the right to challenge jurors: "The trial of all crimes . . . shall be by an impartial jury of freeholders of the vicinage, with the requisite of unanimity for conviction, of the right of challenge and other accustomed requisites . . . ." 1 ANNALS OF CONG. 435 (1789). The amendment was altered in the Senate to eliminate the specific references to the common law features of the jury trial for reasons that are unclear because there are no records of the Senate debates on the sixth amendment. *See* F. HELLER, THE SIXTH AMENDMENT 31–33 (1951). It does not appear, however, that the reference to challenges was removed because the Senate did not consider it an appropriate appendage to the jury trial. Madison wrote that the explicit vicinity requirement was the only feature of the common law jury that was specifically objected to by the Senate. *See* 1 LETTERS AND OTHER WRITINGS OF JAMES MADISON 491, 492–93 (1865). Rather, it seems likely that the Senate's editing of the Madison version rested on the "assumption that the most prominent features of the jury would be preserved as a matter of course." Williams v. Florida, 399 U.S. 78, 123 n.9 (1970) (Harlan, J., concurring).

As a matter of logic, the impartiality of the jury is as much a part of the seventh as of the sixth amendment jury trial guarantee, and as much a part of due process in a civil as in a criminal

based on a reading of history that has been subject to revision and correction. More than four decades later, contrary to the implications of *Stilson*,[38] the Court in *Swain* found that from the time of the first jury trials, peremptory challenges were allowable in noncapital felonies.[39] *Swain*'s approach to the importance of the peremptory challenge is so radically different from *Stilson*'s—not only in its reading of history but generally—that it could be read as a virtual overruling of *Stilson*.

Even in *Stilson*, moreover, the Court acknowledged that the peremptory challenge had always been considered necessary in a capital case.[40] Yet the purpose of the peremptory to promote impartiality applies equally to noncapital cases—and of course, since almost all felonies were capital cases in English history, historically the peremptory was broadly applicable. Finally, quite aside from the impartial jury guarantee, the peremptory challenge is inherent in the jury trial right itself, a position that the *Stilson* Court did not consider. In *Lewis v. United States*, the Court said: "The right of challenge comes from the common law with the trial itself, and has always been held essential to the fairness of trial by jury."[41]

Given the importance of the peremptory challenge, then, "any system that prevents or embarrasses the full, unrestricted exercise of that right of challenge must be condemned."[42] The limited voir dire does prevent and

---

case. Yet it might be argued that the importance of the defendant's belief in the fairness of the jury, the explicit impartiality guarantee in the sixth amendment (not repeated in the seventh), and the fact that biases and prejudices are more likely to be at work in the heated facts of a criminal case, make the constitutional basis of peremptories more certain in that context. The number of peremptory challenges is generally significantly greater in criminal cases. *Compare* FED. R. CRIM. P. 24 *with* FED. R. CIV. P. 47(a); the difference could be read as a recognition that they are more important to the criminal trial, or could be merely a matter of history. At any rate, legislators and rulemakers everywhere have assumed the peremptory challenge as part of due process and jury trial procedure in civil cases.

The Third and Tenth Circuit Courts of Appeals have recognized the centrality of the peremptory challenge to the civil trial in Kiernan v. Van Schaik, 347 F.2d 775 (3d Cir. 1965), and Photostat v. Ball, 338 F.2d 783 (10th Cir. 1964). Both reversed jury verdicts in personal injury cases because defects in the voir dire procedure impaired counsel's ability to exercise peremptory challenges. In *Kiernan*, the court refused to ask questions about the connection with or general knowledge of the insurance business by the prospective jurors. The basis for the trial court's ruling was that such questions were in aid of the peremptory challenge, and voir dire could be directed only at questions that would be the basis for cause challenges. The Third Circuit found this an "erroneous principle," and held the peremptory challenge and the concomitant right to ascertain information for its exercise through voir dire to be necessary to the fairness of a civil trial. In *Ball*, somewhat ambiguous questions were asked by the judge on voir dire, resulting in the failure of four jurors to reveal information about their own prior automobile accidents. While implicitly acknowledging that these facts, if known, would not have necessitated removing the jurors for cause, the Tenth Circuit held that the failure to bring forth the prior accident information interfered with the exercise of the peremptory challenge, and that "the denial or substantial impairment of the statutory right of peremptory challenge is prejudicial to the constitutional right to a fair and impartial jury." 338 F.2d at 786.

38. In holding that "[t]he number of challenges is left to be regulated by the common law" or congressional enactments, 250 U.S. at 586, the *Stilson* Court necessarily presumed that the common law heritage of peremptory challenges was of rather limited scope.

39. 380 U.S. at 212 n.9.

40. 250 U.S. at 586.

41. 146 U.S. 370, 376 (1892).

42. Pointer v. United States, 151 U.S. 396, 408 (1893).

embarrass the right of challenge because it leaves the parties without access, provided by the judicial system, to a reasonable amount of information for making challenges. Full voir dire is, moreover, peculiarly necessary to the peremptory challenge, as compared with the challenge for cause.

For one reason, many of the issues on which questioning is done for the exercise of peremptories differ from those around which challenges for cause are formed. This, of course, means that the peremptory simply requires that additional questions be asked. *Brundage v. United States*[43] illustrates this point: At issue was the trial court's refusal to question the prospective jurors fully on the issue of mental illness, when there was an insanity defense. The judge had informed the prospective jurors that

> lack of mental capacity to commit the offense charged had been raised as a defense and that the burden was on the government to prove mental capacity to commit the offense. They were then asked whether any of them had a fixed view point on the subject of mental incapacity and if each and every one of them had an open mind and would listen to the evidence and base their verdict on the law of the case as given to them by the court.[44]

These questions are all very well for the cause challenge, but trial counsel wanted to "delve further on the question of mental illness," and to ask "particularly whether mental illness had affected any of the jurors' lives in any way either through friend, relative or acquaintance and whether they were acquainted with any psychiatrists, psychologists or other specialists in diseases of the mind and whether they had any experiences or preconceptions so far as the general character of insanity in a criminal case."[45] While none of the questions sought by counsel, except the last, would even arguably elicit answers that could be the basis for a strike for cause, answers to all of them would be extremely helpful in determining whether to exercise a peremptory challenge.[46]

Secondly, even on the issues that might be the basis either of a peremptory or of a challenge for cause, more exploration is needed for the peremp-

---

43. 365 F.2d 616 (10th Cir. 1966).
44. *Id.* at 618.
45. *Id.*
46. Another example may aid in the explication of this point. One piece of received wisdom about jury selection is that people who are good at dealing with others generally make the best jurors. Thus, a person who worked alone most of the time might not be considered appropriate by a particular litigant. If voir dire were limited to very basic information about jurors, the litigant might know only that a prospective juror was, for example, a mathematician, infer that she works alone, and exercise a peremptory on that basis. Yet before such a challenge was entered by a litigant who wanted only gregarious people on his jury, should he not be allowed to ask whether in fact the prospective juror works alone, how long she has done so, how she feels about it, what her hobbies are? One purpose of the peremptory is to allow the party to choose a jury that appears fair and impartial to him. His notions and psychological judgments about the kind of people he wants on the jury may be strictly intuitive and even irrational, but he should be given access to the information to exercise the judgments meaningfully.

tory. Racial bias is an example. When questioned about racial bias, the potential juror very quickly denies it or denies that it would influence her in deciding the case. Thus ends the inquiry for the challenge for cause. But for the exercise of his peremptories, the litigant would continue on in this vein: Does the person know any blacks socially? Does she believe in affirmative action, interracial marriage, busing?[47] The prospective juror's demeanor in answering these questions, as well as the answers, may give much basis for striking peremptorily, though no cause challenge could be made. It is simply in the very nature of the peremptory that deeper, further-ranging questions are necessary for its meaningful exercise.

III. Constitutional Problems Caused by Limiting Voir Dire

For reasons bound up with due process of law and fortified by equal protection considerations, the limited voir dire is far from a mere failure to preserve a procedural nicety. Limiting voir dire creates a situation in which the ability of a person to choose a jury by any method other than through a "meaningless ritual"[48] "depends on the amount of money he has."[49] The poor litigant is left with the answers to a few short questions as the basis for exercising his challenges. The wealthy makes his jury selection on much sounder grounds. For a substantial fee, jury investigation services will compile dossiers on all of the prospective jurors, including information such as party, church, social and other affiliations, family configurations, employment records, and financial standing.[50] Very rich lit-

---

47. United States v. Bowe, 360 F.2d 1 (2d Cir. 1966), illustrates the practical difference between the kinds of questions which might be asked for a challenge for cause and for peremptories. The defendant sought to inquire about the membership of the prospective jurors in specific organizations such as the Ku Klux Klan and the Minute Men. But the Second Circuit Court of Appeals found sufficient the trial court's questions as to whether any of the venire had "any bias or prejudice against a person who is a member of the Negro race;" whether any of them was "a member of any organization which is opposed to equal rights under the law or is opposed to racial equality and religious equality;" and whether "you . . . realize that . . . justice must be dispensed regardless of race, color [or] creed. . . . Is there anybody who has any feeling about this subject that suggests that he or she should be excused from jury service in this case?" Id. at 9. The appellate court characterized this as a "thorough and straightforward examination." Id.

　　Bowe is also a good example of the difference between court- and counsel-conducted voir dire in that the questions by the court are abstract and unlikely to elicit responses. See text accompanying note 15 supra.

48. Douglas v. California, 372 U.S. 353, 358 (1963).

49. Griffin v. Illinois, 351 U.S. 12, 19 (1956).

50. See Okun, Investigation of Jurors by Counsel: Its Impact on the Decisional Process, 56 Geo. L.J. 839, 851 (1968). The investigation of jurors crops up occasionally in reported cases, although understandably it is a low-visibility process. In Kiernan v. Van Schaik, 347 F.2d 775, 777 (3d Cir. 1965), for instance, one reason given for the denial of certain voir dire examination questions was that "Delaware counsel—including those who appeared in this case—subscribe to the services of an investigating agency which supplies them with information on all prospective jurors in the federal and state courts." In a Third Circuit case, Dow v. Carnegie Ill. Steel Corp., 224 F.2d 414, 430 (3d Cir. 1955), some of the methods employed by the investigative services were revealed: "When jury lists were made up, the investigator obtained copies from various lawyers, then proceeded to converse, usually by telephone, with the various jurors' friends and neighbors, whose names were obtained from street directories. The investigator testified as to the extent of his questioning of those whom

igants eschew these services and hire their own investigators to find out even more revealing information: How is the juror regarded by his neighbors? What bumper stickers does he sport? What magazines does he read? How does he spend his spare time? What are his social habits?[51] Interestingly, the methods of the rich have been replicated by some poor litigants whose political causes make scores of volunteer investigators available to them.[52]

Recently wealthy and "political" defendants have employed social scientists and psychologists to guide their attorneys in decisions about questions for voir dire and the exercise of peremptory challenges. As reported by *New York Magazine* in the case against former Attorney General John Mitchell and former Secretary of Commerce Maurice Stans, the defendants commissioned a "communications" specialist, who ran a poll by telephone in New York City to determine the exposure of the public to prejudicial publicity. In conducting the poll, the specialist allegedly discovered a relationship between the amount of publicity-induced bias among the citizens interviewed and other demographic and ethnic characteristics. Therefore, he advised the attorneys to seek a jury of working-class Catholics, neither rich nor poor ($8,000 to $10,000 annual income), and readers of the *New York Daily News*. To be avoided were the college-educated, Jews, and readers of the *New York Times* and the *New York Post*.[53] As reported in the media, an even more intensive demographic survey was made in the trial of seven anti–Vietnam War demonstrators in Harrisburg, Pennsylvania, in which 850 calls were made in a telephone survey, and then a

he contacted: 'I ask the neighbor if they knew this particular person that is called, and if it is a man, where he is employed, if he is married, if he has any children, whether they'd be old enough to work, and if they did work if the neighbor would know where they worked; if they were younger, were they of school age or still younger than that; about how old the man was; if he owned his own property there; if he knew if he ever had any cases in court litigation; if he had ever been hurt in any accident and if they knew their politics or religion.' "

51. *See* White, *Selecting the Jury*, in SUCCESSFUL JURY TRIALS 121 (J. Appleman ed. 1952).

52. Popular accounts of the major political trials of the early 1970's give some hints of the jury investigation methods. *See, e.g.*, Ungar, *The Pentagon Papers Trial*, ATLANTIC MONTHLY, Nov. 1972, at 22, 25: "Sometimes both sides case the prospective jurors' neighborhoods and find out how and with whom they spend their spare time . . . . As each new group of veniremen was called to the jury box, staff from each side—FBI agents and members of the defense 'law commune'—nearly collided with each other as they scurried in and out of the courtroom to assemble information for the lawyers."

Etzioni, in an article entitled *Science: Threatening the Jury Trial*, Washington Post, May 26, 1974, at C3, col. 1, mentions field investigations of the prospective jurors. *See* Kahn, *Picking Peers: Social Scientists' Role in Selection of Juries Sparks Legal Debate*, Wall St. J., Aug. 12, 1974, at 1, col. 1. A National Lawyers Guild mimeographed instruction sheet tells volunteers, "How to Research Prospective Jurors in Santa Clara County [California]": "In the Registrar of Voters Office, for instance, are voter registration affidavits which contain political party, birthplace, registration date, voter's occupation, petitions signed, changes of registration, etc. In addition, the voter's relatives can be checked, as well as the nature of the petitions which the voter has signed." Volunteer jury investigators are also advised to engage in "Direct Observation," "to check out the prospective juror's car and house for bumper stickers, posters, flags, etc. Don't be intrusive."

53. *See* DiMona, *The Real Surprise of the Mitchell-Stans Trial*, N.Y. MAGAZINE, July 8, 1974, at 31; Etzioni, *supra* note 52; Kahn, *supra* note 52.

sample was chosen for face-to-face interviewing, in order to ascertain the characteristics of local people that correlated with favorable attitudes toward the defense.[54] In the trial of Angela Davis,[55] a team of psychiatrists and

---

54. The jury selection and the activities of the social scientists are described at length in Schulman, Shaver, Colman, Emrich & Christie, *Recipe for a Jury*, PSYCHOL. TODAY, May 1973, at 37. The social scientists trained 45 volunteers from the Harrisburg area to do face-to-face interviewing in the homes of respondents. *Id.* at 40. Two hundred and fifty-two people were interviewed on issues such as: media contact; knowledge of the defendants and their case; the greatest Americans during the past 10 or 15 years; trust in the government (*e.g.*, "Would you say the Government is pretty much run for a few big interests looking out for themselves, or is it run for the benefit of the people?"); ages and activities of respondents' children; religious attitudes and commitment; spare-time activities; organizational memberships; their view of the scale of acceptable antiwar activities; other attitudes potentially related to the trial (*e.g.*, "Do you agree with the statement that 'people should support their country even when they feel strongly that federal authorities are wrong'?"). *Id.* Some of the discoveries about local attitudes were as follows: "Religion was significantly related to all the attitudes that concerned us. . . . Certain religious categories—e.g., Episcopalians, Presbyterians, Methodists, and fundamentalists—were 'bad' enough from our point of view to warrant exclusion from the jury unless there were strong reasons to the contrary. (The 'better' religions were Catholic, Brethren, and Lutheran.)

"Education and contact with metropolitan news media, which usually are linked with liberal attitudes, were associated in our sample with conservatism. College-educated people, especially over 30, were more likely to be Republicans, to be businessmen, to be members of local civic organizations. They were more likely to read metropolitan newspapers, but were also more likely to read conservative magazines. Later we learned that liberal college-educated people and younger college graduates tend to leave Harrisburg for more liberal pastures. This fact was by no means obvious to us or to the defense lawyers before the survey, and it was to play an important part in the jury selection." *Id.*

The same technique, with less success since three of the defendants were convicted of felonious assault, was followed in the Wounded Knee trials, where Native Americans were tried in St. Paul, Minn., for conspiracy and other major crimes in connection with the 1973 armed occupation of Wounded Knee, S. Dak. Kahn, *supra* note 52, at 1, col. 1, reported that: "Before the trial, sixty volunteers, varying from professors to housewives, conducted telephone interviews with 575 people chosen at random from voting lists in the judicial district surrounding St. Paul. Interviewers probed attitudes toward the government, police, and Indians, in an attempt to uncover prejudice. A computer correlated the responses with demographic information—such as age, sex, religion and occupation—to predict what sort of people would make the best jurors from the defense's standpoint.

"The data indicated that persons of Germanic or Norwegian origin would be apt to deal harshly with the defendants, while college-educated jurors were likely to be more lenient. Age, sex and political party seemed in this case to be irrelevant."

As a result of these tactics, the warning has been sounded that: "The jury's impartiality is threatened because defense attorneys have discovered that by using social science techniques, they can manipulate the composition of juries to significantly increase the likelihood that their clients will be acquitted." Etzioni, *supra* note 52, at C3, col. 1 (discussing mainly the Mitchell-Stans jury selection). The allegation of a high probability of success is certainly unproved on the basis of the cases in which such techniques have been used. In the Mitchell-Stans trial itself, the most persuasive juror and the one who led the deliberations to acquittal did not meet the demographic demands of the social scientists in any way. Kahn, *supra* note 52, at 19, col. 5. In the Wounded Knee trials, the defendants were convicted. As discussed earlier, psychological assessments of whether blacks, Catholics, women, salespeople would be appropriate jurors for the defense, for instance, are exactly what lawyers have been making from time immemorial in exercising peremptory challenges. Can it really be said that the addition of social science insights changes the very nature of the process and risks the impartiality of the jury?

In other words, the judgments of a skilled lawyer about the kinds of people he wants on the jury have always been psychological evaluations and there is certainly no evidence so far that the evaluations of the social scientists are essentially different from the kind of assessments attorneys make anyway. Professor Hans Zeisel says, for instance, that when the jury selection process is studied empirically, experienced trial lawyers, unassisted by social scientists, were able to predict accurately how jurors would vote in mock trials. *Id.* Ramsey Clark, former Attorney General of the United States and one of the defense lawyers in the Harrisburg case, has been quoted as saying of the social science research of juries: "I doubt that it is revealing any great secrets of human society which human nature hasn't already detected." *Id.* Finally, the inferences that are drawn about the reactions of an individual, from the fact, for instance, that she is a wealthy reader of the *New York Times* (therefore conservative and respectful of authority), are at best extremely uncertain and, even when her initial reactions are as expected, they will often be tempered by the interplay of personalities and deliberation in the jury room.

55. People v. Davis, Cr. No. 52613 (Super. Ct., Santa Clara Cty., Cal., May 4, 1972).

psychologists observed the lengthy voir dire examination and advised the defense attorneys about making peremptory challenges.[56]

The Government, too, has its methods for overcoming the deficiencies of the voir dire examination and assuring—at least in important cases—that it has sufficient information for choosing a jury. Jurors' tax and criminal records are often available to the prosecutor on an "informal" basis, as are police and FBI agents as investigators.[57] Prosecutors are, moreover, in court daily, and so as the term of jury service progresses, they learn and, in many offices, compile information about the voting and other habits of jurors.[58]

That all of those who can afford to obtain such information do so is, as the Supreme Court said of the right to counsel, evidence for believing that information about prospective jurors is not a "luxury" but a "necessity."[59] If the peremptory challenge is a necessary part of the right to trial by an impartial jury, then the state must provide the means for exercising it meaningfully. The best analogy is to the right-to-counsel cases. The sixth amendment guarantees counsel; therefore, as a matter of due process, the state must furnish lawyers to those unable to afford them: "[R]eason and reflection require us to recognize that in our adversary system of criminal justice, any person haled into court, who is too poor to hire a lawyer, cannot be assured a fair trial unless counsel is provided for him."[60] Knowledge about the background of jurors is necessary to selection of an impartial jury;

---

56. *See* Sage, *Psychology and the Angela Davis Jury*, HUMAN BEHAVIOR, Jan. 1973, at 56–61; Robinson, *How Psychology Helped Free Angela*, EBONY, Feb. 1973, at 44.

57. The practice of using the juror's tax records came to light in United States v. Costello, 255 F.2d 876 (2d Cir.), *cert. denied*, 357 U.S. 937 (1958), in which the prosecuting attorneys involved testified that because this was a tax evasion case, they sought the records to make sure that the jurors did not have tax problems of their own. *See* Okun, *supra* note 50, at 853 n.54.

For a case in which surfaced the use of the FBI to investigate prospective jurors, *see* Best v. United States, 184 F.2d 131 (1st Cir. 1950); Okun, *supra* note 50, at 854. Okun argues that the prosecutor's use of the FBI and the police is far more effective than any investigative tool that the defense might employ, because people are generally more likely to answer questions posed by government agents. *Id.* at 853.

58. In Hamer v. United States, 259 F.2d 274, 280 n.7 (9th Cir. 1958), such a compilation was described: "It lists some two hundred and fifty or three hundred jurors, one on each looseleaf page. Of one juror it said: 'This Juror very poor.—held up jury for 4 hours 11–1.' On each of the other eleven jurors who had sat with this juror there appeared the notation that they had sat on this same jury that R . . . had held up for four hours. (These were the 'twelve times' referred to by the court below that a reference had been made in the book to an individual juror's action in the jury room.) A second juror 'caused the jury to be hung several hours.' The address and business, or the spouse's business, and the age of most jurors were given; how long they had lived in Southern California; their former place of residence; number of children, etc.

"One juror was characterized as inattentive, another as having a hard time staying awake during later stages of trial; another juror listened carefully; 'this juror slept during trial—was excused by the Court;' this juror was attentive to instructions; one was characterized as a strong juror for the government, another as 'too sympathetic to boys in handcuffs;' another as an outstanding juror (after voting four times for conviction in government cases).

"All other comments in the book had to do with juries as a whole—'excellent jury;' 'good attentive jury;' 'verdict in less than 20 min.;' 'took 4 hours on simple case;' etc., 'good jury, quick verdict.' "

Prosecutors' jury books also often include the arrest and conviction records of potential jurors. *See* Losavio v. Mayber, —— Colo. ——, 496 P.2d 1032 (1972); Commonwealth v. Smith, 350 Mass. 600, 215 N.E.2d 897 (1966); People v. Aldridge, 47 Mich. App. 639, 209 N.W.2d 796 (1973).

59. *See* Gideon v. Wainwright, 372 U.S. 335, 344 (1963).

60. *Id.* at 344.

therefore, the state must provide access to this information for those who cannot afford to gather it themselves.

The due process analysis is fortified by the unequal protection of the laws inhering in the disparate effect, on the rich and the poor litigant, of the efforts to limit voir dire. But does it follow from this observation that some means adequate for gathering information must be made available to poor litigants? After all, the law cannot make people "economically equal before its bar of justice. . . . Some can afford better lawyers and better investigations of their cases."[61] Some can also afford the opportunity to be more informed in jury selection than others. Isn't it an irremediable fact of life that the rich will be better served? The answer is yes, but *"differences in access to instruments needed to vindicate legal rights*, when based upon the financial situation of the defendant, are repugnant to the Constitution."[62] Through the equal protection doctrine, courts have been trying for more than two decades to move closer to "[p]roviding equal justice for poor and rich, weak and powerful . . . ."[63] The first case was *Griffin v. Illinois*, in which the Supreme Court found a constitutional violation because indigent defendants could not afford the transcript necessary for an appeal. The analogy is obvious: because of his limited means, the poor person cannot obtain the information necessary to effect his challenges.

In the leading case among *Griffin*'s progeny, *Douglas v. California*, the Court held that counsel must be afforded for a nondiscretionary appeal. A California rule of criminal procedure provided that before an indigent would have counsel on appeal, the appellate court must make "an independent investigation of the record and determine whether it would be of advantage to the defendant or helpful to the appellate court to have counsel appointed."[64] The wealthy litigant, of course, simply hired counsel and filed his brief. The United States Supreme Court found in this procedure a "discrimination against the indigent. For there can be no equal justice where the kind of an appeal a man enjoys 'depends on the amount of money he has.' "[65] California's rule afforded the indigent only "a meaningless ritual," rather than a meaningful procedure.[66] Just so, the perfunctory little voir dire ceremony is a meaningless ritual for the indigent, as compared with the elaborate information available to the wealthy for jury selection. Having established a system for jury selection of which the peremptory challenge is a critical part, the state should equalize the opportunity to make effective use of it.

61. Griffin v. Illinois, 351 U.S. 12, 28–29 (1956) (Burton & Minton, JJ., dissenting).
62. Roberts v. LaVallee, 389 U.S. 40, 42 (1967) (emphasis added).
63. Griffin v. Illinois, 351 U.S. 12, 16 (1956).
64. Douglas v. California, 372 U.S. 353, 355 (1963), *quoting* People v. Hyde, 51 Cal. 2d 152, 154, 331 P.2d 42, 43 (1958).
65. 372 U.S. at 355, *quoting* Griffin v. Illinois, 351 U.S. at 19.
66. 372 U.S. at 358.

Although *Griffin* and *Douglas* are essentially equal protection cases, there is a strand of due process analysis in both. Thus, in *Douglas*, the Court stated: "When an indigent is forced to run this gantlet of a preliminary showing of merit, the right to appeal does not comport with fair procedure."[67] In context, however, the due process argument is not compelling because the Court in *Douglas* found that the state was not required to provide an appeal at all. If the procedure itself is something of a frill, the requirement that it be fair is naturally less convincing.[68] The right of peremptory challenge, however, unlike an appeal, does rest on constitutional guarantees, thus making the argument forceful that its dilution denies due process as well as implicating equal protection of the laws.

IV. Conclusion

Because of the constitutional problems caused by the limitation of voir dire examination, the efforts of those interested in the administration of justice should be directed to expanding its effectiveness for all litigants. This is not to say, however, that it is impossible or wrong to seek ways in which to assure that voir dire in all instances does not go to the extremes it has in a few cases.[69] Experiments are needed in methods for making voir dire quickly productive of information without constitutionally undercutting it. A sworn questionnaire, for instance, might gather from jurors answers to basic questions about themselves with face-to-face inquiry reduced to certain key issues on which the reactions of the individual and observation of her or his manner are important.[70] New York has experimented

---

67. *Id.* at 357.

68. The Supreme Court recognized this in Ross v. Moffit, 94 S. Ct. 2437 (1974), a case in which it refused to extend the *Griffin–Douglas* rationale to discretionary review to the highest state court or to the United States Supreme Court. Specifically, the Court found the due process argument less convincing in a situation where the "defendant needs an attorney on appeal not as a shield to protect him against being 'haled into court' by the State and stripped of his presumption of innocence, but rather as a sword to upset the prior determination of guilt. The difference is significant for, while no one would agree that the State may simply dispense with the trial stage of proceedings without a criminal defendant's consent, it is clear that the State need not provide any appeal at all." *Id.* at 2444.

69. *See, e.g.*, State v. Seale, Cr. No. 15844 (Super. Ct., New Haven Cty., Conn., 1971) (13 weeks of voir dire and examination of 1,550 veniremen; 12 jurors and 2 alternates selected); People v. Manson, Cr. No. A253156 (Super. Ct., L.A. Cty., Cal., 1971) (6-week voir dire, 180 veniremen examined; 12 jurors and 6 alternates); People v. Sirhan, Cr. No. A233421 (Super. Ct., L.A. Cty., Cal., 1971) (6-week voir dire, 250 veniremen examined to pick jury of 12 and 6 alternates). These are, however, the unusual cases. Levit, Nelson, Ball & Chernick, *supra* note 2, at 935, 948, reports on the basis of an extended study in the Los Angeles Superior Courts that: (1) where the attorneys conducted the interrogation virtually without court supervision, the average voir dire took 135 minutes; and (2) where the attorneys and judges shared in conducting the interrogation, the average voir dire took 111 minutes; and (3) where the judge alone conducted the questioning, the average voir dire took 64 minutes. *See* F. MERRILL & L. SCHRAGE, A PILOT STUDY OF UTILIZATION OF JURORS (1970), which found the following data in a Missouri study: the voir dire for civil cases averaged 85 minutes, or only 9% of the total time of the trial.

70. In the context of a report on limiting voir dire examination, an Illinois judicial conference committee recommended giving certain information to attorneys about all jurors so that they would not need to spend the time asking about it. The suggested information was: address, occupation of juror and spouse, employer's name and address, real estate holdings, marital status, and number of children. ILLINOIS JUDICIAL CONFERENCE COMM. ON LIMITATION OF VOIR DIRE EXAMINATION, REPORT 9, JUNE

with an attorney-conducted voir dire that does not involve the judge, except when there are contested questions.[71] Voir dire generally should be
governed by more standard and detailed rules, rather than the present
haphazard procedure, often varying from courtroom to courtroom within
a single building, investing practically unreviewable discretion in the trial
judge for its conduct. Such rules might provide for litigation of the scope
of voir dire in a special hearing tailored to the facts of each case. The idea
of a mini-hearing on the appropriateness of certain areas of voir dire has
been expressed in some recent cases. Justice Marshall in *Ham v. South
Carolina* intimated that before questioning on some issues, a showing
should be made of the likelihood that there was prejudice abroad.[72] In
United States v. Robinson,[73] the Circuit Court of Appeals for the District
of Columbia suggested that an attorney seeking to question prospective
jurors about their attitudes on the law of self-defense should have sought
to present argument and evidence that this was a disfavored doctrine in
the community from which the jurors were drawn. The opinion pointed
out that on some issues, such as racial bias, courts have long judicially noticed likely bias in any community, making unnecessary a hearing on the
relevance or propriety of questions directed toward this issue. Even as to
racial prejudice, however, a hearing as to the scope and type of questions
to be asked might be useful. This need not be a vastly time-consuming
process; during the pretrial period the attorneys would present the areas
and questions they think relevant to revealing bias in the circumstances
of their case. Once the matters to be investigated were agreed upon, the
scope of necessary questions could also be argued and decided.

There is, moreover, an emerging standard for deciding the appropriateness of lines of inquiry. In *United States v. Dellinger*,[74] which reversed
convictions of political activists, the Seventh Circuit Court of Appeals held
that there should have been inquiry as requested by counsel into the jurors'
attitudes on protests against the Vietnam War and the values of the youth
culture, and into the relationship of the jurors to law enforcement officers.
The amount of inquiry should be adequate to create a reasonable assurance

---

12–13 (1958). A more extensive questionnaire would be more revealing and would concomitantly
reduce the need for extended face-to-face questioning. Examples of questions that need not necessarily
be asked in person but whose answers would be revealing are: What magazines do you read? Do you
have any bumper stickers on your car? What do they say? What are your hobbies? What jobs have
you held in the past 10 years?

Face-to-face questioning would then be reserved for the issues on which probing is necessary,
such as prejudice against the litigant or bias arising from the facts of the particular case.

71. Both the New York method and some experiments with it in Los Angeles courts are fully
described in Levit, Nelson, Ball & Chernick, *supra* note 2, at 931–46.

72. 409 U.S. 524, 533 (1973) (Marshall, J., concurring). For a brief description of the case,
see text accompanying notes 8–9 *supra*.

73. 475 F.2d 376 (D.C. Cir. 1973).

74. 472 F.2d 340 (7th Cir. 1972).

that the defendants would receive a trial free from prejudices that might arise against them because of the prospective jurors' beliefs in any of these areas. In *Ham,* the Court also suggested that the scope of the voir dire as to racial prejudice should be "sufficient to focus the attention of prospective jurors on any racial prejudice they might entertain."[75]

Whatever the new forms devised for voir dire, they need not produce exactly as much information as the wealthy litigant can get through private means. As the Supreme Court recently stated in refusing to apply the *Griffin–Douglas* rationale to discretionary review to the highest state court or to the United States Supreme Court, the Constitution does not require the state "to duplicate the legal arsenal that may be privately retained by a criminal defendant . . . ."[76] Application of equal protection principles always involves some linedrawing. Nevertheless, one method of bringing all litigants nearer to parity of information about prospective jurors is to curtail the private investigation of jurors, while expanding voir dire. This could be accomplished by rule of court or by legislation,[77] but should not be accomplished by the device of simply keeping secret in advance the names and addresses of the venire. This information is necessary in advance of trial in order for the litigants to formulate any constitutional objections to the venire.[78] Not only does the unrestrained investigation of jurors create an unequal situation for the exercise of peremptories, but the practice also puts a burden on jury duty that can only in the end make citizens less willing to perform it. The pretrial investigation also raises serious issues of the prospective jurors' right to privacy.[79]

The above suggestions are only sketches of ideas for controlling voir dire without curtailing it as a means of access to information for all litigants. The point of this Essay is that rather than minimizing its importance in the trial, we should recognize voir dire as the historically evolved, constitutionally important instrument that it is. Many years ago Professor Wigmore wrote that voir dire was "beyond any doubt the greatest legal engine ever invented for the discovery of the truth. However difficult it may be for the layman, the scientist, or the foreign jurist to appreciate this, its wonderful power, there has probably never been a moment's doubt upon this point in the mind of the lawyer of experience."[80]

---

75. Ham v. South Carolina, 409 U.S. 524, 527 (1973).
76. Ross v. Moffit, 94 S. Ct. 2437, 2447 (1974).
77. *See* Okun, *supra* note 50, at 865.
78. Townsend v. Ross, 396 F.2d 573 (8th Cir. 1968); State v. Patriarca, 308 A.2d 300 (R.I. 1973), Pollard v. State, 205 S.2d 286 (Miss. 1967).
79. Some have argued that voir dire examination itself involves an unjustifiable invasion of the venireman's privacy. *See* Maxwell, *The Case of the Rebellious Juror,* 56 A.B.A.J. 83 (1970). But at least voir dire is conducted in controlled circumstances where the invasions of privacy can presumably be lessened. On a delicate issue, for instance, the judge may order the prospective juror questioned out of the presence of the other members of the venire.
80. 5 J. WIGMORE, EVIDENCE § 1367 (3d ed. 1940).

Behind the Legal Explosion[*]

John H. Barton[†]

> Too much importance is attributed to legislation, too little
> to customs. . . . I should say that physical circumstances are
> less efficient than the laws, and the laws infinitely less so than
> the customs of the people.[1]

The United States is presently experiencing a legal explosion. As implausible as it may appear, exponential extrapolation of increases over the last decade suggests that by the early 21st century the federal appellate courts alone will decide approximately 1 million cases each year. That bench would include over 5,000 active judges, and the Federal Reporter would expand by more than 1,000 volumes each year.[2] This enormous expansion of the judicial system has been paralleled by increases in the workloads of administrative agencies and legislatures.

But the growth in caseloads and legislative terms is only a symptom of a broader problem: the growing intrusion of law on every aspect of American society. The sources of law have become nearly ubiquitous, including not only the courts, administrative agencies, and governments, but also insurance companies and business management. An individual can take only so many hours of filling out forms before exasperation sets in; a business can tolerate only so much regulation before overhead increases exorbitantly; a regulator can tolerate only so much judicial review before record building replaces the problems at hand. These legal costs are less tangible than those of litigating in clogged courts, but they may be much more serious.

I. Traditional Explanations

A. *Complexity*

What has produced this explosion of law? The easiest explanation is that society has become more complex, so that the number and dispute-potential of transactions have both increased. People more often do things

* Many of the ideas in this Essay derive from discussions with my colleagues Thomas Grey and John Merryman, to whom I am deeply indebted.

† B.S. 1958, Marquette University; J.D. 1968, Stanford University. Associate Professor of Law, Stanford University.

1. A. DE TOCQUEVILLE, DEMOCRACY IN AMERICA 334 (Vintage ed. 1954).

2. The annual number of federal appellate cases has increased from about 5,000 to about 15,000 over the past decade. An exponential projection at this rate of increase yields a caseload of 1 million sometime between the years 2010 and 2015. This rate of increase, when applied to the current number of federal appellate judges and the number of volumes in *Federal Reporter, Second Series,* published in 1973, results in the projections mentioned in the text.

that have traditionally involved the law: sell homes, become divorced, have auto accidents. They also do new things that seem to require law: build nuclear reactors, buy condominiums, eat food additives.

This "complexity" explanation is forceful, but it does not reveal why regulation of all these transactions is needed. The hypothesis does help point out those categories of transactions, such as home sales, that might most usefully be drastically simplified and those categories of disputes, such as liability for automobile accidents, that might be settled more efficiently by nonjudicial bodies.[3] Such reforms, although politically difficult to achieve, would be highly useful for certain specific areas of the law. Outside those areas the complexity hypothesis suggests few practical ways to reduce the intrusiveness of law, short of reducing the complexity of life or the number of interacting people. Neither solution appears likely on the scale needed.

B. *Belief in Individual Helplessness*

A second hypothesis concentrates on the assumption of those who support and issue the new regulations—that society has lost confidence in the individual. The individual is considered unable to determine which drugs or food additives are safe; therefore these substances are regulated. He is believed unable to cope with smooth-talking salesmen; therefore cooling-off periods are established for some consumer contracts and the terms of others are regulated. Closely related to this belief that the individual cannot fend for himself is a belief that he will not give sufficient consideration to the well-being of others. He is thought unable to restrain his actions for the common good; therefore his automobile's emissions and his use of land are regulated.

One must wonder whether the individual is as helpless and thoughtless as the activity of regulatory agencies would indicate. Clearly, reasonable grounds often exist for the imposition of regulation: The individual cannot competently evaluate all the chemicals that pharmaceutical makers and food processors sell to him. Sharp salesmen do victimize many consumers. And, though an individual might be sufficiently concerned for his neighbors' well-being to maintain the appearance of his home, he is unlikely to have enough incentive to control his automobile's emissions without knowledge that similar requirements are imposed on others. Yet, regulation has become too easy. No one knows when regulations derive from genuine new evils in a more heavily-populated, technological society and

---

3. Thus, automobile accident disputes could be transferred to insurance companies and divorces to marriage courts. *See* Hufstedler, *New Blocks for Old Pyramids: Reshaping the Judicial System*, 44 S. CAL. L. REV. 901, 907-08 (1971). The alternate institutions, however, might pose exasperation and nuisance costs as great as those of courts.

when they derive from a perception of man that emphasizes his helplessness rather than his creativity.

The helplessness hypothesis does have the virtue of offering a workable solution. The individual could be given more information and education to make him less helpless. For some problems, particularly in the consumer protection area, this may be the best solution. But with so many transactions and such rapid technological change, the economic and psychological costs of the necessary diffusion of expertise will sometimes be as great as those of regulation. The implied caveat emptor world, in which each must concentrate on looking after his own, is a tense one. There is not enough time to learn everything needed and little chance that education of the public would be of any help in solving such problems as auto emissions. The society's rate of change has validated the assumption that individuals alone cannot always protect themselves. In short, regulatory solutions derived from the helplessness hypothesis are at best partial.

C. *The Economic Critique*

Without explaining the proliferation of law, contemporary economic analysis argues from the central economic theorem that an optimal allocation of resources will be achieved when consumers are free to buy anything they choose (within their incomes) at prices that reflect true costs, including hidden harms to others. Using economic tools, it is relatively easy to show that most new regulations lead to a poor allocation of resources. For example, automobile emission-control standards require automobile owners to make greater expenditures for emission-control devices as well as for gasoline. They also give people the benefit of a cleaner atmosphere. If it were possible to buy and sell atmospheric cleanliness, those who wanted a cleaner atmosphere would be willing to pay automobile owners to install emission-control devices. The market for atmospheric cleanliness would clear at a particular level of expenditure and level of cleanliness. It can be argued that this point is optimal for the society, but only by chance would regulation lead to the same optimal point. Most likely, too much or too little will be spent on emission-control devices. Operating under ideal market conditions, society might have achieved its desired level of atmospheric cleanliness at a lower cost.

Economic analysis does not, however, explain the reasons for regulations. From an economic viewpoint, it is hard not to attribute regulations to the stupidity or the power instinct of the regulators. Sometimes, one can find special-interest groups profiting from the regulation. There are strong pressures on both legislatures and administrative agencies to subsidize various special interests, and the subsidies may be disguised in the form

of regulations. An emission-control device manufacturer may be benefited by new auto emission regulations. An environmental organization's
members will benefit if regulation spreads the cost of conservation over all
of society, rather than only on those who most want such measures.

Thus, the economic critique questions the efficiency and rationality of
regulation and suggests that regulation often implies using the state as a
massive cost redistributor. This critique clearly has roots in 19th-century
economic liberalism and in distrust of government, just as some of the new
regulations have roots in Populism and in a 20th-century faith in government.

The economic critique also offers a way to reemphasize individual or
consumer sovereignty, implicitly rejecting the "human helplessness" viewpoint. Many of those who make the economic critique have responsibly
described ways to improve markets to maximize both individual sovereignty and economic efficiency. Thus, if in the food additive cases, tort
liability for bad effects of chemicals were placed on the manufacturer,
presumably he would then use only those chemicals that increased his
operating profits through sales more than they increased his liabilities.
Under appropriate economic assumptions, this individual optimum then
corresponds to society's optimum. The manufacturers would use only those
chemicals that produce a net benefit to society. In the environmental case,
each polluter would be taxed according to the harm his emissions caused
to others. Thus he would buy pollution-reduction equipment so long as
the tax saved by use of the equipment exceeds the cost of the equipment.
The resulting level of emissions can again be shown to be optimal under
certain economic assumptions. The economic theory is thus a helpful tool,
capable of solving some real problems and always useful in pointing out
potential perversions of the regulatory process.

Application of market improvements, such as those just described, does
not, however, necessarily prevent the explosion of law. In the food additive
case, market improvement would replace one regulatory action by a number of tort actions. The legal burden on those bringing the tort actions is
clearly enormous. The burden on the companies also remains because they
must still carefully monitor all uses of the particular chemical and evaluate potential liabilities. In the environmental example, the single regulatory
action would be replaced by several quasi-regulatory actions to set the tax
formula, by many corporate choices between paying the tax and buying
emission control devices, and by governmental action in collecting the tax.
These substituted decisions may be easier to make fairly, and the business'
decision may accord more closely with routine business practice than the
standard regulatory decisions. The psychological and economic costs of
applying law remain, however, and may be greater for the individual.

Moreover, as shown by the proliferation of exculpatory clauses in form contracts, business may attempt to transfer back to consumers those liabilities imposed under the theory. Efforts to vary these form contracts or to attack them in court could become alternative instruments of aggravation.

A more careful economic analysis might suggest ways to reduce some of these burdens. Economic analysts too frequently ignore them. This is not a necessary feature of economic theory but an omission by those who apply the theory. The omission is serious because it is at the transaction level that the oppressiveness of law becomes heaviest. If transaction costs were considered, it might be more economical, for example, for an agency to make a single decision on a food additive than to require businesses to have to investigate the additive. Although regulation may harass business, the economic substitute could harass as well through complicated planning calculations and negotiations. The effect on society would not be as dramatic as that of a return to caveat emptor, but it would be sufficiently substantial to warrant careful consideration.

The economic analysis also suffers from more profound difficulties. The first is that economic theory defines an optimal allocation that depends on the distribution of income. In place of the vagaries and inefficiencies of regulation, the economic analysts would substitute a market in which each person's vote is effectively weighted by his income. One doubts the desirability of such weighting in areas as human as, say, education or the environment.

The problem with income distribution is more than theoretical, because much regulation reflects a strong redistributive intention. For example, entry to trades and to professions is regulated both to protect the public from incompetent practitioners and to give the practitioners a monopoly. For many of these redistributive regulations, the costs to the public are greater than the benefits conferred on the intended recipients, and the benefits are less equitably distributed than by a direct subsidy to the poor. Moreover, the redistribution is often from the poorer to the richer. One suspects, however, that redistribution even from richer to poorer may seldom be politically feasible unless coupled with regulation. If this suspicion is correct, economic inefficiency and legal aggravations are sometimes reasonably tolerated in return for improved distribution.

Second, economic analysis is unsuitable to a consideration of the full range of factors that motivate people. Under the economic theory, man is a profit maximizer.[4] Although financial value can be assigned to a busi-

---

4. An extreme example is the assumption that the cost of lawbreaking is a pecuniary one to be inserted straightforwardly into profit-maximizing calculations. *See, e.g.,* Becker & Stigler, *Law Enforcement, Malfeasance, and Compensation of Enforcers,* 3 J. Leg. Studies 1 (1974). This assump-

ness reputation or to having a child, the incorporation into economics frequently fails to reflect important aspects of motivation. A description of the way people decide how long to work has proved so difficult that economists have been unable to develop a supply curve for labor that is both theoretically and empirically satisfactory. A man deciding whether to breach his business ethics may have his price, but that price has little relation to the financial benefits of his business reputation. If it is lower the second time the reason is psychological, not economic. For areas in which there are deep human values, economic analysis is inadequate.[5] In many respects law is such an area.

II. A CULTURAL ANALYSIS

The complexity hypothesis, the individual's helplessness hypothesis, and the economic analysis each suggest ways to meet the legal explosion. Their suggested solutions, however, will work only in some cases. More seriously, none comes to grips with the burdensomeness of law.

The paradigm of many of the new forms of law is that of the regulator who makes rules for business in order to protect the public. As already noted, the public is assumed to be relatively helpless and the regulator assumes that he knows how to protect the public.

But what is crucial is how the regulator views the regulated man—the businessman, on whom the legal burden falls most heavily. Regulated man is viewed as confronting two decisions. The first is whether or not to obey the regulation, a decision based on the costs of obedience, the probability of detection of a violation, and the sanction in the event of detection. Assuming he has chosen to obey the regulation, the second decision, determined with the help of his attorney, is how close to the boundary of the regulation he can operate. The regulated individual is expected to respond only to his self-interest and to clear legal requirements. Seldom, as viewed by the regulator, does the regulated individual act sympathetically within the vague area between legal and illegal behavior and never does he obey the spirit of the regulation as opposed to its letter. Assuming this picture represents an accurate description of much behavior under regulation, it constitutes an argument against regulation, for no person can psychologically survive operating much of life this way.

Neither the economic nor the regulatory model captures the classically conceived essence of law—a felt duty to obey because the law or regulation

---

tion may be reasonable for deciding how to pay enforcers and for analyzing business in an extremely corrupt nation, but it is useless for most of the variety of conduct that law seeks to affect.

5. Tribe, *Technology Assessment and the Fourth Discontinuity: The Limits of Instrumental Rationality*, 46 S. CAL. L. REV. 617 (1973).

represents a way of obtaining some common value, such as justice. Under this classical view of law and of human nature, the duty often is not even felt; it may be respected out of habit or a sense of tradition. Even when law proves difficult to obey, this ethical aspect removes its psychological oppressiveness. Though few may agree on the jurisprudential basis for law, it is clear that some such tradition, ethos, or culture moves us in many of our decisions to obey law. It is seldom traditional legal sanctions that make us support our children, stop at red lights, or keep our promises. Many of these decisions are altruistic, benefiting others even at substantial personal cost. A profession often possesses its own particular ethos: scientists believe they should report their research results accurately; lawyers usually place the interests of their clients foremost.

Although the ethos of a society or a group changes over time, it is clearly transmitted from generation to generation by education, and it is possible that the sense of duty to respond to an ethos is supported by genetically-transmitted biological mechanisms.[6] Through progress, or evolution, the ethos often incorporates relatively practical solutions to practical problems. At the same time, humans feel a need to ensure that their ethos is rational, and they have developed elaborate jurisprudential systems to justify that ethos. The economic theory described above is a contemporary example of such a system.

This ethos or culture is broader than law but has traditionally supported law. It is absent from much of our new law.[7] I wish to suggest in this Essay that its absence may help explain why law is proliferating so rapidly and to suggest how greater reliance on ethos might be used as an additional tool to dampen the legal explosion.

At one time—as shown in the work of Aquinas, and even in relatively recent Muslim thought[8]—there was intellectually only one law. The government as lawgiver merely explained and detailed a law derived from the same intellectual source as the prevailing morality. For the citizens, the force of law and the force of ethos were one. Although the traditional philosophical underpinnings had long since decayed, the vision that law and ethos would support one another was shared by such a recent common law philosopher as Cardozo:

> The constant assumption runs throughout the law that the natural and spontaneous evolutions of habit fix the limits of right and wrong. A slight extension of custom identifies it with customary morality, the prevailing standard of right conduct, the *mores* of the time. . . . Life casts the moulds of conduct, which will some day

6. *See* F. HAYEK, *Notes on the Evolution of Systems of Rules of Conduct*, in STUDIES IN PHILOSOPHY, POLITICS AND ECONOMICS 66–81 (1967).
7. *See* F. HAYEK, *The Changing Concept of Law*, in 1 LAW, LEGISLATION AND LIBERTY 72 (1973).
8. *See* A. BOZEMAN, THE FUTURE OF LAW IN A MULTICULTURAL WORLD 62–64 (1971).

become fixed as law. Law preserves the moulds, which have taken form and shape
from life.[9]

[T]he judge is under a duty, within the limits of his power of innovation, to
maintain a relation between law and morals, between the precepts of jurisprudence
and those of reason and good conscience.[10]

Where law and custom are closely coupled, it is the custom or the ethos
that primarily shapes behavior and enforces law.[11] Most men therefore
obey the law, and most dispute settlements coincide closely with the norms
of the law.

The few lawsuits of such a world arise from individual aberrance or
from specific disputes in which the laws or customs are unclear because
they are changing. To reaffirm the common order against the aberrant or
to resolve the doubtful case, the judge is likely to look to the culture to
find persuasive principles. There is a good chance that his resolution will
become a new custom or at least rationalize and legitimate a change in
custom. Thus, law and custom remain in harmony.

This coupling between culture and law is virtually absent from today's
newer fields of law. The possible explanations are so manifold that one
cannot choose between them. The psychological binding force of law has
been reduced by positivism—law is now *expected* to be artificial. There is
no longer a single dominant ethos or set of customs in our society, perhaps
because of secularization within and without schools or because of closer
interaction among different subgroups with specific customs. Thus, corporate executives and environmentalists offer radically different ethical norms
for the same transactions. Many decisions that were once made individually
are now made by bureaucracies that are insulated from outside legal and
social forces that might otherwise tend to influence their ethos. Thus a
highway commission may emphasize its dedication to improving traffic
flow while failing to respond to consumers' or even legislators' calls for
greater attention to environmental effects. Businesses sometimes reject an
ethos on the argument that the profit motive often benefits the common
good and therefore motivations other than the profit motivation may be
bad. The religious, academic, and intellectual communities, which might
propose an ethos for the entire society, seldom do so. Sometimes these
communities reject such functions. Sometimes they volunteer shallow ethical criticisms that lack intellectual consistency or perception of the problems being faced by different elements of the society. Whatever the explanations, it would be useful to examine the historical roots of this hypothe-

9. B. CARDOZO, THE NATURE OF THE JUDICIAL PROCESS 63–64 (1921) (footnote omitted).
10. *Id.* at 133–34.
11. *See* F. HAYEK, *The Results of Human Action but Not of Human Design*, in STUDIES IN
PHILOSOPHY, POLITICS AND ECONOMICS 96, 102 (1967).

sized breakdown of ethos and to look for historical parallels. The breakdown may be typical of any transition period or be peculiar to technological change.[12]

With ethos in disarray, litigation need no longer result exclusively from
aberration or from good faith misunderstanding within a common tradition.[13] Instead, it can derive from profound disagreement between two sectors of society in which each sector's position is supported by that sector's
ethos.[14] Disagreement may be so deep that efforts to persuade are ignored
in favor of legal battle. This legal battle is not viewed by the parties as an
effort to settle a conflict; instead it is a tactical engagement in a sustained
war. Resolution of the legal issues or the conflict becomes secondary to the
creating of publicity for a cause or to obtaining, through procedural devices, delay of a decision.

The judge is faced with strongly conflicting parties who lack a shared
ethos to which he can appeal. He is therefore tempted to avoid or to conceal a value judgment by deciding on procedural grounds if at all possible.[15] This emphasis on procedure is supported by the legal process-think-
ing stressed in the best law schools. Legal growth then becomes procedural
growth, resulting in increasingly complicated rules for the courts, the police, and the administrative agencies. Even when the judge does decide on
substantive grounds, the polarization between litigants is so complete that
his opinion can, at best, help lawyers predict future decisions. It is unlikely to persuade either litigant to modify its ethos.

The lawyer's classic answer is that the legislature is the place to resolve
fundamental value conflicts. When the differences within society are relatively simple, a legislature can sometimes negotiate, as did Parliament during the early 19th-century reform struggles and the Congress during the
North-South struggles of the same period. Once passage of a particular
piece of legislation appears likely, a committee meeting or even a meeting of an entire chamber may be the seat of genuine negotiation and compromise, shaping and accommodating the legislation to as many interests
as possible. But the contemporary legislative process seldom helps to reconcile contradictory value systems. Debate is unlikely to be sufficiently

---

12. It is too easy to blame technology per se. The problem often is not that people are unable to
adapt to technology but that only some adapt to it. For example, such a dramatic and sociologically
important technology as oral contraception has led quickly to a new ethos. That ethos, however, is accepted by only part of the society.

13. It has been stated that litigation was considered "debatable and disturbing" in Korea because
it revealed the failure of politics and therefore the moral failure of the ruler. *See* H. Pyong-Choon, The
Korean Political Tradition and Law 29 (1967).

14. *See* Jaffe, *The Citizen as Litigant in Public Actions: The Non-Hohfeldian or Ideological Plaintiff*, 116 U. Pa. L. Rev. 1033 (1968).

15. *Cf.* F. Hayek, *Nomos: The Law of Liberty*, in 1 Law, Legislation and Liberty 94, 120–
21 (1973) (difficulty of judging in a socialist, *i.e.* welfare, state).

penetrating to achieve consensus. Neither does a legislature often provide a choice between values through referendum. Legislators neither have enough preferences nor wish to express them. Rather a contemporary legislature usually devises packages of open and concealed subsidies that can be supported by a majority of the legislature.[16]

It follows that a legislature will seldom have attempted to resolve the value conflicts that are frequently presented to the judiciary. Even if the legislature has acted, it is most likely to have treated only part of an issue or to have acted ambiguously. A broader consensus is too difficult to achieve. Thus, logically similar transactions are treated differently because the laws were passed at different times—door-to-door sales are drastically distinguished from sales in a store, and carcinogenic food additives from those posing other health hazards. This inconsistency may explain why lawyers are often so unsympathetic to legislation. It lacks the inherently principled character of traditional common law. Sometimes it is impossible—given the absence of a national consensus on how to act—for the legislature to obtain consensus on anything but the need for action. The result, as in economic wage and price controls, is delegation to the executive of both the power to act and the duty to bear the political costs of action. The executive must then define a compromise and draft regulations, which have less moral force than legislation.

But the problem goes beyond the legislature's difficulty in gaining consensus. Regulated man, the addressee of the law, does not share a common ethos with the draftsman and is expected to resist the law on basic value grounds. This expectation is particularly strong when the mythology of the legislative process emphasizes a villain, such as the polluting corporation, the corrupt union, or the exploiting employer. Against such a target, law cannot be discretionary. The law's target cannot be trusted to interpret a statute sympathetically. According to the mythology, only a court can be trusted to do so. Legislation or regulation directed against private interest groups is therefore often marked by great detail, which is believed necessary to prevent evasion but which, in fact, simply encourages lawyers to find ways to comply with the letter of the law while opposing its spirit. Thus, the health warning in cigarette advertising becomes just another page-design hurdle to be surmounted. Legislation directed against public regulatory bodies, each of which has its own ethos, is marked by Kafka-esque procedural restraints. The agencies are expected to be uncooperative, and under the judicial principle of respect for administrative expertise, the courts are not expected to enforce substantive directives against them.

---

16. *See* J. BUCHANAN & G. TULLOCK, THE CALCULUS OF CONSENT (1962).

The dominant modes of legislation and regulation thus create a law that is heavily procedural, often illogical, and seldom ethically persuasive. These characteristics, in turn, encourage litigants to use legal action as an artificial tactic in the confrontation of value systems, and they encourage both litigants and courts to attempt to resolve the confrontations procedurally. The result is a vicious circle.

No resolution is in sight, as law has little chance of influencing or being influenced by custom in such a way that the need for law could become marginal. In spite of interminable hearings designed to insure that the law recipient has an opportunity to express his viewpoint, there remains today an enormous gap between lawmaker and law recipient; the assumptions and language of law have diverged from those of life. For example, corporate management has an ethos that combines a profit motivation with less tangible motivations, such as providing a needed product, advancing technology, or supporting employees. The law offers technical tax rules, securities rules, antitrust rules, and product safety rules. Corporate management speaks in one language; legal boundary conditions are cast in another. The corporate lawyer could be the interpreter, but his memoranda suggesting changes in business practice and his briefs or form contracts designed to protect his client seldom communicate underlying interests. Therefore the corporate ethos is unlikely to adopt or assimilate new law.

Communication between the legal system and the regulatory agency is equally poor. The law asks for little other than procedural form. The substance of the agency's action becomes irrelevant, never subject to judicial discussion and subject to congressional discussion only at budget time or when nominations are considered. The agency's substantive ethos is nearly independent of the legislation under which the agency works and easily diverges from the ethos of Congress or of the public. For example, the SEC's goals in regulating the sale of securities seem diametrically opposed to those of courts applying closely related legislation.[17] The gap between agency and judiciary is equaled only by that between agency and public. Except for some potentially corrupting ex parte contacts between agency and regulated industry, there are relatively few times at which the proponents of one ethos face the proponents of others.

---

17. For example, the two share the power of regulating sales of foreign securities in the United States, but there is some question as to the proper extent of United States jurisdiction over these international transactions. The SEC interprets United States jurisdiction narrowly, with the effect of making foreign access to the United States capital market as easy as possible. *See, e.g.,* SEC Securities Act Release No. 8066 (Apr. 28, 1967), [1966–1967 Transfer Binder] CCH FED. SEC. L. REP. ¶ 77,443. *See generally,* H. STEINER & D. VAGTS, TRANSNATIONAL LEGAL PROBLEMS 967–72 (1968). At the same time, the courts interpret United States jurisdiction broadly, in order to protect the United States investor. *E.g.,* Travis v. Anthes Imperial Ltd., 473 F.2d 515 (8th Cir. 1973); Roth v. Fund of Funds Ltd., 405 F.2d 421 (2d Cir. 1968), *cert. denied,* 394 U.S. 975 (1969); Schoenbaum v. Firstbrook, 405 F.2d 200 (2d Cir.), *rev'd en banc on other grounds,* 405 F.2d 215 (2d Cir. 1968), *cert. denied,* 395 U.S. 906 (1969).

These cultural phenomena help explain the crisis of our legal system. Too many conflicts between different cultural or ethical systems exist that are not resolved through informal means or through the legislature. Points of conflict ranging from school discipline to highway aesthetics have become judicial and administrative affairs. Courts have usually responded procedurally, and agencies by increasing the number of regulations. Thus the complexity of law increases while its rationality and persuasiveness do not. The law becomes more complex and more burdensome precisely because it is separated from custom or ethos. The continuing increase in the complexity of society, the need to accommodate to resource limitations, the continuing divergence of ethics among different institutions, and the increasing intractability of the economy suggest that the trend will continue.

This hypothesis—that law is expanding because it is separated from ethos—suggests a further way to dampen the legal explosion. One cannot, however, simply preach discontinuation of the use of the legal system. Too many real injustices and deep value-conflicts exist. The judiciary does still appear to be the only responsive branch of government. Rather, it is here suggested that the legal system be reorganized to facilitate the emergence of a common ethos and to draw on the force of that ethos. This may be dangerous: government by ethos, though more subtle, can be as tyrannical as government by unjustified law. But we are always affected by ethos or custom. The government must therefore not be allowed to dominate it.

III. How Might Common Ethos Be Developed?

The failure of ethos may appear to be so deeply rooted in the society that no legal reform can help. Yet the Uniform Commercial Code stands as a recent example of successful legal reform through abdication of formal law in favor of informal sanctions and customs.

The field of commercial contracts is one in which the ethos is likely to be especially fair. Business ethics already exist, and reputation is important to a businessman. Since many business relationships last for a number of transactions and provide mutual benefits, there are strong informal sanctions—the businessman who fails to meet his obligations loses business. These informal sanctions are so strong that businessmen view the ability to invoke judicial remedies as relatively unimportant.[18] The draftsmen of the Code thus thought heavy reliance on business custom and honor was reasonable. For example, they eliminated many fairness rules of traditional contract law, and replaced them with the concept of "good faith."[19] This

---

18. *See* Macaulay, *Non-Contractual Relations in Business: A Preliminary Study*, 28 Am. Socio. Rev. 55 (1963).

19. Examples include rules restricting options, Uniform Commercial Code § 2–205, contract modifications, *id.* § 2–209, contracts with open price or quantity terms, *id.* § 2–305, and contract assignments, *id.* § 2–210.

concept was given little definition in the Code[20] but is clearly an invocation of a customary ethic. The resulting law is much more flexible and lies much more lightly upon the society. The reform is probably successful as between businessmen. Whether a similar reform between businessmen and consumers could be successful is doubtful because informal sanctions are sometimes much weaker for consumers than between businessmen. The Uniform Commercial Code distinguishes the consumer contract, and applies more rigid rules to it.

The environmental area provides a much more difficult example because, despite a major legislative effort, there is as yet no single ethos. The 1969 National Environmental Protection Act directed federal agencies to consider the environmental effects of their actions. These hortatory provisions, perceived as unenforceable, indicated that Congress had not yet decided what should be sacrificed for the sake of the environment.

The Act also required each agency to prepare an environmental impact statement (the "NEPA statement") outlining the environmental effects of its intended major actions. Preparation of this statement could have encouraged administrators to incorporate environmental goals in the design of their programs. A sequence of statements analogous to common law judicial opinion could even have helped. As it turned out, however, the statements are of low scientific quality,[21] are sometimes written by consultants (probably with cut-and-paste methods), and are so long that no one reads them. Relatively well-understood but less important issues, such as the effects of heat pollution on individual fish species, receive disproportionately greater attention in contrast to less well-understood issues that are likely to be more important, such as long-term climate change. For the administrator, then, the requirement has created a nuisance instead of an ethos.

The requirement for the statement was, however, seized upon by environmental litigators. Supported by sympathetic judges, environmentalists rapidly developed a body of NEPA law under which new projects could be stalled until the NEPA statement met elaborate formal criteria. Major investments stood idle while the statements were revised. More seriously, the environmentalists' success was only partial. Once the statement met the imposed criteria the project could proceed. Sometimes special congressional exemptions were obtained, as for certain nuclear reactors and, in a closely analogous situation, the Alaskan pipeline. The litigation may have helped

20. " 'Good faith' means honesty in fact in the conduct or transaction concerned." *Id.* § 1-201(19). " 'Good faith' in the case of a merchant means honesty in fact and the observance of reasonable commercial standards of fair dealing in the trade." *Id.* § 2-103(1)(b). If construed only formally, these definitions would not give "good faith" enough content to carry the burden cast upon it in the rest of the Code. *See* Summers, *"Good Faith" in General Contract Law and the Sales Provisions of the Uniform Commercial Code,* 54 VA. L. REV. 195 (1968).

21. *See, e.g.,* Gillette, *Low Marks for AEC's Breeder Reactor Study,* 184 SCI. 877 (1974).

create an environmental constituency; it did not establish an environmental ethos.

A better example of legal stillbirth would be hard to find. The most effective aspect of the legislation, from the environmentalist viewpoint, was the procedural part, which allowed projects to be delayed through legal battles over issues far removed from the conflict.[22] However, as the agencies become more adept at complying with the procedural rules, even the delay potential is likely to be lost. Compliance is essentially formalistic—the contents of the statement have little effect on government decisionmaking or on the goals of the environmental movement. Relatively little attention is given to development of an underlying body of ecological and environmental science that might help both decisionmaker and environmentalist.

If an ethos is to replace or support the law, it must be built on informal ethical standards and sanctions. There are at least two possible supports within agencies and the regulated industries upon which an ethos might be built. First, many upper- and middle-level executives of these organizations are themselves political supporters and beneficiaries of environmental improvement. They would almost certainly support environmental perspectives—even against the short-term interest of their employer—provided they were buttressed by an adequate rationale. An analogous rationale already supports corporate and government expenditures for architectural quality in buildings. Second, engineering and science have ethical traditions of their own. Engineering societies, for example, have developed basic standards for structural safety—even without governmental intervention. The engineering profession could easily place a high value on the environment, just as it does on safety.

These supports were not tapped by NEPA, which tended instead to create a special-purpose legal network separate from the decisionmaking network. Tapping such supports would require assimilation of the environmental network into the regular decisionmaking network. One way would be to make environmental statements matter to the agencies. A careful review process, occurring at least in part in the scientific or engineering community, could evaluate the substance of the NEPA statements. If this review process were coupled with the influence of public opinion on congressional attention at budget time, or substantial judicial review of the substance of the statements, the statements would improve and have greater effect on decisionmaking.[23] Administrators might take pride in solving

---

22. See Heyman et al., *The Challenge of Environmental Controls*, 28 Bus. Law., Special Issue of March 1973, at 9, 22–28 (remarks of Cutler).

23. Justice Douglas may have increased the effectiveness of NEPA statements by giving great weight to their evaluation by the Council on Environmental Quality. Warm Springs Dam Task Force v. Gribble, 94 S. Ct. 2542 (1974).

knotty environmental questions as they do in solving knotty technological questions. This mechanism may already have worked in a few NEPA situations.[24]

Another approach would be a direct effort to gain consensus on environmental issues. Face-to-face meetings between environmentalists and engineers might encourage the mutual understanding and respect that usually come from contact outside the courtroom. The environmentalist might be forced to define his priorities more carefully; the engineer to design to meet those priorities. At a local level, this process might lead to mutually acceptable designs. At a national level, it could produce principles analogous to engineering safety standards or the generally accepted principles of accounting. These principles could encourage those within corporations or agencies who wish to argue for environmental restraint but fear they would appear unbusinesslike before colleagues or shareholders. Such principles could also give courts and Congress the vocabulary needed to regulate substance rather than procedure and to regulate in ways that have ethical content. It might then be possible for a court or Congress to speak to agencies as court speaks to court with confidence that intentions will be understood and subtleties supplied.

Success is uncertain. The differences between the various viewpoints may be so great that it is impossible to develop environmental principles that command relatively broad assent and are understandable by a relatively broad range of decisionmakers. The time required to reach a consensus may be too long for today's world. Even if a consensus is definable, it may not become an effective self-enforcing ethos simply through acceptance by the various groups; an environmental ethos would lack obvious informal sanctions comparable to those supporting business ethics. Development of an ethos might require changes outside the environmental area: evolution of employment customs to grant government and industrial scientists independence similar to that of accountants and academic scientists; adjustment of antitrust laws to protect firms from the lower prices of competitors who are less environmentally responsible; development of ways to ensure that the new ethos creators, who would be important power centers, do not abuse their power.

Two more general social changes would also be necessary. They deserve special attention because they would probably be needed in any situation in which the "new" law is replaced by ethos.

The first change concerns corporate and governmental techniques of dealing with the public. Too often, a business or an agency uses one type

---

24. The outstanding example is the use of sterilized insects for agricultural pest control in the place of insecticides.

of argument in making decisions and another in explaining them to outsiders. This pattern destroys the communication needed for the sharing of
an ethos between insider and outsider. As long as the power company is
evasive about how it estimates future electricity requirements, the environmentalist will suspect the worst and work to prevent construction of any
plant. It is psychologically impossible to eliminate the pattern completely,
but it could be altered sufficiently to give the informed public a reasonable
access to and understanding of corporate and governmental decisionmaking
processes. A public relations presentation and a pro forma public hearing
are not enough. One specific reason why the courts are overused is that
they are among the few places where the agency or corporation can be
cross-examined and where the decisionmaker is expected to listen.

Second, public access would be meaningless without public education.
The educational level of the public is crucial to its ability to accept an ethos
that will change constantly as technology changes. Critical to the development of an ethos is the individual's understanding of the effects his actions
have on others. These effects are much harder to appreciate and evaluate
in today's world than they were in an era of small manufacturing and
face-to-face dealing. An insight into allocative economics, an understanding of the political process, and even a general technological literacy would
have to be as accessible to many educated people as income tax rules, football
strategy, and stock market literacy are now.

The obvious response to all of this is that it is excessively idealistic. Yet,
the legal system is in crisis, and its crisis derives partly from assumptions
that only the government can recognize the public interest, that industry
can recognize only a profit interest, and that the public good is best served
if industry does *not* recognize more than a profit interest. All three assumptions are false. As any lawyer or political scientist can elaborate, much contemporary legislation seeks to benefit a special interest at the expense of
the whole. As any industrial manager can establish, every industry and firm
has its own internal traditions and ethos which drive it well away from
pure profit motivation. And, as most economists would admit, the assumptions behind the theory that the public good is served by pursuit of private
interests are only partly met in today's world of oligopoly, tertiary-sector
employment, and limited information flow. It is unrealistic to ignore either
the negative *or the positive* aspects of the failure of these assumptions.

IV. For Further Thinking

If the hypothesis of this Essay—that law's loss of contact with ethos is
an important cause of law's current crisis—is correct, its implementation
implies the development of new roles for legal academicians.

One new role would be to help create an ethos in particular cases, such as the environmental area just discussed. For example, a lawyer might propose new legislation in antitrust law, in trade secret law, or in the duties of managers to shareholders that would facilitate the emergence of a particular ethos. He might also examine more general ways to support the emergence of an ethos in many areas through congressional reform or modifying the doctrine of judicial deference to administrative expertise.

At a more theoretical level, an academic lawyer might compare different approaches such as those suggested in this Essay. In a particular situation, how does one decide between an ethos-based approach, an economic-incentive-based approach, or a classical regulatory approach? What are the interest balances, the information flow patterns, the transaction patterns, and the mental predispositions that are likely to make one of these legal responses better than another? When would an ethos approach be too inflexible or too likely to serve private interests? Finally, is the hypothesis of this Essay correct? Is there a problem in today's law beyond the numerical increase in transactions absolutely requiring legal intervention? If so, is it really related to a divergence between law and custom? Is it avoidable or is it a necessary aspect of post-industrial society? Might historical comparisons or study of ethically-laden areas of new law, such as desegregation, help answer these questions?

Of the new roles, the most novel is the "private policy lawyer" who would, for example, propose ways for private industry to act in the public interest. Academic lawyers, fearful of decisions that are not tempered by economic competition or by formal government institutions, commonly view the lawyer's function as a value-free one of helping a client achieve his predefined ends. Practicing lawyers, however, often do act in value-laden ways in situations ranging from family counseling to negotiating consent settlements or self-regulation programs. In doing so, they are departing from their professional legal expertise and acting on the basis of a more human and social knowledge. Such action is acceptable so long as it is not coercive. If academic lawyers do begin to reflect on the social structure that underlies or might replace law, they might reasonably suggest directions of industrial self-restraint just as they suggest directions of governmental intervention or self-restraint. The government need not be the only recipient of public-policy thinking.

And for the academic lawyer who works within the traditional pattern, the hypothesis of this Essay suggests a greater sensitivity to the cultural and philosophical motivations of those affected by law. We have properly begun to consider the impacts of psychology on criminal law and of economics on regulatory law and have even seen a commercial law that considers commercial customs. Nevertheless, running through much of our law, especially in the new regulatory areas, there is an insensitivity to and a one-dimensional understanding of the entities affected by the legal system. The law can no longer afford to ignore the full motivations of those it regulates or the ways those motivations evolve under regulation. Until it does respect those motivations, it will remain artificial and oppressive.

The Conscientious Legislator's Guide
to Constitutional Interpretation

Paul Brest*

In 1965, when draft-card burning had become a well-known symbol of protest against the war in Vietnam, Congress amended the Selective Service laws to punish the knowing destruction of draft cards.[1] In *United States v. O'Brien*,[2] the Supreme Court sustained the provision against the claim that it violated the first amendment. Suppose that Congress eventually repeals the provision, but that draft-card burning returns as a popular means of protest and a bill is introduced to reenact the ban. A Congressman is considering whether the bill is constitutional. Does *O'Brien* settle the issue?

In his opinion for the Court, Chief Justice Warren articulated the applicable constitutional standards as follows:

> [A] governmental regulation is sufficiently justified . . . if it furthers an important or substantial governmental interest; if the governmental interest is unrelated to the suppression of free expression; and if the incidental restriction on alleged First Amendment freedoms is no greater than is essential to the furtherance of that interest.[3]

The legislative history of the 1965 amendment did not indicate just what "substantial governmental interests" Congress was seeking to further, but the Chief Justice imaginatively hypothesized a number of possible legitimate concerns, to conclude:

> The many functions performed by Selective Service certificates establish beyond doubt that Congress has a legitimate and substantial interest in preventing their wanton and unrestrained destruction and assuring their continuing availability by punishing people who knowingly and wilfully destroy or mutilate them. . . . We perceive no alternative means that would more precisely and narrowly assure the continuing availability of issued Selective Service certificates than a law which prohibits their wilful mutilation or destruction.[4]

The respondent had argued that even if the law *might* serve legitimate purposes, statements by the bill's proponents indicated that their *actual*

---

* A.B. 1962, Swarthmore College; LL.B. 1965, Harvard University. Associate Professor of Law, Stanford University.

1. 50 U.S.C. § 462(b)(3) (1970 App.), 79 Stat. 586 (1965).
2. 391 U.S. 367 (1968).
3. *Id.* at 377.
4. *Id.* at 380–81.

purpose was to suppress freedom of expression. To this the Court responded:

> It is a familiar principle of constitutional law that this Court will not strike down an otherwise constitutional statute on the basis of an alleged illicit legislative motive. . . .
>
> Inquiries into congressional motives or purposes are a hazardous matter. . . . What motivates one legislator to make a speech about a statute is not necessarily what motivates scores of others to enact it, and the stakes are sufficiently high for us to eschew guesswork. We decline to void essentially on the ground that it is unwise legislation which Congress had the undoubted power to enact and which could be enacted in its exact form if the same or another legislator made a "wiser" speech about it.[5]

O'Brien informs the inquiring Congressman that the anti–draft-card burning measure will survive judicial scrutiny. But does this mean that the measure is constitutional? Once the Court hypothesized legitimate and weighty interests in the integrity of draft cards, it presumed conclusively that Congress enacted the 1965 amendment to further them. It made this presumption largely because it could not, or could not properly, determine otherwise. The Congressman knows his own mind, however. And if he accepts the constitutional standards set out in *O'Brien*, can he properly support the measure if *he* believes that it serves no significant purpose or if *his* objective is to suppress antiwar protest?

There is nothing novel in the notion that legislatures and courts approach constitutional questions from different perspectives. Writing in the latter part of the 19th century, James Bradley Thayer paraphrased Judge Thomas Cooley's earlier observation to the effect that

> one who is a member of a legislature may vote against a measure as being, in his judgment, unconstitutional; and being subsequently placed on the bench, when this measure having been passed by the legislature in spite of his opposition, comes before him judicially, may there find it his duty, although he has in no degree changed his opinion, to declare it constitutional.[6]

Judicial "restraint" may be a matter of comity, reflecting respect for the decisions of a coordinate branch of the federal government or of a state's chief policymaking body. It may flow from the court's inability to separate constitutional questions from related empirical issues beyond its competence or from matters of policy within the legislature's domain. It may also reflect the court's inability to ascertain how the legislative process has actually worked in a particular case. None of these considerations suggests that the legislature should exercise restraint in assessing the constitutionality of its own product.

---

5. *Id.* at 383–84.
6. Thayer, *The Origin and Scope of the American Doctrine of Constitutional Law*, 7 HARV. L. REV. 129, 144 (1893).

This Essay does not address the perennial issue of how restrained or activist the judiciary should be in constitutional matters. Rather, it assumes the perspective of a conscientious legislator, to inquire how he or she can assess the constitutionality of proposed legislation.

I. Two Governing Assumptions

Before examining the question in detail, two assumptions should be made explicit. The first is that legislators are obligated to determine, as best they can, the constitutionality of proposed legislation. The second is that they should consider themselves bound by, or at least give great weight to, the Supreme Court's substantive constitutional holdings.

The first proposition may seem self-evident. It is worth some discussion, however, because so many legislators have assumed the contrary—that their job is to make policy without regard to questions of constitutionality, which rest within the exclusive domain of the courts.[7] Briefly, the following points support the proposition.

First, some provisions of the Constitution are explicitly addressed to legislators. Article I, section 9 provides, "No Bill of Attainder or ex post facto law *shall be passed.*" The first amendment says, "*Congress shall make* no law . . . ," and the fourteenth amendment provides that "*No State shall make* or enforce any law . . . ." Many other provisions are addressed to legislatures by clear implication. For example, it would seem odd if Congress were to legislate without inquiring whether article I or some other provision of the Constitution gave it the authority to do so.

Second, many of the framers of the Constitution and members of the early Congresses expressed and acted upon the belief that Congress should assess the constitutionality of pending legislation, whether or not it might later be subject to judicial review.[8] Third, article VI requires that all legislators and officials "be bound by Oath or Affirmation to support this Constitution . . . ." Although this does not entail that all constitutional questions are open to all institutions at all times,[9] the most obvious way for a legislator to support the Constitution is to enact only legislation that is constitutional.

Fourth, Chief Justice Marshall's classic justification for judicial review in *Marbury v. Madison*[10] was not premised on any special, let alone exclusive, constitutional function of the Court, but simply on its duty to decide the case before it in conformance with the superior law of the Constitution. Other arguments for judicial review have accorded the judiciary a special

---

7. *See* D. Morgan, Congress and the Constitution (1966); Mikva & Lundy, *The 91st Congress and the Constitution*, 38 U. Chi. L. Rev. 449 (1971).
8. *See* D. Morgan, *supra* note 7, at 45–98.
9. *See* Eaken v. Raub, 12 S. & R. 330, 353–54 (Pa. 1825) (Gibson, J., dissenting).
10. 5 U.S. (1 Cranch) 137 (1803).

function, but none implies that its role as constitutional interpreter excludes that of other institutions.[11] (There may, indeed, exist constitutional issues committed to the so-called "political branches" to the exclusion of the judiciary.[12])

Finally, courts often accord a challenged law a "presumption of constitutionality" based partly on the assumption that the legislature has previously passed upon the constitutional questions raised in litigation. Even where judicial deference is attenuated, the courts may lack the institutional capacity to review all aspects of legislative decisions, such as the subjective motivations of lawmakers. If the Constitution is to be applied at all in such cases, it must be applied by the lawmakers themselves.

The only plausible argument challenging legislative duty to consider constitutional questions is premised on institutional incompetence. Many legislators are not lawyers; the legislative process is not structured to allow constitutional questions to be examined systematically or dispassionately; and many constitutional problems arise only as legislation is implemented. Although these points may argue for judicial review, they do not argue against an initial legislative examination. The modern legislative committee, staffed by lawyers and others having expertise in particular areas of policy and law, is competent to consider the constitutional implications of pending measures. If many problems cannot be foreseen or adequately handled, that does not argue against confronting those that can. To be sure, legislatures will seldom engage in the disinterested and detailed analysis that we expect of courts. One can reasonably demand, however, that the lawmaking process take explicit account of constitutional values threatened by pending legislation.

I have deliberately hedged the second assumption. Whether or not one agrees with the Court's rather recent assertion that it is "the ultimate interpreter of the Constitution,"[13] the judiciary is its most skilled, disinterested, and articulate interpreter. For present purposes, therefore, one need not assume that a legislature is bound by judge-made constitutional doctrine. It is sufficient that such doctrine carry a strong presumption of correctness in the legislative chambers.

The interaction of these two assumptions gives rise to the central issue in this Essay. If a legislator were not bound to apply the Constitution himself, a "Legislator's Guide" would merely assist him in predicting whether the courts would uphold a measure if and when it were challenged. In other words, the legislator's view of judicial doctrine would be that of

11. *See* P. BREST, PROCESSES OF CONSTITUTIONAL DECISIONMAKING ch. 9 (forthcoming 1975).
12. *See id.* ch. 13; Scharpf, *Judicial Review and the Political Question*, 75 YALE L.J. 517 (1966).
13. Powell v. McCormack, 395 U.S. 486, 549 (1969). *See also* Cooper v. Aaron, 358 U.S. 1, 18 (1958).

Holmes' "bad man, who cares only for the material consequences which such knowledge enables him to predict."[14] If, on the other hand, the legislator were bound to apply the Constitution but not to defer to judicial decisions, the "Conscientious Legislator's Guide" would consist only of lessons in interpreting the text, history, and structure of the Constitution.[15]

If both assumptions are accepted, however, the legislator must learn not only to interpret the Constitution, but also to interpret judicial decisions interpreting the Constitution. Decisions striking down laws are easy to understand: they mean that the laws are unconstitutional. Decisions *not* striking down laws do not always mean that the laws are constitutional, however, for a court's failure to invalidate may only reflect its institutional limitations. The remainder of this Essay inquires how a legislator seeking to assess the constitutionality of a proposed law can find guidance in judicial decisions without being misled by them.

II. UNCONSTITUTIONAL MOTIVES[16]

Decisions invoking the "familiar principle . . . that this Court will not strike down an otherwise constitutional statute on the basis of an alleged illicit legislative motive"[17] emphasize the evidentiary difficulties of ascertaining subjective intent and the futility of invalidating a law that can be reenacted with a rehearsed legislative history and survive review.[18] Decisions ignoring this "familiar principle" do so covertly or inexplicitly.[19] The Court has never squarely faced the basic, substantive question: If the language and effects of a law pass constitutional muster, should the legislature's reasons for enacting it be germane?

The beginning of an answer lies in the observation that many constitutional provisions, such as those forbidding the enactment of laws abridging speech, deterring interstate movement,[20] and discriminating on the basis of race, are designed to prevent certain effects from occurring. One characterizes as "unconstitutional" a legislator's motive to suppress criticism of government, to prevent indigents from settling in his state, or to thwart racial equality, because he is seeking to bring about the very effects that the Constitution seeks to avert.

---

14. Holmes, *The Path of the Law*, 10 HARV. L. REV. 457, 459 (1897).
15. *See* P. BREST, *supra* note 11, pt. I.
16. I use the terms "motives" and "motivations" interchangeably with "objectives," "purposes," and "reasons."
17. United States v. O'Brien, 391 U.S. 367, 383 (1968).
18. *See id.*; Palmer v. Thompson, 403 U.S. 217 (1971).
19. *See, e.g.*, Epperson v. Arkansas, 393 U.S. 97 (1968); Griffin v. County Sch. Bd., 377 U.S. 218 (1964); Gomillion v. Lightfoot, 364 U.S. 339 (1960).
20. No provision explicitly protects interstate movement. The Court has attributed the right to various clauses or found it implicit in the structure of the Constitution. *See* Shapiro v. Thompson, 394 U.S. 618, 629–31 (1969); Crandall v. Nevada, 73 U.S. (6 Wall.) 35 (1868).

If the Constitution were read to prohibit all laws that produce those effects to any extent whatever, legislative motives might be legally irrelevant: the constitutionality of a measure would simply depend on the effects it produced. Constitutional provisions cannot be construed so absolutely, however. Otherwise a state could not outlaw noisy midnight rallies outside hospital windows or collect a $1 toll on an interstate highway.[21] In practice, legislators necessarily have considerable discretion to compromise constitutional values in the pursuit of the various ends of government.

Notwithstanding this discretion, the conscientious legislator will treat a law's adverse effects on constitutionally protected interests as a cost in the intuitive cost-benefit analysis that underlies the legislative process. The indifferent legislator will simply ignore those effects. But the unconstitutionally motivated legislator will count them as a positive good, and this perverse calculation may even cause him to vote for a measure he would not otherwise support. If a law's effects are constitutionally permissible, an individual whose rights it infringes still has a legitimate grievance if it would not have been adopted but for the legislature's counting the infringement as a benefit. The distinction between stumbling over someone and deliberately kicking him is not new to our jurisprudence.[22]

Despite the Court's reluctance to inquire into legislative motivations, its decisions inform the conscientious legislator that some motives are unconstitutional. For example, the standard enunciated in *O'Brien* indicates that the "suppression of free expression" is not a legitimate governmental interest,[23] and the Court's modern internal security decisions strongly imply that a legislator may not vote for the draft-card destruction law *for the purpose* of suppressing antiwar protest.[24] In *Shapiro v. Thompson*,[25] the Court did not examine the legislators' motives in enacting 1-year residency requirements for welfare assistance; but in rejecting the states' proffered "compelling interest" in preventing "a substantial influx of indigent newcomers," the Court held that "the purpose of inhibiting migration by needy persons into the State is constitutionally impermissible."[26] In *Palmer v. Thompson*,[27] the Court refused, out of institutional concerns, to inquire into the reasons that the City Council of Jackson, Mississippi, closed its public swimming pools in the face of an order to desegregate them. But the Court's prior segregation decisions make clear that a Coun-

---

21. *Cf.* Evansville-Vanderburgh Airport Authority v. Delta Airlines, 405 U.S. 707 (1972); Adderley v. Florida, 385 U.S. 39 (1966); Kovacs v. Cooper, 336 U.S. 77 (1949).
22. O.W. HOLMES, THE COMMON LAW 3 (1881).
23. *See* text accompanying note 3 *supra*.
24. *E.g.*, Brandenburg v. Ohio, 395 U.S. 444 (1969); Herndon v. Lowry, 301 U.S. 242 (1937).
25. 394 U.S. 618 (1969).
26. *Id.* at 629.
27. 403 U.S. 217 (1971).

cil member could not constitutionally vote to close the pools out of opposition to social intermingling between the races.[28] Those decisions also imply that even if the Council's objective were the legitimate one of maintaining order, mere speculation that interracial violence might occur could not justify closing the pools.[29]

So far, I have focused on motives that are inconsistent with constitutional prohibitions. But constitutional grants of authority are also susceptible of exercise for illicit purposes.

It is not peculiar that an exercise of power, which is in terms within an institution's authority and which contravenes no specific prohibition, may nonetheless be ultra vires because of the motives underlying the exercise. The most skilled draftsman can seldom tailor the literal terms of a delegation to coincide precisely with the purposes for which it is made. Therefore, the law typically requires those exercising authority to adhere to the purpose as well as the letter of the grant of power. For example, a trustee who intentionally injures the beneficiary, or aids a third party without regard to the beneficiary's interests, may be held accountable for any resulting loss; while another trustee, whose conduct objectively appears no different but who acted in good faith, is not liable. Many legally cognizable "abuses of authority" by servants, agents, trustees, and public officials consist of conduct lying comfortably within the literal terms of their authority.

In *McCulloch v. Maryland*, Chief Justice Marshall noted that this principle applies to the exercise of constitutionally delegated authority:

> [S]hould Congress, under the pretext of executing its powers, pass laws for the accomplishment of objects not intrusted to the government, it would become the painful duty of this tribunal, should a case requiring such a decision come before it, to say that such an act was not the law of the land.[30]

During the early years of the 20th century, in *Hammer v. Dagenhart*[31] and *Bailey v. Drexel Furniture Co.*,[32] the Court carried out Marshall's threat, holding that the regulation of child labor lay beyond Congress' authority and could not be accomplished under the guise of a tax law or a regulation of interstate commerce. The Court has since taken a more modest

---

28. *See, e.g.,* Griffin v. County Sch. Bd., 377 U.S. 218, 231 (1964): "Whatever non-racial grounds might support a State's allowing a county to abandon public schools, the object must be a constitutional one, and grounds of race and opposition to desegregation do not qualify as constitutional."

29. *Cf.* Watson v. City of Memphis, 373 U.S. 526 (1963); Buchanan v. Warley, 245 U.S. 60 (1917). In these cases the Court rejected such speculations as defenses for maintaining segregated facilities, not for abandoning the facilities entirely. The closing of facilities triggered by the prospect of desegregation presents many of the same constitutional difficulties. *See* Brest, *Palmer v. Thompson: An Approach to the Problem of Unconstitutional Legislative Motivation,* 1971 SUP. CT. REV. 95, 132–33.

30. 17 U.S. (4 Wheat.) 316, 423 (1819).

31. 247 U.S. 251 (1918).

32. 259 U.S. 20 (1922).

view of its competence to supervise Congress' exercise of national powers and a more generous view of their scope. But it has never disavowed the principle implicit in Marshall's "pretext" statement.

A conscientious legislator cannot assume that judicial reluctance to supervise Congress' exercise of its powers means that those powers are plenary. This was Professor Gerald Gunther's point when he urged the Department of Justice to base certain of the public accommodations provisions of the Civil Rights Act of 1964 on the 14th amendment rather than on the commerce clause:

> The proposed end run by way of the commerce clause seems to me ill-advised.
> . . . I know of course that the commerce power is a temptingly broad one. But surely responsible statutory drafting should have a firmer basis than, for example, some of the loose talk in recent newspaper articles about the widely accepted, unrestricted availability of the commerce clause to achieve social ends. . . . The commerce clause "hook" has been put to some rather strained uses in the past, I know; but the substantive content of the commerce clause would have to be drained beyond any point yet reached to justify the simplistic argument that all intrastate activity may be subjected to any kind of national regulation merely because some formal crossing of an interstate boundary once took place, without regard to the relationship between the aim of the regulation and interstate trade. The aim of the proposed anti-discrimination legislation, I take it, is quite unrelated to any concern with national commerce in any substantive sense.
> It would, I think, pervert the meaning and purpose of the commerce clause to invoke it as the basis for this legislation.[33]

Notwithstanding this advice, the public accommodations provisions were based primarily on the commerce clause. And in *Katzenbach v. McClung*,[34] the Court sustained the Act's application to a restaurant in which "a substantial portion of the food it serves . . . has moved in [interstate] commerce."[35] Had Professor Gunther become Mr. Justice Gunther in the interim, he would doubtless have felt constrained by the Court's institutional limitations to join in this decision, although his substantive views had in no way changed.

Even accounting for motives, few exercises of the article I powers are constitutionally controversial.[36] By contrast, some proposed measures to implement Congress' article III powers are quite problematic.

Article III does not require the creation of a lower federal judiciary but merely allows for "such inferior Courts as the Congress may from time to

33. Letter of June 5, 1963, *quoted in* G. GUNTHER & N. DOWLING, CONSTITUTIONAL LAW 336 (8th ed. 1970).
34. 379 U.S. 294 (1964).
35. Pub. L. No. 88–352, § 201(c) (1964), codified at 42 U.S.C. § 2000a(c) (1970).
36. Congressional implementation of the 14th amendment pursuant to § 5 may, however, present similar problems of ultra vires action. *Cf.* Oregon v. Mitchell, 400 U.S. 112 (1970). *But see* Cohen, *Congressional Power to Interpret Due Process and Equal Protection*, 27 STAN. L. REV. 603 (1975).

time ordain and establish." Article III also subjects the Supreme Court's appellate jurisdiction to "such Exceptions, and . . . such Regulations as the Congress shall make." Ever since the Judiciary Act of 1789, Congress has regulated the jurisdiction of federal courts in response to federalistic and procedural considerations, to allocate business between the federal and state judicial systems and to channel federal litigation efficiently.[37]

Over the past several decades, a spate of jurisdictional limitations of a quite different sort have been introduced in the Congress. Generated by disagreement with the substance of particular judicial decisions, these bills typically have sought to eliminate both the Supreme Court's appellate jurisdiction and the original jurisdiction of federal district courts in particular subject areas. For example, the Jenner Bill provided that "the Supreme Court shall have no jurisdiction to review . . . any case where there is drawn into question the validity of," *inter alia,* citations for contempt of congressional committees, the discharge of federal employees "whose retention may impair the security of the United States Government," state regulations designed "to control subversive activities," and decisions "pertaining to the admission of persons to the practice of law."[38] The Tuck Bill would have deprived the Supreme Court and federal district courts of jurisdiction over actions "seeking to apportion or reapportion the legislature of any State of the Union or branch thereof."[39] A rejected section of the Omnibus Crime Control and Safe Streets Bill provided:

> Neither the Supreme Court nor any inferior court ordained and established by Congress under Article III . . . shall have jurisdiction to review or to reverse, vacate, modify, or disturb in any way, a ruling of any trial court of any State in any criminal prosecution admitting in evidence as voluntarily made an admission or confession of an accused if such ruling has been affirmed or otherwise upheld by the highest court of the State having appellate jurisdiction of the cause.[40]

The Court has seldom addressed the constitutionality of provisions like these. The leading case in the area is *Ex parte McCardle,*[41] in which a southern newspaper editor held in military custody petitioned for a writ of habeas corpus, challenging the legality of Congress' Reconstruction program. The Circuit Court for the Southern District of Mississippi denied the writ, and he appealed to the Supreme Court. After the appeal had been argued, Con-

---

37. For example, the Judiciary Act of 1789 created no general federal question jurisdiction; limited diversity jurisdiction to suits involving more than $500, and "between a citizen of the State where the suit is brought and a citizen of another State"; and did not authorize Supreme Court review of all state cases arising under the Constitution, laws, and treaties of the United States.

38. S. 2646, 85th Cong., 2d Sess. (1958).

39. H.R. 11926, 88th Cong., 2d Sess. (1964).

40. S. 17, 90th Cong., 2d Sess. (1968).

41. 74 U.S. (7 Wall.) 506 (1869).

gress, quite obviously wishing to preclude a decision on the merits, repealed the statute under which it had been taken. Chief Justice Chase wrote for the Court, dismissing the case for want of jurisdiction:

> We are not at liberty to inquire into the motives of the legislature. We can only examine into its power under the Constitution; and the power to make exceptions to the appellate jurisdiction of this court is given by express words.
>
> What, then, is the effect of the repealing act on the case before us? We cannot doubt as to this. Without jurisdiction the court cannot proceed at all in any cause. Jurisdiction is power to declare the law, and when it ceases to exist, the only function remaining to the court is that of announcing the fact and dismissing the cause.[42]

This and other opinions are ambiguous. They may imply that Congress has plenary power to restrict federal jurisdiction. Or they may merely reflect institutional limitations, such as judicial incompetence to inquire into congressional motivations, or the supposed inability of federal courts to exercise any jurisdiction not conferred by statute, even if the jurisdictional lacuna is patently unconstitutional.[43]

For the conscientious legislator, the central question must be the purely substantive one, whether particular jurisdictional legislation is consistent with the purposes underlying Congress' article III powers and the roles of the federal judiciary in our constitutional scheme. Although some guidelines have been proposed,[44] the problem demands more systematic analysis than it has received. This much may be ventured, however: If one considers Congress' article III powers in the light of any of their likely reasons for being, it is implausible that Congress' control over federal jurisdiction is plenary. And if one accords the judiciary any special role in interpreting the Constitution, it is implausible that Congress should be able to preclude a constitutional decision by the courts merely because the result would be unpopular. The only serious question that remains is whether Congress may preclude decisions it believes would be constitutionally *incorrect*. An unequivocal answer may never emerge. There can be no answer at all, however, unless the question is approached from the viewpoint of a legislator rather than through the purposefully blinded eyes of a Court.

III. The Rationality Standards

During the first third of the 20th century, the Supreme Court often read the due process clause to demand a substantial justification for legislation

---

42. *Id.* at 514.
43. *See Ex parte* Bollman, 8 U.S. (4 Cranch) 75 (1807).
44. *See, e.g.,* Hart, *The Power of Congress to Limit the Jurisdiction of Federal Courts,* 66 Harv. L. Rev. 1362 (1953); Ratner, *Congressional Power Over the Appellate Jurisdiction of the Supreme Court,* 109 U. Pa. L. Rev. 157 (1960).

that adversely affected economic interests.[45] Since 1937, however, courts have subjected most social and economic legislation to the easily satisfied standard of the rational relation test: the law will be sustained if under any reasonably conceivable state of facts it furthers any reasonably conceivable legitimate objective to any extent.[46]

The Court currently holds that the equal protection clause of the fourteenth amendment requires a substantial justification for laws that classify on racial or certain other "suspect" grounds and also for laws that affect certain fundamental interests.[47] Most legislative classifications challenged under the equal protection clause will be sustained, however, if they might conceivably further some legitimate objective to some extent.[48]

These minimal due process and equal protection standards require some modification in order to be useful to a legislator assessing the constitutionality of a pending bill. It is pointless for a legislator to query whether a bill furthers some conceivable objective. The important question is whether it furthers his objectives or those of his fellow legislators. It is also pointless for a legislator to query whether the law will promote the objectives under any reasonably conceivable state of facts. The relevant facts are those that he believes exist.

With these modifications, do the rationality standards comprehend all that the due process and equal protection clauses usually demand of a legislature? Or are the standards essentially deferential criteria of judicial review, consistent with, or even implying, more rigorous legislative standards? This problem pervades the Court's contemporary equal protection jurisprudence.[49]

Among the legacies of the Warren Court was the notion that legislative classifications adversely affecting certain important interests—most notably those in interstate mobility and voting—were subject to especially strict scrutiny under the equal protection clause.[50] It is not clear why the Court invoked the equal protection clause to strike down state residence requirements that deterred movement from state to state, since interstate mobility has long been regarded as an independent constitutional right.[51] There is

---

45. *See, e.g.*, Adkins v. Children's Hosp., 261 U.S. 525 (1923); Lochner v. New York, 198 U.S. 45 (1905).
46. *See, e.g.*, Williamson v. Lee Optical Co., 348 U.S. 483 (1955).
47. *See, e.g.*, Graham v. Richardson, 403 U.S. 365 (1971) (alienage as suspect classification); Kramer v. Union Free Sch. Dist., 395 U.S. 621 (1969) (franchise as fundamental interest).
48. *See, e.g.*, Dandridge v. Williams, 397 U.S. 471 (1970), *quoted in* text accompanying note 56 *infra*.
49. The Court's post-1937 decisions retreating from economic due process are equally ambiguous in this respect. *Cf.* McCloskey, *Economic Due Process and the Supreme Court: An Exhumation and Reburial*, 1962 SUP. CT. REV. 34.
50. *See* Kramer v. Union Free Sch. Dist., 395 U.S. 621 (1969); Shapiro v. Thompson, 394 U.S. 618 (1969) (interstate mobility). *Cf.* Douglas v. California, 372 U.S. 353 (1963) (access to criminal appeal).
51. *See, e.g.*, Crandall v. Nevada, 73 U.S. (6 Wall.) 35 (1868).

no constitutional right to vote, however. The Court justified the strict equal protection standard in voting cases on the grounds that "the right to exercise the franchise . . . is preservative of other basic civil and political rights,"[52] and that "statutes distributing the franchise constitute the foundation of our representative society."[53]

At least one of the Court's opinions implied that it might extend this special solicitude to other important interests, such as subsistence and education.[54] But over the dissents of Justices Douglas, Brennan, and Marshall, the Burger Court has declined to do so.

In *Dandridge v. Williams*,[55] the Court upheld a provision of Maryland's Aid to Families with Dependent Children (AFDC) program that limited the monthly grant to any one family to $250, regardless of the family's size or computed need. The State contended that the regulation was rationally related to the legitimate purposes of encouraging employment and maintaining equity between families on welfare and those supported by an employed breadwinner. The district court applied a stricter standard, however, and held the provision unconstitutional on the ground that it "overreached" and cut "too broad a swath on an indiscriminate basis as applied to the entire group of AFDC eligibles." The Supreme Court reversed, Justice Stewart writing for the majority:

> If this were a case involving government action claimed to violate the First Amendment guarantee of free speech, a finding of "overreaching" would be significant and might be crucial. . . . But the concept of "overreaching" has no place in this case. For here we deal with state regulation in the social and economic field, not affecting freedoms guaranteed by the Bill of Rights. . . . For this Court to approve the invalidation of state economic or social regulation as "overreaching" would be far too reminiscent of an era when the Court thought the Fourteenth Amendment gave it power to strike down state laws "because they may be unwise, improvident, or out of harmony with a particular school of thought." *Williamson v. Lee Optical Co.*, 348 U.S. 483, 488. That era long ago passed into history. . . .
>
> In the area of economics and social welfare, a State does not violate the Equal Protection Clause merely because the classifications made by its laws are imperfect. If the classification has some "reasonable basis," it does not offend the Constitution simply because the classification "is not made with mathematical nicety or because in practice it results in some inequality." . . . "A statutory discrimination will not be set aside if any state of facts reasonably may be conceived to justify it." . . .
>
> To be sure, the cases . . . enunciating this fundamental standard under the

---

52. Reynolds v. Sims, 377 U.S. 533, 562 (1964).
53. Kramer v. Union Free Sch. Dist., 395 U.S. 621, 626 (1969).
54. Shapiro v. Thompson, 394 U.S. 618 (1969). The implications were evident to many scholarly commentators. *See, e.g.,* J. COONS, W. CLUNE & S. SUGARMAN, PRIVATE WEALTH AND PUBLIC EDUCATION (1970); Michelman, *Foreword—On Protecting the Poor Through the Fourteenth Amendment,* 83 HARV. L. REV. 7 (1969).
55. 397 U.S. 471 (1970).

Equal Protection Clause, have in the main involved state regulation of business or industry. The administration of public welfare assistance, by contrast, involves the most basic economic needs of impoverished human beings. . . . [B]ut we can find no basis for applying a different constitutional standard. . . . [I]t is a standard . . . that is true to the principle that the Fourteenth Amendment gives the federal courts no power to impose upon the States their views of what constitutes wise economic or social policy.[56]

Writing in dissent, Justice Marshall criticized the Court for "focusing upon the abstract dichotomy between two different approaches to equal protection problems":

> Under the so-called "traditional test," a classification is said to be permissible under the Equal Protection Clause unless it is "without any reasonable basis." . . . On the other hand, if the classification affects a "fundamental right," then the state interest in perpetuating the classification must be "compelling" in order to be sustained. . . .
>
> This case simply defies easy characterization in terms of one or the other of these "tests." The cases relied on by the Court, in which a "mere rationality" test was actually used, e.g., *Williamson v. Lee Optical Co.*, 348 U.S. 483 (1955), are most accurately described as involving the application of equal protection reasoning to the regulation of business interests. The extremes to which the Court has gone in dreaming up rational bases for state regulation in that area may in many instances be ascribed to a healthy revulsion from the Court's earlier excesses in using the Constitution to protect interests that have more than enough power to protect themselves in the legislative halls. This case, involving the literally vital interests of a powerless minority—poor families without breadwinners—is far removed from the area of business regulation, as the Court concedes. Why then is the standard used in those cases imposed here? We are told no more than that this case falls in "the area of economics and social welfare," with the implication that from there the answer is obvious.
>
> In my view, equal protection analysis of this case is not appreciably advanced by the *a priori* definition of a "right," fundamental or otherwise. Rather, concentration must be placed upon the character of the classification in question, the relative importance to individuals in the class discriminated against of the governmental benefits that they do not receive, and the asserted state interests in support of the classification.[57]

In *San Antonio School District v. Rodriguez*,[58] the Court applied the rational classification standard to uphold Texas' educational finance system, under which a district's expenditures are heavily dependent on the value of local real property. Writing for the majority, Justice Powell rejected the claim that strict judicial scrutiny was required because of the importance of the interest in education:

---

56. *Id.* at 484–86.
57. *Id.* at 519–21.
58. 411 U.S. 1 (1973).

74 PAUL BREST

[I]f the degree of judicial scrutiny of state legislation fluctuated depending on a majority's view of the importance of the interest affected, we would have gone "far toward making this Court a 'super-legislature.'" . . . We would, indeed, then be assuming a legislative role and one for which the Court lacks both authority and competence.[59]

Again in dissent, Justice Marshall argued for a "spectrum of standards" comprehending

variations in the degrees of care with which the Court will scrutinize particular classifications, depending . . . on the constitutional and societal importance of the interests adversely affected and the recognized invidiousness of the basis upon which the particular classification is drawn.

. . . As the nexus between [a] specific constitutional guarantee and [a] nonconstitutional interest draws closer, the nonconstitutional interest becomes more fundamental and the degree of judicial scrutiny applied when the interest is infringed on a discriminatory basis must be adjusted accordingly.[60]

Justice Marshall emphasized the general importance of education in American society and its relationship to the informed exercise of first amendment rights and the franchise (which he explained was itself a fundamental interest because of its societal importance and relationship to first amendment rights). These considerations, together with the system's wealth-discriminatory impact, led him to conclude that the school finance system was unconstitutional.

Do *Dandridge* and *Rodriguez* reflect the Court's *substantive* position that the equal protection clause demands nothing more than "minimum rationality" in the allocation of welfare and educational benefits, or an *institutional* reluctance to second-guess the legislatures' supposed applications of a more demanding requirement? Even if one analyzes the Court's opinions with the care that is due poetry—and is not due any court's opinions—they remain ambiguous. Justice Powell's assertion that "the Court lacks both authority and competence" may embody a substantive interpretation of the equal protection clause. On the other hand, it may mean only that the Court lacks authority because it is institutionally incompetent.

The equal protection clause neither compels nor forecloses Justice Marshall's suggested interpretation. The framers' immediate concern was with racial inequality. But they used general language; their purposes can be characterized more abstractly; and the clause has long been understood to embody broader principles of fair treatment.[61] Indeed, the foundations of

59. *Id.* at 31.
60. *Id.* at 99, 102–03. *See generally* Gunther, *Foreword—In Search of Evolving Doctrine on a Changing Court: A Model for a Newer Equal Protection*, 86 HARV. L. REV. 1 (1972).
61. *See, e.g.,* Weber v. Aetna Cas. & Sur. Co., 406 U.S. 164 (1972) (discrimination against illegitimates); Reed v. Reed, 404 U.S. 71 (1971) (sex discrimination); Morey v. Doud, 354 U.S. 457 (1957) (exemption of named corporation from general regulation).

Justice Marshall's theory lie in the longstanding doctrine—reaffirmed by the Court in *Dandridge* and *Rodriguez*—that the equal protection clause demands that all classifications serve at least some legitimate objective.[62] Justice Jackson explained the function of this rational classification standard:

> [T]here is no more effective practical guaranty against arbitrary and unreasonable government than to require that the principles of law which officials would impose upon a minority must be imposed generally. Conversely, nothing opens the door to arbitrary action so effectively as to allow those officials to pick and choose only a few to whom they will apply legislation and thus to escape the political retribution that might be visited upon them if larger numbers were affected. Courts can take no better measure to assure that laws will be just than to require that laws be equal in operation.[63]

If Justice Marshall's criterion seems too amorphous to guide decision-making by a nonrepresentative judiciary, it nonetheless speaks to a legislator: As the interests affected by legislation become more important and the classifications more invidious, the parochialism, self-interest, logrolling, and the like, that pervade the political process must yield to generally shared principles of fair treatment. A conscientious legislator might take this view even if there were no equal protection clause. But the provision stands as a reminder of the government's commitment to fairness and provides some counterweight to callousness and expediency. This may not seem like much of a constitutional requirement until one compares it with the modified rational classification standard with which we began. For, unless a legislator is unconstitutionally motivated, he is virtually certain to adopt a provision that serves a legitimate objective to some extent. The very permissiveness of the rationality test may indicate that it is a standard of *judicial* review of a prior decision made on the basis of a more meaningful criterion.

IV. State Regulation of Interstate Commerce

The commerce clause of article I, by negative implication, forbids certain state interferences with interstate commerce.[64] The judicial doctrines concerning state burdens on interstate transportation provide a final example of the divergence between substantive constitutional requirements and standards of judicial review.

The Court has sometimes reviewed state regulations of interstate trans-

---

62. *See, e.g.,* F.S. Royster Guano Co. v. Virginia, 253 U.S. 412, 415 (1920): "[T]he classification must be reasonable, not arbitrary, and must rest upon some ground of difference having a fair and substantial relation to the object of the legislation, so that all persons similarly circumstanced shall be treated alike."

63. Railway Express Agency v. New York, 336 U.S. 106, 112–13 (1949) (concurring opinion).

64. *See* Cooley v. Board of Wardens, 53 U.S. (12 How.) 299 (1851).

portation under the minimal rational relation test.[65] For the most part, however, it has subjected such regulations to a slightly more demanding standard—one sufficiently meaningful to strike down an Arizona law limiting the length of passenger and freight trains (*Southern Pacific Co. v.
Arizona*[66]) and an Illinois requirement that trucks be equipped with con-
toured, rather than conventional straight mudflaps (*Bibb v. Navajo Freight
Lines*[67]). The standard nonetheless accords state regulations a heavy presumption of constitutionality. As the Court wrote in *Bibb*, quoting *Southern Pacific*:

> Unless we can conclude on the whole record that "the total effect of the law as
> a safety measure in reducing accidents and casualties is so slight or problematical
> as not to outweigh the national interest in keeping interstate commerce free from
> interferences which seriously impede it" (*Southern Pacific Co. v. Arizona . . .*)
> we must uphold the statute.[68]

I believe that this noninterventionist criterion is largely a product of
the judiciary's institutional limitations and does not inform the conscientious legislator how he or she should assess the constitutionality of a proposed law that impedes interstate transportation. In a decision upholding
South Carolina's restrictive limitations on the height and weight of trucks
using its highways, the Court noted that

> in reviewing a state highway regulation where Congress has not acted, a court
> is not called upon, as are state legislatures, to determine what, in its judgment, is
> the most suitable restriction to be applied of those that are possible, or to choose
> that one which in its opinion is best adapted to all the diverse interests affected. . . .
> When the action of a legislature is within the scope of its power, fairly debatable
> questions as to its reasonableness, wisdom and propriety are not for the determi-
> nation of courts, but for the legislative body on which rests the duty and respon-
> sibility of decision.[69]

The Court made the same point in a recent decision reversing a judgment
invalidating Arkansas' full-crew train law:

> We think it plain that . . . the District Court indulged in a legislative judg-
> ment wholly beyond its limited authority to review state legislation under the
> Commerce Clause. . . . [T]he question of safety in the circumstances of this
> case is essentially a matter of public policy, and public policy can, under our con-
> stitutional system, be fixed only by the people acting through their elected repre-
> sentatives.[70]

65. *See, e.g.*, South Carolina State Highway Dep't v. Barnwell Bros., 303 U.S. 177 (1938).
66. 325 U.S. 761 (1945).
67. 359 U.S. 520 (1959).
68. *Id.* at 524.
69. South Carolina State Highway Dep't v. Barnwell Bros., 303 U.S. 177, 190–91 (1938).
70. Brotherhood of Locomotive Firemen v. Chicago, R.I. & P.R.R., 393 U.S. 129, 136–38 (1968).

The institutional character of the *Southern Pacific–Bibb* criterion is highlighted by the Court's explanation, at the beginning of the opinion in *Southern Pacific*, that

> [t]he matters for ultimate determination here are the nature and extent of the burden which the state regulation of interstate trains, adopted as a safety measure, imposes on interstate commerce, and whether the relative weights of the state and national interests involved are such as to make inapplicable the rule generally observed, that the free flow of interstate commerce and its freedom from local restraints in matters requiring uniformity of regulation are interests safeguarded by the commerce clause from state interference.[71]

This statement—though perhaps it reads too much like a presumption of *un*constitutionality—essentially declares the substantive constitutional standard. The commerce clause demands some accommodation of local regulatory concerns with the national interest in free interstate trade and movement.[72] A legislator does not achieve a rational accommodation by inquiring, as do the judicial tests, whether a burdensome regulation promotes legitimate state interests to *some* extent. He must assess the relative importance of the regulation to the state and its burden on interstate commerce. To be sure, these are incommensurable values, but the weighing of incommensurables is a daily legislative task. Indeed, it partly is in recognition of the legislature's familiarity with the task, and the judiciary's comparative ineptitude, that the Court has adopted so deferential a standard of judicial review in these cases.

V. Conclusion

I have not addressed the practical problems that confront a legislator whose constitutional obligations conflict with the political demands of his office. Perhaps it is naive to assume that the Constitution will often prevail when political interests are threatened. But it would be premature to assume otherwise, until legislators recognize their duty to interpret the Constitution and learn how to do it. The conscientious legislator must learn not only how to interpret original sources, but how to analyze the opinions of courts—the most systematic and best qualified constitutional interpreters.

---

71. Southern Pacific Co. v. Arizona, 325 U.S. 761, 770 (1945).

72. Professor Terrance Sandalow has suggested that, since Congress has plenary authority to overturn state accommodations in this area, state legislatures may properly favor their local interests more than if their decisions were subject only to judicial review.

Congressional Power to Interpret Due Process and Equal Protection

William Cohen*

Can Congress constitutionally legislate to increase the scope of civil liberty? At first blush, the answer seems readily apparent. Congress can limit the exercise of federal governmental power, creating individual rights that the courts have declared not to be compelled by the Constitution. In federal criminal trials, for example, Congress can provide procedural safeguards that go well beyond the minimum guarantees of the Bill of Rights. Moreover, Congress can exercise its broadly interpreted delegated powers to place similar limits on the powers of the states. The public accommodation provisions of the Civil Rights Act of 1964, for example, were passed by Congress and sustained by the Court on the basis of congressional power to regulate commerce among the states.[1]

It is the thesis of this Essay that the issue of federalism is the major constitutional concern of laws that increase civil rights at the expense of state power. Moreover, the courts have reacted to the federalism concern in an inconsistent manner, depending on the clause of the Constitution invoked by Congress to support the legislation.

In the decades prior to 1937, the doctrine of dual federalism described the consistent judicial response to issues of federal power. Under the doctrine, the Court narrowly construed all of Congress' delegated powers in order to avoid encroaching on powers "reserved" to the states by the 10th amendment.[2] Since 1937, however, it has been difficult even to frame examples of plausible federal legislation that the courts would be likely to invalidate solely on the ground of ultra vires. From 1936 to 1970 no Supreme Court decision invalidated a federal law on the ground that Congress had exercised power that belonged exclusively to the states.[3] The reason for the retreat from an earlier era of judicially drawn limits of federal power to a system in which Congress effectively became the judge of the

* A.B. 1953, LL.B. 1956, University of California at Los Angeles. Professor of Law, Stanford University.
1. *See* Katzenbach v. McClung, 379 U.S. 294 (1964); Heart of Atlanta Motel, Inc. v. United States, 379 U.S. 241 (1964).
2. *See* Stern, *The Commerce Clause and the National Economy, 1933–1946*, 59 HARV. L. REV. 645, 647–52, 659–74 (1946).
3. The 1936 decisions invalidating congressional legislation were United States v. Butler, 297 U.S. 1 (1936), and Carter v. Carter Coal Co., 298 U.S. 238 (1936). The 1970 decision reviving ultra vires was Oregon v. Mitchell, 400 U.S. 112 (1970).

extent of its own power cannot be found in a judicial preference for exercise of power by the federal legislature rather than state legislatures.[4]
Rather, the development has been explained as reflecting the relative competence of Congress, compared to the courts, to draw the murky lines that
mark the outermost boundaries of federal power.[5]

In only one class of cases—involving protection of civil rights under
section 5 of the 14th amendment—has the doctrine of dual federalism re-
emerged as a potential limit on the powers of Congress. Ironically, the
Court's major difficulty with issues concerning the limits of congressional
power to legislate affirmative protection for civil rights arose in the context of the constitutional provision that most clearly would seem to grant
such a power. Section 5 of the 14th amendment empowers Congress to
"enforce, by appropriate legislation," the broad guarantees of freedom
contained in the due process and equal protection clauses of section 1 of
the 14th amendment. The cases of *Katzenbach v. Morgan*[6] and *Oregon v.
Mitchell*[7] produced a lively debate about the scope of congressional power
under section 5.[8] Unfortunately, the dialogue has been accompanied by
more questions than answers. Most interesting of all, the result in *Oregon
v. Mitchell* was that for the first time in a third of a century, a federal law
was struck down on ultra vires grounds—congressional action was invalidated not because of a violation of some specific limitation on Congress'
power but because Congress had exceeded the scope of its delegated powers.

I. The Two Rationales of *Katzenbach v. Morgan*

A. *Section 4(e) of the 1965 Voting Rights Act: Congressional Remedy or Constitutional Interpretation?*

Katzenbach v. Morgan involved the constitutionality of section 4(e) of
the Voting Rights Act of 1965. That provision suspended English-language
literacy tests as a voting requirement for persons who had completed the
sixth grade in a Puerto Rican school where the language of instruction
was other than English.[9] New York's Attorney General argued that, unless

---

4. *E.g.*, despite the broad regulatory power conceded to Congress under the commerce clause, the
Court has adopted a rule of statutory construction that "unless Congress conveys its purpose clearly, it
will not be deemed to have significantly changed the federal-state balance." United States v. Bass, 404
U.S. 336, 349 (1971). A judicial preference for federal power would lead to literal readings of statutes
that resulted in expansion of federal power.
    5. *See* H. Wechsler, *The Political Safeguards of Federalism*, in Principles, Politics and Fun-
damental Law 49–82 (1961).
    6. 384 U.S. 641 (1966).
    7. 400 U.S. 112 (1970).
    8. *See* Bickel, *The Voting Rights Cases*, 1966 Sup. Ct. Rev. 79, 85–101; Burt, *Miranda and
Title II: A Morganatic Marriage*, 1969 Sup. Ct. Rev. 81; Cox, *The Role of Congress in Constitutional
Determinations*, 40 U. Cin. L. Rev. 199 (1971); Engdahl, *Constitutionality of the Voting Age Statute*, 39 Geo. Wash. L. Rev. 1 (1970).
    9. 42 U.S.C. § 1973b(e) (1970). The provision was directed specifically at New York which,
in addition to having a sizable Puerto Rican population, permitted English literacy to be established

the Court were to make an independent determination that the English-literacy requirement was a violation of equal protection, section 4(e) exceeded Congress' power under section 5 of the 14th amendment. Significantly, Justice Brennan's opinion for the Court sustained section 4(e) without reaching the separate question whether, in the Court's independent judgment, New York's literacy requirement violated the equal protection clause. Two related theories were advanced by the Court to sustain the provision. First, Congress might have found that the state had discriminated against Puerto Ricans in the furnishing of governmental services, and that extending them the right to vote was a remedial measure designed to cure that discrimination.[10] Second, Congress might itself have determined that application of the English-literacy requirement was a violation of equal protection; as long as the Court could "perceive a basis" for the judgment, Congress' determination—that New York's withholding of the right to vote from Puerto Ricans with a sixth grade education in Puerto Rican schools denied equal protection—was to be sustained.[11]

The second rationale stirred major controversy. While the Court had given large latitude to congressional judgments about appropriate means to accomplish constitutionally defined ends, it had never before conceded to Congress the task of interpreting the meaning of the constitutional text. Traditionally, in the context of congressional power under section 5 of the 14th amendment, Congress could frame broad remedies for clear violations of section 1, but the Court's role has been to determine whether particular conduct violated section 1. While the Court's first rationale in *Morgan* thus saw extension of voting rights to Puerto Ricans merely as a remedy for other violations of equal protection, the second rationale rested on the crediting of a supposed congressional judgment that the denial of voting rights was itself a denial of equal protection.

Justices Harlan and Stewart, who joined in the only dissenting opinion, rejected both rationales. They dismissed the first theory as inapplicable to the challenged legislation. Since section 4(e) had been introduced from the floor during debate on the Voting Rights Act, there had been no investigation of legislative facts to support a finding of discrimination against Puerto Ricans in the rendering of governmental services.[12] As to the second rationale, their objection was more fundamental. The issue whether New York's denial of voting rights to those subsequently enfranchised by section 4(e) violated equal protection was a judicial question which could not be resolved by Congress. A congressional determination that Spanish-

---

either by passing a literacy test or through completion of the sixth grade of a school in which English was the language of instruction, 384 U.S. at 644–45 nn.2 & 3.

10. *Id.* at 653.
11. *Id.* at 654–56.
12. *Id.* at 669 (dissenting opinion).

speaking citizens are as capable of making informed decisions in elections as English-speaking citizens might have some bearing on that judicial decision, but courts should, in interpreting the equal protection clause, give no more deference to congressional judgments than those of state legislatures:

> . . . [W]e have here not a matter of giving deference to a congressional estimate, based on its determination of legislative facts, bearing upon the validity *vel non* of a statute, but rather what can at most be called a legislative announcement that Congress believes a state law to entail an unconstitutional deprivation of equal protection. Although this kind of declaration is of course entitled to the most respectful consideration, coming as it does from a concurrent branch and one that is knowledgeable in matters of popular political participation, I do not believe it lessens our responsibility to decide the fundamental issue of whether in fact the state enactment violates federal constitutional rights.[13]

B. *Limiting Congressional Power to Interpret the Constitution—Justice Brennan's "Ratchet" Theory*

Beyond the theoretical objection—that the majority stood *Marbury v. Madison* on its head by judicial deference to congressional interpretation of the Constitution—the two dissenters also pointed out that congressional power to interpret the Constitution could be used to dilute as well as to expand the substantive scope of due process and equal protection.[14] Justice Brennan's majority opinion addressed that concern in a footnote:

> Contrary to the suggestion of the dissent . . . § 5 does not grant Congress power to exercise discretion in the other direction and to enact 'statutes so as in effect to dilute equal protection and due process decisions of this Court.' We emphasize that Congress' power under § 5 is limited to adopting measures to enforce the guarantees of the Amendment; § 5 grants Congress no power to restrict, abrogate, or dilute these guarantees. Thus, for example, an enactment authorizing the States to establish racially segregated systems of education would not be—as required by § 5—a measure 'to enforce' the Equal Protection Clause since that clause of its own force prohibits such state laws.[15]

Justice Brennan's "ratchet" interpretation of section 5 presents two problems. First, it does not satisfactorily explain why Congress may move the due process or equal protection handle in only one direction. If Congress' interpretive power is grounded on special legislative competence not possessed by courts, then congressional insistence on English language literacy as a qualification to vote would seem to involve the same special competence as the decision to extend voting rights to those literate in a foreign language. In other words, if Congress is in a better position than

---

13. *Id.* at 669–70 (dissenting opinion).
14. *Id.* at 668 (dissenting opinion).
15. *Id.* at 651 n.10 (majority opinion).

the courts to make some kinds of due process fairness judgments and to balance state interests against the demand for equal protection, that competence should extend to a judgment that the courts have gone too far in expanding the scope of individual rights. Surely, close equal protection and due process judgments require determinations of issues of legislative fact and the balancing of competing interests. Even if the unique history of the 14th amendment prevents Congress from authorizing discrimination against racial minorities, in closer cases why should Congress not be accorded similar competence to judge both what due process and equal protection are and what they are not?

The second and more significant problem with the ratchet theory is the difficulty in determining the direction in which the handle is turning. For example, could a congressional expansion of the power of courts to issue gag orders to the press in criminal cases be justified as an enhancement of fair trial without the necessity of any judicial determination of the freedom of the press issue? Any issue involving competing claims of constitutional rights poses the dilemma of determining whether a particular decision "enforces" or "dilutes" constitutional rights.

Section 4(e) itself illustrates another aspect of the problem of determining whether a congressional enactment dilutes or enforces the 14th amendment. Section 4(e) extended the right to vote only to a limited class of non-English-speaking persons, thereby raising the constitutional question whether those literate in a foreign language—but not extended the vote by section 4(e)—had been subjected to invidious discrimination.[16] In determining that the limitation of section 4(e) to those educated in American-flag schools was valid, Justice Brennan's majority opinion reasoned that the strict scrutiny standard applicable to *denials* of voting rights was inapplicable to the challenge to section 4(e)'s *extension* of voting rights to those previously disenfranchised. The statute then was a "reform" measure, which might "take one step at a time."[17] The Court's reasoning suggests that if the same line had been drawn by the New York legislature, it would have survived an equal protection attack. Would any congressional extension of a new right to a limited class of persons accordingly be defined as a measure enforcing rather than diluting the Bill of Rights, and thus qualify as a congressional definition of equal protection? It is in the very nature of equal protection challenges, however, that one may attack the denial to oneself of benefits extended to others. The Court's opinion, which did scrutinize the reasonableness of the distinctions drawn by section

---

16. A companion case presented the issue of whether New York's English-literacy requirement was valid, but the Court did not reach the issue. *See* Cardona v. Power, 384 U.S. 672 (1966).

17. 384 U.S. at 657.

4(e) (albeit from the standpoint of minimum rationality) suggests a negative answer to the above question: a congressional statute that expands constitutional rights must still be judged by courts to determine whether the law itself makes "forbidden discriminations."[18]

C. *Criticism of the Remedy-Interpretation Distinction of the Dissent*

There are at least as many problems with the position of the dissent as with that of the majority. First is the problem of distinguishing remedial from interpretive statutes. In close cases, hewing the line between permissible remedial measures and impermissible interpretation may depend, not on the substantive sweep of the law, but on the ability of the congressional staff to supply the appropriate testimony in hearings and to draft a statutory preamble picking the proper theory. For the dissenters, section 4(e) failed to qualify as a remedial measure only because of the lack of a congressional factual record or findings. Yet a more ambitious suspension of literacy tests in the Voting Rights Act Amendments of 1970—a nationwide ban on all literacy tests[19]—was unanimously sustained by the Court in *Oregon v. Mitchell.* In that situation, the record in Congress convinced both Justices Harlan[20] and Stewart[21] that Congress could, under section 2 of the 15th amendment, ban all literacy tests in order to remedy racial discrimination in voting.[22] The *Morgan* dissent's remedy-interpretation distinction—at least in the case of congressional bans on literacy tests for voting—would therefore seem to turn on both the ostensible congressional theory and the legislative facts supporting that theory.

The dissent in *Katzenbach v. Morgan* has its own ratchet problem. The dissent concedes the power of Congress to impose more drastic remedies for constitutional violations than those fashioned by the courts. If particular remedies are judicially determined to be indispensible to the protection of constitutional rights, how far may Congress suspend those remedies without providing equivalent substitutes? And how are the courts to deal with a congressional judgment that a substituted remedy is equivalent? Most of the Warren Court's controversial criminal due process decisions, to the extent they require the exclusion of evidence in criminal trials, can be classified as remedial. Those judicial rules could be gutted by a binding congressional determination that the constitutional violation should not be

---

18. *Id.* at 658.
19. 42 U.S.C. § 1973aa (1970).
20. 400 U.S. at 216–17 (concurring in part and dissenting in part).
21. *Id.* at 282–84 (concurring in part and dissenting in part).
22. In fact the Court probably would have sustained the 1970 literacy test ban even were there a total absence of factual data in the record before Congress, since the use of literacy tests to accomplish racial discrimination in voting was a matter of common knowledge. It is difficult to estimate how solid the factual record would have had to have been for Justices Harlan and Stewart to have sustained the more limited literacy test suspension in § 4(e) of the 1965 Act.

accompanied by the remedy of exclusion.[23] The current debate over congressional response to court-ordered school busing to achieve integration makes the point that congressional response to unpopular Court decisions not only can, but probably will, take the form of excising the remedy fashioned by the Court.[24] Civil libertarians, concerned that Justice Brennan's theory can be perverted to justify the destruction of liberty, can find only cold comfort in the dissent's interpretation-remedy distinction, which could give Congress a virtual carte blanche to cut back constitutionally-required "remedies."

II. *Oregon v. Mitchell*: A CONSTITUTIONAL LAW DISASTER AREA

The debate in *Katzenbach v. Morgan* over congressional interpretative power continued in Congress with the 18-year-old vote provisions of the Voting Rights Act Amendments of 1970. Proponents of the legislation argued, although with some diffidence, that Congress had the power to determine that denial of voting rights to those in the 18–20 age group was a discrimination prevented by the equal protection clause.[25] Opponents argued that *Katzenbach v. Morgan* was erroneous in recognizing congressional power to interpret the Constitution, or, at the least, that the *Morgan* theory could not be expanded to outlaw discrimination that did not produce even an arguable constitutional violation.[26] The argument for congressional interpretive power eventuated in the 18-year-old vote provisions of the 1970 Voting Rights Act Amendments,[27] and their constitutional testing in *Oregon v. Mitchell*.

Oregon v. Mitchell is a constitutional law disaster area. By shifting 5–4 majorities, the 18-year-old vote extension was upheld in its application to federal elections and struck down in its application to state elections. Four Justices voted to sustain the 18-year-old vote provision in its entirety; four

23. Significantly, Miranda v. Arizona, 384 U.S. 436 (1966), was decided the same day as *Katzenbach v. Morgan*. The *Miranda* opinion encouraged Congress and the states to develop "procedures which are at least as effective" in protecting the privilege against self-incrimination as those that the Court imposed. For a detailed description of congressional response to that invitation, see Burt, *supra* note 8, at 123–32.

24. State Bd. of Educ. v. Swann, 402 U.S. 43 (1971), struck down a state statute that prohibited "involuntary busing of students." President Nixon squarely based his 1972 proposals to limit school integration and busing on the thesis that something less than a flat ban on all busing "deals with a remedy and not a right." *See* G. GUNTHER & N. DOWLING, CASES AND MATERIALS ON CONSTITUTIONAL LAW 364 (Supp. 1973). *See also* R. BORK, CONSTITUTIONALITY OF THE PRESIDENT'S BUSING PROPOSALS (1972).

25. *See, e.g.,* 116 CONG. REC. 6934–36 (1970) (statement by Professor Archibald Cox). Cox's defense of the 18-year-old vote provision, based on the *Katzenbach v. Morgan* rationale, was accompanied by the caution that "some constitutional scholars would not share my view that Congress can reduce the voting age without a constitutional amendment. Possibly, my reasoning runs the logic of *Katzenbach v. Morgan* into the ground." *Id.* at 6936.

26. Dean Louis Pollak's statement was *a principal position* paper. He argued that *Katzenbach v. Morgan* provided a "modestly plausible" but not an "ultimately persuasive" case for congressional power to reduce the voting age. *Id.* at 6964.

27. 42 U.S.C. § 1973bb–1 (1970).

other Justices voted to invalidate the provision in its entirety. Only Justice Black drew a distinction between federal and state elections, finding an unlimited power to set voter qualifications for federal offices in Congress' power to alter the "times, places and manner"[28] of holding those elections.[29] While that rationale was explicitly[30] or implicitly[31] rejected by the remaining eight Justices, it prevailed because of the 4-4[32] division. It is, of course, an anomaly that *Oregon v. Mitchell* may be cited as a resounding rejection of the very rationale—the distinction between voting qualifications for federal and state elections—that governed the outcome of the case.[33]

A. *Rejection of the Broad View of* Morgan

For our purposes, the most significant nose count is the 5 to 4 rejection of the argument that the *Katzenbach v. Morgan* rationale authorized Congress to extend the right to vote to 18-year-olds in all elections, federal and state. But the contrariety of views of the Justices in the majority on that issue makes it impossible to say just what limitation has been placed on the rationale that Congress' enforcement power in section 5 of the 14th amendment includes the power to give substantive content to the meaning of due process and equal protection.

For Justice Black, the limitation is found in the "whole Constitution," which reserves to the states the power to set voter qualifications in state elections,[34] and in the 13th, 14th, and 15th amendments, which qualify that power only in the case of racial discrimination. Thus, in Justice Black's view, section 4(e) of the Voting Rights Act of 1965 had been upheld in *Katzenbach v. Morgan* to remedy racial discrimination against Puerto Ri-

---

28. U.S. CONST. art. I, § 4, cl. 1.
29. 400 U.S. at 119–24.
30. The opinion of Justice Stewart, joined by the Chief Justice and Justice Blackmun, rejected the argument that "manner" can include voter qualifications, *id*. at 288–89 (concurring in part and dissenting in part), as did that of Justice Harlan, *id*. at 211–12 (concurring in part and dissenting in part).
31. Justice Douglas argued that the Civil War Amendments remove any implication in art. I, § 4, that Congress lacks power to fix voter qualifications in either state or federal elections. *See id*. at 143 (concurring in part and dissenting in part). Justice Brennan's opinion, joined by Justices White and Marshall, relies entirely on congressional power under § 5 of the 14th amendment. *Id*. at 229 (concurring in part and dissenting in part).
32. When added to the votes of the four Justices who would sustain the 18-year-old vote provision in toto, Justice Black's position that Congress could set voter qualifications in federal elections resulted in a 5–4 vote that the law could be applied constitutionally to federal elections. When added to the votes of the remaining four Justices who would have struck down the provisions in their entirety, Justice Black's position that Congress could not set voter qualifications in state elections produced a 5–4 vote that these provisions were unconstitutional as applied to state elections.
33. This problem is common in Supreme Court decisions where there is no Opinion of the Court. *See, e.g.*, National Mutual Ins. Co. v. Tidewater Transfer Co., 337 U.S. 582 (1949). That case upheld the constitutionality of the 1940 revision of the Judicial Code extending diversity jurisdiction to District of Columbia citizens, yet the two rationales that were argued to uphold the statute were rejected by votes of 6–3 and 7–2. Siegmund v. General Commodities Corp., 175 F.2d 952 (9th Cir. 1949), coped with the impact of *Tidewater* as precedent on extension of diversity jurisdiction to territorial citizens: "The reasons assigned by the two groups of Justices who concurred in the result are as applicable to cases involving citizens of territories . . . ." *Id*. at 953.
34. 400 U.S. at 125.

cans.[35] Justice Harlan, on the other hand, took the position that congressional extension of the right to vote to 18-year-olds should be sustained *only* if the Court's decisions applying the 14th amendment to voting rights were sound.[36] He continued to maintain the view he had expressed earlier, however, that the 14th amendment was inapplicable to voting rights, whether voting rights were extended by judicial construction of the equal protection clause or by act of Congress. He further stated his disagreement with the "compelling interest" standard of the "new equal protection," which a majority of the Court had applied in voting rights cases, insisting that legislative classifications should be reviewed only for "plain error."[37] Finally, he argued that *Katzenbach v. Morgan* had been wrongly decided insofar as it permitted Congress to be the judge of the scope of its own powers.[38]

In the context of contemporary decisions of the Court, it is difficult to believe that either the Black or Harlan positions are likely to be adopted by the Court. Contrary to Justice Harlan's position,[39] the Court continues to apply the 14th amendment to denials of the right to vote and to insist on a compelling state interest to justify voting rights denial. Contrary to the position of Justice Black,[40] the Court has, in contexts other than voting rights, continued to expand the reach of the equal protection clause to cases not involving racial discrimination. Both Justices Black and Harlan grounded their views of the limited power of Congress to extend voting rights on an equally limited view of the judicial power in interpreting the equal protection clause—a limited view of judicial power that appears, for the present, to be a lost cause.

Justice Stewart, joined by the Chief Justice and Justice Blackmun, argued that *Katzenbach v. Morgan* could not be read to give Congress power under section 5 of the 14th amendment to do more than "provide the means of eradicating situations that amount to a violation of the Equal Protection Clause."[41] They argued that section 4(e) had been upheld on the alternative ground of remedying discrimination against Puerto Ricans in the fur-

---

35. *Id.* at 129.
36. *Id.* at 152 (concurring in part and dissenting in part).
37. *Id.* at 200–09 (the "plain error" language appears *id.* at 209) (concurring in part and dissenting in part).
38. "Whether a state judgment has so exceeded the bounds of reason as to authorize federal intervention is not a matter as to which the political process is intrinsically likely to produce a sounder or more acceptable result. It is a matter of the delicate adjustment of the federal system. In this area, to rely on Congress would make that body a judge in its own cause. The role of final arbiter belongs to this Court." *Id.* at 209 (concurring in part and dissenting in part).
39. *See* Goosby v. Osser, 409 U.S. 512 (1973) (absentee voting by jail prisoners); Dunn v. Blumstein, 405 U.S. 330 (1972) (durational residency requirement); *cf.* Bullock v. Carter, 405 U.S. 134 (1972) (close scrutiny of candidate filing fees).
40. *See, e.g.,* Weber v. Aetna Cas. & Sur. Co., 406 U.S. 164 (1972) (discrimination against illegitimates); Reed v. Reed, 404 U.S. 71 (1971) (sex discrimination); Graham v. Richardson, 403 U.S. 365 (1971) (discrimination against aliens); *cf.* Frontiero v. Richardson, 411 U.S. 677 (1973) (sex discrimination).
41. 400 U.S. at 296 (concurring in part and dissenting in part).

nishing of public services. Discrimination against Puerto Ricans was an undoubted invidious discrimination. Thus, in their view, nothing in *Morgan* sustained a view of congressional power to "determine as a matter of substantive constitutional law what situations fall within the ambit of the [equal protection] clause, and what state interests are 'compelling.' "[42]

B. *Justice Brennan's Modified Ratchet Theory*

The remaining four Justices rejected the remedy-interpretation distinction. Justice Brennan's opinion reiterated the rationale of his opinion in *Katzenbach v. Morgan*. Here Congress had a sufficient basis to make the determination that denial of the right to vote to those between ages 18 and 21 was a denial of equal protection.[43]

This time, Justice Brennan's opinion elaborating his theory of congressional power under section 5 of the 14th amendment offered a new explanation of the ratchet. The rationale set forth in footnote 10 in *Morgan* had been that section 5 gave Congress power to "enforce" but not to "restrict, abrogate, or dilute" the guarantees of section 1 of the 14th amendment.[44] In *Katzenbach v. Morgan*, Justice Brennan had talked of congressional competence to "weigh . . . competing considerations" to determine whether New York's English-literacy requirement was a violation of equal protection.[45] In *Oregon v. Mitchell*, however, he emphasized Congress' superior capacity to "determine whether the factual basis necessary to support a state legislative discrimination actually exists."[46]

> [A] decision of this Court striking down a state statute expresses, among other things, our conclusion that the legislative findings upon which the statute is based are so far wrong as to be unreasonable. Unless Congress were to unearth new evidence in its investigation, its identical findings on the identical issue would be no more reasonable than those of the state legislature.[47]

This new rationale for the ratchet theory is as unpersuasive as the first. If Congress is a more appropriate forum than the courts for determining issues of legislative fact, it is hard to understand why a congressional determination that there exists a sufficient "factual" basis to find discrimination by the state should, in the absence of new evidence, be entitled to no weight at all. Moreover, this time Justice Brennan tells us that the ratchet may be released—that in some cases Congress can turn back the clock on equal protection and due process on the basis of new evidence. If the last sugges-

---

42. *Id.* at 295–96 (concurring in part and dissenting in part).
43. *Id.* at 246–50 (concurring in part and dissenting in part).
44. 384 U.S. 641, 651 n.10 (1966).
45. *Id.* at 656.
46. 400 U.S. at 248 (concurring in part and dissenting in part).
47. *Id.* at 249 n.31 (concurring in part and dissenting in part).

tion is taken seriously, the Congress does have an ill-defined power to dilute judicially declared protections of section 1 of the 14th amendment.

III. Federalism Versus Individual Rights: A Different Approach to Congressional Enforcement Power

A viable theory concerning the limits of Congress' enforcement power under section 5 of the 14th amendment—one that realistically assesses the different strengths of Congress and the courts—can be formulated. Such a theory has long been invoked in analyzing other aspects of constitutional interpretation. The theory turns partly on considerations of federalism, distinguishing the relative capacity of Congress to draw the lines between national and state power from the courts' sensitivity to the rights of racial, religious, and political minorities.

A. *Congress and the Courts: Institutional Competence to Adjust Different Kinds of Conflicts*

Speaking of the political safeguards of federalism, Professor Wechsler has said:

> Far from a national authority that is expansionist by nature, the inherent tendency in our system is precisely the reverse, necessitating the widest support before intrusive measures of importance can receive significant consideration, reacting readily to opposition grounded in resistance within the states. . . . It is in light of this inherent tendency, reflected most importantly in Congress, that the governmental power distribution clauses of the Constitution gain their largest meaning as an instrument for the protection of the states. Those clauses, as is well known, have served far more to qualify or stop intrusive measures in the Congress than to invalidate enacted legislation in the Supreme Court.
>
> This does not differ from the expectation of the framers quite as markedly as might be thought. For the containment of the national authority Madison did not emphasize the function of the Court; he pointed to the composition of the Congress and to the political processes.[48]

Nonetheless, while the makeup of Congress and its political processes make it the ideal forum for determining when decisions traditionally made at the state level should be supplanted by national solutions,[49] Congress has no institutional competence superior to that of the state legislatures in sec-

---

48. H. Wechsler, *supra* note 5, at 78–79.

49. Burt, *supra* note 8, at 110 n.107, argues, however, that Professor Wechsler's thesis "gave insufficient weight to the critical role of the differing constituencies within the same state to which national and state legislators are responsible." It can also be argued that a number of the specifics on which Professor Wechsler argued his case—such as great leeway in state legislatures' power to set voter qualifications and apportion districts in congressional elections—are no longer true. Full-scale argument on the soundness of the Wechsler thesis is beyond the scope of this Essay. However, at least in cases involving the commerce power, the Court continues to act as if the Wechsler thesis were true. *See, e.g.*, Perez v. United States, 402 U.S. 146 (1971).

ond-guessing the courts as to the minimal content of liberty reflected in the due process and equal protection clauses.

B. *Preventing Congressional Dilution of Civil Liberties*

The concern expressed by most of the separate opinions in *Katzenbach v. Morgan* and in *Oregon v. Mitchell*, whether in majority or in dissent, involves developing a theory by which Congress cannot, through a simple legislative majority, roll back individual liberties which the Court has found to have constitutional dimensions. So long as the scope of congressional authority under the 14th amendment's enforcement clause is tied solely to an attribution of congressional superiority in drawing lines or finding legislative fact, no intellectually defensible argument can be made that Congress possesses wide power to enlarge due process and equal protection but lacks power to dilute them. The ratchet remains a problem even if congressional power is limited to defining "remedies," and courts are made the exclusive interpreters of constitutional provisions. However, a theory that distinguishes between congressional competence to make "liberty" and "federalism" judgments resolves the dilemma. A congressional judgment rejecting a judicial interpretation of the due process or equal protection clauses—an interpretation that had given the individual procedural or substantive protection from state and federal government alike—is entitled to no more deference than the identical decision of a state legislature. Congress is no more immune to momentary passions of the majority than are the state legislatures. But a congressional judgment resolving at the national level an issue that could—without constitutional objection—be decided in the same way at the state level, ought normally to be binding on the courts, since Congress presumably reflects a balance between both national and state interests and hence is better able to adjust such conflicts.

C. Katzenbach v. Morgan *and* Oregon v. Mitchell *as Federalism Conflicts*

The issues in both *Katzenbach v. Morgan* and *Oregon v. Mitchell* concerned federalism. Had the New York state legislature enacted a law extending the right to vote to Puerto Ricans literate in Spanish in a manner identical to section 4(e) of the 1965 Voting Rights Act, it too would have been constitutional.[50] If all states had extended voting rights in federal and state elections to 18-year-olds, a result identical to the 1970 Act could have been accomplished without any substantial constitutional concern. The real issue was whether those decisions could be taken out of the hands of the

---

50. *See* text accompanying notes 17–18 *supra*.

states and made at the national level. By way of contrast, as long as denying the vote to non-English-speaking citizens raised a substantial issue[51] of equal protection under the Court's activist new equal protection theories in voting cases, a congressional statute that permitted the states to require English-language literacy as a requirement for voting would involve issues beyond federalism. A congressional judgment that voting can be restricted in this manner would involve not only the issue of the level of government at which such a decision could be made, but also the issue whether such a restriction on liberty could be accomplished at *any* governmental level. As to the latter judgment, the congressional decision should be accorded no more weight than an identical decision by a state legislature, since Congress possesses no peculiar attributes that make it a more appropriate forum than the state legislatures for resolving such an issue. Similarly, congressional judgments limiting constitutionally required remedies in school segregation cases or dispensing with exclusion in criminal cases of illegally seized evidence should be no more conclusive than identical state statutes.

D. *Comparison of the Liberty-Federalism Theory and the Ratchet Theory*

In many cases, Justice Brennan's ratchet will produce the same results as recognition of the distinction between liberty and federalism decisions. Congressional extensions of due process and equal protection will involve federalism decisions, since the only issue raised will be the level of government empowered to make the decision. Congressional dilutions of due process and equal protection will, by contrast, raise issues of whether *any* level of government can constitutionally make the challenged decision. There are, however, situations in which the ratchet and the liberty-federalism distinction will produce different results. The due process clause of the 14th amendment has, in some instances, been used by the Court as an instrument of federalism to allocate power within the federal system. With reference to issues of choice of law and jurisdiction of state courts, the due process clause has been the analogue of the full faith and credit clause, allocating decisionmaking competence among state courts.[52] In the area of state taxation of interstate business, the more recent cases have replaced the commerce clause with the due process clause as the primary limit on state taxing power.[53] Congress might roll back such due process decisions of the Court in recognizing, for example, increased state taxing power or a larger territorial scope of state court jurisdiction. These congressional decisions would

---

51. *See* cases cited in note 39 *supra.*
52. *See* Home Ins. Co. v. Dick, 281 U.S. 397 (1930); Pennoyer v. Neff, 95 U.S. 714 (1877).
53. *See* National Bellas Hess, Inc. v. Department of Revenue, 386 U.S. 753 (1967); General Motors Corp. v. Washington, 377 U.S. 436 (1964).

not be a dilution of liberty, but simply a rearrangement of power within the federal system.[54]

E. *Comparison of the Enforcement Powers Under the 13th and 14th Amendments*

The closest analogy to the enforcement clause (section 5) of the 14th amendment is the enforcement clause (section 2) of the 13th amendment, which recently has been interpreted by the Court in a manner consistent with the liberty-federalism distinction suggested here. The *Civil Rights Cases*[55] held that section 2 of the 13th amendment permitted Congress to ban private racial discrimination that constituted a "badge of slavery." Congress was not granted free rein, however, in defining badges of slavery. The Court insisted on exercising independent judicial judgment as to the forms of private discrimination that constituted a badge of slavery. That aspect of the *Civil Rights Cases* was overruled in 1968 in *Jones v. Alfred H. Mayer Co.*,[56] which concluded that the enforcement clause gave Congress the ultimate power to make rational determinations as to what are badges and incidents of slavery. Thus Congress could bar private racial discrimination that would not, absent the legislation, violate section 1 of the 13th amendment.[57] The result of the *Jones* decision is to give Congress the same power to outlaw private racial discrimination as state legislatures possess.

Justice Stewart's opinion for the Court in *Jones* did not agonize over the distinction between interpretation and remedy, as did his opinions in *Katzenbach v. Morgan* and *Oregon v. Mitchell*. It is possible to argue that the Court, in fact, had "interpreted" section 1 of the 13th amendment in *Jones* by concluding that it barred private discrimination that is a relic of slavery, and that congressional judgment as to the kinds of discrimination that are relics of slavery merely constitutes appropriate "enforcement."[58] It is treacherous business, however, to bring the Court's opinion in *Jones* within the confines of the interpretation-remedy distinction propounded by Justice Stewart in the 14th amendment cases.

IV. CAN *Morgan* AND *Mitchell* BE RECONCILED?

One difficulty with the liberty-federalism theory is that it will not distinguish the results reached in *Katzenbach v. Morgan* and *Oregon v. Mitch-*

---

54. Despite the "fair play and substantial justice" description of the "minimum contacts" theory of International Shoe Co. v. Washington, 326 U.S. 310 (1945), the power to establish nationwide service in the federal courts suggests that Congress should possess a parallel power to enlarge the scope of service of process in the state courts. *See* P. BATOR, P. MISHKIN, D. SHAPIRO & H. WECHSLER, WECHSLER'S THE FEDERAL COURTS AND THE FEDERAL SYSTEM 1106 (2d ed. 1973).
55. 109 U.S. 3 (1883).
56. 392 U.S. 409 (1968).
57. The holding was reaffirmed in Griffin v. Breckenridge, 403 U.S. 88, 105 (1971).
58. *See* D. ENGDAHL, CONSTITUTIONAL POWER: FEDERAL AND STATE IN A NUTSHELL 247–48 (1974).

ell. As previously indicated, if consistently applied, the theory would have upheld the 18-year-old vote provisions in their entirety. However, other theories that attempt to reconcile the two cases are unpersuasive.

A. *Distinguishing Racial Discrimination from Other Discriminations*

An obvious distinction between the two cases is that *Morgan* deals with racial discrimination in voting while *Mitchell* deals with nonracial voting lines. In the last century, however, in defining the theoretical breadth of the enforcement power under the 14th amendment, the Court has not drawn sharp lines that depend solely on whether racial discrimination was at issue. The Court's opinion in the *Civil Rights Cases* was consistent in its approach to the 13th and 14th amendments issues—Congress could act to remedy only those conditions independently determined by the courts to run afoul of section 1 of each amendment. Surely, Justice Stewart's summary abandonment in *Jones* of the *Civil Rights Cases'* limited view of congressional power under the 13th amendment fits uneasily with his insistence in *Katzenbach v. Morgan* on maintaining the *Civil Rights Cases'* parallel restriction on the enforcement clause of the 14th amendment.[59] Crediting congressional power to reach private racial discrimination in housing under the 13th amendment creates an anomalous situation with respect to the insistence that private sexual discrimination in employment can be outlawed under the 14th amendment (rather than the commerce clause) only if the Court independently finds sufficient state action plus a denial of equal protection. Of course, the 13th, 14th, and 15th amendments taken as a whole, do evince a particular concern for racial discrimination. However, it is difficult to find a limitation to issues of racial discrimination in section 5 of the 14th amendment. It is significant that only one of the Justices in *Oregon v. Mitchell*—Justice Black—would expand or contract the scope of section 5 depending on whether the federal statute in question dealt with racial discrimination. Thus *Katzenbach v. Morgan* and *Oregon v. Mitchell* cannot be satisfactorily reconciled on the ground that the former involved racial discrimination in voting and the latter did not.

B. *Distinguishing Powers Specifically Reserved to the States from Those Reserved by the 10th Amendment*

An argument can be made that the decisions are harmonized by regarding the specific voter qualification issues in *Oregon v. Mitchell* as a subject in some way especially reserved to decisionmaking by the states. The argument holds that by the structure of the Constitution the states are given

---

59. 109 U.S. at 11–13.

free rein to set voter qualifications. *Katzenbach v. Morgan* can be explained on the basis of congressional power to enforce the explicit ban on racial discrimination in voting contained in the 15th amendment. *Oregon v. Mitchell*, however, deals with congressional power to enforce the less exact requirement of equal protection of the laws. This power is qualified, the argument goes, by the recognition in the Constitution that voting qualifications are set by the states.

So long as the Court's activism in striking down state voter qualifications as violations of the equal protection clause continues unabated,[60] no convincing argument can be made that congressional power under section 5 of the 14th amendment has special limits in all cases dealing with voter qualifications. Of course, the federalism-liberty distinction articulated by this Essay does not suggest that Congress has unlimited power with respect to issues of federalism. Even in dealing with such a conflict, Congress cannot disregard a limitation on federal power where the limitation is more explicit than the 10th amendment's truism that power not delegated to the United States is reserved to the states. Congress could not, for example, provide three United States Senators for California or New York,[61] nor abolish the electoral college and provide for direct presidential elections,[62] nor authorize the transportation of liquor into a state "in violation of the laws thereof."[63] Does the express reservation of state power to set voting qualifications, as provided in article 1, section 2, of the Constitution, set that area aside from the exercise of the federal legislative power as do the express limitations on congressional power in article 1, section 9? Here, Justice Harlan's opinion in *Oregon v. Mitchell* was surely correct that judicial incursions, under the equal protection clause, into the states' freedom to determine voter qualifications were difficult to square with the argument that the Constitution specially preserved the power of the states to set voter qualifications as they saw fit.

C. *Congressional Power to Interpret the Constitution "at the Margin"*

One difference between the two cases does provide a possible point of distinction. The denial of voting rights to those literate in a foreign language was, in itself, an arguable violation of the equal protection clause. On the other hand, the use of age 21 rather than 18 as the dividing line for voter qualification did not involve a substantial equal protection issue. Thus one could argue that in marginal cases, Congress can enlarge the meaning of due process and equal protection. Congress cannot, however,

60. *See* cases cited in note 39 *supra*.
61. *See* U.S. CONST. art. I, § 3, cl. 1; *id.* art. V; *id.* amend. XVII.
62. *See* U.S. CONST. art. II, § 1, cl. 3; *id.* amend. XII.
63. *See* U.S. CONST. amend. XXI, § 2.

declare a state law to be a violation of due process or equal protection when it is clear that it is not. The argument is that the enforcement power under the 14th amendment, insofar as it involves disputed issues of interpreting section 1, is a power to legislate only at the margins.

Even if *Katzenbach v. Morgan* and *Oregon v. Mitchell* can be relatively easily distinguished on this basis, marking the limits of the margin might be quite troublesome in other cases. For example, in *Branzburg v. Hayes*,[64] the Court divided 5–4 in finding no newsman's privilege in the first amendment. Of course, Congress has ample power to protect newsmen from questioning by federal officials and federal courts. Could Congress, under section 5 of the 14th amendment, enact a newsman's privilege in cases involving state officials and state courts? If the issue was "arguable"—for purposes of determining the propriety of congressional interpretative power—prior to the Court's *Branzburg* decision, does the issue continue to be "arguable" after the decision? Does an issue remain "arguable" as long as the Court's authoritative resolution is by a closely divided Court? Obviously, congressional power should neither depend upon whether Congress or the Court was first in the race to cope with the issue, nor vary with the voting breakdown when the Court finishes first. More significant than the issue of how close was the question in *Branzburg* is the Court's primary reason for not finding a newsman's privilege in the first amendment. The Court believed that this would involve drawing difficult lines that could best be drawn by legislatures. That conclusion suggests that if anything remains of the rationale of *Katzenbach v. Morgan*, Congress should have the power to create a newsman's privilege binding against the states.

Prior to the passage of the 26th amendment, the choice of a particular age limit as a voter qualification would at some point—age 45, for example—have presented an arguable 14th amendment violation. The previous age line of 21 was clearly constitutional only because voting rights do not have to be extended to the newborn, and 21 had been the most common choice. The choice of any particular age requirement is thus a matter of legislative linedrawing. The argument for congressional power to establish a newsman's privilege under the 14th amendment—despite the Court's rejection in *Branzburg* of a constitutional foundation for the privilege—suggests that Congress had the power to establish 18 as the appropriate age for voter qualification, regardless of the obvious absence of an arguable equal protection issue.

V. CONCLUSION

The specific issues raised in *Katzenbach v. Morgan* and *Oregon v. Mitchell* are largely obsolete. The unanimous recognition in *Oregon v. Mitchell*

---

64. 408 U.S. 665 (1972).

of congressional power to abrogate all literacy tests for voting puts in the shade the more limited suspension of literacy tests in section 4(e) of the 1965 Voting Rights Act. The 26th amendment moots any debate over the constitutional dimensions of the 18-year-old vote. The uncertainty generated by *Oregon v. Mitchell* will, in all likelihood, cause Congress to shy away from justifying legislation expanding civil rights solely on the basis of congressional power to interpret the 14th amendment. With reference to future racial civil rights legislation, congressional power under the 13th and 15th amendments will obviate any necessity for reliance on section 5 of the 14th amendment. Beyond racial discrimination, alternative sources of congressional power—such as the commerce clause—will almost surely be invoked. If there is a new round of debate in the Court concerning the limit of congressional power under section 5 of the 14th amendment, it is most likely to arise in the context of a congressional attempt to clip the wings of an unpopular due process or equal protection decision of the Court. It is here that the unsatisfying arguments on all sides of the debate are a matter of continuing concern.

It is not difficult to find scholarly opinion that *Oregon v. Mitchell* was wrongly decided, given its conflicting holdings. It is the thesis of this Essay that the holding was wrong insofar as it denied Congress the power to lower the voting age in state elections. Theories defining Congress' enforcement power under section 5 of the 14th amendment as limited to the creation of "remedies" rather than "interpretation," or theories that would limit the function of congressional "interpretation" to marginal cases, are not viable. The only viable judicially-enforceable limit on congressional power is to be found, not in the 10th amendment, but in the more specific restrictions on federal power in the Constitution, including the Bill of Rights. Recognizing the functional distinction between judgments drawing lines as to the allocation of power within the federal system and those establishing the minimum content of constitutionally protected liberty leaves no room for congressional dilution of the Bill of Rights.

A Comment on the Jurisprudence of the Uniform Commercial Code*

Richard Danzig†

> The men who have studied it [the UCC] carefully have found
> their study turning them into enthusiasts. Doubts vanish like
> haze on a summer morning.[1]

Article II of the Uniform Commercial Code is one of those rare statutes which has been drafted by a self-conscious jurisprude:[2] a person at least as reflective about the role of law in society and the relation of lawmaking institutions to each other as he was concerned about the particular lawmaking task at hand.[3] It therefore seems an oversight to leave discussion of the sales portion of the Code to those commercial lawyers for whom it bulks so large.

For those interested in the evolution of legal philosophies, this portion of the Code offers a rich opportunity. It is possible that rather than attempting to describe and then debate legal realism on the basis of its self-conscious, contradictory, and often overblown theoretical corpus, understanding can be better enhanced if attention is paid to the principal work of the leading proponent of that philosophy.[4] His 10 years of law-in-action as Chief

* I am grateful to John Merryman and Jane Collier for careful readings of an earlier draft of this Essay. In addition, this Essay has benefited from conversations I had some years ago on related topics with Art Leff and Harry Wellington of Yale Law School and Duncan Kennedy of Harvard Law School. That these gentlemen will probably have forgotten those conversations underscores the fact that they bear no responsibility for what follows, but it does not lessen my debt to them.

† B.A. 1965, Reed College; B. Phil. 1967, D. Phil. 1968, Oxford University; J.D. 1971, Yale University. Assistant Professor of Law, Stanford University.

1. Statement by Karl Llewellyn to the Law Revision Commission, in New York Law Revision Comm'n, Record of Hearings on the Uniform Commercial Code 27 (1954).

2. This term is not in any dictionary I have seen, but it was a frequent favorite of the man on whom this Essay focuses. See W. Twining, Karl Llewellyn and the Realist Movement 120 (1973).

3. The Uniform Commercial Code reflects, of course, much more than the thought of Karl Llewellyn. For an analysis strongly downplaying his influence in the original drafting, see Mentschikoff, The Uniform Commercial Code, an Experiment in Democracy in Drafting, 36 A.B.A.J. 419 (1950). The original drafts were themselves modified as a result of both legislative revisions, see note 7 infra, and amendments suggested by the Code's "Permanent Editorial Board." But if ever a statute can be taken as suggestive of a legal philosophy this seems to be such a case. Article II was Llewellyn's main area of interest. His wife and disciple was its second most influential author. Both retained substantial influence over the document through the period of the 1962 official text which is quoted in this Essay.

4. The "realist" group was neither so united nor their program so crystallized as to make the view or actions of any one thinker a touchstone for assessing the movement. But Llewellyn stands out, both as the author of "the first self-conscious statement of Realism," see White, From Sociological Jurisprudence to Realism, 58 Va. L. Rev. 999, 1017 (1972) (referring to Llewellyn's article, A Realistic Jurisprudence—The Next Step, 30 Colum. L. Rev. 431 (1930)), and as the author of its definitive defensive piece, Llewellyn, Some Realism About Realism—Responding to Dean Pound, 44 Harv. L. Rev. 1222 (1931).

Reporter of the UCC promise to teach us more about Karl Llewellyn's realist perspective than his lifetime of lectures on law-in-theory. "Realism" in every sense of the word cries for us to take the measure of his jurisprudence at least as much by contemplation of its effect as by analysis of its rhetoric.

A jurisprudential assessment of Article II of the Code ought to be important even to those with no interest in Karl Llewellyn or the realist movement of which he was a part. For if law students are tacitly encouraged to regard statutes as technical arabesques to be analyzed without reference to a theory of law—that is to say, without reference to philosophic, sociological, and economic premises—then they will be stunted in their capacities to self-consciously shape society in their later incarnations as lawyers, legislators, and judges. In focusing on the concepts of law and the role of legal institutions that I believe underlie Article II of the Uniform Commercial Code, I hope to show that it is not sufficient to read this or any other law in a technical sense. The Code is more than a machine manual or a firedrill regulation. It is too important to be left to commercial lawyers.

I

The central argument of this Essay is that Article II of the Uniform Commercial Code is an idiosyncratic piece of legislation because in critical provisions it neither pretends to the substance nor adopts the form of the usual legislative enactment. It is suggested that an appreciation of the jurisprudential theories of the Article's principal drafter makes the unusual aspects of the Code's approach more salient and more understandable. And it is argued that the animating principle behind these theories and this legislative achievement is, paradoxically, and, in some respects unwisely, a renunciation of legislative responsibility and power.

At the outset it should be noted, however, that some of the peculiarities of the Code derive as much from the atypical nature of the problems and persons with which it deals as from the unusual character of Llewellyn's view of the legal process.[5] Commercial law is at the margin of public law. It deals with a subcommunity ("merchants"), whose members occupy a status position distinct from society at large, whose disputes are often resolved by informal negotiation or in private forums, whose relationships tend to continue over time rather than ending with the culmination of single transactions,[6] and whose primary rules derive from a sense of fairness wide-

---

5. Though these paragraphs suggest that the peculiarities of Llewellyn's philosophy and the peculiarities of contract law can in some respects be distinguished, it is a corollary of the argument of this Essay that Llewellyn's unusual view of the legal process was in many respects a result of his lifelong immersion in contract law. There are signs that the man was shaped by his special field, and that his generalizations are extrapolations from it.

6. *See generally* MacNeil, *The Many Futures of Contracts*, 47 So. CAL. L. REV. 691 (1974).

spread—if imprecisely defined—within the commercial community. In this situation the legislature (often ignorant of the actual circumstances that control commerce) is not likely to conceive of itself as the arena for negotiation between competing interest groups; it is not likely, in fact, to see itself as a place where anything is decided. Instead, it often may merely articulate and place the state's imprimatur on private arrangements fabricated outside its halls. It would not be altogether surprising, then, to find that the legislative process associated with the Uniform Commercial Code was more like law-stating than law-making.

The uniformity sought by the Act's proponents undoubtedly further limited the opportunities for legislative activism and even contributed to some of the idiosyncrasies of the legislation's form. If the Code were to be widely adopted, it would have to be easily assimilated into the prevailing ideology and the prevailing law. Individual legislatures were particularly urged to restrict their lawmaking propensities, at least as to enactments within the framework of this Act, and they were restrained from generating a unique legislative history by the prepackaged gloss provided in the form of official commentary.[7]

Characteristics such as these which stem from a code that would be both uniform and commercial suggest that there is more at play in Article II than Llewellyn's jurisprudence. But this Essay suggests that Llewellyn's jurisprudential preferences strongly reinforced these situational factors and that the genius of the Code is derived in large measure from the mesh Llewellyn effected between the pragmatic demands he faced and the jurisprudential views he held.

To bring out the jurisprudential choices implicit in Llewellyn's work, it is helpful to contrast his ideas with the thought of Hart and Sacks as presented in their masterwork, *The Legal Process: Basic Problems in the Making and Application of Law*.[8] This influential work provides a useful foil against which to highlight the originality of Llewellyn's contemporaneous achievement because these three professors reached different positions after starting from a common point of departure and working through a common area of theoretical concern. Each rejected the method of "mechanical jurisprudence,"[9] which they ascribed to a line of influential

---

7. There is, of course, a legislative history behind the UCC quite apart from that written by the framers of the Code. Discussions were most intense in New York. *See, e.g.,* New York Law Revision Comm'n, Record of Hearings on the Uniform Commercial Code (1954) (2 vols.); New York Law Revision Comm'n, Study of the Uniform Commercial Code (1955) (3 vols.); New York Law Revision Comm'n, Report Relating to the Uniform Commercial Code (1956). In addition there are often state annotations to the Code. Their importance is, however, minimized by the official comments.

8. H.M. Hart & A. Sacks, The Legal Process: Basic Problems in the Making and Application of Law (1958).

9. The phrase is Dean Pound's. *See* Pound, *Mechanical Jurisprudence*, 8 Colum. L. Rev. 605 (1908).

legal thinkers from Blackstone to Beale, and instead proselytized for the
view that the law ought to be developed and assessed against the backdrop
of the everyday world within which it operates. Most significantly, while
a majority of their colleagues passed a lifetime immersed in either jurisprudence, constitutional theory, common law analysis, or debate over the
meaning and application of particular statutes, these three thinkers shared
an almost unique concern with the theories of legislation and adjudication
in general. They thus were atypically reflective on what a statutory scheme
should look like, and how it should be read.[10]

Llewellyn's and Hart and Sacks' views of the importance of legislation
are a study in contrasts. Hart and Sacks were preeminently concerned with
the law as a vehicle of growth and with legislatures as maximizers of social
utilities. Their reaction to mechanical jurisprudence was like Bentham's
to Blackstone: they substituted "purpose" for "analogy" as the creative force
in the law; they regarded legislation (in the ideal) as an instrument fabricated to shape society in a manner chosen by the lawmaker, rather than
as a logical corpus derived from inviolable principles.[11]

Llewellyn also rejected Beale and Blackstone, but his was a different
alternative. Instead of regarding law as a body of deduced rules, or as an
instrument chosen by social planners from among a universe of alternatives, Llewellyn saw law as an articulation and regularization of unconsciously evolved mores—as a crystallization of a generally recognized and
almost indisputably right rule (a "singing reason"), inherent in, but very
possibly obscured by, existing patterns of relationships.[12] To him an "immanent law" lay embedded in any situation and the task of the law authority was to discover it. In perhaps the key passage in *The Common Law
Tradition*, Llewellyn quotes Levin Goldschmidt with approval:

---

10. Unfortunately for the analysis offered here this concern did not always flower into a full-
blown, clearly articulated viewpoint. The theoretical writings of both Llewellyn, *see* most significantly
his masterwork, THE COMMON LAW TRADITION (1960), and Hart and Sacks avoid scores of important,
but hard, questions—the former by rhetoric that sometimes contradicts itself and sometimes signifies
nothing, the latter by offering questions where the authors themselves have no answers. Because of
these gaps or contradictions in thought, the contrast that follows is, I am sure, oversimplified. I nonetheless believe that these thinkers offer us two different ways of viewing the law, that the contrast
is fairly drawn, and that it is helpful.

11. *See, e.g.*, H.M. HART & A. SACKS, *supra* note 8, at 118: "[L]aw is concerned essentially with
the pursuit of purposes . . . ;" "[m]ust not [the decisionmaker] inevitably, at least with problems of
any novelty, make a choice among the possible purposes and the possible ways of accomplishing them?"

12. It is notable that the middle position in this trichotomy (Beale—Hart and Sacks—Llewellyn)
is overlooked in the famous dictum of Oliver Wendell Holmes: "The life of the law has not been
logic: it has been experience." O.W. HOLMES, THE COMMON LAW 1 (1881). Though Holmes' writing
undeniably indicates a perception of the role of ethics in the making of law, it seems more than a
curiosity that the foundation statement for legal realism should leave unarticulated what is most important for Hart and Sacks. (Anyone who doubts Holmes' influence on Llewellyn should note the
similarity in title of their masterworks.) As stated, Holmes offers the converse of the position adopted
by Beale and Blackstone. But his aphorism ignores the position earlier adopted by Bentham and later
taken up by Hart and Sacks, McDougal and Lasswell, and others. In their endorsement of Holmes'
position without amendment, the realists afford a clue to the psychology that is reflected in Article II.

> Every fact-pattern of common life, so far as the legal order can take it in, carries within itself its appropriate, natural rules, its right law. This is a natural law which is real, not imaginary; it is not a creature of mere reason, but rests on the solid foundation of what reason can recognize in the nature of man and of the life conditions of the time and place; it is thus not eternal or changeless nor everywhere the same, but is indwelling in the very circumstances of life. The highest task of law-giving consists in uncovering and implementing this immanent law.[13]

This view has strikingly negative implications for an active legislative role. If law exists and needs only to be discovered, it is not necessary or helpful (but indeed probably only burdensome) that the law-articulating agency be democratically elected and politically responsive; to proceed effectively, a lawmaker needs only a capacity for detecting the "situation sense" and a good faith commitment to the exercise of that capacity. Moreover, since law is immanent in "the very circumstances" of time and place, the agency best suited to find it is presumably not one of general inquiry and decision, like a legislature, but rather one with a more particularized insight: that is, a court should declare law by a careful review of "trouble cases" (disputes). As Llewellyn's collaborator, Hoebel, wrote in another context:

> It is the case of trouble which makes, breaks, twists, or flatly establishes a rule, an institution, an authority. . . . [I]f there be a portion of a society's life in which tensions of the culture come to expression, in which the play of variant urges can be felt and seen, in which emergent power-patterns, ancient security drives, religion, politics, personality and cross-purposed views of justice tangle in the open, that portion of the life will concentrate in the case of trouble or disturbance. Not only the making of new law and the effect of old, but the hold and the thrust of all other vital aspects of the culture, shine clear in the crucible of conflict.[14]

Whereas Hart and Sacks would have ethics and economics—the peculiar tools of the legislature—be their primary guides to lawmaking, the methods and messages of sociology and anthropology[15] as he and Hoebel practiced them, figure more substantially in Llewellyn's thought.[16]

---

13. K. LLEWELLYN, *supra* note 10, at 122. *See also id.* at 126–28.

14. E. HOEBEL, THE LAW OF PRIMITIVE MAN 29 (1954), *quoted in* W. TWINING, *supra* note 2, at 161.

15. I have borrowed this shorthand for the different approaches to judicial decisionmaking from B. CARDOZO, THE NATURE OF THE JUDICIAL PROCESS (1922), but in equating sociology and anthropology with a value-free, purely observational, and not purposive orientation, I use the term in a rather different (more modern) sense than Cardozo used it 50 years ago.

16. In any jurisprudential system the role of lawyers is a corollary of first propositions about the nature of law and of the jurisprude's differential assignment of institutional responsibilities to courts, legislatures, etc. Not surprisingly, therefore, Hart and Sacks' and Llewellyn's differing perspectives lead to differences in the importance and scope of the role of the lawyer. To Hart and Sacks the archtypical lawyer is a critical actor and a maximizer. "In small matters as well as large, the lawyer should be a specialist in making the pies of social living larger." H.M. HART & A. SACKS, *supra* note 8, at 202. Trained to view situations with a wider perspective than his client, he is charged with leading his client to recognize that societal advantage may provoke or precondition individual gain. The converse is not assumed: "As counsel for Mrs. Landy, in what mood would you enter the negotiations on her be-

Article II of the Code can profitably be viewed as adapting the philosophy of "immanent law" to a specific context. Just as Llewellyn found the "Cheyenne Way"[17] by the method of value-free observation, Article II frequently speaks as though courts should discover the law merchant from a careful, disinterested examination of custom and fact situations. Article II is not, in the main, an example of legislative lawmaking, it is a guide to law-finding. It does not tell judges the law; it tells them how to find the law. The law is found not in doctrine, not in policy, but in directed exploration of the "fact-pattern of common life."[18] The search is for the "natural law . . . of the life conditions of the time and place . . . ."[19] Consider, for example, the "law" promulgated by Uniform Commercial Code, section 2–609:

> *Right to Adequate Assurance of Performance*
>   (1) . . . When reasonable grounds for insecurity arise with respect to the performance of either party the other may in writing demand adequate assurance of due performance and until he receives such assurance may if commercially reasonable suspend any performance for which he has not already received the agreed return.
>   (2) Between merchants the reasonableness of grounds for insecurity and the adequacy of any assurance offered shall be determined according to commercial standards.

In a 1944 draft of this section Llewellyn offered a comment (later omitted) that is revealing as to his aim and method: "Subsection 2 is technically unnecessary. . . . But there are a number of lines of doctrine in regard to what constitutes a breach, or even an excuse, which make it vital to remind that the intention of this Act is to use the standards not of past decisions but of current commerce."[20]

In telling a court to use current "commercial standards" to determine

---

half with Tempest? In the mood of trying to get Tempest to agree to the highest possible rent, regardless of the risk to him, and of trying to extract in other respects the maximum concessions? Or with the thought that the parties were in some sense co-adventurers, and their opposing interests in the matter of rent and some other items needed to be adjusted in the light of their common interest in the success of Tempest's enterprise. Which approach would be more realistic?" *Id.* at 229. *See also id.* at 263.

For Llewellyn the flow of the attorney-client relationship is in the opposite direction. Since the correct result is immanent in a situation, the client is better placed to perceive it than the lawyer. The lawyer's function is to learn from the client: to become informed about the situation, to cull the information he has gathered, to organize it, and to translate it into terms that will inform the court. (Note again how analogous this position is to that of the anthropologist.) Llewellyn's lawyer is thus more passive in his relations with clients and occupies a less creative role in the legal system than Hart and Sacks would hope. Concomitantly, Llewellyn made it an aim of his drafting methods to have the Code speak in terms which could be directly understood and applied by the layman so as to minimize the intrusion of a lawyer. *See* W. TWINING, *supra* note 2, at 304–5.

17. *See* K. LLEWELLYN & E. HOEBEL, THE CHEYENNE WAY (1941).
18. K. LLEWELLYN, *supra* note 10, at 122.
19. *Id.*
20. UNIFORM REVISED SALES ACT § 99(2), Comment (Proposed Final Draft no. 1, 1944) (italics omitted).

when "reasonable grounds" for insecurity exist, or to assess whether "adequate assurance" or something more excessive is requested, or to decide if supervision of performance is "commercially reasonable," this provision —which is typical of Article II—is doing neither more nor less than asking a court to find "the immanent laws" of "the time and place."

As another example of this jurisprudential perspective, consider the much-discussed unconscionability clause of the UCC:

> (1) If the court as a matter of law finds the contract or any clause of the contract to have been unconscionable at the time it was made the court may refuse to enforce the contract, or it may enforce the remainder of the contract without the unconscionable clause, or it may so limit the application of any unconscionable clause as to avoid any unconscionable result.
>
> (2) When it is claimed or appears to the court that the contract or any clause thereof may be unconscionable the parties shall be afforded a reasonable opportunity to present evidence as to its commercial setting, purpose and effect to aid the court in making the determination.[21]

Many have noted that this section tells a court almost nothing save that unconscionability is bad and that it exists.[22] But these critics tend to treat it as an aberration—as the product of a lapse or of a too frequently compromised drafting procedure. A jurisprudential perspective on the whole of Article II would suggest that section 2–302 provides a naked example of a very general phenomenon. To those who, like Hart and Sacks, see the legislature as an engine of social reform, the vacuity of the clause is woefully disturbing. But if the weight of lawmaking is thought best distributed elsewhere, then the clause serves its purpose. It empowers and directs the courts to "absorb the particular trouble and resolve it each time into a new, usefully guiding, forward-looking, felt standard-for-action or even rule-of-law."[23]

II

The troublesome vacuity of the unconscionability provision underscores not only the passivity of the legislature in the UCC-Llewellyn scheme, but also the singular difficulties that that jurisprudential approach has in dealing with issues involving moral judgments. An allegation of indifference to any moral imperative is an old charge against the realists, and a common charge against the UCC, though the jurisprudential link between the two critiques has been generally neglected. In a famous, but now much discounted attack, Pound (whose thought, though protean, stands in the intel-

---

21. UNIFORM COMMERCIAL CODE § 2–302.
22. For the leading commentary, *see* Leff, *Unconscionability and the Code—The Emperor's New Clause*, 115 U. PA. L. REV. 485 (1967). Contrast the form of § 2–302 with NAT'L CONSUMER LAW CENTER, NAT'L CONSUMER ACT §§ 5.107 & 6.189 (First Final Draft 1970).
23. K. LLEWELLYN, *supra* note 10, at 513.

lectual lineage that leads to Hart and Sacks) charged that the realists conceived of law "as a body of devices for the purposes of business instead of
as a body of means toward general social ends."[24] Llewellyn replied, not by
rejecting Pound's ideal, but rather by arguing that the successful pursuit
of the ideal first required an appreciation of present reality. Realism was
only a method—"a technology"—for comprehending that reality.[25]

A defense which argues "first things first" is frequently appealing, but
it needs always to be tested by a scrutiny of its proponents' actions when
they reach "second things." Section 2–302 and like provisions scattered
throughout the Code provide us with precisely such a second thing in relation to Llewellyn's thought. If law study can at some times justifiably be
focused narrowly on the "is" rather than the "ought,"[26] surely the same
cannot be said of lawmaking. One may fairly ask to what extent and in
what manner a sense of any moral imperative is reflected in these provisions.

The rhetoric surrounding the Sales Article is strikingly amoral. Llewellyn spoke about the Code, and Article II is written, as though the insights required for this lawmaking job were not born of any reflection on
the gap between the real and the ideal, but rather through the acquisition
of intimate familiarity with "current commerce." Thus in his *Keynote
Memorandum, Re: Possible Uniform Commercial Code*,[27] Llewellyn spoke
of the Code as a means of regularizing "a very considerable body of commercial law which is very largely non-political in character."[28] And the
beginning of the Code echoes this orientation by cataloguing the "underlying purposes and policies of this Act" as:

> (a) to simplify, clarify and modernize the law governing commercial transactions;
> (b) to permit the continued expansion of commercial practices through custom,
>   usage and agreement of the parties;
> (c) to make uniform the law among the various jurisdictions.[29]

Taken on the basis of these pretensions, one might suppose that the Code
belies Llewellyn's defense of realism—the second step seems never to come.
In fact, however, the situation is more complicated than that. The Code is

---

24. Pound, *The Call for a Realist Jurisprudence*, 44 HARV. L. REV. 697 (1931).
25. "What realism was, and is, is a method, nothing more, and the only tenet involved is that
the method is a good one . . . . Realism is not a philosophy, but a technology." K. LLEWELLYN, *supra*
note 10, at 510.
26. Llewellyn, in *Some Realism About Realism—Responding to Dean Pound*, *supra* note 4,
at 1236, defended the "[*t*]*emporary* divorce of Is and Ought for purposes of study" (italics in the
original).
27. Memorandum from Karl N. Llewellyn to the Executive Committee on Scope and Program,
National Conference of Commissioners on Uniform State Laws, *Re: Possible Uniform Commercial
Code, reprinted in* W. TWINING, *supra* note 2, at 524–29.
28. *Id.* at 524. *See also id.* at 528.
29. UNIFORM COMMERCIAL CODE § 1–102(2). *See also* PERMANENT EDITORIAL BOARD FOR THE
UNIFORM COMMERCIAL CODE, REPORT NO. 1, in UNIFORM COMMERCIAL CODE, at xiv (1962 official text)
(stating the criteria for considering amendment of the Code).

not oblivious to ethical concerns. However clearly section 2–302 signals a legislative void, by its very existence it evidences the draftsman's commitment to the notion that a moral referent is relevant to adjudication. What the clause lacks in legislative prescription it charters the judge to provide by other means.

It is the choice of means that is troublesome. The Code appears to be predicated on an assumption that perception of an ideal can be effected by the same "technology" used to secure an appreciation of the real. Ethical questions are relevant, but they are regarded as posing problems of discovery rather than choice. The premise appears to be that values have an objectively ascertainable existence and a near universal acceptance and thus can be judicially discovered just as a "reasonable price" can be ascertained by reference to a market.

Thus, for example, if a seller is charged with breaching an implied warranty of fitness for a particular purpose, the courts are directed by section 2–316(3)(c) to assess a claimed exclusion of the warranty according to contemporary usage, and usage is to be discovered, according to section 1–205, Comment 5, by attention to the mores "currently observed by the great majority of decent dealers, even though dissidents ready to cut corners do not agree." Who are "commercially decent dealers"? What, at the margins, are the indices of decency and indecency? What if "decent" practices, as a judge perceives them, are not those of the "great majority," but instead those of the dissidents? The presumption appears to be that what is "commercially decent" and what is "unconscionable," what is "good faith" and what is bad faith, what is good law and what is bad law will be self-evident to one who carefully studies the situation. It is apparently an axiom of this approach that "good law" cannot be described for courts, but they will know it when they see it.[30]

This approach is disturbing on several counts. First, insofar as the approach is workable, it tends to confine the impact of the law to a reaffirmation of the predominant morals of the marketplace. Practices well below the market's moral median may be constrained, but since the median is the standard, by definition it will be unaffected. Further, this approach seems to encourage exactly that which "realism" was supposed to discourage: a

30. This axiom surfaces very visibly in Llewellyn's retrospective comment on UNIFORM COMMERCIAL CODE § 2–207. The section provides that: "[A] definite and seasonable expression of acceptance or a written confirmation which is sent within a reasonable time operates as an acceptance even though it states terms additional to or different from those offered or agreed upon, unless . . . [*inter alia*] they materially alter it . . . ." Llewellyn later explained the logic behind this provision as follows: "What has in fact been assented to specifically, are the few dickered terms, and the broad type of the transaction, and but one more. That one thing more is a blanket assent (not a specific assent) to any *not unreasonable or indecent* terms the seller may have on his form, which do not alter or eviscerate the reasonable meaning of the dickered terms." K. LLEWELLYN, *supra* note 10, at 370 (emphasis added).

projection of a judge's values onto the scene before him, and then a "discovery" of them as though they existed in an objectively determinable way. The Code approach masks critical choices as technical assessments and allocates them to decisionmakers (judges) of low visibility and low responsibility from the standpoint of the larger public. Here again the perspective offered by Hart and Sacks provides a helpful contrast. These thinkers reason from the premise that there is no self-evidently right answer to an ethical question. From this they infer that the resolution of such questions requires choice, and to them choice ought, wherever feasible, to be made in a self-conscious, visible way by those sensitive to the majority's validation or repudiation of their choices through the electoral process: that is, by legislators. Beyond this, because assessments of reasonableness, unconscionability, materiality, and the like can be expected to vary unpredictably from judge to judge, the Llewellyn approach seems paradoxically to undermine that very certainty and consistency in the law that the Uniform Commercial Code was dedicated to obtaining.

Lastly, an emphasis on the discovery of moral propositions is costly because it tends to focus attention on those considerations which are salient for the parties at hand, at the expense of attention to larger concerns of which the disputants are perhaps unconscious. That is, the methodology itself encourages lawmakers to see law as Pound feared—"as a body of devices for the purposes of business instead of as a body of means toward general social ends."[31]

It could be argued that so narrow a perspective is peculiarly appropriate for a code dealing with the law of contracts. If private vices make public virtues, the maximizing lawmaker may do well to keep his concepts of utility to himself, leaving the parties free to determine their own course. But such a view is by no means compelled by the subject matter. Hart and Sacks begin their text with a commercial law case. Their approach nonetheless leads them to premise their discussion on the question: "to what extent does justice require or permit account to be taken not only of the equities as between the two immediate parties to the dispute but of the effect which one or another decision will have upon the successful functioning of the institutional system as a whole in the future?"[32] For them a primary purpose of the "apparatus of official procedures" is to undertake a "continuous review of . . . private decisions."[33]

Llewellyn himself conceded the importance of a wider perspective. The

---

31. Pound, *supra* note 24, at 708.
32. H.M. HART & A. SACKS, *supra* note 8, at 10.
33. *Id.* at 9. It is interesting that in his academic writings Llewellyn claimed that he shared a concern for the effects of transactions on those other than the parties to the transaction, but, as in his response to Pound about goal orientation, he pleaded that for the moment he lacked the time or knowledge to deal with that dimension. *See* text accompanying notes 34–35 *infra*.

preface to his casebook on sales acknowledges that "[T]he book errs, I think, in too happily assuming the needs of buyers and sellers to be the needs of the community, and in rarely reaching beyond business practice in evaluation of legal rules."[34] As in his response to Pound, Llewellyn's plea was one of first things first. "[Here] again, time for building a wider foundation for judgment has been lacking."[35] And here again one finds the flaw disturbingly replicated when it came time to do the real law work. While Article II speaks the language of "fairness," "good faith," and "unconscionability," nowhere do its terms seem animated by concerns beyond those furthering the interests of the immediate parties, their households,[36] and those creditors, assignees, or bona fide purchasers who come to stand in their shoes.

III

If Llewellyn denigrated the traditional role of the legislature as conceived by thinkers like Hart and Sacks, why then did he write a commercial code and of what vitality is the document? An answer capturing part of the explanation is that he wrote it to clear statute and case law debris from the field so that commercial law could follow the natural flow of commerce. The comment to section 2–101 is revealing:

> This article is a complete revision and modernization of the Uniform Sales Act . . . .
>
> . . . .
>
> The arrangement of the present Article is in terms of contract for sale and the various steps of its performance. The legal consequences are stated as following directly from the contract and action taken under it without resorting to the idea of when property or title passed or was to pass as being the determining factor. The purpose is to avoid making practical issues between practical men turn upon the location of an intangible something . . . .[37]

But this answer is not sufficient for it is clear that Llewellyn's deference to the norms of practice did not leave him without an appreciation for the role of law-agencies, especially courts. To the contrary, he saw courts as the critical agencies for dealing with the "trouble cases"—instances where there

---

34. K. LLEWELLYN, CASES AND MATERIALS ON THE LAW OF SALES, at xv n.3 (1930).
35. *Id.*
36. *See* UNIFORM COMMERCIAL CODE § 2–318.
37. *Id.* § 2–101, Comment. *See also id.* § 2–401, Comment 1, in regard to passing of title. As to the more general point, see the arguments of those who urged adoption of the Code at state bar meetings, legislative hearings, and the like. *E.g.*, Address by William B. Davenport, The Code Approach and Sources of the Law, Institute on the Uniform Commercial Code, House of Delegates, Neb. State Bar Ass'n Annual Meeting, Nov. 12, 1964, printed in 44 NEB. L. REV. 362, 375 (1965): "[P]re-Code sales law more frequently defeat[ed] the reasonable expectations of businessmen than it fulfill[ed] those expectations. So the draftsmen of the Code proceeded on the premise that Article II should fulfill those reasonable expectations, not defeat them. The draftsmen of the Code, in effect, said, 'Let's get rid of a lot of these senseless technicalities of the law that defeat those expectations.'"

was misunderstanding or uncertainty about right standards—that arise in every system. On its most ambitious level Article II's aim, and very possibly its achievement, may be said to have been to coerce courts into reviewing cases *in the manner* Llewellyn thought they ought to be decided. Whereas a code functioned for such diverse thinkers as Frederick the Great, Austin, or Williston as a means of dictating a result,[38] Llewellyn's UCC Article II more often operated as a means of dictating a method. That method was designed to prompt decision not according to the letter or the logic of a statute or a juristic concept but rather according to the "situation-reason."[39]

To achieve this end Llewellyn effected several radical innovations in the form of his legislation. These innovations may be summarized by saying that the provisions of Article II often take the form, not so much of legislation as previously conceived by thinkers like Hart and Sacks, as of a common law decision as Hart and Sacks imagine one would be written. "[L]egislators," remark Hart and Sacks, "characteristically give no reason (if one overlooks legislative history) and courts characteristically do (if one ignores summary *per curiam* decisions). The legislature relies primarily on the authority of its position. The court supplements authority with an effort at justification."[40] But the Code consistently couples each statement of law with a "comment" on precedent and a rationale explaining the reasons for deviation from that precedent. When, for example, section 2–201 announces the formal requirements of a statute of frauds, a comment immediately follows acknowledging that the prior law was different, explaining the drafter's present intent ("[t]he changed phraseology of this section is intended to . . . ."),[41] and concluding with the rationale thought to justify the change ("market prices . . . that are current in the vicinity constitute a . . . check. Thus if the price is not stated in the memorandum it can normally be supplied without danger of fraud . . . .").[42]

More striking still, the legislation buttressed by these "judicial techniques" is itself frequently phrased in what is, by Hart and Sacks' criteria,

---

38. *See* J. FRANK, LAW AND THE MODERN MIND 186–95 (1930).
39. K. LLEWELLYN, *supra* note 10, at 64. Llewellyn also frequently spoke as though an optimum mode of legislative-judicial interaction would be for legislatures to articulate a policy preference in their statutes, and for courts to resolve situations according to the "reason" of the policy. This mode of decisionmaking he termed "the Grand Style" and praised it highly. *See, e.g., id.* at 36–38, 64–72, 373–76.
    Initially my intuition was that Article II of the UCC might profitably be analyzed as an attempt to coerce courts into deciding cases in the Grand Style by means of the devices described in the text. As I examined the "policies" endorsed by Article II, however, I came to the conclusion that at least in this instance Llewellyn was rather like Fuller's Judge Foster. His "penchant for [creating] holes in statutes reminds one of the story . . . about the man who ate a pair of shoes. Asked how he liked them, he replied that the part he liked best was the holes. That is the way [he] feels about statutes; the more holes they have in them the better he likes them. In short, he doesn't like statutes." Fuller, *The Case of the Speluncean Explorers*, 62 HARV. L. REV. 616, 634 (1949).
40. H.M. HART & A. SACKS, *supra* note 8, at 771.
41. UNIFORM COMMERCIAL CODE § 2–201, Comment.
42. *Id.*, Comment 1.

a most common law manner. Hart and Sacks provide a convenient paradigm against which to measure this phenomenon. They suggest a model of law with two poles. At one extreme are legislative enactments: per se rules, rigid in their phrasing and application but modifiable in their long-term implications because of the legislature's powers of amendment and repeal. At the other extreme are court-made common law rules: these are the product of cumulative decisions; they are open-textured so as to admit different judicial applications on an ad hoc basis in different cases, but they are relatively immutable because of a judicial reluctance to overrule prior decisions. Two prototypes of speeding laws illustrate the point. A legislature can limit speeds to 50 miles per hour; a court is not suited to reach so particular a result because there are no logical (others might say "principled") distinctions between 49 and 50 miles per hour. Instead the common law condemns unreasonable speeding—a prohibition that demands ad hoc treatments of each contested case. In Hart and Sacks' view, such different styles of lawmaking are necessary and appropriate responses by legislatures and courts to their different capacities to adapt their laws to changing circumstances. Should technology or circumstance make 50 miles per hour too low a limit, the legislature can amend its standard, while a court that promulgated such a rule would find it difficult to adjust so clearly defined a benchmark.[43]

The Code belies so neat a division of institutional products. Often it speaks in per se terms.[44] But often, also, the promulgated rule is so generalized as to permit only an ad hoc application, as with section 2–206, *Offer and Acceptance in Formation of Contract*:

> (1) Unless otherwise unambiguously indicated by the language or circumstances (a) an offer to make a contract shall be construed as inviting acceptance in any manner and by any medium reasonable in the circumstances . . . .[45]

Section 2–608(2), *Revocation of Acceptance in Whole or in Part* speaks in similar terms:

> (2) Revocation of acceptance must occur within a *reasonable time* after the buyer discovers or should have discovered the ground for it and before any substantial change in condition of the goods which is not caused by their own defects. It is not effective until the buyer notifies the seller of it.[46]

---

43. H.M. HART & A. SACKS, *supra* note 8, at 138–41. Of course, each institution can come to the rescue of the other: courts by interpreting statutes in ways that update them; legislatures by "overruling" case law or displacing common law. This adds flexibility to the total system.

The difficulties that arise when courts establish too specific a rule of law is evidenced by the famous "stop, look, and listen" rule created by Justice Holmes, *see* Baltimore & Ohio R.R. Co. v. Goodman, 275 U.S. 66 (1927), and overruled by Justice Cardozo just 7 years later, *see* Pokora v. Wabash Ry., 292 U.S. 98 (1934).

44. *See, e.g.*, UNIFORM COMMERCIAL CODE §§ 2–205, 2–509, 2–715, 2–718.

45. *Id.* § 2–206.

46. *Id.* § 2–608(2) (emphasis added).

What is "reasonable time"? The Code speaks to this question, but in terms that bear no resemblance to legislation as Hart and Sacks conceive it.

> *Section 1–204. Time; Reasonable Time; "Seasonably."*
>
> (1) Whenever this Act requires any action to be taken within a reasonable time, any time which is not manifestly unreasonable may be fixed by agreement.
>
> (2) What is a reasonable time for taking any action depends on the nature, purpose and circumstances of such action.
>
> (3) An action is taken "seasonably" when it is taken at or within the time agreed or if no time is agreed at or within a reasonable time.[47]

Article II is rife with such open-ended words (none of them referred to in the definitional section)[48] as "reasonable time,"[49] "reasonable medium,"[50] "reasonable grounds,"[51] even "reasonable price,"[52] "reasonable value,"[53] "fair and reasonable cause,"[54] and "material alter[ation],"[55] as well as the notorious "unconscionability."[56] The use of generalized guides to decision (for example, custom and usage) and open-ended terms (reasonableness, good faith, unconscionable), the injection of "official commentary" declaring the intent of the drafters, and, above all, the scarcity of provisions explicit enough to be applied without a consideration of circumstance, compel a court that would use the Code to move beyond the literalism of "mechanical jurisprudence." Llewellyn summarized his approach in *The Common Law Tradition*:

> My argument is that such drafting, by centering the basic question, adding the normal keys to answering and the available clear experience, and suggesting lines of useful further inquiry, would provide something much more certain (as well as much more easily usable) than the hundreds of pages of labyrinthine annotations to the N[egotiable] I[nstruments] L[aw] which hide the law today.[57]

IV

In sum, whereas Hart and Sacks are very conscious of institutional differentiation and assess an institution's performance in part according to whether it exploits its unique capacities, Llewellyn has drafted a statute

---

47. *Id.* § 1–204.
48. *Id.* § 1–201.
49. *E.g., id.* §§ 1–204(2), 2–201(2), 2–205, 2–207(1), 2–309(1), 2–706(2).
50. *E.g., id.* § 2–206(1).
51. *E.g., id.* § 2–609.
52. *E.g., id.* §§ 2–305, 2–709(1)(b).
53. *E.g., id.* § 2–305. As one commentator has remarked, "The word *reasonable,* effective in small doses, has been administered by the bucket, leaving the corpus of the Code reeling in dizzy confusion." Mellinkoff, *The Language of the Uniform Commercial Code,* 77 YALE L.J. 185, 185–86 (1967) (emphasis in original).
54. UNIFORM COMMERCIAL CODE § 2–719, Comment 1.
55. *Id.* § 2–207(2)(d).
56. *Id.* § 2–302. *See also id.* §§ 2–309 & 2–719(3).
57. K. LLEWELLYN, *supra* note 10, at 419 n.39.

that minimizes the differences between the ways courts and legislatures operate. He has delegated legislative decisions to courts, and has phrased a piece of legislation that, save for its comprehensiveness, reads very much like a judicial opinion.

This derogation of the legislative function appears to be premised on the triad of dubious assumptions that self-evident ideal resolutions of situational problems exist, that they can be discovered by careful scrutiny of actual situations, and that once articulated they will be widely accepted. To Hart and Sacks, in contrast, the legislature is especially charged with making law because ethical judgments about the good society and technical observations (derived from economic analysis) about how to reach that society are open to debate and are legitimized only by the democratic character of the institution charged with making them.

It is suggested here that the animating theory of Article II is that law is immanent. The law job is to search it out. There is thus no need for a legislature to create law. The central focus, as in all the writings of the realists, is on courts. Article II is a document whose thrust is not so much to put law on the statute books as it is to coerce courts into looking for law in life.

The Legal Process in Foreign Affairs: Military Intervention–a Testing Case*

Thomas Ehrlich†

In the wake of the United States intervention in Cambodia in April 1970, Secretary of State Rogers sent a memorandum to his departmental advisers urging that, "When crises occur in any area of the world, those in the Department who are most directly involved should be careful to ensure that the legal implications are not overlooked."[1] Secretary Rogers urged particular care in situations involving the potential use of United States armed forces. The memorandum was sent in response to criticisms, in Congress and elsewhere, that legal advice had not been sought in advance of United States ground action in Cambodia. The absence of any references to legal issues in the published portions of the *Pentagon Papers* suggests that the failure was not limited to the Cambodian affair.

This paper suggests procedures by which law may be brought to bear on the process of deciding whether and how to use United States military force short of full-scale war. Particular attention is focused on foreign civil strife, for in the past—and predictably in the future—most decisions by our government on whether to use force have involved such conflicts.[2]

This area of foreign policy is perhaps the most difficult for the legal process. The reason for the difficulty is less the significance of decisions to intervene than the character of the factors involved in the decisions. The United States Government decision in 1968 to support trade preferences for developing countries had a greater impact on our national interests—however defined—than the 1965 decision to land troops in the Dominican

---

* Collaborative efforts with Professor Abram Chayes of Harvard Law School and Professor Andreas F. Lowenfeld of New York University School of Law stimulated many of the themes suggested here. Particular thanks are due to Professor Lowenfeld and to my colleagues Professor John Barton and Professor John Henry Merryman for helpful comments on the Essay in draft form. Finally, I owe a special debt to Professor Alexander George of Stanford for his creative work on decisionmaking in foreign affairs.

† A.B. 1956, LL.B. 1959, Harvard University. Richard E. Lang Dean and Professor of Law, Stanford University.

1. N.Y. Times, June 24, 1970, at 3, cols. 3–5.

2. By civil strife, I mean armed conflict in which the combatants are nationals of a single state. The civil wars in France during the 18th century, in the United States during the 19th century, and in Spain, the Congo, Nigeria, and Yemen during the last two decades are all examples.

In recent years, many scholars have tried to categorize various types of civil strife. In my view, the framework proposed by Professor Richard Falk is particularly useful. *See* Falk, *Introduction*, in THE INTERNATIONAL LAW OF CIVIL WAR (R. Falk ed. 1971). These categorizations are needed to analyze the legitimacy under international law of foreign interventions. For the purposes of this paper, however, such a typology is unnecessary.

Republic. But the factors relevant to intervention issues are both less measurable and less rational than those involved in formulating trade policies. Trade benefits and costs can be measured in ways that are not perceived as possible when the question is whether to send in the marines.

Precisely because of this reality, crises that may lead to the use of force provide a testing case for the legal process in decisionmaking on United States foreign policy. If law and lawyers can have a significant impact in this area, then other areas are a fortiori cases.

I

Although the Vietnam intervention is fresh in our minds, United States military interventions in other lands have occurred mainly within Central America and the Caribbean area. President Theodore Roosevelt issued his famous corollary to the Monroe Doctrine in 1904:

> Chronic wrongdoing, or an impotence which results in a general loosening of the ties of civilized society, may in America, as elsewhere, ultimately require intervention by some civilized nation, and in the Western Hemisphere the adherence of the United States to the Monroe Doctrine may force the United States, however reluctantly, in flagrant cases of such wrongdoing or impotence, to the exercise of an international police power.

Within the next decades, United States marines landed in Cuba, the Dominican Republic, Haiti, and Nicaragua. In each case, what began as a temporary measure turned into a long-term occupation. In each case, United States armed presence was deeply resented. To some Latin American eyes, the United States had made the hemisphere safe from European intervention to preserve the domain for its own.

The pattern of United States military actions that lasted until its replacement by President Franklin Roosevelt's Good-Neighbor policy was generally consistent with traditional international law. Indeed, that pattern—and the pattern of interventions by other Western countries—established the tradition that made the law.

The standard learning[3] is that a nation may aid, in any form it chooses, a regime battling against an "insurgency," but aid to insurgents is precluded as a violation of national sovereignty. Only when and if an insurgency develops into a "belligerency" may a country grant recognition and assistance to the rebels. But the factual premises and normative standards for determining belligerency have never been very clear, and the special nature of recognition further confuses the matter. More troublesome, unilateral determinations by intervening nations have been the rule. Countries that did

---

3. *See, e.g.,* 2 L. OPPENHEIM, INTERNATIONAL LAW § 298, at 660 (7th ed. 1952).

not choose to participate in a conflict could remain neutral. Detailed codes were developed in respect to shipping—where neutrals needed special protection.

The United States usually intervened on the side of the regime in power prior to a civil strife. When this country acted on the side of the rebels, a unilateral declaration of belligerency by the rebels could obviate any problem. Even then, a few troublesome cases arose. Our 1903 involvement in Panama is an unhappy example.[4]

The legal norms with which the legitimacy of particular interventions were traditionally debated are of little utility today. "Sovereignty," "recognition," "insurgency," and "belligerency" were among the key standards. None is of much help, for three interrelated reasons.

First, they appear subject to manipulation in the extreme; whether they are in fact manipulated in any particular case may be less significant than the appearance. A legal norm cannot have much impact if it is viewed as verbal ammunition for either side in a dispute. The meaning of these concepts is clear to some statesmen and scholars, but their clarity is confusion in the eyes of others.

Second, the issues arise so seldom and in contexts so dissimilar that little is possible in the way of reasoned elaboration. "Due process" inherently is no less malleable a term than "sovereignty." But thousands of cases before hundreds of courts have, over time, given substance to the phrase. There are far fewer civil wars, fortunately, and the cultural, political, and social settings are usually sharply different.

Finally, the bias of these concepts toward the status quo is so strong that international law has not provided a modern framework for changing the dimensions of legitimate international activity in this area. Such a framework is essential.

By almost any test, the standard dogma of international law—that an incumbent regime is the only legitimate recipient of assistance—is inadequate in the current world. The case against those traditional rules has been made and remade with persuasiveness and eloquence.[5] Yet I suspect

---

4. In March 1903, the legislature of Colombia rejected an agreement authorizing the United States to construct an isthmian canal. The next month a group of Panamanian residents planned the secession of Panama from Colombia, with at least the tacit support of the United States Government. On October 9, 1903, United States warships were ordered to prevent Colombian troops from landing in the event of a revolt. And on November 3, Secretary of State Hay cabled the United States Consul in Panama: "Uprising on Isthmus reported. Keep the Department fully informed." The Consul replied: "No uprising yet. Reported it will be in the night." The revolution did begin that night and succeeded within a few hours. The Republic of Panama declared its independence on November 4, and the United States recognized the new nation 2 days later. By prearrangement, the Panamanian regime immediately negotiated a new canal treaty that was more favorable to the United States than the previous agreement. See S. MORISON, THE OXFORD HISTORY OF THE AMERICAN PEOPLE 825 (1965).

5. See, e.g., R. FALK, LEGAL ORDER IN A VIOLENT WORLD 109–55 (1968); Farer, *Harnessing Rogue Elephants: A Short Discourse on Intervention in Civil Strife*, 83 HARV. L. REV. 511 (1969);

that the strength of the rules is often underestimated. They are deeply rooted in the psychology of leadership as well as in history. It is much easier for a head of state to explain his government's aid to an existing and therefore "legitimate" foreign regime than to defend aid to foreign insurgents.

The extent of acrimony in the seemingly endless debates of the United Nations Committee on Friendly Relations must give pause to even the most optimistic postulator of new rules. Whether the proposed norms are uniformly endorsed, like "self-determination," or uniformly condemned, like "intervention," the search for agreement on the meaning of such terms has been tortuous. The General Assembly has passed a lengthy resolution that includes a series of hortatory statements concerning the impermissibility of foreign intervention in civil strife.[6] But the very arguments over the meaning of that resolution, in and out of the General Assembly, make it doubtful that the Assembly or any other United Nations organ will produce agreed standards that are both general enough to find broad acceptance and specific enough to have operational consequences.

If agreed norms in this area emerge at all, I suspect they will evolve through case-by-case developments within the broad rubric of Article 2(4) of the United Nations Charter. Its terms provide: "All Members shall refrain in their international relations from the threat or use of force against the territorial integrity or political independence of any state, or in any other manner inconsistent with the Purposes of the United Nations."

This prediction, if it is accurate, puts a great premium on the development by individual nations of procedures for giving content over time, on a case-by-case basis, to the broad prohibition in Article 2(4). Many have commented that the prohibition is in danger of disregard whatever the issue. Certainly this is true in the field of foreign intervention. Yet new normative content can be developed in this area. It must be. What procedures within our own government may be helpful in developing that content?

When decisions arise concerning potential United States military intervention, the problems inherent in a centralized foreign policymaking procedure are accentuated. Policymakers generally have little difficulty in per-

---

Higgins, *Internal War and International Law*, in 3 THE FUTURE OF THE INTERNATIONAL LEGAL ORDER 81 (C. Black & R. Falk eds. 1971).

6. G.A. Res. 2131, 20 U.N. GAOR Supp. 14, at 11, U.N. Doc. A/6014 (1965). After 10 years of debate, the Special Committee on the Question of Defining Aggression finally reached agreement on the text of a draft definition. N.Y. Times, Apr. 13, 1974, at 6, cols. 3–4. The draft marks an important step in developing international agreement on the meaning of "aggression." But its terms inevitably will trigger controversies when applied to specific events. Unfortunately, no dispute-settlement mechanisms are included in the draft to resolve those controversies.

ceiving that an external event or development will damage United States interests. The costs and risks to those interests usually are more apparent than the costs and risks of preventive action. As a result, a consensus favoring action may emerge prematurely. Perceived needs for secrecy and speed generally mean that only a few advisers are involved.[7] The customary checks and balances at work in major decisions on domestic policy—Medicare, air pollution, and the like—are largely absent. Perhaps more critical, no adversary process is at work to ensure full articulation of differing interests and perspectives.

If nothing else is clear it should be that more lawyers in government are not the solution. Some writers (including Dr. Kissinger before he was in office) have suggested that lawyers are often part of the problem—that the legal backgrounds of Secretaries Dulles, Rusk, and Rogers, and others as well, have made them overly concerned with questions of "obligation," and "commitment," or at least overly willing to turn time-bound statements of policy into permanent undertakings imbued with legal implications.[8] But the issue here is not lawyers but legal arrangements.

Legal factors certainly should not be the sole determinant of policymaking in any area of political importance, any more than military, economic, or other factors ought to be the sole determinant. Legal issues ought to be a part of the decisionmaking process, however, and I am concerned because those issues seem to receive relatively short shrift, particularly when military intervention is at issue. The case for that concern is not hard to document. It was true in late 19th-century and early 20th-century foreign policymaking by the United States Government toward Latin America. It was true in the 1965 Dominican Republic crisis. It was true in the 1970 decision to send United States troops into Cambodia. It was true in these and other instances because the existing international norms were inadequate on their substantive merits and self-defining in their procedural applications. Any nation can decide for itself when and if a particular civil strife in some foreign land moves from a rebellion to an insurgency to a belligerency. And there has been no machinery within the United States Government to develop new standards adequate to a new age.

I have no mechanical rabbits to suggest for meeting this challenge. But I believe that important benefits will emerge from attention to ways of promoting advocacy of divergent legal views among government and private lawyers. These benefits are not exclusively related to military inter-

---

7. *See generally* Katzenbach, *Foreign Policy, Public Opinion and Secrecy,* 52 FOREIGN AFF. 1 (1973).
8. *See* G. KENNAN, AMERICAN DIPLOMACY 1900–1950, at 96–100 (1951); Kissinger, *The Viet Nam Negotiations,* 47 FOREIGN AFF. 211, 222–23 (1969).

vention, but they have "testing case" relevance in that context. Three lines of approach seem most promising—within the executive; within the Congress; and within the legal profession.

II

In recent years, a number of case studies have been published concerning United States decisionmaking on whether to use force (and, if so, how much force) abroad.[9] These studies compel the judgment, in my view, that more and better arrangements are needed within the executive branch to ensure what Professor Alexander George has called "multiple advocacy" before the President and Secretary of State.[10] Professor George presents a persuasive case that effective and reasoned decisionmaking is more likely to result when different perspectives are not blurred in the bureaucratic process of preparing the foundation for a presidential decision. President Roosevelt developed a staff of advisers on whom he could count to raise opposing positions and to maintain those positions until the issue reached his desk. The clashes between Harold Ickes and Harry Hopkins are a prime example. Similarly, former Secretary of State Dean Acheson stressed the extent to which President Truman encouraged different officials to bring their different views to him for resolution.[11]

None of the existing formal arrangements in the executive branch is designed to promote this sort of multiple advocacy concerning the legal implications of United States military intervention. The Legal Adviser to the State Department is responsible for considering those implications. But he is also, and primarily, charged with being an advocate for the Department—with defending, in legal terms, the Department's ultimate judgment, whatever that may be.

Some have suggested a legal adviser on international affairs reporting directly to the President.[12] Such an official would weigh the legal aspects of alternative interventionary decisions in terms of developing a sound body of international law. An alternative model, differing more in theory than in practice from the first, calls for a kind of devil's advocate with a man-

---

9. *See, e.g.,* R. Falk ed., *supra* note 2; W. KANE, CIVIL STRIFE IN LATIN AMERICA: A LEGAL HISTORY OF U.S. INVOLVEMENT (1972).

10. George, *The Case for Multiple Advocacy in Making Foreign Policy,* 66 AM. POL. SCI. REV. 751 (1972). *See also* Destler, *Comment: Multiple Advocacy: Some "Limits and Costs,"* 66 AM. POL. SCI. REV. 786 (1972); George, *Rejoinder to "Comment" by I. M. Destler,* 66 AM. POL. SCI. REV. 791 (1972).

11. *See* D. ACHESON, PRESENT AT THE CREATION 733 (1969): "The President gives his hierarchical blessing to platitudes. To perform his real duty must involve the anguish of decision, and to decide one must know the real issues. These have to be found and flushed like birds from a field. The adversary process is the best bird dog."

12. *See* Falk, *Law, Lawyers, and the Conduct of American Foreign Relations,* 78 YALE L.J. 919, 933 (1969).

date to establish an adversary proceeding on the legal implications of alternative proposals.[13] This arrangement would ensure some debate on the law involved in proposed actions. It would reduce the risks that the sharp corners of controversy would be smoothed off as proposals move up a bureaucratic ladder.

The arrangement would have major advantages, but its dangers are obvious. Most important, a devil's advocate too easily could become just that—an advocate of the devil, not a serious proponent of a serious position. Others involved in a particular decision could listen to his arguments with the comfortable knowledge that he was "only doing his job," and was not to be taken seriously.

Another approach would be less mechanical but probably more effective. It would establish within the State Department not a formal mechanism to promote debate from differing perspectives but rather a policy to encourage it. The Legal Adviser would be called on, as a matter of publicly announced policy, to ensure that advocates within—or, if necessary, outside—his office developed the strongest possible legal arguments for conflicting positions. In some situations, this adversary process might involve only two sides; more often, a number of choices should be developed. I am fairly convinced that within a reasonably short time, a practice of preparing opposing legal briefs could become well-ingrained. The value of such a practice could be substantial. It would promote reasoned analysis of legal positions in a way that is unlikely without adversary pressures.

The advantages of multiple-advocacy arrangements are not, of course, limited to lawyers or to legal matters. International trade issues, for example, can be sharpened and clarified by a clash of economists with differing views. The same is true of experts in other disciplines. Further, there is often much to be gained—and little to be lost—from bringing together practitioners in various fields. Coordination is needed to ensure that the clash elucidates rather than clouds an issue. And this is often difficult. But the benefits can be substantial.

Without minimizing the importance of other substantive perspectives, I focus here on law both because it seems to me relatively neglected in foreign policy and because the procedures for ensuring multiple advocacy are themselves part of the legal process in national decisionmaking on foreign affairs.

As Professor George recognizes, the design of multiple-advocacy ar-

---

13. Some have suggested that Undersecretary of State George W. Ball played this role (although not directly regarding legal issues) in the mid-1960's debates on United States policy regarding Southeast Asia. *See* D. HALBERSTAM, THE BEST AND THE BRIGHTEST 491–99 (1972).

rangements can raise formidable bureaucratic problems, especially at administrative levels below that of the Presidential staff. In terms of procedure, the Legal Adviser would need an assistant to coordinate the advocacy—one with adequate leverage to ensure balanced analysis. In terms of
substance, those involved would have to resist the temptation to limit debate to two positions. But I believe that these and other problems could be
overcome and that the results would be more than worth the effort.

The arguments advanced by the Legal Adviser in support of the 1965
Dominican intervention illustrate the dangers of an *ex cathedra* approach.
In April 1965, a military coup overthrew the regime of President Reid Ca-
bral. Almost immediately, the United States landed its troops. The State
Department initially defended the intervention on the ground that the
troops were necessary to protect the lives of United States and other foreign nationals. Rather quickly, however, the stated rationale shifted to a
claim that the United States action was necessary to forestall a Communist
takeover. The Legal Adviser's Office was not substantially involved or consulted either before the intervention or immediately thereafter. It was not
until May 5, 1965—more than a week after the landing of American marines—that the Legal Adviser released a brief on *The Legal Basis for U.S.
Actions in the Dominican Republic.*[14] The opinion was prepared because
of intense pressure from outside the executive branch, particularly within
Congress, for some statement about the law of the matter.

In my view, the Dominican intervention was a tragic mistake. But even
after the United States decision to use force, much might have been done
by lawyers. If the opportunity had been available for the Legal Adviser's
Office to prepare opposing legal arguments—to take advantage of the clash
of opinions—before or during the crisis, I have no doubt that the most
persuasive case in support of intervention would have been framed exclusively in terms of protecting United States citizens and, perhaps, foreign
nationals, much as was done in the Congo rescue operation.[15] One can
question whether the United States should ever intervene militarily to save
its own citizens on foreign shores, but there is substantial support for such
action in traditional international law. A publicly announced legal position along this line might have put some brake on United States involvement in succeeding days, when it became clear that United States citizens
and other non-Dominicans were safe. A policy to ensure a clash of opposing legal positions would almost certainly have produced that result.

The actual opinion of the Legal Adviser seems to conclude that uni-

---

14. *See* Dep't of State, *Memorandum: Legal Basis for U.S. Actions in the Dominican Republic,*
in 111 CONG. REC. 11119 (1965). The final version was revised on May 7, to take into account the
May 6 resolution of the OAS.

15. *See* Ehrlich, *The Measuring Line of Occasion*, 3 STAN. J. INT'L STUDIES 27, 35 (1968).

lateral military intervention is appropriate whenever any one of three circumstances exists—whenever nationals of any foreign country are in danger; whenever it is possible that a regional organization might act; and whenever Communists are involved. I have suggested elsewhere a legal analysis that, in my view, would have been more persuasive and would have created a narrower precedent.[16] My point here is that if the legal arguments put forth to defend the action had been subject to adversary debate before the event, the intervention might not have occurred; or—if it had—the precedent could have been sharply narrowed. Such bad lawyering weakens not only the position of the United States in world affairs, but the position of international law as well.

Another unhappy illustration of the same point is a memorandum issued by the Secretary of State on May 1, 1973, in defense of continued United States bombing of Cambodia,[17] notwithstanding the cease-fire agreement negotiated with North Vietnam 3 months earlier.[18] Article 20 of that agreement calls for the withdrawal of all foreign armed forces from Cambodia. The air strikes on Cambodia represented, according to the memorandum, "a meaningful interim action to bring about compliance with this critical provision in the Vietnam agreement."

The opinion was released only after intense pressures by the Congress for some executive branch legal analysis of the air strikes. In prior weeks, justification by the State Department had been demanded, but the Department had refused. Finally, the opinion was issued. In this case, I know of no sound way in which the United States' actions could be defended in law. The argument that one nation's alleged violation of its commitment provides legal support for bombing another country cannot withstand analysis in international law. The opinion was widely viewed by legal scholars as well as by Congressmen as unpersuasive.

The very fact that no credible legal case could be made for the United States actions may have helped to convince some Congressmen that the bombing should be halted—even though cessation required a step by Congress that had never previously been taken.[19] If the Legal Adviser's Office had been required much earlier to state publicly the basis in law for the United States action—to prepare a kind of legal prospectus—the action

---

16. *Id.* at 36.
17. N.Y. Times, May 1, 1973, at 10, cols. 3–8.
18. The cease-fire agreement is printed in 68 Dep't State Bull. 169 (1973).
19. *See* Second Supplemental Appropriations Act § 307, 87 Stat. 99 (1973): "None of the funds herein appropriated under this Act may be expended to support directly or indirectly combat activities in or over Cambodia, Laos, North Vietnam and South Vietnam or off the shores of Cambodia, Laos, North Vietnam and South Vietnam by United States forces, and after August 15, 1973, no other funds heretofore appropriated under any other Act may be expended for such purpose." The Act was passed and signed by President Nixon after his veto of a version calling for an immediate cutoff of funds was sustained. *See* 1973 U.S. Code Cong. & Ad. News 1985 (President's veto message).

might have been avoided or terminated sooner. At the least, it would have been subject to more searching legal analysis than actually occurred.

By contrast, the Cuban missile crisis illustrates the advantages of affirmative efforts to explore various approaches to particular legal issues.[20] It shows the substantial role that law and lawyers can have in even the most volatile emergency if a multiple-advocacy process is encouraged. Over the course of the 13-day period in which competing strategies were debated within the President's advisory group on the crisis—a group that included a number of lawyers—conflicting legal positions were reviewed as part of the design of competing "scenarios." Those positions ranged from that of Dean Acheson, who said that international law is essentially irrelevant at the time of such crisis, to that of Deputy Attorney General Katzenbach, who claimed that either an air strike or blockade could be supported under international law as self-defense, to that of Acting Legal Adviser Meeker, who argued that the only use of force justifiable in law was a quarantine, and further that a quarantine was valid only if backed by the Organization of American States.[21]

The point here is the value of multiple advocacy of opposing views. The details of various arrangements to promote such advocacy are less significant than that some arrangements exist. Indeed the advantages may be maximized when a number of different arrangements are used.[22]

III

It is, in my view, even more important that new governmental arrangements be encouraged outside the executive branch. As a practical matter, this means legislative arrangements, since there is little likelihood of substantial involvement by the judiciary. Courts were asked to pass on legal issues involving United States participation in the Vietnam War, but they consistently refused. On grounds of either lack of standing or the "political question" doctrine, the courts stopped short of considering the constitutional legitimacy of the war in the absence of a specific declaration of

---

20. *See* A. CHAYES, THE CUBAN MISSILE CRISIS (1974).

21. Ambassador Adlai E. Stevenson went even further and advocated removal of the United States missiles from Turkey and Greece, though published accounts are unclear whether he made that case as a matter of law or of politics.

22. Currently, public debate on intervention issues sometimes can be generated, but only with difficulty and usually well after the decision has been made. When the United States mined the harbor of Haiphong in the spring of 1972, one of my colleagues and I wrote to the State Department Legal Adviser questioning the action on grounds of international law. The Legal Adviser responded, and excerpts from his response were ultimately published. 66 AM. J. INT'L L. 836 (1972). Subsequently, both our initial letter and a rejoinder were also published. 67 AM. J. INT'L L. 325 (1972). Taken together, the letter, response, and rejoinder focus and frame some of the key legal issues involved in considering the legitimacy of the United States action. Regardless of how one resolves the legal questions, most will agree that the arguments ought to have been exposed to public scrutiny, and much more quickly than was actually the case. But it took some effort to ensure that our initial letter and rejoinder to the Legal Adviser's response were also published.

war by Congress. There are some signs that this practice may have weakened. The order by a federal district court in August 1973 to halt United States bombing in Cambodia is a significant example, though that order was reversed on appeal.[23]

Still, a number of important factors militate against a significant impact by the judiciary on the process of policymaking in international affairs. Concerning decisions involving the potential use of force, perhaps the most important factor is timing. Even assuming a willingness on the part of a court to review the legality of a military intervention, such review will almost certainly come only after, rather than before, the fact. Declaratory judgments are unlikely. Further, the restraints on judicial involvement in this area, developed under the "political question" rubric, make it unlikely—and many say improper—for a court to consider the constitutional issues raised by these cases. Congress is, therefore, the only governmental possibility, apart from the executive branch, for guidance on questions concerning military intervention.

In the wake of American involvement in Southeast Asia, a great deal of controversy has been focused on the meaning and implications of the constitutional provision that Congress alone may "declare war." Rather than reexamine that controversy, I turn to what seems to me a pressing requirement: that Congress widen and sharpen the debate on what the international law is and what it should be relative to any particular situation that may involve United States military intervention. Whatever arrangements are designed to encourage multiple advocacy within the executive branch, it is probable that most decisions on intervention will not be subject to a full adversary debate in that forum. But if the Congress is given the facts of a situation, and allowed some time to consider them, such debate is much more likely.

In November 1973 the Congress adopted—over the President's veto—a joint resolution "Concerning the War Powers of the President and Congress."[24] It is designed to limit the circumstances in which the President may deploy United States armed forces in foreign hostilities without legislative sanction. This was the latest round in a series of efforts begun in the 1960's to provide statutory limits on the deployment of United States armed forces by the President in the absence of congressional authorization. The

---

23. The district court's ruling is found in two separate opinions: Holtzman v. Schlesinger, 361 F. Supp. 544 (E.D.N.Y.) (standing) and Holtzman v. Schlesinger, 361 F. Supp. 553 (E.D.N.Y.) (justiciability), *rev'd*, 484 F.2d 1307 (2d Cir. 1973) (holding dispute political question and non-justiciable), *vacation of circuit order refused*, 414 U.S. 1307 (Marshall, Circuit Justice), *circuit order vacated*, 414 U.S. 1316 (Douglas, Circuit Justice), *district order stayed*, 414 U.S. 1321 (1973) (Marshall, Circuit Justice). *See also* Mitchell v. Laird, 476 F.2d 533 (D.C. Cir.), *withdrawn by Order of Court*, 476 F.2d XXVIII (1973).
24. H.R.J. Res. 542, 93d Cong., 1st Sess., 119 Cong. Rec. 170 (1973).

resolution was a compromise between the differing views of many in and out of Congress. President Nixon stated in his veto message that two key provisions in the resolution were "clearly unconstitutional."[25] More than two-thirds of the Congress disagreed. The current status of those provisions is thus unclear. The constitutionality and wisdom of their terms have been argued and reargued at length. But another provision in the resolution—section 4—has particular relevance here, although it received little attention in the public debates, and no one questions its constitutionality. Within 48 hours after deploying United States armed forces in foreign hostilities, the President is required to submit a report on the circumstances and justifications of the intervention, including a legal analysis.

No one can expect preparation of a carefully reasoned, fully developed legal brief within 2 days after a decision to use military force. But precisely for that reason, the requirement can have several useful effects.

First, a reporting requirement will press government lawyers to examine the legal ramifications of possible alternative courses of action in advance of a crisis. International conflicts have occasionally occurred in which the United States could not have foreseen the likelihood of military action. But such situations are relatively rare. In most cases that have involved actual or potential uses of United States military force, policy planners had some warning; prior legal analysis would have been possible, had lawyers been consulted, just as there was contingency planning by the military and the State Department desk officers in these situations.

Second, and closely related, as a crisis develops the reporting requirement will encourage the President and his political and military advisers to involve lawyers in the process of determining whether and when to use force—and how much force to use. The need for legal justification to support the decision will be a strong incentive for analysis of legal considerations as part of the overall decisionmaking process.

The Cuban missile crisis erupted suddenly, for example, but lawyers in the State and Defense Departments had previously worked through the basic legal considerations. The presence of Soviet missiles had not been considered likely by the executive branch, but the possibility that some set of circumstances might warrant United States intervention had been

25. Message from President Nixon to the House of Representatives, Oct. 23, 1973, 1973 U.S. CODE CONG. & AD. NEWS 3808. One of the two provisions requires withdrawal of United States forces from foreign hostilities within 60 to 90 days unless the Congress authorizes an extension. The other requires such a withdrawal immediately upon passage of a concurrent resolution by Congress. The veto message stated that both provisions are unconstitutional, that the Constitution can be altered only by amendment, and that "any attempt to make such alterations by legislation is clearly without force." President Nixon implied, therefore, that he would ignore the provisions should a situation arise in which their terms are applicable. When the resolution was adopted over the President's veto, however, the White House refused to state whether it would obey the statute in those or any other circumstances. See N.Y. Times, Nov. 8, 1973, at 1, col. 8. The resolution does include a severability provision.

foreseen. As a result, preliminary legal analyses were prepared covering some of the key issues. The Legal Adviser's Office in the State Department published the basic legal justification of the quarantine within 12 hours after it was announced.[26] On the whole, that justification withstood scrutiny in the period that followed. But it could not have been written in half a day without careful preparatory work.

Even in the unexpected explosion of the 1973 Middle East War—when prior warnings were not available—lawyers could and should have been engaged during the war in the process of examining alternative peacekeeping arrangements. Yet, from all accounts, State Department lawyers were isolated from policymaking in the matter.[27]

It is true, of course, that if a President's lawyers are only clever but not wise, they can verbalize legal justifications without substantive legal content. Perhaps the reporting provision in the "war powers" resolution is better viewed, therefore, as an opportunity rather than a requirement. But it should, at the least, pressure a President and his advisers to articulate a legal basis for United States intervention and to think through that basis in advance.

It is sometimes suggested that postevent justifications are worth little. But this view misses a fundamental reality of policymaking.

> [T]he requirement of justification suffuses the basic process of choice. There is continuous feedback between the knowledge that the government will be called upon to justify its action and the kind of action that can be chosen. The linkage tends to induce a tolerable congruence between the actual corporate decision-process, with its interplay of personal, bureaucratic, and political factors, and the idealized picture of rational choice on the basis of objectively coherent criteria. We may grant a considerable latitude for evasion and manipulation. But to ignore the requirement of justification too long or to violate its canons too egregiously creates, in a democracy, what we have come to call a "credibility gap." The ultimate consequence is to erode the capacity of the government to govern.[28]

Even if one concludes—erroneously, I believe—that the legal analyses required under the "war powers" resolution will have little impact on decisionmaking within the executive branch, they should still focus intervention issues within a framework that promotes public debate. One can expect the arguments to be rebutted and executive branch lawyers to re-

---

26. *See* Dep't of State, *Memorandum: Legal Basis for the Quarantine of Cuba*, in A. CHAYES, T. EHRLICH, & A. LOWENFELD, INTERNATIONAL LEGAL PROCESS, Doc. Supp. 552–58 (1968).

27. After Dr. Kissinger became Secretary of State, he appointed his personal lawyer, Carlyle Maw, as the Department's Legal Adviser. In spite of Dr. Kissinger's previously disparaging view of the role of lawyers in foreign affairs, *see* note 8 *supra* and accompanying text, Mr. Maw accompanied the Secretary during most of his "shuttle diplomacy" in the Middle East, and apparently had a more significant role in peacemaking than had any Legal Adviser since Herman Phleger, who held that office when John Foster Dulles was Secretary of State.

28. A. CHAYES, *supra* note 20, at 103.

spond to the rebuttals. The process should produce far more informed
analysis of policy issues in their legal dimensions than now occurs.

The resolution does not, by its terms, require congressional involvement in the analysis of intervention issues before—as opposed to after—
United States troops are engaged in foreign hostilities. But for the reasons
I have indicated the reporting requirement in the resolution should make
such involvement more likely. No one can be sure, of course, how much
legislative impact participation would have in any particular case. A lesson from the Indochina War of two decades ago, however, suggests that
the impact can be substantial.

Until 1954, all Indochina was a French colonial possession. But in the
spring of that year, a bloody civil war was taking place within Vietnam.
On March 20, the French Chief of Staff arrived in Washington with a
message that Indochina would fall unless the United States intervened.
France sought United States military action to turn the tide. Strong support for American intervention came from the Chairman of the Joint
Chiefs of Staff, Admiral Radford. He viewed the potential fall of Vietnam
as a first step toward the loss of Indochina and ultimately all of Southeast
Asia. It was essential, he argued, that what was later called the first domino
not be allowed to fall. The French forces in Vietnam would have to be
buttressed by the United States.

Admiral Radford prepared a detailed plan of military action to aid the
French. President Eisenhower called on Secretary of State John Foster
Dulles and Admiral Radford to meet with eight congressional leaders—
five senators and three representatives—to review the intervention plan.
The meeting was held on April 3, 1954. Radford presented his scheme and
Dulles endorsed it.[29]

But the congressional leaders unanimously opposed United States intervention. All agreed that the unilateral use of force by the United States
would be a disaster. They insisted on a multilateral effort if any effort
were to be made at all. Although the arguments were probably rooted primarily in political considerations, they might well have been framed in
legal terms. Certainly the Congressmen were influenced by the multilateral
support through the United Nations of the United States intervention in
Korea.

There are some ironies in the whole affair, particularly that Senator

<hr>

29. One recent analysis claims that Dulles really wanted to scuttle the Radford plan. *See* R.
RANDLE, GENEVA 1954, 63–65 (1969). According to this theory, Dulles arranged the meeting with
legislative leaders to prove to the United States military establishment that Congress would not permit
United States intervention. This effort to make Dulles appear less of a hawk, but more of a Machiavelli,
seems implausible in light of other reports of his stated support for an American use of force. Most
accounts conclude that Dulles supported the Radford plan because he saw it as essential to check a
Communist chain reaction through Indochina. *See* George, *The Case for Multiple Advocacy in Making
Foreign Policy, supra* note 10, at 771 n.67.

Lyndon B. Johnson was one of the most vocal opponents of the plan. April 3, 1954, has been called "The Day We Didn't Go to War"[30] by Chalmers M. Roberts. Others have suggested that Mr. Roberts over-dramatized the confrontation with congressional leaders. But no one disputes that key figures in the executive branch were prepared to intervene and that a handful of Congressmen raised a series of counterarguments that the President found compelling. In my own view, the decision not to intervene in Indochina was correct, at least if one divorces that decision from the events of a decade later. Even if one disputes that verdict, I think it hard to dissent from the proposition that congressional judgment brought a valuable dimension to the decisionmaking process.[31]

Contrast the process of decisionmaking in April 1954 with the process in March 1969 when the United States began to bomb Cambodia. For 13 months the intervention remained a secret from the public and from most of Congress. The President obviously knew about the massive bombings, yet in April 1970 he claimed that the United States invasion at that time was the first involvement by the American military in Cambodia. Presumably, many in the State Department were wholly unaware of the United States' actions during the 13-month period. The State Department Legal Adviser stated in May 1970 before a bar association meeting that the United States had not intervened until the previous month.[32] It might be that most in Congress would have approved the bombing of Cambodia if it had been announced publicly in the spring of 1969. It is conceivable that a sound legal case for the bombing could have been presented and that the case would have been accepted by Congress as by the President. But the opportunity never came. As a result, the kind of countervailing congressional pressures that prevailed in 1954 never had a chance to be expressed.

The persuasive legal case that the United States made for the quarantine during the Cuban missile crisis was premised in major measure on the operation of multilateral as opposed to unilateral decisionmaking processes. The quarantine would be authorized by a regional arrangement, the Organization of American States, acting under a multilateral agreement, the Rio Treaty. It appears that in 1954 the congressional leaders advocated a similar collective approach if any action were to occur. I do not suggest that they argued primarily on the law. Whether or not the Congressmen pressed their case in terms of law, morality, or practical politics is less sig-

30. Roberts, *The Day We Didn't Go to War*, 11 THE REPORTER, Sept. 14, 1954, at 31. *See also* R. RANDLE, *supra* note 29, at 63–65.
31. Gen. Matthew Ridgway, Army Chief of Staff, also opposed the plan, and his arguments were an important factor in the ultimate decision not to intervene.
32. Stevenson, *United States Military Actions in Cambodia: Questions of International Law*, 62 DEP'T STATE BULL. 765 (1970).

nificant than that the President found it important to seek their counsel.

Too often in the recent past there have been inadequate opportunities for such advice to be given. The "war powers" resolution is an important step forward. It underscores the desires of Congress for involvement in decisionmaking. The resolution may be a sufficient catalyst to promote congressional consultation before as well as after an intervention decision. Only experience will tell.

IV

Finally, I think that members of the legal profession have an opportunity and an obligation in this field. Unfortunately, in the realm of international law, the organized bar in general and the American Bar Association in particular are best known for their stands against American involvement in international arrangements—the Genocide Convention is a prime example. On the rare occasions when the bar in the United States has focused its attention on matters of international law, its leaders have generally been content to confine themselves to platitudes favoring world peace through world law.

An opportunity exists to do much more—to organize and promote focused debate on legal issues involving particular military interventions. Some legal institutions—local bar associations and law schools—meet this responsibility. The Association of the Bar of the City of New York, through the Hammarskjöld Forum, is a prime example. But sadly, such institutions are rare. One should not expect resolutions on the merits of intervention issues. But it is reasonable to expect that those institutions seek out qualified advocates for opposing positions and press them to present their views. Insight and understanding will emerge in the clash of opinions.

"We must not make a scarecrow of the law," wrote Shakespeare in *Measure for Measure*, "setting it up to fear the birds of prey, and let it keep one shape till custom make it their perch, and not their terror."[33] For too long, the international law on foreign intervention has kept one shape; now there is little left but rhetoric. It is up to all of us in the legal profession to engage in the creative process of designing a new shape. In this area of law, more than others, process is substance. Creative procedures are needed to ensure reasoned deliberations on any actual or proposed new interventions. Lawyers can and should contribute to those procedures and deliberations.

---

33. Act II, scene i.

Personal Injury Accidents in New Zealand and the United States: Some Striking Similarities*

Marc A. Franklin†

On April 1, 1974, New Zealand's Accident Compensation Act went into effect, abolishing virtually all lawsuits for personal injury. Such injuries are now handled through an insurance system financed from several different sources. Briefly stated, the scheme contains three separate parts. All workers are covered for personal injuries on and off the job under a plan financed by employers along the lines of workmen's compensation. Injuries attributable to motoring are financed from a fund produced by charges on motoring. Nonmotoring injuries sustained by nonworkers are covered from general revenue sources. All personal injury actions for accidental harm are abolished.[1]

Although much has been and will be written about the new system, little has been written about accidents and accident law in New Zealand before its advent. The Royal Commission that proposed the revolutionary change[2] offered little empirical evidence to bolster what were essentially arguments on principle as to how the society should respond when accidental injury befalls a citizen.[3] Although the Commission did note some shortcomings

* The research for this Essay was undertaken while the author was a Fulbright-Hays Research Scholar in residence at Victoria University of Wellington, in Wellington, New Zealand.

Several New Zealanders were most helpful in facilitating my access to data. For obvious reasons, several in the insurance industry have preferred anonymity. Among those who may be mentioned, four stand out: F. Findlay and J. Frasier at the National Health Statistics Centre in Wellington; S. Cole, Medical Records Officer, Hutt Hospital; and Ian B. Campbell, then Secretary of the Workers' Compensation Board, now Safety Director of the Accident Compensation Commission. In addition, many persons working at the various branches of the Department of Statistics were helpful in locating and developing data.

† A.B. 1953, LL.B. 1956, Cornell University. Professor of Law, Stanford University.

1. See Palmer, *Compensation for Personal Injury: A Requiem for the Common Law in New Zealand*, 21 AM. J. COMP. L. 1 (1973), and articles cited in note 1 therein. *See also* Note, *The End of a Faulted System: New Zealand Adopts a No-Fault Approach to Personal Injury Compensation*, 1973 L. & Soc. ORDER 679. These pieces were written at a time when it appeared the Act would exclude coverage of nonworkers unless they were hurt in motor vehicle accidents. The bill was subsequently amended and coverage extended to this group before the Act went into effect. Accident Compensation Amendment Act (No. 2), 1973, N.Z. Stat. no. 113, § 37 (adding the "Supplementary Scheme," §§ 102A–102D, to the principal act). A summary of the current Act may be found in Campbell, The Accident Compensation Act (Victoria Univ. of Wellington, Industrial Relations Centre, Occasional Papers in Industrial Relations No. 9, 1974). *See also* 29 N.Z. NEWS, June 1974, at 2–3.

2. The Commission had originally set out to study only possible changes in the workers' compensation system. ROYAL COMM'N OF INQUIRY, COMPENSATION FOR PERSONAL INJURY IN NEW ZEALAND 11 (1967).

3. Palmer & Lemons, *Toward the Disappearance of Tort Law—New Zealand's New Compensation Plan*, 1972 U. ILL. L.F. 693. Palmer & Lemons noted "the lack of empirical data on the performance of the existing tort system." *Id.* at 739.

in the existing law, such as the lack of provision for rehabilitation, their emphasis was on a philosophy of community responsibility that rejected the traditional reliance on litigation.[4]

The Commission's failure to delineate the personal injury accident picture in New Zealand before the change presents an inadequate basis for evaluating the efficacy of the new system. This study seeks to remedy the problem by reviewing the nature and frequency of personal accidents suffered in 1970.[5] This will provide a baseline for later efforts to study the new system, including such questions as whether a new legal response to accidents may produce new patterns of accident occurrence. Although new patterns are unlikely when the potential harmers are the same group as the potential victims, as in motor vehicle situations, they become plausible in cases where one is rarely the victim of one's own carelessness, such as those involving medical treatment, maintenance of commercial property, and manufacture of consumer products.

Despite obvious differences between the two countries, New Zealand and the United States have remarkably similar accident patterns. This strengthens the view that New Zealand's experience with its new system cannot be ignored in future consideration of changes in accident law in this country.[6]

I. Introduction

To make the accident data meaningful one must first gain some understanding of New Zealand. This Article will emphasize aspects most relevant to an understanding of accident data.

New Zealand is essentially two islands, the North Island and the South Island, separated by a narrow strait. The country, 1,500 miles east of Australia, stretches nearly 1,000 miles north-south, but is so narrow that no point is more than 70 miles from a seacoast. With a population of 2.8 million, comparable to Iowa, and an area of 103,736 square miles, roughly the same as Colorado, it has a population density of about 28 persons per square

---

4. See ROYAL COMM'N OF INQUIRY, supra note 2, at 39–41.

5. Unless otherwise indicated, data for New Zealand will all refer to the calendar year 1970. At the time this study was conducted, accident data and hospital records were being put into final shape for that year. Up through 1973 no dramatic changes had occurred to mar the usefulness of the 1970 data. In 1974 New Zealand was affected by the oil supply problems that affected this country, and motor vehicle data for 1974 will surely be unusual in both countries as a result. 29 N.Z. NEWS, May 1974, at 3.

It should also be noted at the outset that there has been no attempt at pinpoint accuracy. As will be seen, some of the data permit only the most general analysis. Where the records indicate that a complete count is being offered, precise numbers have been used. Even so, other impediments to precision remain. See note 43 infra.

6. Naturally one must know more about the society and culture of each country before asserting total comparability. The only attempt being made in this Article is to determine whether the two countries are comparable from an accident standpoint.

mile, approximately that of Kansas.[7] The two islands differ in density: the North Island has 42 percent of the area, 70 percent of the population, and a density of 45 persons per square mile, similar to Mississippi. The South Island, famed for its scenic beauty, is mountainous and even less crowded, with about 14 persons per square mile, similar to Arizona.

The population is roughly two-thirds urban.[8] The three largest population centers, Auckland, Wellington, and Christchurch, account for almost half the total population of New Zealand, with the Auckland metropolitan area composing nearly half of that. Thus, although New Zealand as a whole is sparsely populated by American standards, its population is largely urban.[9]

The New Zealand population closely resembles that of the United States in vital statistics. The life expectancies and the age and sex distributions are virtually identical.[10] Maoris, the group of Polynesians who came to New Zealand several centuries before the Europeans, now account for 8 percent of the population. There are other subgroups of Polynesians among the recent immigrants to New Zealand but the overwhelming majority of the country, more than 90 percent, is of European stock, virtually all from the British Isles.[11] In both countries, then, there are similar proportions of nonwhite population, and national figures reflect a composite of different health and accident data for whites and nonwhites.[12]

Although the sizes of the work forces in the two countries are proportionate,[13] only 28 percent of New Zealand women are in the labor force as compared to 38 percent in the United States.[14] Thus any compensation

7. N.Z. DEP'T OF STATISTICS, NEW ZEALAND OFFICIAL YEARBOOK 65 (1972) (using data from 1971 census) [hereinafter cited as YEARBOOK 1972]. An extraordinary variety of data concerning New Zealand may most conveniently be found in the annual editions of the Yearbook. New Zealand's demography and legal system are discussed in Bernstein, *No-Fault Compensation for Personal Injury in New Zealand*, in HEW, REPORT OF THE SECRETARY'S COMMISSION ON MEDICAL MALPRACTICE 836 (1973).
8. YEARBOOK 1972, *supra* note 7, at 58.
9. The average density in the United States is 57.5 persons per square mile. Of the total population, 73.5% is considered to be urban. U.S. DEP'T OF COMMERCE, STATISTICAL ABSTRACT OF THE UNITED STATES 1973, at 5, 17 [hereinafter cited as 1973 STATISTICAL ABSTRACT].
10. See N.Z. DEP'T OF STATISTICS, NEW ZEALAND OFFICIAL YEARBOOK 100 (1973) [hereinafter cited as YEARBOOK 1973] for life-expectancy comparisons as of 1967–68. The 0–4-age group makes up 8.4% of the American population and 10.5% of New Zealand's; the 5–24-year figures are 37.4% and 38.7%; the 25–44-year figures are 23.7% and 23%; the 45–64-year figures are 20.5% and 19%; and the over-64 figures are 9.9% and 8.5%. *Compare* 1973 STATISTICAL ABSTRACT, *supra* note 9, at 31, *with* YEARBOOK 1972, *supra* note 7, at 1038. Women make up 51% of the population in New Zealand and 50% in the United States. *Id.*
The causes of mortality are also similar in both countries. The cancer and accident rates are virtually identical; the vascular disease rate is somewhat higher in New Zealand, but the American heart disease rate is substantially higher. *Compare id.* at 100, *with* 1973 STATISTICAL ABSTRACT, *supra* note 9, at 61. This last difference alone accounts for the entire difference in mortality rates from all causes (884 deaths per 1,000 in New Zealand to 940 per 1,000 in the United States). *Id.*
11. See YEARBOOK 1972, *supra* note 7, at 81; Bernstein, *supra* note 7, at 837.
12. *Compare* YEARBOOK 1972, *supra* note 7, at 81, 1038, *and* Bernstein, *supra* note 7, at 837, *with* 1973 STATISTICAL ABSTRACT, *supra* note 9, at 29.
13. The labor force is roughly 40% of the population in both countries. *Compare* NEW ZEALAND POCKET DIGEST OF STATISTICS 12 (1972), *with* 1973 STATISTICAL ABSTRACT, *supra* note 9, at 5, 220.
14. *Compare* YEARBOOK 1972, *supra* note 7, at 839, *with* 1973 STATISTICAL ABSTRACT, *supra* note

scheme covering only workers or motor vehicle accident victims would have excluded many adults from coverage.[15]

One pervasive difference between the two countries is the levels and distribution of income and consequent living patterns. The range of incomes in New Zealand is extremely narrow: in the income year 1970–71, 99 percent of the individual tax returns filed reported incomes from all sources of under 10,000 New Zealand dollars.[16] Almost 90 percent of the returns showed income under $4,000, with a median income of approximately $2,400. This suggests a narrow range of income that creates slight differentiations in standards of living. Accumulations of wealth are further inhibited by a highly progressive income tax that reaches a maximum of 67 percent at the $12,000 level.[17]

Another critical difference between the two countries relates to the financing and distribution of health care services. For medical care in New Zealand, the government pays the physician a flat rate for each patient, depending on the nature of the service rendered, and the physician is free to charge the patient an additional amount. In 1938, when this system was introduced, the flat fee amounted to perhaps three-fourths of the total fees received. By 1970 this amount, 75 cents, was only one-third of the average charge.[18] Patients are free to choose any general practitioner. These physicians account for virtually three-fourths of all physician care. Patients usually go to specialists only when referred by a general practitioner. The government also makes partial fee payments to specialists in addition to paying for virtually all drugs and medications prescribed by physicians.[19]

Substantial differences also exist in the financing of hospital care. New Zealand has a network of public hospitals that are completely free in all

---

9, at 219. A larger number of American women are divorced, separated, or widowed and must work, and the dearth of daycare centers and preschools in New Zealand further reflects a cultural resistance to women entering the labor force. *See* W. SUTCH, WOMEN WITH A CAUSE 149–53 (1973).

15. Accidents in the home are also a major cause of death and injury. *See* text accompanying notes 48 & 76 *infra*. In New Zealand, however, a non-wage earner will have fewer out-of-pocket expenses than in this country because he is not required to pay hospital expenses. *See* text accompanying note 20 *infra*.

16. *See* Palmer & Lemons, *supra* note 3, at 696. During the period under discussion a New Zealand dollar was worth $1.12 in U.S. currency. *See* Bernstein, *supra* note 7, at 839 n.8.

17. *See id.* at 837. *See also* YEARBOOK 1973, *supra* note 10, at 767. Although the dollar levels of income are substantially higher in the United States than in New Zealand, and the income tax rates are substantially higher in New Zealand than in the United States, it is difficult—and beyond our scope —to draw conclusions about standards of living in the two countries. International comparisons of car ownership, television ownership, telephones, and similar measurable goods are presented in *id.* at 954. From another perspective, however, it is undoubtedly significant to know that 43% of the national budget goes to welfare and social services as against 7% for defense. Bernstein, *supra* note 7, at 837.

18. Much of the data relating to health care services may be found in ROYAL COMM'N OF INQUIRY, SOCIAL SECURITY IN NEW ZEALAND, especially at 392–480 (1972). *See also* Bernstein, *supra* note 7, at 839–44.

19. *See* Bernstein, *supra* note 7, at 840–41.

respects to all residents.[20] The hospitals are administered by 30 regional hospital boards and are financed almost entirely by allocations from the central New Zealand government derived from the income tax. The hospital patient is treated by members of the hospital staff and does not choose his physician. First priority for admission, of course, is given to accident victims and emergency cases, with additional patients chosen from among the waiting lists. In urban areas there are long waiting lines for elective surgical procedures.[21]

There are numerous private hospitals in New Zealand, but they are generally much smaller than the public hospitals and account only for 15 percent of the available beds.[22] These private hospitals serve two basic functions: they provide geriatric services and they permit patients awaiting elective surgery to avoid the queue and select a particular surgeon.[23] Private hospital patients are subsidized $9.00 per day for surgical treatment.[24] In recent years the growth of hospital insurance has made the private hospital option more attractive.[25]

Since no private hospital in New Zealand has an emergency department,[26] all seriously injured accident victims who require hospitalization are brought to public hospitals. Most persons who suffer fairly minor accidental injury think first of the public hospital, rather than of a physician, because few individual practitioners are equipped to take X-rays or to diagnose or treat serious injuries.[27] All these facts make the public hospitals an

20. Under the new Accident Compensation Act, the Supplementary Scheme applies to persons not otherwise covered under the Earners' Scheme or the Motor Vehicle Scheme. This would include such persons as "tourists and visitors, children, students, housewives, and retired people." This scheme is financed from general taxation. 29 N.Z. NEWS, June 1974, at 2–3. *See also* note 1 *supra*.

21. Interview with J. Allan, Administrative Officer, Wellington Hospital, in Wellington, N.Z., Feb. 7, 1973.

22. YEARBOOK 1973, *supra* note 10, at 142.

23. *Id*. at 143 (reporting that 73% of all patients in private hospitals on the date of the 1971 census were over 65 years of age, compared with 42% in the public hospitals).

24. *Id*. at 141.

25. The membership of the largest medical care society grew from 10,000 in 1965 to 190,000 in 1972. Attachment to letter from Peter A. Smith, General Manager, Southern Cross Medical Care Society, to author, May 21, 1973, on file in Stanford Law Library.

26. Private hospitals cannot afford to staff or equip such a service and also cannot afford to keep beds open in anticipation of the arrival of an accident victim. Interview with Gordon Lee, General Secretary, New Zealand Private Hospitals Association, and General Secretary, Medical Association of New Zealand, in Wellington, N.Z., Feb. 13, 1973.

27. Dixon, Emery & Spears, *Casualty Department Utilization Survey*, 71 N.Z. MED. J. 272–76 (1970). This is a study of utilization of casualty services in Dunedin. The authors conclude that patients come to public hospitals rather than to practitioners because they perceive that hospitals have better technical facilities and expertise. The study found no evidence for the proposition that hospitals are favored because their services are free whereas a practitioner charges a fee. Nevertheless some health sources interviewed did suggest that the price differential might influence the choice though people would be most reluctant to admit it.

Even if a patient does go to a general practitioner first, that practitioner will send the patient to the hospital in all cases involving suspected fractures, foreign objects, head injuries, or orthopedic problems. The practioner will treat only bruises and lacerations or injuries requiring minor suturing. Interview with Gordon Lee, *supra* note 26.

excellent place to study accident victims and the types of accidents they suffer.[28]

II. INCIDENCE OF ACCIDENTAL INJURIES

We turn now to a profile of the accidental deaths and injuries in New Zealand during 1970. The data gathered in New Zealand are grouped according to the International Classification of Diseases, a system utilized throughout the world.[29] The next Part summarizes the financial aspects of personal injury accidents in New Zealand.

Deaths and injuries will be discussed separately for several reasons. Data on deaths are the most accurate accident statistics in any country; a separate death certificate is required and the condition is relatively easy to report and analyze. Furthermore, American data for deaths are classified by external cause;[30] thus we can make extensive comparisons of accidental deaths in the two countries. The injury data are less reliable for comparison purposes because injuries in the United States are not classified by external cause.[31] Moreover, even in New Zealand, where data are available to indicate how many accident victims were admitted to the hospital, we cannot tell how many were seriously injured.[32] In addition, some victims with serious injuries may not be admitted to the hospital. These vagaries muddy the analysis of data on accidental injuries.

A. Deaths

The most striking initial observation about accidental deaths[33] is that although national rates throughout the world ranged from 18 to 78 per

---

28. As will be seen later, there is no convenient way to study emergency patients who are not subsequently admitted. *See* text accompanying note 57 *infra*.

29. Both countries basically follow WORLD HEALTH ORGANIZATION, MANUAL OF THE INTERNATIONAL STATISTICAL CLASSIFICATION OF DISEASES, INJURIES, AND CAUSES OF DEATH (8th rev. 1967). New Zealand has certain additions that permit other information to be obtained. *See* note 81 *infra*. In the case of the United States more extensive adaptations have been made, although accident data are little affected. *See* U.S. PUBLIC HEALTH SERVICE, INTERNATIONAL CLASSIFICATION OF DISEASES, ADAPTED FOR USE IN THE UNITED STATES (Pub. No. 1693, 1967).

Accident data are coded in two ways: according to the external cause of death (the "E" code), and from the standpoint of medical symptoms (the "N" code). Our primary focus will be on the external causes as the more helpful indicator.

30. American mortality data under the International Classification of Diseases by E code have been supplied by the National Center for Health Statistics of the Public Health Service of the Department of Health, Education, and Welfare. Some of the data are for 1969 and will be published in NATIONAL CENTER FOR HEALTH STATISTICS, HEW VITAL STATISTICS OF THE UNITED STATES II, pt. A (1969). Other unpublished data apply to 1970 and will appear in another forthcoming volume. Letter from Sandra K. Surber, Office of Information, Nat'l Center for Health Statistics, to author, Mar. 14, 1974, on file in Stanford Law Library.

31. Presumably it is too costly to assemble the massive information that is required.

32. A significant number of accident patients in New Zealand are admitted solely for observation and are released shortly thereafter. *See* text accompanying notes 70–72 *infra*.

33. Throughout this study, some E-code classifications are excluded for all purposes because they do not comport with our conventional understanding of the word "accident." Thus, E950-959, covering suicides and attempted suicides, has been excluded. Also, E960-969, covering homicides and other purposely inflicted injuries on other persons, have been excluded. Accidents occurring during legal in-

100,000 population in 1970, the United States and New Zealand had the same rate—56 per 100,000 population.[34] The sex and age ratios are also quite similar.[35] In both countries accidents are the primary cause of death for a large segment of the population.[36]

The two countries are also similar in that motor vehicle fatalities far exceed all other accidental causes of death, accounting for 42 percent of the total in New Zealand and 47 percent in the United States.[37] New Zealand has a higher rate of motor vehicle deaths in proportion to both vehicles registered and miles driven, but a lower figure in proportion to population.[38] Looking past the gross motor vehicle figures, we find great comparability of sex, age, and activity of those killed.[39]

tervention, E970–978, are also excluded. A fourth category, E980–989, covering injuries in which it has been "undetermined whether accidentally or purposely inflicted," is generally thought to include suspicious but unproven suicidal behavior and has been excluded. Finally, injuries resulting from the operations of war, E990–999, have been excluded. The net result is that for this study accidental injuries include E800–949.

34. NATIONAL SAFETY COUNCIL, ACCIDENT FACTS 20 (1972 ed.) [hereinafter cited as ACCIDENT FACTS 1972]. Such countries as the Dominican Republic, the Philippines, Thailand, and Ceylon have low accident rates while France and Austria are at the upper end of the range. Clustered around 56 are such countries as Hungary, Australia, Canada, Czechoslovakia, and Finland. Not all industrialized countries are on the high side. Thus England, Japan, and Sweden range between 35 and 43. A few figures are for years other than 1970. *Id.*

35. Males accounted for 64% of the 1,586 accidental deaths in New Zealand. N.Z. NAT'L HEALTH STATISTICS CENTRE, DEP'T OF HEALTH MEDICAL STATISTICS REP., PART I—MORTALITY AND DEMOGRAPHIC DATA 1970, table 13 (1970) [hereinafter cited as Table 13]. The American figure in 1969 was 69%, NATIONAL SAFETY COUNCIL, ACCIDENT FACTS 14 (1973 ed.) [hereinafter cited as ACCIDENT FACTS 1973].

As to accident death by age, in the 0–4 group both countries report 6%; for the 5–14 group both report 7%; for the 15–24, 25–44, and 45–64 groups, the United States reports 21% each, while New Zealand reports 20%, 19%, and 16%, respectively. For the 65–74 group, the United States figure is 9%, while New Zealand's is 7%. New Zealand's 75-plus population provides 26% of its accidental deaths while the American figure is 15%. This high accidental death rate for the 75-plus population in New Zealand is attributable to a strikingly high rate of fatal falls among elderly women, discussed in the text accompanying note 41 *infra. Compare* Table 13, *supra, with* ACCIDENT FACTS 1973, *supra,* at 11.

36. In the United States, accidents are the leading cause of death among all persons aged 1–44. ACCIDENT FACTS 1973, *supra* note 35, at 9 (using 1969 data). In New Zealand, accidents are the leading cause of death for persons between the ages of 2 and 34. Table 13, *supra* note 35. In both countries, accidents accounted for roughly 6% of all deaths in the year 1970. *Compare id. with* 1973 STATISTICAL ABSTRACT, *supra* note 9, at 61.

37. *Compare* Table 13, *supra* note 35, E810–823, *with* NATIONAL SAFETY COUNCIL, ACCIDENT FACTS 3 (1971 ed.) [hereinafter cited as ACCIDENT FACTS 1971].

38. The rate per 10,000 vehicles is 5.6 in New Zealand and 4.9 in the United States. The rate per 100,000 population is 23.2 for New Zealand and 26.9 for the United States. The rate per 100 *supra* note 7, at 315, *with* 1973 STATISTICAL ABSTRACT, *supra* note 9, at 552. The total mileage driven in New Zealand is estimated for the year 1970 at "8277.079 million miles." Letter from A. Darroch, Road Safety and Publicity Section, Road Transport Division, Ministry of Transport, to author, Apr. 19, 1974, on file in Stanford Law Library. The death rates per 100,000 population for most European countries tend to range between 20 and 27. *See* ACCIDENT FACTS 1972, *supra* note 34, at 71. The New Zealand rate per population is lower because New Zealanders have only 316 passenger cars per 1,000 people, as compared with a figure of 434 per 1,000 Americans. Comparable figures for other countries are Australia, 311; Canada, 308; Sweden, 285; and United Kingdom, 209. *See* YEARBOOK 1973, *supra* note 10, at 954.

39. In both countries males accounted for 73% of motor vehicle fatalities. *Compare* Table 13, *supra* note 35, at E810–819, *with* National Center for Health Statistics, Deaths from Motor Vehicle Accidents, by Person Injured, Cause of Death, Color and Sex: U.S. 1970, Table 298, Nov. 7, 1973 (unpublished table on file in Stanford Law Library) [hereinafter cited as Table 298].

In both countries the largest group of fatalities occurred in the 15–24 age group, with the 25–44 group second, and the 45–64 group following. All age groups were represented to virtually the same

Falls are the second most frequent cause of accidental death in both countries, but in New Zealand falls account for 28 percent of all accidental deaths, nearly twice the American figure.[40] One possible explanation is that females in New Zealand account for 63 percent of the fall fatalities and 88 percent of these women were aged 75 and over, while in the United States, just under 50 percent were females and 72 percent were 75 or older.[41]

After these first two causes, drowning ranks third in both countries, with fire ranking fourth.[42] Taken together, deaths from motor vehicle accidents, falls, drowning, and fire account for approximately three-fourths of all accidental deaths in both countries.[43]

So far we have been analyzing accidental deaths according to external causes as grouped by the International Classification of Diseases. Another important statistic is the location of the accident. Both New Zealand and the United States have data available on fatal accidents occurring at work and in the home.

---

extent in both countries except that in the United States the 15–24 age group accounted for 30% of the motor vehicle deaths and the 25–44 group 25% of the deaths, while in New Zealand the figures were 34% for the former group and 22% for the latter group. *Compare* Table 13, *supra* note 35, at E810–819, *with* ACCIDENT FACTS 1971, *supra* note 37, at 60.

In both countries, collisions with pedestrians accounted for roughly 18% of all fatalities and noncollison (loss of control) cases accounted for 20% of all fatalities. In general the collison-noncollision figures in the two countries were quite comparable except that in the United States collisions between motor vehicles were more frequent, while in New Zealand, collisions with objects other than motor vehicles were more frequent. *Compare* Table 13, *supra* note 35, *with* Table 298, *supra* (in using the latter Table, 5,619 unspecified accidents [E819] were eliminated to obtain the percentages; there were no unspecified motor vehicle deaths in New Zealand).

Pedestrians accounted for 16% of fatalities in New Zealand as against 19% in the United States. *Compare* N.Z. ROAD TRANSPORT DIVISION, MINISTRY OF TRANSPORT, MOTOR ACCIDENTS IN NEW ZEALAND: STATISTICAL STATEMENT FOR CALENDAR YEAR 1970, at 35, *with* ACCIDENT FACTS 1971, *supra* note 37, at 45.

40. *See* Table 13, *supra* note 35, at E880–887. The American figure is 15%. National Center for Health Statistics, Deaths and Death Rates for Each Cause, by Color and Sex: United States, 1969, Table 204, Mar. 18, 1972 (unpublished table on file in Stanford Law Library) [hereinafter cited as Table 204].

41. *See* sources cited in note 40 *supra*. Other data show that of the 16,926 fatal falls in 1970, 8,192 or 48% were sustained by women. Of this group, 5,932 or 72% were aged 75 or over. National Center for Health Statistics, Deaths from Each Cause by 5-Year Age Groups, Color, and Sex: United States 1970 (unpublished table on file in Stanford Law Library). Thus, women 75 and over accounted for 55% of New Zealand's fatal falls, as against 35% in this country. *See* note 50 *infra*.

42. Fire is very unimportant as a cause of death in New Zealand—perhaps because there are relatively few high-rise buildings and most burning structures can be evacuated with no loss of life. Another explanation is a suggested correlation between incidence of fires and the large number of electrical appliances per house in this country. *See* Emmons, *Fire and Fire Protection*, 231 SCI. AM., July 1974, at 21.

43. The actual numbers of deaths resulting from motor vehicle accidents, falls, drowning, and fire in New Zealand are 654, 440, 147, and 30, respectively; these total 1,271 or 80% of the 1,586 accidental deaths. Table 13, *supra* note 35, at E830–832, 910. For the United States, the respective figures are 55,791, 17,827, 7,699, and 7,163. The total is 88,480 or 76% of the 116,385 accidental deaths reported in the United States. *See* Table 204, *supra* note 40. It is interesting to note that the National Safety Council estimates projected 54,800, 17,500, 7,300, and 6,700, totaling 86,300 or 76% of the projected 114,000 deaths. ACCIDENT FACTS 1971, *supra* note 37, at 6. This remarkable accuracy in estimation is found throughout the data.

One substantial disparity in death data concerns the category "surgical and medical complications and misadventures." In its mortality data, New Zealand reports only 2 such deaths in 1970, while the United States reports 2,572, proportionately 20 times as many. *Compare* Table 13, *supra* note 35, at E930–936, *with* Table 204, *supra* note 40. Obviously different reporting criteria are involved, probably due to the difficulty of deciding whether a death is attributable to a condition that required the medical or surgical procedure or was brought about by the procedure.

Turning first to industrial accidents, New Zealand's death rate is less than half the American rate.[44] This difference cannot be explained by a simple comparison of those engaged in manufacturing and nonmanufacturing jobs in the two countries,[45] nor by a more detailed analysis of the relative importance in each economy of the statistically more dangerous industries. The United States has a higher death rate not only for industry as a whole, but also for individual industries.[46] Moreover, the injury rates for industrial accidents provide still more unresolved mysteries.[47]

An analysis of fatal accidents in the home shows remarkable similarities: in both countries they account for about one-fifth of all accidental deaths, half as many as the motor vehicle, and yield the same death rate.[48] Falls are the major cause of home fatalities in both countries; over four-fifths of the victims of this type of fatal accident are over 65.[49] In New Zealand falls account for almost two-thirds of the home fatalities, followed distantly by poisonings. In the United States falls account for just over one-third of home deaths, followed fairly closely by fires.[50]

44. In New Zealand, 88 workers were killed in a 1970 labor force of 1,100,000, yielding a death rate of 8 per 100,000 workers. *See* letter from E. Harris, in N.Z. DEP'T OF STATISTICS, MONTHLY ABSTRACT OF STATISTICS 1 (Supp. July 1973) [hereinafter cited as MONTHLY ABSTRACT]. In the United States, the figure is 18 deaths per 100,000 workers for 1970. *See* ACCIDENT FACTS 1971, *supra* note 37, at 29.

45. Employees involved in manufacturing make up one-fourth of the total labor force in each country and the ratio of accidental deaths in manufacturing to total industrial deaths is almost identical in each. In New Zealand there were 11 deaths out of 275,000 manufacturing workers and 77 deaths among 825,000 nonmanufacturing workers. For the death statistics, *see* MONTHLY ABSTRACT, *supra* note 44, at 1. The labor force statistics may be found in YEARBOOK 1972, *supra* note 7, at 841. In the United States the figures are 19 million manufacturing workers with a death rate of 9 per 100,000 and 60 million workers in nonmanufacturing jobs with a death rate of 21 per 100,000. ACCIDENT FACTS 1971, *supra* note 37, at 29. In both, as will be noted, the death rate among manufacturing workers is just less than half that of nonmanufacturing workers.

46. Grouping all industry into seven categories—agriculture, mining and quarrying, manufacturing, building and construction, transportation and public utilities, commerce, and services—in 1970 the United States had an industrial death rate in each sector at least twice as great as the corresponding rate in New Zealand. Moreover, in two sectors that are among the most dangerous in terms of death rates, building and construction and agriculture, the labor force comprised a larger share of total employment in New Zealand than the United States. For New Zealand fatality rates, *see* MONTHLY ABSTRACT, *supra* note 44, at 1. For New Zealand employment data, *see* YEARBOOK 1972, *supra* note 7, at 972. For American fatality rates, *see* ACCIDENT FACTS 1971, *supra* note 37, at 23; for employment data, *see* 1973 STATISTICAL ABSTRACT, *supra* note 9, at 228, 233.

Since the higher industrial death rate in the United States cannot be explained by the manufacturing-nonmanufacturing composition of the economy nor by the increased relative importance of "dangerous industries" in the United States, a likely hypothesis is that, as a whole, the American work force is engaged in activities of greater risk—such as construction of higher buildings, deeper mines, mechanized agriculture, or work involving asbestos, and plastics, and other dangerous substances—than are New Zealanders, so that the higher risk of death is spread throughout many activities and cannot be isolated.

47. *See* text accompanying note 80 *infra*.

48. Fatal home accidents in New Zealand total 330. This is determined from Table 13, *supra* note 35. The 330 known home fatalities represent 21% of the total accidental death figure of 1,586, 50% of the motor vehicle figure of 655, and a death rate of 12 per 100,000 population.

The home fatality figure in the United States can be determined from estimates that show home deaths totaling 26,500, or 23% of the accident total of 114,000, 48% of the motor vehicle figure of 54,800, and a death rate of 13 per 100,000. *See* ACCIDENT FACTS 1971, *supra* note 37, at 80–84.

49. For New Zealand, the figures are 184 persons over the age of 65 killed in falls, or 88% of the total killed in home falls (209). Table 13, *supra* note 35, at E880–887. The United States figures are 7,700 out of 9,600, or 80%. ACCIDENT FACTS 1971, *supra* note 37, at 84.

50. Falls account for 63% of all accidental deaths in the home—209 out of 330. Poisonings of

B. *Injuries*

As indicated earlier, nonfatal injury data in each country are imperfect and attempts to compare them compound the problems. Unfortunately, there is no good indicator of the severity of the injury of those hospitalized, nor can we identify serious injuries suffered by those who are treated as hospital outpatients.[51] In the United States the difficulty of estimating the number of victims of nonfatal accidents may be insuperable because of the definitional problems and enormous numbers involved.[52] Nevertheless, some specific comparisons can be made.

In New Zealand, accident victims make up almost one-fifth of the total number of patients admitted to hospitals, almost double the figure in the United States.[53] There are also clear differences between the two countries in terms of hospital stays. In New Zealand the average hospital stay is approximately 16 days for all conditions; for accident victims the average is 12.5 days.[54] In the United States the average stay is 7.8 days for all conditions and 8.4 days for accident injuries.[55] This shorter stay in the United States is reflected in most injury subcategories.[56] The difference may reflect differing medical attitudes toward recuperation. Also, the absence of out-

---

all types are a distant second with 54 or 14% of home deaths. Table 13, *supra* note 35. In the United States, falls account for 36% of all fatal home accidents, with fire ranking second at 21%. ACCIDENT FACTS 1971, *supra* note 37, at 81. In this country the death rate from accidental home falls has dropped sharply between 1960 and 1970 and has been attributed to "improved medical treatment of the injured and better and safer housing for the elderly." *Id.* at 84.

51. The Dixon study, *supra* note 27, did not discuss severity of injuries.

52. As one example of the difficulty, motor vehicle injuries in 1970 are estimated at 2,000,000 in ACCIDENT FACTS 1971, *supra* note 37, at 40, and 5,100,000 in 1973 STATISTICAL ABSTRACT, *supra* note 9, at 553.

53. The New Zealand figure, 47,497, is 19% while the American rate is 10% of all patients. *Compare* N.Z. NAT'L HEALTH STATISTICS CENTRE, MEDICAL STATISTICS REPORT PART III, HOSPITAL AND SELECTED MORBIDITY DATA, 1969 & 1970, at 5 [hereinafter cited as MEDICAL STATISTICS REPORT, Part III], *with* 22 MONTHLY VITAL STATISTICS REPORT, no. 6, at 3 (Supp. Sept. 14, 1973) (1971 data) [hereinafter cited as VITAL STATISTICS]. Perhaps American hospitals may undergo greater use for procedures unrelated to accidents. Given a more advanced medical capability, one would expect treatment of increasingly sophisticated ailments, while in New Zealand one might expect a more basic health care in which accident admissions loom larger.

The hospitalization data all speak of patients "discharged" during 1970. This will include some who were admitted during 1969 and discharged during 1970, but this is probably counterbalanced by those admitted in 1970 but discharged in 1971, so there is every reason to treat the discharged category as virtually synonymous with the injured category. All E-code data concerning injuries are organized by discharge date.

54. MEDICAL STATISTICS REPORT, PART III, *supra* note 53, at 5 (1969 data).

55. VITAL STATISTICS, *supra* note 53, at 5. It may be significant that New Zealand admits so many possible concussion cases for observation, because without these short admissions the New Zealand average stay would be substantially longer and the disparity even greater—unless a similar practice is generally followed in the United States. This appears unlikely because intracranial injury (excluding skull fracture), N850–854, constituted only 9% of accident discharges in this country as against 21% in New Zealand. *Compare id.* at 3 *with* MEDICAL STATISTICS REPORT, PART III, *supra* note 53, at table 3 (1970 data). *See* text accompanying note 70 *infra*.

56. Dissecting the gross accident-stay figure, the average stay for all fractures in New Zealand is 21.2 days, while in the United States it is 11.7 days. For the major category of intracranial injuries the average New Zealand stay is 4.6 days, in the United States it is 5.8 days. Finally, for lacerations and open wounds the average stay in New Zealand is 7.3 days, 5.3 days in the United States. *Compare id.* at 127 *with* VITAL STATISTICS, *supra* note 53, at 5. The greater average length of stay in New Zealand hospitals is noted by Bernstein, *supra* note 7, at 842, but he offers no explanation.

of-pocket cost to the hospital patient in New Zealand removes one factor that may deter the continuation of hospital care in the United States.

Attempts to identify "serious" injuries failed. Just as it is clear that not all hospital admissions are serious cases,[57] so it is also clear that some serious injuries, such as fractures and other disabling injuries, are not recorded in New Zealand's hospital admission statistics. Unfortunately, centralized records are not kept for nonhospitalized accident victims, nor does any sampling service attempt to gather these data nationally. In an effort to learn more about nonhospitalized victims, I surveyed all 30 regional hospital boards, but most were able to tell little about those who used hospital accident and emergency facilities.[58]

Survey responses indicate that the number of first-time users of hospital emergency services in New Zealand annually totals one-eighth of the population.[59] Motor vehicle victims made up 7 percent of this group; two-fifths of these traffic victims were admitted as inpatients.[60] Perhaps 15 percent of all who sought emergency services were ultimately admitted.[61] Thus the high motor vehicle admission figure suggests that all cases other than motor vehicle would produce a 12-percent admission rate.[62] The 40-percent and 12-percent figures give a rough indication of the number of emergency service patients whose injuries are serious enough to require further hospitalization.

But these data tell us little about those accident victims who are not admitted. In a search for more information, a study was undertaken of the accident and emergency records of one medium-sized urban hospital. Six weeks in 1970 were chosen to represent typical periods of the year. The

57. The most obvious stumbling block here is a definition of the word "serious." There is no generally accepted technique for achieving this kind of measurement and the New Zealand data were no exception.

58. Copies of the one-page questionnaire I sent to the secretaries of each of the 30 regional boards and the 20 responses received are on file in the Stanford Law Library. M. Franklin, Survey of N.Z. Regional Hospital Boards, Apr. 24, 1973.

There is no institution comparable to our National Health Survey that produces such volumes as VITAL STATISTICS, *supra* note 53. The study of Dunedin emergency facilities by Dixon, Emery & Spears, *supra* note 27, gives raw numbers but does not discuss severity or cause of injury.

59. The 20 regional boards that did respond represent a population area of some 2,400,000 and reported 283,414 first visits to accident and emergency departments in 1970. *See* M. Franklin, *supra* note 58. Extrapolating from this for the population groups of the areas that did not respond would add another 50,000, suggesting some 333,000 users of such services in the year 1970, virtually all due to accidents.

Persons with bad head colds are effectively discouraged from using emergency facilities. Interview with J. Allan, Administration Officer, Wellington General Hospital, in Wellington, N.Z., Feb. 7, 1973.

60. These figures are derived from reports of the seven or eight regional boards that were able to provide such information. M. Franklin, *supra* note 58.

61. If 333,000 patients made first appearances in accident and emergency wards in 1970 and some 47,497 accident inpatients were discharged during that year, *see* note 53 *supra*, we can estimate that 15% of all who sought emergency services were ultimately admitted.

62. The 12% admission rate is arrived at by extrapolating from the figures reported in note 59 *supra*, and from the fact that 10,557 hospital inpatients were motor vehicle accident victims, *see* text accompanying note 68 *infra*.

extrapolated results suggest that of 333,000 first emergency attendances, some 17,000 victims had fractured limbs that were treated in fracture clinics.[63] Virtually all other serious injuries were admitted. This permits us to estimate that 55,000–60,000 persons suffered disabling accidental injuries.[64]

There are also some data available on nonfatal hospitalized accidental injuries that distinguish between transportation and nontransportation accidents.[65] Turning first to transportation accidents, we note that the motor vehicle accident is overwhelmingly important in both countries.[66] In New Zealand, the Ministry of Transport keeps motoring records and classifies motor vehicle injuries as serious or minor. Investigating police officers are to report an injury as "serious" in all cases involving "fractures, concussion, severe cuts and lacerations, severe general shock necessitating medical treatment, and any other injury involving detention in hospital."[67]

In light of the reporting requirement—especially the last clause—one would expect that "serious" injuries for 1970 would total more than the 10,557 who were hospitalized as a result of motor vehicle accidents, plus unhospitalized fractures.[68] Yet the Ministry's tally for serious injuries is 8,468 of the 20,791 persons injured by motor vehicle accidents in the year 1970.[69] The discrepancy might be explained by the fact that half of the

63. This study indicated an average of 520 weekly visits to the emergency department for a daily average of about 75. One-fourth of these patients had X-rays taken to determine whether limbs were fractured. Positive results were observed in one-fifth of the X-rays, suggesting that perhaps 5% of all who appeared at the accident and emergency department had fractures that required treatment at the outpatient fracture clinic. See M. Franklin, Survey of Hutt Hospital, Lower Hutt, N.Z. (unpublished survey on file in Stanford Law Library). These may well have been serious injuries in the sense that they impeded people from carrying on their normal activities for some period. Note also that these data do not include persons appearing with multiple injuries, including fractures, who would probably have been admitted without waiting for the results of X-rays.

64. Roughly 47,500 patients were admitted to hospitals as a result of accidental injuries. See note 53 supra. By subtracting the 6,000 (two-thirds of 9,000) who had been admitted for observation only and whose diagnoses were negative, see text accompanying note 71 infra, and then adding the estimated 17,000 limb fracture cases who were not admitted but were still serious, see note 63 supra, we obtain a total of between 55,000 and 60,000 disabling accidental injuries for the year 1970.

65. As was the case with accidental deaths, there are several ways to categorize data on nonfatal hospitalized accidental injuries. The first is along the lines of the International Classification of Diseases. New Zealand uses a refinement that identifies the location of nontransportation accidents, such as the home or a recreation area. The refinement involves using the fourth digit code for place of occurrence in nontransport accidents as found in the WORLD HEALTH ORGANIZATION, MANUAL OF THE INTERNATIONAL STATISTICAL CLASSIFICATION OF DISEASES, INJURIES, AND CAUSES OF DEATH 511 (7th rev. 1955). This is used for E-code classifications E825-827, E850–929.

Other agencies collect specific accident data related to particular activities, such as motoring and working. These do not always refer to hospitalization, so that cross reference is not possible, but such data may nevertheless prove useful—especially for comparative purposes.

66. In New Zealand, motor vehicle accidents accounted for 10,799 hospitalized victims. Rail accidents accounted for 99, water transportation accidents accounted for 201, and air transportation accidents accounted for 30 accident victims, making a total of 330 transportation injuries not involving motor vehicles. See N.Z. National Health Statistics Centre, Dep't of Health, Causes of Death 1970, By Sex and Age Groups (unpublished table on file in Stanford Law Library) [hereinafter cited as 1970 E-Code Table]. See also ACCIDENT FACTS 1971, supra note 37, at 74–78.

67. See Traffic Accident Report, Form 4169, Instruction No. 2 (on file in Stanford Law Library) (this is the prescribed form to be filled out following all motor vehicle accidents).

68. There is no way to estimate how many of the unhospitalized fractures were attributable to motor vehicle injuries.

69. N.Z. ROAD TRANSPORT DIVISION, MINISTRY OF TRANSPORT, supra note 39, at table 22.

hospitalized motor vehicle accident victims are admitted either for suspected brain concussion or suspected skull fractures.[70] Two-thirds of these prove negative and the patients are discharged within 2 days; three-fourths are released within 3 days.[71] Interviews suggested that these admissions are not considered serious by the staff.[72] It seems likely that when a policeman prepares his report and learns that the victim was released from the hospital without positive findings, he reports the injury as "not serious," despite the instructions.[73] This would tend to bring the two sets of figures more closely into line. All motor vehicle accidents combined entail an average hospital stay of 11.8 days. If those who are discharged in 1 or 2 days are subtracted, the stays of remaining patients average 17 days.[74]

When motor vehicle injuries are categorized by age they do not parallel the age distribution for motor vehicle deaths. The most substantial disparity occurs in the 15–24-year-old group, which accounts for one-third of the motor vehicle deaths but almost half of the hospital admissions due to motor vehicle accidents.[75]

We turn now to nontransportation accidents. Of the 28,502 accidents, 23,637 can be described by location, of which just over half occurred in the home.[76] This makes the domestic accident the most common cause of accident hospitalization in New Zealand. Although falls account for two-fifths of all domestic accidents, victims of falls account for over two-thirds of all hospital days attributable to domestic accidents.[77]

Next to the home, places of recreation and sport are the most common locales for accidental injuries. The number of accidents, however, is much smaller: these places yield only 4,000 hospitalizations annually.[78]

Location aside, the largest nontransportation category of injuries involves falls, resulting in one-fourth of all hospitalized accident victims in

70. N.Z. Dep't of Health, Motor Accidents by N-Code Study for 1970 (unpublished study on file in Stanford Law Library). Those admitted for skull fracture and intracranial injuries (E800–804, 850–854) numbered 5,417. *Id.*

71. This is derived from a study of the 9,286 cases involving such suspected injuries but not limited to the motor vehicle cases. *See* N.Z. Ministry of Health, Public Hospitals 1970: Intracranial Injury N850–854 (unpublished table on file in the Stanford Law Library), for information leading to those results.

72. Interview with K. Wardill, Medical Superintendent, Wellington General Hospital, in Wellington, N.Z., Feb. 7, 1973.

73. Interview with R. Henry, Director, Road Safety and Publicity Section, Road Transport Division, Ministry of Transport, in Wellington, N.Z., Apr. 18, 1973.

74. This result is obtained by using the data for motor vehicle accidents from the unpublished 1970 E-Code table, *supra* note 66, and then subtracting the information on motor vehicle short-stays for observation obtained from N.Z. Dep't of Health, Motor Accidents by N-Code Study for 1970, note 70 *supra*.

75. N.Z. ROAD TRANSPORT DIVISION, MINISTRY OF TRANSPORT, *supra* note 39, at table 33.

76. The reason for the disparity is that 4,865 accidents were coded "place not specified." There were 12,238 home accidents. *See* 1970 E-Code Table, note 66 *supra*, at E850–929.

77. *See* 1970 E-Code Table, *supra* note 66, at E880–887, indicating that domestic fall victims accounted for 110,680 of the 163,042 total hospital days attributable to domestic accidents.

78. *Id.* at E850.4–929.4.

New Zealand, and an average stay of 19.3 days. Falls within the home account for almost half this group.[79]

In the area of work-connected injuries, it is difficult to get data except through industrial injury figures. In 1970, 68,000 such accidents led to 88 deaths, 11 cases of permanent-total disability, 1,012 cases of permanent-partial disability, and 66,734 cases of temporary disability.[80]

Industrial injury data do not reveal how many injured workers were subsequently hospitalized, but it seems probable that no more than 5,000 of the 47,000 hospitalized accident victims—barely one-tenth—were hurt on the job.[81] Many of the larger companies in New Zealand maintain their own nursing staffs to treat injured employees and send them to the hospital only in serious cases.[82]

Although the death rate from industrial accidents in New Zealand is substantially lower than in this country, the accident frequency rate is twice as high in New Zealand.[83] Moreover, based on more limited data, New Zealand appears to have both a higher rate of permanent disabilities per 100,000 man-hours of exposure and a greater injury severity rate than the United States.[84] The convergence of all four measures leads to the hypothesis that technological differences between New Zealand and American industry cause a greater number of accidents to occur in New Zealand, but also result in relatively fewer fatalities.[85]

---

79. The exact figure is 44%. *Id*. at E880–887.

80. Only 74 of these 88 death cases have been closed as of April 1974. *See* Letter from E. Harris, N.Z. Dep't of Statistics, to author, Apr. 11, 1974, on file in Stanford Law Library.

81. Using New Zealand's fourth-digit figures we can calculate that there were 1,540 farm injury cases (excluding those in the home) plus 2,238 injuries on mining and industrial premises for a maximum of 3,778 hospitalized cases. 1970 E-Code Table, *supra* note 66, at E850–929. During the first 3 months of 1971, only 4% of the industrial injuries reported led to admission as hospital inpatients. Letter from E. Harris, *supra* note 80.

82. Interview with Ian B. Campbell, Secretary, Workers' Compensation Board, in Wellington, N.Z., May 23, 1973.

83. The New Zealand rate is 38.8 injuries per 1,000,000 man-hours worked. *See* letter from E. Harris, *supra* note 80 (enclosing Table I of the forthcoming volume on Industrial Injuries for the year 1970). Those American companies reporting to the National Safety Council have a rate of 8.87 per 1,000,000 man-hours. ACCIDENT FACTS 1971, *supra* note 37, at 26. But those who do not report to the National Safety Council have substantially higher rates—perhaps double that of reporting companies. *Id*. at 27. Even so, the American rate would be far below that of New Zealand.

84. Although data limitations make a complete and conclusive comparison of the two countries impossible, general inferences can be drawn. First, the 1970 permanent-disability rates (permanent disabilities per 100,000 man-hours of exposure) for the United States in manufacturing, building and construction, wholesale and retail trade, and public utilities were approximately three-fourths of the corresponding rates for New Zealand in 1969. For New Zealand, *see* N.Z. DEP'T OF STATISTICS, IN-DUSTRIAL INJURIES 1968 & 1969, tables 35 & 36 (1973); for the United States, *see* U.S. BUREAU OF LABOR STATISTICS, DEP'T OF LABOR, INDUSTRY RATES BY INJURY 1970, at 7–17 (1972). With respect to injury-severity rates for the two countries in these same industries, the United States rate is less than half that of New Zealand in manufacturing and in public utilities, and less than three-fourths that of New Zealand in building and construction and in wholesale and retail trade. *Id*.

85. Perhaps technological factors inherent in the New Zealand and United States economies cause a higher accident-frequency rate in New Zealand than in the United States, but relatively fewer fatalities. New Zealand's industry is less mechanized, so that relatively many workers are injured, and some seriously, but relatively few are killed. This is consistent with the death and accident frequency rates for the two countries and with the statistics on permanent impairment and injury severity. More detailed and comprehensive data are necessary before any more definite conclusion can be drawn.

In both countries, it appears that temporary disabilities produce the overwhelming number of reported workers' compensation cases.[86] The distribution of injuries in terms of parts of the body is also similar in both countries.[87]

C. *Conclusion*

The conclusions that may be drawn from these figures on accidental death and injury are limited but important. Although the two countries are by no means identical in their accident profiles, the data clearly reflect substantial similarities on several levels: types of accidents that predominate, demographic characteristics of persons involved in the various types of accidents, and types of injuries suffered by victims of these accidents. This similarity is not necessarily limited to the United States and New Zealand. Indeed, all countries having a certain level of population concentration, industrialization, and wealth may exhibit similar accident patterns, despite many other cultural differences. The similarity between New Zealand and the United States in accident profile, however, indicates that we should watch closely the New Zealand scheme as we continue to rethink our approach to personal injury compensation in this country.

III. Remedies and Costs

This Part attempts to identify the amounts and sources of dollars that flowed to accident victims in New Zealand as a result of accidental injuries sustained during 1970.

At the time, New Zealand's personal injury law generally conditioned liability on a showing of negligence.[88] Although strict liability for defective products had not developed in New Zealand, two aspects of New Zealand law were more favorable to plaintiffs than was the American system: by statute New Zealand has adopted "pure" comparative negligence[89] and, further, workers retained their negligence actions against employers. The damage categories were nominally the same in both countries although pain and suffering recoveries were much lower in New Zealand.[90] New Zealand

---

86. The New Zealand figure is 98% (66,734 of 67,831 closed cases). *See* letter from E. Harris, *supra* note 80 (enclosing table 36 to be published in Industrial Injuries—1970 Volume). In the United States the figure exceeds 95%. *See* U.S. Bureau of Labor Statistics, *supra* note 84, at table IA. These disabilities averaged 15 days in New Zealand, letter from E. Harris, *supra* note 80, and 24 days in the United States. Accident Facts, *supra* note 37, at 28.

87. For New Zealand the figures are head injuries 9%; trunk 21%; upper limb 40%; lower limb 23%. Monthly Abstract, *supra* note 44, at 6. For the United States the figures are head 12%; trunk 26%; upper limb 33%; lower limb 23%. Accident Facts 1971, *supra* note 37, at 30.

88. *See, e.g.,* A. Davis, The Law of Torts in New Zealand (1951); R. Mulholland, Introduction to the New Zealand Legal System 120–28 (1972); J. O'Keefe & W. Farrands, Introduction to New Zealand Law 277–318 (2d ed. 1973).

89. The Contributory Negligence Act of 1947, 2 N.Z. Stat. Reprint 1908–57, no. 3, at 755.

90. The point is made by some examples from Auckland Law Society, Records of Jury Verdicts in Actions for Damages for Personal Injury or Death (author's summary of records on file in Stanford

commonly used the American jury system in personal injury cases while following English substantive law.

Most personal injury claimants retained attorneys. The attorney was compensated by a fee for service. The contingent fee was not explicitly used.[91] One eminent lawyer, who prefers to remain anonymous, has stated, however, that the fees tended to cluster at 7 or 8 percent of the amount recovered.

In terms of financial responsibility, New Zealand had compulsory third-party motor vehicle liability insurance with unlimited coverage.[92] Each guest was covered up to a limit of $15,000.[93] The rate for this insurance was set by a government panel and in 1970 was $7.90 per year for each passenger vehicle. The insurance industry is privately operated with over 60 companies writing liability insurance[94] but a company was obligated to accept compulsory third-party coverage if it was selected by the registrant. Partly because of this inability to choose liability risks, virtually all of the liability insurers organized the Motor Vehicle Third Party Pool to share the burdens of defending third-party claims made against their insureds.[95]

A. *Adversary Proceedings*

During 1970, 21,900 vehicles in New Zealand were involved in 13,300 injury accidents leading to 21,446 injuries and fatalities.[96] Given this num-

Law Library), covering local jury verdicts from 1968 to 1972. One plaintiff was described as a "total wreck"—a 36-year-old fruiterer who suffered a fractured skull with loss of memory and intelligence; severed optic nerve with loss of peripheral vision; personality changes; infection in skull that led to meningitis and hypersexuality; unemployable. The jury award was $64,555 before reduction for contributory negligence. *Id.* no. 158.

In a case classified as "serious," a clerk, 44, was rendered paraplegic with no bladder control or sexual function; had back pains and swelling feet; no hope of recovery; employed by former "understanding" boss with an economic loss of $1,500–2,000 per year. The jury awarded $40,000 before consideration of contributory negligence. *Id.* no. 138.

An example from wrongful death provides some idea of economic-loss measurement. A draughtsman, 46, left a widow, 46, and four children, 15, 13, 10, 1. He earned $2,350 after taxes. The jury awarded $20,000. *Id.* no. 113.

Bernstein, *supra* note 7, at 839 states: "Juries tend to be niggardly by American standards. Even taking into account the relative prices and earnings levels, jury awards as published in newspapers would seem to be about a third or a fourth of comparable American judgments."

91. *See In re* C., [1963] N.Z.L.R. 259.

92. Transport Act of 1962, 1962 N.Z. Stats. no. 135, at 975. *See* J. O'KEEFE & W. FARRANDS, *supra* note 88, at 319.

93. Transport Amendment Act of 1963, no. 62 § 4(1), 1963 N.Z. Stats. no. 62, § 4(1), at 543. It has been suggested that this coverage was created because of the practice of many hospital boards in sending letters to passengers who had been hurt in automobile accidents indicating that legal liability might exist in such cases and therefore that hospital benefits might not be payable. Interview with K. Wardill, Superintendent, Wellington Hospital, Wellington, N.Z., Feb. 7, 1973.

94. *See* DEP'T OF STATISTICS, N.Z. INSURANCE STATISTICS: 1970–71, at 8–9 (1972) (listing 67 insurers writing "accident" coverage).

95. The insurers were free to select risks on applications for comprehensive policies and to use differential rates.

The only significant company that has remained outside the Pool is AA Mutual, a company run by the New Zealand Automobile Association. This company insured one-third of the motor vehicles in the country, virtually all of them private passenger vehicles. The Pool, then, accounted for the other two-thirds and virtually all commercial vehicles.

96. This figure includes only the accidents in which at least minor personal injury, such as

ber of injuries and the existence of the pure comparative negligence rule, one might expect a large number of claims. But when one subtracts the cases in which the injuries were perceived to be too minor to bother with and the approximately 4,000 one-car accidents,[97] many of which undoubtedly involved only the driver, and the cases in which an injured party perceived himself to be totally at fault, many potential claims are eliminated. In fact, 8,000 accidents involving 9,415 potential claims were reported to insurers. Virtually half these possible claims have already been closed with no payment made, almost always because no claim was made.[98] Payments have been made to 4,126 claimants totaling $8 million, an average payout of $2,000 per claim.[99] Of the 829 claims that remained open in 1974, estimated liability had been set at $3,400,000—an average of $4,100. Although larger cases do take longer to close, experience indicates that insurers in New Zealand, as elsewhere, tend to overestimate open liability. It is likely that payments in these cases will not exceed $3,000,000, for a total automobile payout of less than $11,000,000.[100]

Contributory negligence has a significant effect on the dollar recoveries in both settlements and jury verdicts. In one set of closing data it appeared that contributory negligence reduced recovery in 14 percent of the cases by a median figure of 25 percent. A study of the 32 plaintiffs' verdicts in motor vehicle cases in Wellington between 1967 and 1970 reveals that the jury found contributory negligence in 10 of the cases with a median reduction in recovery of 50 percent.[101] These 32 cases yielded an average of $6,446 per case, suggesting also that bigger cases went to trial—at which contributory negligence may have been a major issue—while smaller cases were much more likely to be settled.

The other major source of tort litigation in New Zealand is the indus-

---

bruises and scrapes, were reported. *See* N.Z. ROAD TRANSPORT DIVISION, MINISTRY OF TRANSPORT, *supra* note 39, at 2, 35.

97. Unpublished chart supplied by N.Z. Ministry of Transport, May 23, 1973 (on file in Stanford Law Library).

98. Of the 4,460 potential claimants whose files were closed with no payment, it appears that no more than 4 or 5 went to court.

99. Based on a large sample of about two-thirds of 4,126 successful claimants, it appears that a total of 85 went to trial.

100. To this figure must be added the sums paid guests in excess of the $15,000 covered by the compulsory policy. Excess liability coverage was available as part of the comprehensive policy. But a study of one large insurer suggested that payouts under this clause of the comprehensive policy amounted to less than 3% of the total amount paid under the compulsory coverages, or a national figure of less than $330,000.

101. *See* Wellington District Law Society, Record of Jury Awards in Actions Heard in Wellington from Jan. 1967 for Damages from Personal Injury or Death (author's summary of the records on file in Stanford Law Library). The book, which runs through December 11, 1970, reports only cases in which plaintiffs obtained verdicts.

A similar study for Auckland does not separate motor vehicle claims from other types of claims; however, it does disclose that of the 98 plaintiff's verdicts returned between 1968 and 1972, 36 involved reductions for contributory negligence. Auckland Law Society, *supra* note 90. Comparing this with the Wellington figures for all negligence awards reveals almost the same percentage—27 of a total of 70 cases—in which the recovery was reduced because of contributory negligence.

trial injury. As of 1974, some $9,400,000 had been paid by employers as a result of industrial injuries arising in 1970.[102] Of this, $1,660,000 was paid for tort liability.[103] Some $4,600,000 had been paid in the form of weekly compensation payments. A smaller amount was paid in lump-sum settlements of the compensation claims so that a total of $6,000,000 was paid for lost wages under the compensation part of the system. Recent reports suggest that $1,000,000 of the total figure of $9,400,000 was paid by insurance carriers to hospitals as reimbursement for medical services rendered. Since accidents without time loss are excluded from this analysis and some of these did involve medical expenses, the actual medical reimbursement figures are undoubtedly substantially higher than this. The average payment made per reported work accident, including both compensation and tort damages, was $139. This amounted to 3 weeks' wages based on the wage scales of males injured in 1970.

Other personal injury tort liability in New Zealand was largely theoretical. For 1970, no more than 60 arguably serious medical malpractice claims were made and the total payout from physicians' malpractice carriers was less than $150,000.[104] Hospital liability payouts for 1970 were no more than $35,000.[105] Malpractice insurance premiums in 1970 ranged between $17 and $28 per year per physician.

There is no special category of landowners liability insurance in New Zealand. The only other major liability coverage is public liability insurance. This plays a small role in the work of the insurance industry and most of that relates to property damage. Based on one large insurer's experience, it seems likely that no more than $300,000 was paid in 1970 for personal injuries under this coverage. When this is added to the malpractice payments, we see that total insurance payments for personal injury liability, aside from motor vehicle and industrial injuries, were less than $500,000 for the year 1970. There is no reason to think that payments are made by uninsured defendants in New Zealand any more frequently than in the United States.

B. *Other Sources*

Among government sources of aid to personal injury victims, the overwhelmingly most important was the free access to public hospitals, which

---

102. *See* Letter from E. Harris, *supra* note 83, for all information concerning industrial injury data.
103. Of the 16 workers' compensation cases tried in Wellington in which contributory negligence was found, 8 involved reductions for contributory negligence of 15% or less and 12 were reduced 33.3% or less. *Compare* these figures *with* the motor vehicle figures in the text accompanying note 101 *supra*.
104. Interviews with Mr. McLeod, of the Medical Protection Society, and Mr. James, of the Medical Defense Union, in Wellington, N.Z., May 10, 1973. Of the 71 verdicts in the Wellington study, *supra* note 101, 37 were motor vehicle cases, 32 were workers' compensation cases, one involved water skiing, and one involved the firing of a shotgun.
105. Interview with R. Clark, Claims Manager, State Insurance Office, in Wellington, N.Z., May 21, 1973. All but one of the hospital boards were represented by the State Insurance Office.

in 1970 was valued at an average of $27 per day.[106] Multiplying the per diem figure by the number of days spent in hospitals by accident victims yields a figure of $15,661,593 allocated to hospital victims plus an unknown amount in physicians' fees. As noted earlier, some of this is reimbursed from liability insurance sources but it is not clear how much.

The only other significant governmental benefit program, social security sickness benefits, is available to workers who have been unable to work because of temporary incapacity not due to a work-related accident. Data suggest that some $1,100,000 went to 4,850 accident victims in 1970 under this provision.[107]

Private insurance is a significant source of aid because New Zealanders are among the highest per capita purchasers of life insurance in the world.[108] Drawing on data from one large life insurer, we can estimate that $2,820,000 in life insurance payments were the result of fatal accidents that occurred in 1970.[109]

Another significant private insurance source is personal accident and sickness insurance. Again, based on a study of several insurance companies, we can estimate that almost 75 percent of the payouts were attributable to accident claims rather than sickness claims and that the amount paid for accidents in 1970 was $2,574,000.[110] Using one company's figure of $150 as the average payout would suggest that 17,160 accident victims received payments from this source.[111]

Private hospital insurance was of minor importance in New Zealand in 1970. The leading company estimates that no more than $32,000 was paid to accident victims for private medical bills incurred during 1970.[112]

Finally, we may note that sick leave as part of a collectively bargained agreement was virtually nonexistent in 1970.[113] Although the government had such a policy private industry did not generally have such coverage

---

106. Interview with J. Wilson, Department of Health, in Wellington, N.Z., May 9, 1973. The $27 figure is a weighted average for 1970 between urban hospitals at $28 and rural hospitals at $25.

107. SOCIAL SECURITY DEP'T, REPORT FOR THE YEAR ENDED 31 MARCH 1971, at 12, 13, 31 (1971) (the dollar payment figure was derived by multiplying the amount paid out for sickness benefits in 1970 from table 26 by the percentage from table 9 that represents the ratio of accident benefits to all sickness benefits). Another program pays invalid benefits to persons permanently and totally disabled. In 1970, 22 accident victims became eligible to receive payments for an indefinite period under this program. *Id.* at 10.

108. *See* INSTITUTE OF LIFE INSURANCE, 1971 LIFE INSURANCE FACT BOOK 101 (1971).

109. All companies providing life insurance data were able to exclude suicides from accident figures. Five percent of the claims made involved accidental deaths. DEP'T OF STATISTICS, *supra* note 94, at 12, suggests that $47 million was paid during 1970. Industrial life insurance was of little significance in 1970, accounting for perhaps 5% of the payouts attributable to ordinary life insurance. *Id.*

110. *See id.* at table 17 (averaging the total payout figures for 1969–70 and 1970–71).

111. Accident and medical insurance were also available under provisions of the motor vehicle comprehensive policy but both were limited in amount and subject to exclusions that made the total payouts insignificant.

112. Letter from Peter A. Smith, General Manager, Southern Cross Medical Society, to author, May 21, 1973.

113. Interview with H. Duncan, Legal Officer, Department of Labour, in Wellington, N.Z., May 15, 1973.

and even within government it was estimated that 90 percent of the claims
made were attributable to sickness rather than accident.[114]

When we combine all of these figures we learn that $44,000,000 in money
and services has flowed and will flow from various sources in New Zealand
to aid victims who suffered accidents in 1970 and their families.[115]

This study has considered two distinct aspects of New Zealand's accident experience. First, we compared the data on accident occurrence in
New Zealand and the United States and concluded that remarkable similarities existed. Next, we explored New Zealand's legal and social responses
to the problems of accidental injuries. Although that part was not explicitly
comparative, it is clear that enormous differences exist between the two
countries in the nature of the legal and social responses. It thus seems clear
that when persons in this country consider New Zealand's experience under
its new accident compensation system, the primary concerns must be how
that system is working there, how it would work here, and whether the
changes it would bring to our legal approach to accidents are acceptable to
the American public. It is also clear, however, that the New Zealand experience cannot be summarily dismissed—we are too similar in the ways in
which we kill and injure ourselves.

---

114. Interview with J. Frasier, Ministry of Public Works, in Wellington, N.Z., May 15, 1973.
115. As developed in this Part, the following may be identified as major sources of funds
to victims:

Motor vehicle liability payments	$ 8,000,000
Motor vehicle—estimated liability	3,000,000
Payments to guests under comprehensive policy	330,000
Workers' compensation payments to date	9,400,000
Workers' compensation—estimated liability	734,000
Medical malpractice payments	185,000
Public liability payments (personal injury only)	300,000
Hospital services	15,660,000
Social security sickness benefits (accidents only)	1,100,000
Personal accident insurance	2,574,000
Personal hospital insurance (accidents only)	32,000
Life insurance	2,800,000
Total	$44,115,000

Life insurance payments totaling $2,800,000 have been included even though they would
necessarily be made at some time, and the fatal accident only accelerated that payment. To the extent we are interested in how much money victims' families had to call upon after the accident, this
amount should be counted. To the extent we are concerned with benefits that flowed because of accidents that would not have changed hands otherwise, life insurance payments should be excluded.

The estimated liability figure for workers' compensation is a guess. We know that 145 claims
are still open and that 14 of these are death claims. MONTHLY ABSTRACT, *supra* note 44, at 1. Some
undeterminable number will fail at common law. Some common law recoveries will be reduced by
contributory negligence. Since these are probably serious cases, generous allowances should be made.
I have estimated that the average death case payment will be $15,000 ($210,000) and the remaining
131 will involve average payments of $4,000 ($524,000) for a total of $734,000. (These are higher
than the average motor vehicle estimated liability averages because some payments are due in virtually
every case.)

The hospital service figure raises a double-counting problem. We know that insurers have reimbursed hospitals in some workers' compensation and motor vehicle cases, but we do not know
how much. Based on the workers' compensation data and on an extrapolation from the Wellington
Hospital Board's experience, a fair guess for 1970 would be $2 million.

The Rulemaking Power of the Supreme Court: A Contemporary Crisis

Jack H. Friedenthal*

In 1934 the Congress invested the United States Supreme Court with the power to promulgate rules governing procedure in all actions in federal trial courts.[1] Prior to that time, since 1842, the Court had clearly had the power to provide rules for suits in equity and admiralty, but in actions at law each federal court had been required by statute to follow those procedural rules in the state in which the particular federal court was located.[2] The 1934 statute was the result of a struggle that began in Congress as far back as 1885,[3] by legislators who favored a single system of procedure applicable to all cases and under the control of the Court.

Such judicial rulemaking power, now adopted in a number of states,[4] is attractive as a means of obtaining meaningful and necessary reform of antiquated procedural rules that can otherwise be altered only through legislation. The legislative process seems particularly unsuited both to wholesale reform of court procedures and to technical adjustment of specific regulations. First, legislators must be educated by proponents of a bill as to the need for its adoption. If judges or court personnel desire specific reforms, they may be forced to assume the role of partisan lobbyists and engage in political infighting—which should be avoided if courts are to remain, and appear to the public to remain, independent and objective arbiters. Second, legislators, even when sensitive to the need for reform, are often influenced by special interest lobbyists, including members of various elements of the bar itself. Such lobbyists may pressure legislators to alter crucial parts of a proposed reform bill, thereby limiting or destroying its overall effectiveness.

An excellent example[5] of the impact of special interest lobbying is provided in New York, where in 1962 the state legislature approved a com-

* A.B. 1953, Stanford University; LL.B. 1958, Harvard University. Professor of Law, Stanford University.

1. 28 U.S.C. § 2072 (1971).
2. Act of Aug. 23, 1842, ch. 188, § 6, 5 Stat. 516, 518. See 4 C. WRIGHT & A. MILLER, FEDERAL PRACTICE AND PROCEDURE: CIVIL, § 1002, at 35 (1969).
3. Id. at 38–39.
4. Arkansas is the state that most recently granted rulemaking power to its supreme court. See ARK. STAT. ANN. § 27–137 (Temp. ed. 1973). Courts in other states have possessed such power for many years. See, e.g., ARIZ. REV. STAT. §§ 12–109 to –111 (1956); MINN. STAT. ANN. §§ 480.051–.058 (1971). In some judisdictions the power is established by the state constitution. See, e.g., MICH. CONST. art. VI, § 5; N.J. CONST. art. VI, § 2, ¶ 3.

prehensive procedural reform bill that took effect in September 1963. The
original proposal would have included all of the modern discovery devices
in use under the Federal Rules. However, the state negligence bar vigorously objected. As a result, a compromise was reached whereby one of the
most useful discovery tools, interrogatories to parties, was omitted from
the legislative package. This, in turn, brought a number of strong protests
from the state governor and members of the bar. In response the legislature
quickly enacted provisions for interrogatories, while assuaging the objections of the negligence bar by prohibiting their use in negligence or wrongful death cases.[6] This limitation—politically convenient but legally unwarranted—has been adversely criticized both by courts and commentators.[7]

By way of contrast, judges, particularly those with lifetime tenure, are
less susceptible to many of the political pressures that can affect the actions
of elected officials. Thus, when given the power to do so, such judges are
freer to make procedural changes despite special interest opposition. The
results of the Supreme Court's rulemaking power have been spectacular.
As first promulgated in 1938, the Federal Rules of Civil Procedure established uniform procedures for all civil cases in federal courts,[8] swept away
antiquated pleading requirements,[9] and instituted a comprehensive set of
pretrial discovery rules[10] that have revolutionized trial practice. The success
of the rules—acclaimed by judges, lawyers, and commentators almost without opposition[11]—is underscored by the fact that they have been emulated,
in whole or substantial part, in nearly every state.[12] Yet it is doubtful that
these alterations in federal procedure could have been made by Congress
in the face of opposition from trial attorneys. Prior to the adoption of the
rules, each federal court was required by statute in jury trial actions to
follow the procedural rules of the state in which it was located.[13] The prospect of learning an additional set of rules for cases in federal courts generated substantial opposition to the rules,[14] opposition that Congress, unlike
the Supreme Court, appeared unlikely to resist.[15]

---

5. For a general discussion of the matter, *see* 3A J. WEINSTEIN, H. KORN & A. MILLER, NEW
YORK CIVIL PRACTICE ¶ 3130.01–.02, at 31-477–83 (1973).
6. N.Y. CIV. PRAC. § 3130 (McKinney 1970).
7. *See* 3A J. WEINSTEIN, H. KORN & A. MILLER, *supra* note 5, ¶ 3130.01–.02, at 31-477–83.
8. *See* FED. R. CIV. P. 1.
9. *See* FED. R. CIV. P. 8–12.
10. *See* FED. R. CIV. P. 26–37.
11. *See, e.g.*, 4 C. WRIGHT & A. MILLER, *supra* note 2, § 1008, at 65; Clark, *Two Decades of
the Federal Civil Rules*, 58 COLUM. L. REV. 435, 443 (1958).
12. Among the states that have adopted the rules within the past 3 years are Ohio, *see* PAGE'S
OHIO REV. CODE, Ohio R. Civ. P. (Supp. 1974); Tennessee, *see* TENN. CODE ANN., Tenn. R. Civ. P.
ch. 1 (Supp. 1974); and Vermont, *see* VT. STAT. ANN., Vt. R. Civ. P. (1971).
13. Act of June 1, 1872, ch. 255, § 5, 17 Stat. 197.
14. Indeed some congressmen advocated enactment of a statute to void the rules on this ground.
See Chandler, *Some Major Advances in the Federal Judicial System, 1922–1947*, 31 F.R.D. 307,
506–07 (1963).
15. Senate discussions of the rules revealed substantial hostility among Senate leaders. Had a
vote been required it would probably have gone against the rules. *Id.* at 511.

In the federal system, as well as in many states, the judicial rulemaking powers are not wholly independent of legislative control; proposed rules must be presented to Congress 90 days prior to their effective date.[16] This permits Congress to take action if it finds the proposals unsatisfactory. Ordinarily, however, it is unrealistic to expect members of Congress to study proposed new rules, let alone to approve or disapprove of them formally.[17] Thus it is hardly surprising that until recently Congress was so indifferent to such proposals that the Court's rulemaking powers had begun to seem virtually unlimited.[18] This situation changed dramatically with regard to the recently proposed Federal Rules of Evidence.[19] Controversial sections of these rules evoked substantial protests from members of the public as well as from congressmen. As a result, Congress enacted a statute[20] requiring specific legislation before the rules can go into effect. Thus the President as well as Congress has been given a role in the rulemaking process.

The occurrence of such a congressional response is less significant than its level.[21] By passing the bill requiring congressional approval of the rules, rather than taking a milder approach (such as approving a resolution requesting the Court to withdraw the rules pending further study), Congress reentered the rulemaking arena. This action may have spelled the end of the autonomous role held by the Supreme Court for the past 40 years.[22]

What specifically caused this turnabout? What, if anything, can or should be done to restore to the Court the full rulemaking powers it previously enjoyed and exercised with, on the whole, remarkable success? It is to these questions that this Article turns.

I. The Role of Judges in the Rulemaking Process

It is necessary to recognize the inherent dangers in granting rulemaking powers to the highest appellate court in a judicial system. First, judges on such a court are busy and cannot be expected to have the time to draft re-

---

16. 28 U.S.C. § 2072 (1971).

17. Unless and until a proposed rule gives rise to a major political controversy, such indifference seems inevitable. As Mr. Justice Frankfurter stated in his dissent in Sibbach v. Wilson, 312 U.S. 1, 18 (1941): "In this view little significance attaches to the fact that the Rules, in accordance with the statute, remained on the table of two Houses of Congress without evoking any objection . . . and thereby automatically came into force. Plainly the Rules are not acts of Congress and can not be treated as such. Having due regard to the mechanisms of legislation and the practical conditions surrounding the business of Congress when the Rules were submitted, to draw any inference of tacit approval from non-action by Congress is to appeal to unreality."

18. For 40 years, from the time the Court was given rulemaking powers until the submission of the proposed Rules of Evidence, Congress had never challenged any rule approved by the Court. *See* N.Y. Times, Jan. 6, 1973, § 1, at 14, col. 2.

19. Rules of Evidence for United States Courts and Magistrates, 34 L. Ed. 2d lxi–cciv (1972).

20. Pub. L. No. 93–12, § 1 (Mar. 30, 1973).

21. The fact that the House favored the bill by a vote of 399 to 1, *see* N.Y. Times, Mar. 15, 1973, § 1, at 19, col. 1, gives some indication of the level of the members' disenchantment.

22. For a discussion of the newly imposed limitations on the Court's rulemaking powers with respect to the rules of evidence, *see* text accompanying notes 69–74 *infra*.

form proposals; they therefore delegate that task to commissions, usually composed chiefly of legal scholars and senior lawyers, whose work sometimes reveals an ignorance of the day-to-day practice of attorneys actively engaged in litigation. Although some individual judges do consider major policy matters at length,[23] the tendency of most judges is to accept the commission's final draft without serious scrutiny and independent judgment of many of the detailed rules.[24]

Second, appellate judges are somewhat removed from the trial scene. Therefore, even were they not pressed for time, they would be forced to rely to some extent on the views of others as to how reforms should be accomplished. At times this may have the unfortunate result of creating an atmosphere in which neither the drafting committee nor the judges accept the ultimate responsibility for justification of the final product.[25]

The current rulemaking crisis in the federal system is due, at least in part, to a failure of the Supreme Court to recognize and avoid these dangers through direct supervision of the product of the Advisory Committee on the Federal Rules of Evidence. As Mr. Justice Douglas stated in his dissent from the Supreme Court's approval of the Evidence Rules:

> [T]his Court does not write the Rules, nor supervise their writing nor appraise them on their merits, weighing the pros and cons. . . . Those who write the Rules are members of a Committee named by the Judicial Conference. The members are eminent; but they are the sole judges of the merits of the proposed Rules, our approval being merely perfunctory. In other words, we are merely the conduit to Congress. Yet the public assumes that our imprimatur is on the Rules, as of course it is.[26]

It seems clear that the Justices relied completely on the work of the Advisory Committee and were so lulled into complacency by Congress' 40 years of acquiescence regarding proposed rules[27] that they believed that no matter how controversial the changes, or how poorly they might be presented, the rules would take effect without serious congressional challenge.

It is important to note that the Court had a different attitude from 1935, when it first appointed[28] what was to become a standing Advisory Com-

---

23. *See, e.g.,* Supreme Court Order Amending the Federal Rules of Civil Procedure, 383 U.S. 1031, 1032–37 (1966) (Black, J., dissenting); Supreme Court Order Amending the Federal Rules of Civil Procedure, 368 U.S. 1012, 1012–14 (1961) (Douglas, J., dissenting).

24. *See* text accompanying note 26 *infra.*

25. Mr. Justice Douglas, in his dissent from the Court's approval of the proposed Rules of Evidence, commented on the knowledge of the Justices as follows: "We are so far removed from the trial arena that we have no special insight, or meaningful oversight to contribute. The Rules of Evidence—if there are to be some—should be channeled through the Judicial Conference whose members are much more qualified than we to appraise their merits when applied in actual practice." 34 L. Ed.2d lxvi (1972) (dissenting opinion).

26. *Id.*

27. *See* note 18 *supra.*

28. Order Appointing Committee to Draft Unified System of Equity and Law Rules, 295 U.S. 774 (1935).

mittee[29] over which the Court had exclusive control, until 1956, when for reasons unarticulated, the Court ordered the Committee discharged.[30] Although the Justices generally deferred to the Committee's expertise during that period, they at least read and, when appropriate, rejected proposed alterations.[31] After 1956 an important change occurred regarding the appointment and responsibility of such advisory bodies. Pursuant to a statute enacted in 1958[32] with the Court's endorsement,[33] the duty to study the operation of current rules of procedure and to suggest changes was placed in the hands of the Judicial Conference consisting of the Chief Justice of the United States plus a number of appellate and trial judges from the various federal courts. In turn the Judicial Conference appointed a number of advisory committees including an Advisory Committee on Civil Rules and a special committee to draft the rules of evidence.

The removal of the direct connection between the advisory committees and the Court appears to have caused deterioration both in the product presented by such committees for the Court's approval and in the level of supervision exercised by the Court. As discussed below, both the 1970 revisions to the Federal Rules of Civil Procedure and the proposed Federal Rules of Evidence provide striking examples of this phenomenon.

II. The Results of Inadequate Judicial Supervision over Rulemaking

The blame for the current distrust of the Supreme Court's rulemaking authority should be shared by members of the bar and, in particular, by those legal scholars who carefully monitor judicial reform. No one warned the Court and the Advisory Committees of the impending breakdown of the rulemaking process. This breakdown resulted from two obvious weaknesses: (1) the failure of the Advisory Committees to discuss fully the reasons justifying major proposals and (2) the insertion of major alterations at the last minute so that they appeared for the first time as approved without any opportunity for public comment.

A. *Difficulties with the 1970 Revisions of the Work Product Rules*

In 1970 the Federal Rules of Civil Procedure regarding discovery were thoroughly revamped. Particular attention was paid to rules governing the work product doctrine. The alterations made in the work product rules

---

29. *See* Order Continuing Advisory Committee, 314 U.S. 720 (1942).
30. Order Discharging Advisory Committee, 352 U.S. 803 (1956).
31. For a discussion of specific Advisory Committee proposals rejected or altered by the Court, *see* 4 C. Wright & A. Miller, *supra* note 2, §§ 1004, 1006, at 48–49 & n.80, 53–56; Clark, *supra* note 11, at 442.
32. Act of July 11, 1958, 72 Stat. 356, *amending* 28 U.S.C. § 331 (1948).
33. *See* 4 C. Wright & A. Miller, *supra* note 2, § 1007, at 57 & n.12.

contained several important flaws, but because these specific changes, unlike some of the proposed evidence rules, did not contain deep-seated emotional issues, the new provisions quietly slipped past Congress and went into effect. The work product doctrine was initially established by the Supreme Court in the famous case of *Hickman v. Taylor*[34] and was developed through subsequent, and sometimes inconsistent, lower federal court decisions, which created an air of uncertainty as to when the doctrine applied.[35] One of the chief reasons for adopting a written rule was elimination of such uncertainty.[36] Unfortunately, the rule as promulgated is imprecise in a number of aspects and requires judicial interpretation.

Consider, for example, the fundamental question of what information the new rule was intended to include. As written[37] the rule pertains only to discovery of "documents and tangible things" and does not prohibit one party from taking the deposition of the opposing party's counsel to determine the substance of an oral statement made by a witness to counsel during preparation for trial. Yet the Court in *Hickman*, in establishing the work product doctrine, was quite clear in pointing out the need for protection against just such discovery:

> But as to oral statements made by witnesses to Fortenbaugh, whether presently in the form of his mental impressions or memoranda, we do not believe that any showing of necessity can be made under the circumstances of this case so as to justify production. Under ordinary conditions, forcing an attorney to repeat or write out all that witnesses have told him and to deliver the account to his adversary gives rise to grave dangers of inaccuracy and untrustworthiness. No legitimate purpose is served by such production. The practice forces the attorney to testify as to what he remembers or what he saw fit to write down regarding witnesses' remarks. Such testimony could not qualify as evidence; and to use it for impeachment or corroborative purposes would make the attorney much less an officer of the court and much more an ordinary witness. The standards of the profession would thereby suffer.[38]

---

34. 329 U.S. 495 (1947).

35. *See* Advisory Committee's Note on Rule 26(b)(3), in REPORT OF THE JUDICIAL CONFERENCE OF THE UNITED STATES, OCTOBER SESSION, 1969, 48 F.R.D. 481, 499–503 (1969).

36. See *id.*

37. FED. R. CIV. P. 26(b)(3): *"Trial Preparation: Materials.* Subject to the provisions of subdivision (b)(4) of this rule, a party may obtain discovery of documents and tangible things otherwise discoverable under subdivision (b)(1) of this rule and prepared in anticipation of litigation or for trial by or for another party or by or for that other party's representative (including his attorney, consultant, surety, indemnitor, insurer, or agent) only upon a showing that the party seeking discovery has substantial need of the materials in the preparation of his case and that he is unable without undue hardship to obtain the substantial equivalent of the materials by other means. In ordering discovery of such materials when the required showing has been made, the court shall protect against disclosure of the mental impressions, opinions, conclusions, or legal theories of an attorney or other representative of a party concerning the litigation.

"A party may obtain without the required showing a statement concerning the action or its subject matter previously made by that party. Upon request, a person not a party may obtain without the required showing a statement concerning the action or its subject matter previously made by that person. If the request is refused, the person may move for a court order."

38. 329 U.S. at 512–13. If anything, the Justices' opinions indicated the need for greater protection of an attorney's oral recollections of an interview with a witness than of a witness' written

In commenting on the language of *Hickman,* the Advisory Committee simply noted that "[t]he *Hickman* opinion drew special attention to the need for protecting an attorney against discovery of *memoranda* prepared from recollection of oral interviews."[39] Thus the Advisory Committee, by referring only to "memoranda," inexplicably misrepresented the full thrust of the *Hickman* decision.

It is certainly open to a party currently seeking discovery to argue that the new rule supersedes *Hickman* and limits work product protection to discovery of tangible items. This argument can be supported by noting that prior to the adoption of the new federal rule, commentators[40] had discussed the problem at issue and had sometimes criticized similar state work product statutes for having too limited a coverage. The Advisory Committee can be charged with knowledge of these comments, since it cited some of these authorities with respect to closely related matters.[41] Furthermore, another section of the same rule dealing with discovery of expert information[42] grants protection from discovery by deposition and interrogatory as well as from discovery by demand for reports and other tangible items. Except for cases involving experts, it thus appears that the Advisory Board and the Supreme Court intended to narrow the scope of the work product doctrine to discovery of tangible items. Such a position seems unsound in light of the arguments made in the *Hickman* case, and it is highly unlikely that the federal courts will adopt a narrow work product interpretation. Regardless of the relative merits of the rule the problem illustrates the fact

statement. As Justice Jackson said in his concurring opinion, *id.* at 516–17: "To consider first the most extreme aspect of the requirement in litigation here, we find it calls upon counsel, if he has had any conversations with any of the crews of the vessels in question or of any other, to 'set forth in detail the exact provision of any such oral statements or reports.' Thus the demand is not for the production of a transcript in existence but calls for the creation of a written statement not in being. . . .

". . . I can conceive of no practice more demoralizing to the Bar than to require a lawyer to write out and deliver to his adversary an account of what witnesses have told him. Even if his recollection were perfect, the statement would be his language, permeated with his inferences. Every one who has tried it knows that it is almost impossible so fairly to record the expressions and emphasis of a witness that when he testifies in the environment of the court and under the influence of the leading question there will not be departures in some respects. Whenever the testimony of the witness would differ from the 'exact' statement the lawyer had delivered, the lawyer's statement would be whipped out to impeach the witness. Counsel producing his adversary's 'inexact' statement could lose nothing by saying, 'Here is a contradiction, gentlemen of the jury. I do not know whether it is my adversary or his witness who is not telling the truth, but one is not.' Of course, if this practice were adopted, that scene would be repeated over and over again. The lawyer who delivers such statements often would find himself branded a deceiver afraid to take the stand to support his own version of the witness's conversation with him, or else he will have to go on the stand to defend his own credibility—perhaps against that of his chief witness, or possibly even his client."

39. REPORT OF THE JUDICIAL CONFERENCE OF THE UNITED STATES, OCTOBER SESSION, 1969, *supra* note 35, at 502 (emphasis added).

40. *See* D. LOUISELL, MODERN CALIFORNIA DISCOVERY § 10.11, at 312–13 (1963); Friedenthal, *Discovery and Use of an Adverse Party's Expert Information,* 14 STAN. L. REV. 455, 476–77 (1962); Note, *Aspects of the Minnesota Rule Prohibiting Discovery of Work-Product and Expert Conclusions,* 48 MINN. L. REV. 977, 983–86 (1964).

41. *See* Advisory Committee's Note on Rule 26(b)(4), in REPORT OF THE JUDICIAL CONFERENCE OF THE UNITED STATES, OCTOBER SESSION, 1969, *supra* note 35, at 504–05.

42. FED. R. CIV. P. 26(b)(4).

that the Advisory Committee was guilty of careless draftsmanship and insufficient analysis[43] and that the Supreme Court failed to remedy these deficiencies before approving the rule.

At least two other defects in the work product rule can be attributed in part to the fact that they were inserted at the last minute without sufficient opportunity for outside comment. As we will later see, this same treatment resulted in Congress' distaste for the proposed rules of evidence. One such defect appears in a clause directing courts to "protect against" disclosure of an attorney's mental impressions and legal theories. Even before the *Hickman* decision, the question of the protection of such matters had been hotly debated. In 1946, the Supreme Court rejected an Advisory Committee proposal that would have barred courts from ordering discovery of any writing that reflected "an attorney's mental impressions, conclusions, opinions, or legal theories."[44] Many states, in enacting work product rules, have resolved the matter by adopting language similar to the 1946 proposal.[45] Elsewhere this wording has been omitted, leaving the courts free to require disclosure if sufficient good cause is shown.[46] The new federal rule, as originally drawn and circulated to the public, did not contain such a clause, and the matter was not discussed in the Advisory Committee's comments.[47] As finally proposed and adopted, however, the new rule contains the ambiguous "protect against" language. The Advisory Committee's notes are far from clear as to precisely what was meant, although on balance they seem to indicate that such discovery is to be barred.[48] If that were the intent

43. The history of the discovery rules indicates that the failure to encompass other forms of discovery in the new work product rule was inadvertent. This appears from the fact that at the time the new rule was drafted a major concern was to eliminate uncertainty regarding discovery of tangible items. Prior to the 1970 alterations, FED. R. CIV. P. 34 had prohibited discovery of any documents or tangible items in the control of an opposing party without a showing of good cause. The *Hickman* case limited discovery of work product unless good cause could be demonstrated. Although documents were sought in *Hickman*, the court failed to discuss or mention rule 34. Therefore, when documents or other tangible items fell within the scope of work product, the courts were in a quandary. Did *Hickman* require a different "good cause" than did rule 34, and if so, what was the difference? The new rules solved the problem by eliminating the general good-cause requirement in rule 34 and by encompassing it in the new regulation governing only work product. In concentrating on these matters, however, the Advisory Committee apparently overlooked the effect of the work product doctrine on other forms of discovery.

44. For the full text of the proposal and a detailed discussion of its history, *see* 4 J. MOORE, FEDERAL PRACTICE ¶ 26.63[6] (2d ed. 1972).

45. *See, e.g.,* CALIF. CIV. PRO. CODE § 2016(b) (West 1955); MD. R. P. 410d; MICH. GEN. CT. R. 306.2.

46. *See* IND. R. TR. P. 26(b)(2).

47. *See* COMMITTEE ON RULES OF PRACTICE AND PROCEDURE OF THE JUDICIAL CONFERENCE OF THE UNITED STATES, PRELIMINARY DRAFT OF PROPOSED AMENDMENTS TO RULES OF CIVIL PROCEDURE FOR THE UNITED STATES DISTRICT COURTS RELATING TO DEPOSITION AND DISCOVERY, 43 F.R.D. 211, 224–28 (1967).

48. The sole relevant comment of the Advisory Committee is as follows: "Subdivision (b)(3) . . . goes on to protect against disclosure of the mental impressions, conclusions, opinions, or legal theories concerning the litigation of an attorney or other representative of a party. . . . The courts have steadfastly safeguarded against disclosure of . . . [these matters]. In enforcing this provision . . . the courts will sometimes find it necessary to order disclosure of a document but with portions deleted . . . . Under . . . [rules allowing discovery of interrogatories or admissions of a party] a

it is difficult to understand why the rule does not say so. Surely courts and litigants are entitled to a clear determination of whether the section creates a flat prohibition on discovery.[49] The matter is not without practical significance, for if such discovery is improper, then an attorney, whenever feasible, will be wise to take a witness' written statement on a question and answer basis, since the questions will reveal the attorney's theories and discovery of the answers alone often will not be meaningful.

The second defect is the unfortunate last-minute inclusion of a novel clause providing that any witness who has given a written statement to one of the parties may, upon demand, obtain a copy of that statement.[50] Except in the rarest of cases, a nonparty witness will learn of his right to receive a copy of his statement only if he is informed by the attorney for one of the parties whose attempts to obtain the statement from the party who controls it have been thwarted by the work product rule. In such circumstances the attorney will encourage and aid the witness in demanding a copy of the statement in order to learn its contents. Hence whenever a witness is friendly to the side seeking disclosure, the work product rule will be undercut. On the other hand, if the witness is friendly to the litigant who controls the statement, disclosure will be thwarted. It is absurd and unfair to adopt a rule permitting discovery to be determined by the witnesses' feelings regarding the parties.

The Advisory Committee did not fully consider this drawback. In its comments the Committee merely notes that the right of a witness to obtain his statement can be justified on many of the same grounds that justify a provision permitting a party to obtain a copy of any statement he has given to an opponent.[51] The analogy, however, is superficial. A statement of a party can be introduced at trial by an opposing party to prove the truth of any assertions contained in the statement.[52] Admission does not depend on whether the party who made the statement is called as a witness.[53] The statement of a litigant used by an opponent naturally tends to have a sub-

---

party and his attorney or other representative may be required to disclose, to some extent, mental impressions, opinions, or conclusions. But documents or parts of documents containing these matters are protected against discovery by this subdivision. Even though a party may ultimately have to disclose in response to interrogatories or requests to admit, he is entitled to keep confidential documents containing such matters prepared for internal use." REPORT OF THE JUDICIAL CONFERENCE OF THE UNITED STATES, OCTOBER SESSION, 1969, *supra* note 35, at 502.

49. There are substantial arguments against imposing an absolute ban on discovery of an attorney's legal theories and contentions regarding his case. *See* Cooper, *Work Product of the Rulesmakers,* 53 MINN. L. REV. 1269, 1284–93 (1969).

50. For the exact text of this clause, *see* note 37 *supra.*

51. The Advisory Committee's entire substantive comments on the clause are as follows: "Many, though not all, of the considerations supporting a party's right to obtain his statement apply also to the nonparty witness. Insurance companies are increasingly recognizing that a witness is entitled to a copy of his statement and are modifying their regular practice accordingly." REPORT OF THE JUDICIAL CONFERENCE OF THE UNITED STATES, OCTOBER SESSION, 1969, *supra* note 35, at 503.

52. C. McCORMICK, EVIDENCE § 262 (2d ed. 1972).

53. *Id.*

stantial impact on a trier of fact, particularly a jury. It is not unreasonable therefore to rule that in any case where such a statement exists, good cause exists for its production.

On the other hand, a statement by an ordinary witness is normally considered inadmissible hearsay, which cannot be introduced into evidence by any party in order to prove the truth of the facts asserted.[54] Such a statement can be introduced only if the witness is called to the stand and, under oath, offers testimony inconsistent with the prior statement—and even then only for the limited purpose of showing that the witness is not reliable.[55] Obviously, such a statement, even when introduced at trial, does not have the same impact as does the statement of a party. But assuming arguendo that it would have an important effect on the case and would result in unfairness to one of the litigants, the special clause is not designed as a remedy, since it does not allow discovery by the party who would be injured;[56] the clause provides only for disclosure to the witness himself. It is not at all clear what purpose this serves other than to aid witnesses in planning their testimony at trial so as to avoid embarrassment.[57] Exposing inconsistencies and other faults in testimony is one of the major purposes of trial, and the discomfort of witnesses has never before been considered too high a price for arriving at the truth.

B. *Problems with the Proposed Rules of Evidence*

A study of the work of the Advisory Committee which drafted the proposed evidence rules reveals that the same two faults that plagued the rule-making process with regard to the alteration of the work product rules also were responsible for the major defects in the evidence rules. The Advisory Committee Notes are strangely inadequate. Major questions and objections are often ignored or glossed over as if they had not been given due consideration. Furthermore, some of the most controversial provisions were not included in the initial draft that the Committee circulated for comment by interested persons; instead the provisions first appeared in the final document as already approved by the Court. Not only did this procedure curtail the discussion so necessary to ensure the soundness of the proposals in their final form, but it also eroded the public image of the Court and tended to rob it of support even from those who ultimately might have approved of the proposals.

---

54. *Id.* § 251.
55. *Id. But see* CAL. EVID. CODE § 1235 (West 1966), which provides that a prior inconsistent statement may be introduced for the truth of the matters it contains.
56. In such a case, the party seeking discovery would normally be able to establish sufficient good cause to avoid the work product prohibition, and thus would not require the cooperation of the witness.
57. *Cf.* C. WRIGHT, LAW OF FEDERAL COURTS § 83 (2d ed. 1970).

Much of the present controversy revolves around the treatment of privileged communications.[58] For example, proposed rule 505, although preserving the right of an accused in a criminal action to prevent his spouse from testifying against him, omits the more general common law privilege which prohibits one spouse in any type of proceeding from revealing confidential communications received from the other spouse during marriage. This omission was acknowledged by the Advisory Committee in its preliminary draft in 1969.[59] The Committee's cryptic comments were, however, woefully inadequate in explaining such a substantial, although by no means clearly improper, deviation from universal practice. As the Committee stated:

> The traditional justifications for privileges not to testify against a spouse and not to be testified against by one's spouse have been the prevention of marital dissension and the repugnancy of requiring a person to condemn or be condemned by his spouse. 8 Wigmore §§ 2228, 2241 (McNaughton Rev. 1961). These considerations bear no relevancy to marital communications. Nor can it be assumed that marital conduct will be affected by a privilege for confidential communications of whose existence the parties in all likelihood are unaware. The other communication privileges, by way of contrast, have as one party a professional person who can be expected to inform the other of the existence of the privilege. Moreover, those privileges are essentially and almost exclusively verbal in nature, quite unlike marriage.[60]

Subsequent to this initial draft, the Advisory Committee received comments from distinguished members of the bar urging that the marital communications privilege be included, on the ground that privacy ought to be

---

58. The Court's rules regarding privilege have provoked two kinds of objections. First, specific provisions have been challenged for the way they grant or fail to grant privileged status to various items of evidence. Some of these challenges are discussed in the text of this Essay. *See* notes 59–69 *infra* and accompanying text. Second, promulgation of *any* set of privilege rules has been labeled improper, as beyond the powers of the Court granted in the Rules Enabling Act, 28 U.S.C. § 2072 (1971). *See* New York Trial Lawyers Committee on the Proposed Rules of Evidence, Recommendation and Study Relating to the Advisory Committee's Preliminary Draft of the Proposed Federal Rules of Evidence 30–32 (1970); N.Y. Times, Feb. 1, 1973, § 1, at 9, col. 1; *id.*, Mar. 15, 1973, § 1, at 19, col. 1. The Act proscribes rules that "abridge, enlarge or modify any substantive right." In recent action, the House of Representatives has approved a bill that would require an Act of Congress before any Court rule regarding privilege could take effect. *See* note 70 *infra* and accompanying text.

It should be noted that objections to the proposed rules regarding matters other than privilege have been made. For example, a number of persons took issue with proposed Rule 803(24), permitting as an exception to the hearsay exclusion, "[a] statement not specifically covered by any of the [23 specifically stated] foregoing exceptions but having comparable circumstantial guarantees of trustworthiness." *See* N.Y. Times, Jan. 6, 1973, § 1, at 14, col. 2; *id.* Mar. 15, 1973, § 1, at 19, col. 1. On February 6, 1974, the House of Representatives passed H.R. 5463, 93d. Cong., 1st Sess. (1973), a set of evidence rules for federal courts. The hearsay rules of H.R. 5463 closely parallel those proposed by the Supreme Court; however, a counterpart to rule 803(24) was omitted. *See generally* notes 70–74 *infra* and accompanying text.

59. Committee on Rules of Practice and Procedure of the Judicial Conference of the United States, Preliminary Draft of Proposed Rules of Evidence for the United States District Courts and Magistrates 92–93 (1969).

60. *Id.*

preserved in such a vital area of personal relationships;[61] the notion that one spouse could be forced to reveal the other's confidential admission regarding commission of a tort seemed, at least to some, extremely unwise. The Advisory Committee in its final draft failed even to acknowledge these important arguments; indeed the Committee's comments on the matter were practically identical to those in the original draft distributed 4 years earlier.[62] Given this kind of treatment, it is hardly surprising that omission of the marital communications privilege has been one of the most frequently cited reasons for congressional refusal to accept the rules.[63]

It is in regard to rule 509, the so-called state secrets privilege, that the greatest emotions have been aroused concerning the propriety of any one of the new rules. As originally written,[64] rule 509 was not controversial. In accord with established federal decisions,[65] it provided protection for secret information concerning national defense or the international relations of the United States. The rule spelled out reasonable procedures permitting only the head of the department affected, normally a cabinet officer, to claim the privilege. But by the time rule 509 appeared in its final form—already approved by the Court—it had been substantially expanded. In addition to state secrets, the rule now provided a privilege for "official information" defined in extremely broad terms.[66] Furthermore, such a privilege could be asserted "by any attorney representing the government." The amended proposal would have allowed government agencies at the lowest level to raise the privilege in any civil or criminal case, in an attempt

61. *See, e.g.,* New York Trial Lawyers Committee on the Proposed Federal Rules of Evidence, *supra* note 58, at 42, 48, 142–43.

62. *See* Advisory Committee's Note to Rule 505, 34 L. Ed. 2d cxv–cxvi (1972).

It is important to note that not all public suggestions did inevitably receive a negative response from the Advisory Committee. For example, in arguing for the retention of a general doctor-patient privilege which was replaced by a psychotherapist-patient privilege, the New York Trial Lawyers Committee relied primarily on the fact that poor and rural patients utilized general practitioners to deal with emotional problems. *See* New York Trial Lawyers Committee on the Proposed Federal Rules of Evidence, *supra* note 58, at 39–40, 46–48, 138–39. Although the Advisory Committee continued to reject inclusion of a wholesale doctor-patient privilege, it redefined psychotherapist to include any physician while engaged in treating emotional disorders, including drug addiction. *Compare* the rule as originally proposed, Rule 5–04(a)(2), in Committee on Rules of Practice and Procedure of the Judicial Conference of the United States, *supra* note 59, at 85, *with* the final draft of Rule 504(a)(2), 34 L. Ed. 2d cxi (1972).

63. *See, e.g.,* N.Y. Times, Jan. 6, 1973, § 1, at 14, col. 2; *id.,* Feb. 1, 1973, § 1, at 9, col. 1; *id.,* Feb. 9, 1973, § 1, at 16, col. 1; *id.,* Mar. 15, 1973, § 1, at 19, col. 1.

64. Committee on Rules of Practice and Procedure of the Judicial Conference of the United States, *supra* note 59, at 100–02 (1969).

65. *See* United States v. Reynolds, 345 U.S. 1 (1953).

66. Proposed Rule 509(a)(2) defines official information as follows: " 'Official information' is information within the custody or control of a department or agency of the government the disclosure of which is shown to be contrary to the public interest and which consists of: (A) intragovernmental opinions or recommendations submitted for consideration in the performance of decisional or policymaking functions, or (B) subject to the provisions of 18 U.S.C. § 3500, investigatory files compiled for law enforcement purposes and not otherwise available, or (C) information within the custody or control of a governmental department or agency whether initiated within the department or policymaking functions, or (B) subject to the provisions of 18 U.S.C. § 3500, investigatory files to the public pursuant to 5 U.S.C. § 552 [the so-called Freedom of Information Act]." 34 L. Ed. 2d cxx (1972).

to keep hidden a substantial amount of material that previously had routinely been subject to disclosure.[67]

It is difficult to believe that the Supreme Court would knowingly have approved of such an important, far-reaching rule without giving the public an opportunity to read it and respond. In this case the Court's utter reliance on the discretion of a drafting committee ended in disaster. The anger of those who objected to the rule was hardly soothed by revelations that the "official information" provisions had been submitted by the Department of Justice,[68] obviously in its own self-interest. The apparent attempt of the Justice Department to slip this rule past Congress, plus the failure of the Court to intercede, could not help but result in skepticism concerning the continuing ability of the Court to supervise and control rulemaking activities.[69]

III. Conclusion

The shortcomings of the 1970 work product rule probably would have been prevented had the Supreme Court properly attended to its rulemaking functions; similarly, if the 1970 errors had been analyzed and exposed, the Supreme Court would undoubtedly have exercised more diligence with regard to the proposed rules of evidence, perhaps avoiding the current crisis with Congress. The Court cannot continue to hold the rulemaking power unless it ceases to be a "mere conduit" for the work of others. The Court should refuse even to consider rules that have not been circulated to the public for a sufficient period to allow for critical comment. It should automatically recommit rules to the Judicial Council whenever formal Advisory Committee comments fail to answer criticisms and objections. If members of the Court cannot find time to undertake these tasks themselves, certainly they could employ a clerk, who would be answerable directly to the Justices, to do so. Finally, the members of the Court, no matter how busy they might be, must spend some time independently reviewing the substance of rules before approving them. Had they done so in the past, the obvious errors discussed above would not, in all likelihood, have been overlooked.

The failure of the Court to reestablish firm control over rulemaking would be unfortunate, for, as was noted at the outset, legislation is generally

---

67. Consider, for example, the effect of the proposed rule on cases such as Abel Inv. Co. v. United States, 53 F.R.D. 485 (D. Neb. 1971) (suit to recover a tax refund), in which the courts have required the Internal Revenue Service to disclose to plaintiff-taxpayers relevant internal IRS memoranda and reports, routinely prepared prior to litigation.

68. The admission was publicly made by Court of Appeals Judge Albert B. Maris, Chairman of the Judicial Conference's Standing Committee on Practice and Procedure, who had a large hand in drafting the rules. *See* N.Y. Times, Feb. 8, 1973, § 1, at 13, col. 1.

69. This skepticism was reinforced when alteration of Rule 509 proved not to be an isolated instance; a number of other important changes in the rules appeared for the first time in the final draft as approved by the Court and transmitted to Congress. *See* N.Y. Times, Feb. 8, 1973, § 1, at 13, col. 1; *id.*, Feb. 9, 1973, § 1, at 16, col. 1.

a less satisfactory way to obtain procedural reform. However, Congress now appears less inclined to trust the Court's judgment in the future. On February 6, 1974, the House of Representatives passed a bill[70] to establish a comprehensive set of federal evidence rules, based generally on the rules approved by the Supreme Court, but with a number of significant differences—particularly in the area of privileges.[71] Although the bill contains a special new enabling act permitting the Supreme Court to amend the evidence rules,[72] some important limitations have been imposed. First, any amendment can be vetoed by a resolution of either the House or the Senate,[73] and, second, an amendment creating, abolishing, or modifying a privilege cannot take effect without a formal Act of Congress.[74] One must hope that it is not already too late for the Court to reestablish public confidence in its rulemaking activities and that congressional tempers aroused by the Supreme Court's evidence proposals will not result in additional legislation terminating or limiting the Court's rulemaking responsibilities with regard either to evidence or to other areas of practice and procedure.

---

70. H.R. 5463, 93d Cong., 1st Sess. (1973).
71. *See* 120 CONG. REC. 543–70 (daily ed. Feb. 6, 1974).
72. *See id.* at 567, setting forth proposed 28 U.S.C. § 2076.
73. *Id.*
74. *See id.* at 567–68, setting forth the substance, discussion, and approval of this limitation. The reasons for special treatment of privilege rules are discussed in note 58 *supra*.

San Benito 1890: Legal Snapshot
of a County*

Lawrence M. Friedman†

About 90 miles south of San Francisco, and about 25 miles inland from Monterey Bay, is the northern edge of San Benito County. The county is about 70 miles long and averages 21 miles in width. Much of the land is mountainous; in the southern part of the county lies an area of dramatic peaks and outcroppings, which has been set aside as Pinnacles National Monument. About 18,000 people live in San Benito County, in the towns or on farms, ranches, and vineyards in the fertile valleys. The economy historically and presently rests on agriculture although New Idria was once an important quicksilver mine.

Until 1874 the county was merely an inland portion of Monterey County. This political arrangement, however, did not please the settlers in San Benito. Monterey was not far away, as the crow flies, but the coastal range made access difficult. A rather intense political struggle between the two county factions ended in 1874, when the legislature carved a new county, San Benito,[1] out of the eastern part of Monterey.

The county seat of San Benito County is Hollister, founded in 1872. It is by far the largest town in the county with a present population of roughly 8,000. Hollister lies in the northwest part of the county, in an area of strong seismic activity. It has suffered considerable damage over the years. One serious earthquake on April 24, 1890, brought about considerable loss of property and, we are told, led to the death of Mrs. D. W. Gilmore, who was so affected by the tremors that she sank into a state of weakness and, despite the efforts of the doctors, died shortly thereafter.[2] West of Hollister at the northwest edge of the county is the town of San Juan Bautista, with a 1970 population of just over 1,000. San Juan is famous for its beautiful mission, founded in 1797; the mission fronts on a plaza which it shares with a group of 19th-century buildings, carefully restored and open to the public. No other town in the county is at all sizable. The climate is mild—very dry

* The research on this Essay was supported by National Science Foundation Grant GS 33821. I wish to thank E. Allan John, Jr., Marilyn Epstein, Marc Warsowe, and Robert Percival for their great help with the research on which this article is based.

† B.A. 1948, J.D. 1951, L.L.M. 1953, University of Chicago. Professor of Law, Stanford University.

1. Ch. 87, [1874] Cal. Stat.; see HISTORY OF SAN BENITO COUNTY 79–80 (1881).
2. San Benito Advance, Apr. 25, 1890, at 3, col. 4.

and rather hot in summer; winters are cooler, but never cold, and there is, on the average, some 13 inches of rain. The climate has always been praised as exceedingly healthful: "no chills and fever, no epidemic diseases"; no malaria brought on by the "atmosphere."[3] The hills are brownish-gold in summer and velvety green in winter. To the casual passerby, it seems as if the hand of man has hardly disturbed them in their beauty.

San Benito is untroubled, too, by urban congestion. In 1890, the populace was even thinner. Census-takers in that year counted 6,412 people within the county. Hollister township had 2,700 population; 1,234 of these lived in the town itself. The town of San Juan Bautista had less than 500 inhabitants. The county was growing rather slowly, compared with certain other parts of California. Between 1880 and 1890, San Benito had grown about 15 percent—from 5,584 to 6,412; the town of Hollister increased from 1,034 to 1,234; in the same decade, Los Angeles tripled its population.[4] There were more men than women in the county (3,640 against 2,772), an unmistakable sign of a new community with a transient population. Most of the 1890 population was native born. About 1,355 of the residents were foreign born. The largest contingent came from Ireland. There was a large group of Germans and Canadians, and a considerable group from Portugal and the Azores. Only 85 Chinese remained (242 had been recorded in 1880), along with a handful of Indians and blacks.[5]

In 1890, San Benito, small as it was, had been a full-fledged county for 16 years. This meant it was entitled to a full panoply of political and legal offices: a superior court, justice courts, a board of supervisors, a sheriff, a district attorney, treasurer, coroner, superintendent of schools, and so on.[6] What role in the life of the community did these officials, and the law of California, play in 1890? Despite earthquakes and the ravages of time, the raw data for an answer lie in the back room of the county courthouse, in heavy folios or in dusty files. These legal records, along with the yellowed pages of Hollister's weekly newspapers, and a scattering of other sources, give us a lively snapshot of the law at work in this small community, 10 years before the turn of the century.

Neither in 1890 nor today is San Benito County a law unto itself, nor is it isolated from the rest of California. Today, highway connections are excellent, and San Benito is, of course, bound to the outside world by telephone and telegraph, radio, movies, and television. No passenger trains stop in the county today, but there is bus service and an airport for private planes. In 1890, Hollister had a post office, express and telegraph offices, and "a

---

3. HISTORY OF SAN BENITO COUNTY, *supra* note 1, at 11.
4. U.S. DEP'T OF THE INTERIOR, REPORT ON POPULATION OF THE UNITED STATES AT THE ELEVENTH CENSUS: 1890, pt. I, at 72 (1895).
5. *Id.* at 404, 437, 491, 612–13.
6. The fundamental law in force in 1890 regulating county government was ch. 75, [1883] Cal. Stat.

commodious passenger and freight depot." Travel, of course, was slower, but Hollister was a station on the Tres Pinos branch of the Northern Division of the Southern Pacific Railroad[7] and enjoyed stagecoach service as well. It was not too arduous a trip to go to San Francisco, and leading citizens sometimes traveled to the city to see the opera and the sights. Telephone service was not yet available in San Benito, but toward the end of the year merchants were discussing bringing in some lines.[8]

In many other ways the world came to San Benito. In January, 1890, "two Frenchmen with a couple of bears" performed on the street of Hollister; in March "three traveling photographers" arrived to rake in stray dollars; in May 75 bicyclists pedaled some hundred miles from San Francisco; in June the Pawnee Indian Medicine Company held an enormous show in Hollister, admission 25 cents. There were plays and circuses, and the Fourth of July was celebrated with a gala. Lou Johnstone's Minstrels performed in San Juan on July 25. In October the "ladies of the Presbyterian Church" gave a concert at which Enrico Tomasso, "the celebrated baritone," appeared; the performance brought in some 60 dollars for the church. Hollister had an "Opera House," as was so often the case with old towns of the West. In Hollister's opera house, in 1890, there was indeed no opera to be seen. But a costume ball was held in February (competing perhaps with the gospel temperance meeting of the W.C.T.U.), and another ball in April, when a Mrs. Blum of San Jose came to town "with a full assortment of costumes." In October the opera house held a boxing match: Gonzalez, the heavyweight, fought Billy Shannon of San Francisco; but the Charity Ball in late November, featuring the Hollister String Band, was held elsewhere, in the Odd Fellows Hall.[9]

In another sense, too, the community was far from isolated. It was a melting pot of foreigners and Americans. It was a rare person who had actually been *born* in San Benito; probably 95 percent of the adult population had come as immigrants or strangers. Newcomers were of all sorts and conditions: thieves and tramps, laborers and farmers, even professionals, like young Dr. W. F. Mitchell, a graduate of the College of Physicians and Surgeons in New York, who arrived in Hollister and joined up with Dr. J. H. Tebbetts in the practice of medicine. People constantly entered the county, bringing with them the flavor of their state or country of origin. People also constantly left. It was a small but heterogeneous population.

For every full-fledged county, the state of California mandated a set of

7. McKENNEY DIRECTORY CO., SAN JOSE CITY DIRECTORY 812 (1889) [hereinafter cited as SAN JOSE CITY DIRECTORY] (the Directory includes listings for San Benito County).
8. Hollister Free Lance, Dec. 26, 1890, at 3, col. 2.
9. These accounts are collected from various editions of the San Benito Advance. *See* Jan. 24, 1890, at 2, col. 3; Feb. 21, 1890, at 3, col. 5; Mar. 28, 1890, at 3, col. 3; Apr. 4, 1890, at 3, col. 3; May 16, 1890, at 3, col. 3; July 11, 1890, at 2, col. 1; July 25, 1890, at 3, col. 5; Oct. 3, 1890, at 3, col. 2; Oct. 10, 1890, at 2, col. 5; Nov. 28, 1890, at 2, col. 3.

judicial institutions. At the base were the justice courts. In the smaller counties, justices depended on fees; sometimes, as the newspapers dryly recounted, business was bad: "One solitary drunk illumined the gloom that has settled over the justice courts, this weak [*sic*]. Judge Lee returns thanks . . . for $3 in fees, earned this year. At this rate, he figures that in 8 years and 10 months he will . . . save enough money to purchase a cord of firewood."[10] These courts had jurisdiction over civil cases if the amounts or damages claimed amounted to less than $300. In criminal cases, their jurisdiction extended to petit larceny, assault and battery, breaches of the peace, and "all misdemeanors punishable by fine not exceeding five hundred dollars, or imprisonment not exceeding six months, or by both."[11] There were four justice courts sitting in San Benito: one in Hollister, another in San Juan Bautista, and two in outlying districts. Despite the complaints about fees, the jobs were eagerly sought after: no less than four candidates ran for the office of Justice of the Peace of Hollister Township in 1890; in San Juan Township there were three candidates, and the winner had a 12-vote margin.[12] Unlike judges of the superior court, the justices did not have to be lawyers, although some were. The justice of the peace in San Juan, until his defeat in November, 1890, was a barber.[13]

The superior court was the trial court of general jurisdiction. It handled important cases—all felonies and those misdemeanor and civil cases that exceeded the limit of the justice courts. James F. Breen was judge of the superior court.[14] He ran for reelection in 1890 and defeated his opponent, Craig, by about 200 votes out of a total of 1,600. Five attorneys in the county regularly advertised their services in the newspapers;[15] these five dominated practice in the county's courts, although outside attorneys had a share of the business. F. A. and M. D. Hyde of San Francisco, "Attorneys in Land Cases," solicited business in the pages of the *San Benito Advance*[16];

10. *Id.*, Mar. 28, 1890, at 3, col. 2. The justices in cities and larger towns were salaried. CAL. CODE CIV. PRO. §§ 97, 103 (Newmark 1889).

11. *Id.* §§ 112, 115.

12. The election returns are in Minutes of the Board of Supervisors, San Benito Cty., vol. 3, Nov. 1890, at 52–60.

13. CAL. CODE CIV. PRO. § 159 (Newmark 1889). W.G. Lee, Hollister Justice of the Peace, is listed in the city directory as "attorney-at-law and Justice of the Peace." SAN JOSE CITY DIRECTORY, *supra* note 7, at 826. Leon Bullier is listed as a barber. *Id.* at 850.

14. Occasionally, Judge John Reynolds, a Superior Court Judge of Santa Clara County, took Breen's place—for example, in handling the estate of E.J. Breen, since Judge Breen, a brother of the deceased, was one of the executors. *In re* Estate of Breen, Probate No. 201 (Super. Ct., San Benito Cty., Cal., 1890).

15. An 1895 directory of attorneys listed seven attorneys for the county, all except one practicing in Hollister. CAL. ATTORNEYS DIRECTORY 68 (1895). Five of these were practicing in 1890 and were the only local attorneys to practice in superior court. Others may have appeared in justice court, since there are occasional references to such men in the newspapers or other sources. For example, R.E. Boyn and John Fletcher are listed in the directory as "attorneys-at-law" in Hollister. SAN JOSE CITY DIRECTORY, *supra* note 7, at 814–15. The *Advance* refers to a Joseph Lahiff as a "rising young lawyer." San Benito Advance, Feb. 7, 1890, at 3, col. 3.

16. *See, e.g.*, San Benito Advance, Jan. 3, 1890, at 1, col. 1.

so did C. H. Wyman, "Land and Mine Attorney," of Stockton, California, who boasted of "eighteen years practical experience in land business."[17] While no large firms practiced in Hollister, there were two 2-man partnerships: Montgomery and Scott,[18] and Briggs and Hudner.

The superior court was the highest court sitting in the county. A losing party could, of course, appeal to the California Supreme Court. The Supreme Court, however, was far away—and so were the federal courts in San Francisco, whose work barely affected the people of San Benito County.[19] The legislature in Sacramento enacted laws for the state as a whole, and these often profoundly affected San Benito—rules about courts and county government, and rules of land law, divorce, tort, crime and punishment. Closer to home, the board of supervisors provided day-to-day governance of the county. Hollister and San Juan had municipal governments, and there were many local officials—constables, a county clerk, district attorney, assessor, coroner, county treasurer, and superintendent of schools among others. Most of these offices were elective and were hotly contested.[20] In March, 1890, Deputy Sheriff Frank Chamberlain resigned his job to become a bartender;[21] but most political jobs were not full-time, and were valued for the money or prestige they brought in.

The county board had five members and met, on the average, about once a week. William Palmtag, a merchant of Hollister, owner of vineyards, and a pillar of the community, acted as chairman.[22] The board's main functions were administrative. It passed on claims against the county, tax matters, payment of officials. Roads and highways were perhaps the board's biggest concern. The board established roads, let contracts for building and repair, and levied the "road tax," under which able-bodied men could either work a few days a year on county roads or pay a poll tax. In 1890, the road tax was fixed at $2, levied on "each able-bodied man between the ages of 21 and 55."[23] The board also concerned itself with the

---

17. *Id.*, Feb. 7, 1890, at 1, col. 1. A San Francisco firm appeared as counsel for defendant in Sanford v. Fay, Civil No. 651 (Super. Ct., San Benito Cty., Cal., July 17, 1890).

18. In December, 1890, the firm of Montgomery and Scott dissolved, and Scott formed a partnership with M.T. Dooling. Hollister Free Lance, Dec. 26, 1890, at 2, col. 5.

19. Examination of federal court archives for northern California turned up only one federal case in which a litigant came from San Benito County. Southern Pac. R.R. v. Breen, Civil No. 10672 (N.D. Cal. 1890), a quiet-title action involving the Breen who sat as superior court judge in San Benito County. Another land dispute, begun long before 1890, was still in progress in 1890 in the federal courts in San Francisco. Hollister Free Lance, Dec. 19, 1890, at 3, col. 2. Since federal court records do not always show the county of origin of litigants, possibly one or two more federal cases came out of San Benito County in 1890. But it is clear that the federal courts played a small role at best in the legal life of the county.

20. Minutes of the Board of Supervisors, San Benito Cty., vol. 3, Nov. 1890, at 52–60.

21. San Benito Advance, Mar. 28, 1890, at 3, col. 2.

22. On Palmtag, *see generally* J. GUINN, HISTORY OF THE STATE OF CALIFORNIA AND BIOGRAPHICAL RECORD OF SANTA CRUZ, SAN BENITO, MONTEREY AND SAN LUIS OBISPO COUNTIES 584–85 (1903). Palmtag's father, Christian, was an immigrant from Baden, Germany.

23. CAL. POL. CODE § 2652 (Newmark 1889); Minutes of the Board of Supervisors, San Benito Cty., vol. 2, Jan. 7, 1890, at 553; G. NASH, STATE GOVERNMENT AND ECONOMIC DEVELOPMENT 120–23 (1964).

168   LAWRENCE M. FRIEDMAN

state of the courthouse and jail. The board exercised some legislative powers
—for example, it passed, and tinkered with, ordinances "for the destruction
of squirrels and gophers,"[24] which were a constant menace to crops. The
board also handled the rudimentary welfare services of the county. Since
San Benito County was too small for a poor farm, indigents were handled
"out-of-doors," that is, outside any institution. On March 17, 1890, the board
awarded a 1-year contract "for burying the pauper dead" to G. C. Rue, a
carpenter, fixing payment at "$16 per body, including the coffin and all
conveyance and burial"; on April 10, the board granted $40 to a G.A.R.
(Grand Army of the Republic) post for the relief of John W. Spader; on
October 8, Dr. J.H. Tebbetts was granted $30 "for relief of Mrs. Day."
On November 6, the clerk was ordered to "notify all persons on the County
Poor List to appear before the board on Tuesday, December 2, 1890, and
show cause why their several allowances should not be discontinued." For
all that appears, however, no one was dropped from the rolls.[25]

Only fragments survive of the records of the justice courts. These, however, together with newspaper accounts and documents preserved in cases
appealed to superior court, give some idea of these lower courts at work.
The justice courts had, on the whole, a more important part to play in the
legal life of the community than, say, small claims courts do today. Proceedings could be formal; parties were often represented by attorney; and
a jury was occasionally convened.[26]

Most cases in justice court were probably humdrum and routine, but
sometime a colorful incident took place in court or had its echo there. The
Advance recounted these with gusto. Two attorneys in Selma, near Fresno,
got into a dispute and made a bet, each laying a $10 gold piece on the jus-
tice's desk, "for him to act as a stakeholder." The wily judge fined them
$10 each for contempt, and pocketed the money.[27] Closer to home, in Hol-
lister, a "hungry man from Merced" wandered into Cargin's restaurant
and "mildly asserted that he could eat 150 Eastern oysters in twenty minutes." The wager was on, again for $20. He ate the first 50 "with a relish,"
the next 50 "were swallowed reluctantly," and the last 50 "were forced
down." But was the time 20 minutes—or 21? A dispute broke out, and
"the great feat" was bound to be "ventilated in one of the Justice Courts."[28]

---

24. Minutes of the Board of Supervisors, San Benito Cty., vol. 2, May 8, 1889, at 502; *id.*, June 4,
1889, at 506; *id.*, vol. 3, July 6, 1891, at 115.
25. *Id.*, vol. 2, Mar. 17, 1890, at 574; *id.*, Apr. 10, 1890, at 585; *id.*, Oct. 8, 1890, at 634; *id.*,
Dec. 2, 1890, at 52.
26. People v. Scott (J.P. Ct., San Benito Township, Cal., Oct. 22, 1890) (manuscript records
at 72); Hollister Free Lance, Nov. 28, 1890, at 3, col. 1 (recording a dispute between two neighbors
in San Juan; one neighbor charged another with assault: "Two Hollister lawyers are engaged to argue
the matter in the Justice Court").
27. San Benito Advance, Mar. 14, 1890, at 2, col. 3.
28. *Id.*, Feb. 7, 1890, at 3, col. 4. Whether the case ever reached the court is unknown.

The superior court was a more serious place. Its civil volume was not excessively heavy. Thirty-one civil cases were filed during the year, some quite routine. Frances M. Moore and Etta A. Sowle, in separate actions, alleged that their husbands could not support them and applied for the right to conduct a millinery business as "sole traders";[29] these were uncontested, *ex parte* suits. Other cases—not necessarily turning on large sums of money—were bitterly contested, and the court handled them carefully. *Freitas v. Thomas*[30] was a wage claim by a "roustabout," who worked in defendant's hotel. The case began in justice court and went from there to superior court on appeal. Plaintiff won a judgment of $56.50. An intelligent, cautious opinion, six pages of neat longhand, appears in the files under Judge Breen's signature. Essentially, plaintiff's view prevailed.

The superior court also handled probate matters. Eighteen estates were opened during the year, 13 testate and 5 intestate. Clearly only a minority of those who died in the county left estates large enough for probate. In addition, the court handled guardianships of minors and the affairs of incompetents, such as old Abraham Weiser, a veteran of the Mexican War.[31] Insolvency matters also fell within the court's jurisdiction.[32] For example, Douglass Brothers, a firm of merchants, petitioned in November 1889 for a declaration of insolvency. An assignee was appointed and in June 1890 accounts were settled in the Superior Court. Creditors received a dividend of 14⁷⁄₁₀ percent.[33] The court also admitted aliens to citizenship. Naturalization was shared with the federal courts, but few if any residents of Hollister bothered to seek out the federal courts in San Francisco since the matter could be handled close to home. Similarly it was in San Benito superior court that resident aliens, like Isaiah Archibald, a subject of Queen Victoria, and Samuel Stone, a subject of the "Empire of Russia," filed their intentions to become citizens.[34]

Apparently, the superior court tried no more than five or six criminal cases during the year. When a murder case was dismissed in February, the *Advance* remarked that the calendar of the superior court had been "cleared of criminal cases."[35] This, however, gives a wholly misleading view of criminality in San Benito County. The pages of the two weekly newspapers recorded a depressing catalogue of crime and punishment. Some of

29. *In re* Moore, Civil No. 639 (Super. Ct., San Benito Cty., Cal., Mar. 1, 1890); *In re* Sowle, Civil No. 640 (Super. Ct., San Benito Cty., Cal., Mar. 1, 1890). A "sole trader" was not liable for her husband's debts nor he for hers. CAL. CODE CIV. PRO. §§ 1811–21 (Newmark 1889).

30. Civil No. 636 (Super. Ct., San Benito Cty., Cal., Feb. 7, 1890).

31. *In re* Estate of Weiser, Probate No. 189 (Super. Ct., San Benito Cty., Cal., 1890).

32. At the time no federal bankruptcy act was in force. California's insolvency law was ch. 175, [1880] Cal. Stat.

33. *In re* Douglass Bros., Insolvency Proceedings Records, vol 1, at 319 (Super Ct., San Benito Cty., Cal., June 18, 1890).

34. Declarations of Intention, Nos. 299, 300 (San Benito Cty., Cal., 1890).

35. San Benito Advance, June 6, 1890, at 3, col. 3.

this found its way into the records of the superior court; more flowed into
the justice courts; other crimes and criminals escaped detection and judgment. In February, for example, a Chinese cook disappeared from the
farm on which he lived, leaving behind a disordered room and traces of
human blood. Foul play seemed obvious. The Six Companies of San Francisco offered a $200 reward for recovery of the body. Local officials made
"great efforts to clear up the mystery," but the search was abandoned in
March.[36] The papers are full of accounts of vandalism, of mysterious
thefts—horses, bicycles, money. In June, the Marshal and a Constable Mc-
Donald were on the lookout for a "brute" who had recently "committed a
felonious assault" in another place, "and is supposed to be headed this way."
In January burglars broke into a home and "carried off everything but the
stove."[37]

For those arrested, justice was swift. The formalities of due process were
more or less observed. Criminal process was efficient: there was no backlog of cases. California law allowed criminal process to begin with a complaint sworn out before a magistrate.[38] In San Benito County, criminal
cases normally began and ended in the justice court. Serious cases, however, were committed to the county sheriff after preliminary hearing; the
district attorney would then file an information in the superior court.[39]
Indictment by grand jury was never used. The 1889 grand jury, for example, was "not . . . called upon to find any indictments" or inquire "into
any criminal cases"; instead, the jury examined county finances, the state
of county buildings ("the courthouse has materially settled in the center,
causing cracks in the ceiling") and recommended that "[p]atent seats be
placed in the closets in the rear of the building."[40]

After the information was filed, matters proceeded quickly. Most criminal matters were handled in hours and days, more complex cases in perhaps a month or two, never in years. Albert Jeffrey was tried on July 19,
1890, for forging checks. He was an orphan who had been raised by the
Breens, one of the most prominent families in the county. The defendant
came into court without a lawyer; the court appointed an attorney on the
spot. The clerk handed the lawyer a copy of the information and read the
original. The boy pleaded guilty. He was asked "if he had any legal cause
to show why judgment should not be pronounced against him." When he

---

36. Another mysterious disappearance was reported in October 1890. This was a Hollister farmer
who turned out to have gone on a binge. *Id.*, Oct. 17, 1890, at 3, col. 4.
37. *Id.*, June 6, 1890, at 3, col. 3; *id.*, Jan. 10, 1890, at 3, col. 3.
38. CAL. PENAL CODE § 806 (1889 Desty); C. FAIRALL, CRIMINAL LAW AND PROCEDURE OF
CALIFORNIA 283 (1902).
39. CAL. PENAL CODE § 809 (1889 Desty).
40. San Benito Advance, Jan. 3, 1890, at 2, col. 3. The grand jury for 1890 made a similar
report, claiming this time that the courthouse needed a whole new foundation. *Id.*, Dec. 19, 1890,
at 2, col. 4.

replied "that he had none," the judge ordered him sent to San Quentin. All this took less than a day.[41]

Process was swift even for defendants who pleaded not guilty and demanded a jury. On August 21, 1890, the district attorney filed an information charging Ysidro German with robbery. He was arraigned on September 4, 1890, at 10:00 a.m. German appeared with his lawyer. The information was read to him and the case continued until 2:30 p.m. German's attorney moved to set aside the information; the motion was denied. He filed a demurrer, which the court overruled. He then pleaded not guilty. Trial was set for September 16, 1890, at 10:00 a.m. Since it appeared "that there are no jurors in attendance," the court ordered "that a special venire for 25 good and lawful jurors be issued returnable on September 16, 1890, at 10:00 a.m."[42]

On September 16, the clerk wrote the names of the 25 jurors on pieces of paper, put them in a box, and drew out names at random. Two jurors were excused "on account of a physical infirmity" and two more names were drawn. Each side challenged two jurors; more names were drawn, completing the jury. The trial began. Seven witnesses testified for the state and three for the defendant. The case was continued to the next morning. At 10:00 a.m., September 17, arguments were concluded, the court charged the jury, and the jury retired to deliberate. By 4:00 p.m. the jury returned with its verdict: not guilty. It was less than a month since the process began.

In *People v. Jose Sierras*,[43] a man named John Kelley was robbed on November 23, 1890. Certain coins (including a $15 gold piece), tobacco, and other articles of personal property were taken. A day later, one Manuelo Gonzalez accused Sierras and Jose Cebellos, filing a complaint before a justice of the peace. On the next day, the justice issued a warrant. The defendants appeared and after the hearing were bound over to answer charges in superior court. Bail was set and the district attorney filed his information in superior court on December 13. The jury assembled on January 10, 1891, and the trial began on January 12; by January 13, the trial was over, again with a verdict of not guilty. The whole process had run its course less than 2 months from the time the crime was committed.

These cases moved along smoothly, but they do not seem unfair—neither excessively slapdash nor unnecessarily technical. In the last two cases, perhaps by coincidence, a jury of middle-class whites acquitted Mexican defendants. Perhaps jurors took the ideal of openmindedness rather seriously. Moreover, criminal justice was not yet highly professionalized. Scientific

41. People v. Jeffrey, Crim. No. 73 (Super. Ct., San Benito Cty., Cal., July 19, 1890); Minutes and Orders, Super. Ct., San Benito Cty., vol. 3, 1890, at 597–98.
42. People v. German, Crim. No. 43 (Super. Ct., San Benito Cty., Cal., Sept. 17, 1890).
43. Crim. No. 77 (Super. Ct., San Benito Cty., Cal., Jan. 13, 1891).

detection played little role in San Benito. Today the professionals, starting
with the police, screen out most of the obvious cases (guilty or innocent). In
1890, in San Benito, trial by jury played a more important part in "filtering"
out the innocent.

The Court System: Some General Considerations

Courts perform many functions in different societies. They settle disputes, they enforce rules of social control, they check and review actions
of other branches of government; they may also busy themselves with routine administrative matters, registering and storing information (probating
wills, collecting debts) and legitimizing statuses (changing names, granting uncontested divorces). Not *all* courts perform all of these functions,
and the mix of functions is different in different societies. In small face-to-
face societies, for example, dispute settlement is apt to be a very prominent
function. Courts are open and easily accessible; justice is lay justice, swift
and cheap. The courts of tribal societies are perhaps the most striking example. Wise men, elders, or chiefs gather under a tree or in some public
space. People come to them with troubles and disputes; the court resolves
matters in such a way as to restore harmony to the group, using norms
drawn from the general moral sense of the community. Lloyd Fallers has
described one such system in Uganda. Here "litigation is a preeminently
public activity . . . ." It is "popular," the courthouse is always crowded,
and everyone from "gray-haired elders" to "wide-eyed boys" and "nursing
mothers" are in the audience. The onlooker listens intently; since "something like one in every ten adult males is likely to appear in court as a principal . . . every year, the lessons learned . . . will find ready application."[44] But the audience is itself a judge of the case: the public must be
convinced that decisions are wise and just. In this type of court legal and
social rules coincide; no sharp distinction is made between legal and non-
legal norms.

The formal courts of modern societies are at the other end of the scale.
These courts distinguish sharply between legal and nonlegal rules; they
are expensive, slow, and technical. Because of this, it is not easy, by and
large, to approach these courts without professional help. The judges are
specially trained in the logic and doctrine of law; their style of decision
tends to be rather remote from the hopes, feelings, and values of ordinary
citizens. Courts, especially appellate courts, take pains to isolate clear-
cut "issues" of law and fact before deciding a case. They sift these issues in
terms of (legal) rights and wrongs; they do not try to assess the social
background of the dispute or to take it on themselves to restore whatever
social fabric has been ripped by acrimony. Courts like those in Uganda

---

44. L. FALLERS, LAW WITHOUT PRECEDENT 22 (1969).

seem well suited to small communities, where people know each other, respect authority, and more or less agree about the norms that should govern their lives. Life in the modern world, especially in big cities, does not meet these conditions. In any event, society does not seem to place much weight on courts as agencies for patching up disputes of everyday life.

In many regards, the courts of San Benito County fell between the two types. The county had a small population; county judges—certainly justices of the peace in their districts—were bound to know a great deal about the community and to know many constituents personally. No judge in a big city today could possibly have such knowledge. As in tribal courts, justice was swift and cheap and courts were easily accessible. There was one justice court for every 1500 inhabitants. The courts were not overburdened. Court costs were low. We have no information about lawyers' fees, but people sued for such small amounts that one must conclude that cost was not so great a barrier as it is today. On the other hand, San Benito County was emphatically not a "traditional" society. It was raw and new. Hardly anyone had lived in the county very long. It had no "traditions" handed down from generation to generation. Of course, American society had customs, traditions, and norms; most residents shared these. But there was a transient, floating element in San Benito. Community opinion operates best on people who stay put, in stable settings, and who must please their neighbors if they want to get along. Against the deviants of San Benito, public opinion alone would not be enough.

At any given time, the county swarmed with birds of passage. In the eyes of settled citizens, many of the transients were plainly undesirable— vagrants, "tramps,"[45] thieves, fakers, and quick-buck salesmen who traveled about the countryside. San Benito needed the skills, labor, and capital of newcomers; but strangers were strangers, and it was always a question whether they would play a harmful or a beneficial role. In such a community, courts could not behave like courts in small but traditional societies. The leading citizens of San Benito valued the law because it protected them and their property against aggressive attack and because it exerted control over underlings and undesirables. They did not see law as an efficient, ethical tool for resolving disruptive disputes, as an agent of social harmony and peace. Law was an extension of physical and social struggle.[46]

One indicator of the legal culture was the low esteem enjoyed by men

---

45. The newspapers constantly complained about the "tramps." Arrest and prosecution of tramps and vagrants was also a political issue—but largely because of the cost to the county. In 1889, 52 men were imprisoned for vagrancy at a cost to the county of nearly $300. San Benito Advance, Feb. 14, 1890, at 2, col. 2.

46. Compare the account in Cohn, *Some Notes on Law and Change in North India*, in LAW AND WARFARE 139 (P. Bohannan ed. 1967) (manipulative use of litigation in an Indian community following the sudden intrusion of British law).

of the law. Like most states of the union, California elected its judges. Elections were partisan and, as we noted, sharply contested. Judges did not have safe seats in San Benito. Of the two weekly newspapers published in the county, one was strongly Democratic, the other strongly Republican. They regularly heaped insults onto each other. The Democratic *Advance* complained of "sewers of campaign slander" in the Republican *Free Lance*.[47] But the *Advance* was quite slanderous itself, even in the criticism of judges. The *Advance*, writing about a federal judge, recommended that he retire; he was not regarded as "above suspicion."[48] More surprising was a bitter attack on the California Supreme Court—a "rotten institution," which evoked a "fierce wave of disgust and contempt" and which was suspected (said the *Advance*) of "fraud, bribery, and corruption." What touched off this attack was the case of a San Francisco "Mongolian" named Lee Chuck who twice successfully appealed his conviction of murder, at a cost of $20,000: "[I]t would be interesting to know how much, if any of the $20,000 was apportioned to the judges of the Supreme Court. . . . [T]he working majority of [the] Supreme Court is composed of second rate shysters, imbeciles or knaves."[49] Judicial office was, apparently, no different from other political office; it was fair game for any type of partisan attack.[50] The newspapers seemed totally innocent of any notion of the majesty and awesomeness of law. No doubt citizens had ideas about fair trials and fair play and some pride in their legal system; at the same time, they knew it cynically as a powerful weapon of social control, a magnificent instrument for insuring power and wealth.

Dry legal records, no less than the flamboyant stories in the newspapers, make clear that San Benito was two nations: there were those who "belonged," and the others, the outsiders, the undesirables. Naturally, those who belonged controlled the levers of government. A small group of businessmen and lawyers ran the county. William Palmtag, chairman of the board of supervisors, was partner in a liquor and cigar business. His firm acted as agent for various shipping lines,[51] he was also a prominent rancher. He owned 320 acres of land, and his 80 acres of vineyard yielded up to 30,000 gallons of wine each year.[52] Roderick Shaw, the county clerk, was local agent for Wells Fargo and dealt in insurance.[53] Judge Breen and his

---

47. San Benito Advance, Oct. 10, 1890, at 2, col. 1.
48. *Id.*, Jan. 24, 1890, at 2, col. 1.
49. *Id.*, Mar. 21, 1890, at 2, col. 2. The majority of the court was Republican, including Chief Justice W. Beatty. CALIFORNIA BLUE BOOK OR STATE ROSTER 1891, at 106 (1891). The cases are People v. Lee Chuck, 74 Cal. 30, 15 P. 322 (1887), and People v. Lee Chuck, 78 Cal. 317, 20 P. 719 (1889).
50. Federal judges, though appointed, were viewed as no less political, no less subject to partisan abuse.
51. SAN JOSE CITY DIRECTORY, *supra* note 7, at 830.
52. CALIFORNIA AS IT IS 111–12 (5th ed. 1888).
53. SAN JOSE CITY DIRECTORY, *supra* note 7, at 834.

family were prominent landowners. Politics and law were forms of business for these men, ways to advance their own interests. There was, one would guess, little sense of community in San Benito, only a kind of boosterism; men loved not the town so much as the idea of profits and rising land values. Outsiders, drifters, undesirables were a constant source of danger and trouble. Toward the community of outsiders and failures, those who would never be accepted, the tone of the *Advance* is always sardonic and contemptuous: "Two Mongolian highbinders battered each other at the opium joint of Hong Chung Tuesday night."[54] A Chinese cook, it was reported, died when he celebrated Chinese New Year with too much "lightning extract."[55] "Dozing topers around the stoves of town saloons are treated to doses of snuff. The succeeding fits of sneezing are wonderful aids to sobering up."[56]

Underlying the suspicion and contempt was an attitude that the world was raw and risky. Strangers were not to be trusted. When the circus arrived, and the tents went up, within an hour "numerous gambling and robbing games were running full blast." There was a floating class of idle, vicious ne'er-do-wells—so the leading citizens believed. Juan Trujillo, arrested for stealing a horse, was described in the *Advance* as "an impecunious Spaniard who has been leading a vagrant life in the community for some time." Drunkenness was apparently very common; the *Advance* treats it in its characteristic tone of sarcastic disgust, blaming it for all sorts of antisocial manifestations. In September, a drunk caused a fire in a hay pile at the rear of a saloon. In the same month, "some drunken brute" was found lighting matches and fumbling at the door of the sheriff's house; he got away. In November, the election officials in Quien Sabe were drunk and failed to fill out their tally sheets correctly.[57] W. D. Andrews, a veterinary surgeon, was arrested in Gilroy (in Santa Clara County) walking the streets naked at an early hour. At first, people thought he was insane, but "the opinion of the court and the physicians is that he is suffering from the effects of a protracted debauch, and that he will be all right in a few days."[58]

Insanity and despondency were distressingly common. William Patterson, formerly a night watchman in Hollister, died in an insane asylum. Once, "in quelling a bar room row," he was "struck on the head with a beer glass." He became insane from the effects of this blow.[59] The news-

---

54. San Benito Advance, Sept. 12, 1890, at 3, col. 3.
55. *Id.*, Dec. 19, 1890, at 3, col. 3.
56. *Id.*, Jan. 24, 1890, at 3, col. 3.
57. *Id.*, Nov. 7, 1890, at 3, col. 4.
58. *Id.*, July 18, 1890, at 3, col. 4. *See also* Hollister Free Lance, Dec. 5, 1890, at 3, col. 3 (a woodchopper who seemed insane and frightened householders may be "suffering more from an overdose of Hollister whiskey, than from any other cause").
59. San Benito Advance, May 30, 1890, at 3, col. 4.

papers recorded five or six suicides—one man depressed by "business re-
verses," the wife of a prominent citizen brooding over her illness and those
of her mother and brother, another woman unable to face life as a "hopeless invalid."[60] These suicides too suggest a cruelly stratified, naked society,
one which lacked institutions and traditions to sustain those who failed in
life, or in business, or who found their sufferings pointless.[61] This was the
other side of the coin of mobility—the darker half of an open society,
where immigrants could rise to respectability and fortune, and a barren
flat could become a metropolis, almost overnight.

It is striking how law, law and order, court cases, justice, and crime
command space in the 4-page weeklies. Legal process was a game, a weapon, and an entertainment. The anonymous copy editors recorded the seamy
side of life with enormous relish—how, at Panoche, after "a little row,"
Thomas Craycroft "sampled one of George Berg's fingers with his grind-
ers"; the index finger of Berg's left hand was badly mangled, and Craycroft was charged with mayhem.[62] Here one man suffered great pain, and
another faced prison, but to the *Advance* the whole incident is a kind of
joke. It is as if its readers are spectators at a kind of Punch and Judy show.
The better folks, the successful folks, sit and watch; puppets from a different social world carouse, quarrel, and beat each other. They are dragged
off to judgment at the end, while the audience howls and slaps its thighs.

What are we to make of San Benito? Its towns bear, in the first place,
little resemblance to the idyllic, mythic picture of the American small
town: perhaps more culture and variety than one might guess, but also
generous helpings of violence, depravity, and insanity. Society is mobile
but also, at any given moment, highly stratified. Nor does our county fit
very well a more sophisticated idyll painted by David Potter in a provocative essay. Potter tries to explain the success (until recently) of American
government, by arguing that Americans have been "remarkably homogeneous," that the values they shared "were far more important . . . than
the values on which they disagreed," and, most important, that they lived
in small towns which were "strong" and "cohesive communities." These
communities could be cruel toward outsiders and toward deviants, but this
was less important than the strength and solidarity they imparted to institutions, and indeed to social life.[63]

---

60. These episodes appear in *id.,* Mar. 21, 1890, at 2, col. 4; *id.,* May 30, 1890, at 3, col. 4; *id.,*
July 25, 1890, at 3, col. 4; *id.,* Nov. 7, 1890, at 3, col. 2.
    61. *See* M. LESY, *Conclusion* in WISCONSIN DEATH TRIP (1973).
    62. San Benito Advance, Nov. 21, 1890, at 3, col. 3; *id.,* Dec. 19, 1890, at 3, col. 3.
    63. Potter, *Social Cohesion and the Crisis of Law,* in HISTORY AND AMERICAN SOCIETY 390 (D.
Fehrenbacher ed. 1973) (a collection of essays by David M. Potter).

The picture suffers from a certain imprecision. What is "homogeneous"? What is "community"? What is "cohesiveness"? Not that Potter is clearly wrong about San Benito; but neither is he clearly right. The quality of life seems on the whole grimmer and more destructive than he would concede, and the data does not suggest any obvious cohesiveness and strength. But we cannot get inside people's heads, and we cannot compare the results of social arrangements in San Benito with others that were never tried. San Benito was a county at the western edge of the nation, quite new in comparison with small towns in the East, South, and Middle West. It may be atypical, yet similar deviance and madness have been recorded elsewhere. Legal records and newspapers are, of course, biased toward the pathological. But their testimony at least raises questions about the quality of life in the smaller communities and casts doubt on the thesis of "community."

What of the role of *law* in San Benito? First, its sheer importance, relatively speaking, is obvious and striking. Our indicators are crude at best, but they suggest that law, government, and legal process were central to the lives and careers of "insiders." A leading citizen was likely to be active in local government; a lawyer had public as well as private practice. Citizens were more prone to use the courts, for attack or defense, than today. Law was a ubiquitous presence for the "outsider" too—the sheriff and the justices stood over his shoulder, armed with the clubs of the law. Yet the role of the court as moral steward seems far less than in tribal societies or in some socialist systems. One role of the law, much diminished since 1890, was that of entertainer. The crudity and vulgarity of some aspects of life, reflected in justice court dockets and repeated in the press, no doubt amused the better folks in this landlocked community, like the saloons and costume balls, or the French bears and Swiss bellringers passing through town. But this was a by-product only. The main function of the system was to keep order, while allowing the economy to grow. The criminal side was part of this system. It existed not to amuse but to control; not to divert, but to suppress.

Do We Have an Unwritten Constitution?*

Thomas C. Grey†

In reviewing laws for constitutionality, should our judges confine themselves to determining whether those laws conflict with norms derived from
the written Constitution? Or may they also enforce principles of liberty
and justice when the normative content of those principles is not to be found
within the four corners of our founding document? Excluding the question
of the legitimacy of judicial review itself, that is perhaps the most fundamental question we can ask about our fundamental law.

I. The Pure Interpretive Model

For many years this most basic question has not much engaged the explicit attention of constitutional scholars or of the courts or judges themselves, with at least one important exception. That exception was Mr. Justice
Black. Throughout his long and remarkable career on the bench, the most
consistently reiterated theme of his constitutional jurisprudence was the
need for fidelity to the constitutional text in judicial review, and the illegit-
imacy of constitutional doctrines based on sources other than the explicit
commands of the written Constitution.[1]

It now appears that as a final mark of Mr. Justice Black's achievement,
his jurisprudential view of constitutional adjudication may be returning to
favor. In the last few years, distinguished commentators on constitutional
law have begun to echo Mr. Justice Black's central theme, criticizing constitutional developments in terms that have scarcely been heard in the scholarly community for a generation.

The criticism has centered around the new "fundamental interest"
branch of equal protection doctrine, and the emerging libertarian right of
privacy in familial and sexual matters. The strand of criticism that I wish
to focus on here has not alleged the impolicy of the new doctrines, or their
lack of internal coherence or principled articulation—those are the familiar
themes of contemporary constitutional commentary. Rather it has urged
that because the new developments rest on principles not derived by normal

* I would like to thank Professors John Ely and Hans Linde for their thoughtful comments on
an earlier draft of this Essay.
† A.B. 1963, Stanford University; LL.B. 1968, Yale University. Associate Professor of Law, Stanford University.
1. *See, e.g., In re* Winship, 397 U.S. 358, 377 (1970) (Black, J., dissenting); Griswold v. Connecticut, 381 U.S. 479, 507 (1965) (Black, J., dissenting); Rochin v. California, 342 U.S. 165, 174
(1952) (Black, J., concurring); Adamson v. California, 332 U.S. 46, 68 (1947) (Black, J., dissenting).

processes of textual interpretation from the written Constitution, they represent a wholly illegitimate mode of judicial review.

This is the strand of criticism that sounds in the jurisprudence of Mr. Justice Black. It has been put most forcefully by Solicitor General (then Professor) Bork:

> [T]he choice of "fundamental values" by the Court cannot be justified. Where constitutional materials do not clearly specify the value to be preferred, there is no principled way to prefer any claimed human value to any other. The judge must stick close to the text and the history, and their fair implications, and not construct new rights.[2]

Mr. Bork calls this the requirement of "neutral derivation" of constitutional principle, and makes clear that he regards it as additional to the requirement of "neutral application" of principle so much debated in the 1950's and 1960's.[3]

In a thoughtful and stimulating review and extension of that familiar "neutral principles" debate, Professor Hans Linde has likewise urged a return to the commands of the constitutional text as the sole legitimating source for judicial review:

> The judicial responsibility begins and ends with determining the present scope and meaning of a decision that the nation, at an earlier time, articulated and enacted into constitutional text . . . .[4]

The last example of this recent trend that I will cite—though not the last I could cite—is Professor John Ely's powerful assault on the Supreme Court's recent decision in the Abortion Cases.[5] Professor Ely charges that in those decisions, based on a right of "privacy" drawn by no imaginable arts of construction or interpretation from the constitutional text, the Court has violated its "obligation to trace its premises to the charter from which it derives its authority." He goes on:

> A neutral and durable principle may be a thing of beauty and a joy forever. But if it lacks connection with any value the Constitution marks as special, it is not a constitutional principle and the Court has no business imposing it.[6]

Professor Ely takes care to characterize the Bork and Linde articles as "espousing the general view of constitutional adjudication espoused here."[7]

---

2. Bork, *Neutral Principles and Some First Amendment Problems*, 47 IND. L.J. 1, 8 (1971).
3. *Id.* at 7.
4. Linde, *Judges, Critics, and the Realist Tradition*, 82 YALE L.J. 227, 254 (1972). Professor Linde has urged the same viewpoint with respect to the application of state constitutional provisions. Linde, *Without "Due Process": Unconstitutional Law in Oregon*, 49 ORE. L. REV. 125 (1970).
5. Roe v. Wade, 410 U.S. 113 (1973); Doe v. Bolton, 410 U.S. 179 (1973).
6. Ely, *The Wages of Crying Wolf: A Comment on* Roe v. Wade, 82 YALE L.J. 920, 949 (1973) (footnote omitted).
7. *Id.* at 949 n.147. Professor Ely disagrees, however, with many of Mr. Bork's criticisms of the Warren Court.
For other recent constitutional commentary in which the Bork-Ely-Linde view is expressed or

I do not think that the view of constitutional adjudication outlined by these commentators is sufficiently broad to capture the full scope of legitimate judicial review. It seems to me that the courts do appropriately apply values not articulated in the constitutional text, and appropriately apply them in determining the constitutionality of legislation.

This view, it seems to me, tacitly underlies much of the affirmative constitutional doctrine developed by the courts over the last generation. The trouble is that the view has been too tacit. It has not been clearly stated and articulately defended, as basic constitutional doctrine should be. Nor, for that matter, has the opposing general view received adequate theoretical statement and defense—except by Mr. Justice Black. Unfortunately, the professional world concerned with constitutional law has not taken Mr. Justice Black's theoretical position sufficiently seriously. Perhaps there was too much of a tendency to accept at face value the great Justice's pose as a rather old-fashioned and simple-minded country lawyer, with sound intuition and a good nose for the concrete issues, but lacking any claim to jurisprudential sophistication.

If the articles by Messrs. Bork, Linde, and Ely mark the emergence of an important trend—as I suspect they do—this basic theoretical issue will no longer be swept under the rug. These critics simply cannot be dismissed as unsophisticates or out-of-date legal primitives.

The truth is that the view of constitutional adjudication that they share with Mr. Justice Black is one of great power and compelling simplicity. That view is deeply rooted in our history and in our shared principles of political legitimacy. It has equally deep roots in our formal constitutional law; it is, after all, the theory upon which judicial review was founded in *Marbury v. Madison.*[8]

The chief virtue of this view is that it supports judicial review while answering the charge that the practice is undemocratic. Under the pure interpretive model (as I shall henceforth call the view in question), when a court strikes down a popular statute or practice as unconstitutional, it may always reply to the resulting public outcry: "We didn't do it—you did." The people have chosen the principle that the statute or practice violated, have designated it as fundamental, and have written it down in the text of the Constitution for the judges to interpret and apply. The task of interpretation of the people's commands may not always be simple or mechanical; there is no warrant to condemn Mr. Justice Black or his allies with the

---

implied, *see* Epstein, *Substantive Due Process by Any Other Name: The Abortion Cases,* 1973 SUP. CT. REV. 159; Winter, *Poverty, Economic Equality, and the Equal Protection Clause,* 1972 SUP. CT. REV. 41.

8. 5 U.S. (1 Cranch) 137 (1803).

epithet "mechanical jurisprudence." But the task remains basically one of interpretation, the application of fixed and binding norms to new facts.[9]

II. BEYOND INTERPRETATION

The contrary view of judicial review, the one that I espouse and that seems to me implicit in much of the constitutional law developed by the courts, does not deny that the Constitution is a written document, expressing some clear and positive restraints upon governmental power. Nor does it deny that part of the business of judicial review consists of giving effect to these explicit commands.

Where the broader view of judicial review diverges from the pure interpretive model is in its acceptance of the courts' additional role as the expounder of basic national ideals of individual liberty and fair treatment, even when the content of these ideals is not expressed as a matter of positive law in the written Constitution. It must at once be conceded that such a role for our courts is more difficult to justify than is the role assigned by the pure interpretive model. Why, one asks, are the courts better able to discern and articulate basic national ideals than are the people's politically responsible representatives? And one recalls Learned Hand's remark that he would find it "most irksome to be ruled by a bevy of Platonic Guardians, even if I knew how to choose them, which I assuredly do not."[10]

These grave difficulties no doubt explain, although they do not excuse, the tendency of our courts—today as throughout our history—to resort to bad legislative history and strained reading of constitutional language to support results that would be better justified by explication of contemporary moral and political ideals not drawn from the constitutional text. Of course, this tendency of the courts in no way helps to establish the legitimacy of noninterpretive judicial review. Indeed, standing alone it tends to establish the opposite; for if judges resort to bad interpretation in preference to honest exposition of deeply held but unwritten ideals, it must be because they perceive the latter mode of decisionmaking to be of suspect legitimacy.

However, the tendency to slipshod history and text-parsing does not

---

9. The pure interpretive model should not be confused with *literalism* in constitutional interpretation, particularly with "narrow" or "crabbed" literalism. The interpretive model, at least in the hands of its sophisticated exponents, certainly contemplates that the courts may look through the sometimes opaque text to the purposes behind it in determining constitutional norms. Normative inferences may be drawn from silences and omissions, from structures and relationships, as well as from explicit commands. Thus I do not see the sort of constitutional reasoning described by Professor Charles Black in his STRUCTURE AND RELATIONSHIP IN CONSTITUTIONAL LAW (1969) as necessarily going beyond the interpretive model.

What distinguishes the exponent of the pure interpretive model is his insistence that the only norms used in constitutional adjudication must be those inferable from the text—that the Constitution must not be seen as licensing courts to articulate and apply contemporary norms not demonstrably expressed or implied by the framers.

10. L. HAND, THE BILL OF RIGHTS 73 (1958).

stand alone. The courts do not only effectuate unwritten ideals and values covertly. Rather, in a very large proportion of their important constitutional decisions, they proceed in a mode that is openly noninterpretive. If this assertion seems at first glance surprising, it may be so partly because of the way in which constitutional law is taught in our law schools.

In the academic teaching of constitutional law, the general question of the legitimacy of judicial review is addressed largely through the vehicle of *Marbury v. Madison*. Students examine the arguments made for judicial review by Chief Justice Marshall, and perhaps contrast them with some of the counterarguments of later judges or commentators. The discussion concludes with the point that, whatever the validity of those arguments as an original matter, history has firmly decided in favor of judicial review. Thereafter, debates about judicial review focus on the question of how "activist" or how "deferential" *it* should be. *It* is always assumed to be the single unitary practice established and justified in *Marbury*.

This seems to me a seriously misleading way of proceeding. *Marbury* defends (and its detractors attack) what I have here called the pure interpretive model of judicial review. The case itself involves the close interpretation of a technical and explicit constitutional provision, which is found, upon conventional linguistic analysis, to conflict with a statute. The argument for judicial review as a general matter is made in terms appropriate to that sort of case. Chief Justice Marshall's stress is on the *writtenness* of the Constitution, and on its supremacy in cases of clear conflict with ordinary law.[11] His heuristic examples all involve obvious conflicts between hypothetical (and unlikely) statutes on the one hand, and particularly explicit constitutional commands on the other.[12]

All this makes *Marbury* a most atypical constitutional case, and an inappropriate paradigm for the sort of judicial review that has been important and controversial throughout our history, from *Dred Scott*[13] to the *Legal Tender Cases*[14] to *Lochner*[15] to *Carter Coal*[16] and on to *Brown v. Board of Education*,[17] *Baker v. Carr*,[18] and the Death Penalty[19] and Abortion[20] cases in our own day. In the important cases, reference to and analysis

---

11. 5 U.S. (1 Cranch) 137, 176–78 (1803). Although the argument proceeds in terms of instances of purely interpretive judicial review, the underlying principle—that the courts must give precedence to constitutional law over ordinary law—is not itself found in or easily inferred from the text. Nevertheless, the argument for that principle still seems to be in the interpretive mode, based as it is on the intentions inferable from the framers' adoption of a written constitution.

12. For example, Marshall asks rhetorically whether the courts should enforce a statute generally imposing a duty on exports from a state, or an avowed bill of attainder or ex post facto law. *Id.* at 179.

13. Dred Scott v. Sanford, 60 U.S. (19 How.) 393 (1857).

14. 79 U.S. (12 Wall.) 457 (1871).

15. Lochner v. New York, 198 U.S. 45 (1905).

16. Carter v. Carter Coal Co., 298 U.S. 238 (1936).

17. 347 U.S. 483 (1954).

18. 369 U.S. 186 (1962).

19. Furman v. Georgia, 408 U.S. 238 (1972).

20. Roe v. Wade, 410 U.S. 113 (1973); Doe v. Bolton, 410 U.S. 179 (1973).

of the constitutional text plays a minor role. The dominant norms of decision are those large conceptions of governmental structure and individual
rights that are at best referred to, and whose content is scarcely at all specified, in the written Constitution—dual federalism, vested rights, fair procedure, equality before the law.

The question of the legitimacy of this very different sort of judicial review is scarcely addressed, much less concluded, by the arguments of *Marbury v. Madison*. To approach that question, we might better examine the
debate between Justices Chase and Iredell in *Calder v. Bull*.[21] And if exposure to the matchless rhetoric of John Marshall is desired, *Fletcher v. Peck*[22]
provides an excellent example. In that case, the Georgia statute is struck
down on two alternative grounds. The first is a strained interpretation
of the contract clause, comparable in flimsiness to some of the poorer interpretive efforts of the Warren Court. The second ground is expressed in the
Court's conclusion that the statute violates "general principles which are
common to our free institutions"—in particular, the principle of the in-
violability of vested rights.[23] Conspicuously absent is a dissent arguing
that this principle is nowhere stated in the constitutional text. Indeed, the
other opinion in the case—that of Justice Johnson—expresses agreement
with the result on the ground of "general principles," but disavows the
strained reading of the contract clause.[24]

The parallel between *Fletcher* and most contemporary judicial review
is striking. Today, the Court will formally invoke one of the majestic
generalities of the Constitution, typically the due process or equal protection clause, as the textual basis for its decision. Even this much specificity
is not always vouchsafed us. Thus we are told of the constitutional "right
to travel" that the Court has "no occasion to ascribe the source of this right
to . . . a particular constitutional provision."[25] And in the Abortion Cases,
the Court's reference to the textual cover for the "right of privacy" is strikingly casual:

---

21. 3 U.S. (3 Dall.) 386 (1798). Chase: "I cannot subscribe to the omnipotence of a state legislature, or that it is absolute and without control, although its authority should not be expressly restrained by the constitution, or fundamental law of the State. . . . There are certain vital principles
in our free republican governments, which will determine and overrule our apparent and flagrant
abuse of legislative power . . . ." *Id.* at 387–88 (majority opinion).

Iredell: "It is true, that some speculative jurists have held, that a legislative act against natural
justice must, in itself, be void; but I cannot think, that under such a government, any court of
justice would possess a power to declare it so. . . .

"[T]he ideas of natural justice are regulated by no fixed standard; the ablest and the purest
men have differed upon the subject; and all that the court could properly say, in such an event,
would be, that the legislature, possessed of an equal right of opinion, had passed an act which, in
the opinion of the judges, was inconsistent with the abstract principles of natural justice." *Id.* at
398–99 (concurring opinion).

22. 10 U.S. (6 Cranch) 87 (1810).

23. *Id.* at 139.

24. *Id.* at 143 (concurring in part).

25. Shapiro v. Thompson, 394 U.S. 618, 630 (1969) (footnote omitted).

> This right of privacy, whether it be founded in the Fourteenth Amendment's concept of personal liberty and restrictions upon state action, as we feel it is, or, as the District Court determined, in the Ninth Amendment's reservation of rights to the people, is broad enough to encompass a woman's decision whether or not to terminate her pregnancy.[26]

It should be clear that in these cases the Court is quite openly *not* relying on constitutional text for the content of the substantive principles it is invoking to invalidate legislation. The parallel reliance on the ninth amendment and the due process clause in the Abortion Cases is instructive on the point. The ninth amendment on its face has no substantive content.[27] It is rather a license to constitutional decisionmakers to look beyond the substantive commands of the constitutional text to protect fundamental rights not expressed therein. In this case at least, the due process clause is being used in the same way.

Much of our substantive constitutional doctrine is of this kind. Where it arises "under" some piece of constitutional text, the text is not invoked as the source of the values or principles that rule the cases. Rather the broad textual provisions are seen as sources of legitimacy for judicial development and explication of basic shared national values. These values may be seen as permanent and universal features of human social arrangements—natural law principles—as they typically were in the 18th and 19th centuries. Or they may be seen as relative to our particular civilization, and subject to growth and change, as they typically are today. Our characteristic contemporary metaphor is "the living Constitution"—a constitution with provisions suggesting restraints on government in the name of basic rights, yet sufficiently unspecific to permit the judiciary to elucidate the development and change in the content of those rights over time.

This view of constitutional adjudication is at war with the pure interpretive model. As Mr. Justice Black said often and forcefully enough, he had no truck with the notion of changing, flexible, "living" constitutional guarantees.[28] The amendment process was the framers' chosen and exclusive method of adopting constitutional values to changing times; the judiciary was to enforce the Constitution's substantive commands as the framers meant them.

This is not to say that the interpretive model is incompatible with one

---

26. Roe v. Wade, 410 U.S. 113, 153 (1973). Students of the aesthetics of pseudo-interpretation may debate whether or not this formulation is preferable to the Court's celebrated shuffle in Griswold v. Connecticut, 381 U.S. 479 (1965), through the "emanations" and "penumbras" of the Bill of Rights.

27. "The enumeration in the Constitution, of certain rights, shall not be construed to deny or disparage others retained by the people." The uses and limits of the ninth amendment as a "source" of constitutional rights are analyzed by Mr. Justice Goldberg in Griswold v. Connecticut, 381 U.S. at 486 (concurring opinion).

28. *See, e.g.,* Harper v. Virginia Bd. of Elections, 383 U.S. 663, 670 (1966) (Black, J., dissenting).

limited sense of the concept of a "living" constitution. The model can contemplate the application of the framers' value judgments and institutional
arrangements to new or changed *factual* circumstances.[29] In that sense, its
proponents can endorse Chief Justice Marshall's view of the Constitution
as "intended to endure for ages to come, and consequently, to be adapted
to the various crises of human affairs."[30]

But the interpretive model cannot be reconciled with constitutional doctrines protecting unspecified "essential" or "fundamental" liberties, or "fair
procedure," or "decency"—leaving it to the judiciary to give moral content
to those conceptions either once and for all or from age to age. That sort
of "interpretation" would drain from the interpretive model its animating
strength. Once it was adopted, the courts could no longer honestly defend
an unpopular decision to a protesting public with the transfer of responsibility: "We didn't do it—you did." No longer would the Court's constitutional role be the technical and professional one of applying *given* norms
to changing facts; instead the Court would assume the large and problematic role of discerning a society's most basic contemporary values.

III. The Implications of the Pure Interpretive Model

Let me now give some examples, confined to the area of individual
rights, of the numerous and important substantive constitutional doctrines
which seem to me unjustified under a consistently applied pure interpretive
model of judicial review. First and most obvious is virtually the entire body
of doctrine developed under the due process clauses of the 5th and 14th
amendments. If those clauses can be seen as having any specific normative
content attributable to their framers, it is probably only that given to them
by Mr. Justice Black.[31] In his view, due process requires only that depriva-
tions of life, liberty or property be authorized by law duly enacted, rather
than carried out by arbitrary executive action. A slightly more ambitious,
though highly implausible, narrow interpretation is that adopted by the

---

29. Presumably it is in this sense that Professor Linde can describe judicial review as "a task of
construing the *living* meaning of *past* political decisions" without any sense of internal inconsistency.
He notes that some constitutional provisions "obviously contemplate changing applications in step
with economic and technological developments, or with changes in the relation of the individual to
social agencies." Linde, *Judges, Critics, and the Realist Tradition, supra* note 4, at 254–55 (emphasis
added).

Similarly, Professor Ely argues: "Surely the Court is entitled, indeed I think it is obligated, to seek
out the sorts of evils the framers meant to combat and to move against their fundamental twentieth century counterparts." Ely, *supra* note 6, at 929 (footnote omitted).

30. McCulloch v. Maryland, 17 U.S. (4 Wheat.) 415, 427 (1819).

31. *See In re* Winship, 397 U.S. 358, 377–85 (1970) (dissenting opinion). As Mr. Justice Black
notes in that opinion, his separate position that the 14th amendment incorporates the Bill of Rights
is not based on construction of the due process clause alone, but on "the language of the entire first
section of the Fourteenth Amendment, as illuminated by the legislative history surrounding its
adoption." *Id.* at 382 n.11.

pre-Civil War Supreme Court—that the clause prohibits departures from the settled course of procedure familiar in the English courts in 1791.[32]

On the interpretive model, then, all the rest of due process doctrine must go. First, what many regard as the core of due process doctrine—its flexible requirement of "fundamentally fair" procedures in criminal and civil proceedings—cannot be reconciled with the interpretive model. These doctrines are developments of the "living constitution" concept *par excellence.*[33] In addition, everything that has been labeled "substantive due process" would be eliminated. It is these doctrines on which the proponents of the interpretive model have most often focused their attacks. Much of the force behind their position derives from the deeply felt opposition to the constitutionalization of laissez-faire economics epitomized by *Lochner v. New York,*[34] and they typically unite in opposition to contemporary doctrinal developments that remind them too much of *Lochner.*[35]

A striking point often overlooked by contemporary interpretivists is that the demise of substantive due process must constitutionally free the federal government to engage in explicit racial discrimination. There is no textual warrant for reading into the due process clause of the fifth amendment any of the prohibitions directed against the states by the equal protection clause.[36]

Equally strikingly, the application of the provisions of the Bill of Rights to states cannot be justified under an interpretive model—unless one strains to accept, as the Court clearly has declined to do, the flimsy historical ev-

---

32. Murray's Lessee v. Hoboken Land & Improvement Co., 59 U.S. (18 How.) 272, 277 (1856).
33. *See, e.g., In re* Winship, 397 U.S. 358, 377 (1970) (Black, J., dissenting); Goldberg v. Kelly, 397 U.S. 254 (1970) (Black, J., dissenting).
34. 198 U.S. 45 (1905).
35. It now seems that the ultimate punchline in the criticism of a constitutional decision is to say that it is "like *Lochner*." Professor Ely has even minted a generic term, "to *Lochner*," to describe whatever-it-was-so-awful-the-Court-did-in-*Lochner*. Ely, *supra* note 6, at 944. *Cf.* Winter, *supra* note 7, at 102: "Make no mistake about it, *Lochner v. New York* is alive and well in *Shapiro v. Thompson.*"
    Lochner is only one of thousands of decisions in the history of the Court that invoke a noninterpretive mode of constitutional adjudication; if it was a bad decision, as I think it was, it by no means follows that the general mode of adjudication it represents is illegitimate. There are many bad decisions in the mode of pure interpretation.
    It is an often overlooked point that Mr. Justice Holmes in his classic *Lochner* dissent did not use the case as an occasion to reject noninterpretive adjudication generally, or even substantive due process as such; quite the contrary: "I think that the word liberty in the Fourteenth Amendment is perverted when it is held to prevent the natural outcome of a dominant opinion, *unless it can be said that a rational and fair man necessarily would admit that the statute proposed would infringe fundamental principles as they have been understood by the traditions of our people and our law.*" 198 U.S. at 76 (emphasis added).
36. *See* Bolling v. Sharpe, 347 U.S. 497, 499 (1954). Since *Bolling,* the Court has often applied equal protection doctrine to the federal government "under" the fifth amendment due process clause. *See, e.g.,* Shapiro v. Thompson, 394 U.S. 618 (1969), in which the Court invalidated a District of Columbia statute as a violation of due process, while relying upon the equal protection clause to invalidate similar state statutes. Since *Bolling*—at least as far as I have been able to discover—the Court has never even seriously discussed the possibility that the fifth amendment due process clause might not fully incorporate the requirements progressively imposed on the states under the equal protection clause.

idence that the framers of the 14th amendment intended this result.[37] Freedom of speech, freedom of religion, and the requirement of just compensation in the taking of property, as well as the procedural provisions of the
fourth, fifth, sixth, and eighth amendments must then no longer be seen as
federal constitutional restraints on state power.

All of the "fundamental interests" that trigger "strict scrutiny" under
the equal protection clause would have to be discarded, if the interpretive
model were to control constitutional adjudication. Most obviously, the large
body of doctrine that has grown up around the interests in the franchise
and in participation in the electoral process could not stand. If the values
implicit in the equal protection clause are limited only to those that its
framers intended at the time of enactment, the clause clearly does not speak
to questions of eligibility for the franchise or of legislative apportionment.[38]

Thus far, it seems to me there is little room for disagreement that the
premises of the pure interpretive model would require the conclusions I
have drawn from it. For those who have not yet had enough, and coming
to slightly more doubtful matters, there is serious question how much of
the law prohibiting state racial discrimination can survive honest application of the interpretive model. It is clear that the equal protection clause
was meant to prohibit *some* forms of state racial discrimination, most obviously those enacted in the Black Codes. It is equally clear from the legislative history that the clause was *not* intended to guarantee equal political
rights, such as the right to vote or to run for office, and perhaps including
the right to serve on juries.[39]

It is at least doubtful whether the clause can fairly be read as intending
to bar any form of state-imposed racial segregation, so long as equal facilities are made available. Professor Bickel's careful study of the legislative
history revealed little evidence of intent to prohibit segregation, which at
the time was widespread in the North.[40] Professor Bickel did conclude that
the original understanding of the amendment was consistent with the decision in the School Segregation Cases, but only in the sense that the general language of the clause *licensed* the courts (and Congress) to enforce

---

37. The Court's refusal to adopt the "incorporation" theory is clear both from its refusal to apply
the requirements of grand jury indictment and civil jury trial to the states, and from its statements in
"selective incorporation" cases. *See, e.g.*, Duncan v. Louisiana, 391 U.S. 145, 149 (1968), which held
that due process required the states to provide jury trial in serious criminal cases *because* "trial by
jury in criminal cases is fundamental to the American scheme of justice . . . ." For the controversy
over the intent of the framers, *compare* Fairman, *Does the Fourteenth Amendment Incorporate the
Bill of Rights?*, 2 STAN. L. REV. 5 (1949), *with* Adamson v. California, 332 U.S. 46, 68 (1947) (Black,
J., dissenting).

38. The numerous dissenting opinions of Mr. Justice Harlan in voting and reapportionment
cases put the point beyond doubt. *See, e.g.*, Carrington v. Rash, 380 U.S. 89, 97 (1965) (Harlan, J.,
dissenting); Reynolds v. Sims, 377 U.S. 533, 589 (1964) (Harlan, J., dissenting).

39. *See generally* Bickel, *The Original Understanding and the Segregation Decision*, 69 HARV. L.
REV. 1 (1955).

40. *Id.* at 58.

evolving ideals of racial justice.[41] Yet this is a classic invocation of the notion of the "living constitution," and as such is not permitted by the interpretive model.

Finally, under the interpretive model, modern applications of the provisions of the Bill of Rights based on their capacity to grow or develop with changing social values would have to be discarded. Prominent among the discarded doctrines would be the prevailing view that the eighth amendment's prohibition of cruel and unusual punishments must be "interpreted" in light of society's "evolving standards of decency."[42] It is doubtful that much of modern first amendment doctrine could be defended on the basis of value choices attributable to the framers,[43] and similar doubts must cast a shadow on some of the law of the fourth amendment.[44] The doctrine that the sixth amendment guarantees appointed counsel for indigent defendants[45] is likewise in serious jeopardy, if historically intended meaning must be the only legitimate guide in constitutional adjudication.[46]

While one might disagree with this rough catalogue on points of detail, it should be clear that an extraordinarily radical purge of established constitutional doctrine would be required if we candidly and consistently applied the pure interpretive model. Surely that makes out at least a prima facie practical case against the model. Conservatives ought to be cautious about adopting any abstract premise which requires so drastic a change in accepted practice, and liberals presumably will be dismayed by the prospect

---

41. *Id.* at 62–65.
42. *See, e.g.,* Trop v. Dulles, 356 U.S. 86, 101 (1958).
43. *See generally* L. LEVY, LEGACY OF SUPPRESSION (1960).
44. *See, e.g.,* Katz v. United States, 389 U.S. 347 (1967), in which the Court extended fourth amendment coverage to the recording of oral statements by electronic devices. Justice Black filed a lone dissent arguing—from an interpretive stance—"[s]ince I see no way in which the words of the Fourth Amendment can be construed to apply to eavesdropping, that closes the matter for me. . . . I will not distort the words of the Amendment in order to 'keep the Constitution up to date' or 'to bring it into harmony with the times.'" *Id.* at 373 (dissenting opinion).
45. Johnson v. Zerbst, 304 U.S. 458 (1938).
46. The instances of noninterpretive judicial review I have mentioned fall into three general groups. First are those instances where the courts have created (or found) independent constitutional rights with almost no textual guidance. Examples are the contemporary right of privacy, and the older liberty of contract. Second are those instances where the courts have given general application to norms that the constitutional text explicitly applies in a more limited way. Examples are the application of equal protection and contract clause principles to the federal government, and the application of the Bill of Rights to the states—"under" the conveniently all-embracing due process clauses. The third type is the extension or broadening of principles stated in the Constitution beyond the normative content intended for them by the framers. Examples are the School Segregation Cases, and the extension of the fourth amendment to cover eavesdropping.
Most of the ire of proponents of the pure interpretive model has been directed against the first of these types of noninterpretive review. However the other two types are equally illegitimate, given the logic of the interpretive model. The advantage of placing a controverted case in the third rather than the first grouping is that it is usually possible to argue, with at least a shadow of plausibility, that extension of a specific constitutional prohibition really involves only the application of old norms to changed facts, and not a change in the norms themselves. *See, e.g.,* the majority opinion in Griswold v. Connecticut, 381 U.S. 479 (1965), for an implausible attempt to base a nontextual right of marital privacy on an "interpretation" of various provisions of the Bill of Rights—thus converting a Type 1 case into a "less suspect" Type 3 case.

of any major diminution in the courts' authority to protect basic human rights.

IV. Beyond Interpretation: A Program of Inquiry

The uncomfortable results of adopting the interpretive model do not by themselves make a wholly satisfying argument for judicial review that goes beyond interpretation. Constitutional adjudication going beyond the norms implicit in text and original history requires its own affirmative justification. In this short Essay, I can only suggest the several levels on which this inquiry might proceed, and hint at some of the directions it might take.

A. *The Question of Practical Wisdom*

First, one must consider the question of the wisdom and prudence of putting—or more accurately *leaving*—in the hands of judges the considerable power to define and enforce fundamental human rights without substantial guidance from constitutional text and history. How one views this question depends largely on how one evaluates the practical results, over the long run, of the exercise of this power. Arguments about institutional competence and the general propensities of judges become relevant here. Familiar in this context is the argument made in varying forms by constitutional commentators from Alexander Hamilton to Alexander Bickel that it makes some sense to give the final—or nearly final—say over the barrier between state and individual to the "least dangerous branch," the one that possesses neither purse nor sword.[47] But much can be said the other way, particularly through assignment in the name of popular sovereignty, and through allusion to *Lochner* and its ilk.

B. *The Jurisprudential Question*

Second, one can ask the jurisprudential question whether as a general matter the defining and enforcing of basic rights without external textual guidance is essentially a judicial task. Judges may be fine folk, but if what they are doing when they engage in judicial review on the basis of changing and unwritten moral principles is not adjudication, then they are sailing under false colors. For they have consistently told us that judicial review is genuinely incident to their traditionally assigned task of deciding litigated cases according to law.

A rigorously positivist jurisprudence would hold that judicial decision not directed by the articulate command of a determinate external sovereign is not truly adjudication. Rather it is a species of legislation. But this sort

---

47. *See* The Federalist No. 78, at 504–05 (E. Earle ed.) (A. Hamilton); A. Bickel, The Least Dangerous Branch 23–28 (1962).

of positivist also views the entirely traditional judicial task of common law development through case-by-case decision as a form of legislation.[48] If common law development is an appropriate judicial function, falling within the traditionally accepted judicial role, is not the functionally similar case-by-case development of constitutional norms appropriate as well? Granted that the supremacy of constitutional law over legislation, when contrasted with the formally inferior status of common law, makes a great difference. But the difference is in the hierarchical status of the judicial decision—which turns on a question of *authority*—and not in the intrinsic nature of the task.

C. *The Question of Lawful Authority*

The question of authority is the third level of inquiry into the justification for noninterpretive judicial review. Even if this mode of judicial review produces good results in the eyes of some beholders, and even if it is not intrinsically unjudicial, there remains the question whether in our Constitution we have actually granted this large power to our judges.

In resolving this issue of legal authority, there seems to me only one plausible method of inquiry. We must apply the conventional and accepted categories of legal argument—original understanding, judicial precedent, subsequent history, and internal consistency—and see if they support judicial review that goes beyond interpretation.

I believe that when these tests are applied, constitutional adjudication of the sort objected to by Mr. Justice Black and the other proponents of the pure interpretive model will be seen to be a lawful and legitimate feature of our system of judicial review. Full development of the argument must await another occasion; it necessarily requires lengthy and detailed historical documentation. But a brief sketch may be useful here.[49]

For the generation that framed the Constitution, the concept of a "higher law," protecting "natural rights," and taking precedence over ordinary positive law as a matter of political obligation, was widely shared and deeply felt. An essential element of American constitutionalism was the reduction to written form—and hence to positive law—of some of the principles of

---

48. I do not endorse this positivist analysis. It seems to me that traditional common law decision and constitutional decision according to the noninterpretive mode both can be seen as decision of cases according to law. The law in question consists of the generally accepted social norms applied in the decision of the cases, norms that are—contrary to the positivists' position—best seen as "part of the law," quite independent of their promulgation through defined lawmaking procedures. *See* Dworkin, *The Model of Rules,* 35 U. CHI. L. REV. 14 (1967); Wellington, *Common Law Rules and Constitutional Double Standards: Some Notes on Adjudication,* 83 YALE L.J. 221 (1973).

49. I have set out my sketch as a simple narrative, lacking the detail, the qualifications, and the analysis of conflicting evidence that the full argument requires. I have also left out any documentation, on the theory that incomplete and necessarily misleading citation of sources is worse than none at all. The full-scale development of the historical argument sketched here awaits the completion of a forthcoming article.

natural rights. But at the same time, it was generally recognized that writ-ten constitutions could not completely codify the higher law. Thus in the framing of the original American constitutions it was widely accepted that there remained unwritten but still binding principles of higher law. The ninth amendment is the textual expression of this idea in the federal Con-stitution.

As it came to be accepted that the judiciary had the power to enforce the commands of the written Constitution when these conflicted with or-dinary law, it was also widely assumed that judges would enforce as con-stitutional restraints the unwritten natural rights as well. The practice of the Marshall Court and of many of its contemporary state courts, and the writings of the leading constitutional commentators through the first gen-eration of our national life, confirm this understanding.

A parallel development during the first half of the 19th century was the frequent attachment of unwritten constitutional principles to the vaguer and more general clauses of the state and federal constitutions. Natural-rights reasoning in constitutional adjudication persisted up to the Civil War, particularly with respect to property and contract rights, and increasingly involving "due process" and "law of the land" clauses in constitutional texts. At the same time, an important wing of the antislavery movement developed a natural-rights constitutional theory, built around the concepts of due process, of national citizenship and its rights, and of the human equality proclaimed in the Declaration of Independence.

Though this latter movement had little direct effect on pre-Civil War judicial decisions, it was the formative theory underlying the due process, equal protection, and privileges and immunities clauses of the 14th amend-ment. Section 1 of the 14th amendment is thus properly seen as a reaffirma-tion and reenactment in positive law of the principle that fundamental human rights have constitutional status.

The late 19th century saw the most controversial phase in our history of unwritten constitutional law, with the aggressive development by state and federal judges of constitutional principles protecting "liberty of contract" against labor regulation, and restraining taxation and the regulation of prices charged by private business. The reaction to this tendency marked the beginning of sustained intellectual and political attack on the whole concept of unwritten constitutional principles.

Politically, emergent and eventually dominant social forces continued to press for the legislation that was being invalidated under these consti-tutional principles. Intellectually, the 18th-century philosophical frame-work supporting the concept of immutable natural rights was eroded with the growth of legal positivism, ethical relativism, pragmatism, and histor-icism.

Under the combined assault of these social and intellectual forces, the courts retreated from the doctrines of "economic due process," abandoning them in the 1930's. However, although the more sweeping attack on the whole tradition of unwritten constitutional principles gained some important adherents within the judiciary and still more among academic critics, it did not ultimately prevail.

For at almost the same time as the doctrines protecting the laissez-faire economy were passing out of constitutional law, the judiciary began the active development of new civil libertarian constitutional rights whose protection was deemed "essential to the concept of ordered liberty"—for example, rights against state governments of freedom of speech and religion, rights to "fundamentally fair" proceedings, and rights to familial autonomy in childrearing and education.

The last generation has seen further development of constitutional rights clearly—and sometimes avowedly—not derived by textual interpretation, notably the right of privacy, the right to vote, the right to travel, and generally the rights resulting from application of "equal protection of the laws" to the federal government. The intellectual framework against which these rights have developed is different from the natural-rights tradition of the founding fathers—its rhetorical reference points are the Anglo-American tradition and basic American ideals, rather than human nature, the social contract, or the rights of man. But it is the modern offspring, in a direct and traceable line of legitimate descent, of the natural-rights tradition that is so deeply embedded in our constitutional origins.

To summarize, there was an original understanding, both implicit and textually expressed, that unwritten higher law principles had constitutional status. From the very beginning, and continuously until the Civil War, the courts acted on that understanding and defined and enforced such principles as part of their function of judicial review. Aware of that history, the framers of the 14th amendment reconfirmed the original understanding through the "majestic generalities" of section 1. And ever since, again without significant break, the courts have openly proclaimed and enforced unwritten constitutional principles.

V. CONCLUSION

I recognize that there are a host of controversial assertions in this little historico-legal sketch. Had the natural-rights arguments that played so large a role in the American Revolution passed out of fashion and favor when the Constitution was framed? Was not the ninth amendment meant merely to express a principle of federalism? How clear are the natural-rights, anti-slavery origins of the 14th amendment?

Perhaps the most significant question raised is not one of historical fact so much as of legal principle and political theory. Conceding the natural-rights origins of our Constitution, does not the erosion and abandonment of the 18th-century ethics and epistemology on which the natural-rights theory was founded require the abandonment of the mode of judicial review flowing from that theory? Is a "fundamental law" judicially enforced in a climate of historical and cultural relativism the legitimate offspring of a fundamental law which its exponents felt expressed rationally demonstrable, universal, and immutable human rights?

These questions remain to be debated and further investigated before the legitimate pedigree of noninterpretive judicial review can be established. I certainly make no claim that they have been answered here. I have only argued in this Essay that very little of our constitutional law of individual rights has any firm foundation in the model of judicial review which traces from *Marbury v. Madison* to the jurisprudence of Mr. Justice Black. And I have suggested that the reflexive resort to variants of this model, so common a rhetorical response of constitutional scholars in the *Lochner* era, seems to be reviving today, and therefore requires more direct critical scrutiny than it has had in the recent past.

Learned Hand and the Origins of Modern First Amendment Doctrine: Some Fragments of History*

Gerald Gunther†

This Essay grows out of my research for a biography of Judge Learned Hand.[1] My main purpose is to put into print significant portions of the largely unpublished correspondence between Judge Hand and two other major contributors to the evolution of first amendment doctrine, Justice Oliver Wendell Holmes and Professor Zechariah Chafee, Jr. Sixteen of their letters—the first group between Hand and Holmes, the second between Hand and Chafee—constitute the Appendix to this Essay.[2] Here I want not only to sketch the background and describe the substance of the exchanges, but also to offer my tentative interpretation of their meaning and impact.

I believe these are letters of historical fascination and continuing importance. They are fascinating for their behind-the-scenes glimpses of personal interactions and intellectual struggles in the formative era of free speech law, little more than a half century ago. They are important because the writers then debated at a level of analytical sophistication and philosophical insight not surpassed in judicial opinions or academic commentary to this day. And they are especially important because they illuminate the quite different speech-protective formulas advanced by Hand and Holmes—formulas that have recently coalesced in unanticipated ways to form the core of today's first amendment doctrine.

This correspondence centering on Learned Hand throws light on two major themes, one beginning to be explored in the literature, the other more

* © 1975 by Gerald Gunther.
† A.B. 1949, Brooklyn College; M.A. 1950, Columbia University; LL.B. 1953, Harvard Law School; William Nelson Cromwell Professor of Law, Stanford Law School.
  1. My work on the biography of Judge Hand rests on indispensable assistance from two sources: The William Nelson Cromwell Foundation (Whitney North Seymour, Esq., Chairman), whose grant (assisted by the Ford Foundation) supports much of my work; and Norris Darrell, Esq., Judge Hand's literary executor, who asked me to do the biography and who has given me access to the treasure that is the Hand Papers.
  2. These letters are published with the kind permission of Professor Grant Gilmore, Justice Holmes' biographer and literary executor, Norris Darrell, Esq., Judge Hand's literary executor, and the Harvard Law Library. I want also to acknowledge the encouragement of Mr. Zechariah Chafee, III, Professor Chafee's son, and the research assistance of James H. Andrews of the Stanford Law School Class of 1976. My work on this Essay—and on the biography generally—has been immensely facilitated by the talents and efforts of a superb archivist, Mrs. James H. Chadbourn, Curator of Manuscripts and Archives, Treasure Room, Harvard Law Library. Her work in organizing the Hand, Holmes, and Chafee Papers, among others, should serve as a model for all manuscript custodians.

novel. The first pertains to the perceptions and contributions of Justice Holmes at the time of the Supreme Court's first significant encounter with first amendment problems, in cases involving agitation against United States participation in World War I. In the spring of 1919, Justice Holmes announced the clear and present danger test in the Court's opinion in *Schenck v. United States.*[3] The correspondence between Hand and Holmes confirms what revisionist commentators have recently suggested:[4] that Holmes was at that time quite insensitive to any claim for special judicial protection of free speech; that the *Schenck* standard was not truly speech-protective; and that it was not until the fall of 1919, with his famous dissent in *Abrams v. United States,*[5] that Holmes put some teeth into the clear and present danger formula, at least partly as a result of probing criticism by acquaintances such as Learned Hand.

The second theme pertains to the meaning and persistence of Learned Hand's *Masses* alternative for the solution of seditious speech problems. In 1917, District Judge Hand decided *Masses Publishing Co. v. Patten,*[6] holding that the radical magazine *The Masses* could not be banned from the mails under the World War I Espionage Act. It was a rare judicial effort to stem the mounting tide of suppression of dissent, in an articulation of first amendment values and an elaboration of free speech doctrine announced 2 years before the Supreme Court's first opportunity to grapple with the same issues.

These letters make clear what has long been doubted or ignored: that the *Masses* approach was indeed a distinctive, carefully considered alternative to the prevalent analyses of free speech issues. According to the usual arguments, the punishability of speech turned on an evaluation of its likelihood to cause forbidden consequences. Varying formulations—"natural and probable" consequences and "bad tendency" were the favorites—authorized suppression upon different showings of the closeness of speech to

---

3. 249 U.S. 47 (1919).

4. To me, the most provocative and intellectually satisfying stimulus to the modern reexamination of Holmes was a superb essay by my colleague Yosal Rogat, *The Judge as Spectator*, 31 U. CHI. L. REV. 213 (1964). *See also* his two-part article, Rogat, *Mr. Justice Holmes: A Dissenting Opinion*, 15 STAN. L. REV. 3 & 254 (1962–63). That article carefully examines Holmes' civil liberties opinions outside the first amendment area and notes, *id.* at 307, "that even when compared with his contemporaries Holmes had some striking insensitivities." I believe, as this Essay indicates, that this observation is applicable to Holmes' first amendment opinions as well, and I hope that Rogat will develop this theme in a future piece.

For the most careful recent critical analysis of the background and content of some of Holmes' first amendment opinions, *see* Ragan, *Justice Oliver Wendell Holmes, Jr., Zechariah Chafee, Jr., and the Clear and Present Danger Test for Free Speech: The First Year, 1919*, 58 J. AM. HIST. 24 (1971). *See also* Ginsburg, *Afterword to Ernst Freund and the First Amendment Tradition*, 40 U. CHI. L. REV. 243 (1973); Kalven, *Professor Ernst Freund and Debs v. United States*, 40 U. CHI. L. REV. 235 (1973). On changing assessments of Holmes, *see* S. KONEFSKY, THE LEGACY OF HOLMES AND BRANDEIS (1956); and White, *The Rise and Fall of Justice Holmes*, 39 U. CHI. L. REV. 51 (1972).

5. 250 U.S. 616, 624 (1919) (dissenting opinion).

6. 244 F. 535 (S.D.N.Y.), *rev'd*, 246 F. 24 (2d Cir. 1917).

illegal action. But all of those approaches shared the common characteristic of requiring factfinders—typically, juries—to assess circumstances and to guess about the risks created by the challenged speech.

Learned Hand thought this characteristic of the prevalent formulas too slippery, too dangerous to free expression, too much at the mercy of fact-finders reflecting majoritarian sentiments hostile to dissent. Instead, he urged, in *Masses* and for several years thereafter, the adoption of a strict, "hard," "objective" test focusing on the speaker's words: if the language used was solely that of direct incitement to illegal action, speech could be proscribed; otherwise, it was protected.

In the received wisdom about our first amendment tradition, *Masses* has been overshadowed by the clear and present danger criterion that emerged 2 years later, in the Holmes opinions in *Schenck* and *Abrams*. The tendency has been to view the *Masses* approach as a precursor of clear and present danger, essentially similar to Holmes' test. It has seemed to me for some time that sharp differences are perceptible on the face of the Hand and Holmes opinions. But not until these letters became available was there convincing evidence that the differences were from the beginning deeply felt and clearly perceived. When I prepared an edition of my constitutional law casebook a few years ago, before I began my research in the Hand Papers, I included *Masses* as the only principal case that was not a Supreme Court decision,[7] and I called attention to the differences between the *Masses* incitement test and clear and present danger.[8] At that time, I feared—and others admonished me—that I might be exaggerating the differences, that I might be reading too much into the words of the opinions.

The correspondence removes those doubts. Hand was fully aware of the distinctiveness of his approach. He adopted it with considerable concern and thought, and he persisted in urging it despite the coolest reception from the profession. Perhaps most intriguingly, the correspondence demonstrates that Hand was among the very few who did not wholly join the chorus of libertarian acclaim for Holmes' dissent in *Abrams*. Instead, in his letters to Chafee, he lucidly and persuasively articulated flaws in the clear and present danger test and continued for some years to advocate the *Masses* alternative.

In the early 1920's, Hand gave up. He was resigned to seeing his analysis condemned to oblivion. Yet he proved a better prophet than he knew. Clear and present danger did indeed become the dominant libertarian doctrine for the three decades after *Schenck*: it was increasingly invoked

---

7. G. GUNTHER & N. DOWLING, CASES AND MATERIALS ON CONSTITUTIONAL LAW 1070 (8th ed. 1970).
8. *Id.* at 1069, 1073, 1111.

in Supreme Court opinions and widely hailed in off-the-Court commentaries, led by those of Zechariah Chafee, Jr. But in the late 1950's, the popularity of clear and present danger waned. The Supreme Court set off in new directions; and the perceptions and doctrines of its new outlook proved to be strikingly similar to those Learned Hand had urged from 1917 to 1921. Indeed, today's operative first amendment doctrine, as first enunciated in *Brandenburg v. Ohio* in 1969,[9] can be viewed as a coalescing of the best features of the two contending approaches: Hand's incitement analysis has become a central theme; elements of Holmes' clear and present danger test provide additional safeguards for free expression.

THE CORRESPONDENCE IN CONTEXT

I. *The* Masses *Decision, 1917*

A. *The background of* Masses.

The letters printed here span a period of less than 3 years, from the summer of 1918 to the spring of 1921. According to the traditional view of the intellectual history of the first amendment, that brief span is ample to encompass all high points of the formative years: in 1918, the crest of prosecutions under the World War I Espionage Act;[10] in the spring of 1919, the Supreme Court's raising of the banner of the "libertarian" clear and present danger test in *Schenck v. United States*;[11] in the fall of 1919, the elaboration of that standard in Holmes' *Abrams* dissent;[12] at the end of 1920, the publication of the book that was to guide speech-protective thinking for a generation, Zechariah Chafee, Jr.'s *Freedom of Speech*.[13] But these letters cannot be viewed adequately in their historical and legal contexts without reaching back a year earlier, to the summer of 1917, when Learned Hand decided *Masses Publishing Co. v. Patten*. For it was in *Masses* that Hand first articulated the alternative approach to freedom of expression problems that he urged upon Holmes before *Schenck* and that he adhered to throughout these letters, even after Holmes' *Abrams* dissent.

To what extent may Congress suppress criticism of government? For more than a century after the demise of the Sedition Act of 1798, there

---

9. 395 U.S. 444 (1969).
10. Act of June 15, 1917, ch. 30, 40 Stat. 217, *as amended*, Act of May 16, 1918, ch. 75, 40 Stat. 553. According to the Reports of the Attorney General for 1918 and 1919, 1,956 persons were prosecuted under the Espionage Acts of 1917 and 1918, of whom 877 were convicted. Z. CHAFEE, FREEDOM OF SPEECH 387 (1920). *See also* ESPIONAGE ACT CASES 81 (W. Nelles ed., Nat'l Civil Liberties Bureau 1918).
11. 249 U.S. 47 (1919).
12. Abrams v. United States, 250 U.S. 616, 624 (1919) (dissenting opinion).
13. Z. CHAFEE, *supra* note 10.

was little occasion for federal courts to confront that question.[14] But soon after America's entry into World War I, Congress revived the issue by enacting the Espionage Act of 1917.[15] The Act did not purport to prohibit seditious libel in so many words, but its administrators soon sought to achieve that effect. The most important provisions were directed at those who "willfully cause or attempt to cause insubordination, disloyalty, mutiny, or refusal of duty, in the military or naval forces of the United States" and those who "willfully obstruct the recruiting or enlistment service of the United States."[16] And another section declared publications violating those provisions "nonmailable."[17] As Postmaster General Albert Sidney Burleson—and soon, prosecutors—read the statute, criticism of government policies could constitute the prohibited interference with military activities if disruption was the natural and reasonable effect of the dissident speech.[18]

One of the first publications to feel the bite of the new law was Max Eastman's *The Masses*, "a monthly revolutionary journal" with a circulation of over 20,000. Thomas G. Patten, the New York Postmaster, acting under orders of the Postmaster General, notified *The Masses* early in July that its forthcoming issue would be excluded from the mails under the Espionage Act. *The Masses* promptly sought a preliminary injunction against Patten. As a result of that motion, Learned Hand became one of the first judges required to interpret the Act. His decision of July 24, 1917— less than 6 weeks after enactment of the law—granted the injunction.[19]

---

14. Though the federal courts were largely silent, the attention to first amendment issues in the legal literature was greater than is commonly realized. *See generally* D. Rabban, The Meaning of the First Amendment in the Generation Before World War One, May 31, 1974 (unpublished seminar paper, on file with author, Stanford Law School). For example, several commentators took a broader view of the first amendment than that endorsed by Justice Holmes in Patterson v. Colorado, 205 U.S. 454, 462 (1907)—that the major thrust of the provision was to protect against prior restraints. *See, e.g.*, T. COOLEY, CONSTITUTIONAL LIMITATIONS 603–04 (7th ed. 1903); Biklé, *The Jurisdiction of the United States Over Seditious Libel*, 41 AM. L. REG. 1 (1902); Schofield, *Freedom of the Press in the United States*, 9 AM. SOCIOL. SOC'Y: PAPERS AND PROCEEDINGS 67, 99–102 (1914). *See also* the treatment of first amendment problems in E. FREUND, POLICE POWER (1904); T. SCHROEDER, FREE SPEECH FOR RADICALS (1916); L. WHIPPLE, THE STORY OF CIVIL LIBERTY IN THE UNITED STATES (1927).

15. Act of June 15, 1917, ch. 30, 40 Stat. 217.

16. *Id.* ch. 30, tit. 1, § 3, 40 Stat. 219.

17. *Id.* ch. 30, tit. 12, § 1, 40 Stat. 230.

18. *See* W. Nelles ed., *supra* note 10.

19. 244 F. 535 (S.D.N.Y.), *rev'd*, 246 F. 24 (2d Cir. 1917).

The Hand Papers reveal that this injunction action was not Learned Hand's first contact with Max Eastman's efforts to combat suppression of his magazine. About a year before the Postmaster General's ban, there was an effort to exclude *The Masses* from newsstands in New York City's subway and elevated stations. A state legislative committee scheduled hearings on that exclusion. Max Eastman asked Learned Hand for a statement opposing that ban; Judge Hand promptly complied.

Eastman wrote Hand that if the Judge would send him a statement "that you believe The Masses ought to be on those stands, it will be the favor of a lifetime." Letter from Max Eastman to Learned Hand, June 26, 1916, on file in the Hand Papers, Box 20, Folder 1, Harvard Law Library, Treasure Room. Hand complied the next day, in a statement akin to some of the views expressed in his judicial opinion a year later. Letter from Learned Hand to Max Eastman, June 27, 1916, on file in the Hand Papers, Box 20, Folder 1, Harvard Law Library, Treasure Room. Hand wrote: "I have your letter of

It was a remarkable decision—remarkable even decades later; especially remarkable given the practical and doctrinal climate of the times,
so strikingly inhospitable to dissent. Radicals preaching pacifism, conscientious objection, or worse, were anathema in wartime America.[20] And
constitutional interpretation offered no shelter. There was doubt that the
first amendment applied to postpublication sanctions: the Supreme Court's
sparse announcements had embraced the Blackstonian view that freedom
of expression was protected solely against prior restraint.[21] And beyond
that niggardly view of the first amendment, many Court statements appeared to give the government virtually total discretion in controlling the
mails.[22] Moreover, the Government's arguments for suppressing speech
under a statute prohibiting acts such as interference with recruiting reflected the customary legal thinking of the day: punishability of speech
turned on its probable effect or tendency, on assessments of causation and
consequences; talk of the "natural and reasonable effect of the publication" was a characteristic way of framing the question. Most of those who
viewed such a standard as too speech-restrictive did not quarrel with the
emphasis on guessing about the consequences of speech. Their rejoinder
to arguments about bad tendencies and probable effects was to urge a
narrower, closer cause-effect relationship represented by formulations such
as "direct and immediate"—or "clear and present danger."

B. *Hand's contribution in* Masses.

Hand's analysis stepped outside of that framework. He conceded that
speech could indeed cause effects harmful to the war effort; but he did

the 26th asking me to say that I think 'The Masses' ought not to be excluded by Ward & Gow from
the newsstands. I answer unhesitatingly that I think it ought not. I do not often see your paper, and
as you probably can guess, I do not feel sympathy with your approach to the question of social and
economic reörganization, or the means by which you seek to bring it about. That I prefer another
way, does not blind me to the wisdom of giving you the chance to persuade men of yours. I have
never seen anything in 'The Masses' which did not have a sincere and genuine relation to these absolutely legitimate purposes. You will forgive my saying that parts of it have at times been extremely
repellant to me, though never what you did yourself, but that in my judgment has nothing to do
with this matter. Yours is a way, whether it is a good way or a bad way, of getting men to think and
feel about those things on which it is most important that they should think and feel. I can conceive no
possible defence for excluding you except either that such matters must not be discussed, or that they
must be discussed only in a way which accords with the common standards of taste. One alternative
is tyrannous absolutism, the other, tyrannous priggism." I do not know whether Hand's letter was
entered into the record of the legislative hearings in 1916, or whether the Judge apprised the parties of
the statement when the injunction proceeding came before him a year later.

    Max Eastman and Learned Hand met on at least one occasion: Eastman recalled in one of his
autobiographical volumes that Judge Hand introduced an Eastman lecture on radicalism before "New
York's exclusive woman's club," the Colony Club. M. EASTMAN, ENJOYMENT OF LIVING 481–82 (1948).
In the 1920's, Eastman became a leading anti-Stalinist; and in his later years, he joined the staff of *The
Reader's Digest*. N.Y. Times, Mar. 26, 1969, at 1, col. 1.

    20. *See* Z. CHAFEE, THIRTY-FIVE YEARS WITH FREEDOM OF SPEECH 4–7 (1952). *See also* P. MUR-
PHY, THE CONSTITUTION IN CRISIS TIMES 1918–1969, at 21–28 (1972); P. MURPHY, THE MEANING OF
FREEDOM OF SPEECH 23–27 (1972).

    21. *See* especially Justice Holmes' opinion for the Court in Patterson v. Colorado, 205 U.S. 454,
462 (1907).

    22. *See, e.g.,* Public Clearing House v. Coyne, 194 U.S. 497 (1904); *In re* Rapier, 143 U.S.
110 (1892); *Ex parte* Jackson, 96 U.S. 727 (1877).

not think that tightening the required chain of causation was an apt or effective method of protecting speech. To second-guess enforcement officials about probable consequences of subversive speech was to him a questionable judicial function: judges had no special competence to foresee the future. Moreover, even if predictions about the consequences of words were thought to be appropriate court business, the task would ordinarily fall not to the judge but to the jury, a body reflecting majoritarian sentiments unlikely to be conducive to the protection of dissent in wartime.

Hand's solution to the problem of an appropriate and effective judicial role was to focus on the speaker's words, not on their probable consequences. Instead of asking in the circumstances of each case whether the words had a tendency or even a probability of producing unlawful conduct, he sought a more "absolute and objective test" focusing on "language"[23]—"a qualitative formula, hard, conventional, difficult to evade,"[24] as he said in his letters. What he urged was essentially an incitement test, "a test based upon the nature of the utterance itself":[25] if the words constituted solely a counsel to law violation, they could be forbidden; all other utterances were permissible. As he put it in *Masses*:

> [T]o assimilate agitation, legitimate as such, with direct incitement to violent resistance, is to disregard the tolerance of all methods of political agitation which in normal times is a safeguard of free government. The distinction is not a scholastic subterfuge, but a hard-bought acquisition in the fight for freedom . . . . If one stops short of urging upon others that it is their duty or their interest to resist the law, it seems to me one should not be held to have attempted to cause its violation.[26]

It was an extraordinarily speech-protective interpretation of the Espionage Act. On its face, it was only statutory interpretation: Hand raised no doubts about the scope of congressional power; he purported to be dealing simply with legislative purpose.[27] But it was legislative purpose read in the context of constitutional values—values expressed in a manner as noble as any we have on the books. In the *Masses* case itself, that articulation of values was simply used to justify the narrow interpretation of the statute.[28] But that Hand's position on the scope of permissible dissent in a free society became for him a constitutional norm as well emerges quite clearly from his letters. His statement of democratic values is notable for

23. Letter from Learned Hand to Zechariah Chafee, Jr., Dec. 3, 1919, on file in the Chafee Papers, Box 4, Folder 20, Harvard Law Library, Treasure Room [hereinafter cited as Appendix Doc. No. 9].
24. Letter from Learned Hand to Zechariah Chafee, Jr., Jan. 2, 1921, on file in the Chafee Papers, Box 4, Folder 20, Harvard Law Library, Treasure Room [hereinafter cited as Appendix Doc. No. 15].
25. Letter from Learned Hand to Zechariah Chafee, Jr., Jan. 8, 1920, on file in the Chafee Papers, Box 4, Folder 20, Harvard Law Library, Treasure Room [hereinafter cited as Appendix Doc. No. 11].
26. 244 F. at 540.
27. *Id*. at 538.
28. As Hand said in the passage immediately following that setting forth his incitement standard: "If that be not the test, I can see no escape from the conclusion that under this section every political agitation which can be shown to be apt to create a seditious temper is illegal. I am confident that by such language Congress had no such revolutionary purpose in view." *Id*. at 540.

several reasons: the *Masses* articulation contrasts sharply with the lack of similar sensitivity in Holmes' early confrontations with the same issues in *Schenck* and the companion cases in the spring of 1919; Hand's eloquence bears comparison with Holmes' much-quoted words when he at last began to exhibit a similar awareness in the *Abrams* dissent in the fall of 1919; and, most important, the values emphasized by Hand in *Masses* inspired his partially successful appeals to Holmes before *Abrams* and his continuing disagreements with Holmes in the post-*Abrams* letters.

Hand's technique in *Masses*, though statutory interpretation in form, was in substance an effort at judicial delineation of areas of protected speech. Criticism and agitation that fell outside of the narrow bounds of direct incitement or advocacy of illegal action should be immune from suppression, no matter what the circumstances, no matter what the changing perceptions of impassioned juries. This delineation did not rest simply on judicial fiat: Hand justified it as rooted in values that he saw as essential to a free society—values that his judicial responsibility authorized him to articulate candidly and forcefully.

Hand's technique is well illustrated by his handling of the statutory ban on willfully causing insubordination in the armed forces. Instead of second-guessing the Government's practical causation argument, he accepted it as empirically accurate—but insisted that it was a standard inconsistent with free speech values. The Government justified application of the statute to antiwar speech by arguing "that to arouse discontent and disaffection among the people with the prosecution of the war and with the draft tends to promote a mutinous and insubordinate temper among the troops."[29] That, Hand conceded, was "true: men who become satisfied that they are engaged in an enterprise dictated by the unconscionable selfishness of the rich, and effectuated by the tyrannous disregard for the will of those who must suffer and die, will be more prone to insubordination . . . ."[30] But predictions about the possible impact of speech, plausible as they were, would not do as a legal standard consistent with free speech values:

> [T]o interpret the word "cause" so broadly would . . . involve necessarily as a consequence the suppression of all hostile criticism, and of all opinion except what encouraged and supported the existing policies, or which fell within the range of temperate argument. It would contradict the normal assumption of democratic government that the suppression of hostile criticism does not turn upon the justice of its substance or the decency and propriety of its temper. Assuming that the power to repress such opinion may rest in Congress in the throes of a struggle for

29. *Id*. at 539.
30. *Id*.

the very existence of the state, its exercise is so contrary to the use and wont of our people that only the clearest expression of such a power justifies the conclusion that it was intended.[31]

The "normal assumption of democratic government," the "use and wont of our people," or, as Hand put it earlier in the opinion, the "right to criticise either by temperate reasoning, or by immoderate and indecent invective, which is normally the privilege of the individual in countries dependent upon the free expression of opinion as the ultimate source of authority"[32]—those were the sources of the values articulated in *Masses*. They were sources derived from history and philosophy—especially the latter. Hand's invocation of history was essentially impressionistic:[33] he actually had little acquaintance with the history of American civil liberties, or indeed with American history generally. His inclinations in his historical reading ran to Europe. It was the underpinning of philosophy and political theory that truly ran deep: in the eloquent articulation of values, the voice was that of Billings Learned Hand, Harvard undergraduate specializing in philosophy, and Learned Hand, lawyer and judge of an inescapably philosophical bent of mind.

But how were those values to be translated into effective law by a judge skeptical of the speech-protective capacity of doctrine, yet persuaded that doctrine might do some good? If an adequate legal standard "could become sacred by the incrustations of time and precedent," he suggested in one of his letters, "it might be made to serve just a little to withhold the torrents of passion to which I suspect democracies will be found more subject than for example the whig autocracy of the 18th century."[34] For Hand, the best hope for avoiding the "suppression of the free utterance of abuse and criticism of the existing law, or the policies of the war,"[35] lay not in analogies to the law of criminal attempts or to legal doctrines of causation, but rather in an "objective" scrutiny of the challenged speech to determine whether the words in question were those of incitement or counselling to illegal action:

> [T]here has always been a recognized limit to such expressions, incident indeed to the existence of any compulsive power of the state itself. One may not counsel or

---

31. *Id.* at 539–40.
32. *Id.* at 539.
33. *See, e.g.,* Letter from Learned Hand to Zechariah Chafee, Jr., Jan. 2, 1921, Appendix Doc. No. 15, *supra* note 24: "Indeed, how baffling [this subject] is I never quite realized till I had been over your pages. I kept feeling,—did I write you so before?—that in writing my own opinion . . . it was well that I knew no more than I did. Like the heathen I was saved by my invincible ignorance . . . ." *See also* Appendix Doc. No. 9, *supra* note 23, and Letter from Learned Hand to Zechariah Chafee, Jr., Dec. 3, 1920, on file in the Chafee Papers, Box 4, Folder 20, Harvard Law Library, Treasure Room [hereinafter cited as Appendix Doc. No. 14].
34. Hand to Chafee, Jan. 2, 1921, Appendix Doc. No. 15, *supra* note 24.
35. 244 F. at 540.

advise others to violate the law as it stands. Words are not only the keys of persuasion, but the triggers of action, and those which have no purport but to counsel
the violation of law cannot by any latitude of interpretation be a part of that public
opinion which is the final source of government in a democratic state . . . . To
counsel or advise a man to an act is to urge upon him either that it is his interest
or his duty to do it. While, of course, this may be accomplished as well by indirection as expressly, since words carry the meaning that they impart, the definition
is exhaustive, I think, and I shall use it. Political agitation, by the passions it arouses
or the convictions it engenders, may in fact stimulate men to the violation of law.
Detestation of existing policies is easily transformed into forcible resistance of the
authority which puts them in execution, and it would be folly to disregard the
causal relation between the two. Yet to assimilate agitation, legitimate as such, with
direct incitement to violent resistance, is to disregard the tolerance of all methods
of political agitation which in normal times is a safeguard of free government.[36]

"Direct incitement," "direct advocacy" of illegal action—these were the
strict standards Hand insisted upon. They were standards focused more on
the content than on the effect of the speech. They were standards that
would have protected much of the unpopular speech condemned by the
prevailing doctrines—and by Holmes' clear and present danger test of the
Schenck era. For Hand, the question was not whether "the indirect result
of the language might be to arouse a seditious disposition, for that would
not be enough," but whether "the language directly advocated resistance to
the draft."[37]

The libertarian nature of this standard is illustrated by Hand's application of it to passages in *The Masses* praising conscientious objectors and
those, like Emma Goldman and Alexander Berkman, who were in jail for
conspiring to induce persons not to register for the draft. To most judges—
including the circuit court of appeals that reversed Hand, and to Justice
Holmes in the spring of 1919—admiration of such "martyrs" encouraged
emulation and contributed at least indirectly to violation of law; and that
was enough to justify punishment. Not so for Hand. He conceded that the
"martyrs" were indeed held up "to admiration, and hence their conduct to
possible emulation."[38] And he noted: "It is plain enough that the paper
has the fullest sympathy for these people, that it admires their courage,
and that it presumptively approves their conduct. . . . [M]oreover, these
passages, it must be remembered, occur in a magazine which attacks with
the utmost violence the draft and the war."[39] Still, it was not enough, for
the objective standard was not satisfied:

> That such comments have a tendency to arouse emulation in others is clear enough,
> but that they counsel others to follow these examples is not so plain. Literally at

36. *Id.*
37. *Id.* at 542.
38. *Id.* at 541.
39. *Id.* (paragraphing omitted).

least they do not, and while, as I have said, the words are to be taken, not literally, but according to their full import, the literal meaning is the starting point for interpretation. One may admire and approve the course of a hero without feeling any duty to follow him. There is not the least implied intimation in these words that others are under a duty to follow. The most that can be said is that, if others do follow, they will get the same admiration and the same approval. Now, there is surely an appreciable distance between esteem and emulation; and unless there is here some advocacy of such emulation, I cannot see how the passages can be said to fall within the law. If they do, it would follow that, while one might express admiration and approval for the Quakers or any established sect which is excused from the draft, one could not legally express the same admiration and approval for others who entertain the same conviction, but do not happen to belong to the society of Friends . . . . Surely, if the draft had not excepted Quakers, it would be too strong a doctrine to say that any who openly admire their fortitude or even approved their conduct was willfully obstructing the draft.[40]

Here was a strict, literal, perhaps even strained doctrine in the interest of speech protection. The approach had its problems. As contemporaries recognized,[41] it could not easily deal with the indirect but purposeful incitement of Marc Anthony's oration over the body of Caesar. Although Hand recognized that advocacy could be accomplished by "indirection," he insisted on starting with the "literal meaning" of the words and never completely explained how far beyond he was willing to go. Nor did he fully deal with the problem of the harmless inciter, the speaker explicitly urging law violation but with little realistic hope of success. That problem was not clearly confronted until *Brandenburg v. Ohio* in 1969.[42] But Hand's eloquent assertion of a rule protecting all critical speech falling short of direct incitement was nevertheless an extraordinary achievement, not only for its time but, as the Supreme Court was implicitly to recognize decades later, for ours as well.

C. *The response to* Masses.

For Hand, the response to *Masses* was painfully disappointing. As he recalled to Chafee more than 3 years later, "it seemed to meet with practically no professional approval whatever."[43] The most formal indication of that disapproval soon appeared in the official reports. Within 2 weeks of Hand's order, Circuit Judge Charles M. Hough took the unusual step of writing an opinion continuing a stay of Hand's injunction pending appeal.[44] Hough, the widely admired, tough-minded son of a brigadier

---

40. *Id.* at 541–42.
41. *See, e.g.,* Letter from Zechariah Chafee, Jr., to Learned Hand, Mar. 28, 1921, on file in the Hand Papers, Box 15, Folder 26, Harvard Law Library, Treasure Room [hereinafter cited as Appendix Doc. No. 16]: "Your test is surely easier to apply although our old friend Marc Anthony's speech is continually thrown at me in discussion."
42. 395 U.S. 444 (1969).
43. Appendix Doc. No. 14, Dec. 3, 1920, *supra* note 33.
44. Masses Publishing Co. v. Patten, 245 F. 102 (2d Cir. 1917).

general, was "never tortured by doubt."[45] He was readily attracted to the
Postmaster's position on what Hough called "indirect incitement,"[46] and
he was openly skeptical of Hand's contrary approach:

> [I]t is at least arguable whether there can be any more direct incitement to action
> than to hold up to admiration those who do act. Oratio obliqua has always been
> preferred by rhetoricians to oratio recta; the Beatitudes have for some centuries
> been considered highly hortatory, though they do not contain the injunction "Go
> thou and do likewise."[47]

When the case came before the full circuit court of appeals a few
months later, the criticism of Hand's position was not limited to its vulnerability as to the Marc Anthony problem. Judge Henry Wade Rogers' opinion reversed Hand's order outright.[48] Rogers[49] did not have a mind as strong
and brilliant as Hough's, but his capacities were adequate to reflect the
mainstream of contemporary legal thinking. Most of his opinion read like
an administrative law essay: he emphasized the broad discretion of the
Postmaster General,[50] after recalling the contemporary black-letter law
about the virtually unlimited power of Congress to exclude matter from
the mails.[51] But Rogers did ultimately reach the problems of the appropriate legal standards governing criticism of national policies and their application to the contents of *The Masses*. These questions seemed to him the
easiest ones in the case. He noted Hand's incitement test and replied: "This
court does not agree that such is the law. If the natural and reasonable effect
of what is said is to encourage resistance to a law, and the words are used in
an endeavor to persuade to resistance, it is immaterial that the duty to resist
is not mentioned, or the interest of the persons addressed in resistance is
not suggested."[52] Nor did he find it "necessary that an incitement to crime
must be direct."[53] And so it was easy to conclude "that, considering the natural and reasonable effect of the publication, it was intended willfully to
obstruct recruiting; and even though we were not convinced that any such
intent existed, and were in doubt concerning it, the case would be governed
by the principle that the head of a department of the government in a

---

45. Veeder, *Charles Merrill Hough*, in 5 DICTIONARY OF AMERICAN BIOGRAPHY pt. 1, at 249 (rev.
ed. 1958). Van Vechten Veeder, a contemporary of Hand and Hough, was a District Judge for the
Eastern District of New York. *See* text accompanying note 56 *infra*.
46. Masses Publishing Co. v. Patten, 245 F. at 105.
47. *Id*. at 106.
48. Masses Publishing Co. v. Patten, 246 F. 24 (2d Cir. 1917).
49. Clark, *Henry Wade Rogers*, in 8 DICTIONARY OF AMERICAN BIOGRAPHY pt. 2, at 97 (rev. ed.
1958). Rogers—like Charles E. Clark, the author of the biographical sketch—came to the Second
Circuit from the deanship of Yale Law School.
50. 246 F. at 32–33.
51. *Id*. at 27–30.
52. *Id*. at 38.
53. *Id*.

doubtful case will not be overruled by the courts in a matter which involves his judgment and discretion, and which is within his jurisdiction."[54]

The rejection of Hand's position was not limited to official statements from the bench. As Hand wrote to his friend and sometime patron, the distinguished New York lawyer and civic leader Charles C. Burlingham:

> I think all this building,[55] plus Veeder,[56] is against me, although Ward[57] does not commit himself. Gus[58] thinks of it as nothing more than another instance of my natural perversity.[59]

The widespread repudiation of Hand's *Masses* approach may have had a temporary impact on the Judge's career as well as on his personal and professional pride. As he recalled to Chafee later: "The case cost me something, at least at the time . . . ."[60] That "cost" may have been the added shadow cast on Hand's opportunity for promotion to the Second Circuit in 1917.[61]

Yet, despite these frustrations, Learned Hand remained content with and committed to his *Masses* position. As he wrote to Burlingham in October, after reporting his cousin Gus' comment that *Masses* represented "nothing more than an instance of my natural perversity":

> [T]he perversity is there all right and God knows how much my subconscious self, which is no doubt a cross-grained critter, may have been fooling with my cerebral centres, but I never was better satisfied with any piece of work I did in

---

54. *Id.* at 39.

55. The reference is to the quarters of the federal courts in Manhattan—the United States District Court for the Southern District of New York and the United States Circuit Court of Appeals for the Second Circuit.

56. Van Vechten Veeder was a judge of the United States District Court for the Eastern District of New York.

57. Henry G. Ward was a judge of the Circuit Court of Appeals. A month after this letter was written, Ward joined in reversing Hand's *Masses* decision. Ward, however, did not go as far as the majority: rather than joining Judge Rogers' opinion, he wrote a separate concurrence, emphasizing that the Espionage Act reached only writings printed with "the intention of advising resistance to the law." 246 F. at 39 (concurring opinion).

58. Augustus N. Hand, Learned Hand's cousin and lifelong friend, was a judge of the United States District Court for the Southern District of New York. Three years after Learned Hand's appointment to the Circuit Court of Appeals in 1924, Augustus Hand followed him to the Second Circuit.

59. Letter from Learned Hand to Charles C. Burlingham, Oct. 6, 1917, on file in the Hand Papers, Box 100, Folder 26, Harvard Law Library, Treasure Room.

60. Appendix Doc. No. 14, Dec. 3, 1920, *supra* note 33.

61. Hand was not named to the Second Circuit until 1924. The slim chance for promotion in 1917 that the *Masses* decision may have helped to extinguish existed because of a vacancy caused by the retirement of Judge Alfred C. Coxe. For a letter urging Hand's name for that vacancy, *see* Letter from Lawrence E. Sexton to President Wilson, July 5, 1917 (less than 3 weeks before Hand's *Masses* decision), on file in the Hand Papers, Box 100, Folder 26, Harvard Law Library, Treasure Room. C. C. Burlingham urged Hand's promotion both before and after the *Masses* ruling. *See* Charles C. Burlingham to Attorney General Thomas W. Gregory, Nov. 28, 1917, on file in the Hand Papers, Box 100, Folder 26, Harvard Law Library, Treasure Room: "I venture to write you once more about the appointment of a successor to Judge Coxe. . . . [Hand's] logical power and his wide and deep legal learning are greatly needed in the Court. No other District Judge can compare with him in these respects."

my life. I do not mean that I was pleased with it as a judicial performance, but with the result. There is a bit of it that is arguable, no doubt; in the main outlined [*sic*] I have been very happy to do what I believe was some service to temperateness and sanity.[62]

Learned Hand's self-deprecating remark about pride in "result" rather than "judicial performance" is a characteristic one; but in fact, he took pride in both. As his letters demonstrate, his years of effort to spread the message of his *Masses* opinion had a twofold aim: to heighten sensitivity to the importance of protecting free expression values; and to urge his special doctrinal implementation of that sensitivity. If "result" signifies some progress toward the former goal, surely the "judicial performance" is the source of the lasting strength of the doctrinal approach of *Masses*. It is time to turn to the letters printed in the Appendix to examine in somewhat greater detail Learned Hand's values-cum-doctrine campaign.

II. *An Encounter on a Train, Summer 1918*

The first round of Hand's campaign was fired a year after *Masses*. The target of this initial volley was Supreme Court Justice Oliver Wendell Holmes; and the aim was not to urge the *Masses* doctrine in detail—no Espionage Act case was yet before the Supreme Court—but to persuade Holmes of the importance of special sensitivity to free speech values. It was an eloquent but utterly failing effort.

The first confrontation between Hand and Holmes on issues of free speech was a chance one, brief but revealing. Hand and Holmes shared a train ride from New York City most of the way to Boston, on Wednesday, June 19, 1918. Holmes, at the end of the Supreme Court Term, was on his way to his Beverly Farms, Massachusetts, residence; Hand was travelling to his summer home in Cornish, New Hampshire, across the Connecticut River from Windsor, Vermont. They talked about the majority's right to suppress dissent. Echoes of that conversation are preserved for us because Hand, on brooding about it in New Hampshire, decided he "gave up rather more easily"[63] than he should have and decided to restate his position for Holmes; and Holmes promptly replied.

That exchange—Documents 1 and 2 in the Appendix—reveals that a year after *Masses*, months before *Schenck,* Holmes and Hand were indeed very far apart: Hand argued the case for protecting the dissenter; Holmes disagreed. That was a gap in values all the more remarkable because Hand and Holmes shared a common philosophical outlook in most respects.

62. Letter from Learned Hand to Charles C. Burlingham, Oct. 6, 1917, *supra* note 59.
63. Letter from Learned Hand to Oliver Wendell Holmes, June 22, 1918, on file in the Holmes Papers, Box 43, Folder 30, Harvard Law Library, Treasure Room [hereinafter cited as Appendix Doc. No. 1].

Neither believed in absolutes or eternal truths; both were skeptics, or at least seemed to be;[64] and both doubted the effectiveness as well as the legitimacy of judicial restraints on majority sentiments.[65] Yet from those premises Hand was able to derive arguments for the protection of minority views, more than a year before Holmes arrived at a parallel conclusion in his *Abrams* dissent.

The dispute between Hand and Holmes that first emerges in this 1918 exchange and that persists throughout these letters is remarkable, too, at another, more personal, level. To find Hand disagreeing with Holmes, strongly and persistently, is extraordinary. Although the skeptical Hand did not often suffer from hero worship, his admiration, even idolatry, of Holmes permeates his public and private statements. It was an uncharacteristic veneration, exceeding even that for some of his Harvard professors such as James Bradley Thayer.[66] To Hand, Holmes was "the epitome of what a judge should be,"[67] a continuous object of "affection," "a dear friend, a wise guide and the example of all that I most cherish."[68] Plainly, only a most important, most deeply held belief could spur the 46-year-old Hand, 9 years a district judge, to do battle with a Justice more than three decades older, with almost three decades more experience on the bench. Only a matter of utmost significance could move Hand to challenge—and to persist in challenging—a man for whom he felt an affection and respect second only to that he felt for the father who had died when Learned Hand was a teenager.

What emerges from Hand's 1918 letter is the credo that spurred his doctrinal implementations in *Masses* and thereafter—a credo Holmes was unable to accept until late in the following year, and was never able to implement as effectively. "Opinions are at best provisional hypotheses, incompletely tested. . . . So we must be tolerant of opposite opinions or varying opinions by the very fact of our incredulity of our own."[69] So

---

64. For a sophisticated questioning of Holmes' alleged skepticism, *see* Rogat, *The Judge as Spectator, supra* note 4, at 250–56. After finding neither genuine humility nor skepticism in Holmes, Rogat suggests that those who speak of Holmes' skepticism are really reacting to his uninterested detachment: "To a remarkable degree, Holmes simply did not care." *Id.* at 255.

65. For example, both Holmes and Hand were early opponents of the economic due process doctrines that flourished at the beginning of the 20th century. *Compare* Holmes' famous dissent in Lochner v. New York, 198 U.S. 45, 74 (1905), *with* Hand's article, *Due Process of Law and the Eight-Hour Day*, 21 HARV. L. REV. 495 (1908).

66. *See, e.g.*, Hand, *Foreword to Williston's Life and Law*, in THE SPIRIT OF LIBERTY 140 (2d ed. I. Dilliard 1953); *cf.* L. HAND, THE BILL OF RIGHTS 77 (1958).

67. Letter from Learned Hand to Oliver Wendell Holmes, Mar. 7, 1921, on file in the Holmes Papers, Box 43, Folder 30, Harvard Law Library, Treasure Room.

68. Letter from Learned Hand to Oliver Wendell Holmes, Mar. 8, 1933, on file in the Holmes Papers, Box 43, Folder 30, Harvard Law Library, Treasure Room. *See also* Letter from Learned Hand to Felix Frankfurter, Dec. 2, 1916, on file in the Holmes Papers, Box 43, Folder 30, Harvard Law Library, Treasure Room (on a Holmes opinion "that nearly makes me cry with envy from its own beauty").

69. Appendix Doc. No. 1, *supra* note 63.

Hand insisted in the face of Holmes' defense of the right of the majority to suppress the minority. Deference to majoritarianism was ordinarily central to Hand's beliefs as well; but in the area of freedom of expression, he could not follow that customary guide. Yes, silencing "the other fellow when he disagrees" was indeed "a natural right," but it was not a right that society and the law could afford to acquiesce in:

> Only, and here we may differ, I do say that you may not cut off heads . . . because the victims insist upon saying things which look against Provisional Hypothesis Number Twenty-Six, the verification of which to date may be found in its proper place in the card catalogue. Generally, I insist, you must allow the possibility that if the heads are spared, other cards may be added under that sub-title which will have, perhaps, an important modification.[70]

It was a Hand argument strikingly similar to the hallowed defense of free speech that Holmes ultimately presented in his *Abrams* dissent:

> Persecution for the expression of opinions seems to me perfectly logical. If you have no doubt of your premises or your power and want a certain result with all your heart you naturally express your wishes in law and sweep away all opposition . . . . But when men have realized that time has upset many fighting faiths, they may come to believe even more than they believe the very foundations of their own conduct that the ultimate good desired is better reached by free trade in ideas—that the best test of truth is the power of the thought to get itself accepted in the competition of the market, and that truth is the only ground upon which their wishes safely can be carried out. That at any rate is the theory of our Constitution.[71]

That "theory of our Constitution" had not yet revealed itself to Holmes in 1918. Then, he could see only the "perfectly logical" aspects of persecuting dissenters. The "but," the qualification about the uncertainty of received opinions and the need for a free trade in ideas that Hand urged in 1918, was not yet congenial to Holmes. Yet, characteristically, Holmes tried to meet Hand's 1918 argument with the assertion that "I agree with it throughout."[72] A year later, after *Schenck* and *Debs*, Holmes would wholly fail to see any difference between his standard and Hand's *Masses* alternative.[73] But in June 1918, he did admit to one difference from Hand, one "qualification"—an all-important one. Free speech, he insisted, "stands no differently than freedom from vaccination."[74] And that, of course, could be readily overridden by the majority, as the decision Holmes had joined 13 years earlier, in *Jacobson v. Massachusetts*,[75] had made clear. In Holmes'

---

70. *Id.*
71. 250 U.S. 616, 630 (1919) (dissenting opinion).
72. Letter from Oliver Wendell Holmes to Learned Hand, June 24, 1918, on file in the Hand Papers, Box 103, Folder 24, Harvard Law Library, Treasure Room [hereinafter cited as Appendix Doc. No. 2].
73. *See* notes 83 & 116–18 *infra* and accompanying texts.
74. Appendix Doc. No. 2, *supra* note 72.
75. 197 U.S. 11 (1905).

letter, the overriding emphasis is on what Hand called the "natural right" to kill the opponent.[76]

In short, Holmes was not truly ready to "agree" with Hand that majorities legitimately may be curbed. He believed that the majority's right is all; there is no recognition of any limitation on that "natural right" stemming from the uncertain nature of "truth" or the demands of a democratic society. As Holmes saw it in 1918, occasions "when you cared enough" to stop the dissident might indeed be rare, "but if for any reason you did care enough you wouldn't care a damn for the suggestion that you were acting on a provisional hypothesis and might be wrong. That is the condition of every act."[77]

Within months, the philosophical battlelines drawn between Holmes and Hand were to be translated into concrete doctrinal differences. In March 1919, it fell to Holmes to write for the Supreme Court in its first encounters with the provisions of the Espionage Act of 1917 that Hand had tried to construe narrowly in *Masses*. These encounters produced the first statement of the clear and present danger test.

But the clear and present danger test of the spring of 1919 was not a useful libertarian doctrine. Rather, it was little more than a manifestation of the philosophical underpinnings revealed by Holmes in June 1918— a philosophy that would recognize no real justification for limiting the right of the majority to "kill" the dissident minority. And perceiving no such justification, Holmes understandably—and to Hand's regret if not surprise—found no compelling reason to elaborate satisfying doctrinal safeguards for free speech.

III. Schenck-Frohwerk-Debs *Before the Supreme Court, Spring 1919*

On March 3, 1919, the Supreme Court decided *Schenck v. United States*.[78] One week later, decisions were handed down in *Frohwerk v. United States*[79] and *Debs v. United States*.[80] In each case, the Court was unanimous: speaking through Justice Holmes, it affirmed convictions under the 1917 Espionage Act in all three cases.

Schenck enunciated the clear and present danger test; *Frohwerk* and *Debs* applied it. Clear and present danger, as it has come down through the years of praise from libertarian commentators such as Zechariah Chafee, Jr., stands for the view that speech cannot be punished unless it creates an immediate risk of harm. Three of the letters below[81] are from the

---

76. *See* Appendix Doc. No. 1, *supra* note 63.
77. *Id.*
78. 249 U.S. 47 (1919).
79. 249 U.S. 204 (1919).
80. 249 U.S. 211 (1919).
81. *See* Appendix Docs. Nos. 3–5 and accompanying notes *infra*.

period immediately before and after *Schenck* and *Debs*. They confirm and amplify what some modern commentators[82] have begun to appreciate: that in its origin, clear and present danger reflected neither special sensitivity to free speech values nor special concern for tailoring doctrine to implement those values. Rather, Holmes, at the time of *Schenck* and company, is revealed as not having moved at all from his 1918 position of blindness to any justification for curtailing majority suppression of dissent. He was at that point immune to any persuasion that special doctrine, such as that enunciated in *Masses*, was needed to protect free speech.

That imperviousness characterized Holmes' thinking throughout the spring of 1919, both before and after the *Schenck* trilogy of cases. While the cases were pending, for example, Hand tried to induce Holmes to think about the *Masses* formulation. His efforts were of no avail. After *Debs*, Hand expressed his criticism of that decision. His arguments appeared to make no impact. Quite simply, Holmes did not yet get the point.[83] By the end of the spring, Learned Hand could reasonably conclude that the campaign he had begun with *Masses* was a failure. As he wrote to another critic of *Debs*, Professor Ernst Freund of the University of Chicago Law School: "I own I was chagrined that Justice Holmes did not line up on our side; indeed, I have so far been unable to make him see that he and we have any real differences . . . ."[84]

In Hand's first approach to Holmes during that spring of 1919, just before the decisions were handed down, Hand reminded Holmes of the *Masses* opinion. Holmes, it seems, had read it at some earlier point. But the best he could do now, a week before *Schenck*, was to acknowledge that he did not have "the details in my mind."[85] All that Hand received was a perfunctory acknowledgment: Holmes assumed he would "come to a different result" but praised Hand's forcefulness and "admirable form."[86]

Not surprisingly, then, there is no hint of Hand's message, either of philosophy or of doctrine, in *Schenck* or *Frohwerk* or *Debs*. The only recognition of a first amendment concern is in one brief passage in *Schenck*; the other cases merely refer to *Schenck* as dispositive of the constitutional

---

82. *See* note 4 *supra*.

83. Indeed, Holmes said so in so many words. *See* Letter from Oliver Wendell Holmes to Learned Hand, Apr. 3, 1919, on file in the Hand Papers, Box 103, Folder 24, Harvard Law Library, Treasure Room [hereinafter cited as Appendix Doc. No. 5]: "I don't quite get your point." Compare Harry Kalven's recent comment about *Debs*, a comment I would apply to the entire spring 1919 trilogy: "It was for Holmes a routine criminal appeal." Kalven, *supra* note 4, at 238.

84. Letter from Learned Hand to Ernst Freund, May 7, 1919, on file in the Hand Papers, Box 21, Folder 1, Harvard Law Library, Treasure Room. The letter is printed in full in Ginsburg, *supra* note 4, at 244.

85. Letter from Oliver Wendell Holmes to Learned Hand, Feb. 25, 1919, on file in the Hand Papers, Box 103, Folder 24, Harvard Law Library, Treasure Room [hereinafter cited as Appendix Doc. No. 3].

86. *Id.*

objections. The *Schenck* passage contains the famous clear and present danger formulation:

> The question in every case is whether the words used are used in such circumstances and are of such a nature as to create a clear and present danger that they will bring about the substantive evils that Congress has a right to prevent. It is a question of proximity and degree.[87]

Later Holmes elaborations infused some requirement of immediacy of danger into that formula, although Holmes himself never addressed such complicating questions as the requisite seriousness of the anticipated harm.[88] But one is hard put to find any suggestion of immediacy, as contrasted to the more remote "bad tendency," in *Schenck*. In the spring 1919 cases, Holmes spoke interchangeably of the present danger and the natural tendency of the words. He took his stand within the framework of the Government arguments that the Second Circuit had accepted in *Masses*: words could be punished if they risked bad consequences. If he sought to confine the pursuit of chains of potential causation more tightly than those who talked of "probable" effects and of "bad tendencies," the effort is not perceptible on the face of *Schenck* and even less so in *Frohwerk* and *Debs*.

Indeed, to Holmes in *Schenck*, the applicability of the first amendment to postpublication sanctions was still in doubt. All he would concede was that it "well may be that the prohibition of laws abridging the freedom of speech is not confined to previous restraints, although to prevent them may have been the main purpose."[89] And all he could offer by way of analogy was the inapt "shouting fire in a theatre" example.[90] He concluded: "If the act [speaking, or circulating a paper], its tendency and the intent with which it is done are the same, we perceive no ground for saying that success alone warrants making the act a crime."[91] What "intent" had to do with a constitutional test purportedly focusing on the consequences of speech was never made clear, here or in later cases.

In *Schenck*, at least, the antiwar documents that provoked the prose-

---

87. 249 U.S. at 52.
88. *See, e.g.*, Yosal Rogat's critique of some "defects" in the Holmes formulation, including the comment: "[A] legislature is subject to constitutional limitations when, as in [Gitlow v. New York, 268 U.S. 652 (1925)], it prohibits the advocacy of a specific doctrine, but the question is not one of measuring 'proximity' to a specified act. Since the legislature has itself designated the point at which words become unlawful, the question is no longer how *close* words come to achieving certain consequences. In *Gitlow*, Holmes was confronted by, and evaded, the difficulty of applying his *Schenck* remark without modification to this different kind of problem." The important question in such a case, Rogat argues—and I agree—may well be not "proximity," but "which 'evils' a legislature may prohibit." Rogat, *The Judge as Spectator*, *supra* note 4, at 217. Only with Brandeis' superb concurrence in Whitney v. California, 274 U.S. 357, 372 (1927), did libertarian justices begin to confront the complex questions avoided in the Holmes opinions.
89. 249 U.S. at 51–52.
90. *Id.* at 52. On the inaptness of the analogy, *see, e.g.*, G. GUNTHER & N. DOWLING, *supra* note 7, at 1068; Kalven, *supra* note 4, at 236.
91. 249 U.S. at 52.

cution were "circulated to men who had been called and accepted for military service."[92] That was not true in either *Frohwerk* or *Debs*; but Holmes showed no greater hesitation about affirming the convictions in those cases. In *Frohwerk*, he added to the "shouting fire" analogy the equally inapt point that men like Hamilton or Madison would not have found suppression of the "counselling of a murder" to be an abridgment of free speech.[93] And when it came to the permissible interpretation of the defendants' words, Holmes' approach was in particularly striking contrast to Hand's strict, language-oriented analysis in *Masses*. Frohwerk, for example, had deplored draft riots in language, as Holmes put it, "that might be taken to convey an innuendo of a different sort."[94] And the position of Holmes' later defenders that clear and present danger contained a strong immediacy element in the spring of 1919[95] is hard to credit when one reads in *Frohwerk* that "it is impossible to say that it might not have been found that the circulation of the paper was in quarters where a little breath would be enough to kindle a flame."[96]

But the spring 1919 case most clearly insensitive to free speech concerns, and the one that aroused the strongest contemporary protests, was the prosecution of the Socialist leader and soon-to-be presidential candidate, Eugene V. Debs. As Holmes described Debs' speech, its main theme "was socialism, its growth, and a prophecy of its ultimate success."[97] But Holmes added: "[I]f a part or the manifest intent of the more general utterance was to encourage those present to obstruct the recruiting service and if in passages such encouragement was directly given, the immunity of the general theme may not be enough to protect the speech."[98] Again, as in *Frohwerk*, Holmes was willing to speculate about damaging innuendoes: "[Debs] said that he had to be prudent and might not be able to say all that he thought, thus intimating to his hearers that they might infer that he meant more . . . ."[99] Other parts of the speech, Holmes added, "had only [an] indirect though not necessarily ineffective bearing on the offences alleged."[100] Yet from these fragments, Holmes concluded, a jury could find "that one purpose of the speech, whether incidental or not does not matter, was to oppose not only war in general but this war, and that the

---

92. *Id.* at 49.
93. 249 U.S. at 206.
94. *Id.* at 207.
95. *See, e.g.,* Chafee's explanation of Holmes' course in 1919, Z. CHAFEE, FREE SPEECH IN THE UNITED STATES 86 (1941): "Looking backward, . . . we see that Justice Holmes was biding his time until the Court should have before it a conviction so clearly wrong as to let him speak out his deepest thoughts about the First Amendment."
96. 249 U.S. at 209.
97. 249 U.S. at 212.
98. *Id.* at 212–13.
99. *Id.* at 213.
100. *Id.* at 214.

opposition was so expressed that its natural and intended effect would be to obstruct recruiting."[101] Again, "natural tendency and reasonably probable effect"[102]—a formulation hardly different from that of the Government in the wartime prosecutions or of the Second Circuit in *Masses*—was enough to send Debs to jail. As Harry Kalven recently reminded us, it was "somewhat as though George McGovern had been sent to prison for his criticism of the [Vietnam] war."[103] *Schenck* is rightly read together with *Debs* (and with *Frohwerk*); and Kalven was right to find that the Holmes of these cases "shows no sensitivity to accommodating a tradition of political dissent, a sensitivity which had so characterized Hand's opinion two years earlier in [*Masses*], and makes no effort to suggest the parameters of improper criticism of the war."[104]

That it is accurate to deny any free speech sensitivity in the Holmes opinions of the *Schenck* period, despite the traditional view that would have it otherwise, is confirmed by the exchange of letters between Hand and Holmes soon after *Debs*.[105] Learned Hand was so distressed by *Debs* that he was moved to renew his campaign for greater protection of speech. He had little hope of success: his views, he told Holmes, were "already fast receding in the seas of forgotten errors."[106] Achieving adoption of his *Masses* approach seemed now a hopeless venture: "I bid a long farewell to my little toy ship which set out quite bravely on the shortest voyage ever made."[107] Nevertheless, despite the repeated frustrations, Hand made another effort to persuade Holmes, in March 1919. It was to be Hand's final direct appeal to Holmes—though by no means Hand's last effort to urge the *Masses* approach, as the later exchanges with Chafee demonstrate.[108]

In his March 1919 letter to Holmes, Hand begins by saying that "Debs was guilty under any rule conceivably applicable."[109] That comment is hard to credit: it differs from the tenor of his remarks to others, and it is impossible to believe that Debs' statements would have been punishable under the direct incitement test of *Masses*. That opening passage is best seen as an expression of Hand's extraordinary deference to Holmes, as an effort to seem to agree with the result while trying to persuade the master of

---

101. *Id.* at 214–15.
102. *Id.* at 216.
103. Kalven, *supra* note 4, at 237.
104. *Id.* at 237–38.
Kalven's characteristically perceptive comments on Holmes are but a small sample of the great loss suffered by all of us by the recent death of that most astute of modern commentators on the first amendment.
105. Letter from Learned Hand to Oliver Wendell Holmes, (late Mar.) 1919, on file in the Holmes Papers, Box 43, Folder 30, Harvard Law Library, Treasure Room [hereinafter cited as Appendix Doc. No. 4]; Appendix Doc. No. 5, Apr. 3, 1919, *supra* note 83 (Holmes and Hand).
106. Appendix Doc. No. 4, [late Mar.] 1919, *supra* note 105.
107. *Id.*
108. *See* notes 141–65 *infra* and accompanying text.
109. Appendix Doc. No. 4, *supra* note 105.

the error of his reasoning. The thrust of Hand's letter is sharply in contrast with Holmes' approach. Clear and present danger, like "natural and probable consequences," was a test of causation, a test calling for guesses about the future impact of words. As in *Masses*, Hand does not disagree that words may have practical consequences; rather, he denies that mere risk of consequences can justify legal culpability:

> In nature the causal sequence is perfect, but responsibility does not go pari passu. I do not understand that the rule of responsibility for speech has ever been that the result is known as likely to follow. It is not—I agree it might have been—a question of responsibility dependent upon reasonable forecast . . . . The responsibility only began when the words were directly an incitement.[110]

Hand suggested this as a test validated by history. But as in *Masses*, it was not truly a standard that rested on extensive reading in American history. Rather, it was a legal standard that was primarily a reflection of Hand's appreciation of free speech values.

But there was far more than the detached philosopher behind the incitement approach. It was an approach prompted, too, by Hand's practical awareness of the risks to speech if juries were permitted to punish on the basis of guesses about intent or reasonable consequences:

> All I say is, that since the cases actually occur when men are excited and since juries are especially clannish groups . . . it is very questionable whether the test of motive is not a dangerous test. Juries won't much regard the difference between the probable result of the words and the purposes of the utterer. In any case, unless one is rather set in conformity, it will serve to intimidate—throw a scare into—many a man who might moderate the storms of popular feeling. I know it did in 1918.[111]

This practical concern, and the reference to Postmaster General Burleson's "legal irresponsibility" in terrorizing some of the press,[112] reveal some important differences between Hand and Holmes. In Holmes, one finds the detached observer, the ironical philosopher of the June 24, 1918, letter.[113] Holmes is the Olympian, relatively unconcerned stoic watching mankind fight its battles from afar. There were ample detachment and skepticism in Hand's makeup as well. But there was also greater feeling, greater concern with what we now call "chilling effects," greater agony about the real-life impact of legal doctrine. It is a difference well illustrated by the respective reactions of Hand and Holmes to prosecutions such as that of Debs. Both were sideline observers; but Hand cared more about the injuries inflicted in the arena. Neither supported the prosecutions; but while

110. *Id.*
111. *Id.*
112. *Id.*
113. Appendix Doc. No. 2, *supra* note 72.

Holmes viewed them simply as additional illustrations of mankind's fol-
lies, to Hand they were genuine tragedies.[114]

Holmes' quite different perspective on the appropriate legal standards
emerges clearly from his reply to Hand's comment on *Debs*.[115] The basic
theme of his answer to Hand is accurately stated at the beginning of the
letter: in response to Hand's advocacy of a word-oriented incitement test—
in contrast to a cause-and-effect orientation—Holmes states: "I don't quite
get your point."[116] And as if to emphasize Holmes' lack of awareness of distinctions quite plain to more concerned contemporary observers, he responds to Hand's reference to incitement by quoting the full clear and present danger test from *Schenck*, adding the remarkable comment: "I don't
see how you differ from the test as stated by me."[117]

But it is the final portion of the passage that may best illustrate the primi-
tiveness of Holmes' first amendment thinking at that time. Holmes points
out that Hand had after all agreed in *Masses* that words may constitute a
violation of the statute, without proof of an actual obstruction. And he
adds: "So I don't know what the matter is, or how we differ so far as your
letter goes."[118] But very much was the matter. Of course Hand agreed that
words could sometimes be punishable. Virtually all commentators agreed
on that point. But Holmes thought that shared premise was the end of the
problem. In fact, it was only the beginning. The real challenge was to
articulate a standard that, while reaching some words, would protect most
criticism of government. The *Masses* incitement test was one such effort.
Clear and present danger at the time of *Schenck*, it seems evident, was not.
How could it be, when Holmes simply failed to see the problem?

IV. *The* Abrams *Dissent and Hand's Continued Adherence to the* Masses *Approach, 1919–21*

Eight months after the *Schenck* trilogy, Justice Holmes began to get
the point: in *Abrams v. United States*,[119] he put forth his now famous
elaboration of first amendment doctrine. It was as if the message of critics
such as Learned Hand were having a delayed impact; but it was only a
partial impact. Holmes' dissent in *Abrams* is a classic primarily because
of its eloquent concluding passages, with their emphasis on the "free trade
in ideas" as "the theory of our Constitution." Those passages are indeed

114. On Holmes' views, *see, e.g.*, 2 HOLMES-POLLOCK LETTERS 7, 11, 15 (M. Howe ed. 1941);
1 HOLMES-LASKI LETTERS 190–91, 197 (M. Howe ed. 1953). Hand's views surface repeatedly in the
letters printed in the Appendix.
115. Appendix Doc. No. 5, Apr. 3, 1919, *supra* note 83.
116. *Id.*
117. *Id.*
118. *Id.*
119. 250 U.S. 616, 624 (1919) (dissenting opinion).

218

GERALD GUNTHER

a response to the first part of Hand's message: the need to appreciate the values of free speech, the legitimate claim of free speech to special legal protection. But as to the second part of the Hand message, on the need for adequate doctrinal implementation of free speech values, the Holmes dissent is considerably less satisfying. And Hand clearly was not satisfied.

Justice Clarke's majority opinion affirming the conviction of the defendants in *Abrams* dismissed the constitutional objections as "definitely negatived" by *Schenck* and *Frohwerk*.[120] And it is indeed difficult to perceive any significant differences in tenor between the Clarke opinion and those of Holmes in the spring. But Holmes, joined by Brandeis, now dissented. There were two strands to his argument; and his dissent does not fully disentangle the strands. In part, Holmes rested on statutory interpretation; in part, he relied on constitutional argument—clear and present danger infused with a new immediacy element.

The statutory argument arose because the *Abrams* defendants had been charged under the 1918 amendments to the Espionage Act, not under the 1917 provisions applied in *Masses* and the *Schenck* trilogy. Among the new offenses designated in the May 1918 amendments was urging the curtailment of the production of materials necessary to the prosecution of the war with Germany, with intent to hinder the prosecution of that war.[121] Holmes managed to read a strict specific intent requirement into that provision. The *Abrams* defendants were "anarchists" who had urged a general strike to oppose American military intervention against the Russian revolution. Stopping war production to impede American forces in Russia might indeed have the effect of interfering with the war with Germany; but, Holmes insisted, since the German war was not the immediate target of the defendants, the requisite specific intent had not been shown.[122] Learned Hand had some difficulty with that reading of the intent requirement, as two of his letters to Chafee illustrate.[123]

But the statutory issue was not the critical one. It was the elaboration of clear and present danger as a constitutional test that made the *Abrams* dissent doctrinally significant. Holmes insisted that the *Schenck* trilogy was "rightly decided":

---

120. *Id.* at 619.
121. Act of May 16, 1918, ch. 75, § 3, 40 Stat. 553, *amending* Act of June 15, 1917, ch. 30, tit. 1, § 3, 40 Stat. 217, 219.
122. 250 U.S. at 626–27, 628–29 (dissenting opinion).
123. *See* Appendix Doc. No. 9, Dec. 3, 1919, *supra* note 23; Appendix Doc. No. 15, Jan. 2, 1921, *supra* note 24.
In the first letter, Hand expressed great doubt about Holmes' reading of the specific intent requirement: "[O]n the facts [in *Abrams*] it seems to me very questionable whether the decision was not correct. At first, upon reading the opinion, I was quite sure the majority was wrong, but the distinction seems to me pretty tenuous between the purpose to encourage resistance to the United States and merely to prevent the United States from overthrowing the Bolshevik party." In the second letter, about a year later, Hand moved somewhat closer to Holmes' approach on the intent issue and expressed his revised position by offering a hypothetical jury charge.

I do not doubt for a moment that by the same reasoning that would justify punishing persuasion to murder, the United States constitutionally may punish speech that produces or is intended to produce a clear and imminent danger that it will bring about forthwith certain substantive evils that the United States constitutionally may seek to prevent.[124]

Again, the inapt "persuasion to murder" analogy of *Frohwerk* appears. And once more, intent and actual risks are alternative ingredients, without any explanation of the relevance of intent to a standard emphasizing the dangerous consequences of words. But despite the continuing obscurity in Holmes' approach, some passages at last injected a genuine immediacy ingredient into clear and present danger and sharply distinguished Holmes' *Abrams* requirements from the remote consequences adequate for conviction under a "bad tendency" standard:

It is only the present danger of immediate evil or an intent to bring it about that warrants Congress in setting a limit to the expression of opinion where private rights are not concerned . . . . I think that we should be eternally vigilant against attempts to check the expression of opinions that we loathe and believe to be fraught with death, unless they so imminently threaten immediate interference with the lawful and pressing purposes of the law that an immediate check is required to save the country.[125]

For Holmes, Abrams' pamphlets were "poor and puny anonymities"[126] —though one would think not more so than some of the materials he had found punishable a few months earlier. And Holmes now saw the force of the historical argument he had been oblivious to earlier: the first amendment did not leave "the common law as to seditious libel in force. History seems to me against the notion. I had conceived that the United States through many years had shown its repentance for the Sedition Act of 1798, by repaying fines that it imposed."[127] Holmes left many questions unanswered; but the *Abrams* dissent did at last provide a real basis for regarding clear and present danger as a speech-protective doctrine.

The balance of these letters[128] deals with Learned Hand's reaction to *Abrams*. These are the most novel, intriguing, and revealing portions of the correspondence. The most striking theme that emerges from this final group is a complex, profoundly important reaction by Hand: he welcomes the *Abrams* dissent for its values; he does not accept its doctrine. To have Holmes at last recognize that free speech is worthy of special protection was gratifying; but, more important, clear and present danger, even in its revised form, was less attractive to Hand than his own "hard" and "objec-

---

124. 250 U.S. at 627 (dissenting opinion).
125. *Id.* at 628, 630 (dissenting opinion).
126. *Id.* at 629 (dissenting opinion).
127. *Id.* at 630 (dissenting opinion).
128. *See* Appendix Docs. Nos. 6–16 and accompanying notes *infra*.

tive"[129] incitement test of *Masses*. Writing to Holmes, Hand simply acknowledged his appreciation of finding added judicial support for his own special concern for speech.[130] With Holmes' short reply,[131] the Hand-Holmes correspondence about the first amendment ended: Hand thought it pointless to pursue his advocacy of the *Masses* approach vis-à-vis Holmes. But that he did not abandon it and indeed elaborated it is the clear message of the remaining correspondence, with Zechariah Chafee, Jr.[132]

Learned Hand's post-*Abrams* letter of November 25, 1919,[133] was his last to Holmes on first amendment issues. He was pleased with the dissent, "especially with the close," and "quite confident" that "in the end your views must prevail, after people get over the existing hysteria."[134] He was obviously encouraged by the fact that the free speech values he had articulated since *Masses* had at last found their way into the United States Reports—encouraged "because I had found so little professional support for my own beliefs which would always have been expressed so, had I had the power to express them."[135]

Hand's letter withheld any further criticism of Holmes, and Holmes gracefully acknowledged Hand's praise.[136] But Hand was not in fact uncritical. His satisfaction with Holmes' closing passages could not overcome his deep reservations about the doctrinal implementation. They were reservations especially difficult to contain because the underlying practical problems were more pressing than ever. As Hand told Holmes, "the merry sport of Red-baiting goes on, and the pack gives tongue more and more shrilly."[137] Hand ended his letter to Holmes with an especially characteristic and powerful line:

> For men who are not cock-sure about everything and especially for those who are not damned cock-sure about anything, the skies have a rather sinister appearance.[138]

Pervasive skepticism, genuine openmindedness, persistent self-doubt, not being "damned cock-sure about anything"—these were indeed appropriate characterizations of Learned Hand's makeup throughout his life.[139]

---

129. *See* Appendix Doc. No. 15, *supra* note 24; text accompanying notes 23–24 *supra*.

130. Letter from Learned Hand to Oliver Wendell Holmes, Nov. 25, 1919, on file in the Holmes Papers, Box 43, Folder 30, Harvard Law Library, Treasure Room [hereinafter cited as Appendix Doc. No. 6].

131. Letter from Oliver Wendell Holmes to Learned Hand, Nov. 26, 1919, on file in the Hand Papers, Box 103, Folder 24, Harvard Law Library, Treasure Room [hereinafter cited as Appendix Doc. No. 7].

132. *See* notes 141–65 *infra* and accompanying text.

133. Appendix Doc. No. 6, *supra* note 130.

134. *Id.*

135. *Id.*

136. Appendix Doc. No. 7, Nov. 26, 1919, *supra* note 131.

137. Appendix Doc. No. 6, Nov. 25, 1919, *supra* note 130.

138. *Id.*

139. *See* Gunther, *Introduction*, in THE SPIRIT OF LIBERTY—THE LEARNED HAND CENTENNIAL EXHIBIT AT THE HARVARD LAW SCHOOL 1–3 (Harvard Law School Library 1972). For brief personality

All the more extraordinary, then, is Hand's persistence in identifying the flaws in Holmes' clear and present danger standard and in adhering to his *Masses* approach in the years immediately following *Abrams*. With the judge he most respected impervious to his arguments, with no real hope that his own "little toy ship"[140] would ever again float, Hand was nevertheless sufficiently persuaded of the legal and practical importance of the issue to continue the articulation of his position for a while longer. But that articulation was now addressed to Chafee rather than Holmes.

The Hand-Chafee letters[141] seem to me especially important contributions to the intellectual history of first amendment doctrine. This remarkable exchange came about quite fortuitously—almost as accidentally as the chain of circumstances that was fast making Chafee the country's foremost expert on the first amendment. Chafee wrote Hand less than a month after *Abrams*. The men were not acquainted; they apparently did not meet throughout the period of this 16-month exchange.[142] The correspondence began with an invitation to Hand to join Holmes and Brandeis as guests of the Harvard Liberal Club of Boston to honor "the stand taken by the two Harvard men on the United States Supreme Court on the question of freedom of speech,"[143] in the *Abrams* dissent.

By then, at the end of 1919, Zechariah Chafee, Jr., had begun to build a reputation as a scholar of civil liberties. It was a recently developed interest with him; but at a time when few academics—or judges or lawyers—were concerned with the first amendment, even 2 or 3 years' exposure to the field was enough for incipient prominence. Chafee was an unlikely candidate for that role. The soft-spoken New Englander had left his Providence law practice in 1916 to teach at Harvard. "[T]wo accidents"[144] brought him into contact with free speech problems. He was asked to teach a course on injunctions against torts. He decided to follow Dean Roscoe Pound's footsteps and discuss in that course the problem of enjoining libels. He started to read cases about liberty of the press. He found little that was useful in the decisions through 1916. Then he came across *Masses*. And, as he told Hand in 1920: "It was really your opinion in the Masses case that started me on my work."[145]

---

and biographical sketches of Learned Hand, *see* Dilliard, *Introduction*, in I. Dilliard ed., *supra* note 66; Shanks, *Introduction*, in THE ART AND CRAFT OF JUDGING—THE DECISIONS OF JUDGE LEARNED HAND 1–28 (H. Shanks ed. 1968).

140. Appendix Doc. No. 4, (late Mar.) 1919, *supra* note 105 (Hand to Holmes).
141. *See* Appendix Docs. Nos. 8–16 and accompanying notes *infra*.
142. Indeed, in their first exchange, each erred in writing the other's name: Chafee's first letter to Hand is addressed to "Judge Learned B. Hand"; Hand's response is to "Chaffee," not "Chafee." Letter from Zechariah Chafee, Jr., to Learned Hand, Dec. 2, 1919, on file in the Hand Papers, Box 15, Folder 26, Harvard Law Library, Treasure Room [hereinafter cited as Appendix Doc. No. 8]; Hand to Chafee, Dec. 3, 1919, Appendix Doc. No. 9, *supra* note 23.
143. Appendix Doc. No. 8, *supra* note 142.
144. Z. CHAFEE, *supra* note 20, at 1.
145. Letter from Zechariah Chafee, Jr., to Learned Hand, Oct. 25, 1920, on file in the Hand

But Chafee might have remained solely a teacher of equitable remedies had it not been for another "accident." Harold Laski, then a Harvard tutor and occasional contributor to *The New Republic,* urged Chafee to use some of his research on the Espionage Act cases for a piece for the magazine.[146] Chafee agreed: "[T]he prospect of $75 was a sharp spur to an assistant professor. It was the first cash I earned by writing."[147] From that beginning grew longer articles for the *Harvard Law Review.*[148] Then Walter Lippmann encouraged Chafee to turn his work into a book. *Freedom of Speech* was the result; Chafee's reputation was made; and the reputations of Oliver Wendell Holmes and the clear and present danger test were immeasurably enhanced.

Irony abounds in the fact that Zechariah Chafee, Jr., was the addressee of Learned Hand's most careful and, to me, most compelling elaboration of the *Masses* approach. Chafee was the single most important publicist for Holmes' clear and present danger test: it was Chafee's writing, more than anyone else's, that made clear and present danger for so long the rallying point of libertarians; and it was Chafee who defended Holmes and clear and present danger against all attackers for more than three decades.[149] Yet, Chafee also was the primary audience for Hand's explanation of the major alternative approach. There is additional irony: the single most important book spreading the gospel of clear and present danger was Chafee's 1920 volume, *Freedom of Speech*; yet the occasion for some of the Hand-Chafee correspondence was Chafee's decision to dedicate this Holmes-praising book to Learned Hand. What is more, Chafee proves to hold a secret preference for the *Masses* approach,[150] even while publicly advocating the clear and present danger test so effectively. Perhaps it is the ultimate irony that Hand wrought better than he knew: though he had lost hope that his test would ever be accepted, he persisted for several years in elaborating its advantages to Chafee and in identifying some of the shortcomings of clear and present danger; and these private messages to Chafee contained the lessons that the Supreme Court ultimately learned in the 1950's and 1960's, after decades of unsatisfying experimentation with clear and present danger.[151]

Papers, Box 15, Folder 26, Harvard Law Library, Treasure Room [hereinafter cited as Appendix Doc. No. 12].

146. *See* Chafee, *Freedom of Speech*, 17 THE NEW REPUBLIC 66 (1918).
147. Z. CHAFEE, *supra* note 20, at 3.
148. *See* Chafee, *A Contemporary State Trial*—The United States *versus* Jacob Abrams et al., 33 HARV. L. REV. 747 (1920); Chafee, *Freedom of Speech in War Time*, 32 HARV. L. REV. 932 (1919).
149. The best-known defense during Chafee's later years was his Book Review, 62 HARV. L. REV. 891 (1949) (reviewing A. MEIKLEJOHN, FREE SPEECH AND ITS RELATION TO SELF-GOVERNMENT (1948)). The Book Review is reprinted in ASSOCIATION OF AMERICAN LAW SCHOOLS, SELECTED ESSAYS ON CONSTITUTIONAL LAW 1938–1962, at 618 (1963).
150. *See* note 154 *infra* and accompanying text.
151. *See* notes 182–97 *infra* and accompanying text.

The legend on the dedication page of Chafee's *Freedom of Speech* illustrates some of these ironies:

TO

LEARNED HAND
UNITED STATES DISTRICT JUDGE
FOR THE SOUTHERN DISTRICT OF NEW YORK
WHO DURING THE TURMOIL OF WAR
COURAGEOUSLY MAINTAINED
THE TRADITION OF ENGLISH-SPEAKING FREEDOM
AND GAVE IT NEW CLEARNESS AND STRENGTH
FOR THE WISER YEARS TO COME[152]

A strange phenomenon indeed: the chief publicist for clear and present danger dedicating his book to the author of the *Masses* alternative.

Hand's letters gave Chafee ample basis to know that *Masses* and clear and present danger were quite different approaches. In his private letters, Chafee even acknowledged for many years that *Masses* would have been a preferable standard; he saw the shortcomings of Holmes' test. As he wrote to Hand in the last of these letters, "Holmes' distinction would prove unworkable in many cases. The Jury would go over it rough shod."[153] But only once to my knowledge did he ever prefer the *Masses* approach in public: "I still like better Judge Learned Hand's phrase in the suit to get The Masses back into the mails, 'direct incitement to violent resistance' . . . ."[154] But, characteristically, he added: "Yet these are only minor variations."[155]

Of course, they were not "minor." What, then, prompted Chafee to advocate Holmes' test in his writings? What moved him to take the lead for years in conveying the impression that *Masses* was not all that different from clear and present danger? I am not certain of the answer. In part, Chafee may not have fully appreciated the differences: there is some sup-

152. Z. CHAFEE, *supra* note 10, at iii.
153. Appendix Doc. No. 16, Mar. 28, 1921, *supra* note 41. *See also* Chafee's comments to his old friend (but intellectual adversary on the subject of Holmes and clear and present danger), Alexander Meiklejohn, in a letter accompanying the manuscript of the well-known book review noted *supra* note 149. Chafee wrote in order to convey to Meiklejohn "a greater awareness of the serious difficulties involved in your own position [of which you would have been aware] if you had read more widely in the legal materials" and to give him "a better understanding of the reasons which led Holmes to formulate his clear and present danger test." Letter of Zechariah Chafee, Jr., to Alexander Meiklejohn, Nov. 23, 1948, on file in the Chafee Papers, Box 2, Folder 16, Harvard Law Library, Treasure Room. Chafee's comments included the following passages: "Hand's opinion in the Masses case is just as important for me as the opinion of Holmes in the Schenck case, to which you naturally pay a great deal of attention. . . . Holmes could not possibly have convinced his colleagues that all speech which tended to produce evasion of the draft was immune. Hand had tried to draw the line pretty close to express words, but the court which reversed him felt that this did not sufficiently take care of the Mark Anthony problem. Holmes evidently had similar worries. My own inclination is to agree with Hand, but I can see the reasonableness of a different point of view."
154. Z. CHAFEE, *supra* note 20, at 9.
155. *Id.*

port for that view in the letters. Perhaps, too, Chafee became an unwitting captive of the Holmes mythology he had created. And perhaps some of the explanation rests on pragmatic grounds: Holmes' *Schenck* and *Abrams* language was on the Supreme Court books; *Masses* was not; one might as well make the most of the second best. The author of *Masses* himself understood Chafee's emphasis on Holmes in that light. As Hand wrote Chafee at the beginning of 1921:

> You have, I dare say, done well to take what has fallen from Heaven and insist that it is manna rather than to set up any independent solution. "Immediate and direct" is all we have; for God's sake let us not look it in the mouth.[156]

Yet Hand's understanding did not compel emulation: Chafee might make the most of the "manna" that had "fallen from Heaven"; Hand would persist in arguing that *Masses* was a distinctive and a preferable approach.

But Chafee's perceptions and motivations are not the central issues; Hand's thinking after *Abrams* is. And what is entirely clear from the Hand-Chafee correspondence is that Hand himself did not view the differences between *Masses* and clear and present danger as "minor." Within a week after Hand's congratulatory letter to Holmes on the *Abrams* dissent, Hand told Chafee, after expressing his delight that the Holmes dissent had appeared:

> I do not altogether like the way Justice Holmes put the limitation. I myself think it is a little more manageable and quite adequate a distinction to say that there is an absolute and objective test to language. I daresay that it is obstinacy, but I still prefer that which I attempted to state in my first "Masses" opinion, rather than to say that the connection between the words used and the evil aimed at should be "immediate and direct."[157]

That proved to be no offhand remark. When Chafee suggested some variations in the doctrine,[158] Hand was stirred into producing one of the most careful restatements of the *Masses* approach.[159] And once again, his restatement is joined with a critique of clear and present danger:

> It seems to me, I own, that the test of immediacy and directness, while in application it may be about the same as the other I shall suggest is not, strictly speaking, correct; I say this with a genuine diffidence. I prefer a test based upon the nature of the utterance itself. If, taken in its setting, the effect upon the hearers is only to counsel them to violate the law, it is unconditionally illegal . . . .
>
> As to other utterances, it appears to me that regardless of their tendency they should be permitted. The reason is that any State which professes to be controlled

---

156. Appendix Doc. No. 15, Jan. 2, 1921, *supra* note 24 (Hand to Chafee).
157. Appendix Doc. No. 9, Dec. 3, 1919, *supra* note 23.
158. Letter from Zechariah Chafee, Jr., to Learned Hand, Jan. 6, 1920, on file in the Hand Papers, Box 15, Folder 26, Harvard Law Library, Treasure Room [hereinafter cited as Appendix Doc. No. 10].
159. Appendix Doc. No. 11, Jan. 8, 1920, *supra* note 25.

by public opinion, cannot take sides against any opinion except that which must express itself in the violation of law. On the contrary, it must regard all other expression of opinion as tolerable, if not good. . . .

. . . [N]othing short of counsel to violate law should be itself illegal. There could be no objection to the rule of the Supreme Court, tendency plus a purpose to produce the evil, even though the words did not come to the objective standard, if one were sure of the result in practical administration. The chance that the State would lose any valuable opinion by suppressing those whose purpose was to produce a violation of law, while they kept on the safe side of counselling it, seems to me much too thin for practical estimate. My own objection to the rule rests in the fact that it exposes all who discuss heated questions to an inquiry before a jury as to their purposes. That inquiry necessarily is of the widest scope and if their general attitude is singular and intransigeant, my own belief is that a jury is an insufficient protection. I think it is precisely at those times when alone the freedom of speech becomes important as an institution, that the protection of a jury on such an issue is illusory. The event seems to me to have proved this.

Therefore, to be a real protection to the expression of egregious opinion in times of excitement, I own I cannot see any escape from construing the privilege as absolute, so long as the utterance, objectively regarded, can by any fair construction be held to fall short of counselling violence. That much actually sinister utterance will pass, is undoubtedly true, but the whole institution presupposes a balance of evils. In taking sides I suppose one will range oneself according to one's degree of natural scepticism about opinions in general. For myself I think our chief enemies are Credulity, and his brother Intolerance.[160]

For a while, the Hand-Chafee exchange rested with that letter of early 1920. Then, in the fall of that year, Chafee asked Hand for permission to dedicate *Freedom of Speech* to him;[161] and despite Hand's obvious delight,[162] the Judge, on reading the book, was moved once again to defend *Masses* and criticize the *Abrams* dissent, more eloquently and more elaborately than ever.[163] In what may be the single most impressive letter of the correspondence, Hand comments, for example:

I am not wholly in love with Holmesy's test and the reason is this. Once you admit that the matter is one of degree, while you may put it where it genuinely belongs, you so obviously make it a matter of administration, i.e. you give to Tomdickandharry, D.J., so much latitude [here Learned Hand wrote and struck out "as his own fears may require," and continued] that the jig is at once up. Besides even their Ineffabilities, the Nine Elder Statesmen, have not shown themselves wholly immune from the "herd instinct" and what seems "immediate and direct" to-day may seem very remote next year even though the circumstances surrounding the utterance be unchanged. I own I should prefer a qualitative formula, hard, conventional, difficult to evade. If it could become sacred by the incrustations of time and precedent it might be made to serve just a little to withhold the torrents of

160. *Id.*
161. Appendix Doc. No. 12, Oct. 25, 1920, *supra* note 145.
162. *See* Appendix Docs. Nos. 13–15 and accompanying notes *infra*.
163. Appendix Doc. No. 15, Jan. 2, 1921, *supra* note 24.

passion to which I suspect democracies will be found more subject than for example the whig autocracy of the 18th century. . . .[164]

It is a splendid letter to crown a sparkling sequence. Again and again— not only on *Masses* versus clear and present danger, but also on the appropriate interpretation of the intent provisions of the 1918 amendments to the Espionage Act and on deportation problems—Hand reveals a striking combination of qualities of the judicial craftsman and the concerned libertarian. And there is, too, a glimpse of the warm and modest and charming human being, expressing a final delight at Chafee's dedication of the book:

> [Y]ou have made *me* feel very happy, and you have pleased three little girls too, who I am glad to say have never regarded their father hitherto as much more than an elderly man with a not wholly reliable amiability, though buttressed with a taste for buffoonery.[165]

EPILOGUE—THE BELATED VINDICATION OF HAND'S *Masses* APPROACH

> I can't help wondering whether a good many years from now when you are old and I am dead, you may not pick up the book and reading the first page, smile with some amusement and some regret. You really will have nothing personal to regret, even if you would not then think of repeating it, but still if I were there then—and perhaps I shall come back to plague you for your thoughts, because ghosts have no respect for freedom of opinion—I should feel a little as though I have passed off on you some false coin.[166]

So wrote Learned Hand to Zechariah Chafee, Jr., at the beginning of 1921, in a delightful last paragraph of his final letter in this series. It was characteristically self-deprecating, but with a serious undercurrent. Hand had advocated his *Masses* approach for the last time; he had no real hope that it would ever re-emerge. As he wrote to civil liberties lawyer Walter Nelles 2 years later, "I have not much hope that my own views as stated in the Masses case would ever be recognized as law."[167] From the reaction to *Masses* in the years immediately after the decision, it seemed indeed destined to be viewed as "false coin."[168] And Chafee, in fact, did not adhere to the dedication on the first page of his 1920 book. In 1941, Chafee published *Free Speech in the United States*, a revised and expanded version of *Freedom of Speech*. In the revision, the dedication was not to Learned Hand but to former Harvard President Abbott Lawrence Lowell.[169] Chafee had

---

164. *Id.*
165. *Id.*
166. *Id.*
167. Letter from Learned Hand to Walter Nelles, Apr. 20, 1923, on file in the Hand Papers, Box 33, Folder 6, Harvard Law Library, Treasure Room.
168. Appendix Doc. No. 15, Jan. 2, 1921, *supra* note 24 (Hand to Chafee).
169. Z. CHAFEE, *supra* note 95, at v.

understandable reasons for the change.[170] But the disappearance of Learned Hand from Chafee's dedication page in 1941 had a symbolic significance as well. By then, *Masses* seemed forgotten, clear and present danger had made its way into Supreme Court majority opinions, and the Holmesian phrase had become the rallying point for libertarians.

It was always a standard more popular than sturdy. Holmes had added more memorable rhetoric in another classic dissent to join *Abrams*, in *Gitlow v. New York*.[171] But what real subtlety and substance clear and present danger achieved came primarily from an opinion that was not only "classic" but meaty, that of Justice Brandeis in *Whitney v. California*.[172] During the decade after Chafee's 1941 book appeared, clear and present danger came under increasing attack.[173] It flourished largely in contexts far from its origins in the problems of allegedly seditious speech.[174] And when the Court returned to this context with the prosecution of Communist Party leaders under the Smith Act,[175] in *Dennis v. United States*,[176] clear and present danger proved of little help in the protection of free speech values.

Debate still continues about the source of the debacle of the *Dennis* case: whether the wounds were inflicted by the Vinson Court, or whether the episode simply exposed the inherent vulnerabilities of the Holmes standard. At any rate, the Vinson Court in *Dennis* restated clear and present danger in a manner draining it of most of the immediacy emphasis it had attained over the years. And by many, Learned Hand is better remembered for his participation in this restatement than for his *Masses* opinion. Thirty-two years after *Schenck*, Chief Justice Vinson explicitly adopted the reformulation of clear and present danger put forth by Learned Hand, by then Chief Judge of the Court of Appeals for the Second Circuit: "In each case, [courts] must ask whether the gravity of the 'evil,' discounted by its improbability, justifies such invasion of free speech as is necessary to avoid the danger."[177]

<hr/>

170. Lowell, as Harvard President in the early 1920's, had helped protect Professor Chafee against alumni attacks on some of his libertarian writings—especially his criticisms of the *Abrams* prosecutions. *See* A. SUTHERLAND, THE LAW AT HARVARD 250–59 (1967); Chafee Papers, Harvard Law Library, Treasure Room, *passim*. *See generally* Prude, *Portrait of a Civil Libertarian: The Faith and Fear of Zechariah Chafee, Jr.*, 60 J. AM. HIST. 633 (1973). As Chafee put it in his dedication of the 1941 book, Lowell had helped assure that "No One Could Breathe the Air of Harvard and Not Be Free." Z. CHAFEE, *supra* note 95, at v.
171. 268 U.S. 652, 672 (1925) (dissenting opinion).
172. 274 U.S. 357, 372 (1927) (concurring opinion); *see* note 88 *supra*.
173. *See, e.g.*, A. MEIKLEJOHN, *supra* note 149, at 47–50; P. FREUND, ON UNDERSTANDING THE SUPREME COURT 27–28 (1949); Wechsler, *Symposium on Civil Liberties*, 9 AM. L. SCH. REV. 881 (1941).
174. *See, e.g.*, Learned Hand's review of the cases in his opinion in Dennis v. United States, 183 F.2d 201, 209–12 (2d Cir. 1950), *aff'd*, 341 U.S. 495 (1951). An excerpt of the Hand critique in *Dennis* is quoted in text accompanying note 179 *infra*.
175. 18 U.S.C. § 2385 (1970) (*originally enacted* as Act of June 28, 1940, ch. 439, §§ 2(a), 5, 54 Stat. 671).
176. 341 U.S. 495 (1951).
177. *Id.* at 510, *quoting with approval* 183 F.2d 201, 212 (2d Cir. 1950).

The later years of Learned Hand are not the focus of this Essay: this is
not the place to explore fully the Judge's performance in *Dennis*. Several
factors may explain Hand's articulation of a standard which was less protective than *Schenck* (as interpreted in the *Abrams* dissent) and obviously
less so than *Masses*. For one, as his letters make clear, Hand had never liked
the *Schenck* standard. As he said explicitly a few years after *Dennis*, in a
wry aside about Holmes' formulation: "Homer nodded."[178] But more basic
forces were no doubt at work. Hand as Circuit Judge in 1950 was not writing on a blank slate as he had in *Masses*; he was now compelled to try to
make sense of what the Court had done with the *Schenck* standard in the
intervening decades. And Hand was plainly puzzled: his conclusion that
the cases were ultimately unhelpful had ample basis in the Supreme Court
opinions. As Hand said in *Dennis*, after tracing the emergence of clear and
present danger in a variety of cases of the 1930's and 1940's:

> The opinions in all these cases did however repeat the rubric of Schenck v. United
> States, though none of them attempted to define how grave, or how imminent the
> danger must be, or whether the two factors are mutually interdependent. More-
> over, the situation in all was wholly different from that in the preceding decisions.
> It is one thing to say that the public interest in keeping streets clean, or in keeping
> a register of union leaders, or in requiring solicitors to take out licenses, will not
> justify interference with freedom of utterance . . . ; but it is quite another matter
> to say that an organized effort to inculcate the duty of revolution may not be re-
> pressed. It does not seem to us therefore that these decisions help towards a solution
> here.[179]

Perhaps most basic of all were Hand's growing doubts that courts could
truly aid in preserving freedom of expression in times of crisis. That skepticism was far deeper in his later years than it had been during World War
I.[180] By the time of his Holmes Lectures in 1958, he had come to view the
first amendment as one of a set of moral adjurations, not as a judicially
enforceable norm.[181]

But it is the post-*Dennis* course of decisions that presents the ultimate
irony: a belated adoption by the Supreme Court of aspects of the *Masses*
approach—long after Hand himself had lost confidence in it, after the rise
and decline of *Schenck*'s clear and present danger standard, after Hand
had contributed to *Schenck*'s disintegration. This long-delayed vindication
of *Masses* came in the post-*Dennis* Smith Act cases, especially *Yates v.
United States*[182] and *Scales v. United States*,[183] in response to the nadir of

178. L. HAND, *supra* note 66, at 59.
179. 183 F.2d at 209.
180. *See, e.g.*, Hand, *Chief Justice Stone's Concept of the Judicial Function*, in I. Dilliard, ed.,
supra note 66, at 201; Hand, *The Contribution of an Independent Judiciary to Civilization*, in *id.*, at
155.
181. *See, e.g.*, L. HAND, *supra* note 66, at 56–77.
182. 354 U.S. 298 (1957).
183. 367 U.S. 203 (1961).

modern civil liberties protection in *Dennis*. It came at the hands of Justice John Marshall Harlan, who wrote the prevailing opinions in those cases.

That Justice Harlan rekindled the torch lit and carried by Hand from 1917 to 1921 is fitting. At the time of *Yates*, Justice Harlan had recently come to the Supreme Court from the Second Circuit. He was at the beginning of what was to become an increasingly distinguished career as a thoughtful interpreter of the first amendment.[184] And he reinvigorated free speech protection in the post-*Dennis* years by exhibiting the best qualities of judicial craftsmanship so long associated with Learned Hand. Harlan found a way to curtail prosecutions under the Smith Act even though the constitutionality of the Act had been sustained in *Dennis*. He did it by invoking techniques very similar to those applied by Hand in *Masses* to the World War I Espionage Act: he read the statute in terms of constitutional presuppositions; and he strove to find standards "manageable" by judges and capable of curbing jury discretion. He insisted on strict statutory standards of proof emphasizing the actual speech of the defendants—a variation on the "hard," "objective," words-oriented focus of *Masses*. Harlan claimed to be interpreting *Dennis*. In fact, *Yates* and *Scales* represented doctrinal evolution in a new direction, a direction in the *Masses* tradition.

In *Yates*, Harlan propounded a variation on Hand's incitement test. The defendants had challenged the trial court's instructions on the ground that they provided inadequate guidance to the jury on the distinction between abstract doctrine and advocacy of action. They objected that the trial judge had failed to charge that the defendants' advocacy must be "of a kind calculated to 'incite' persons to action for the forcible overthrow of the government."[185] The Government replied "that the true constitutional dividing line is not between inciting and abstract advocacy of forcible overthrow, but rather between advocacy as such, irrespective of its inciting qualities, and the mere discussion or exposition of violent overthrow as an abstract theory."[186]

Justice Harlan rejected the Government's argument. He found the trial court's charge defective because it had withdrawn from the jury's consideration "any issue as to the character of the advocacy in terms of its capacity to stir listeners to forcible action."[187] Evil intent was not adequate under the Smith Act; only advocacy that constituted an "effort to instigate action" was punishable.[188] And, he insisted, the evidence must be carefully scru-

184. *See* Gunther, *In Search of Judicial Quality on a Changing Court: The Case of Justice Powell*, 24 STAN. L. REV. 1001, 1004–14 (1972).
185. 354 U.S. at 312.
186. *Id.* at 313.
187. *Id.* at 315.
188. *Id.* at 318. Justice Harlan added: "The distinction between advocacy of abstract doctrine and advocacy directed at promoting unlawful action is one that has been consistently recognized in the opinions of this Court . . . . We need not, however, decide the issue before us in terms of constitutional compulsion, for our first duty is to construe this statute. . . . The essential distinction is

tinized to assure that the speaker had explicitly urged illegal action. Echo-
ing concerns about juries similar to those voiced by Hand years earlier,
Harlan added: "Vague references to 'revolutionary' or 'militant' action
of an unspecified character, which are found in the evidence, might in
addition be given too great weight by the jury in the absence of more precise instructions."[189] As Harlan elaborated in *Scales* in 1961, 4 years after
Yates, the Smith Act required "strict standards in assessing the adequacy of
the proof needed to make out a case of illegal advocacy."[190]

A few years later, in the 1969 decision in *Brandenburg v. Ohio*,[191] the
Warren Court built on *Yates* and *Scales* to produce its clearest and most
protective standard under the first amendment. And *Brandenburg* continues to be adhered to by the Burger Court.[192] *Brandenburg* rests ultimately on the insight Learned Hand urged without success at the end of
World War I. The *Brandenburg* per curiam emphasized that laws affecting first amendment rights "must observe the established distinction between mere advocacy and incitement to imminent lawless action."[193] That
was hardly an "established" distinction. Indeed, that was precisely the distinction Holmes has sought to discredit in the *Gitlow* dissent with the
deprecating comment: "Every idea is an incitement."[194] An incitement-
nonincitement distinction had only fragmentary and ambiguous antecedents in the pre-*Brandenburg* era; it was *Brandenburg* that really "established" it; and, it was essentially an establishment of the legacy of Learned
Hand.

In one sense, *Brandenburg* combines the most protective ingredients of
the *Masses* incitement emphasis with the most useful elements of the clear
and present danger heritage. As the Court summarized first amendment
principles in *Brandenburg*—purporting to restate, but in fact creating—:

> [T]he constitutional guarantees of free speech and free press do not permit a State
> to forbid or proscribe advocacy of the use of force or of law violation except where
> such advocacy is directed to inciting or producing imminent lawless action and is
> likely to incite or produce such action.[195]

---

that those to whom the advocacy is addressed must be urged to *do* something, now or in the future,
rather than merely to *believe* in something." *Id*. at 318, 319, 324–25.

189. *Id*. at 327.
190. 367 U.S. at 232.
191. 395 U.S. 444 (1969).
192. For a recent reliance, *see* Hess v. Indiana, 414 U.S. 105 (1973) (per curiam reversal of
disorderly conduct conviction of demonstrator who had said: "We'll take the fucking street later [or
again]"; the reversal eschews overbreadth and vagueness grounds and relies primarily on the failure to
meet the *Brandenburg* incitement requirements: "At best, . . . the statement could be taken as counsel for present moderation; at worst, it amounted to nothing more than advocacy of illegal action at
some indefinite future time." *Id*. at 108.
193. 395 U.S. at 449 n.4.
194. 268 U.S. 652, 673 (1925) (dissenting opinion). Contrast Justice Brandeis' far greater sensitivity to the potential utility of the incitement concept—a sensitivity unmatched among early proponents
of clear and present danger. As Justice Brandeis stated in his concurring opinion in Whitney v. California, 274 U.S. 357, 376 (1927): "The wide difference between advocacy and incitement, between
preparation and attempt, between assembling and conspiracy, must be borne in mind."

The incitement emphasis is Hand's; the reference to "imminent" reflects a limited influence of Holmes, combined with later experience; and the "likely to incite or produce such action" addition in the *Brandenburg* standard is the only reference to the need to guess about future consequences of speech, so central to the *Schenck* approach. Under *Brandenburg*, probability of harm is no longer the central criterion for speech limitations. The inciting language of the speaker—the Hand focus on "objective" words —is the major consideration. And punishment of the harmless inciter is prevented by the *Schenck*-derived requirement of a likelihood of dangerous consequences.

And so, via Justice Harlan and the Supreme Court majority at the end of the Warren era, the language-oriented incitement criterion, so persistently urged by Hand in *Masses* and in these letters, has become central to the operative law of the land. *Brandenburg* is the most speech-protective standard yet evolved by the Supreme Court. Learned Hand would no doubt be surprised, and surely pleased, at this belated vindication. In 1921, Hand could not "help wondering whether a good many years from now when you are old and I am dead,"[196] his *Masses* contribution might seem trivial. *Masses*, he anticipated, would vanish. Its test might be seen as "some false coin."[197] But Learned Hand's analysis was precious metal, never "false coin"; the problem always lay in the eyes of the appraisers. Hand made sense in 1917 and 1918, in 1920 and 1921. Now, we have come to appreciate it.

APPENDIX

Document No. 1. *Learned Hand to Oliver Wendell Holmes, June 22, 1918*[198]

Windsor, Vermont

June 22, 1918.

Dear Mr. Justice

I gave up rather more easily than I now feel disposed about Tolerance on Wednesday. Here I take my stand. Opinions are at best provisional hypotheses, incompletely tested. The more they are tested, after the tests are well scrutinized, the more assurance we may assume, but they are never absolutes. So we must be tolerant of opposite opinions or varying opinions by the very fact of our incredulity of our own. (This may be left for deduc-

---

195. 395 U.S. at 447.
196. Appendix Doc. No. 15, Jan. 2, 1921, *supra* note 24.
197. *Id.*
198. Letter from Learned Hand to Oliver Wendell Holmes, June 22, 1918, on file in the Holmes Papers, Box 43, Folder 30, Harvard Law Library, Treasure Room, *printed in full* in 1 HOLMES-LASKI LETTERS, *supra* note 114, at 159 n.2.

---

tive demonstration in accord with the inexorable rules of formal logic by E.D.W., C.J. U.S.Sup.Ct.).[199]

You say that I strike at the sacred right to kill the other fellow when he disagrees. The horrible possibility silenced me when you said it. Now, I say, "Not at all, kill him for the love of Christ and in the name of God, but always realize that he may be the saint and you the devil. Go your way with a strong right arm and a swift shining sword, in full consciousness that what you kill for, and what you may die for, some smart chap like Laski may write a book and prove is all nonsense." I agree that in practical application there may arise some difficulty, but I am a philosopher and if Man is so poor a creature as not to endure the truth, it is no concern of mine. I didn't make him; let the Galled Jade wince, speaking reverently of course.

I sat under the Bo Tree and these truths were revealed unto me. Tolerance is the twin of Incredulity, but there is no inconsistency in cutting off the heads of as many as you please; that is a natural right. Only, and here we may differ, I do say that you may not cut off heads, (except for limited periods and then only when you want to very much indeed), because the victims insist upon saying things which look against Provisional Hypothesis Number Twenty-Six, the verification of which to date may be found in its proper place in the card catalogue. Generally, I insist, you must allow the possibility that if the heads are spared, other cards may be added under that sub-title which will have, perhaps, an important modification.

All this seems to me so perfectly self-evident, self-explanatory and rigidly applicable to the most complicated situations that I hesitate to linger upon it, lest I should seem tolerant of any different of opinion concerning it.

I greatly enjoyed my good fortune in meeting you on the train.

Faithfully yours,
Learned Hand.

Document No. 2. *Oliver Wendell Holmes to Learned Hand, June 24, 1918*[200]

Beverly Farms, Mass.
June 24, 1918

Dear Hand

Rarely does a letter hit me so exactly where I live as yours, and unless you are spoiling for a fight I agree with it throughout. My only qualification,

199. Chief Justice Edward Douglass White. White's opinions typically had a surface appearance of formal logic but were widely thought to be unsatisfactory. *See, e.g.,* McBain, *Edward Douglass White,* in 10 DICTIONARY OF AMERICAN BIOGRAPHY, pt. 2, at 96, 97 (rev. ed. 1958): "There was no crystal clarity in his reasoning processes and his sentences were long, labored, and involved."

200. Letter from Oliver Wendell Holmes to Learned Hand, June 24, 1918, on file in the Hand Papers, Box 103, Folder 24, Harvard Law Library, Treasure Room, *quoted in part* in Ragan, *supra* note 4, at 28.

if any, would be that free speech stands no differently than freedom from vaccination. The occasions would be rarer when you cared enough to stop it but if for any reason you did care enough you wouldn't care a damn for the suggestion that you were acting on a provisional hypothesis and might be wrong. That is the condition of every act. You tempt me to repeat an apologue that I got off to my wife in front of the statue of Garrison on Commonwealth Avenue, Boston, many years ago. I said—If I were an official person I should say nothing shall induce me to do honor to a man who broke the fundamental condition of social life by bidding the very structure of society perish rather than he not have his way—Expressed in terms of morals, to be sure, but still, his way. If I were a son of Garrison I should reply—Fool, not to see that every great reform has seemed to threaten the structure of society,—but that society has not perished, because man is a social animal, and with every turn falls into a new pattern like the Kaleidoscope. If I were a philosopher I should say—Fools both, not to see that you are the two blades (conservative and radical) of the shears that cut out the future. But if I were the ironical man in the back of the philosopher's head I should conclude—Greatest fool of all, Thou—not to see that man's destiny is to fight. Therefore take thy place on the one side or the other, if with the added grace of knowing that the Enemy is as good a man as thou, so much the better, but kill him if thou Canst. All of which seems in accord with you. If I may repeat another chestnut of ancient date and printed in later years—When I say a thing is true I mean that I can't help believing it—and nothing more. But as I observe that the Cosmos is not always limited by my Cant Helps I don't bother about absolute truth or even inquire whether there is such a thing, but define the Truth as the system of my limitations. I may add that as other men are subject to a certain number, not all, of my Cant Helps, intercourse is possible. When I was young I used to define the truth as the majority vote of that nation that can lick all others. So we may define the present war as an inquiry concerning truth. Of course you won't suspect me of thinking with levity on that subject because of my levitical speech. I enjoyed our meeting as much as you possibly could have and should have tried to prolong it to Boston but that I feared my wife would worry.

Sincerely Yours
O. W. Holmes

Document No. 3. *Oliver Wendell Holmes to Learned Hand, Feb. 25, 1919*[201]

Supreme Court of the United States,
Washington, D.C.

Feb. 25, 1919

Dear Judge Hand

Instead of the letter I intended to write to you some new work makes it necessary that I should confine myself to a word. I read your Masses decision—I haven't the details in my mind and will assume for present purposes that I should come to a different result—but I did want to tell you after reading it that I thought that few judges indeed could have put their view with such force or in such admirable form.

Sincerely yours

Hon. Learned Hand   O. W. Holmes

Document No. 4. *Learned Hand to Oliver Wendell Holmes, (late Mar.)* 1919[202]

JUDGE LEARNED HAND'S CHAMBERS

Dear Mr. Justice

I have read Debs v. U.S. and the other case[203] and this is positively my last appearance in the role of liberator. I haven't a doubt that Debs was guilty under any rule conceivably applicable. As to the rule actually laid down my dying words are these, now already fast receding in the seas of forgotten errors, and a crazy Saragossa that would be, wouldn't it? All the mad freaks of past contrivance.

The thing against which the statute aims is positive impediments to raising an army. Speech may create such by its influence on others' conduct. In nature the causal sequence is perfect, but responsibility does not go pari passu. I do not understand that the rule of responsibility for speech has ever been that the result is known as likely to follow. It is not,—I agree it might have been,—a question of responsibility dependent upon reasonable forecast, with an excuse when the words, had another possible effect. The responsibility only began when the words were directly an incitement. If I am wrong about that, it is mere matter of history. I confess I have no present access to the history.

---

201. Letter from Oliver Wendell Holmes to Learned Hand, Feb. 25, 1919, on file in the Hand Papers, Box 103, Folder 24, Harvard Law Library, Treasure Room.

202. Letter from Learned Hand to Oliver Wendell Holmes, (late Mar.) 1919, on file in the Holmes Papers, Box 43, Folder 30, Harvard Law Library, Treasure Room, *quoted in part* in Ginsburg, *supra* note 4, at 243.

203. Frohwerk v. United States, 249 U.S. 204 (1919).

Assuming that I am not wrong, then it was a question of extending the responsibility, and that was fairly a matter of better and worse. All I say is, that since the cases actually occur when men are excited and since juries are especially clannish groups,—are they societates perfectae?,—it is very questionable whether the test of motive is not a dangerous test. Juries wont much regard the difference between the probable result of the words and the purposes of the utterer. In any case, unless one is rather set in conformity, it will serve to intimidate,—throw a scare into,—many a man who might moderate the storms of popular feeling. I know it did in 1918.

The rule coupled w. Burleson's[204] legal irresponsibility certainly terrorized some of the press whose voices were much needed.

There, that is all! Absolutely and irrevocably all in saecula saeculorum! I bid a long farewell to my little toy ship which set out quite bravely in the shortest voyage ever made.

I was amused at the Harrison law decision,[205] which showed the vast importance of the sacred doctrine of "Imputation." That means the "Mystery" or "Sacrament" of being able to impute to Congress purposes you know they didn't have.

Sincerely yours
L. Hand

Document No. 5. *Oliver Wendell Holmes to Learned Hand, Apr. 3, 1919*[206]

Supreme Court of the United States,
Washington, D.C.

April 3, 1919

Dear Judge Hand

Since your letter came I have been so busy propagating new sophistries &c. that I haven't had time to defend the old ones. And now I am afraid that I don't quite get your point. As to intent under the Espionage Act I believe I have said nothing except to note that under the instructions the jury must be taken to have found that Debs's speech was intended to obstruct and tended to obstruct—and except further that evidence was held admissible as bearing on intent. Even if absence of intent might not be a defence I suppose that the presence of it might be material. Leaving that on one side, you say "the responsibility only began when the words were

---

204. Albert Sidney Burleson—Postmaster General of the United States, 1913–1921—was responsible for mail bans such as that challenged in the *Masses* case.

205. *See* United States v. Doremus, 249 U.S. 86 (1919).

206. Letter from Oliver Wendell Holmes to Learned Hand, Apr. 3, 1919, on file in the Hand Papers, Box 103, Folder 24, Harvard Law Library, Treasure Room, *quoted in part* in Ragan, *supra* note 4, at 39, and in Ginsburg, *supra* note 4, at 243–44.

directly an incitement"—I am afraid I do not know exactly what history you have in mind—but I don't see how you differ from the test as stated by me Schenck v. U S (March 3, 1919). "The question in every case is whether the words used are used in such circumstances and are of such a nature as to create a clear and present danger that they will bring about the substantive evils that Congress has a right to prevent. It is a question of proximity and degree."—I haven't time even now to recur to your decision but I take it that you agree that words may constitute an obstruction within the statute, even without proof that the obstruction was successful to the point of preventing recruiting. That I at least think plain. So I don't know what the matter is, or how we differ so far as your letter goes. With which I send you my blessing and don't hold you bound by your adieu to this stage.

As to the Harrison Drug Act, (*between ourselves*) I am tickled at every case of that sort as they seem to me to confirm the ground of my dissent in the Child Labor case last term. Hammer v. Dagenhart, 247 U.S. 257, 277. Also I think the drug act cases rightly decided. In my opinion Congress may have what ulterior motives they please if the act passed in the immediate aspect is within their powers—though personally, were I a legislator I might think it dishonest to use powers in that way.

Yours sincerely
O. W. Holmes

Document No. 6. *Learned Hand to Oliver Wendell Holmes, Nov. 25, 1919*[207]

JUDGE LEARNED HAND'S CHAMBERS

Dear Mr. Justice

I was greatly pleased with your dissent in the Abrams case, especially with the close which, if I may say so, was in your very highest vein. I am quite confident that whether it is avowed or not, in the end your views must prevail, after people get over the existing hysteria. It will not be the first time that you have formed the law by a minority opinion. I also agree with enthusiasm with your analysis of motive & intent about which there has been much too meagre discussion in the books. It was with a strong emotion that I read your words, stronger because I had found so little professional support for my own beliefs which would always have been expressed so, had I had the power to express them. I cannot help feeling like thanking

207. Letter from Learned Hand to Oliver Wendell Holmes, Nov. 25, 1919, on file in the Holmes Papers, Box 43, Folder 30, Harvard Law Library, Treasure Room.

you, even though I recall the annoyance it gives me when anyone undertakes to thank me for what I may say in an opinion. I always want to answer, "You fool, *I* didn't do it, it just came that way, quite simply and inevitably. If you thank me, you only show that you haven't the remotest idea of what I am doing." So I shall refrain—expressly anyway.

Meanwhile the merry sport of Red-baiting goes on, and the pack gives tongue more and more shrilly. I really can't get up much sympathy for the victims, but I own to a sense of dismay at the increase in all the symptoms of apparent panic. How far people are getting afraid to speak, who have anything really worth while to say, I don't know, but I am sure that the public generally is becoming rapidly demoralized in all its sense of proportion and toleration. For men who are not cock-sure about everything and especially for those who are not damned cock-sure about anything, the skies have a rather sinister appearance.

Nov. 25, 1919   Faithfully yours
Mr. Justice Holmes   Learned Hand

Document No. 7. *Oliver Wendell Holmes to Learned Hand, Nov. 26, 1919*[208]

Supreme Court of the United States,
Washington, D.C.

Nov. 26, 1919

My dear Judge

Your letter gives me the greatest pleasure and I am very much obliged to you for writing to me. Sympathy and agreement always are pleasant but they are much more than that when they come from one that I have learned to think of as I do of you. Accept my thanks.

Ever sincerely yours
Hon. Learned Hand   O. W. Holmes

---

208. Letter from Oliver Wendell Holmes to Learned Hand, Nov. 26, 1919, on file in the Hand Papers, Box 103, Folder 24, Harvard Law Library, Treasure Room.

Document No. 8. *Zechariah Chafee, Jr. to Learned Hand, Dec. 2, 1919*[209]

LAW SCHOOL OF HARVARD UNIVERSITY
CAMBRIDGE, MASS.

Judge Learned B. Hand,   December 2, 1919.
New York City,
Dear Sir,

The Harvard Liberal Club of Boston is anxious to make some public recognition of the stand taken by the two Harvard men on the United States Supreme Court on the question of freedom of speech, and a dinner is to be given in their honor on January 12 at the Boston City Club. We should like very much to have you come as the guest of the Liberal Club and be one of the speakers. . . . Our endeavor is to gather a number of thoughtful speakers who will consider the proper limits of discussion at the present time. . . .

I suppose the Abrams decision was the same kind of shock to you that it was to me. At all events Holmes' dissent is bound to win against the unreasoning majority opinion as the years go on, and I console myself occasionally with Browning's "baffled to fight better." If the Circuit Court of Appeals had only sustained you, one of the worst pages in our history might not have been written. I am glad to think of Holmes, Brandeis, and yourself, all Harvard Law School men.

Sincerely,
Zechariah Chafee, Jr.

Document No. 9. *Learned Hand to Zechariah Chafee, Jr., Dec. 3, 1919*[210]

JUDGE LEARNED HAND'S CHAMBERS
My dear Mr. Chaffee:

I have your letter of December second. It does not seem likely that I shall be able to get away to Boston at the time you mention, January twelfth, but I should like to do so and I will advise you some time early next month as to what the chances are. I do not think, however, that I had better make a speech. If you are going to have Justices Holmes and Brandeis there, and if they are going to speak, I should hardly feel like adding my mite to their plenitude.

209. Letter from Zechariah Chafee, Jr., to Learned Hand, Dec. 2, 1919, on file in the Hand Papers, Box 15, Folder 26, Harvard Law Library, Treasure Room.
210. Letter from Learned Hand to Zechariah Chafee, Jr., Dec. 3, 1919, on file in the Chafee Papers, Box 4, Folder 20, Harvard Law Library, Treasure Room.

I am not much surprised at the Abrams case, although the doctrine laid down seems to be what you so well call the "tendency" doctrine, which seems to me entirely destructive of any genuine freedom. I must say, however, that on the facts it seems to me very questionable whether the decision was not correct. At first, upon reading the opinion, I was quite sure the majority was wrong, but the distinction seems to me pretty tenuous between the purpose to encourage resistance to the United States and merely to prevent the United States from overthrowing the Bolshevik party.

Nevertheless, nothing could be more needed than Justice Holmes's opinion. I am delighted that it appeared. Naturally it is some comfort to find myself not in a judicial minority of one. I think I will look over the case more carefully once again, just for curiosity.

I do not altogether like the way Justice Holmes put the limitation. I myself think it is a little more manageable and quite adequate a distinction to say that there is an absolute and objective test to language. I daresay that it is obstinacy, but I still prefer that which I attempted to state in my first "Masses" opinion, rather than to say that the connection between the words used and the evil aimed at should be "immediate and direct."

May I say what great pleasure I had in your article in the June number of the "Review,"[211] and that I have heard it highly praised by most competent opinion? I must discount my own pleasure, as you treated me so well, but Graham Wallas and Benjamin Cardozo, both high authorities, have each expressed themselves in high praise of it, and I have no doubt there are many others. I wish I had known half as much as you do about the subject when I wrote my opinion, I could have made it so much better. But you know the conditions under which we have to decide these questions. I sometimes think that I never have learned any law since I left the School, and I am condemned by my own limitations when I come to take up a great subject like this. I think I can also say, without exceeding proper deference, that it would have been a great advantage to us all if, when the final dissent was written, it could have been written with your historical perspective.

Faithfully yours,
Learned Hand

Zechariah Chaffee, Jr., Esq.
Harvard Law School.
December 3, 1919

———

211. Chafee, *Freedom of Speech in War Time, supra* note 148.

Document No. 10. *Zechariah Chafee, Jr. to Learned Hand, Jan. 6, 1920*[212]

LAW SCHOOL OF HARVARD UNIVERSITY
CAMBRIDGE, MASS.

January 6, 1920

Dear Judge Hand,

. . . I was very much interested in what you wrote me about Judge Holmes's test and your own, and have been wondering whether it is possible to embrace them both in defining the constitutional limits of speech. Suppose we divide utterance as you do in the Masses case into

(1) political agitation

(2) incitement to resistance to law or violation of law.

If the policy behind the First Amendment is the attainment of truth through discussion, can (2) be excluded from its scope since the inciter wants a smash and not discussion? On the other hand can we say that (1) is protected subject to Holmes's test of "clear and present danger"?

Of course the 1917 Espionage Act, properly construed, did not touch (1) at all.

The broadest possible view (short of absolute license for speech) would be this:—

(1) can never be punished;

(2) can be punished only if it satisfies the danger test. This seems to me the right view as a matter of expediency, but I doubt whether Congress is so closely restricted (apart from Supreme Court decisions on the matter, which show amazing readiness to treat much of (1) as if it were (2), and then smite it even if there is no danger).

Hoping that you can come, I am

Sincerely,

Zechariah Chafee, Jr.

_____

Document No. 11. *Learned Hand to Zechariah Chafee, Jr., Jan. 8, 1920*[213]

JUDGE LEARNED HAND'S CHAMBERS

Dear Mr. Chafee:

I am sorry to say that I have got myself tied up in a calendar with cases set every day which will prevent my going to Boston. I ought to have remembered the dinner when I was doing this, but frankly, I did not think of it. . . .[214]

---

212. Letter from Zechariah Chafee, Jr., to Learned Hand, Jan. 6, 1920, on file in the Hand Papers, Box 15, Folder 26, Harvard Law Library, Treasure Room.

213. Letter from Learned Hand to Zechariah Chafee, Jr., Jan. 8, 1920, on file in the Chafee Papers, Box 4, Folder 20, Harvard Law Library, Treasure Room.

214. By this time, Chafee had advised Hand that Holmes would not be able to come to the dinner

As to the general question to be discussed, I should hardly feel like making a speech. In the first place, I have some doubt about the propriety of a judge's taking sides on such matters anyway. In this especial question it so happens that I have expressed myself officially in opinions which have met with almost unanimous disapproval by other Federal judges, and it seems to me pretty clearly inappropriate that I should take part in what certainly may have the appearance of a protest against those which prevailed. I think I at any rate am disqualified, whether or not the same is to be said of other judges.

My view of the matter is about like this. The State,—you see, I still cling to the old nomenclature,—must regard with disapproval all conduct which tends to produce any violation of its laws. It may, and in my judgment must, permit a great deal of such conduct,—utterances,—notwithstanding their tendency, that is, notwithstanding the probability that it may produce a violation of law. This tolerance, however, depends upon the fact that the utterances in question may have some other result than to produce the evil against which the law is directed. Utterances which can have no other results than to do this may therefore be unconditionally forbidden. It seems to me, I own, that the test of immediacy and directness, while in application it may be about the same as the other I shall suggest is not, strictly speaking, correct; I say this with a genuine diffidence. I prefer a test based upon the nature of the utterance itself. If, taken in its setting, the effect upon the hearers is only to counsel them to violate the law, it is unconditionally illegal. By "counsel" I mean to persuade them that their interest or duty lies in violating the law. It may be that that analysis is inadequate, but it is the only one I have been able to find.

As to other utterances, it appears to me that regardless of their tendency they should be permitted. The reason is that any State which professes to be controlled by public opinion, cannot take sides against any opinion except that which must express itself in the violation of law. On the contrary, it must regard all other expression of opinion as tolerable, if not good. As soon as it does not, it inevitably assumes that one opinion may control in spite of what might become an opposite opinion. It becomes a State based upon some opinion, as against any opinion which may get itself accepted, but it has been indubitably the presupposition of democratic states, however little they have lived up to it.

If so, nothing short of counsel to violate law should be itself illegal.

—"I fear that Hamlet is to be left out of the play"—and that Brandeis would probably also be absent. Renewing his urging that Hand attend, Chafee had written: "So I hope very much that you can come, and should especially like to meet you myself. Not only your liberty of the press opinions but technical discussions . . . always make me say, here's the Harvard Law School way of looking at legal problems." Letter from Zechariah Chafee, Jr., to Learned Hand, Dec. 5, 1919, on file in the Hand Papers, Box 15, Folder 26, Harvard Law Library, Treasure Room.

There could be no objection to the rule of the Supreme Court, tendency plus a purpose to produce the evil, even though the words did not come to the objective standard, if one were sure of the result in practical administration. The chance that the State would lose any valuable opinion by suppressing those whose purpose was to produce a violation of law, while they kept on the safe side of counselling it, seems to me much too thin for practical estimate. My own objection to the rule rests in the fact that it exposes all who discuss heated questions to an inquiry before a jury as to their purposes. That inquiry necessarily is of the widest scope and if their general attitude is singular and intransigeant, my own belief is that a jury is an insufficient protection. I think it is precisely at those times when alone the freedom of speech becomes important as an institution, that the protection of a jury on such an issue is illusory. The event seems to me to have proved this.

Therefore, to be a real protection to the expression of egregious opinion in times of excitement, I own I cannot see any escape from construing the privilege as absolute, so long as the utterance, objectively regarded, can by any fair construction be held to fall short of counselling violence. That much actually sinister utterance will pass, is undoubtedly true, but the whole institution presupposes a balance of evils. In taking sides I suppose one will range oneself according to one's degree of natural scepticism about opinions in general. For myself I think our chief enemies are Credulity, and his brother Intolerance.

Sincerely yours,

Learned Hand

Zechariah Chafee, Jr., Esq.
January 8, 1920.

Document No. 12. *Zechariah Chafee, Jr. to Learned Hand, Oct. 25, 1920*[215]

81 IRVING STREET
CAMBRIDGE

October 25.

My dear Judge Hand,

The time is, I am glad to say, rapidly approaching when my book on Freedom of Speech goes to press. Would you give me the great pleasure of dedicating it to you? It was really your opinion in the Masses case that

---

215. Letter from Zechariah Chafee, Jr., to Learned Hand, Oct. 25, 1920, on file in the Hand Papers, Box 15, Folder 26, Harvard Law Library, Treasure Room.

started me on my work. I feel more and more that it was a staggering task to solve the problem as you did at the very outset of the War, with so few precedents and in such pressure and excitement, and also that if your view had only been followed a living public opinion might have developed in this country on the ultimate purposes of the War, which since the armistice we have fatally lacked. I have spoken of your judgment at length in the body of the book, but I should like to place my opinion of it at the very start.

Sincerely,

Zech Chafee Jr.

Document No. 13. *Learned Hand to Zechariah Chafee, Jr., Oct. 28, 1920*[216]

JUDGE LEARNED HAND'S CHAMBERS

New York,
October 28, 1920

Dear Mr. Chafee

Your letter has really thrown me in more embarrassment than I have felt for long, indeed as an old lady would say, I am all upset. That you should select me to dedicate your book to fills me with an unaccountable measure of pleasure. Especially, do I feel this in view of the very slight accord which my opinions ever received from the profession at large. It was indeed scarcely necessary to ask my consent to what I should deem to be a very great honor, but as you have done so, I give it with content and indeed with a sense of great humility. You must know that we who have left the School always look back to it as the "fountain of honor." It is from there that we hope to get approval, and it is by their standards that we wish our work to be judged. It follows that they are likely to be the best judges of its quality.

I cannot conclude without expressing my thanks to you for your kindness and repeating my very genuine sense of the unfitness which I have for the signal honor you mean to give me.

Sincerely yours
Learned Hand

---

216. Letter from Learned Hand to Zechariah Chafee, Jr., Oct. 28, 1920, on file in the Chafee Papers, Box 4, Folder 20, Harvard Law Library, Treasure Room.

Document No. 14. *Learned Hand to Zechariah Chafee, Jr., Dec. 3, 1920*[217]

JUDGE LEARNED HAND'S CHAMBERS

Dear Mr. Chafee

[Chafee had written Hand to say that the book was off the press and on its way to Hand, with its dedication to Hand for his work in the *Masses* case. Chafee had apparently once again praised the *Masses* case in his letter of November 30, which is not preserved. Hand responds:] . . . The case cost me something, at least at the time, and, as you know, it seemed to meet with practically no professional approval whatever. I kept up my hopes till Debs's case and when the whole court affirmed that without laying down anything like what I thought was the rule, I confess I began to wonder whether I had not got some kind of wrong squint on the subject.

Later things turned a little the other way, but your very generous, and, I must believe, exaggerated, recognition of my views has been by far the most whole-hearted support I have ever got. It may interest you to know that when I was suddenly faced with the decision, I looked back with the greatest regret at my wasted days. "Here," I thought, "if you only knew enough, there is a place to state correctly, based on scholarship, what is the right rule. You don't know your job; you don't know anything about the history of the subject, and you must fire off your own funny ideas about what ought or oughtn't to be." If then I could have tapped the resources of the H.L.S. I should have been a happy man. However there was nothing very peculiar in that; I feel it so often, and when a book like Williston comes out, I frankly annex it and seek to learn no more. I dare say yours in its field will take its own stand as a similar authority. I shall surely read it, and if anything occurs to me that seems worth saying I shall take great pleasure in letting you have it.

With renewed thanks and the hope of an early meeting I am

Sincerely yours
Learned Hand

December 3, 1920.

---

217. Letter from Learned Hand to Zechariah Chafee, Jr., Dec. 3, 1920, on file in the Chafee Papers, Box 4, Folder 20, Harvard Law Library, Treasure Room.

Document No. 15. *Learned Hand to Zechariah Chafee, Jr., Jan. 2, 1921,* [Learned Hand's draft][218]

New York
Jan. 2, 1921

My dear Mr. Chafee

My life here is so full of interruptions that I have only just finished reading "Freedom of Speech" and that too without that chance for a continuous perusal which it deserves, instead of in disconnected snatches now and then. It has more than justified all the hopes I had for it, and it will stand for an indefinite time as the most complete and satisfactory exposition of one of the most baffling subjects in the law. Indeed, how baffling it is I never quite realized till I had been over your pages. I kept feeling,—did I write you so before?—that in writing my own opinion, which you have so kindly noticed, it was well that I knew no more than I did. Like the heathen I was saved by my invincible ignorance, and now that you ask me to suggest any deficiencies in your work I can really do nothing, certainly I can bring nothing that I do not carry from its covers.

As you so often point out, the decision in any given case will depend upon the relative values which the tribunal places on the importance of illumination in general through discussion, and the immediate purpose which is in danger. I doubt whether men will ever succeed at once in feeling intensely the necessity of accomplishing this thing, here and now, and in retaining enough detachment to remember that a precedent is a precedent and that the first taste of blood is often the greatest danger. There will be a few who can at least believe of themselves that they combine the two, but their fellows will always put them in the church of Laodicea, and relatively that is really the place for them—in my judgment the most honorable place of all.[219] In any event the result is that we must be content to worry through with as little inconsistency as possible, making prayerful protestations where we must, and securing heartfelt accord when there is

218. Letter from Learned Hand to Zechariah Chafee, Jr., Jan. 2, 1921. The draft reproduced here is on file in the Hand Papers, Box 15, Folder 26, Harvard Law Library, Treasure Room. *See also* copy of letter on file in the Chafee Papers, Box 4, Folder 20, Harvard Law Library, Treasure Room.

219. The reference to the "church of Laodicea" may warrant some amplification, both because it may be as obscure to others as it was at first to me, and because it is a charming and apt allusion in describing Learned Hand's courageous, concerned, yet characteristically self-doubting effort to steer a road between immediate societal needs and long-term threats to civil liberties.

The reference is to Chapter 3 of *Revelations*. *Revelations* 3:14–16 states: "And unto the angel of the church of the Laodiceans write . . . I know thy works, that thou art neither cold nor hot: I would thou wert cold or hot. So then because thou art lukewarm, and neither cold nor hot, I will spue thee out of my mouth."

In the New Testament, that description of "neither cold nor hot" but "lukewarm" is one of condemnation. Hand accepts that description as applicable to his stance—and takes pride in it, for that "neither cold nor hot" position was for him "the most honorable place of all."

no need for protecting those who talk unpalatably—that is, when they have no chance of success.

I am not wholly in love with Holmesy's test and the reason is this. Once you admit that the matter is one of degree, while you may put it where it genuinely belongs, you so obviously make it a matter of administration, i.e. you give to Tomdickandharry, D.J., so much latitude [here Learned Hand wrote and struck out "as his own fears may require," and continued] that the jig is at once up. Besides their Ineffabilities, the Nine Elder Statesmen, have not shown themselves wholly immune from the "herd instinct" and what seems "immediate and direct" to-day may seem very remote next year even though the circumstances surrounding the utterance be unchanged. I own I should prefer a qualitative formula, hard, conventional, difficult to evade. If it could become sacred by the incrustations of time and precedent it might be made to serve just a little to withhold the torrents of passion to which I suspect democracies will be found more subject than for example the whig autocracy of the 18th century. We know very little yet about enormous aggregations such as our present U.S. How can we catch this fly and preserve it in amber? What sanctified ritualistic phrase shall fix the place where discussion ends and words may ex cathedra be said to have no power to enlighten? You have, I dare say, done well to take what has fallen from Heaven and insist that it is manna rather than to set up any independent solution. "Immediate and direct" is all we have; for God's sake let us not look it in the mouth.

Next as to Uncle Henry Clayton.[220] Did I tell you that I always felt a little responsible? We were glad enough to get anyone who could legally sit on a bench, and he was fish because he swam into the net. Then I turned the D. Atty loose on him as usual, and lo! a cause célèbre to the honor of no one. But wasn't it a little *over* irresponsible? I fear I am not free from blame. On the law of that case in the Supreme Court I have reflected a little since reading your article in the H.L.R. and now your chapter, and you have brought me around. At first I was even guilty of what seems to be the universally conceded solecism that the Russian expedition was a part of the war. In that you assure me that only poor Wigmore is with me, respectable enough company usually, but a bit toqué here. Well, will this content you? I am charging the jury vice Uncle Henry and without his racy gift of speech. I say: "you must find that the defendants intended to impede the war, and to do so you must decide either that they had that purpose, which in your places I should find they had not, or that they knew

220. District Judge Henry D. Clayton—former Congressman from Alabama and author of the Clayton Anti-Trust Act—had presided at the *Abrams* trial. Chafee severely criticized Clayton's conduct of the trial. *See, e.g.,* Chafee, *A Contemporary State Trial*—The United States *versus* Jacob Abrams *et al., supra* note 148.

that in stopping the production of munitions till the Russian expedition was given up, the war against Germany would inevitably be impeded. If you think that they understood that they could not stop munitions here without that result, that knowledge is enough special intent under the statute. As to the Russian expedition itself I charge you that while you may not review the wisdom or necessity of including a diversion,—if it was intended to be a diversion, in Siberia, or of the release of Czecho-Slovaks who might be made to fight, the U.S. must show you that it was intended by those who directed it as a part of the war w. Germany, and they have showed nothing whatever about it. They might show it perhaps by calling those who directed it and letting them tell you how it was a part of the war. If they had you would have had to take their word for it, however mistaken as strategy you thought it, unless some one satisfied you that they might not be telling you the truth about their own purposes. As no one has told you anything about it, I must take that phase of it from you."

There, am I orthodox? Does there lurk a heresy somewhere in there? Further, I will not go; "Gott hilfe mich, ich kann nicht anders." I have forgotten whether he "hilfs" or "hilfes" mich. That Uncle Henry is a lazy, violent, ignorant old political hack is true; that he is a rather engaging, worldly wise shrewd old codger by no means devoid of charm, and with some talent for getting under the wire w. the C.C.A. is also true. Amen, he is not coming up again, and he takes his rank with judges of his kidney of the past. You have given him the only immortality he will ever get except from his dishonest Clayton Act. By the way I am doubtful of that severity of taste which left out "Judge Clayton produced the Clayton Act."

Item, Deportations. My God, but I never knew they were like that. That comes of never reading the papers, I suppose. Croly says it was all in his sheet, but at that time I was too mad with their intransigance about the Treaty to do them justice in anything. Your doubts about the constitutionality of any deportation, as distinct from exclusion, law, I think I don't share. On the whole I believe that while the justification for freedom of speech is public enlightenment, historically the "right,"—though I join you in hating the word,—is vested in the speaker constitutionally, and our legislatures can engage ad lib. in obscurantism, provided they don't infringe on an individual who can cry out. Now it is inhuman enough, and it has filled me with loathing to have to recognize it, but it is the fact that if I come here and don't get out my "papers" I stay on sufferance. Quite seriously, I don't think we judges could intervene if they deported all aliens who ate with their knives. After all a court which doesn't recognize the post "as of common right" is not going to strain at gnats like deportations.

But you are quite right only to slide over the constitutional aspect. The law's the thing, and a devilish hateful one. In a recent case I squirmed horribly and finally broke the "head hold" that that damned Lopez case[221] had on me, for there was a miserable dishonest ground of deportation which certainly held for aught I could do. Lord, it will go against the grain if I have to let a man be deported for his opinions. But we shall see, we shall see. . . .

Well, you will be glad at last that I have nothing more to say. You have I think done a notably admirable thing,—naturally I am prejudiced,—and you have preserved so excellent a good-humor and so much moderation that the book should have influence now in these less excited time. The work must have been severe and the material hard to get in convenient and condensed form. How did you manage to find the time? That is where you active fellows with jobs who write books puzzle me.

But the thing which is nearest to me is what will be least important to your other readers, that you selected me for a very great honor. I must confess I can't help feeling a little danger in it. It is well and admirable to yield to enthusiasm, but I can't help wondering whether a good many years from now when you are old and I am dead, you may not pick up the book and reading the first page, smile with some amusement and some regret. You really will have nothing personal to regret, even if you would not then think of repeating it, but still if I were there then,—and perhaps I shall come back to plague you for your thoughts, because ghosts have no respect for freedom of opinion,—I should feel a little as though I have passed off on you some false coin. Whatever *you* may come to feel I don't know, but you have made *me* feel very happy, and you have pleased three little girls too, who I am glad to say have never regarded their father hitherto as much more than an elderly man with a not wholly reliable amiability, though buttressed with a taste for buffoonery.

Sincerely yours
Learned Hand

---

221. Lopez v. Howe, 259 F. 401 (2d Cir. 1919), *appeal dismissed & cert. denied*, 254 U.S. 613 (1920). In *Lopez*, the Second Circuit had broadly interpreted a statutory provision governing the deportation of aliens found to be "advocating or teaching anarchy." Judge Rogers refused to limit the provision to "violent" anarchists and held that it covered "philosophical" anarchists as well: "The fact that he is only a philosophical anarchist, and not an advocate of a resort to force and revolution, makes him, in the opinion of Congress, none the less a dangerous presence. . . . If the government considers his presence undesirable, because of his advocacy of a doctrine which it regards as inimical to civilization, it must have the power to send him out of the country . . . ." 259 F. at 404.

Document No. 16. *Zechariah Chafee, Jr., to Learned Hand, Mar. 28, 1921*[222]

LAW SCHOOL OF HARVARD UNIVERSITY,
CAMBRIDGE, MASS.

March 28, 1921

My dear Judge Hand:

. . . . How far, for the sake of protecting ourselves from an obviously bad man, shall we lay down a general rule which will also include persons whose wickedness is less certain. Of course, when you can put a high board fence around the bad men as you can for murder and many other overt acts, we can handle them very well; but in the sedition cases, the attempt to draw a boundary seems to baffle us all. I agree with you that Holmes' distinction would prove unworkable in many cases. The Jury would go over it rough shod. Thomas Reed Powell feels this even more strongly than I do. Your test is surely easier to apply although our old friend Marc Anthony's speech is continually thrown at me in discussion. After all, we ought to take the best test we can find even though it will sometimes break down, and then prevent its breaking down by using channels outside the law to produce greater tolerance in Judges and jurors and the public at large, so that when the next emergency arises we shall be better prepared. . . .

Yours sincerely,
Zech Chafee Jr.

---

222. Letter from Zechariah Chafee, Jr., to Learned Hand, Mar. 28, 1921, on file in the Hand Papers, Box 15, Folder 26, Harvard Law Library, Treasure Room.

Some Choice-of-Law Problems Posed by Antiguest Statutes: Realism in Wisconsin and Rule-Fetishism in New York

Moffatt Hancock*

> The essence of the judicial process is the determination of the case in hand and nothing more. There is no legal power in a court to bind itself or any other court—whether the judges remain the same or are changed—to any course of decision of indeterminate future cases.
>
> Joseph Walter Bingham[1]

In the recent case of *Neumeier v. Kuehner*,[2] a majority of the New York Court of Appeals adopted the astonishing methodology of laying down three relatively narrow rules[3] apparently intended to furnish the correct solution for *all* choice-of-law cases involving antiguest statutes. These rules are not condensed summaries of the court's prior decisions;[4] they purport to resolve in advance hypothetical cases that the court has never before decided. These narrow rules are *obiter dicta* of the most extravagant kind. Moreover, some of the results they prescribe are flatly contrary to the considered decisions of other state courts, of which certain well-reasoned decisions of the Supreme Court of Wisconsin are good examples.[5] This article

* B.A. 1933, University of Toronto; J.D. 1936, Osgoode Hall Law School; S.J.D. 1940, University of Michigan. Marion Rice Kirkwood Professor of Law, Stanford University.

1. Bingham, *Credo*, in My Philosophy of Law: Credos of Sixteen American Scholars 20–21 (1941).

2. 31 N.Y.2d 121, 286 N.E.2d 454, 335 N.Y.S.2d 64 (1972).

3. "1. When the guest-passenger and the host-driver are domiciled in the same state, and the car is there registered, the law of that state should control and determine the standard of care which the host owes to his guest.

"2. When the driver's conduct occurred in the state of his domicile and that state does not cast him in liability for that conduct, he should not be held liable by reason of the fact that liability would be imposed upon him under the tort law of the state of the victim's domicile. Conversely, when the guest was injured in the state of his own domicile and its law permits recovery, the driver who has come into that state should not—in the absence of special circumstances—be permitted to interpose the law of his state as a defense.

"3. In other situations, when the passenger and the driver are domiciled in different states, the rule is necessarily less categorical. Normally, the applicable rule of decision will be that of the state where the accident occurred but not if it can be shown that displacing that normally applicable rule will advance the relevant substantive law purposes without impairing the smooth working of the multi-state system or producing great uncertainty for litigants." *Id.* at 128, 286 N.E.2d at 457–58, 335 N.Y.S.2d at 70.

4. For references to the court of appeal's prior choice-of-law decisions involving antiguest statutes, *see* the most recent of such decisions, Tooker v. Lopez, 24 N.Y.2d 569, 249 N.E.2d 394, 301 N.Y.S.2d 519 (1969).

5. *See* notes 20–38 *infra* and accompanying text.

demonstrates several such contrarieties resulting from the *Neumeier* rules, as well as the unsoundness of the actual decision in the *Neumeier* case. But before mounting this attack, it is necessary to describe briefly the realistic choice-of-law methodology adopted by many state courts during the past ten years, with the New York Court of Appeals playing a leading role.

I. The Background and Methodology of *Babcock v. Jackson*

Prior to the critical commentarial writing of the late Professor Brainerd Currie and those who supported him,[6] conflict of laws was generally regarded as a unique, self-contained, and exclusive discipline. Its major concern was the problem of choice confronting a court in a case in which the facts were connected both with the forum and with another state whose domestic rule for such a case differed from that of the forum. Normally, these different domestic rules promoted one or more different policies. But the traditional discipline of conflict of laws attached almost no significance to the policies or practical effects of domestic rules. The discipline was supposed to have its own paramount policy objectives, the most important of which was the construction of an interstate and international system that would secure, so far as possible, uniform and predictable results in all choice cases, wherever they might be litigated.[7] Some commentators also professed to believe that an important policy objective was to effectuate the reasonable expectations of the parties concerning the law that should govern their conduct.[8]

As for the idealistic objective of constructing an international system, the picture of judicial practice was, of course, decidedly discouraging. For example, Canada, though linked to the United States by ties of trade, tourism and a common legal background, had and has a doctrinal approach to torts choice-of-law cases entirely different from and seemingly antithetical to the traditional doctrines adopted by courts in the United States.[9] As for the construction of an interstate system that would produce uniform and predictable results, the outlook was equally gloomy. True, all state

---

6. For a brief summary of Currie's views, *see* Currie, *Comment*, in Symposium, *Comments on Babcock v. Jackson, A Recent Development in Conflict of Laws*, 63 Colum. L. Rev. 1212, 1233–43 (1963). For a fuller discussion, *see* B. Currie, Selected Essays on the Conflict of Laws (1963). For examples of supportive writing, *see* Hancock, *Three Approaches to the Choice-of-Law Problem: The Classificatory, the Functional and the Result-Selective*, in XXth Century Comparative and Conflicts Law 365–79 (K. Nadelmann ed. 1961); Traynor, *Is This Conflict Really Necessary?*, 37 Texas L. Rev. 657 (1959).

7. *See, e.g.*, Restatement of Conflict of Laws 699 (1934); M. Hancock, Torts in the Conflict of Laws 54–61 (1942); Goodrich, *Public Policy in the Law of Conflicts*, 36 W. Va. L.Q. 156, 162–69 (1930).

8. *See, e.g.*, Rheinstein, *The Place of Wrong: A Study in the Method of Case Law*, 19 Tul. L. Rev. 4, 17–20 (1944).

9. *See* Hancock, *Torts Problems in Conflict of Laws Resolved by Statutory Construction: The Halley and Other Older Cases Revisited*, 18 U. Toronto L.J. 331 (1968).

courts began the analysis of tort choice cases with the proposition that prima facie the law of the state of injury should control. But where, because one or more of the parties were domiciled or doing business in the forum, a judge concluded that its pertinent rule should control instead, he could resort to any one of several overriding principles to justify application of the forum's rule.[10] In short, when a judge perceived that a case fell clearly within the policy-determined scope of a rule of the forum, the traditional system was flexible enough to permit him to apply that rule. But since the system attached no explicit significance to the policies of domestic rules, it was a haphazard, hit-or-miss system under which courts sometimes enforced the pertinent rule of the state of injury and sometimes rejected it by adopting an overriding principle. Neither interstate uniformity nor predictability was achieved; the overall picture was one of uncertainty and confusion.

With ruthless realism, Currie critically analyzed and described the uncertain and curious workings of the traditional system. He persuasively demonstrated that, in certain types of cases, application of the pertinent domestic rule of the state of injury was absurd because the facts of those cases did not bring into play any of the policies that the rule was supposed to effectuate. He urged courts to begin their analysis of choice-of-law cases with a careful examination of the policies and practical effects of each of the pertinent domestic rules.[11] In the celebrated case of *Babcock v. Jackson*,[12] the New York Court of Appeals adopted this suggestion in principle, though the opinion contained some arguments that Currie considered irrelevant.[13] In that case the host-driver and injured guest-passenger were both domiciled in New York, whose legislature had three times refused to enact an antiguest statute; the injury was inflicted in Ontario, whose antiguest statute prohibited any recovery. The most notable achievement of Chief Judge Fuld's majority opinion was his demonstration that none of the policies of the Ontario antiguest statute supported its application to the instant case.[14] On the contrary, the case fell squarely within the policy range of New

---

10. By classifying the rule of forum law as procedural or remedial, the judge could invoke the overriding principle that the forum's remedial rules should be followed. By classifying the rule of forum law as contractual (in cases involving carriers' or employers' liability) he could invoke the overriding principle that the forum's rule should prevail because the contract was made there. If these overriding principles seemed inappropriate, he could invoke the principle that the "public policy" of the forum should prevail in its courts, especially where the rights of its citizens were involved. *See* B. CURRIE, *supra* note 6, at 181; R. LEFLAR, AMERICAN CONFLICTS LAW 212 (1968).
    11. *See* B. CURRIE, *supra* note 6, at 77–187.
    12. 12 N.Y.2d 473, 191 N.E.2d 279, 240 N.Y.S.2d 743 (1963).
    13. *See* Currie, *supra* note 6.
    14. So far as the statute was designed to protect host-drivers from liability to guest-passengers, it should not be applied for the benefit of host-drivers domiciled in New York. So far as it was intended to protect insurance companies against collusive claims supported by the false testimony of host-drivers, it should not be applied for the benefit of insurers of New York domiciliaries. (It might have been added that if the statute had a policy of protecting insurance defense counsel from the

York's rule permitting the injured guest to recover for ordinary negligence.

Despite its apparent novelty, the methodology suggested by Currie and adopted in *Babcock v. Jackson* received a remarkably warm reception from advocates and judges in other states. It was adopted in torts cases in which the facts and issues of law were quite different from those of *Babcock v. Jackson*[15] and in contracts cases as well.[16] It is important to note that when judges in other states adopted this methodology, they must have foreseen that it was certain to present a type of problem that did *not* arise in the *Babcock* case.[17] For there it was easy to show that the facts fell within the policy-determined scope of the New York rule and outside that of the Ontario antiguest statute. But if the host-driver had been domiciled in Ontario, a plausible argument could have been made for the application of its statute to protect him from liability. Such application would, however, have subverted the policy of the New York rule to secure compensation for the New York domiciliary. But the obvious possibility of having to resolve this and other true-conflict cases[18] did not deter judges from adopting the new methodology because its realistic approach to the rule-choosing problem seemed to be a great improvement over the crude undiscriminating formulas of the traditional system. Moreover, the courts of other states that adopted the methodology of the *Babcock* case have subsequently encountered a variety of true-conflict cases and, with some commentarial guidance, have succeeded in resolving them to their satisfaction.[19]

II. Some Unsound Results Prescribed by the *Neumeier* Rules

Yet now a majority of the New York Court of Appeals has announced in the *Neumeier* case that the policy-centered methodology, proposed by Currie and sponsored by the court in *Babcock v. Jackson*, is not really necessary for the satisfactory resolution of choice problems involving antiguest statutes because all the various patterns of facts and laws can be disposed of by three relatively narrow rules. But, as previously noted, some of the

hazards of defending collusive lawsuits, this was for the benefit of Ontario counsel only.) For a recent study of the scanty legislative history of the Ontario antiguest statute, *see* Baade, *The Case of the Disinterested Two States:* Neumeier v. Kuehner, 1 Hofstra L. Rev. 150, 152–56 (1973).

15. *See* the cases cited in R. Weintraub, Commentary on the Conflict of Laws 234 n.36 (1971).

16. *See, e.g.,* Lilienthal v. Kaufman, 239 Ore. 1, 395 P.2d 543 (1964).

17. *See, e.g.,* Wilcox v. Wilcox, 26 Wis. 2d 617, 133 N.W.2d 408 (1965).

18. A true-conflict case—as distinguished from a no-conflict or false-conflict case—is one in which the facts fall within the policy-determined scope of the pertinent rule of one state and also within the policy-determined scope of the pertinent, divergent rule of another state, as in the hypothetical example discussed in the text. A false-conflict or no-conflict case is one in which the facts fall within the policy-determined scope of the pertinent rule of one state only, although the facts have some contact with another state whose pertinent rule is different, as in *Babcock v. Jackson*.

19. *See* Hancock, *Anti-Guest Statutes and Marital Immunity for Torts in Conflict of Laws: Techniques for Resolving Ostensible True-Conflict Cases and Constitutional Limitations,* 1 Dalhousie L.J. 105 (1973).

results thus prescribed are patently inconsistent with considered decisions reached by other state courts using the *Babcock* methodology. The following discussion of fact-law patterns in four cases will demonstrate the shortcomings of this rule-oriented approach.

A. Heath v. Zellmer, Conklin v. Horner, *and Rule One*

In *Heath v. Zellmer*[20] the essential facts, somewhat simplified, were as follows: Indiana had an antiguest statute requiring proof of "wanton or wilful misconduct";[21] Wisconsin had none. Guest-passengers domiciled in Indiana, riding with a host-driver also domiciled there,[22] were injured in Wisconsin in a collision with a second car driven by a Wisconsin domiciliary. The injured Indiana guest-passengers sued the Wisconsin driver of the second car, alleging his ordinary negligence; the Wisconsin driver claimed contribution from the Indiana host-driver, alleging that her ordinary negligence had been a partial cause of the guest-passengers' injuries. Under Wisconsin domestic law, if the guest-passengers' injuries had been caused by the ordinary negligence of the host-driver combined with that of the driver of the second car, the host-driver would have been compelled to pay a share of the damages proportionate to her fault. Calling for the application of the Indiana antiguest statute, the Indiana host-driver demanded complete immunity from such contribution unless she were shown to have been guilty of "wanton or wilful misconduct." As the Wisconsin court pointed out, application of the Indiana antiguest statute could have resulted in throwing the entire burden of the damages on the Wisconsin driver even though the ordinary negligence of the Indiana host-driver "might be . . . the principal cause of the accident."[23]

In addition to Wisconsin's policy of protecting its citizens from having to bear the entire burden of the damages, the court found several other Wisconsin policies to be involved. Wisconsin's law imposing civil liability on host-drivers for ordinary negligence was intended to be both punitive and deterrent; why should the Indiana host-driver enjoy an immunity not enjoyed by Wisconsin citizens? Moreover, enforcement of the Wisconsin rule would ensure that bills for medical services furnished by Wisconsin doctors and hospitals to transient guest-passengers of limited means would be fully paid. Finally, the court declared that it was unwilling to discrim-

---

20. 35 Wis. 2d 578, 151 N.W.2d 664 (1967).
21. IND. ANN. STAT. § 9-3-3-1 (Burns 1973).
22. The host-driver was actually domiciled in Ohio, whose antiguest statute was similar to that of Indiana. *See* OHIO REV. CODE ANN. § 4515.02 (Page 1972). But the car driven by her was owned by her father who was domiciled in Indiana. His insurer defended against the claim for contribution. The court stated twice that the Indiana antiguest statute had a policy of protecting the host and *his* insurer from liability. *See* 35 Wis. 2d at 591–92, 151 N.W.2d at 669–70.
23. 35 Wis. 2d at 601, 151 N.W.2d at 675.

inate against nonresidents as compared to residents in providing compensation for highway traffic injuries inflicted in Wisconsin.

As for the important policy of the Indiana antiguest statute to prevent collusive lawsuits, the court dismissed it as irrelevant to a suit brought in a Wisconsin court.[24] But it recognized that enforcement of the Wisconsin rule would subvert Indana's policy of protecting the "kindly host" from the embarrassment of litigation. Nevertheless, the seven judges were unanimous in their decision to enforce the Wisconsin law. Indeed, it is difficult to imagine that any court would be willing to subvert so many interests of the forum in order to advance a single policy of another state's antiguest statute. Yet rule one of the *Neumeier* case indicates that the New York Court of Appeals would do just that.[25] The most charitable explanation for this result is that the court simply failed to foresee the case of a two-car collision raising the contribution issue. That is one of the pitfalls that lie in wait for judges who undertake to promulgate rules for cases they have never actually considered.

---

24. *See* 35 Wis. 2d at 591 n.4, 151 N.W.2d at 669 n.4. The court noted that defendant's automobile was registered and insured in Indiana with an Indiana-domiciled insurance company but did not suggest that these facts gave rise to any interest of Indiana. Some judges (misled by commentators) have professed to find that the state in which a host defendant's car was garaged and insured had a strong interest in the application of its antiguest statute because his insurer had supposedly calculated its premiums with the antiguest statute in mind. *See, e.g.,* Pryor v. Swarner, 445 F.2d 1272, 1277 (2d Cir. 1971). This assumption as to the calculation of premiums is erroneous. In fixing premiums, insurance actuaries do not and cannot take into account such uncertain and miniscule factors as the potential application of particular rules of domestic law. To make statistically reliable forecasts of future losses, they must necessarily use a vast body of highway accident loss experience, including hundreds of claims that did not involve antiguest statutes at all. The premium paid by the host-driver in the *Heath* case would have been derived from a forecast (based on past loss experience) of the total losses expected to be incurred by all cars garaged in the same rating territory in Indiana, regardless of what rules of law might affect the outcome of individual lawsuits or the settlement of individual claims. *See* Morris, *Enterprise Liability and the Actuarial Process,* 70 YALE L.J. 554 (1961). As for the suggestion (sometimes made) that decisions for the plaintiff in cases like *Heath v. Zellmer* may result in higher insurance rates in the future for the various rating territories of the antiguest statute state, Morris demonstrates that the impact of such decisions would be either very slight or totally insignificant. In any event, there is a formidable and comprehensive argument against any consideration of policies designed to protect insurers or their counsel or to depress insurance rates in choice cases. If the host-defendant were not insured, such policies would be irrelevant. Even where the host-defendant is insured, such policies should not be considered. It would be grossly unfair to the plaintiff that his chances of recovery should be diminished because the host-defendant was insured. It is not a proper function of liability insurance to provide additional defenses for insured defendants in choice-of-law cases.

25. *See* note 3 *supra.* This rule is also inconsistent with a prior New York supreme court appellate division decision with a similar fact pattern—Rye v. Kolter, 39 App. Div. 2d 821, 333 N.Y.S.2d 96 (1972).

Heath v. Zellmer appears to fall within rule one because the owner of the automobile in which the injured guest-passengers were riding was domiciled in Indiana, the state of their domicile. *See* note 22 *supra.* The rules could not have been intended to exclude the important liability of automobile owners whose cars are being driven by others.

Though the driver and the passengers were domiciled in different states (*see* note 22 *supra*), the case does not fall within rule three because rule three is intended to apply only to cases where the laws of the "different states" are different. Suppose for example that the driver and passenger are domiciled in different states, each of which imposes liability for ordinary negligence, but the injury occurs in an antiguest statute state. Such a case would be virtually indistinguishable from *Babcock v. Jackson,* yet rule three, if applicable, would require enforcement of the antiguest statute, an absurd result.

In *Conklin v. Horner*,[26] a host-driver domiciled in Illinois, whose anti-guest statute required a showing of "wilful and wanton misconduct,"[27] was sued by a guest-passenger, also domiciled there, for injuries sustained in Wisconsin. Since no second car was involved, the influential argument that application of the Illinois statute would throw the entire burden of the guest-passenger's damages upon a Wisconsin citizen was not available. If the court had applied the Illinois statute, the burden of the damages would have fallen upon the injured Illinois guest-passenger. However, as the court pointed out, the three other Wisconsin interests involved in *Heath v. Zellmer* were likewise involved in the *Conklin* case. And, again, as in *Heath v. Zellmer*, only one policy of the Illinois antiguest statute, that of protecting its host-driver citizen from liability, came into conflict with the three Wisconsin policies.

To resolve that conflict, the court employed two techniques of reconciliation. First, relying upon a commentarial survey of a line of Illinois cases,[28] the court observed that, in construing the words "wilful and wanton misconduct," the Illinois courts had consistently restricted the protection given to host-drivers by the antiguest statute. Hence, the court concluded that the degree of conflict between the Wisconsin rule and the Illinois statute was not as great as a literal reading of the statute would have indicated and therefore that it was justified in giving enforcement of the Illinois statute a low priority. This analysis might have been fruitfully expanded as follows: Illinois' domestic law reflected a conflict between two sharply divergent sets of policies. For the benefit of most victims of traffic accidents, liability was imposed for ordinary negligence. This rule effectuated three policies: it deterred negligent driving; it compensated the injured and the dependents of the dead; and it attempted to ensure that the costly services of therapeutic creditors to indigent victims would be paid for.[29] On the other hand, in a relatively small number of cases, the antiguest statute permitted two contrary policies—the protection of kindly hosts from liability and the prevention of collusive lawsuits—to prevail over the other three general ones. The line of Illinois domestic decisions narrowing the operation of the antiguest statute showed that the Illinois

---

26. 38 Wis. 2d 468, 157 N.W.2d 579 (1968).

27. ILL. REV. STAT. ch. 95½ § 9–201 (1957), *as amended*, ILL. REV. STAT. ch. 95½ § 10–201 (1971).

28. 54 Nw. U.L. REV. 263, 267 (1959). The court also considered the decision in Spivak v. Hara, 69 Ill. App. 2d 22; 216 N.E.2d 173 (1966).

29. In cases having the fact-law pattern of *Babcock v. Jackson*, judges have pointed out that a decision in favor of the plaintiff rendered by the court of the parties' common domicile (which has no antiguest statute) actually advances certain policies of the state of injury *other than those of its antiguest statute. See* Macey v. Rozbicki, 18 N.Y.2d 289, 295, 221 N.E.2d 380, 383, 274 N.Y.S.2d 591, 595 (1966) (Keating, J., concurring); Beaulieu v. Beaulieu, 265 A.2d 610, 615 (Me. 1970). In *Heath v. Zellmer*, the court pointed out that Indiana highway accident law apparently supported the three policies set out in the text *except* where injury or death was suffered by a guest-passenger. *See* 35 Wis. 2d 578, 591–92, 151 N.W.2d 664, 670 (1967).

judges had been resolving this conflict by advancing the three more general policies at the expense of the two supported by the statute. The *Conklin* case presented an analogous problem in that the Wisconsin court had to resolve a conflict between one policy of the antiguest statute and several policies of Wisconsin law similar to the three broader policies of Illinois domestic law. Since the Illinois judges had consistently subverted the policies of their own antiguest statute, the Wisconsin judges were fully justified in doing likewise.

The court's second technique of reconciliation was the better-law analysis, which it had already discussed in *Heath v. Zellmer.*[30] Relying upon Leflar's persuasive analysis of an analogous hypothetical case,[31] the court had there concluded that the Wisconsin rule imposing liability upon host-drivers for ordinary negligence was the better law for two reasons. First, antiguest statutes were both harsh and anachronistic: "the . . . era that produced them is past and current feeling is that they are both unfair to guests and contrary to the enterprise liability, spread-the-loss concept that prevails in the automobile tort area today."[32] Second, judges in states where they were in force had protested against them by consistently narrowing their effect.[33] Despite some abstract commentarial criticism,[34] the better-law analysis has apparently made a strong appeal to judges in Wisconsin and elsewhere.[35] Like the policy-determined state interest analysis that has brought it into favor as a technique of reconciliation, better-law analysis represents a trend toward greater realism in the decisions of choice cases. There is no reason why judges should always indulge the polite fiction that one state's law is just as fair and well-adjusted to modern conditions as that of another.

The decision in *Conklin v. Horner* is supported by decisions of courts in other states using a policy-determined methodology in cases involving the same fact-law pattern.[36] Nevertheless, the first rule promulgated in the

30. *Id.* In the cases discussed in this Essay, the better-law analysis has been used to resolve a true-conflict between divergent pertinent rules. *See* note 18 *supra* and accompanying text.

Although the facts of these cases fell within the policy-determined scope of the pertinent and divergent rules of two concerned states, it would obviously have been impossible to apply both rules simultaneously. The resolution of such true-conflict cases by means of one or more techniques of reconciliation, such as the better-law analysis, is probably the most important problem confronting courts that employ state-interest analysis.

31. Leflar, *Conflicts Law: More on Choice-Influencing Considerations*, 54 CALIF. L. REV. 1584, 1593 (1966).

32. 35 Wis. 2d at 603–04, 151 N.W.2d at 676.

33. The following studies strongly support the observation that antiguest statutes have been narrowly construed: Comment, *Recent Construction of the Colorado Guest Statute*, 33 ROCKY MT. L. REV. 374, 392 (1962); Comment, *Judicial Nullification of Guest Statutes*, 41 S. CAL. L. REV. 884 (1968); 40 CAN. B. REV. 284 (1962).

34. *See, e.g.*, B. CURRIE, *supra* note 6, at 153–54.

35. *See, e.g.*, Schneider v. Nichols, 280 Minn. 139, 158 N.W.2d 254 (1968); Clark v. Clark, 107 N.H. 351, 222 A.2d 205 (1966).

36. *See, e.g.*, Arnett v. Thompson, 433 S.W.2d 109 (Ky. 1968); Gagne v. Berry, 112 N.H. 125, 290 A.2d 624 (1972). *See also* the New York cases in note 37 *infra*.

Neumeier case is totally inconsistent with these decisions.[37] More importantly, the first two *Neumeier* rules reject, by implication, all reconciliation techniques such as the better-law analysis and the technique of showing that the courts of an antiguest statute state have consistently narrowed its operation.[38]

B. Cipolla v. Shaposka *and Rule Two*

The much discussed case of *Cipolla v. Shaposka*[39] involved the following pattern of facts and laws. Delaware had an antiguest statute requiring proof of "intentional or wilful or wanton misconduct."[40] Pennsylvania had none. A guest-passenger domiciled in Pennsylvania brought suit there against his host-driver domiciled in Delaware. The accident had occurred in Delaware. The argument for applying the Pennsylvania rule was strong and simple; the plaintiff called upon the courts of his home state to enforce its ordinary negligence rule for his benefit.

What, for the Pennsylvania court, was the significance of Delaware domestic law? Like that of Illinois in the *Conklin* case, it reflected two sharply divergent sets of policies. For the benefit of most victims of traffic accidents, liability was imposed for ordinary negligence; this rule effectuated the same policies as the analogous Illinois rule.[41] In a purely domestic case involving a host-driver defendant, however, Delaware law would have subverted these policies in favor of the two narrow policies of the antiguest statute. But this was *not* a purely domestic case. The Pennsylvania court had a strong claim for advancing the compensatory policy of its own rule. And since Delaware law reflected two sharply divergent sets of policies, the court was surely entitled to recognize that a decision for the plaintiff, advancing Pennsylvania's policy, would also advance the three more general policies of Delaware law. The court was further entitled to recognize that since the litigation was not in a Delaware court, only one policy of the antiguest statute—that of shielding the kindly host from the unpleasantness and risks of litigation—would be subverted by a decision for the plaintiff. Thus, the court might have held that a decision to apply the Pennsylvania rule, while subverting only one policy of the antiguest statute, would have advanced the Pennsylvania compensatory policy and several Delaware policies as well.

In a brilliant dissenting opinion, Mr. Justice Roberts urged his colleagues

---

37. *See* note 3 *supra.* Rule one is also inconsistent with two New York appellate division cases with a law-fact pattern similar to *Conklin v. Horner. See* Bray v. Cox, 39 App. Div. 2d 299, 333 N.Y.S.2d 783 (1972); Fosillo v. Matthews, 30 App. Div. 2d 1049, 295 N.Y.S.2d 327, *aff'g* 59 Misc. 2d 539, 299 N.Y.S.2d 872 (1968).

38. For fuller discussion of reconciliation techniques, *see* Hancock, *supra* note 19.

39. 439 Pa. 563, 267 A.2d 854 (1970).

40. DEL. CODE ANN. tit. 21, § 6101(a) (1953).

41. *See* text accompanying note 29 *supra.*

to reject the Delaware antiguest statute because a recent Delaware choice-of-law decision[42] showed that "Delaware itself limits the scope of its policy and the protection it will give to its resident-hosts."[43] He also urged that the conflict between Delaware and Pennsylvania policies should be resolved by adopting the better law (Pennsylvania's rule) for the reasons advanced in the Wisconsin decisions.

Unfortunately, the majority of the court rejected Mr. Justice Roberts' valuable suggestions for resolving the conflict of policies and applied the Delaware antiguest statute. Like the majority of the New York Court of Appeals in the *Neumeier* case, they seem to have been obsessed with the desire to decide the case by adopting a narrow rule practically identical with the second rule of the *Neumeier* case.[44] The *Cipolla* case appears to be the only example of the fact-law pattern there presented in which a state court has applied the antiguest statute.[45] Two other state courts have dealt with the same fact-law pattern,[46] and, for various reasons, have enforced the ordinary negligence rule of the plaintiff's domicile, which was also the forum.

Again we note that the second rule promulgated in the *Neumeier* case would reject by implication all techniques for resolving policy conflicts such as the better-law analysis and the technique of showing that the courts of antiguest statute states have consistently restricted the operation of such statutes. More significantly, the *Neumeier* rules would also ignore, by implication, an important phenomenon brought to light by policy-centered analysis: when a person not domiciled in an antiguest statute state is injured in such a state, a decision to enforce the rule of his home state imposing liability for ordinary negligence will actually advance several general policies of the antiguest statute state that are contrary to those of the statute. This result becomes possible because the domestic law of the antiguest statute state reflects a conflict between two sharply divergent sets of policies.

C. Neumeier v. Kuehner *and Rule Three*

When *Neumeier v. Kuehner*[47] arose, Ontario's antiguest statute required injured guest-passengers or the dependents of deceased ones to prove gross

---

42. Friday v. Smoot, 58 Del. 488, 211 A.2d 594 (1965).
43. 439 Pa. at 576, 267 A.2d at 861.
44. "[I]t seems only fair to permit a defendant to rely on his home state law when he is acting within that state. . . . Inhabitants of a state should not be put in jeopardy of liability exceeding that created by their state's laws just because a visitor from a state offering higher protection decides to visit there." *Id.* at 567, 267 A.2d at 856–57. For the second *Neumeier* rule, *see* note 3 *supra*.
45. A federal court decided against the plaintiff in the virtually identical case of Pryor v. Swarner, 445 F.2d 1272 (2d Cir. 1971). The opinion is seriously weakened by its reliance on the fallacious reasoning discussed in note 24 *supra*.
46. Foster v. Leggett, 484 S.W.2d 827 (Ky. 1972); Schneider v. Nichols, 280 Minn. 139, 158 N.W.2d 254 (1968).
47. 31 N.Y.2d 121, 286 N.E.2d 454, 335 N.Y.S.2d 64 (1972).

negligence. A host-driver domiciled in New York drove into Ontario and picked up a guest-passenger domiciled there to accompany him on a short trip within the province. When their car was struck by a train at a railroad crossing, both were killed. The wife and administratrix of the deceased guest-passenger brought a suit for wrongful death damages[48] against the estate of the deceased host-driver,[49] whose estate was insured.

The fact-law pattern of this case differed from all those previously discussed because New York, the state whose law would have favored the guest-passenger's recovery, had no direct interest of the usual kind in awarding compensation to the family of a deceased guest-passenger domiciled and killed in Ontario.[50] Nevertheless, through careful analysis of the policies of the pertinent rules of Ontario and New York, a very strong argument could have been marshalled for the plaintiffs' recovery. The key to this argument is the recognition that Ontario domestic law reflected a conflict between two sharply divergent sets of policies. For the benefit of most dependent wives and children whose husbands and fathers were killed in traffic accidents, liability was imposed for ordinary negligence. This rule doubtless had some effect as a deterrent of careless driving, but its most important purpose was compensation of the decedent's dependents to prevent them from becoming public charges and to alleviate their drastic loss of economic support. Had the deceased host-driver been domiciled in Ontario and so entitled to the protection of its antiguest statute, these policies would probably[51] have been subordinated, in an Ontario court, to those of the statute. But the host-driver was *not* domiciled in Ontario and, the suit having been brought in New York, neither he nor his estate could, by any stretch of the legal imagination, be brought within the policy range of the Ontario antiguest statute.[52] Thus, with the antiguest statute and its policies completely removed from consideration, the court should have given effect

---

48. This suit was *not* brought on behalf of the decedent's estate but on behalf of his distributees, *i.e.*, his wife and children, to recover fair and just compensation for the pecuniary injuries to them resulting from his death. *See* N.Y. Est., Powers & Trusts §§ 4–1.1, 5–4.1, 5–4.3, Commentary to § 5–4.1 (McKinney 1957). The choice-of-law issue was raised by the plaintiff's motion to dismiss the defendant's affirmative defense that the Ontario antiguest statute should be applied.

49. The plaintiff also sued the Canadian National Railway whose train was involved in the fatal accident. Counsel for the railway contended that the Ontario antiguest statute should be applied. Its interest in making this contention is not explained in the opinion of the court of appeals nor in those of the lower courts. For a full discussion of this complex question, *see* Baade, *supra* note 14, at 156–61.

50. A majority of the appellate division held that New York's liability-for-ordinary-negligence rule imposed upon Kuehner, a New York citizen, a duty and standard of careful driving with a corresponding liability, even though his failure to meet that standard caused injury in an antiguest statute jurisdiction to a person domiciled there. *See* Neumeier v. Kuehner, 37 App. Div. 2d 70, 72, 322 N.Y.S. 2d 867, 868–69 (1971), *overruled*, 31 N.Y.2d 121, 286 N.E.2d 454, 335 N.Y.S.2d 64 (1972).

51. It must be borne in mind that the Ontario courts have consistently narrowed the operation of the statute, so that it has a number of loopholes permitting plaintiffs to recover *without* proving gross negligence. *See* 40 Can. B. Rev. 284 (1962).

52. *See* note 14 *supra*.

to the compensatory policy of Ontario law by enforcing its law of wrongful death, including its standard of ordinary negligence. This compensatory policy was one of serious concern to that province because the deceased guest-passenger and his dependents were all domiciled there. While this rule-choosing analysis would have advanced an important policy of Ontario law other than those of the antiguest statute, it would not have subverted any of that statute's policies, nor would it have subverted any policy of New York.[53]

Would it have been anomalous for the New York court to have enforced Ontario's law of wrongful death (including its standard of ordinary negligence) while rejecting its antiguest statute? Not at all. In *Babcock v. Jackson*, the New York Court of Appeals rejected the Ontario antiguest statute because its enforcement to protect a New York citizen in a New York court would not have advanced any of the statute's policies. At the same time, the court held that if the issue had related to the manner in which the defendant had been driving his car when the accident occurred, the propriety of his conduct would have been judged according to the Ontario rules of the road. In the *Neumeier* case, Ontario had a strong concern for the effectuation of certain laws and policies quite different from the policies of the antiguest statute that, for the *Neumeier* fact-law pattern, were irrelevant.

From the foregoing rule-choosing analysis, there emerged a further formidable argument for the plaintiff. If the New York court were to enforce the antiguest statute against the Ontario plaintiffs, its decision would be unjustifiably discriminatory. As the *Babcock* case and others showed,[54] a New York court would not have enforced the antiguest statute against a plaintiff domiciled in New York. Doubtless a court may, with justification, treat persons not domiciled in the forum state less generously than it treats those who are, if it does so to advance the interests of another state or country. But, as we have seen, enforcement of the antiguest statute in the *Neumeier* case would not have advanced any of the statute's policies; on the contrary, it would have subverted Ontario's policy of compensating its domiciliaries for the loss of their breadwinner.[55]

---

53. We cannot, of course, say of New York law (as we can of Ontario law) that it reflected *two* conflicting sets of policies, one set of which would have been subverted in purely domestic cases. There was nothing in New York law to suggest that when, in a New York domestic case, an injured guest-passenger recovered damages for ordinary negligence, some unseen policy favoring host-defendants was being subverted. New York had no such policy. Moreover, as far as appears from the case, New York's wrongful death law was the same as Ontario's.

54. Tooker v. Lopez, 24 N.Y.2d 569, 249 N.E.2d 394, 301 N.Y.S.2d 519 (1969); Macey v. Rozbicki, 18 N.Y.2d 289, 221 N.E.2d 380, 274 N.Y.S.2d 591 (1966).

55. The critical reader may be inclined to ask whether a decision against the New York host-defendant in the *Neumeier* case would not be discriminatory because, presumably, an Ontario host-defendant would receive the protection of the antiguest statute under the same circumstances. Of course it would. But discrimination against the New York host-defendant would be justified because the decision would advance policies of Ontario law other than those of the antiguest statute and would not subvert any other policies of New York or Ontario law, whereas a decision in favor of the New

Strange as it may seem, a majority of the *Neumeier* court decided to enforce the Ontario antiguest statute. Their opinion evinces a strong desire to establish the narrow rules previously referred to. These rules had already been suggested by the author of the *Neumeier* opinion in a concurring opinion delivered in a prior case,[56] and the third rule pointed to the result reached in the *Neumeier* case.[57] At no point does the opinion recognize the importance of Ontario's policies other than those of the antiguest statute. Nowhere does the opinion recognize that, with the widest rational application given to the policies of the antiguest statute, the host-driver and his estate were beyond its scope.[58] On the contrary, the opinion tries to suggest, in a carefully guarded statement, that a decision for the plaintiffs would subvert some unspecified policy of the statute.[59] The argument that a decision against the Ontario plaintiffs would subject them to indefensible discrimination is casually dismissed with the abstract statement that such discrimination is the result "of the existence of disparate rules of law in jurisdictions that have diverse and important connections with the litigants and the litigated issue."[60]

III. Conclusion: Future of *Neumeier v. Kuehner* and Its Rules

Despite the foreseeable consequence of raising a difficult choice problem in true-conflict cases, the policy-centered, state interest methodology sponsored by the opinion in the *Babcock* case was adopted by judges in other states with remarkable rapidity. Obviously, they preferred this more realistic methodology to the traditional one that, while giving a limited priority to the law of the state of injury, retained sufficient flexibility to permit a judge to apply the pertinent rule of the forum by the use of an overriding principle. Though flexible, the traditional methodology was confusing and highly inarticulate.

Soon after adopting the new state interest methodology, the Supreme

York host-defendant would subvert Ontario's policies other than those of the antiguest statute without advancing any other policies of New York or Ontario law.

56. Tooker v. Lopez, 24 N.Y.2d 569, 584–85, 249 N.E.2d 394, 404, 301 N.Y.S.2d 519, 532–33 (1969) (Fuld, C.J., concurring).

57. *See* note 3 *supra*. For a cogent and penetrating criticism of these rules and of the actual decision in *Neumeier v. Kuehner, see* Sedler, *Interstate Accidents and the Unprovided for Case: Reflections on Neumeier v. Kuehner*, 1 HOFSTRA L. REV. 125 (1973).

58. Yet the majority opinion of the appellate division had very clearly made this point. *See* 37 App. Div. 2d 70, 71, 322 N.Y.S.2d 867, 868–69 (1971).

59. New York "has no legitimate interest in ignoring the public policy of a foreign jurisdiction—such as Ontario—and in protecting the plaintiff guest domiciled and injured [*sic*] there from legislation obviously addressed, at the very least, to a resident riding in a vehicle traveling within its borders." 31 N.Y.2d at 125–26, 286 N.E.2d at 456, 335 N.Y.S.2d at 68.

60. *Id.* at 126, 286 N.E.2d at 456, 335 N.Y.S.2d at 68. Judge Bergan's dissent, *id.* at 132–33, 286 N.E.2d at 460, 335 N.Y.S.2d at 73, was based in part upon the ground of unfair discrimination against the decedent and his family. For further discussion of unfair discrimination in choice-of-law cases, *see* B. CURRIE, *supra* note 6, at 445–583; Hancock, *supra* note 9, at 340–46.

Court of Wisconsin encountered two true-conflict fact-law patterns involving antiguest statutes in the *Heath* and *Conklin* cases. An approach similar to that of the Wisconsin court was adopted by Mr. Justice Roberts in
his dissenting opinion in the *Cipolla* case, which exemplified a third true-
conflict fact-law pattern involving an antiguest statute. The judges who
wrote these opinions refused to adopt the rigid and dogmatic position—supported by some of Currie's earlier articles[61]—that in a true-conflict case the
court should invariably prefer the pertinent rule of the forum. Instead,
adopting commentarial suggestions, they made use of two techniques of
reconciliation: the better-law analysis and the technique of studying purely
domestic cases to see what judicial treatment the pertinent disparate rules
had received in their home states. These well-considered opinions offer
valuable guidance to all courts concerned with true-conflict torts cases,
especially those involving antiguest statutes. Furthermore, they are supported by decisions of other state courts applying state interest analysis to
identical fact-law patterns in somewhat less elaborate opinions.[62] Yet the
actual decision reached in each of these three well-reasoned opinions is
contrary to the rules announced in the *Neumeier* case. Moreover, those rules
appear to reject by implication the techniques of reconciliation employed
in the three opinions. Finally, application of the rules in the *Neumeier* case
itself resulted in an unsound decision.

What impact will the rules of the *Neumeier* case and the actual decisions
have upon future decisions of courts in other states using interest analysis?
In answering this question, it must be borne in mind that the traditional
place-of-injury doctrine operated in practice as a very flexible methodology
because of the availability of broad overriding principles to be used as escape devices. It seems unlikely that judges who have only recently eman-
cipated themselves from the more flexible traditional system will be eager
to put their necks under the yoke of the relatively narrow and rigid *Neumeier* rules. Surely they will be even less inclined to do so when they realize
that these rules purport to decide cases that the New York Court of Appeals
has never actually considered and that other state courts have reached contrary results in well-reasoned opinions.

As for the actual decision in the *Neumeier* case, the reasoning of the
majority is highly vulnerable at several points. Nowhere does the opinion
explain why the Ontario antiguest statute should be extended to protect
the estate and the insurer of a host-driver domiciled in New York. And it
totally fails to meet the vigorous criticism of the dissent that the decision

61. *See* B. CURRIE, *supra* note 6, at 181–82, 184. For a later and somewhat different statement
of his views, *see* Currie, *supra* note 6, at 1241–43.
62. *See* notes 35 & 46 *supra*.

unfairly discriminates against the plaintiffs and their decedent because they were domiciled in an antiguest-statute jurisdiction.[63]

The most significant question raised by the *Neumeier* majority opinion is not whether courts of other states will follow its narrow rules or its actual decision; obviously they are most unlikely to do so. Much more significant is the question whether the New York Court of Appeals itself will actually follow the narrow rules in future cases. One judge dissented from the majority opinion and two others, while concurring in the result, declined to endorse the rules, saying: "It is undesirable to lay down prematurely major premises based on shifting ideologies in the choice of law."[64] It is to be hoped that on reflection other members of the court will share this sentiment and return to the orthodox practice of deciding one case at a time. It is also to be hoped that the Court of Appeals will rejoin the mainstream of state court adjudication in the choice-of-law field by giving some attention to the decisions of other courts that, following the lead of *Babcock v. Jackson*, have adopted state-interest analysis.

---

63. *See* note 59 *supra.*
64. 31 N.Y.2d at 130, 286 N.E.2d at 459, 335 N.Y.S.2d at 71 (Breitel, J., concurring).

Some Reflections on the Control of the Publication of Appellate Court Opinions

J. Myron Jacobstein*

Since the early 19th century American legal scholars have warned against the uncontrolled proliferation of law reports. An article published in 1824 complained:

> [T]he multiplication of reports, emanating from the numerous collateral sources of jurisdiction, is becoming an evil alarming and impossible long to be born [*sic*]. It has of late increased enormously in every mode of increase; the establishment of new tribunals; the increased habit of reporting; and the prolix method adopted by the reporters. All these reports are considered to be entitled to respect in a greater or less degree, and they come upon us from every quarter in an overwhelming flood, intermingled with digest, compends, and essays, without number. Such has been this increase, that very few of the profession can afford to purchase, and none can read all the books which it is thought desirable, if not necessary, to possess. By their number and variety they tend to weaken the authority of each other, and to perplex the judgment. No system ought to be adopted, which should prevent our searching for the lights of jurisprudence in every quarter whence a ray can be derived, but we surely may avoid something of the perplexity and confusion of false lights.[1]

More than a century and a half later a distinguished modern jurist in strikingly similar language repeated the complaint, saying:

> [U]nlimited proliferation of published opinions constitutes a burden and a threat to a cohesive body of law. . . . [T]here are limits in the capacity of judges and lawyers to produce, research and assimilate the sheer mass of judicial opinions. These limits are dangerously near at present and in some systems may already be exceeded. . . . Common law in the United States could be crushed by its own weight if present trends continue unabated.[2]

In fact, numerous articles[3] appeared subsequently in legal periodicals and bar association proceedings commenting on the problem. Nearly all

---

* B.A. 1946, Wayne State University; M.S. 1950, Columbia University; J.D. 1953, Chicago–Kent School of Law. Professor of Law and Law Librarian, Stanford University.
1. Bliss & White, *The Common Law*, 10 N. AM. REV. (n.s.) 411, 433 (1824).
2. Joiner, *Limiting Publication of Judicial Opinions*, 56 JUDICATURE 195, 196 (1972).
3. One author wryly noted that lawyers will soon need to concern themselves with exercising control over the number of articles devoted to reducing the number of judicial opinions. O'Connell, *A Dissertation on Judicial Opinions*, 23 TEMP. L.Q. 13, 14 n.3 (1949).

reiterate the theme that the growing number of published court opinions is threatening to destroy our system of American jurisprudence.[4]

This article seeks to (1) summarize the problems associated with the flood of reported decisions and the proposals for the limitation of published opinions; (2) summarize the opposition to such proposals; (3) examine why the dire predictions of collapse have not as yet been fulfilled; and (4) examine the effectiveness of the rules on publication of opinions implemented by the United States courts of appeals, and California Supreme Court.

I. PROPOSALS FOR REDUCING THE VOLUME OF REPORTED OPINIONS

Three methods have been consistently urged for the control of the number of published opinions: (1) codification, (2) the writing of shorter opinions, and (3) selective reporting.

A. *Codification*

The earliest recommendations for limiting the number of appellate court reports sought methods for the codifying of the common law in a manner similar to that of the Justinian and Napoleonic Codes. Justice Story, for example, after warning of the "[c]alamity which threatens us, of being buried alive, not in the catacombs, but in the labyrinths of the law,"[5] offered a solution:

> I know indeed of one adequate remedy, and that is by a gradual digest under legislative authority of those portions of our jurisprudence, which under the forming hand of the judiciary shall from time to time acquire scientific accuracy. By thus reducing to a text the exact principles of the law, we shall, in a great measure, get rid of the necessity of appealing to volumes which contain jarring and discordant opinions; and thus we may pave the way to a general code, which will present . . . the most material rules to guide the lawyers . . . .[6]

Although similar appeals for codification[7] continued to appear for the hundred years following Justice Story's proposal, recent writers seldom

---

4. Nearly all the literature on this subject is concerned with the writing and publication of appellate court opinions. For a comprehensive analysis on the publication of trial court decisions in the federal system, *see* Vestal, *A Survey of Federal District Court Opinions: West Publishing Company Reports*, 20 Sw. L.J. 63 (1966); Vestal, *Publishing District Court Opinions in the 1970's*, 17 LOYOLA L. REV. 673 (1971); Vestal, *Reported Federal District Court Opinions, Fiscal 1962*, 4 HOUSTON L. REV. 185 (1966); Vestal, *Reported Opinions of the Federal District Courts: Analysis and Suggestions*, 52 IOWA L. REV. 379 (1966). It is also interesting to note that the Federal Bar Association of New Jersey has recently announced a subscription service for the unreported decisions of the United States District Court in New Jersey.

5. *Judge Story's Address*, 1 AM. JURIST 1, 31 (1829).

6. *Id.*

7. There is no generally accepted definition of "codification." As used here, the term means a legislatively enacted law that becomes the primary source of authority and supersedes all previous law whether statutorily or judicially created. For a concise summary of the problem of defining codification, *see* L. SCARMAN, A CODE OF ENGLISH LAW? 4–7 (1966).

mention codification as a solution, reflecting most likely the experience and history of the Restatements.[8]

B. *Shorter Opinions*

Concurrent with the criticism that too many opinions are being published has been the constant plea for shorter opinions. The argument is that if judges could be persuaded to be less prolix and more willing to place a premium on conciseness, a substantial part of the problem would be solved.[9] In recent years, however, there appears to have been less faith placed in this solution. Perhaps the realization has developed that not all judges can write opinions in the style of Oliver Wendell Holmes, Jr., as well as an awareness that self-constraint is the only means of enforcement.[10]

C. *Selective Reporting of Opinions*

Lord Coke, faced in 1777 with a total of roughly 30 volumes of reported decisions, warned judges not to report all decisions.[11] This admonishment to avoid writing opinions for cases that do not make a substantial contribution to the body of the law has been repeated innumerable times.[12] It has been suggested that under this criterion three-fourths of the opinions presently published would remain unpublished.[13]

It is evident that if a court undertakes to adopt the selective publication of its opinions, standards are necessary to determine which opinions should be published and which should not.[14] At least one set of standards for the publication of the appellate court opinions has been suggested. Under these

---

8. An account of the reception of the *Restatements* may be found in E. POLLACK, FUNDAMENTALS OF LEGAL RESEARCH 364–66 (4th ed. J. Jacobstein & M. Mersky 1973).

9. For articles supporting this position, *see Report of the Special Committee on Reports and Digests*, 2 A.B.A.J. 618 (1916); Dillon, *Law Reports & Law Reporting*, 1886 A.B.A. REP. 257; Leach, *The Length of Judicial Opinions*, 21 YALE L.J. 141 (1911); McComb, *A Mandate from the Bar: Shorter and More Lucid Opinions*, 35 A.B.A.J. 382 (1949); Warren, *The Welter of Decisions*, 10 ILL. L. REV. 472 (1916); Winslow, *The Courts and the Papermills!*, 10 ILL. L. REV. 147 (1915). *But see* Peterson, *Court Opinions and Reports*, 86 CENT. L.J. 428 (1918).

10. This, indeed, was recognized in a recent report of the Committee on Judicial Opinions of the Pennsylvania Bar Association, which concluded: "The subject of the style of judicial opinions was discussed at some length in Committee sessions, but it was finally decided that it would serve no useful purpose to attempt to make recommendations concerning literary style to be employed by individual judges in writing opinions, although it was recognized that literary style may affect the length as well as the readability of opinions in many instances." Haas, *Some Comments on the Report of the Committee on Judicial Opinions*, 35 PENN. B. ASS'N Q. 365, 366 (1964).

11. 3 COKE'S REP. iii (1777). The 30-volume estimate is derived from Warren, *supra* note 9, at 472.

12. For articles supporting this position, *see, e.g.,* ANNUAL REPORTS OF THE COMMITTEE ON REPORTS AND DIGESTS OF THE A.B.A. (1884–1948); *Opinions of Courts: Should Number Published Be Reduced?*, 34 A.B.A.J. 668 (1948); Davis, *The Case for the Case Lawyer*, 3 MASS. L.Q. 99 (1916); Winters, *Reducing the Volume of Published Opinions*, 20 FLA. L.J. 250 (1946).

13. Warren, *supra* note 9, at 475.

14. The suggestion for the selective publication of opinions has always raised the question as to who should decide which opinions to publish—the courts or someone else, such as a panel of lawyers. *See, e.g., Current Topics*, 15 CENT. L.J. 41 (1882); Winters, *supra* note 12. As will be seen in Part IV, current practice is to have the decision made by the court.

standards the court's decision is published if (1) the opinion lays down a new rule of law or alters or modifies an existing rule; (2) the opinion involves a legal issue of continuing public interest; (3) the opinion criticizes existing law; or (4) the opinion resolves an apparent conflict of authority.[15]

II. CRITICISM OF SELECTIVE LAW REPORTING

Of the proposals discussed, the present consensus appears to be that selective reporting of opinions is the only effective means of solving the problems presented by excessive opinion writing. However, the view that there is no effective way of enforcing selective publication has frequently been expressed. The specter of private publishers publishing unreported decisions has always haunted the legal profession. It may be that any attempt to prohibit such publication would be unconstitutional.[16] While court opinions may be a matter of public record, courts appear to have the power to prohibit the citation of unpublished opinions.[17]

While the majority of the bar undoubtedly favors the limitation of published court reports (at least as measured by the literature on this subject), a number of writers have warned that selective law reporting has its own shortcomings. The objections raised may be classified in four categories: (1) cases are more likely to be decided correctly on the law when there are written opinions;[18] (2) the writing of opinions is a means of convincing the bar, litigants, and the public that the cases have been carefully considered, and thus results in increased respect for the courts;[19] (3) the law becomes more certain and understandable when there are written opinions;[20] and (4) there is no satisfactory method of selecting which cases are to be published and which omitted.[21]

Until recently there has been no way to assess the potential success of efforts to limit the number of decisions. However, the United States courts of appeals and the California Supreme Court have recently implemented rules limiting publication of opinions. These rules now afford an oppor-

---

15. COMMITTEE ON USE OF APPELLATE COURT ENERGIES OF THE ADVISORY COUNCIL ON APPELLATE JUSTICE—STANDARDS FOR PUBLICATION OF JUDICIAL OPINIONS 15–17 (Federal Judicial Center Research Series No. 73–2, Aug. 1973) [hereinafter cited as STANDARDS FOR PUBLICATION].

16. *See* O'Connell, *supra* note 3, at 16.

17. In Jones v. Superintendent, Virginia State Farm, 465 F.2d 1091, 1094 (4th Cir. 1972), it was held that the courts of appeals' screening procedure and disposition by unreported memorandum decisions, though imperfect, accorded with due process and the courts' duty as article III judges.

18. *Cf.* Jenkins, *Courts: Sufficiency of Opinions*, 9 OKLA. L. REV. 171 (1956).

19. "Another office of the opinion is to give assurance to a litigant that his appeal has received fair consideration." *Id.* at 173.

20. "The function [of the court] is not declaring justice between man and man, but of settling the law. The court exists, not for the individual litigant, but for the indefinite body of litigants whose causes are potentially involved in the specific course at issue. The wrongs of aggrieved suitors are only algebraic symbols from which the court is to work out the formula of justice." CARDOZO, JURISDICTION OF THE COURT OF APPEALS OF THE STATE OF NEW YORK § 6 (2d ed. 1909).

21. Winters, *supra* note 12, at 252.

tunity for testing the effectiveness of selective reporting in solving the problems created by the indiscriminate publication of opinions.

III. Why the Predicted Collapse of the Judicial System by Unlimited Court Opinions Has Not Yet Occurred

The literature on court reporting is abundant with dire predictions related to the flood of opinions. It is interesting to ponder why our judicial system still functions, with court opinions still performing a dominant role. It is also puzzling to note that the American Bar Association, after forming a Committee on Law Reports and Digests in 1884 which then issued annual reports for nearly 65 years, abolished this Committee in 1948. In a similar pattern, the number of articles on the subject published in legal periodicals has declined dramatically during the past decade and a half. Nearly all the articles now published are written by judges or are reports of the federal and various state judicial councils. It is clear that the impetus has changed from the lawyer's complaints of too many books to buy and shelve to that of judges and court administrators concerned with the rapidly growing number of docketed cases.

But what seems puzzling at first glance becomes less so as one searches for the reasons for this apparent drop in interest by lawyers. A part of the answer can perhaps be found in a change in the structure of the legal profession and in the response of private lawbook publishing companies. The last 20 years have seen rapid growth, not only in the number of lawyers, but also in the development of specialization among individual practitioners and within law firms. The number of sole practitioners has been declining and the size of large firms increasing.[22] This growth of specialization among lawyers has been reflected in the greater availability of specialized subject court reports, a phenomenon not always noted by those concerned with the volume of published judicial opinions. The number of such sets is astonishing. It has recently been estimated that sales of special subject reporters, such as those by the Commerce Clearing House, Prentice-Hall, and the Bureau of National Affairs, now approximate those of the traditional court reports, such as those by the West Publishing Company and the Lawyers Co-operative Publishing Company.[23]

Lawyers who are primarily involved with corporate law, taxation, and the regulated industries are really not concerned about the expanding number of volumes in the National Reporter System, or of their state reports. Their needs for access to cases in their fields of practice are met by the

---

22. *Cf.* Hazard, *Rethinking Legal Ethics* (Book Review), 26 Stan. L. Rev. 1227, 1229 (1974).
23. Sandza, *Lawbook Publishing: A $145-Million-a-Year Business*, Juris Doctor, Feb. 1974, at 31.

specialized subject reporting services. The fear so frequently expressed in the past that lawyers would not be able to find space in their libraries for all of the reports is not applicable to this group. It is rather those lawyers whose practice is primarily involved with criminal law, landlord-tenant, domestic relations, and other areas common to the sole practitioner or the average small firm that must still rely on the standard sets of court reports.

IV. The Efforts to Limit the Publication of Appellate Court Opinions by Court Rule

A. *United States Courts of Appeals*

The soaring caseload of the United States courts of appeals has long been of concern to those interested in court administration. It has been predicted that the total caseload for the 10 federal circuits will have increased from nearly 4,000 in 1960 to nearly 14,000 by 1975.[24] The writing of opinions has been ranked as the second most significant cause of delay in appellate courts.[25] The impact of the growing caseload on the courts can best be ascertained by reading the poignant opinion[26] of Chief Judge Brown of the Fifth Circuit, in which he explains the reasons for the adoption of a rule limiting the number of published opinions.[27]

The Fifth Circuit has attacked this problem through its adoption of Rule 21. Under this rule the court may determine that when certain criteria are met and when an opinion would have no precedential value, an order or judgment may be affirmed or enforced without an opinion. In similar fashion pursuant to a recommendation by the Judicial Conference, all of the circuits have adopted new guidelines for the publication of their opinions.[28] While the wording differs in each circuit, basically each provides for three possibilities: (1) Opinion: When a pending case meets the standards set by the *Standards for Publication of Court Opinions* it will be designated "For publication"; (2) Memorandum: A written reasoned disposition of a case not intended for publication; (3) Order: Any other disposition by the court. Any disposition which is not for publication will not be regarded as a precedent.

In some circuits the decision to publish is made by the writer of the opinion, in others by a majority of the panel. Provision is also made either for mandatory designation for publication, when an opinion has been pub-

---

24. NLRB v. Amalgamated Clothing Workers, 430 F.2d 966, 969 (5th Cir. 1970).
25. Standards for Publication, *supra* note 15, at 1.
26. NLRB v. Amalgamated Clothing Workers, 430 F.2d 966 (5th Cir. 1970).
27. The question whether a written opinion is required must be kept separate from the question of publishing opinions after they are written. *See* Standards for Publication, *supra* note 15, at 2.
28. Federal Judicial Center, Annual Report 6 (1973). Each circuit has issued a Plan for Publication of Opinions. These are on file at the Stanford Law Library.

lished by the district court or an administrative agency, or for the periodical listing of unpublished orders in the *Federal Reporter*.[29] The impact of these new rules is revealed by an examination of the statistics for the first 11 months of 1973, when 2,708 cases were decided without the writing of opinions, 1,477 case opinions were written but not published, and 4,563 opinions were published.[30]

While it cannot be denied that these new rules have effectively reduced the number of opinions judges have to write and the number of published opinions available for precedential purposes, the impact of these rules on the administration of justice must also be considered. Has the reduction of the burden on the judges created other problems? A recent U.S. Supreme Court case may already signal one danger of the absence of a written opinion. In *Taylor v. McKeithen*[31] the Court had before it a case involving the 1970 reapportionment of the Louisiana legislature. The federal district court had adopted a plan of its special master over a counterplan of the state attorney general. The court of appeals under its new rules reversed without opinion. The Supreme Court granted certiorari and then vacated the judgment below. In so doing, the Court noted that the court of appeals may have based its decision on the belief that the district judge's action in adopting the special master's plan was unconstitutional. Such a decision would raise a substantial federal question. Without, however, a court of appeals' opinion setting forth its reasoning, the Supreme Court felt the need to vacate the judgment below because "this record does not fully inform us of the precise nature of the litigation and we have not had the benefit of the insight of the Court of Appeals . . . ."[32]

B. *California Supreme Court*

Since 1964, when the California Supreme Court adopted Rule 976, "Publication of Court Opinions,"[33] the California courts of appeal opinions have received limited publication. Under Rule 976 the California Supreme Court could order an opinion not published. In 1972, this rule was modified and stricter standards for the publication of opinions adopted. Under the modified rule, no opinions are to be published unless they conform to

---

29. *See, e.g.*, 488 F.2d 1056 (5th Cir. 1974). The importance of this provision cannot be overstated. The danger of having a published trial court opinion followed by an unpublished appellate court opinion is obvious. Several years ago Professor Howard Williams of the Stanford Law School called to my attention that the opinion *In re* Estate of Humphrey, 254 F. Supp. 33 (D.D.C.), *rev'd sub nom.* Humphrey v. Tolson, 384 F.2d 987 (D.C. Cir. 1966), had been reversed by an unpublished order of the court of appeals. It was not until an inquiry was made of the West Publishing Company that the court released the order for publication.
30. *Increase Continues in Federal Appeals Courts' Caseload*, 60 A.B.A.J. 566 (1974).
31. 407 U.S. 191 (1972).
32. 407 U.S. at 194. For a similar decision in a state court, *see* Rosenthal v. Scott, 131 So. 2d 480 (Fla. 1961).
33. CAL. SUP. CT. (CIV.) R. 976 (West 1964), *as amended* (West Supp. 1974).

the criteria set forth. In addition, the courts of appeal must affirmatively indicate that an opinion is for publication.[34] Since 1964, 58 percent of the cases of the California courts of appeal have not been reported. This figure increased to 71 percent in 1971.[35] However, since no rule forbade citing unreported cases, this practice became prevalent and indeed advantageous to some attorneys.[36] The California Supreme Court then made the next logical move when it adopted Rule 977,[37] which prohibits the citation of unpublished opinions of the courts of appeal.

V. CONCLUSION

The unrest among lawyers opposed to the limitation of appellate court opinions, nevertheless, continues. A proponent of the rules has argued recently that the substance of the rules is necessary for ". . . the preservation of *stare decisis* as a workable doctrine, [with] fairness, reliability and efficiency . . . ."[38] An opponent illustrates the contrary view through illustration of a case in which a used car dealer was convicted for "spinning back" odometers on cars he sold.[39] The court of appeal affirmed but did not publish the opinion. The author emphasizes the potential usefulness that the publication of this opinion would have had as a deterrent to such practices by used car dealers. He then quotes Professor Phillip B. Kurland's statement that "efficiency measured solely by productivity is as likely to be destructive of the functions of law in a democratic society as the inefficiency it replaces . . . ."[40] A recent poll of Los Angeles lawyers on their attitudes toward the new practice of restrictive publication of court of appeal opinions revealed that those polled voted two-to-one against the practice and in favor of the publication of all court of appeal written opinions.[41] A bill[42] introduced into the California Legislature that would require all opinions to be published caused heated arguments before the Senate Judiciary Committee.[43] Another example of a negative reaction to the failure to publish an opinion occurred when the California court of appeal held that traffic

---

34. *Id.*
35. Seligson & Warnlof, *The Use of Unreported Cases in California*, 24 HASTINGS L.J. 37 (1972).
36. The Compendium, May 1973 (Poopsheet from Courtroom Compendium). This is a service reporting California cases on search and seizure. The editor, commenting on revised Rule 976, noted that "subscribers from all over the state report winning case after case in trial courts by citing unpublished opinions."
37. CAL. SUP. CT. (CIV.) R. 977 (West Supp. 1974).
38. Seligson & Warnlof, *supra* note 35, at 53.
39. Kanner, *The Unpublished Appellate Opinion: Friend or Foe?*, 48 CAL. ST. B.J. 386 (1973). *See also Publish or Perish: The Destiny of Appellate Opinions in California*, 13 SANTA CLARA LAW. 756 (1973).
40. Kurland, *The Lord Chancellor of the United States*, Trial, Dec. 1971, at 11.
41. Los Angeles Daily J., Jan. 8, 1974, at 1, col. 4.
42. Calif. S. 2246 (1974). This bill was amended on June 5, 1974 to provide for the publication of opinions not in the Official Reports in a new series to be called Civil or Criminal Memorandum Reports.
43. Los Angeles Daily J., June 14, 1974, at 1, col. 5. The Committee voted 13–2 against the bill.

violators have a statutory right to representation by an attorney.[44] A columnist in the *Palo Alto Times* noted the financial impact this ruling could have on local government finances and quoted the lawyer for the successful appellant as saying, "I'm sure that's why the judges wouldn't have their opinion published."[45]

It is evident that the solution to the problem of the proliferation of appellate court reports has not as yet been found. The position of those opposed to the selective writing and publication of appellate decisions has some merit. Yet it is difficult to deny the reasoning of those who maintain that the continued publication of all opinions "constitutes a burden and a threat to our cohesive body of law."[46] Essentially two separate issues require consideration. The first is the increasing number of cases being heard by appellate courts. If we assume for the moment a sufficient number of judges are available to alleviate the time pressure on each judge in his writing of opinions, then at least this issue could be eliminated. The ever-increasing number of written decisions, however, would remain. The problem would now be the same as that which troubled the bar in earlier years—the concern over too many bound volumes of reports and the excessive time needed in researching the law. Nonetheless, this concern may be more amenable to solution. As noted in Part III of this Article, the increasing availability of subject court reports is already serving the needs of many lawyers. A further expansion of this method of court reporting could undoubtedly be undertaken where needed. Other means for the more efficient publication of court reports are also available, such as the use of microforms, computer data banks, and other techniques now being perfected by information scientists.

Rather than continuing the battle over the reporting of decisions, our efforts should be devoted to the following three concerns: convincing the Congress and the state legislatures that more judges are needed; achieving an agreement that only some opinions shall serve as precedents, with others available for persuasive purposes; and stimulating a willingness by the courts to explore and utilize new methods to make all decisions of our appellate courts available for consultation by any interested party. Until then we remain in danger of repeating, by design or otherwise, the behavior of the Roman Emperor Gaius Caligula, who passed many new laws that were never published. When the people complained, he "had the law posted up, but in a very narrow place and in excessively small letters, to prevent the making of a copy."[47]

---

44. CAL. PENAL CODE § 987 (West Supp. 1974).
45. Palo Alto Times, Sept. 27, 1973, at 22, col. 3.
46. Joiner, *supra* note 2, at 195.
47. SUETONIUS, THE LIVES OF THE TWELVE CAESARS 192 (J. Gavorse ed. 1931).

A Primer on Heroin

John Kaplan*

I. The Geography, Pharmacology, and History of Heroin

A. *The Opium Poppy*

The opium poppy (*Papaver somniferum*) grows under a wide variety of climatic conditions, though it seems to prefer a warm, dry climate. Its growth is presently illegal in the United States, as in most other countries, and its cultivation, where legal, is limited by a network of international agreements.

Legally or not, however, the plant is grown on a large scale in several areas of the world. In India the plant is grown lawfully as a cash crop for the medical drugs that may be obtained from it and, so far as we know, diversion to other illegal uses is not common. In central Turkey opium has been cultivated for centuries and is the basis of the local cuisine. Its leaves are eaten in salad and the oil from its seeds, like the olive oil in Spanish cuisine, is an important ingredient in traditional cookery. The plant is also an important cash crop, with the government, in theory, buying up the entire production of opium for medical uses. But here—as in other areas where there is a shortage of police resources, a cultural tradition of opium growing, and a large supply of cheap rural labor—the illegal market flourishes. The monetary return from the Turkish illegal market is enough to make diversion to illegal uses a serious problem.[1] This diversion has been so serious that the United States Government for 2 years expended a considerable amount of resources to persuade the Turkish government to ban growth of the plant altogether.[2] In areas of Pakistan, Afghanistan,[3] and the "Golden Triangle" of Laos, Burma, and Thailand—areas effectively outside the power of any of those embattled governments—the poppy is grown entirely for the illegal market.

B. *Morphine and Heroin*

Opium is the dried exudate of the flower of the poppy and has been known for several thousand years as a folk medicine, healer of pain, and

---

* A.B. 1951, LL.B. 1954, Harvard University. Professor of Law, Stanford University.

1. Land, *Turkey's View of the New Opium War*, The Journal, Sept. 1, 1974, at 5, col. 1 (Addiction Research Foundation, Toronto).

2. Anderson, *U.S. Warns Turkey on Opium Growing*, San Francisco Chronicle, Sept. 9, 1974, at 37, col. 5; Linton, *Opium Furor*, The Journal, Sept. 1, 1974, at 1, col. 5 (Addiction Research Foundation, Toronto).

3. *See* McLaughlin & Quinn, *Drug Control in Iran: A Legal and Historical Analysis*, 59 Iowa L. Rev. 469, 502 (1974). *See also* 25 U.N. ECOSOC 4–5, 8–9, U.N. Doc. E/CN. 7/550, E/CN. 7/AC. 10/1 (1972).

giver of pleasure. Originally it was drunk in various potions, but with the introduction from the New World of smoking as a method of drug use, the opium pipe came into widespread use—the smoker often mixing the opium with another New World import, tobacco.

In 1803 the active ingredient of opium, a white, crystalline powder responsible for the great bulk of opium's pharmacological effects, was first isolated. Appropriately, it was named "morphine" after Morpheus, god of sleep.[4] In 1898 heroin was produced from morphine by a relatively simple chemical manipulation. Although heroin was originally believed to have all the therapeutic qualities of morphine without the most serious side effect of that drug—its addicting quality—experience quickly showed that heroin was every bit as addictive as morphine and about 2 to 2.5 times as strong on a per weight basis.[5]

The addict seems to prefer heroin to morphine for several reasons. First, since it acts more quickly, the time lag between injection and action is that much shorter. Second, many addicts report that injections of morphine lead to an unpleasant tingling sensation in the fingers and toes.[6] Of perhaps most importance, heroin is more easily available than morphine on the illegal market in the United States, since both the illegal seller and smuggler prefer it. Heroin, being more concentrated, can be concealed more easily than an equivalent dosage of morphine.[7]

Fifty years after the isolation of morphine, another major technological development occurred, having a profound influence on the opiate problem. The invention of the hypodermic syringe in 1853 allowed administration of the drug in far more concentrated form. Although morphine and heroin

---

4. COMMISSION OF INQUIRY INTO THE NON-MEDICAL USE OF DRUGS, FINAL REPORT 300 (1973) [hereinafter cited as CANADIAN COMMISSION].

5. Blaine, Bozzetti, & Ohlson, *The Narcotic Analgesics: The Opiates*, in DRUG USE IN AMERICA, APP., VOL. 1: PATTERNS AND CONSEQUENCES OF DRUG USE 60, 62 (Nat'l Comm'n on Marihuana and Drug Abuse 1973) [hereinafter cited as PATTERNS AND CONSEQUENCES OF DRUG USE].

The precise reason for this increased "strength" is somewhat complex. Heroin is not simply a concentrate of morphine—indeed, a pound of morphine yields about 1.2 pounds of heroin. Moreover, heroin quickly breaks down into morphine when it enters the bloodstream. Apparently heroin also acts somewhat more quickly than morphine, probably because it can cross the blood-brain barrier more easily.

6. *Id.* at 62. The high concentration of morphine near the site of injection causes the release of histamines, which in turn cause the tingling. Since heroin is better distributed in the bloodstream before it breaks down into morphine, the histamines are not released and hence the tingling does not occur.

7. In addition to morphine and heroin, the opiate family contains several other important members. Codeine, an extremely valuable medical drug, is a relatively minor constituent (0.5%) of opium. Meperidine (Demerol), Jaffe, *Narcotics Analgesics*, in THE PHARMACOLOGICAL BASIS OF THERAPEUTICS 237, 255–56 (4th ed. L. Goodman & A. Gilman eds. 1970), and methadone, *id.* at 260, are both synthetic drugs quite close in pharmacological action to the natural opiates. In addition to these most common opiates, a host of other relatives are already known—some being up to 1,000 times as powerful, on a per weight basis, as morphine.

All of the opiates have roughly similar effects, and may be substituted for one another by addicts—though for various reasons some choose one over another when many are available. Pharmacologists use the terms "opiate" and "narcotic" interchangeably, despite the efforts of legislatures to include within the latter definition cocaine—a stimulant—and marihuana—a hypnotic, or mild hallucinogen.

can be smoked or eaten, injection is the preferred means by which addicts in the United States take the drug. Injection is the most efficient method; smoking destroys much of the drug and eating allows the gastric juices to destroy some of the drug and the liver to neutralize much of what is absorbed. These factors might perhaps be less important were the drug cheaper, but present street prices in the United States[8] make it the rare American addict who can afford the luxury of using any means other than injection.[9] Injection is also attractive because it minimizes the timelag between administration of the drug and its effect; indeed, injection into a vein—a process addicts call "mainlining"—causes the drug to take effect almost instantaneously. Moreover, many addicts desire the "rush" that the injected drug gives them as it takes effect all at once. And, since intravenous injection provides the fastest connection between drug taking and its desired effects, of all modes of administration, injection creates the most immediate reinforcement and thus the most powerful psychological conditioning effects. It is this conditioning that greatly complicates the problem of addiction.[10]

C. *Evolution of Opiate Regulation*

Although the addictive effect of opium has long been known, the social problem of opiate, or narcotics, control is of relatively recent origin. In the 19th century, addiction was for the first time conceived of as a social problem rather than as a personal health problem.[11] In the United States, national concern over opiate addiction first occurred after the Civil War, when physicians' use of the relatively new drug, morphine, injected by the still more novel hypodermic needle, to treat large numbers of battlefield injuries, resulted in a sizeable number of morphine addicts. The problem was, however, regarded almost exclusively as medical in nature—another of the many types of war injuries—and morphine, the drug that both caused and alleviated the symptoms of the addiction, remained freely available.[12]

The next major development in the public awareness of narcotics came in the wake, not of war, but of one of our recurrent racial problems. The Chinese coolies who, in the 1860's, had been brought here to build the western railroads remained in the United States and competed with white

---

8. The average daily dose is 55 milligrams and the current street price is approximately $0.55 per milligram. The average cost per day per addict is therefore $30. Holahan, *The Economics of Heroin*, in DEALING WITH DRUG ABUSE 255, 290–91 (Drug Abuse Survey Project 1972) [hereinafter cited as Drug Abuse Survey Project].

9. Interestingly, in Iran and Hong Kong where heroin, though illegal, is far cheaper than in the United States, the drug is much more often smoked than injected.

10. *See* text accompanying notes 37–38 *infra*.

11. *See* E. BRECHER, LICIT AND ILLICIT DRUGS 3–7 (1972). For additional information on early drug use, *see* C. TERRY & M. PELLENS, THE OPIUM PROBLEM chs. 1 & 2 (1928).

12. Blaine, Bozzetti, & Ohlson, *supra* note 5, at 60. *See also* C. TERRY & M. PELLENS, *supra* note 11, at 69.

Americans for employment positions. Although whites ascribed a series of unpleasant practices to the Chinese, their smoking of the exotic drug, opium, received disproportionate attention. It was thought that prohibition of opium smoking would not only stigmatize a practice associated with the despised minority, but would also deprive the Chinese of this drug in the United States and so cause their return to China. A parallel hope was that insofar as opium provided the Chinese with their energy and ability to tolerate hardship—a very different view of the drug's effect from what is generally held today—its prohibition would deprive the aliens of an unfair advantage over American workmen.[13]

The wave of resentment against Chinese triggered the first major American legislation in the narcotics field—the anti-opium legislation in the Western states, which began with a San Francisco ordinance of 1875 forbidding the keeping of opium dens.[14] Congress in turn gradually extended the prohibitions on opium smoking. In 1883, it raised the tariff on smoking-opium (a prepared, relatively mild form of the drug);[15] in 1887, prohibited the importation of such opium by Chinese;[16] and in 1909, completely banned its importation.[17] While the impact of these laws has not been carefully investigated, it has been argued that their two principal effects were to shift use from smoking-opium to morphine[18] and to create a class of illegal opium smokers.

Although the stringency of the campaigns against opium smoking continued to grow, Congress, responding to quite different pressures, laid down the general outlines of our present narcotics policy in the Harrison Act of 1914.[19] In part because of our unique relationship with China, the nation felt to be most victimized by the opium traffic, the United States had earlier taken a major part in the international negotiations that resulted in the Hague Convention of 1912,[20] outlawing the international nonmedical opium traffic. The international concern highlighted the virtually nonexistent control the United States exercised over its internal opiate traffic— apart from the restrictions on smoking opium. And opium smoking was a relatively minor cause of opiate addiction here. "Tonics" and patent medicines were virtually unregulated, and many contained opiates. It was said that the largest group of addicts consisted of middle class white women[21] who did not even know they were addicted. They only knew that their

---

13. *See generally* E. SANDMEYER, THE ANTI-CHINESE MOVEMENT IN CALIFORNIA (1973).
14. E. BRECHER, *supra* note 11, at 42–43.
15. Act of Mar. 3, 1883, ch. 121, §§ 2499, 2502, 22 Stat. 488, 491–95.
16. Act of Feb. 23, 1887, ch. 210, § 1, 24 Stat. 409.
17. Act of Feb. 9, 1909, ch. 100, § 1, 35 Stat. 614.
18. *Cf.* E. BRECHER, *supra* note 11, at 45–46.
19. Act of Dec. 17, 1914, ch. 1, 38 Stat. 785.
20. D. MUSTO, THE AMERICAN DISEASE ch. 2 (1973).
21. *See* E. BRECHER, *supra* note 11, at 17–19.

"tonic," taken regularly, prevented the sickly feeling that came on whenever they missed their medicine.

The Harrison Act made illegal the importation, sale, or possession of opiates except within medical channels. Within the general prohibition on opiate use, the law permitted a physician to prescribe opiates "in the course of his professional practice only."[22] Such a drug could be obtained legally only pursuant to a physician's prescription, and detailed inventory and recordkeeping requirements were established to prevent diversion.[23]

Even more important than the Harrison Act itself were its implementing policies and regulations. The Act left open the issue of whether a physician could prescribe narcotics simply in order to "maintain" an addict. The authorities enforcing the Act immediately took the position that "in the course of professional practice" did not comprehend mere maintenance of addicts on opiates and they began prosecutions of physicians who implemented a contrary interpretation.[24] These prosecutions not only eliminated those "script doctors" who gave out the drug promiscuously but deterred physicians who might attempt to maintain addicts under medical supervision. For a while, the authorities tolerated, indeed encouraged, the prescription of maintenance doses for addicts by specialized clinics beyond the control of individual private practitioners, but gradually these were closed down.[25] It is by no means clear even today whether law enforcement agencies closed the clinics because of abuses that cropped up or because of the agencies' generally prohibitionist philosophy; nevertheless, by 1925 there were no legitimate sources of opiates for addicts.[26]

From that time until the 1960's, the national narcotics policy changed only in the direction of gradual increases in the penalty structure. Thereafter, the only significant changes were the repeal of certain minimum sentences, expanded civil commitment provisions, and a slight relaxation of the prohibition on medical maintenance of addicts.

The effects of 60 years of this policy are subject to some dispute. Several facts are quite clear, however. First, the type of addict has changed dramatically from the pre-Harrison days, when opiate addicts were primarily middle class and middle-aged women from rural areas or small towns. These addicts were takers of oral morphine or opium and certainly not regarded as particularly criminal. Within 15 years after the passage of the Harrison Act, addicts were much more likely to be male, urban, lower

---

22. Act of Dec. 17, 1914, ch. 1, § 2(a), 38 Stat. 785, 786.
23. *Id*. ch. 1, § 3, 38 Stat. 785, 787–88.
24. D. MUSTO, *supra* note 20, at 121–23.
25. *Id*. at 151–82.
26. None, that is, other than those available to ease the pain of short-term withdrawal. *Id*. at 181.

class, and young.[27] They were injectors of heroin and a serious criminal problem not only with respect to the violations of the drug laws inherent in being an addict, but also with respect to property crimes.

A considerable part of this transition can be explained by the change in the legal treatment of opiates. Since the Harrison Act cut off all legitimate sources of the drug, addicts had to rely on smuggled drugs. The difficulties of concealment increased the popularity of more powerful opiates such as heroin as compared with morphine or opium. Finally, the criminality of addicts rose in part because the price of the drug had gone up so enormously that sustaining a habit required considerably more money than most addicts could earn through honest work.[28]

We must balance against these changes the fact that the per capita percentage of addicts in the population almost certainly decreased.[29] Nonetheless, it is hard for any observer comparing the situation just prior to the Harrison Act with that existing at any time after 1930 to say that opiates were not far more of a problem in the later years.

II. HEROIN USE AND ITS EFFECTS

With this brief sketch as background, we turn to a number of questions relevant to the formulation of public policy in the narcotics area. As this Essay will indicate, the answers to questions such as "How harmful is heroin?" or "Why do people use heroin?" are themselves affected by existing public policy. Nonetheless, we will first consider why, given the serious legal and medical consequences, people in the United States today use heroin.

A. *The Reasons for Addiction*

There are many reasons for the use of heroin, the simplest being that many users are heroin addicts and hence will go through withdrawal without the drug.[30] There is no doubt that opiates are addicting: somehow, after

27. *Cf.* Ball, *Two Patterns of Opiate Addiction*, in THE EPIDEMIOLOGY OF OPIATE ADDICTION IN THE UNITED STATES 81, 93–94 (J. Ball & C. Chambers eds. 1970) [hereinafter cited as EPIDEMIOLOGY OF OPIATE ADDICTION].

28. For a discussion of some of the immediate effects of the passage of the Harrison Act, *see* E. BRECHER, *supra* note 11, at 50–55.

29. The level of addiction in 1900 has been estimated at 10–20 times the current level of addiction. Saper, *The Making of Policy Through Myth, Fantasy and Historical Accident: The Making of America's Narcotics Laws*, 69 BR. J. ADDICT. 183, 184 (1974). It has also been estimated at twice the present rate. C. TERRY & M. PELLENS, *supra* note 11, at 41, estimated the number of addicts in 1920 to be 264,000. Current estimates range from 250,000–300,000. *See* note 57 *infra* and accompanying text. This is despite a population increase from 106 million in 1920 to 210 million in 1973. *See* U.S. DEP'T OF COMMERCE, STATISTICAL ABSTRACT OF THE UNITED STATES 1973, at 5.

30. This paper does not deal with the many nonaddict users of heroin. There may be as many of these as there are addicts but the data on the nonaddict population is far less complete than on the addicted group. They also, for reasons that will later appear, come to attention much less often than do addicts.

use on a highly variable number of occasions, the body of the user adjusts biochemically to the drug, so that, thereafter, a cessation of drug use is accompanied by unpleasant physical symptoms—nausea, running nose, gooseflesh, and cramps.[31] Nevertheless, blaming the persistency of opiate addiction simply on fear of withdrawal is insufficient. Most heroin addicts today do not in fact go through any serious withdrawal when they stop using the drug.[32] The heroin currently available in the United States is of such low quality and is used in such low dosage that in many areas police departments report that months go by without their seeing a classic case of heroin withdrawal among those arrested.[33]

Moreover, simple fear of withdrawal does not explain the phenomenon of readdiction. It is far easier to bring an addict through withdrawal than to keep him from becoming readdicted. Long before the Harrison Act, when addiction was regarded simply as a sickness, it had been noted that the relapse rate after treatment approached 100 percent.[34] Nor was the criminal law, after 1914, a more effective agent of cure. The vast majority of addicts imprisoned for several years for crimes arising out of heroin use would go through withdrawal within the first few days after arrest, only to return promptly to heroin use upon their release.[35]

Although there is some evidence for a biochemical cause of the readdiction phenomenon,[36] the relapse rate is equally well explained by a psychological-conditioning theory.[37] During his period of addiction, the addict has used heroin many times to stave off the discomfort of withdrawal and to obtain a feeling of well-being. In psychological terms, the behavior of heroin injection has been consistently rewarded over a sizeable period and hence, by a process of operant or Skinnerian conditioning, the addict will tend to engage in this behavior whenever the cues of discomfort are present.

---

31. Dimijian, *Contemporary Drug Abuse*, in A. GOTH, MEDICAL PHARMACOLOGY 324, 327 (4th ed. 1968); Jaffe, *Drug Addiction and Drug Abuse*, in L. Goodman & A. Gilman eds., *supra* note 7, at 276, 287–88.

32. *Cf.* Way, *Contemporary Classification, Pharmacology, and Abuse Potential of Psychotropic Substances*, in DRUGS AND YOUTH 27, 30 (J. Wittenborn, H. Brill, J. Smith & S. Wittenborn eds. 1969).

33. *Id.* at 28; private communication from undercover narcotics agent to editors of *Stanford Law Review*, in San Jose, Cal., Nov. 14, 1974. Even in its classic form, heroin withdrawal is simply not *that* serious. Pharmacologists compare it to having a bad case of flu for a few days. Organizations such as Synanon insist that people who come to them take no medication to ease withdrawal pains. And, unlike the case of alcohol and barbiturates, no fatalities have been unambiguously traced to heroin withdrawal. Glaser & Ball, *Death Due to Withdrawal from Narcotics*, in EPIDEMIOLOGY OF OPIATE ADDICTION, *supra* note 27, at 263, 286–87.

34. *Cf.* E. BRECHER, *supra* note 11, at 66.

35. *Id.* at 66–78.

36. *See, e.g., id.* at 68. Under this theory opiate use causes a permanent change in the biochemistry of the addict. Even though the most obvious manifestations of addiction have disappeared once the addict has been through withdrawal, this theory asserts that there persists a biochemical change causing periods of tension, depression, anxiety, and a craving for opiates that make it virtually impossible to effect any permanent cures.

37. *See* Wikler, *Conditioning Factors in Opiate Addiction and Relapse*, in NARCOTICS 85 (D. Wilner & G. Kassenbaum eds. 1965).

Moreover, the mere lack of ability to perform the heroin-using response does not extinguish the behavior. Only the use of heroin over a long period without rewarding consequences can do this.

In addition to operant conditioning, another type of conditioning has a significant bearing on the relapse problem. During an addict's life on the street, he will begin to feel the onset of withdrawal many times—typically just before injecting heroin. Gradually, the stimuli of the streets become associated (or paired) with the feeling of withdrawal, just as in Pavlov's well-known experiment the sound of the bell became associated with the appearance of food, triggering salivation in the dog. As a result of this classical, or Pavlovian, conditioning, a former addict, abstinent for years— or even under a maintenance dosage of methadone—can suddenly feel all of the symptoms of withdrawal. This not only activates the first conditioning mechanism and the use of heroin, but also causes a serious discomfort that can only be relieved by a heroin injection. The mere approach to his former "scoring area," the sight of an "outfit," or "works," even reading about addiction, all can produce physiological symptoms indistinguishable to the ex-addict from those of withdrawal.[38]

Another phenomenon also helps explain the low rate of success for almost all methods of treating addicts. After treatment, which usually involves some prolonged period of incarceration either in a prison, a hospital or, nowadays, a therapeutic community, the ex-addict will eventually be released, usually back into the milieu he knew best before his incarceration —typically the addict subculture in an area of high heroin use. In psychological terms, his associates "model" heroin use. Often they will offer him the drug and consider it a friendly challenge to break down his resolve to stay "clean." In short, the addict is released into the so-called "sustaining conditions" of heroin use.

There are, to be sure, other reasons why people use heroin. One is simply that they enjoy it. Part of the reason is pharmacological; the drug gives a pleasurable "high," at least to some of its users.[39] Another explanation for heroin use is related to this pleasure theory. Heroin addicts—coming from the underprivileged segments of our population[40]—have enormous problems coping with our society and arguably use the drug in an effort to kill the pain of their life situation.

38. *Id*. at 88–89.

39. There are assertions in the literature that heroin use is pleasurable only before it causes addiction and that, thereafter, an addict takes the drug solely to avoid withdrawal. *See, e.g.*, CANADIAN COMMISSION, *supra* note 4, at 787. There is reason to doubt this, however; interviews with heroin addicts reveal that a sizeable number continue to find their drug use quite pleasurable. *See id*. at 308.

40. *Cf*. Ball, *supra* note 27, at 81–94. After all, the primary medical value of narcotics is to relieve pain. This theory also purports to explain why the groups in our society that one might expect to be most pained—the underprivileged, particularly the black or Chicano slum dweller, coping with a society in which opportunity is denied them—have the highest risk of heroin addiction. *Id*. One problem with this explanation is the lack of empirical evidence that people who use heroin or become heroin addicts feel greater pain with the world than those who do not.

Another, often neglected, reason why users enjoy heroin turns on socio-logical rather than pharmacological factors. Under this explanation, it is the lifestyle that exerts the main attraction to the addict; the drug effect is secondary. For some, being a heroin addict provides an attractive alterna-tive—at least initially—to an otherwise complex way of life. Insofar as society accepts that the addict must steal to support his habit, he has, in some sense, a license to steal. Indeed, the addict typically accepts the so-cietal view that stealing or selling drugs to support his habit is no sin over and above that of addiction itself. The heroin addict, moreover, often has no problem of existential choice. His daily routine is preestablished: "scor-ing" heroin and stealing or hustling enough money to do it.[41]

B. *Why Prevent Heroin Use?*

Having briefly outlined the reasons for heroin use, the next question is why should society attempt to prevent such use. In asking this question, we must be careful not to fall prey to circular reasoning. Certainly, at least to some extent, the reasons for opposing heroin use are themselves conse-quences of a system that attempts to prevent such use. At each point, then, it will be well to ask what would be the result of heroin use per se—that is, were the legal system to allow the drug to be freely available. The answers are considerably different from those indicated by observations of heroin addicts in today's world.

The objections to heroin use fall into four major categories: those based on the health of the user; those based on his lowered productivity; those based on the crimes that heroin causes him to commit; and those based on the asserted immorality of heroin use.

1. *Health of the user.*

Examination of just how harmful heroin is to the health of the user produces some surprising information. Undoubtedly, under the post–Harrison Act system of heroin prohibition,[42] addiction to heroin can cause enormous damage to the physical and mental health of the user. These effects are so great, however, that they rarely are isolated from the harm that would be caused were the drug freely available.

Heroin prohibition itself creates a number of problems. First, by turn-ing the addict into an outlaw, the law makes it more difficult for him to seek medical treatment for any ailment, whether or not caused by his ad-diction. Not only does he risk being turned in to the police, but he faces the requirement that a physician treating an addict withdraw him from narcotics. Moreover, the far higher price of heroin, a clear consequence

---

41. *See generally* Preble & Casey, *Taking Care of Business—the Heroin User's Life on the Street,* 4 INT'L J. ADDICT. 1 (1969).
42. *See* notes 22–26 *supra* and accompanying text.

of its illegality, may force the addict to compromise his nutrition and the conditions of sanitation under which he lives. The difficulties of obtaining the illegal drug and the higher likelihood of detection in society-at-large tend to force him into a tight addict subculture, which in turn encourages unsanitary practices such as sharing of needles, a major contributor to the spread of diseases such as hepatitis, which are endemic among heroin addicts.[43]

Surprisingly, however, the best estimates of the damage caused by heroin to its user under conditions of free availability indicate that the drug is a relatively safe one. A standard medical text reports:

> There is no evidence that the opiates produce organic central nervous system damage or other pathology, even after decades of continuous use. An 84-year-old physician who was a morphine addict was found to exhibit no evidence of mental or physical deterioration after continuous use for sixty-two years.[44]

Moreover, studies of heroin and morphine addicts have indicated that they seem to have no health problems that are not shared by the general population.[45] Finally, comparison with alcohol and tobacco, both of which do cause serious health problems, makes it clear that when freely available, heroin is simply in a different, and less damaging, league, so far as damage to the health of the drug user is concerned.[46]

Despite this, there are individual health reasons for caution concerning the use of heroin. First is the so-called overdose problem. Until recently this would have been high on the list of law-caused hazards of heroin addiction, since the lack of regulation—as distinguished from prohibition—of heroin sales causes wide variations in the potency of the drug sold by different dealers or by the same dealer at different times, thus increasing the possibility of an accidental overdose.[47] However, new evidence indicates that what is called the overdose death is often the result either of using heroin in combination with alcohol or barbiturates, or of an allergic reaction either to heroin or to one of the materials with which it is "cut," rather than the result of an unusually large dose.[48] Still, until this problem is solved,

---

43. Jaffe, *supra* note 31, at 286.
44. Dimijian, *supra* note 31, at 326.
45. E. BRECHER, *supra* note 11, at 23–25. There are, to be sure, certain complications of injecting any substance. These, however, are no different from those of the diabetic who must inject insulin. And in the case of heroin, the use of the needle is in great part a consequence of the legal regulation that has made it too expensive to take the drug by other routes.
46. Dimijian, *supra* note 31, at 326.
47. It was the prevailing view that the wide variations in the potency of street drugs had resulted in many deaths—so many as to be, in New York City, the largest cause of death in the 15- to 35-year-old age bracket. N.Y. Times, Dec. 30, 1970, at 31, col. 3, *cited in* E. BRECHER, *supra* note 11, at 102 n.8. It is certainly true that in times of scarcity heroin may be far more diluted than in normal times.
48. E. BRECHER, *supra* note 11, at 109–14. This may explain why the death rate of British heroin addicts is perhaps as high as 28 times that of similar nonaddicts in the general population, even though addicts in England are maintained under conditions that more closely approximate free availability than does the situation in the United States. *See* May, *Narcotics Addiction and Control in Great Britain,*

the health dangers of heroin present reason for caution, entirely apart from those far greater dangers that exist only where the drug is prohibited.

2. *Lowered productivity of the addict.*

The next major reason for the societal interest in discouraging addiction is the view that the addict's social productivity is destroyed or greatly damaged by his addiction. Whether or not one agrees that society has the right to require a minimum level of productivity from its members,[49] it is extremely difficult to tease out just how much of the productivity problem is due to addiction itself and how much is brought about by our method of legal regulation.[50] Entirely apart from any productivity loss occasioned by the drug itself, our legal regulation clearly makes the problem a great deal worse. The addict must expend considerable energy, which perhaps could otherwise be devoted to productive uses, in obtaining the drug and in avoiding detection. Moreover, the arrests and other types of law enforcement harassment which are part of the addict's life further decrease the likelihood of his maintaining a steady job.

Probably the most important factor contributing to the addict's decreased productivity is the constant variation in the availability of heroin, which prevents an addict from stabilizing his dosage. One of the characteristics of opiates, and of all other addicting substances, including alcohol, barbiturates, and tobacco, is the development of tolerance,[51] necessitating a gradually increasing dose of the drug in order to cause a constant effect. Despite this phenomenon, it appears that heroin addicts with free access to the drug can stabilize their doses—though at a relatively high level—and can often function relatively normally once they have reached this level.[52] The vari-

---

in Drug Abuse Survey Project, *supra* note 8, at 345, 386; *cf.* text accompanying notes 79–82 *infra*. On the other hand, this may simply be a statistical artifact caused by an underlying condition correlated with, but not caused by, heroin addiction.

49. Of course, one might deny that coercion of social productivity from its citizens is an appropriate function of government. The prevailing view holds that in a free country the government should be able to insist only that we perform certain civic duties, such as paying our taxes or, if called, serving in the military, that we do not harm others, and that, perhaps, despite John Stuart Mill, we do not harm ourselves—at least in certain ways.

It is not usually thought that in a free country the government should also require its citizens to be productive. First of all, definitions of what is productive labor incorporate so many value judgments—many of which are dubious at best—that they are quite unworkable. Second, though some nations do define productivity and punish as "parasites" those who, without excuse, are unproductive, we take some pride that we do not. Of course, one need not uphold the punishment of "parasites" in order to assert that government may appropriately prevent the use of substances which would impair the social productivity, however reasonably defined, of large numbers of citizens. Indeed, though this issue deserves a considerably greater discussion than it has received, whatever the merits of the respective positions, virtually all governments have taken the view that they do have such right and the only debate seems to be whether the exercise of this right in particular instances is worth its cost.

50. To complicate the inquiry, the heroin addict is likely to have far lower than average job skills and was likely to have been in educational difficulty even before he first used heroin. *See generally* J. Ball, Chambers, & M. Ball, *The Association of Marihuana Smoking with Opiate Addiction in the United States*, 50 J. CRIM. L.C. & P.S. 171 (1968).

51. *See* Jaffe, *supra* note 31, at 286–87.

52. *Id.* at 286.

ations in the availability of heroin under a system of prohibition prevent stabilization and often leave the addict either suffering the onset of withdrawal or else nodding or euphoric from an overdose.

Unfortunately, we do not know the extent to which heroin addiction per se is incompatible with social productivity. We certainly do know of many individuals, some quite eminent, who were addicted to morphine for many years and yet led productive lives.[53] It is interesting too that of those known to have been productive under American conditions, many have been physicians, insulated from the worst effects of the prohibition by their professional access to opiates.[54] Still, the best we can say is that some—perhaps even a sizeable percentage of—opiate addicts can be quite productive. There is evidence, on the other hand, to suggest that while addicts are able to hold down steady employment under conditions of relatively free availability, their employment tends to be at a somewhat lower level than would have been predicted from their social class and educational attainments.[55]

3. Commission of property crimes.

Probably the most significant reason for the concern about heroin addiction in the United States today is the heroin addict's need to violate the law in order to raise sufficient funds to support his habit.[56] There is some dispute about the total amount of money heroin addicts must obtain through criminal purposes, since neither the total number of addicts nor their average habit is accurately known. Nonetheless a rough estimate indicates that there are 250,000 addicts whose average daily consumption of heroin retails for about $30 per day.[57] The best estimates suggest that 60 percent of this $2.5 billion per year is obtained through consensual crimes, such as prostitution and heroin sales, while most of the remainder comes from the commission of property crimes, such as burglary, shoplifting, and other "hustles."[58] The figure of approximately $1¼ billion obtained from thefts is an impressive one. In fact, however, an accurate estimate would require at least doubling this amount, since the cost of "fencing" is high and the

---

53. See E. BRECHER, supra note 11, at 33–36 (pre–Harrison Act addicts in the United States).
54. Id. at 33–41.
55. Cf. J. O'DONNELL, NARCOTICS ADDICTS IN KENTUCKY (Public Health Serv. Pub. No. 1881, 1969), discussed in E. BRECHER, supra note 11, at 129–34.
56. There are, to be sure, some heroin addicts who can feed their habits without violating any criminal law other than those which outlaw the use or possession of heroin itself. In general, such addicts do not come to public attention and they are probably relatively few in number. One would expect them to be concentrated in certain occupations that either produce an extremely high income for sporadic work, such as that of a rock musician, or that permit access to a supply of opiates at far below market rates, such as that of a physician or pharmacist. The physician's drug of addiction is generally the synthetic opiate meperidine, better known by its trade name, Demerol. See generally Garb, Drug Addiction in Physicians, 48 ANESTHESIA & ANALGESIA 129 (1969).
57. Holahan, supra note 8, at 291.
58. Id. at 292.

heroin addict rarely receives more than one-third of the value of his non-cash thefts.[59] Assuming, generously, that half his thefts are in cash, heroin addicts must steal about $2.5 billion per year simply to buy their drug.

There is, of course, a serious methodological problem in concluding that the legal system's treatment of heroin is responsible for the high criminality of addicts. The fact is that most heroin addicts were criminals before they first used heroin.[60] Nevertheless, virtually every commentator examining the problem has concluded that the urgent demands of addiction cause addicts to commit crimes to afford heroin and that the amount they must raise is enormously inflated because of the prohibition on commerce in the drug. The morphine equivalent of $30 worth of heroin is available through legal medical channels for about $0.20.

4. *Opposition on moral grounds.*

Finally, apart from any direct harm to the addict or to society, the prohibition of heroin is supported on moral grounds related both to pleasure and free will. Many people do not approve of a heroin user's deriving pleasure from his drug, because they feel that such pleasure is artificial and unearned. Moreover, addiction to a drug is a denial of another of our putative values—the free will of the individual to do either good or evil. Insofar as a society allows addiction, it is being forced to acknowledge that people may not be in control of their own actions, let alone their own destinies. Nevertheless, although it is likely that every society attempts to force its moral values on at least some of its deviants, there are reasons to argue that the vindication of the society's moral feelings at the expense of a sub-group is not a sufficient reason for the criminalization of certain conduct[61] —especially where the practical disadvantages of such a course may be enormous.

III. SOLUTIONS TO THE ADDICTION PROBLEM

The mere demonstration, however, that the present method of regulation has the practical disadvantages of increasing the number of crimes addicts commit and exacerbating both their health problems and lack of social productivity, does not by any means settle the issue of whether the system should be changed. It may well be that a different legal structure—

---

59. *Id.*
60. Tinklenberg, *Drugs and Crime*, in PATTERNS AND CONSEQUENCES OF DRUG USE, *supra* note 5, at 242, 262. It is at least possible that if not addicted they might simply steal just as much and enjoy a much higher standard of living. Indeed, it has been argued—perhaps not seriously—that the lowered productivity of some heroin addicts simply prevents them from stealing as much as they would were they drug free. Epstein, *Methadone: the Forlorn Hope*, 36 PUB. INTEREST 3, 12 (1974).
61. In any event, the moral argument is not generally heard on the issue of whether to prohibit heroin, perhaps because of the preponderance of practical arguments on one side or the other. Nonetheless, a variant of the moral argument is important in the debates over methadone maintenance.

one that made heroin freely available, for example—would cause an increase in the level of addiction serious enough to outweigh its advantages in terms of the addict's improved health and productivity and lowered criminality. There is no a priori reason for confidence on this matter. It is admittedly possible that those who today would not use heroin because of the legal consequences, the inconveniences of addiction, the social controls against the use of this drug, and the difficulties of obtaining a supply would not use it even if it were legal and available. On the other hand, the basic teaching of economics is that when the price, which reflects the risk of apprehension and the cost of information, goes down, the amount sold goes up. In short, we must balance the additional damage to and by the individual addict in our system of prohibition against the damage that would be caused if the bars to addiction were lowered.

A. *Free Availability of Heroin*

Some estimate as to the percentage of the population that would become addicted if heroin were as freely available as alcohol would be helpful in weighing the advantages of this alternative system. Here, again, we can make only the most limited of guesses. During the latter stages of our involvement in Vietnam, where heroin was, as a practical matter, freely available, some 20 percent of the ground troops became addicted to the drug.[62] Extrapolating this figure for the general, noncombatant population is extremely difficult, however. The boredom and unpleasantness of life, together with the lack of nondrug satisfactions for Americans in Vietnam, all might be expected to push toward drug use. It is also possible, however, that 20 percent is too low a figure, since there is no evidence that heroin use had stabilized by the end of our involvement. Had the troops been there considerably longer with no law enforcement inhibition of heroin use, the percentage of addicts might have grown considerably.

Nor can we use the figure for physicians' addiction—which is estimated at 10 to 20 times[63] that of other classes of adult Americans—as an estimate of the possible addiction that might be expected in the general population were heroin freely available. On the one hand, physicians typically work under greater pressure than do most of the rest of the population, a factor that might incline them toward greater use of drugs. On the other hand, because of their training and personalities, physicians as a class may be better able than most to appreciate the danger of drugs and also to exercise self-discipline. If so, their vulnerability to addiction might actually be con-

62. Cranston, *Legislative Approaches to Addiction Among Veterans: The Nation's Unmet Moral Responsibility*, 4 J. DRUG ISSUES 1 (1974).
63. Little, *Hazards of Drug Dependency among Physicians*, 218 J. AM. MED. ASS'N 1533 (1971).

siderably below that of the general population, though their greater access to the drug causes a higher addiction rate. Finally, both state and federal investigators do their best to assure that physicians' access to opiates is by no means completely free; and the sanctions to the physician caught misusing opiates may be severe indeed.

The ability to predict the extent of heroin addiction in a society in which the drug would be freely available is made especially difficult by the resultant availability of the drug to the young. Even if one were to conclude that the adult population would overwhelmingly resist the blandishments of the drug, a different result might obtain for the young population, who are traditionally more experience-seeking, more present-oriented, and more willing to take risks than the adult population. It is here that the addicting nature of the drug is crucial: heroin use begun in youth is likely to carry on into adulthood, leading to a continuous and unpredictable growth in the addict population so long as we are unable to cure the condition.

It would thus seem that the uncertainties as to both the consequences of heroin addiction and the projected extent of addiction are such that no responsible formulator of public policy should advocate free availability of heroin in preference even to the current, seriously deficient legal scheme. Moreover, although we will probably gain considerably more information relating to both of these variables, it is most unlikely that we will be able to convince ourselves in the foreseeable future that such a risk would be worth taking.[64]

B. *Increased Law Enforcement of Prohibition*

Our unwillingness to face the unknown evil—that of free heroin availability to the population-at-large—does not necessarily mean that we must continue to endure fully that which we do know—the complete criminalization of heroin as effectuated today. A full appreciation both of the present costs, to the addict and to society, of our heroin prohibition and of the magnitude of the dangers and uncertainties in allowing the free availability of heroin prompts an examination of alternative courses.

One obvious alternative contemplates a greater component of law enforcement so as to make the prohibition work. Although increased resources devoted to the law enforcement effort have in the past simply increased the risk and expense of supplying heroin, so that the inelasticity of demand for

---

64. Moreover, the heroin problem would not disappear even if we were certain that addiction is completely harmless to the individual and society once heroin is made freely available. A responsible policymaker might well decide that the vulnerability of the population to an interruption of the heroin supply is a sufficient reason to oppose free availability of the drug. Though such a possibility is not likely, we cannot ignore the consequences of, for example, a strike in the heroin-producing industry or some natural disaster interrupting the supply of heroin to a society in which 70% of the population is addicted.

heroin among addicts resulted in higher prices and more stealing by addicts, it is reasonable to believe that the demand for heroin is not completely inelastic. Drastically raising the price of heroin through law enforcement might lower the overall social cost of heroin addiction. Thus, if an addict required $10,000 per day for his habit instead of $100, he might simply have to give up the use of the drug.

Such increased law enforcement effort to choke off the supply of heroin might be directed at three different points in the chain of supply: at the point of sale within the United States; at the point of entry into the United States; and at the point of production outside the United States. So far as prevention of sale within the United States is concerned, it is not necessary to reject the role of law enforcement entirely to assert that we have passed the point of diminishing returns in that area. If our police were untainted by corruption, if they were not distracted by many other problems, if there were no constitutional guarantees of privacy, and if we were willing to put vast amounts of additional resources into infiltration of the addict subculture and into surveillance and other forms of intrusion into privacy, we might be able to push the cost of heroin beyond the limit of the earning capacity of most addicts. Past experience, however, indicates that we are simply unable or unwilling to do this.

Nor can we be much more sanguine about the second possibility—preventing the smuggling of heroin into the United States. Here we encounter the stark fact that the total requirement of all American addicts for a year is, under today's conditions, probably less than 10 tons. When this is contrasted with the 100 million tons of freight brought into the United States and with the more than 200 million people who cross the American borders each year, the magnitude of the interdiction task becomes clear.[65] This is not to say that we cannot improve our performance in this matter. At present the estimate is that less than 5 percent of the heroin entering the United States is seized at the borders.[66] We can perhaps do better than this, but it is hard to believe that we can more than double or triple the percentage. Hence, the price of the drug would by no means be pushed out of the range most addicts could afford, and society would end up paying for the higher price in increased thefts.

The third and final method of curtailing the supply is preventing the production of heroin outside the United States. The only feasible method of such prevention is control of poppy cultivation,[67] either by buying up

---

65. E. BRECHER, *supra* note 11, at 92–93.
66. *Id.* at 93.
67. In theory this could take place at any one of a number of steps, from the cultivation of the poppy to the transformation of morphine into heroin. In fact, prevention of the latter operation is infeasible; the chemistry of heroin production is too simple and the ingredients not derived from the opium poppy, primarily anhydrous acetic acid, are too widely available. *See The Heroin Labs of Marseille,* 1 DRUG ENFORCEMENT 10 (1973).

the entire crop[68]—which is unfeasible because of possible leakage—or by forbidding opium poppy cultivation—which is complicated by serious problems of international cooperation.

The failure of attempts to erect barriers against diversion in underdeveloped countries indicates that simply banning poppy cultivation altogether may be a superior solution. The Iranian experience with enforcement of a total ban shows that within a few years such a ban is workable even in the face of widespread opium use.[69] But Iran found that prohibition in one country is insufficient without the cooperation of its neighbors: smuggled heroin from Afghanistan and Turkey made up for the opium on the Iranian market. The negative effects of the smuggled heroin[70] forced Iran to repeal the ban on opium cultivation.

There can be no workable ban on cultivation without international cooperation. But there are serious obstacles to such cooperation. First, the products of the opium poppy are extremely important in medicine.[71] Second, although opium growing is not crucial to the overall economies of these countries, it is often quite important as a cash crop in those areas where it is cultivated. One approach providing hopeful incentive to nations to encourage an opium ban in the face of their farmers' opposition is a crop substitution program—replacing poppies with other commercial crops.[72] Unfortunately, this approach faces both the inertia of rural populations towards substituting for a commercially and culturally important crop, and the unsuitability of opium-growing regions for the cultivation of other crops. The American effort to induce Turkey to substitute for opium was the most publicized such attempt. But, although the United States spent over $30 million, the Turkish ban was in effect for only 2 years[73] and the extent of its enforcement was probably considerably exaggerated.

There are numerous other problems with attempting to prevent the

---

68. At present prices this would not be impossible. Indeed, it would cost far less than does the criminalization of heroin today. There are several problems, however, with such a course. First of all, our own agricultural production during the 1950's graphically demonstrated the effect of government subsidies on farm production. Moreover, even if no increase in production occurred, chances are that no matter how reasonable a price were offered opium producers for their crop, the illegal market could simply bid higher on the relatively small amount it required. Farmers would thereby maximize their income by delivering most of their production to the opium-purchasing department while withholding enough for the illegal market to maintain the status quo.

69. *See generally* McLaughlin & Quinn, *supra* note 3.

70. The change in supply led to the growth of organized criminal gangs, a sharp rise in the price of drugs, and a drain upon Iran's foreign exchange resources.

71. Often there are no adequate substitutes for natural opiates, so that denying ourselves their benefits constitutes a serious step.

72. Phares, *The Simple Economics of Heroin and Organizing Public Policy*, 2 DRUG ABUSE L. REV. 129, 139 (1973). Permitting states that have sufficient control over their rural populations to control diversion of opium products is another method. But, national pride being what it is, it is hard to imagine many nations admitting that they do not fall into this category—or of our setting up some system to adjudicate the matter. Indeed, nations where opium is cultivated do not, in general, have an opium problem—and they do have many other problems that they regard as urgent, such as energy needs and industrial development.

73. *See* Anderson, *supra* note 2, at 37, col. 7.

growth of the opium poppy. Chief among them is the relative smallness
of the illegal market in the United States. The entire illegal American
market could be satisfied by the production from 25 square miles of opium-
producing land.[74] As a result, our efforts to prevent the growth of opium
would have to be successful not only in areas such as Turkey, Iran, and
India, where the governments have a reasonable degree of control over their
populations, but also in areas such as the Golden Triangle and Afghanistan, where the plant is cultivated by tribes uncontrolled by any government.

The final reason for pessimism concerning both the interdiction of heroin at our borders and the suppression of opium cultivation is the fact that
accomplishment of either of these goals—and the resultant choking off of
the supply of heroin—might well do us no good. There exist substitutes
for heroin that are up to 1,000 times as strong. These substitutes are not
very difficult to synthesize from widely available industrial chemicals and,
as one might gather, are far easier than heroin to smuggle.[75] The most
likely result of cutting off the supply of heroin thus would be the production and importation of synthetics. That this has not yet happened is some
indication as to just how ineffective our efforts against heroin itself have
been.

Our attempts, then, to lessen substantially the damage done by heroin
addiction through reducing the supply of the drug are hardly promising.
This does not mean, however, that such steps are without value. In fact,
for all their costs, restrictions upon supply differentiate our present system
from that of free availability, which we are unwilling to attempt. Moreover, the restrictions on supply have had one major consequence that can
be looked upon only as favorable: 4 years ago, based on cure rates of
heroin addiction one might have predicted that we would be saddled with
a massive problem of heroin addiction among veterans returning from
Vietnam. In fact, this has not happened, and studies indicate an extremely
low usage of heroin among those who had been addicted in the Far East.[76]

There are various reasons for this. First, the sustaining conditions of
addiction, the friends who use the drug, the sight of needles and other
"works," and the easy acceptance, indeed encouragement, of heroin use,
were not thrust upon them. Second, the alternatives to addiction in the
United States were vastly different from those in Vietnam. Additionally, the
Vietnam addicts for the most part were not injectors but sniffers of heroin
—a consequence of the low price and availability of heroin there. As a result,

74. Marks, *The Heroin Problem: Policy Alternatives in Dealing with Heroin Use*, 4 J. DRUG
ISSUES 69, 73 (1974).

75. *See* Jaffe, *supra* note 31, at 278.

76. *See* Robins, *A Follow-Up Study of Vietnam Veterans' Drug Use*, 4 J. DRUG ISSUES 61, 62–63
(1974).

conditioning effects were considerably less important in causing a relapse into heroin use. Finally, and probably most importantly, because of restrictions on the supply of the drug, heroin was simply not as available to the Vietnam addict in the United States. In other words the cost of the drug—in both financial and informational terms—was higher in the United States than in Vietnam. The veterans were not part of the addict subculture in the United States: they had not grown up in areas where heroin use was endemic; they did not know the right people. Presumably, they could have joined the addict subculture by spending some time in our jails or prisons, but for most of them this price for heroin was too high to pay.

C. *Price Discrimination Between Two Markets: Addict versus Nonaddict*

1. *Theoretical basis and practical effects.*

The existence of a heroin-addict subculture points up the crucial dilemma in controlling the supply of the drug. A rational policy might separate the market for heroin into two distinct markets—that of addicts and that of nonaddicts who would nonetheless use heroin.[77] In this second category would be the experimenters, the thrill-seekers, the curious, and the weak, many of whom—though we have no idea how many—would eventually become addicted. It is very likely that the relative inelasticity of the demand for heroin among addicts is not at all paralleled among the non-addicted users. Indeed, in view of the competition from other drugs—many of which are as euphoric as heroin—and of other activities, it is likely that demand for heroin among nonaddicts is quite elastic.

It is arguable then, that the most sensible heroin policy would be to make the drug as expensive as possible to the nonaddicts whose demand for the drug would therefore drop, while at the same time making it as cheap as possible to the addict, whose demand remains constant within a wide price range. Certainly there is today a sizeable difference in cost between the two markets insofar as the nonaddict generally incurs greater "costs" in obtaining information and faces more difficulties in convincing a "pusher" that he is not a narcotics agent. Once we attempt to go further than this and create a price difference as well, we come up against the problem faced by the price-discriminating monopolist who tries to sell in two different markets at two different prices. Both the addicts' need for money and their indifference to the criminal law are such that heroin would tend to seep out of the low-priced addict market into the higher-priced market for nonaddicts.

Keeping the two markets apart would be one of the great dilemmas of

---

77. For this formulation of the problem, I am indebted to Mark H. Moore. *See* Moore, *Policies to Achieve Discrimination of the Effective Price of Heroin*, 63 AM. ECON. REV. 270 (1973).

heroin policy. There are, nevertheless, some means that could exert pressure in this direction. For instance, the concentration of law enforcement resources could make it especially dangerous for addicts to sell to nonaddicts. Toward this end, agencies might attempt to keep the addict subculture geographically compact by "hassling" small sales when they took place outside an informally designated area; they might investigate with special vigor reports of addicts' selling to nonaddicts and pass the word along that they will make no sentencing deal—or will make harsher ones—in such cases; and they might even use undercover agents posing as nonaddicts willing to pay over-market prices, in an effort to instill greater caution in such sales.

Nonetheless, it is doubtful that we could do much to further raise the price of heroin in the nonaddict market; we could, however, do a great deal to lower it in the addict market. The ultimate step would be to give heroin free to the addict—or, what is almost the same, to sell it to him at its true cost. If, somehow, we could solve the problem of diversion into the nonaddict market, this course would have several major advantages: first, it would lessen the demand for *illegal* heroin among addicts and hence make the overall demand for the illegal drug more elastic. As a result, law enforcement attempts to impose costs and risks upon the supplier would be more effective in lowering the supply—since the lower demand would be insufficient to make the risk worth taking—rather than in simply raising the price of the drug and the profitability of dealing in it.

Moreover, to the extent that we were to replace heroin of variable quality with that of stable quality, addicts could stabilize their doses and lead more normal and healthy lives. And insofar as we were to replace high-priced with low-priced heroin, we would free the addict of the need to steal to feed his habit.

2. *Lowering costs to addicts while preventing leakage.*

There are several possible methods of giving addicts low-cost legal heroin and yet at the same time restricting the leakage into the nonaddict market. These methods are all loosely grouped under the general heading of "the British system."

Dispensing and use under staff inspection. The first and most obvious method of providing heroin to addicts only would be to have the dispensing authority, usually conceived of as a physician or a medical clinic, determine the appropriate dose for the addict and give him the heroin to be used in the presence of a dispensing agent. Of course, in such a system there would remain the possibilities that members of the dispensing staff would be corrupted or that addicts somehow would work out a method of pretending to use the heroin and subsequently sell at least part of it. Although these problems are real, the major problem in requiring the addict to use the drug in the presence of the dispensing authority is simply that the active life of heroin in the bloodstream is only about 6 hours.[78] As a result, the addict would have to return to the dispensing authority several times a day to inject his heroin. The resulting inconvenience would discourage an addict from accepting the heroin under these conditions and, even if he were prepared to do so, would make it almost impossible for him to lead any sort of a normal life—unless, of course, the number of dispensing authorities were extremely high. Although a dispensing clinic in every neighborhood would lessen the problem of inconvenience, it would exacerbate the problem of diversion of the drug through corruption or theft from one of the many facilities.

The system in Britain: evolution of heroin by prescription. The system described above, though referred to by many as "the British system," has never been implemented in Britain—or, for any length of time, anywhere else. The actual system in Britain allows the dispensing authority to give addicts a prescription for heroin, which can be filled at a local pharmacy, 1 day's supply at a time.[79] Unfortunately, under this policy the addict can—and often does—sell part of his supply. For some time, the British did not conceive of this possibility as a serious problem. Individual physicians were entrusted to prescribe only the amount the addict needed to sustain his own habit, thus leaving him with no surplus to sell. Moreover, the British addict was very different from the post–Harrison Act American addict. He had typically become addicted because of medical treatment,[80] very much like the Civil War casualty in the United States. Since the British addict was not a member of an addict subculture and not likely to be particularly criminally inclined, it was unlikely that he would either attempt to get more than his needs from the physician or sell part of his supply to others. Moreover, authorities felt that not enough people were interested in purchasing or using heroin to provide a market for any addict who had the drug to sell.

All of this changed, however, around the early 1960's when supposedly a relatively small number of American-style addicts appeared in Britain, fleeing the harsh Canadian law.[81] The appearance of these addicts, combined with a considerable degree of naïveté on the part of some British physicians, led in a short time to the destruction of the British system as

78. *See* DeLong, *The Drugs and their Effects,* in Drug Abuse Survey Project, *supra* note 8, at 62, 77, 86.
79. *See* May, *supra* note 48, at 365.
80. *Id.* at 348.
81. E. BRECHER, *supra* note 11, at 123.

it then existed: in practice physicians could often be tricked or otherwise
induced into prescribing considerably more than these addicts needed and
the addicts were not only willing and eager to sell their surplus, but also
able to find ready buyers[82] among the new arrivals and previously unad-
dicted natives in the subculture that they frequented.

Between 1964 and 1968 the number of British addicts increased more
than fivefold, and while the total number amounted to less than 3,000, the
trend was so alarming that major changes were made in the British system.[83] Of these the most important was the requirement that heroin be
prescribed not by private physicians but by clinics specifically set up for
the purpose. These clinics were to be staffed by experts in heroin addiction, who would be considerably more suspicious of addicts' stated requirements. Moreover, the clinic staffs have attempted gradually to lower
the addicts' dosages, often with the ultimate aim of withdrawing them
completely from opiates.[84] So far as one can tell, the adoption of the clinic
system has been successful in halting the explosive growth of heroin addiction. The number of addicts in Britain remains at about 1 percent of the
American total, and even on a per-addict basis the social cost of addiction
in Britain is far smaller.[85]

One might think that similar clinics dispensing heroin to addicts would
be the principal hope for the United States in lowering the social cost of
heroin addiction. In fact, this is not the case. A technological development
has intervened, promising sizeable lowering in the costs of heroin addiction
with considerably fewer risks of diversion than are entailed by the heroin-
clinic system. This technological development has been the introduction
of methadone—a synthetic opiate developed in Germany during World
War II—to maintain heroin addicts.[86]

D. Methadone Maintenance

Methadone is pharmacologically similar to heroin except for two major characteristics. First, it can be taken orally far more easily than can
heroin; second, its effects last for a little over 24 hours—about 4 times
as long as those of heroin.[87] It may very well be that there are other important differences between heroin and methadone—though space does not
permit the discussion here of this much-debated issue.[88] In any event, these
two major differences make it much easier to prevent the diversion of

82. Jaffe, *supra* note 31, at 306.
83. May, *supra* note 48, at 352.
84. *Id.* at 354–68.
85. *Id.* at 386–90.
86. A. GOTH, *supra* note 31, at 317.
87. Dimijian, *supra* note 31, at 327–28.
88. For a thorough discussion of the problems and promise of methadone maintenance, *see* E.
BRECHER, *supra* note 11, at 135–82.

methadone than of heroin. It is considerably more practical to have the addict drink his methadone mixed with orange drink once a day than to have him report 4 times a day for his injection. Moreover, after the addict is stabilized on methadone and permitted to take several days' supply of the drug home with him, the fact that the drug is dissolved in the drink, and impractical to inject, makes it much more difficult to sell to nonaddicts though it still has value in staving off the withdrawal symptoms of addicts.

There are, however, several reasons why conclusions as to the efficacy of methadone maintenance under American conditions are still tentative. First, methadone maintenance is very new; the first published evaluation of a program is less than 10 years old.[89] Second, there are enormous variations among the programs, which exist in almost all sizeable American cities. Some give all addicts methadone and provide virtually no other services.[90] Others regard methadone merely as a method of "hooking" an addict so that he may be treated for his underlying psychological problems—both those antedating and those caused by his addiction. Finally, there are sizeable variations in the reliability of data among programs.[91]

Despite these variations, a number of general statements may be made which seem to apply to most, if not all, of the programs. First, methadone maintenance seems to be more successful with addicts who are poor, Spanish-speaking, or black, older, and abusers only of heroin, rather than with middle-class, white, younger addicts who have a history of abuse of other drugs such as LSD, amphetamines, barbiturates, and alcohol.[92] Second, though the considerable variation from program to program allows one to make a case for better or for worse results, it seems that methadone maintenance "works" for between 30 and 50 percent of the addicts who undergo treatment.[93]

Probably the most impressive statistic is that in the most carefully studied methadone programs the arrest rate of addicts has dropped dramatically. For instance, in one program where the addicts averaged two arrests per year before admission, the overall arrest rate of those who entered the program was reduced to about one-third of this figure, while among those who remained in the program at the time of the study, arrests had been cut to less than one-fifth the previous rate.[94] Indeed, one

---

89. Dole & Nyswander, *A Medical Treatment for Diacetylmorphine (Heroin) Addiction*, 193 J. AM. MED. ASS'N 80 (1965).

90. DeLong, *Treatment and Rehabilitation*, in Drug Abuse Survey Project, *supra* note 8, at 200–01.

91. *Cf.* S. Wilmarth & A. Goldstein, Therapeutic Effectiveness of Methadone Maintenance Programs in the Management of Drug Dependence of the Morphine Type in the United States, Dec. 31, 1973, at 3–4 (World Health Org. Rev. Draft).

92. *See* DeLong, *supra* note 90, at 204.

93. S. Wilmarth & A. Goldstein, *supra* note 91, at 26, 80 fig. 2.

94. *Id.* at 61 table 4 (based on reports of the Santa Clara County Methadone Maintenance Program).

methadone program reported that of those remaining in treatment for periods of from 1 to 8 years, the arrest rate has been reduced to 1½ percent of the rate of those originally seeking treatment.[95]

E. *Remaining Problems and Possible Solutions*

The optimistic conclusions about methadone programs are, of course, subject to challenge on methodological grounds.[96] But even if we accept at face value all of the assertions of benefit in methadone maintenance we still need more effective ways of lowering the social costs of heroin addiction. For a variety of reasons, less than half the heroin addicts remain in methadone programs—though evidence indicates that virtually all try it.[97] Moreover, even for the percentage of addicts who adapt successfully to methadone there are reasons to continue the search for a solution.[98] Methadone maintenance involves an ever-present danger of diversion. Sometimes this is accidental, as where the addict's children mistakenly drink his "orange juice," with sometimes fatal results. More often the diversion is deliberate, as where the addict, needing money or as a favor, sells or gives away some of his methadone supply.

Even if advances in technology produce a new, longer-lasting heroin substitute that ameliorates the problem of diversion, there remain other reasons for dissatisfaction with the maintenance of addicts on opiates. First, there are side effects to all the opiates—and though these may seem trivial compared with the effects of heroin under our present prohibition, they are nonetheless a public health problem—especially since we are by

---

95. *Id.* (based on reports of New York City Methadone Maintenance Treatment Programs).

96. It is possible that the use of the overall arrest rates of those entering the programs is misleading because those who previously had least often been arrested were most likely to remain in the programs. And we do know that older addicts tend to "mature out" and are less often arrested as they near 30 years of age. Moreover, perhaps the lowering of arrest rates was caused by the fact that the police devoted less attention to, or otherwise ignored, crimes by those addicts enrolled in methadone programs.

Similar methodological problems exist with respect to virtually every positive finding as to methadone maintenance, with the possible exception of those verified by urinalysis. Prior to undergoing methadone treatment, the addict typically used heroin 3 times per day. Urinalysis data indicate reductions so drastic that the results are couched in terms of mean number of weeks abstinent from heroin (22 for those in treatment 1 year) or of percent abstinent in the previous week (80% after 1 year). *See, e.g.,* S. Wilmarth & A. Goldstein, *supra* note 91, at 87 fig. 9 (Santa Clara Methadone Maintenance Program); *id.* at 89 fig. 11 (Illinois Drug Addiction Program); Epstein, *supra* note 60.

97. *Id.* at 5. Perhaps heroin gives them an unknown something that they consider very important and that is lacking in methadone; perhaps they need the addict's lifestyle so much that even the advantages of easy, lawful access to methadone do not compensate for having to live straight; perhaps they find some of the side effects of methadone too unpleasant—even though they would seem less serious than the effects of heroin.

98. Tests have already begun on a synthetic opiate with a life in the blood stream of about 3 times that of methadone. E. Brecher, *supra* note 11, at 161 n.†. With such a drug it becomes more practical to allow administration under the eyes of the program staff—thus sharply limiting diversion. If such a longer-acting opiate proves usable, it will ameliorate another disadvantage of methadone as a maintenance drug: toward the downside of the methadone effect, near the end of a 24–28-hour period following the last dose, those in the programs are most likely to use heroin. A longer-acting opiate, at the very least, would lessen the number of such vulnerable periods.

no means sure of the differing long-term effects of these drugs on various addict groups, such as pregnant women or those with alcohol problems.

The moral overtones of the methadone issue considerably complicate the public health problems posed by methadone programs. The twin affronts to our values inherent in drug-induced pleasure and in the denial of free will by addiction are involved in methadone maintenance as well as in heroin addiction. As a result, the moral issue leads to the common complaint that methadone merely "substitutes one addiction for another." If nothing else, this causes political opposition that prevents such programs from being fully effective. There is also opposition to methadone maintenance from other points on the political spectrum. For example, some civil rights and minority group organizations protest that methadone programs merely keep addicts in the thrall of the government.[99]

Again, technology may be able to provide alternatives to overcome the opposition. There already exists a family of chemicals called narcotic antagonists. Unlike methadone, which is primarily a substitute for heroin, these prevent heroin from taking effect in the body. Although most heroin addicts in experimental programs would not continue taking the narcotic antagonists and hence relapsed into addiction, some of those who continued the treatment were cured. While the addicting nature of methadone is thus a great advantage in keeping the addicts on treatment, there is reason to expect that scientific progress in this area will lead to a feasible method of keeping former addicts on narcotic antagonists.[100] This will have several advantages over methadone maintenance as a method of coping with heroin addiction: it will not only avoid the side effects of addiction, but will also help extinguish the conditioned response of using heroin. Nor does our search for a technological solution cease here. There already are reports of a vaccine that "immunizes" monkeys against heroin.[101] If the reports are accurate, it may be that immunization can be used on humans as a permanent narcotic antagonist.

IV. CONCLUSION

Although there are drugs more harmful to the individual than heroin, no other drug so unfortunately interacts with its legal regulation to cause such social havoc. As dismal as our present system may be, the proposals for

---

99. *See, e.g.,* Uncle Sam the Pusherman, 9–10 (undated) (pamphlet distributed by Drug Research Project, San Francisco, Cal.); Medical Comm. on Human Rights, Methadone, the Other Side of the Coin (undated).

100. *See* DeLong, *supra* note 90, at 233–36. We are gradually hearing more about longer-acting narcotic antagonists and even of methods of delivering such drugs over a long period of time through surgical implants. *See* E. BRECHER, *supra* note 11, at 160.

101. *Anti-heroin Injections Successful in Immunizing a Monkey to Dope,* 11 CONNECTION 5, 6 (1974).

legal reform present their own unique problems: the possibility of a soaring addiction rate and its uncertain consequences, in a system of free availability; the inevitable diversion of heroin to the nonaddict population, where the system dispenses the drug to those addicted; the uncertain results of methadone maintenance.

In light of the inadequacies of these alternative "solutions," the optimism over technical possibilities is hardly surprising. But we should keep in mind that though technology is improving in this area, we have been disappointed too often in the past by technological solutions to social problems. It is likely that those who abuse heroin will abuse another drug if their first-choice drug is somehow denied them—and, from their point of view, the change may not be an improvement.

There are other reasons for extreme caution in embracing the technology being offered us. If one can alter the chemistry of a heroin addict, why not that of an alcoholic, or someone with too hot a temper? And if we can, as a society, chemically enforce compliance with our heroin laws through such methods, will the political powers see any reason not to attempt this with marihuana users? If Prohibition was repealed because it was unenforceable, perhaps we are now at the point of having the means to do the job right. Obviously, before we go much further in the heroin area we will have to develop controls on how much we can do with our only partially willing patients. As yet we have hardly begun to think about the matter.

Politics and Health Care in China:
The Barefoot Doctors

Victor H. Li*

On the eve of the establishment of the People's Republic in 1949, China faced some enormous problems in the health area. More than a century of nearly continuous foreign and civil war had drained the country and dislocated the entire society. Economic disruption, malnutrition, and breakdown of health services produced a situation in which, for example, some 30 percent of the children died before the age of 5, and rampant diseases such as smallpox, cholera, tuberculosis, and malaria sapped the strength of the survivors.[1]

China also lacked adequate resources to deal with these problems. The bare subsistence economy yielded little surplus that could be invested in other areas. What surplus there was had to be divided in response to demands for increasing food and industrial production, developing military strength, and providing a range of social services—of which health care was only one aspect.[2] In terms of personnel, China had between 20 and 40 thousand physicians in 1949.[3] This small group had to care for a gigantic population while carrying on teaching, research, and other professional work.

The problems confronting China were not just material and physical, but intellectual as well. The basic model for a "modern" health care system was centered around relatively highly trained professionals applying sophisticated technology and often using complex equipment and medicines. This model had many advantages in terms of producing quality medical

* B.A. 1961, J.D. 1964, Columbia University; LL.M. 1965, S.J.D. 1971, Harvard University. Lewis Talbot & Nadine Hearn Shelton Professor of International Legal Studies, Stanford University.

1. For descriptions of pre-1949 conditions, *see* J. HORN, AWAY WITH ALL PESTS, AN ENGLISH SURGEON IN PEOPLE'S CHINA: 1954–1969 (1971); Bowers, *The History of Public Health in China to 1937*, in PUBLIC HEALTH IN THE PEOPLE'S REPUBLIC OF CHINA 26 (M. Wegman, Tsung-yi Lin & F. Purcell eds. 1973); Worth, *Health in Rural China: From Village to Commune*, 77 AM. J. HYGIENE 228 (1963).

2. Western observers do not know the actual amounts expended for health since Chinese government budgets are generally not available and aggregate local and individual spending is difficult to calculate. One study estimates central government spending on health in 1966 to be about 1.2% of gross national product or 4% of the central budget. Heller, *The Strategy of Health-Sector Planning*, in M. Wegman, Tsung-yi Lin & F. Purcell eds., *supra* note 1, at 62, 69.

3. STAFF OF SENATE COMM. ON LABOR AND PUBLIC WELF., HEALTH POLICIES AND SERVICES IN CHINA, 1974, 93d Cong., 2d Sess. (Comm. print 1974) (report prepared by Leo A. Orleans for the Subcommittee on Health of the Committee on Labor and Public Welfare of the United States Senate [hereinafter cited as L. ORLEANS]); Chu-yuan Cheng, *Health Manpower: Growth and Distribution*, in M. Wegman, Tsung-yi Lin & F. Purcell eds., *supra* note 1, at 139; Sidel, *Medical Personnel and Their Training*, in MEDICINE AND PUBLIC HEALTH IN THE PEOPLE'S REPUBLIC OF CHINA 153 (J. Quinn ed. 1973) [hereinafter cited as J. Quinn].

and health care, but in many ways it did not meet Chinese needs. The training of new professionals required a considerable investment of time and resources. Consequently, only a limited number of such persons could be added to the work force each year. In addition, the professionals tended to work in urban areas where facilities were available and where individuals or social units could afford to pay the high cost of care. The professionals also stressed curative rather than preventative services. This meant that the urban areas—or about 15 percent of the Chinese population —received most of the benefits of the new health care system. Such a situation obviously presented great political and philosophical difficulties to a regime stressing egalitarianism and drawing much of its support from the peasantry. Was there a different model—one that could establish a health care system more quickly and inexpensively while ensuring a more equitable distribution of benefits across the entire population?

Less than 25 years later, American visitors returning from China favorably compare the level of health care in China with that in our own country.[4] Clearly something quite dramatic is happening there. The striking point is not which country might be "doing better," but rather that a comparison of Chinese and American health conditions can be made given the deplorable conditions and the limited resources available in China in 1949. Examination of the present health situation in China not only reveals the achievements produced in the span of one generation, but also illustrates the evolution of a developmental model that alters the role of the professional in Chinese society.

I. Progress in Health Care

Some of the Chinese accomplishments during the past 25 years were due to the "peace dividend" that accompanied the establishment of a stable government. Social and economic recovery followed the termination of physical strife.[5] Agricultural production increased, leading to improved nutrition and health. In addition, although a poor country, China has invested considerable resources in the health sector. By 1966, for example, approximately 180,000 physicians had graduated from medical school, and another

    4. See, e.g., J. Galbraith, A China Passage 112 (1973); Sidel, The Health Workers of Fengsheng Neighborhood of Peking, 43 Am. J. Orthopsych. 737 (1973); P. Lee, Medicine and Public Health in the People's Republic of China—Observations and Reflections of a Recent Visitor, Aug. 22, 1973 (paper prepared for Medical Staff Conference, School of Medicine, University of Cal., San Francisco). See also China Report: Health Care in the World's Most Populous Country, 109 Can. Med. Ass'n. J. 150L (1973) (report of Canadian medical delegation to China); Medicine in China, 12 Eastern Horizon 1 (1973).
    5. See generally China's Developmental Experience (M. Oksenberg ed. 1973); Joint Economic Committee of the United States Congress, People's Republic of China: An Economic Assessment, 92d Cong., 2d Sess. (1972). On health work, see generally D. Lampton, The Politics of Public Health in China: 1949–1969 (1974) (unpublished dissertation in Stanford University Library).

500,000 assistant doctors, nurses, and pharmacists had completed secondary level medical education.[6] Scarce financial resources were also stretched as far as possible. Labor-intensive methods, such as the antipest campaigns, achieved desired results through mass mobilization of manpower—a resource China had in abundance. The emphasis on sanitation, inoculation, health, education, and other prevention work also raised the standard of health in a relatively quick and inexpensive manner.

A. *Training of Paramedics*

The most innovative and far-reaching effort to provide better health care for the entire population, however, has been the training of a large cadre of new paramedical workers—the barefoot doctors[7]—most of whom are located in the rural areas.[8] There are about one million barefoot doctors at present, or 1 per 800 population. The target is 1 barefoot doctor per 500 population. A few began work in the health sector during the 1958 Great Leap Forward, while others started in the mid-1960's. The great bulk, however, were trained in the past several years in response to Mao's May 26, 1965 directive "in medical and health work, to put the stress on the rural areas."[9]

The range of training and skill of the barefoot doctors is wide, so much so that it is sometimes confusing to identify the entire group by one label.[10] In general, prospective barefoot doctors have graduated from junior high school and are about 20 years old; about half are women. Most are given 3 to 6 months of classroom and clinical training in a nearby hospital, although some receive only 2 months while others receive 2 years of initial training. (Although not a great deal of training, it might be compared to

---

6. L. ORLEANS, *supra* note 3, at 24–25.

7. This name comes from the fact that rice field workers do not wear shoes in the wet paddies. Hence being "barefoot" symbolizes a paramedic who also engages in agricultural work.

8. In the past several years, China has published a great deal of material on the barefoot doctors, including numerous technical manuals and pamphlets and a magazine focusing on the Chinese paramedic, BAREFOOT DOCTORS MAGAZINE. *See generally* U.S. DEP'T OF HEALTH, EDUC. & WELF., A BIBLIOGRAPHY OF CHINESE SOURCES ON MEDICINE AND PUBLIC HEALTH IN THE PEOPLE'S REPUBLIC OF CHINA: 1960–1970 (1973). Some examples of descriptive articles are: Yu Yang, *'Barefoot Doctors': An Army of New Doctors*, 23 CHINA RECONSTRUCTS, Apr. 1974, at 6; Ling Yang, *Medical Network in a Mountain Country*, 16 PEKING REV., Aug. 24, 1973, at 17, & Sept. 4, 1973, at 49; *The 'Barefoot Doctors'*, 18 CHINA RECONSTRUCTS, Mar. 1969, at 34.

9. On the development of rural health care, *see* Rifkin, *Health Care for Rural Areas*, in J. Quinn ed., *supra* note 3, at 141; Chung Ko, *Medicine and Public Health in Chung-shan Hsien*, Chung-kuo Hsien-wen (Peking), June 26, 1973 (trans. in JOINT PUBLICATIONS RESEARCH SERVICE [hereinafter cited as JPRS] No. 60,569, Nov. 16, 1973).

10. Portions of the materials presented below were gathered by a group of eight health specialists, China specialists, and filmmakers who visited China during the summer of 1973. The members of the group were: Jay Jia Hsia, psychology and child development, Educational Testing Service; Che-tsao Huang, educational technology and communications, York College of the State University of New York; Michael Gao; Diane Li, filmmaker, Stanford University; Mary L. New, biostatistics, Springhurst Community Health Center; Peter K. New, medical sociology, University of Toronto School of Medicine; Virginia L. Wang, health education and rural development, Johns Hopkins University; and myself. A monograph and a film are forthcoming.

that of medical corpsmen in the American military.) Thereafter, the bare-foot doctors return each year for additional training of about 1 month (again the lower and upper limits of this training range from 2 weeks to 3 months) to upgrade skills and learn new techniques. In terms of professional functions, the barefoot doctors stress preventive work: sanitation, pest control, health education, family planning, immunization, and the like. They also carry out simple curative work, ranging from first aid and distribution of various pills and medicines, to minor surgery and treatment of some diseases. As their skills improve and as prevention work becomes fully developed, the curative aspect of the barefoot doctors' work is likely to increase in importance.[11]

A look at the more advanced barefoot doctors gives an indication of the best work, particularly in the curative area, that paramedical personnel can now do and of the level of skill others may attain in the future. The School of Public Health in Shenyang (formerly Mukden, Manchuria) offers a 6-month training program for barefoot doctors. Entering students first go through 3 days of orientation and political study during which they discuss why they are entering health work, whom they should serve, and what their attitudes should be. Thereafter, they study a wide variety of medical problems and treatment—including acupuncture and other Chinese medical techniques, treatment of diseases common to the local area, and public health education—with about one-half of the training time devoted to clinical work.[12]

Some of the barefoot doctors at the August One commune near Shenyang had received 2 years of initial training at the Shenyang School of Public Health. Interviews with both students and faculty reveal that the work of the barefoot doctor includes diagnosis and treatment of respiratory, digestive, urinary, and circulatory disorders, as well as providing vaccinations, obstetric and pediatric services, and a narrow range of surgical and

---

11. See, e.g., *Two Barefoot Doctors Succeeded in Curing Over 500 Cases and Made a 7-Year Paralytic Stand Up Again*, Chung-kuo Hsien-wen (Peking), June 28, 1973 (trans. in JPRS, *supra* note 9, No. 60,673, Dec. 3, 1973).

12. The course of study is as follows: (1) Anatomy and physiology—7 days; including the study of a corpse. (2) Microbiology—2–3 days; investigation of the origins and transmission of diseases. (3) Herbs—7 days; identification, preparation, and use of the 40 most common herbs of this province. (4) Western style medicines and drugs—7 days. (5) Acupuncture and other Chinese medical techniques—10 days. (6) Emergency techniques and first aid—2 days; bandaging, splinting, and stopping of bleeding. (7) Treatment of diseases common to the local area—2½ months. The students learn to diagnose and treat some bronchial and respiratory diseases, hypertension, some infectious diseases, childhood diseases, pneumonia, influenza, measles, worms, intestinal disorders, and similar matters. They are able to recognize but not to treat problems such as ulcers and appendicitis. They also learn about the prevention of tuberculosis, and how to give inoculations for all childhood diseases, scarlet fever, measles, polio, smallpox, cholera, diphtheria, pertussis and tetanus, and encephalitis. (8) Obstetrics and gynecology—3–6 days; including 10–12 hours on family planning, and observing, but not performing, abortions and implacement of IUD's. (9) Chinese medicine—10–12 days; training in addition to the study of herbs and acupuncture mentioned earlier. (10) Public health education—3 days; learning about sanitation, waste control, and hygiene.

psychiatric care. Table 1, taken from these interviews, lists the specific diagnostic and treatment areas that barefoot doctors were said to handle.[13]

B. *Financing the System*

The cost of establishing and maintaining the barefoot doctor system is shared among the state, the local unit, and the individual seeking medical care. In the rural areas,[14] the state usually pays for the salaries of professional health workers such as physicians and nurses, the building and equipping of regular hospitals, and the training of the barefoot doctors. At the local level, each individual contributes about one percent of his income to a commune cooperative medical fund; this amount is matched by a similar contribution from the commune. The fund pays for the salaries of the barefoot doctors and the operation of their clinics. In addition, an individual seeking medical assistance is sometimes required to pay a small sum for each visit and for some medicines.

To give a concrete example, 31 barefoot doctors serve the 22,000 members of the Four Seasons Evergreen commune near Hangchou. These paramedics were trained at a nearby hospital at state expense. Ten of them now work in a commune clinic that was constructed and equipped through a grant from the commune's capital accumulation fund. The others work in health stations located at each of the 10 brigades that make up the commune. The brigades converted rooms to health stations at their own expense. In 1969, a cooperative medical fund was set up. About 18,000 persons joined,[15] each paying the equivalent of 75 cents a year. The brigades matched this amount, yielding a total fund of $27,000. Fifteen percent of the fund was used to pay the salaries of the 10 commune-level barefoot doctors. (Salaries of brigade barefoot doctors were paid from brigade operating expenses.) The remaining 85 percent paid for supplies and one-half the cost of medicines (with the individuals receiving the medicine paying the other half) used by all barefoot doctors. Although the small fund was divided among many purposes and persons, enough money had accumulated after the first year to reduce to 50 cents the yearly contribution of individuals.

---

13. Unfortunately, since the information was gathered during a visit of only a few days, there was no adequate way of determining exactly which items were recognized and diagnosed but not treated by the barefoot doctors, or how skillfully the treatments were carried out. Nevertheless, the lists are impressive and consistent with each other. The table was prepared by Virginia L. Wang.

14. For industrial workers, the factory establishes a labor insurance fund, equal to 3% of the payroll, which provides benefits such as retirement, compensation for injuries, maternity leave, death benefits, and funeral expenses. In addition, this fund pays for a factory clinic and for all medical expenses of workers and half the medical expenses of dependents. *See Labour Insurance Regulations of the People's Republic of China*, in IMPORTANT LABOUR LAWS AND REGULATIONS OF THE PEOPLE'S REPUBLIC OF CHINA 11–31 (enlarged ed., Peking: Foreign Languages Press, 1961). Government cadres have their own cooperative health plan.

15. The other 4,000 were local factory workers, cadres, and their dependents, who were already covered by some other health insurance plan.

TABLE 1
DIAGNOSTIC AND TREATMENT AREAS OF BAREFOOT DOCTORS
WHO HAVE HAD 2 YEARS OF TRAINING

According to Barefoot Doctors	According to Faculty of Shenyang School of Public Health

Surgical treatment
  Sutures
  Removal of lipoma
  Biopsy
	Surgical treatment
	  Sutures
	  Vasectomies

Respiratory system
  Upper respiratory infection
  Bronchitis
  Pneumonia
  Mild tuberculosis
  Emphysema
  Pleuritic lesions
	Respiratory system
	  Upper respiratory inflammation
	  Bronchitis
	  Lobal bronchitis
	  Pulmonary diseases

Digestive system
  Acute and chronic gastritis
  Peptic ulcer
  Dysentery colitis
  Upper gastrointestinal bleeding
	Digestive system
	  Acute gastritis
	  Peptic ulcer
	  Acute colitis
	  Obstructive intestinal diseases
	  Acute pancreatitis
	  Cirrhosis of the liver (rarely seen)

Urinary tract
  Kidney diseases
  Puerilitis
  Bladder infection
  Cystitis
	Urinary tract
	  Urinary tract infections

Circulatory system
  Mild high blood pressure
  Arteriosclerotic heart diseases
  Rheumatic heart diseases
  Mild puriculitis
  Tachycardia
	Circulatory system
	  Rheumatoid heart disease
	  Arthritis
	  Coronary heart disease (rarely handled by barefoot doctors)
	  Arteriosclerosis (rarely handled by barefoot doctors)

Nervous system
  Mental depression
  Nervous weakness
  Mild mental breakdown
	Nervous system
	  (not mentioned)

Pediatrics
  Pneumonia
  Bronchitis
  Simple indigestive diseases
  Rickets
  Convulsion
  Tonsilitis
  Pharyngitis
	Pediatrics
	  Acute infectious diseases
	  Pneumonia
	  Pertussis

According to Barefoot Doctors	According to Faculty of Shenyang School of Public Health
Laryngitis	
Measles	
Eczema	
Chicken pox	
Middle ear infection	
Eye infection	
Trachoma	
Conjunctivitis	
Eye injury	
Emergency care	Emergency care
Appendicitis	General accidents
Diagnosis	
Trauma	
Female problems	Obstetrics
Menstrual problems	Family planning
External inflammation	Regular delivery
	Prenatal care
	Postnatal bleeding
	Toxemia of pregnancy
	Other female problems
Ear, nose and eye	Ear, nose and eye
(not mentioned)	Middle ear infection
	Eye diseases
	Acute rhinitis
Vaccination	Vaccination
Smallpox	(not mentioned)
Tuberculosis	
Polio	
Diphtheria, pertussis & tetanus	
Japanese B Type encephalitis	
Others	Others
(not mentioned)	Schistosomiasis

Through sharing costs and using simpler techniques and equipment, China has been able to go a long way with limited resources. This has been achieved, in part, by the policy of spreading the expense of training health workers over many years. By shortening the first period of training for the barefoot doctors and by emphasizing clinical education methods, the initial outlay is kept relatively small. In subsequent years, additional sums can be invested gradually to improve their skills.

Still another factor has been the effort to fully utilize available resources. For example, China's approach to disposal of garbage and human wastes differs substantially from the costly procedure employed in the United

States. A sanitation station in a town in suburban Shanghai employs 94 persons to collect garbage, to clear public toilets, and to sweep the streets, as well as to handle environmental conservation and pest control work. The waste materials collected by the unit are fermented and then sold as fertilizer to nearby farmers. The income from sales not only pays for all salaries, but also pays for the construction of more and better toilets—which in turn will yield more wastes to be collected and sold—and for the support of the conservation and pest control programs.

II. PROFESSIONALISM AND EGALITARIANISM

The presence of one million new health workers has already greatly improved health services, particularly in the rural areas. A thought about the future is provoking. By 1980, for example, each of these million persons will have had a total of a year of additional training beyond the initial period of study, plus 10 years or more of practical experience—and at that time will be only about 30 years old. Thus it would seem that China has come far in solving the critical problem of how to establish a viable health care system for a large but poor population.

The barefoot doctor system is interesting not only because of its role in changing the quality and kind of health care, but also because it illustrates a number of other important aspects of contemporary Chinese social philosophy and practice. As mentioned earlier, the desire for more equal distribution to all persons of the benefits of modern technology was a major reason behind Mao's 1965 call to shift health resources from the urban to the rural sector and to increase the total amount of resources being devoted to health work. This was obviously not an easy decision to reach; 1965 was 16 years after Liberation. The reliance upon a massive number of low level paramedics went against the traditional model for developing a health care system and against the preferences of the health professionals. Nevertheless, on the eve of the Cultural Revolution, Mao reasserted the importance of the principle of egalitarianism, and took the necessary steps—and the attendant risks—to create a radical new system by which his principles could be put into actual practice in the health area.

A. *"Dilution" in the Context of Health Care*

More generally, the crucial role played by the barefoot doctors in helping to bring sophisticated medical and health technology to the public is one example of a widespread movement in China to make directly useful to and usable by the masses many kinds of specialized knowledge. Similar "dilution" of complex matters and training of paraprofessionals occurs in the effort to disseminate agricultural technology and those aspects of industrial technology necessary to establish commune-level factories. A substantial portion of primary and secondary education deals with teaching technical information that can be put to immediate practical use in the local area. From a different perspective, having the masses themselves take direct part in formulating and implementing programs in art, social work, and even politics involves "dilution" and the training of "paratechnicals."

An important aspect of this "dilution" is the need to reduce the complexity of specialized knowledge, so that persons with only limited training can properly utilize the information. In the health area this is accomplished in a number of ways. One general principle is that a person does not need 4 to 10 years' formal medical training to handle many medical and health problems. It is true that a highly trained physician can almost always give better treatment than the barefoot doctor and that a paramedic is likely to make more errors, especially when he is inexperienced. On the other hand, the realistic alternative in China to treatment by paramedics is often no treatment at all—not a very attractive choice. The effort, therefore, is to train paramedics to an initial level of minimally acceptable competence, then to upgrade skills gradually through continuing education and work experience. Training is simplified by stressing the practical aspects of how to handle a problem, rather than dwelling on theoretical concepts or giving complicated explanations. In addition, since training takes place locally, a paramedic need study only those problems that are important in his local area. Considerable research is also being done to develop techniques and equipment that can be used by persons having limited skills and resources. For example, experiments are being conducted in which tonsilitis can be treated by cauterization with a heating element dipped in an herbal solution. A barefoot doctor can carry out this procedure relatively easily, while he probably cannot perform a tonsillectomy requiring general anesthesia, an operating table, and other supporting items. Another example is the production of portable equipment such as X-ray machines, made even more portable since they can be powered by a bicycle-operated electrical generator.

The barefoot doctor is at the bottom of a multi-tiered system. When sufficiently difficult problems arise, persons with greater training and skill assume responsibility. Professional personnel at the county hospital not only train the barefoot doctors, but also handle cases referred by them. The same training/referral relationship is repeated between the county hospital and larger urban hospitals, and between urban hospitals and major hospitals and research centers.

While developing simpler technology and equipment is an important aspect of "dilution," a more fundamental social issue is the means by which and extent to which persons possessing specialized knowledge should be made accountable to the general public. Stated most broadly, we live in a world of rapidly growing functional specialization. Because the complexity of specialized knowledge is beyond the grasp of ordinary members of the public (or even specialists in other areas), how is the general public to participate in any decisionmaking process that governs the use of specialized knowledge? Put another way, a specialist, by virtue of his greater knowledge about a subject, may feel that he "knows better" than an ordinary member of the public and therefore should have a greater say in decisions that concern that subject. This assertion of professional dominance produces a serious dilemma: on the one hand, the use of knowledge is maximized—a desirable result—while on the other hand the public loses control of the specialist—an undesirable result. In the latter case, the specialist may become increasingly isolated from the public and begin to develop an elitist attitude. In due course he may become unresponsive to the public, and eventually feel responsible not to the public but only to himself or to other fellow specialists.

The dilemma can also be stated in the converse. While broad public participation in various specialized areas (such as health programs) is desirable since it enhances local interest and support, the wishes of the public may often conflict with the considered technical judgment of the (health) professionals. In Chinese translation, while favoring the mass-line approach, there are still contradictions between red and expert, that is, between those who are ideologically advanced but lacking in technical expertise, and those who are technologically proficient but politically naive.

The barefoot doctor is an example of the Chinese effort to resolve the contradiction of how to utilize specialized knowledge without developing the negative aspects of professionalism. This is accomplished in a number of ways. To begin with, members of the local community participate extensively in the barefoot doctor program. Subject to some restrictions, they select the persons who will receive barefoot doctor training. The selection process is apt to be quite careful and successful, since the selectors are picking the person who will return and treat *them*. (This is quite different from a medical school admissions committee selecting who will be trained to go treat *others*.) The community also takes part in formulating local health policies, since decisionmaking at the commune level is done by a general committee not divided along functional lines, and since a considerable portion of the health program is locally funded. In addition, mass pest control or sanitation campaigns not only accomplish results at low cost, but also enable the public to be active participants in health work, rather than merely observers or recipients.

At the same time, the barefoot doctor strongly identifies with the local community. First, he is working in his native area. Second, the "doctor-patient" relationship is especially close, since all of his patients are relatives and friends with whom he has a great deal of nonmedical contact. Moreover, since he lives in the community and generally cannot move to another area, he cannot easily escape being criticized for carelessness or callousness in his work. Thus, rather than functioning in a physically and emotionally detached professional manner, the barefoot doctor is fully integrated into the community.

Perhaps even more important, the barefoot doctor is supposed to engage in health work part time only and takes part in regular agricultural labor the remainder of his working time. This helps him "maintain his class standpoint"; that is, the barefoot doctor must not forget what harsh manual labor is like, and must not develop elitist attitudes because he now possesses greater knowledge and skills. By remaining in the fields, he not only becomes more accessible to the community, but also develops greater understanding of local and individual problems. In this sense, perhaps, plowing is really a medical activity. Last, but far from least, the barefoot doctor's income is basically the same as the income of other full-time peasants. This practice again emphasizes the fact that the barefoot doctor is a regular member of the community who happens to work in the health area, rather than a health specialist who happens to be employed in a particular locale. It also enables a poor community to afford the services of skilled or semi-skilled persons.

The overall effect of such a structure is that the barefoot doctor acts as a bridge between the local community and the health specialists. Ideally he will not develop elitist tendencies since he is firmly rooted in the local community. At the same time, his level of professional skill will constantly improve. As a bridge, the barefoot doctor can explain local concerns and conditions to the specialists and can help the specialists implement programs more effectively in the local area. For example, the rapid success of the family planning effort in China is due, to a considerable degree, to the fact that the principal local advocate of the program is a person the community knows and trusts, the barefoot doctor.[16] Moreover, the barefoot doctor is constantly present within the community to supply contraceptives, allay misgivings, reinforce positive attitudes, and treat physical side effects resulting from the practice of birth control.

To complete the picture, China also tries to control the negative aspects

---

16. Although there is controversy over this matter, the current birth rate appears to be about or slightly under 20 per thousand. *See, e.g.*, L. ORLEANS, EVERY FIFTH CHILD: THE POPULATION OF CHINA (1972); Pi-chao Chen, *Population Planning: Policy Evolution and Action Programs,* in M. Wegman, Tsung-yi Lin & F. Purcell eds., *supra* note 1, at 236; *cf.* J. AIRD, ESTIMATES AND PROJECTIONS OF THE POPULATION OF MAINLAND CHINA: 1953–1986 (1968).

of professionalism by acting directly on the health specialists. There is a great deal of explaining to these persons regarding why they should heed the wishes of the masses, follow the mass-line, and serve the people.[17] One might cynically say that such propaganda is merely cosmetic; or one might laud the effort and say that attitudes can be changed through proper education. More concretely, in recent years a substantial number of physicians have been assigned to practice medicine in rural areas.[18] In this way they are better able to understand the living conditions of the peasants and also can train and back up the barefoot doctors. Finally, it appears that about half of the present medical students are former barefoot doctors. If this trend continues, and if the medical student–barefoot doctor can "maintain his class standpoint" after graduation, then the character of the Chinese medical profession will greatly change within a generation.

B. *Analogy to Law: Public Participation in Legal Decisionmaking*

The Chinese ideal of full public participation is reflected in contexts other than those of health problems. The area of law presents perhaps the most graphic illustration of the effort in China to reduce the role of the professionals and to engage the masses in political-legal work. In 1956, at the height of the stress on legality, the Chinese said that there were only 3,500 lawyers in the entire country; no subsequent statement has claimed a higher number.[19] While this figure may be somewhat understated—the actual number may be closer to 10,000—it is nonetheless a stark contrast to the current count in the United States of 400,000 lawyers serving a population only one-fourth the size of China's. There are similar, though less drastic, limitations on the number of professional and bureaucratic workers in other legal sectors. For example, in 1964 in one suburban county east of Canton, approximately 300 policemen covered a population of over half a million persons.[20]

How does the Chinese legal system function with so few professionals? A large part of the answer is that a great number of laymen and parapro-

17. *See, e.g.*, MEDICAL WORKERS SERVING THE PEOPLE WHOLEHEARTEDLY (Peking: Foreign Languages Press, 1971); *Hospital on the Road of Revolutionization*, 18 CHINA RECONSTRUCTS, Mar. 1969, at 11; *Our Experiences in Serving the Former Poor and Lower-Middle Peasants*, 1968 CHINA'S MEDICINE 286; *Resolutely Implement Chairman Mao's Great Call "In Medicine and Health Work, Put the Stress on the Rural Areas,"* 1968 CHINA'S MEDICINE 744.

18. "By the end of 1972 more than 50 percent of China's professional medical workers and medical appropriations were serving the countryside at the county level and below." Hsin Hua-wen, *Commune Hospitals Grow*, 22 CHINA RECONSTRUCTS, Nov. 1973, at 2. Orleans states that as of 1973, "300,000 city medical workers and medical school graduates went to live and work in the countryside, and almost 400,000 medical personnel made tours of the rural areas in mobile medical teams," although some of these transfers may not have been permanent. L. ORLEANS, *supra* note 3, at 30.

19. *See* COHEN, THE CRIMINAL PROCESS IN THE PEOPLE'S REPUBLIC OF CHINA, 1949–64: AN INTRODUCTION 440 (1968); TAO-TAI HSIA, GUIDE TO SELECTED LEGAL SOURCES OF MAINLAND CHINA 51 (1967); SHAO-CHUAN LENG, JUSTICE IN COMMUNIST CHINA: A SURVEY OF THE JUDICIAL SYSTEM OF THE CHINESE PEOPLE'S REPUBLIC 135–36 (1967).

20. Li, *The Public Security Bureau and Political-Legal Work in Hui-Yang, 1952–64*, in THE CITY IN COMMUNIST CHINA 61 (J. Lewis ed. 1971).

fessionals, mostly unpaid, also take part in political-legal work. Thus, at about the same time that China stated that it had only 3,500 lawyers, it also described how 94,000 procuratorial correspondents[21] (members of the public who help the procurators uncover and investigate violations of law), 246,500 people's assessors[22] (who serve for 20 days each year as a kind of juror in most trials of first instance), and 157,966 mediation committees, or about one million lay mediators,[23] were also engaged in legal or quasi-legal work. The extent of public participation can also be seen at the level of the urban neighborhood.[24] Groups of about 3,000 persons form themselves into residents' committees, each of which is divided into 10 or 15 residents' small groups. Under each residents' committee there are a number of other functional bodies such as the mediation committee, the security defense committee (which assists in police work), the women's affairs committee, and the militia. All of these units are run by residents who are elected by their neighbors and generally serve without pay. The residents' small group elects one to three "officials," the chief of whom also serves as a leader of the residents' committee; about 10 persons are elected to each of the other committees. Analysis of these figures reveals that about seven percent of the local adults serve in some capacity in the neighborhood apparatus.

Moreover, the work done at the neighborhood level is not trivial. These persons may mediate disputes, assist in police work, manage several small neighborhood factories and farms, operate day-care centers, kindergartens, and adult education classes, take part in planning extracurricular activities for students, carry out public health and sanitation work, and run the "small group study sessions" that do everything from discussing Chairman Mao's writings to criticizing the work style of some local government official to implementing the family planning program. This is public participation carried virtually to its logical extreme, with local people using their own human and material resources to take care of a large portion of their needs. Even granting the limitations of such participation, particularly in the area of formation of major policies, this arrangement leads to real local influence over decisionmaking at the local level[25]—just as the major role played by the needs of the local people strongly influences the training and orientation of barefoot doctors.

---

21. *See* Hsia, *supra* note 19, at 37–38.
22. *See* SHAO-CHUAN LENG, *supra* note 19, at 88.
23. *See id.* at 91–93; COHEN, *supra* note 19, at 121–31, 141–53.
24. *See generally* COHEN, *supra* note 19, at 98–199; Lubman, *Mao and Mediation: Politics and Dispute Resolution in Communist China*, 55 CALIF. L. REV. 1284 (1967).
25. On the mass-line, *see generally* M. SELDEN, THE YENAN WAY IN REVOLUTIONARY CHINA (1971); J. TOWNSEND, POLITICAL PARTICIPATION IN COMMUNIST CHINA (1967). *See also* Li, *Law and Penology: Systems of Reform and Correction*, in M. Oksenberg ed., *supra* note 5, at 144; Li, *The Role of Law in Communist China*, 44 CHINA Q. 66 (1970).

III. CONCLUSION

In this Essay, I have tried to illustrate the politics of professionalism in China by describing that country's active and thoughtful effort to find means of delivering extensive health services at low cost and of training health professionals who are specialists without being elitists. In this instance, the potential clash between the ideological imperatives of mass control and egalitarianism on the one hand and the technical requirements of functional specialization on the other appears to have been resolved in a manner beneficial to both sides. Experts have not been rejected but, instead, have played a major role in training a new generation of health workers who in due course will be at the same time red and expert. In the process, a great many services will have been delivered despite limited resources.

This is not to suggest that this model is being implemented in China without difficulty, or that reality and the ideal model coincide. Several situations in which implementation of this model may encounter serious problems in the future come to mind. For example, on the economic side, the small amounts paid by the individual and the commune to the cooperative medical fund have been adequate because the stress has been on the inexpensive, labor-intensive prevention work, rather than on curative medicine. In the not too distant future, the demand for curative services will increase as the public learns more about medical treatment and as the barefoot doctor becomes more knowledgeable and skillful. The question then will become, "From what source will the money come to pay for new equipment and facilities and for more expensive medicines?" On the political side, it remains to be seen whether China will be able to resist the lure of professionalization. That is, there will undoubtedly be considerable pressure to have the barefoot doctors engage in health work on a full-time basis, since there is probably more health work to be done than they now handle. If the barefoot doctors begin to do more professional work and less manual labor, might they develop the negative aspects of professionalism?

While the barefoot doctors appear to be an exciting social experiment, I am not suggesting that this model of development is necessarily adaptable to or suitable for other societies. Such a model is based on a whole grid of social and ideological factors—particularly the commitment to the mass-line and the willingness to accept temporary losses when professionalism is first downplayed—that may not be present or even desired in another society. Transplanting is a difficult business. We must remember that in most cases a single thread of social practice from one society cannot be extracted without bringing with it the whole social fabric, nor can a single thread be inserted into another society without disturbing its entire pattern.

Some Preliminary Notes on the American Antitrust Laws' Economic Tests of Legality

Richard S. Markovits*

Although there has been considerable debate about whether the legality of various practices under the American antitrust laws depends solely on their economic or also on their political or social consequences, it has always been assumed that the relevant economic test or tests were unambiguous and well-established. Unfortunately, this assumption is unwarranted. Indeed, most antitrust commentators—including many who believe that the Sherman[1] and Clayton Acts[2] contain a strictly economic test of legality—have never bothered to articulate the standard in question. Moreover, those few who have tried to be more specific have tended to drift among four tests which they assume are operationally equivalent. Unfortunately, despite the fact that they share the (dubious) assumption that the American antitrust laws were designed to prevent behavior that would increase the deviation between the relevant firm's or industry's actual performance and its perfectly competitive counterpart, these four tests have considerably different legal implications.

This Essay will examine these four tests and propose some alternatives that are more consistent with the language of the antitrust acts, the regulatory framework into which they are set, and the goals they are designed to achieve. The analysis will be divided into four parts. The first delineates the basic functional distinctions which should underlie any interpretation of the Sherman and Clayton Acts. The second examines the ambiguity, inconsistency, and nonfunctionality of the four "deviation from perfectly competitive results" tests. The third describes and explains the justification for the economic tests I think the antitrust laws should be held to contain. And the fourth examines how the tests would operate in practice by describing how they structure the legal analysis of horizontal mergers and reciprocity.

---

* A.B. 1963, Cornell University; Ph.D. 1966, London School of Economics; LL.B. 1968, Yale University. Associate Professor of Law, Stanford University.
    1. 15 U.S.C. §§ 1–7 (1970).
    2. *Id.* §§ 12–27.

I. Three General Ways in Which a Seller's Behavior Can Increase His Profits: An Analysis of Their Character and a Preliminary Statement of Their Status in American Law

There are three general ways in which business practices can increase their employers' profits. First, a practice may increase a seller's profits by enabling him to increase his basic competitive advantage[3] (BCA) over his rivals or to reduce his fixed costs, that is, by increasing the extent to which he is a natural monopolist.[4] Practices can enable sellers to increase their natural monopoly position either by reducing the variable or fixed costs of producing or distributing a particular product or by shifting the demand curve they face by changing the physical character of their product, its image, or the amount of information communicated about its value, price, or availability.

Second, a practice can increase a seller's profits by enabling him to take better advantage of the natural monopoly position he enjoys, that is, by enabling him to take better advantage of the demand and cost curves he faces. Lump-sum fees, conventional price discrimination, tying agreements, reciprocal trading agreements, and vertical price and territorial restraints may all increase profits in this manner,[5] though they will frequently perform the other two basic functions as well.

Third, a practice can increase a seller's profits by reducing the attractiveness of the offers against which he has to compete, for example, by inducing his rivals to reduce the attractiveness of their offers or by reducing the number of competing products produced by independent rivals (by deterring price competition by independent producers of rival products, by eliminating established rivals, by inducing such rivals to reduce the number of products they offer, the amount of capacity they maintain, and/or the number of distributive outlets they operate, or by preventing the entry of potential competitors).[6]

---

3. The basic competitive advantage of a particular seller in his relationship to a particular customer is equal to the sum of (1) the difference between his marginal costs and those of his closest rival in their dealings with this customer and (2) the extra money this buyer would be willing to pay to obtain his product rather than that of his closest rival.

4. In this Essay, I will use the term "natural monopoly" in a rather expanded sense. In particular, I will say that a seller has a natural monopoly to the extent that he has a basic competitive advantage over his rivals in his dealings with a particular customer or can earn supernormal returns without relying on threats or promises to deter his actual and potential rivals from expanding.

5. See, e.g., Markovits, The Nonleverage Functions, Competitive Impact, Legality, and Welfare Effects of Reciprocal Trading Agreements (forthcoming); Markovits, Vertical Integration and Its Surrogates: A Functional, Legal, and Policy Analysis (forthcoming); Markovits, Tie-ins, Leverage, and the American Antitrust Laws, 80 Yale L.J. 195 (1970); Markovits, Tie-ins, Reciprocity, and the Leverage Theory, 76 Yale L.J. 1397 (1967).

6. Before proceeding, I should note that mergers may also enable sellers to realize additional profits by reducing the barriers to expansion they face. If the first function described in the text is referred to as "increasing (private) static efficiency," this function might be called "increasing dynamic efficiency." In the text that follows, I will ignore this possibility since this function will almost always be procompetitive.

Of course, individual practices may increase a seller's profits in more than one of the ways just described. Thus a merger (1) may increase the participating firms' natural monopoly (by reducing their costs or enabling them to produce more attractive products), (2) may enable them to take better advantage of their natural monopoly positions (for example, by facilitating their use of tie-ins), and (3) may reduce the attractiveness of the offers against which the merging firms must compete (for example, by freeing them from each other's competition or by enabling them more easily to detect secret price-cutting by others). Nevertheless, it will be useful to keep these categories separate when analyzing the legal implications of the various economic tests that have at times been employed or advocated in the antitrust context.

Let's proceed, then, to analyze the status of these various functions under the American antitrust laws. On the one hand, the Sherman Act was clearly designed to prevent firms from acting together to increase their profits by reducing the attractiveness of the offers against which they must compete. On the other hand, nothing in the Sherman Act suggests that it was meant to overturn the traditional American policy of allowing firms to lower their costs or increase the attractiveness of their products, that is, to increase their basic competitive advantages and fixed cost-advantages. Thus, (1) the term "agreement in restraint of trade"—which had no consistent common law meaning—appears to have been interpreted by most post-Sherman Act courts to refer to an agreement that was not motivated by a legitimate business purpose, that is, to refer to an agreement whose profitability depended on its tendency to reduce the attractiveness of the offers against which its participants had to compete; and (2) the phrase "monopolize or attempt to monopolize" seems always to have referred to single-firm behavior that fits the above description.[7] This policy of encouraging firms to lower their costs and improve their products would also seem to imply the legitimacy of the second function just described, that is, would also seem to imply that firms should be allowed to take advantage of their basic competitive advantages even at their customers' expense through any means they wish (at least so long as their choice does not reduce the attractiveness of their rivals' offers). Moreover, although the Clayton Act's "lessening competition" language does not focus on the motivation of the firms in question, it has always been assumed that the two acts should be interpreted to draw the same basic functional distinction. In short, although the Clayton Act may reach further than the Sherman Act, it probably shares its predecessor's assumption that only the function of reducing the quality of rival offers is

---

7. *See* Bork, *The Rule of Reason and the Per Se Concept: Price Fixing and Market Division*, 74 YALE L.J. 789 (1965).

inherently suspect under the American antitrust laws. However, before proceeding to describe the way in which these acts should be interpreted, it
will be useful to examine the four economic tests of antitrust legality that
various commentators have read into the Clayton and Sherman Acts.

II. Four Common Economic Tests of Antitrust Legality

This section explores the four economic tests of antitrust legality that
have often been articulated and applied in the antitrust literature.[8] Although
all derive from the Clayton Act's "lessening competition" language, they
have been used as much in Sherman Act as in Clayton Act discussions. As
we shall see, although various commentators seem to have assumed that the
four tests are operationally equivalent, they do in fact differ significantly
from each other. Admittedly, however, all four do share the dubious assumption that the legality of any practice or event under the antitrust laws
depends on its impact on the results of the competitive process—more particularly, on the extent to which the price, quality, and/or quantity of the
output of the firms in question, the profits of these sellers, or the welfare
of the buyers concerned deviate from their perfectly competitive counterparts. This section examines these tests to determine (1) whether they are
as comprehensive and unambiguous as is normally supposed, (2) whether
they make the legality of various practices turn on the functional distinctions just articulated, and (3) whether they are consistent with each other.

A. *The (P-MC) Test*

According to one definition sometimes used in antitrust discussions, the
legality of any act covered by the antitrust laws depends on whether it
widens the gap between the actual price and the actual marginal cost of
the product concerned, that is, between the actual and (short-run) perfectly
competitive price.[9] Unfortunately, this test is far from satisfactory, for it is
arbitrary, ambiguous, and noncomprehensive. Its arbitrary character reflects the fact (1) that it is based on one of several possible definitions of
the intensity of price competition and (2) that it does not directly consider
investment competition.[10] Its ambiguity and/or noncomprehensiveness
arises because (1) it does not indicate how practices that change the product
concerned should be treated, (2) it does not speak to situations involving

---

8. Sometimes in the mistaken belief that they represented an operationalization of the type of
"deterioration of rival offer" test I will eventually propose. *See* notes 30–35 *infra* and accompanying
text.
9. Thus, a horizontal merger that induced the merging sellers to increase their across-the-board
prices from $10 to $12 and left their marginal cost unchanged at $8 would clearly violate the
(P-MC) test.
10. For a discussion of these problems, *see* Markovits, *Fixed Input (Investment) Competition
and the Variability of Fixed Inputs (Investment): Their Nature, Determinants, and Significance*, 24
Stan. L. Rev. 507, 522–25 (1972).

lump-sum fees,[11] and (3) it does not provide standards for acts that increase the (P-MC) gap charged to some customers or for some products while decreasing the gap that prevails in relation to other customers or products.[12]

Second, this test is not based in any way on the functional distinction delineated in the first section. Indeed, it neither draws the line I have suggested nor treats each of the three functions consistently. Admittedly, the (P-MC) test would condemn virtually all practices that benefit their employers by reducing the attractiveness of competing offers—though even here exceptions might arise in across-the-board pricing situations.[13] However, the (P-MC) test will often not be directly applicable to practices that enable a seller to take better advantage of his natural monopoly position (since such practices will usually involve lump-sum fees, price discrimination, or more than one product). Moreover, the (P-MC) test will also not treat practices that increase a seller's natural monopoly power in any consistent fashion. Thus, on the one hand, under a (P-MC) test the legality of practices that change the attractiveness of products would depend on their functionally fortuitous effect on the (P-MC) margin. On the other hand, such a test would usually condemn a practice that functioned by lowering its employer's marginal costs—except in the unusual case in which at least 100 percent of the cost reduction was passed on. In short, the (P-MC) test does not treat the various functions we have described either consistently or in the manner I have recommended.

Third, the (P-MC) test will often produce results that are inconsistent with those of the other deviation tests that have been employed. Thus, since MC is equated with actual marginal costs at each point in time, such a test would condemn a practice that functioned by lowering its employer's costs even if it induced (smaller) reductions in prices that benefitted the consumers of the products in question, that is, even if it increased unit output and buyer welfare. Indeed, on this interpretation, such a test would also condemn practices that increased (P-MC) gaps by increasing the attractiveness of the products their employer produced—regardless of whether such practices benefitted or harmed this seller's customers. In short, the (P-MC) test is arbitrary and noncomprehensive; it is not based on any functional distinctions, much less on reasonable ones; and it will often produce results that are inconsistent with those of the other deviation tests that have been recommended.

---

11. Literally interpreted, the (P-MC) test would make variations in lump-sum fees irrelevant. Obviously, however, such an interpretation would produce results that are entirely inconsistent with the test's rationale.

12. For a discussion of the additional problems posed by practices that affect different buyers differently, *see* Markovits, *Tie-ins, Leverage, and the American Antitrust Laws, supra* note 5, at 247–48.

13. Since a practice that reduces the attractiveness of some of the offers against which a seller must compete may increase the quantity he can sell at lower prices without changing his demand curve at higher prices, it may thereby induce him to lower his across-the-board price.

B. *The Unit-Output Test*

According to the unit-output test, the legality of a practice would depend on its impact on the unit sales of the product or products directly affected[14] or, more precisely, on whether it reduced the gap between the product's actual and competitive outputs (the output that would result if price equalled marginal cost).[15] Let's proceed to analyze the ambiguity and functionality of the unit-output test as well as its consistency with the other "deviation from perfectly competitive results" tests that have been proposed. First, the unit-output test produces ambiguous results when applied to practices that either change a product or increase the output of some products while decreasing the output of others. However, unlike the (P-MC) test, the unit-output test is not ambiguous when applied to practices that involve lump-sum fees or that increase the prices charged some buyers while decreasing the prices charged others. Second, the unit-output test is not functionally consistent or desirable. Thus, even if the unit-output test could be applied in a simple way to practices that increase a seller's natural monopoly by enabling him to change his product, its image, or the extent to which the public is aware of its attributes, it would have no general implications about their legality, for under a unit-output test the legality of such practices would presumably depend on whether any related increase in demand was more than offset by any associated increase in price. By way of contrast, a unit-output test would rarely forbid practices that increase natural monopoly by lowering costs since such cost reductions will usually lead to price reductions and unit-output increases.[16]

The legality of most practices that enable a seller to take advantage of his natural monopoly position would also be uncertain under a unit-output test. Thus, since the effect of price discrimination on total sales will vary from case to case, the unit-output test would not justify declaring this practice either per se lawful or per se unlawful. Nor would any general rule be justified for tie-ins that function by reducing the amount of buyer and seller surplus destroyed as a result of the tendency of supramarginal cost pricing to reduce unit sales, since such agreements would tend to increase the unit sales of the tying product but decrease the unit sales of the tied product.[17] The legality of vertical price and territorial restraints that func-

---

14. For an instance in which this test has been employed, *see* Bowman, *Tying Arrangements and the Leverage Problem*, 67 YALE L.J. 19, 25 (1957).

15. Thus, since the merger described in note 9 *supra* would reduce the unit sales of the sellers in question (since fewer people will be willing to buy their products at the higher price) without changing their competitive outputs, it would also violate the unit-output test described in the text.

16. An issue might arise where the cost reduction made it profitable in the short run for a seller to reduce his prices to an extent that caused some rivals to exit since such departures might decrease unit output by enabling the seller in question to raise his price above its original level in the long run.

17. *See* Markovits, *Tie-ins, Reciprocity, and the Leverage Theory*, *supra* note 5, at 1413-23. Of course, if such ambiguous cases were settled by determining the effect of the tie-in on the total variable costs incurred on the two products, the practices would probably be upheld in most cases.

tion in this way would also be uncertain—at least until one determined what other changes the sellers in question would introduce if these restraints were forbidden. In general, then, a unit-output test would not produce any clear rules about the legality of practices that function by enabling their employers to take better advantage of their given natural monopoly positions. However, since practices that function solely by deterring competition or eliminating competitors will generally induce their employers to raise their prices, the unit-output test would probably condemn practices that operate exclusively in this way (though as we noted, exceptions will be possible in this case as well).[18]

Finally, the unit-output test is also not consistent with the other deviation tests that have been proposed. Thus, as we have already noted, unlike the (P-MC) test, the unit-output test would almost always[19] avoid the absurdity of condemning practices that operate by reducing marginal costs. Indeed, the unit-output test would also frequently produce different results from the buyer-welfare test since, for example, a shift from conventional single pricing to lump-sum pricing or some more complicated, related scheme (perhaps involving tie-ins or reciprocity) may simultaneously increase unit output (by decreasing per unit price) and decrease buyer welfare.

C. *The Seller-Profit Test*

Obviously there is no reason for making the legality of a particular practice depend on whether it turned out to be individually profitable (since it would be far more efficient to make such a practice per se unlawful on the assumption that it would be individually profitable if adopted). However, some commentators[20] have assumed that the legality of practices other than mergers depends on whether their general adoption would increase the gap between actual and competitive or normal profits, other things being equal.[21]

As with the first two tests, the seller-profit test may be somewhat am-

---

18. *See* note 13 *supra*.

19. As we saw, the (P-MC) test would condemn such practices whenever their employers responded to the cost reduction in question by reducing their price by a smaller absolute amount. On the other hand, since such cost reductions will always lead to some price reductions in the short run, the unit-output test would condemn such practices only if (1) they reduced their employers' short-run maximizing prices sufficiently to induce them to set nonpredatory prices that would cause some of their competitors to exit in the long run, (2) this exit enabled the remaining employers of the practice in question to charge higher prices in the long run than they would have charged had they not engaged in the practice in question, and (3) the (discounted) reduction in their long-run unit sales exceeded the associated increase in their short-run unit sales.

20. In fact, in an earlier article, I used such a test myself in order to operate on a basis that least favored my conclusion that the per se rule against tie-ins should be rejected. *See* Markovits, *Tie-ins, Leverage, and the American Antitrust Laws, supra* note 5, at 250.

21. Thus, the legality of a group of competitors' offering reciprocity agreements to their various customers might be said to depend on whether the practice increased the profits of the sellers in question. Similarly, one might analyze the legality of allowing all alternative suppliers to enter into tying agreements with a particular buyer by assessing the likely effect on the profits his best-placed supplier could earn by supplying him.

biguous since it is not clear whether gross profits or supernormal profits are meant to be determinative. Unfortunately this ambiguity may be crucial in some cases, for practices that change industry investment and industry profits in the same direction may increase a seller's gross profits while decreasing his supernormal profits, or conversely.

Moreover the seller-profit test would not treat each of the three functions described in the first section consistently. Thus, although a generalized seller profit test would tend to condemn practices that increase each seller's ability to take advantage of his natural monopoly, it might have the opposite effect if the general availability of the practices reduced the best-placed supplier's competitive advantage. Similarly, since a series of reciprocity or tying agreements which reduce the costs or improve the products of all firms operating in a market might leave them better or worse off, such a test would not treat consistently practices which function by increasing a seller's natural monopoly power. Of course, since rational sellers will not engage in behavior designed to reduce competition or eliminate competitors unless they expect it to increase their profits, such acts would be condemned by a generalized seller-profit test.

Nor would such a seller-profit test be consistent with the other deviation tests that have been proposed. Thus, since reciprocity, tie-ins, etc. may increase buyer welfare at the same time that they increase seller profits, a seller-profit test will sometimes produce different results from a buyer-welfare test. As we have seen, the unit-output and (P-MC) tests are too ambiguous in relation to such practices to permit any meaningful comparisons. In short, the type of seller-profit test I have just described is neither unambiguous nor consistent either functionally or with its deviation siblings.

D. The Buyer-Welfare Test

The fourth test commentators have sometimes adopted is the buyer-welfare test.[22] According to this test, regulated behavior would violate the antitrust laws if and only if it seemed likely to move buyers further from the position they would occupy in a perfectly competitive market, that is, if it seemed likely to injure the buyers directly affected.[23] Although like its predecessors this test is also consistent with the Clayton Act's "lessening competition" language, its support derives from two related sources as well: (1) the test's focus on the apparent proximate goal of the antitrust laws (to protect consumers) and (2) the (mistaken) belief that any act that injures

---

22. See, e.g., Bork, A Reply to Professors Gould and Yamey, 76 YALE L.J. 731, 732 (1967).
23. The horizontal merger described in note 9 supra would clearly violate a buyer-welfare test since the customers of the merging firms would obviously be injured by the price rise that the merger would cause.

the actor's customers must also worsen resource allocation and economic performance.[24]

Although the buyer-welfare test is not ambiguous,[25] it does have its predecessors' other failings. Thus, the buyer-welfare test also fails to generate any clear rules about the legality of the basic functions first described. For example, under this standard, the treatment of practices that increase their employer's natural monopoly power would depend on the way in which they produced this result. On the one hand, since practices that operate exclusively by reducing costs will usually tend to benefit their employer's customers (since reductions in marginal costs will usually induce price reductions directly, while reductions in fixed costs will tend to induce additional quality-increasing investments that raise quality and reduce prices as well), such practices would not usually be condemned under a buyer-welfare test.[26] On the other hand, since practices that increase a seller's natural monopoly power by enabling him to change his product, product image, or product exposure will have a more uncertain effect on his various customers (since the associated shift in his demand curve may be accom-

---

24. Many people believe that any act that harms the actual and potential consumers of the seller or sellers directly involved must also worsen economic performance in some more general sense—except perhaps to the extent that the profits the sellers thereby obtain provide a desirable incentive for product improvements and cost reductions that ultimately will work to the benefit of consumers as a class. In fact, however, many practices that injure directly-affected buyers by reducing the quality of the offers against which the sellers in question have to compete may improve the allocation of resources, even if they do not increase the productive efficiency of the firms in question. After all, the customers of the sellers in question are only one subset of all those affected by the behavior concerned: the dollars won and lost by the sellers directly involved, by the other producers from whom resources were withdrawn or to whom resources flowed, and by the potential buyers of other products whose prices may have been affected are equally weighty on allocative grounds (though they may be weighted differently for distributional purposes). Indeed, although there are valid allocative reasons for desiring reduction in prices (which will incidentally benefit the consumers in question), anticompetitive events that increase prices in markets in which prices were originally low relative to marginal costs may very well reduce resource misallocation—even if they do not reduce costs or generate product improvements.

Thus, on allocative grounds, it may be desirable to allow practices that increase their employer's allocative efficiency even if they injure the buyers directly involved—at least in industries in which price is relatively close to marginal cost. In fact, even if income distribution is considered, I suspect that it would be desirable to have a presumption in favor of events that seem likely to create static efficiencies in less-than-typically monopolistic industries even if they may also tend to worsen rival offers—at least to the extent that it would be expensive or self-defeating for defendants to demonstrate such efficiencies in a public forum. This conclusion obviously underlies my desire to qualify the deterioration test with an allocative-efficiency defense even in those cases in which the event or practice injures the buyers most directly affected. *See* text accompanying note 37 *infra*.

I should emphasize, however, that I would simultaneously recommend a substantial increase in the government's efforts both to reduce the number of Sherman Act violations private firms commit and to prevent further deteriorations in the attractiveness of rival offers in less competitive markets, particularly where no static or dynamic efficiency seems to be involved. Although this goal could be achieved by increasing the budget of the antitrust division, it could also be attained if the Division stopped attacking the host of practices that firms engage in to take better advantage of their given natural monopolies or to increase the extent of their natural monopolies by reducing their costs or changing the substance, product images, or exposure of the goods or services they sell.

25. At least if one places an equal weight on the average dollars won and lost by those buyers whom the practice benefits and harms.

26. Of course, to the extent that a practice that reduces a seller's costs makes it profitable, even in the short run, for him to charge prices that cause other firms to exit, it may be against his customers' interests in the long run.

panied by either a decrease or an increase in the amount of consumer surplus his operations generate),[27] their legality would be uncertain under a
buyer-welfare test.

The legality of practices that increase a seller's profits by enabling him
to take better advantage of his original monopoly position would also be
uncertain under a buyer-welfare test, since practices that function exclusively in this way can either harm or benefit the buyers directly affected.
Thus, a full-requirements tie-in that functions by reducing the amount of
transaction surplus any given amount of nonmarginal cost pricing destroys
may harm the consumers in question by making it profitable for the seller
concerned to remove consumer surplus that would otherwise be too expensive to eliminate. On the other hand, such agreements may actually benefit
the consumers they affect if (1) these consumers are in a position to bargain
for some of the savings in transaction costs and/or gross transaction (total
buyer and seller) surplus they generate or (2) their general availability
improves inferior suppliers' absolute positions. Admittedly, however, with
rare exceptions,[28] practices that function exclusively by deterring competition or eliminating competitors will be condemned by the buyer-welfare
test.

Finally, the buyer-welfare test would often produce different results
from those that would be generated by the other deviation tests just described, for a given event can increase buyer welfare, (P-MC), and seller
profits at the same time or can increase buyer welfare while reducing unit
output.[29]

In short, we have now seen that at least three of the deviation tests just
described will sometimes be ambiguous; that none of them treats the functions described in section one in a consistent manner (much less draws the
functional distinctions I have advocated); and that none of them is consistent with any of the others.

III. The Sherman and Clayton Acts' Economic Tests of Legality: Two Proposals

This section will describe a set of functional interpretations for the Sherman and Clayton Acts and explain why they should be adopted. As I have
already indicated, the four tests conventionally used all assume that some-

---

27. Such practices may also either improve or worsen the terms received by those buyers who
do not end up patronizing him since his terms may influence the attractiveness of the offer they
receive from their eventual suppliers.

28. See note 13 supra.

29. Thus, a meter-pricing tie-in that replaces a pure lump-sum pricing agreement can simultaneously increase the buyer's profits (by enabling him to share in the savings it achieves or by
increasing the attractiveness of the offers against which his best-placed supplier must compete) while
decreasing the number of times he uses the machine in question (by increasing the private cost to him
of each use).

thing should be said to violate the antitrust laws if and only if it increases the extent to which the results of the competitive process deviate from their perfectly competitive counterparts. In fact, however, the language of the Sherman Act, the general character of American regulatory policy, and the goals of the antitrust laws all seem to require that both the Sherman Act and the Clayton Act be interpreted very differently, that is, according to the functional distinctions described in the first section.

Let's begin with the language of the Sherman Act. As Professor Bork has shown, according to the main tradition of Sherman Act interpretation, the phrase "agreement in restraint of trade" refers to agreements that were not ancillary to some legitimate purpose—to agreements that were not undertaken in order to reduce competition.[30] Translated into our functional framework, this fact suggests that the Sherman Act's proscription of agreements in restraint of trade[31] should be held to proscribe those acts and only those acts whose (prospective) profitability depends on their tendency to reduce the attractiveness of the offers against which the actors in question have to compete. Obviously, the Sherman Act's proscription of "monopolization" and "attempts to monopolize" could be interpreted similarly to prohibit single-firm action which would not have been undertaken but for its expected tendency to reduce the attractiveness of such competing offers. In comparison with the various "deviation from perfectly competitive results" tests, such functional interpretations have the further advantage of being more consistent with the pro-natural monopoly strain of American policy, which encourages firms to lower their costs and improve their products by allowing them to take advantage of the competitive advantages they thereby obtain. This pro-natural monopoly policy is reflected (1) in the fact that conventional innovations are not condemned by the antitrust laws (and indeed may even be given patent protection), (2) in the fact that opponents of particular practices have frequently felt it necessary to demonstrate either that they represent "unfair methods of competition"[32] or

---

30. Bork, *supra* note 7. Unfortunately, the common law seems never to have given this term any consistent meaning. *Id.* at 784.

31. The Sherman Act may not prohibit unsuccessful *attempts* to engage in contracts, conspiracies, or agreements in restraint of trade. *See* Markovits, *Oligopolistic Pricing Suits, the Sherman Act, and Economic Welfare* (pt. 2), 26 STAN. L. REV. 717, 742 (1974). I should hasten to admit that one might also interpret the Sherman Act to forbid all behavior whose "primary purpose" was to suppress competition, that is, to worsen the offers against which the actors in question had to compete. Under this interpretation, horizontal mergers which function "primarily" by suppressing competition would be illegal under the Sherman Act, even if they generate enough static efficiencies to be profitable on this account as well. Although it is certainly possible to argue that such a result was intended when the Sherman Act was passed, since at that time no other antitrust legislation was available for use against such mergers, I suspect that the profitability of almost every merger for monopoly depended on its suppressive effect, that is, that most such mergers would be condemned under my interpretation as well. In any case, it seems to me that the passage of the Clayton Act eliminates the need to use such a vague test in Sherman Act cases.

32. The phrase derives from § 5 of the Federal Trade Commission Act, 15 U.S.C. § 45 (1970).

that they "intrude an alien and irrelevant factor"[33] into the competitive process, as well as (3) in the fact that a "superior skill, foresight and industry" defense has been recognized in Sherman Act litigation.[34]

Admittedly, however, the Clayton Act probably should be interpreted somewhat differently from the Sherman Act. Not only does the Clayton Act seem to require a lower probability of the forbidden effect, it also seems to shift the focus away from the specific intent of the actors in question toward the general effect of their behavior on the relevant market.[35] However, there is no reason why the Clayton Act's "lessening competition" language should not be given an interpretation that is similar to the Sherman Act interpretation just proposed. Thus, one could say that an event lessened competition if on balance it reduced the attractiveness of the offers against which the actor in question *and his fellow competitors* had to compete in those cases in which they were best-placed (in individualized pricing markets) or in general (in across-the-board pricing situations). Under such a test, some behavior that would not violate the Sherman Act would be prohibited by the Clayton Act—behavior whose profitability did not depend on its reducing the attractiveness of the offers against which the actors in question competed (but which nevertheless did on balance reduce the attractiveness of the offers against which the actors in question and their rivals had to compete). Such an interpretation would not do violence to the language of the Clayton Act and would conform with the conventional assumption that the Sherman Act and the Clayton Act reflect the same general policy. Moreover, such an interpretation would produce results which are preferable on ultimate policy grounds to those that would be generated by any of the deviation tests previously described.[36]

Before concluding, I would like to suggest two additional qualifications that might be made to this general "deterioration of rival offer" test. Indeed, despite the fact that neither is implied by the language of the Clayton Act, I would prefer adopting the stronger of these two qualifications. First, one could qualify such a general deterioration test to allow any act that benefits the consumers of the seller in question, despite its tendency on balance to reduce the attractiveness of the offers against which the actor and his rivals compete. Obviously, such a test would be more consistent with the apparent proximate goal of the antitrust laws (benefitting the consumers of the regulated firms). Moreover, it may also appeal to those who believe that the Clayton Act's "lessening competition" language should be interpreted to contain a "deviation from perfectly competitive results" test of legality.

---

33. FTC v. Consolidated Foods, 380 U.S. 592, 594 (1965).
34. United States v. Aluminum Co. of America, 148 F.2d 416, 430 (2d Cir. 1945).
35. In particular, the Clayton Act condemns various practices "where the effect . . . may be to lessen competition . . . ." 15 U.S.C. § 13 (1970).
36. *See* note 24 *supra.*

The second qualification relates to the possible conflict between the American regulatory system's "antitrust" and pro-natural monopoly policies. In most cases, these two policies will not conflict. However, in individual instances they may, for practices that function in the first instance by enabling their employer to increase his basic competitive advantage or to take better advantage of given competitive advantages may injure buyers by reducing the attractiveness of the offers against which he must compete, that is, by disadvantaging marginal and potential competitors. According to the second qualification, one would strike the balance in these cases of conflict in favor of the pro-natural monopoly policy, even in those instances in which the behavior in question would or did on balance injure the actor's and his rivals' customers. In other words, one could qualify such a general deterioration test by allowing particular acts that reduce the attractiveness of the offers against which the actor or his rivals must compete when they are best-placed, even if the practices in question do injure these firms' customers, whenever this deterioration can be attributed to the behavior's capacity to increase the actor's relative allocative efficiency. In addition to being more consistent with America's pro-natural monopoly policy, this qualification would also promote the antitrust laws' ultimate goal of improving the performance of the economy. Moreover, such a qualification would have two further effects that some might find advantageous: first, it would increase the similarity between the Sherman Act's and Clayton Act's treatment of ancillary restraints; and second, it would increase the similarity between the treatment of efficiencies achieved through internal growth and controls and efficiencies achieved through contractual growth and controls. It is difficult to reconcile such a qualification with the "lessening competition" language of the Clayton Act. Nevertheless, given the vagueness of congressional intent in this area and the fact that many practices covered by the Clayton Act are likely to be as allocatively efficient as those that are not, I think that a good case could be made for a court to adopt the second as well as the first qualification just described. Of course, I must admit that this result is probably not consistent with the tenor of most academic discussion of such issues—though it may be more consistent with prevailing judicial attitudes than those discussions would suggest.[37]

IV. The Deterioration of Rival Offer Test: Some Suggestive Applications

This section will try to make the "deterioration of rival offer" test somewhat more concrete by applying it to particular practices covered by the antitrust laws. The analysis will focus on the Clayton Act version of the

---

37. *See* notes 32–34 *supra*.

deterioration test, which will require consideration of all the ways in which the behavior in question could deteriorate rival offers rather than just those that relate to the rival offers against which the individual actors in question must compete.

However, before proceeding it will be useful to develop a distinction which relates to the way in which any given event or practice should be analyzed under the Clayton Act. In particular, it seems to me quite clear that the legality of at least some practices covered by the Clayton Act should not be analyzed on an individual firm-by-firm basis. For example, I think that it would be totally improper to make the legality of a particular firm's employing tying agreements depend on the impact of its tie-ins analyzed individually, that is, to analyze each firm's use of tie-ins on the assumption that the legality of its rivals' use of tie-ins would have to be separately determined. Such an approach would be objectionable because it would convert the courts into handicappers authorized to establish a rule that would allow marginal firms, but not nonmarginal firms, to offer tie-ins to the same buyers.[38] At a minimum, then, one should focus on the impact of allowing all possible suppliers to offer tying agreements to a particular subset of a market's buyers. Indeed, it would probably be even more practical and appropriate to focus on the impact of allowing such agreements to be employed throughout an entire market.

Obviously, the rationale for this approach will apply to far more practices than tie-ins. In particular, this more generalized focus is clearly applicable to such other vertical contractual practices as reciprocity, resale price maintenance, and vertical territorial restraints, and is probably applicable to vertical mergers as well.[39] On the other hand, it also seems clear that practices involving the kind of oligopolistic and predatory conduct condemned by the Sherman Act should be individually analyzed. Moreover, although I am not entirely satisfied with my own reasoning on this subject, I suspect that for three reasons the legality of any horizontal merger should probably be individually determined as well. First, two of the major determinants of the legality of such mergers—the extent to which the merging firms previously constrained each other (were each other's closest

---

38. For a previous statement of this point, *see* Markovits, *Tie-ins, Leverage, and the American Antitrust Laws, supra* note 5, at 245.

39. Admittedly, one of the concerns that has led to the attack on vertical integration—the concern that independents will be frozen out of supplies or distributive outlets—may become more serious as the percentage of integrated investment increases. However, this concern rests on the assumption that the integrated sellers will engage in either individual or collective predatory behavior, (sacrificing short-run profits by refusing to supply a nonintegrated rival or by refusing to distribute his goods), that is, that they will use their vertical integration to conceal a subsequent Sherman Act violation. Accordingly, one might handle this problem by attacking such subsequent illegal behavior when it occurs. Of course, to the extent that such subsequent violations are expensive or difficult to detect or prove, it might be appropriate to adjust vertical integration law to deter such conceivably related behavior.

competitors for various buyers' patronage) and the extent to which their merger increased their static and dynamic efficiency—will obviously vary from case to case. Second, the extent to which horizontal mergers increase the amount of legal and illegal oligopolistic behavior[40] may depend on the preexisting structure of the relevant markets. And third, unlike vertical practices but like clear Sherman Act violations, horizontal mergers will tend to reduce the attractiveness of rival offers directly. Thus, in the end, my distinction between events that should be individually analyzed and practices that should not corresponds to the distinction between behavior that can reduce the attractiveness of rival offers directly and behavior that will do so only indirectly (that is, behavior whose profitability cannot depend on its producing such an effect).

Let us proceed, then, to analyze the way in which one would apply a "deterioration of rival offer" test to an individual event (a horizontal merger)[41] and a general practice (reciprocity)[42] respectively. In general, the legality of any individual event or universal practice under the Clayton Act will depend on (1) its effect on the average number of independent products against which producers must compete (when they are best-placed to serve a particular customer) as well as (2) its effect on the quality of the offers made by the relevant independent rivals. The first effect will, in turn, depend (a) on the impact of the event or practice on the total amount of products, capacity, and distributive outlets present in the industry in question as well as (b) on its impact on the average amount of such quality-or-variety-increasing investments in the hands of each of the surviving firms. The second effect on the quality of the offers made by such independent rivals will depend on (a) its impact on the competitiveness of the remaining independent products with each other, (b) its impact on the cost-quality position of each independent product, and perhaps (c) its impact on the amount of oligopolistic pricing that takes place.[43]

Although, as I will show elsewhere in more detail, other factors must be considered as well,[44] the legality of a horizontal merger under such a

---

40. For a discussion of this phenomenon and the distinction in question, *see* Markovits, *supra* note 31, at (pts. 1 & 2).

41. For a fuller discussion of horizontal mergers, *see* Markovits. *Horizontal Mergers, Competition, and the American Antitrust Laws* (forthcoming).

42. For a fuller discussion of reciprocity, *see* Markovits, *The Nonleverage Functions, Competitive Impact, Legality, and Welfare Effects of Reciprocal Trading Agreements, supra* note 5.

43. In what follows, I will proceed on the assumption that the test in question will not have to be adjusted because of the cost of obtaining the relevant information.

44. Although the factors mentioned in the text are likely to be the most important, horizontal mergers may affect the quality of rival offers in at least seven other ways as well. First, where one of the merging sellers would originally have been willing to expand at a level of industry investment that would have precluded anyone else from doing so, a horizontal merger may induce him to restrict his and hence the industry's total investment by increasing the monopolistic investment disincentives he faces. Second, where the merged sellers both belonged to a small group of best-placed potential expanders, their combination may induce the merger partners and one or more of their

Clayton Act test would basically depend on whether its tendency to reduce the attractiveness of the offers against which the merging firms have to compete (by freeing them from each other's competition and thereby reducing the number of independent products against which they have to compete) will be outweighed by any tendency such a merger may have to increase the competitive pressure the merging firms place on their rivals (1) by increasing their static efficiency and thereby improving the price-quality combination they can offer their rivals' customers and/or (2) by decreasing the barriers to expansion they face.[45] More particularly, under

---

rivals not to expand by increasing the oligopolistic investment disincentives they face by reducing the number of independent firms in that position. Third, to the extent that the merger creates static efficiencies for the merging sellers, it may decrease the competition that their rivals give them and each other by reducing the level of industry quality-or-variety-increasing investment (QV) that will deter them from expanding or entering, that is, by reducing the sum of the competitive advantages they would enjoy on the output they would produce or distribute with the additional investments in question. Fourth, to the extent that the merger creates static efficiencies, it may reduce the number of independent products against which the merging company and his surviving rivals will have to compete by inducing some disadvantaged established firms to exit or by deterring some disadvantaged potential competitors from entering, that is, by reducing the number of independent firms that make the QV investments in question. Fifth, where the merging companies and their rivals operate in an individualized pricing market and practice illegal oligopolistic pricing, the merger (1) may decrease the extent to which the merged firm's beatable offers are in fact undercut (by increasing its total sales and thereby its ability to detect secret price cutting from circumstantial evidence relating to sales, by reducing the number of its rivals and hence increasing its ability to identify its undercutter, by increasing the number of products with which it can retaliate and hence by reducing the costs it must incur to inflict any given amount of harm on any undercutter, and finally by increasing its stake in developing a tough reputation and hence the return from retaliating) and (2) may decrease the extent to which the merged firms undercut their rivals' beatable offers (by increasing the number of products against which the firms it undercuts can retaliate). Sixth, where the merging companies operate in an across-the-board pricing market in which illegal oligopolistic pricing is sometimes practiced, their merger (1) may deter them from undercutting (where they are members of the competitive fringe) by increasing the share of any associated retaliation they bear or (2) may deter others from undercutting by increasing the profitability to them of retaliation (where they are less competitive with each other than with the undercutter in question). Seventh and finally, such a merger may tend to decrease the amount of investments the merging firms' rivals make by increasing the retaliation barriers they face, that is, by reducing the cost of such retaliation to the merged companies by giving them two products with which to retaliate and by increasing their share of the benefits generated by any investment restrictions their retaliation causes. I have confined my discussion of these possibilities to this footnote for various reasons. In particular, I have treated the last three possibilities in this manner on the assumption that any illegal subsequent behavior of this kind could be dealt with separately when it occurred. Admittedly, to the extent that such violations are difficult or expensive to detect or prove, one might use merger policy to prevent their occurrence. On the other hand, the third and fourth possibilities have been treated in a note because of my assumption that any deterioration that results from the act's tendency to improve the offers the merging company makes to customers that previously belonged to its rivals should not contribute to its illegality—particularly where an allocative efficiency is involved. Of course, the first two possibilities discussed in this note cannot be dismissed on either of these grounds. Where they apply, they clearly must be considered in any overall analysis of the legality of a horizontal merger. I have confined my discussion of them to this footnote because they cannot be elaborated without introducing a fairly complicated set of concepts which I have developed elsewhere. See Markovits, *Quality-and-Variety-Increasing (QV) Investment and QV Investment Competition: Their Definition and Relation to Conventional Cost-Reducing Investments and Conventional Price (-Variable Input) Competition* (forthcoming). For a discussion of all these factors, *see* Markovits, *supra* note 41.

45. Such a reduction in the barriers to expansion facing the merging firms could improve the quality of rival offers in any of three ways: first, where the merger lowered the barriers to expansion faced by the merging firms below those that would be faced by any other rival at some relevant level of investment, it might increase the competitive pressure the merging firms exerted on others by inducing them to expand their own and their industry's total QV investments; second, where the merger reduced the barriers to expansion facing the merging firms to the level faced by some rival who previously was best-placed to expand the industry's investment beyond some relevant level, the

the test I am proposing, one would weigh these two sets of tendencies against each other by examining their respective impacts on the welfare of the buyers concerned. Thus, under my deterioration test, the major questions one would have to address when analyzing the legality of a horizontal merger would be the following: (1) To what extent were the merging companies each other's closest rivals for the patronage of particular buyers? (2) To what extent would the merger create marginal static efficiencies and thereby enable the merging companies to beat the offers of the firms that originally were their remaining rivals' closest competitors for the patronage of particular buyers? (3) To what extent would the merger tend to increase equilibrium investment in the industry in question by reducing the barriers to expansion the merging companies faced or by creating static efficiencies that would carry over to expansions as well and thereby inducing the merged firm or its rivals[46] to invest additional amounts in the industry in question? And (4) to what extent would the merger tend to reduce equilibrium investment in the industry by increasing the operative monopolistic and oligopolistic investment disincentives by freeing the merging firms from each other's investment competition and creating a new company with a larger market share?

Let's turn, then, to the general practice of reciprocity. As noted above, neither an individual reciprocity agreement nor the general practice of reciprocity will be able to reduce the attractiveness of the offers against which any (best-placed) seller might compete unless its original profitability can be attributed to another source. However, reciprocity which initially does perform an entirely different function may still have the effect of reducing the attractiveness of rival offers if (1) the individual agreements are more profitable for some firms than for others and (2) their general use tends to concentrate the industry in question and/or to reduce its equilibrium level of investment, for example, by disadvantaging and driving out marginal firms or by disadvantaging a potential entrant who would have been (or who continued to be) an effective force in the market in question. Of course, since such agreements will almost always initially improve the terms on which suppliers can supply the relevant buyers without incurring a loss, their employment may improve the offers inferior suppliers make

---

merger might increase the pressure the postmerger firm and this rival exert on each other and their fellow competitors; third, where the merger reduced the barriers to expansion facing the merging firms to the same level as those faced by some small group of rivals that were previously equally-best-placed to expand industry investment beyond some relevant level, the merger might increase the pressure the postmerger firm and its rivals exert on each other and their fellow competitors by inducing several or all of them to expand (by reducing the expansion barriers faced by the merging companies and the spontaneous oligopolistic disincentives faced by the members of this best-placed group). For a discussion of expansion barriers, monopolistic investment disincentives, and spontaneous oligopolistic investment disincentives, see Markovits, *supra* note 44.

46. A reduction in the barriers to expansion faced by one firm may induce others to expand by reducing the monopolistic and oligopolistic disincentives to investment they face.

even when such agreements do reduce equilibrium investment, increase the amount of quality-or-variety-increasing investment in the hands of each surviving firm, or increase the amount of illegal oligopolistic pricing that takes place. In fact, even in the (rare) case in which reciprocity does on balance reduce the attractiveness of such offers, the Clayton Act might not condemn the general practice if my second qualification were adopted, for since most types of reciprocity operate by increasing the allocative productivity of their employers, it will usually be possible to make. out an allocative efficiency defense in any related litigation. Thus, under my deterioration test, the crucial questions in a reciprocity case would be the following: (1) Will the general availability of reciprocity tend to disadvantage and drive out marginal firms or disadvantage and raise the entry barriers faced by effective potential competitors?[47] (2) Will any associated deterioration in the offers of inferior suppliers be offset by the ability of reciprocity to improve the terms on which remaining suppliers can break even on individual transactions? And (3) did the reciprocity agreements in question increase their employers' allocative productivity?

V. CONCLUSION

In this Essay, I have tried to point out the general character of and important differences among the economic tests that have usually been employed to evaluate the legality of various acts under the Sherman and Clayton Antitrust Acts. By using a test that focuses on the functional distinction between reducing the attractiveness of rival offers on the one hand and increasing or taking advantage of competitive advantages on the other, I have also indicated the way in which I would resolve the usually submerged dispute over standards that has influenced many antitrust debates. Although I do not purport to have justified my own conclusions in any definitive way, I hope that their articulation will provide clear alternatives on which future discussions can focus. In any case, this discussion may help prevent the confusion that has so often resulted from the failure of commentators to decide on, or agree on, the standards of legality they were individually or jointly employing.[48]

---

47. The availability of reciprocity might also tend to deteriorate rival offers if it concentrated the industry by causing some firms to shrink and others to expand more rapidly than they otherwise would.

48. One dispute of this kind comes readily to mind. In particular, uncertainty about standards seems to me to have contorted the debate about the legality of such vertical practices as resale price maintenance and vertical territorial agreements. At times the proponents of such vertical agreements seem committed to a unit-output or buyer-welfare standard while at times they appear to be adopting the deterioration test described above. Debates have developed in which opponents have responded to arguments that presuppose a unit-output or buyer-welfare test only to be told in effect that their arguments are irrelevant since a deterioration test should actually be employed.

Legal Education There and Here:
A Comparison*

John Henry Merryman†

The examination of legal education in a society provides a window on its legal system. Here one sees the expression of basic attitudes about the law: what law is, what lawyers do, how the system operates or how it should operate. Through legal education the legal culture is transferred from generation to generation. Legal education allows us to glimpse the future of the society. Those who will man the legal system and will fill those positions of leadership in government and the private sector that seem to fall more frequently to lawyers, at least in Western societies, come out of the law schools. What they are taught and how it is taught to them profoundly affect their objectives and attitudes and the ways in which they will fill these social roles.

The same ideas can be put in a more sociological form. A legal system is a component part (a subsystem) of a social system, and the system of legal education is a component part (a sub-subsystem) of the legal system. The system and its subsystems are organically related and give meaning to each other. A change in any part resounds throughout the whole.

These considerations indicate both the importance and the difficulty of a comparison of systems of legal education. Such a comparison, if well done, throws light on much more than legal education; it tells us something essential and profound about legal systems and the societies in which they operate. But such a comparison requires, if it is to be useful and valid, that what is said about any system of legal education be put into legal and social context. It is difficult enough to do this for one's own society; to do it for all those in two great legal families—civil law and common law—goes beyond the limits of this Essay and the abilities of the author. The most one can hope to do is to suggest general points of contrast that seem to be significant and interesting and to indicate some of the ways in which these differences are related to legal systems and societies.

* Copyright 1974 by John Henry Merryman. I wish to thank Mauro Cappelletti, Thomas Ehrlich, Dietrich Andre Loeber, Inga Markovits, Max Rheinstein, and Robert B. Stevens for their advice and criticisms. An earlier version of this Article was delivered at the Seminar on Comparative Legal Education in Perugia, Italy, in October, 1973. I am indebted to Professor Alessandro Giuliani, who organized the Seminar, for his invaluable help and to the other participants in the seminar for their thoughtful comments.

† B.S. 1943, University of Portland; M.S. 1944, J.D. 1947, University of Notre Dame; LL.M. 1951, J.S.D. 1955, New York University. Sweitzer Professor of Law, Stanford University.

One difficulty is that there is no single system of legal education in civil law nations. Legal education in Italy is not exactly like legal education in Germany or in Ecuador. Generalizations that one might validly make about legal education in France simply do not apply in Spain or Mexico. In this brief Essay I shall of necessity deal in generalities that are, by their nature, only partially accurate for any civil law nation. In deriving these generalizations, I shall depend primarily on my personal contact with legal education and legal educators in several civil law jurisdictions[1] and on a certain amount of hearsay about others. Similarly, legal education is not uniform throughout the common law world. In particular, legal education in England and in the United States are in many ways strikingly different; English legal education often seems more like that in Europe than that in the United States. Here again one must generalize, and this Essay will do so by referring primarily to legal education in the United States.[2]

Even within the United States there are significant variations among law schools. In part these differences are explainable by the large number of schools and their wide distribution among 50 quasi-sovereign states, Puerto Rico, and the District of Columbia, but other factors, described below, are also at work. One result is a universe of legal education in which there are a relatively few "leading" law schools and an informal but generally understood declining rank order below them. The tone is set by the leading schools, where one finds the best students, the most eminent faculty, the largest libraries, the most influential law reviews, the richest curricula (and extracurricula), and the most generous supporting facilities. Most of the other schools try to emulate them, but at a certain point their ability to do so becomes so attenuated that only superficial resemblances remain. The substance of what goes on in the name of legal education at a leading school is accordingly quite different from what goes on at many lesser schools. In describing legal education in the United States I will focus on the objectives and methods of the leading schools. As a result, the picture of American legal education drawn here represents an ideal which only a few schools—possibly 10 or 12—approach. The remaining 200 or so depart more or less drastically from the model in practice, but it is significant that most of them accept that model, seek to conform to it, and regard their deviation from it as an undesirable condition.[3]

---

1. That contact has been most intensive and prolonged in Italy, over a period beginning in 1961 and continuing today, and in Chile from 1966 to 1969, as consultant to the Ford Foundation and the International Legal Center and as Director of the Stanford-Chile Seminar on Legal Education. Contact with legal education has been less intensive, but still direct and significant in Colombia, Costa Rica, France, Germany, Greece, Mexico, and Peru.

2. Much of what is said will also be applicable to some extent to legal education in Canada, Australia, and New Zealand, where there has been a significant tendency to adopt the main features of American legal education.

3. For additional discussions of legal education in the United States, see Currie, *The Materials of Law Study*, 8 J. LEGAL ED. 1 (1955); Stevens, *Law Schools and Law Students*, 59 VA. L. REV. 551

I. HIGHER EDUCATION: THREE FUNDAMENTAL DIFFERENCES

There are certain fundamental differences between the systems of higher education in the United States and those in most civil law countries, and these differences strongly affect the two systems of legal education. I will discuss three such fundamental differences, the first of which might be summed up in the terms "democracy" and "meritocracy." In a sense this first difference results from two major inconsistent forces in higher education: on the one hand there is a desire to make higher education available to everyone without distinction; on the other there is the desire to make the university a place in which academic merit is recognized and rewarded. One ideal leads to the conception of the mass university; the other to the university in which admission and advancement are controlled on the basis of academic aptitude and performance. It is my observation that universities in the civil law world lean in the democratic direction, while meritocracy is the dominant ideal in American universities.[4] This is not to say that merit is totally ignored or devalued in the civil law world, nor that American universities ignore democratic considerations; it is only to suggest a significant difference in emphasis.

Thus, the Faculty of Law at the University of Rome has 12,000 to 15,000 students, while the Stanford Law School has a student body of 450. The difference arises in part from the power of American law schools to exclude applicants on the basis of merit. In a single year Stanford Law School has received more than 3,000 applications for admission, and of these it can admit only 160 and still retain its present size. The principal determinants for admission are totally academic: the student's score on a nationally administered Law School Aptitude Test and the grades received by the student in his undergraduate university education. The American law school does not admit every applicant who meets certain minimum standards; every applicant is in competition with every other applicant for a limited number of spaces, and those with the highest academic qualifications are the ones chosen.

An enormous amount of administrative and faculty time is spent in re-

(1973); Stevens, *Two Cheers for 1870: The American Law School*, in 5 PERSPECTIVES IN AMERICAN HISTORY 405 (C. Fleming & B. Bailyn eds. 1951); PROCEEDINGS OF ASSN. OF AM. L. SCHOOLS, 1971 ANNUAL MEETING, TRAINING FOR THE PUBLIC PROFESSIONS OF THE LAW pt. 1, § 2 [hereinafter cited as THE CARRINGTON REPORT]. For a thoroughly disenchanted view *see* Kennedy, *How the Law School Fails: A Polemic*, 1 YALE REV. L. & SOC. ACTION 71 (1970). For comparative discussions *see* C. EISENMANN, THE UNIVERSITY TEACHING OF SOCIAL SCIENCES: LAW. (rev. ed. 1973); E. SCHWEINBURG, LAW TRAINING IN CONTINENTAL EUROPE, ITS PRINCIPLES AND PUBLIC FUNCTION (1954). Additional readings will be found in D. DJONOVICH, LEGAL EDUCATION: A SELECTIVE BIBLIOGRAPHY (1970); and in C. SZLADITS, BIBLIOGRAPHY OF FOREIGN AND COMPARATIVE LAW (1955, 1962, 1968, Supps. 1970 & 1971).

4. On the increasingly meritocratic character of higher education in the United States, particularly in the professional schools, *see* C. JENCKS & D. RIESMAN, THE ACADEMIC REVOLUTION ch. 1 (1968); Riesman, *Notes on Meritocracy*, DAEDALUS, June 1967, at 897–908.

viewing and evaluating applications for admission in the effort to select
the best possible group of first-year students from the pool of applicants.
It is common for students to apply to several law schools, since they have
no certainty of being accepted at any of them. Because of the competition
among law schools for the best students, and the desire of the best students
to go to the more eminent schools, a student who is denied admission at
Harvard or Yale or Stanford may be admitted to some less highly regarded
school. Thus, there is a tendency for the academic quality of student bodies
to be stratified according to the national reputations of the schools. The
cycle is, to some extent, self-perpetuating, since one of the important factors
in the reputation of a law school is the quality of its student body. Thus,
although there is likely to be a place in some law school for almost any
student, the best students go to the best schools and get the best legal education and move more easily into the best careers.

The situation in many civil law universities is entirely different. There
anyone who has completed certain formal prerequisites and has survived
a certain number of years of prior education is automatically admitted to
the university and to the faculty of law.[5] In the post–World War II period
of mounting affluence, rising expectations, the extension of public primary
and secondary education to greater numbers of people, and the greater
democratization of society in such nations, the old economic and social barriers to university education lost much of their effectiveness. Suddenly,
great floods of students descended on universities with inadequate numbers
of faculty and inadequate libraries, classrooms, and other physical facilities.
This phenomenon provides a partial explanation of the student upheavals
in Paris and other parts of Europe in 1968: too few universities with too
few resources submerged by thousands of students. An adequate explanation of the situation of students in civil law universities would be extremely
complex, but as this example shows, the democratic principle—the notion
that the student is, at a certain stage of his education, entitled as of right to
admission to the university—is an important component of it.

Even among those who favor academic meritocracy, there is wide recognition that it can compound social injustice. Many young people never
reach the point of applying to or attending a university, or of applying to
law school, out of economic or social disadvantage. One's performance on
a Law School Aptitude Test and in an undergraduate university are, to
some extent, functions of one's social and economic background. Even those
who succeed in breaking out of the poverty cycle or surmounting the dis-

---

5. Of course, the flow of students to the civil law university is conditioned by factors that distinguish it from that in the United States: a more rigorous and demanding system of secondary education, and a socio-economic structure that have tended historically to limit access to the university to
a relatively small group (or class) of the population.

advantages imposed on them by racial or social prejudice often begin with a serious handicap. They, unlike more wealthy, more fully assimilated competitors, may have had inferior primary and secondary educational experiences, and may have come from families in which there was little of the sort of intellectual stimulation—little opportunity to develop the kind of reflective minds and studious habits—that university education values. Even though reliance on merit as a criterion for admission to the university is not intended to be undemocratic, meritocracy can operate in an undemocratic way.

This problem has received much attention in the United States in recent years. Universities first attempted to provide enough money to enable poor students to attend their institutions (all of which charge tuition fees and the best of which charge very substantial fees. In most civil law universities, consistent with the democratic approach described above, tuition fees are extremely low and do not in themselves exclude many students). The stated ideal at this stage was that *qualified* students should not be excluded from attending the university by financial considerations. The next major step was an attempt to do something about the possible injustices concealed by the term "qualified." This was accomplished in part by such direct methods as discrimination in the admission process in favor of members of identifiable disadvantaged groups. A more fundamental attack on the same problem attempts to provide equality of opportunity through equal access to quality primary and secondary education and through elimination of poverty, discrimination, and social disadvantage. Some progress has been made, but the injustice inherent in a system of meritocracy in a society in which wealth and prior educational opportunity are unequally distributed is far from completely solved. The continued emphasis on quality itself limits the options; no law school has abandoned academic merit as the basic criterion of admission. Certain minor concessions are made, but most law schools still hope to meet their social obligation by admitting "qualified" minority students. The lack of emphasis on merit in civil law universities greatly reduces the significance of this problem.

A second distinguishing feature of higher education in the civil law world is the minor role played by private universities. Indeed, in most civil law nations private universities do not exist.[6] Instead, universities are maintained and are subject to control by the state, usually through the same ministry that has the responsibility for public elementary and secondary education. In the United States, on the contrary, both private and public uni-

---

6. By private I mean universities supported and maintained primarily by private funds, and not administered under the direct supervision of governmental officials. Private universities in the United States may, and do, seek grants from governmental as well as private sources to finance specific programs.

versities compete with each other for faculty and students, as well as for gifts and grants from individuals, corporations, foundations, and government sources. In this competition, the private universities occupy a position of leadership and have done so throughout the history of the nation. There are excellent and influential public universities, but as a general proposition the private universities set the standard for higher education.

Because the private university is not subject to anything but the most limited form of governmental supervision, it has more freedom to experiment, to innovate, and in general to progress. The autonomy of private universities leads in turn to greater freedom for public universities. Since the major private universities provide the leadership for all of higher education, the other universities, including the public ones, tend to emulate them. Any attempt to establish rigid control over the policies, faculty, curricula, and operations of public universities is met with the objection that such controls will put them at a disadvantage in the competition with private universities and lead in the end to deterioration of the public university. In this way, the autonomy of the private university helps to maintain the autonomy of the public university. The emphasis of the private university upon excellence—that is to say on meritocracy—makes it necessary for the public university to do the same. Otherwise it will lose out in the competition for students, faculty, funds, and prestige. These are powerful considerations.

In a number of civil law nations none but the most trivial reforms seems to be possible without ministerial, and sometimes legislative, action at the highest levels. Uniformity is the rule, so that policies adopted for one university extend to all. The notion of the dynamic university, constantly experimenting and progressing, does not exist. Nor does the notion of academic competition among universities, with each striving for leadership, for the best faculty and students, and for the most distinguished scholarship. Instead, one finds a relatively static and standardized university system.

A final major difference between American and civil law universities is the higher degree of self-consciousness in the United States about the objectives and methods of university education. This characteristic is particularly marked in the law schools. It is significant that a professional association (*The Association of American Law Schools*) and a professional journal (*The Journal of Legal Education* and its predecessor, *The American Law School Review*), concerned solely with legal education, its objectives, methods, and problems, have existed in the United States since the earliest years of the century. Only in common law law schools does one find continuous self-searching about what we are doing, why we are doing it, and how we might better do it. Most who teach in civil law universities are, by comparison, totally unconcerned with such issues. Questions about teaching objectives and methods are considered uninteresting or not open to discussion. One teaches as professors have always taught; one's purposes are the same purposes as they have always been; questions about such matters do not arise. In recent years, things have begun to change in a number of civil law jurisdictions,[7] but the trend is still uncommon.

An obsession with objectives and methods in legal education can easily become excessive, by diverting energy better directed toward other activities (such as scholarship) or problems (such as substantive questions). Still, one wonders about the vitality of a system in which such questions are not even asked. Society, after all, changes, and the legal system either changes with it or becomes increasingly archaic and irrelevant. In turn, the system of legal education either reflects the responses of the legal system to social change or degenerates into something artificial, useless, and perhaps even socially harmful. In a society undergoing substantial change, legal education should be in constant flux.[8]

II. THE GOALS OF LEGAL EDUCATION

The objectives of legal education in the two systems are vastly different. This can be shown through a few generalizations that oversimplify but may be sufficiently instructive to justify the risk. First, legal education in the civil law world is, at bottom, general education, not professional education. It is true that many civil law faculties include some instruction of a technical or professional nature, but courses of this kind typically are recent minor additions to a corpus that is fundamentally liberal in character and outlook. It is not anticipated that all, or even most, of those who attend the faculty of law will become advocates or judges or notaries. Law is merely one of the curricula available to undergraduate students.

This is one reason why legal education in civil law universities seems to

---

7. This trend is most prominent in Latin America, where a variety of programs for reform of legal education have been instituted. The most far-reaching is under way in Chile. All Chilean law faculties are involved in the reform, and their efforts are supported and coordinated through the interuniversity Instituto de Docencia y Investigaciones Juridicas in Santiago. The Instituto is in part an outgrowth of the Stanford-Chile Seminars on Legal Education. In Chile the principal directions of reform are: conversion to active teaching methods; appointment of full-time professors; building law libraries capable of supporting research; increasing the curricular demands on students; expanding the extracurriculum; encouraging empirical and socially responsive research.

Other significant reform efforts are going on in Peru, at the Pontifical Catholic University in Lima, and in Costa Rica. It is unclear whether related efforts at reform in Colombia and Brazil have had any significant effect on legal education in those countries.

8. One who believes that law is immutable will resist the suggestion that the objectives and methods of legal education need periodic reexamination. One who sees law primarily as a conservative, stabilizing social force will find it easier to believe that law is immutable. And one who is by nature or preference conservative will find it easier to see law as a conservative, stabilizing force. Accordingly it is not surprising that the pressure for reform of legal education in civil law countries, where it exists at all, tends to come more from the center or left than from the right.

us to be comparatively "nonprofessional" or "nontechnical." Any movement in the direction of technical or professional education is a movement away from the paradigm. Thus, instruction in civil law faculties is more abstract, more concerned with questions of philosophic than immediate practical importance, more removed from the solution of social problems. University legal education in England shares these characteristics; in this respect it is more like the legal education in the typical European or Latin American university than that in most American law schools. In England and on the Continent the professional side is taken care of after the university: in the *Referendarzeit*, or in apprenticeship with a solicitor, advocate, or notary, or in special advanced professional schools for administrators or judges.

In the United States, legal education is primarily professional education, with some admixture of nonprofessional elements. In part this difference is structural: here legal education is *graduate* education, something undertaken *after* completion of the undergraduate degree requirement. Law is not regularly taught in the university as a liberal or humane subject, or as a social science. One obvious disadvantage of such a system is that the great mass of undergraduates leave the university without any organized exposure to the legal system. Virtually no courses are available for the student who wishes to learn about the legal system, but does not want to spend the additional years in law school.[9]

Recent developments have tended to blur the distinction between liberal or nonprofessional—university legal education in the civil law world and professional legal education in the United States. The introduction of *travaux pratiques* (meetings with teaching assistants to discuss concrete cases as a supplement to the theoretical lectures given by the professor) in France and a number of Latin American universities is only one example of the many ways in which the purity of a liberal legal education is impaired in the civil law world. American law schools continue to demonstrate growing interest in the study of law from the perspectives of the social sciences and the humanities, not merely as desirable components of the education of professional lawyers but in and for themselves.

A second generalization about the objectives of legal education might be put as follows: In the civil law world the practicing lawyer or judge is seen as a technician, as the operator of a machine designed and built by others. In the United States, the practicing lawyer or judge is seen as a sort

9. There has been a good deal of concern about this lacuna and a variety of attempts to deal with it. Currently the tendency is for professors in the law schools to offer occasional undergraduate courses in law. No one is convinced that this satisfies the need, and in all probability more ambitious programs—perhaps even undergraduate majors in law—will soon appear.

of social engineer, as a person specially equipped to perceive and attempt to solve social problems. Lawyers in the United States gravitate toward positions of responsibility in government and the private sector. The advice they give frequently extends beyond technical legal questions to consideration of the broader consequences of alternative forms of action and to advice on how to anticipate and deal with such consequences. Lawyers are seen as key elements of social reform, as experts on making new social programs work.

In other words, the lawyer in the United States is seen as a kind of omnicompetent problem-solver, and the system of legal education, with the self-consciousness described above, earnestly tries to prepare him for this kind of social role. In civil law countries, even though lawyers tend to occupy the same positions in government and in the private sector as they do in the United States, there seems to be less general understanding of this fact and little interest in relating it to legal education. The professional lawyer is thought of as a technician who does important but uncreative and narrowly professional work. Such a view affects civil law legal education in two significant ways: it justifies the prejudice of law faculties who ignore professional training as beneath their dignity and prefer instead to emphasize law as a liberal study; it also reinforces the tendency to approach professional training, wherever it is carried out, as technical education.[10]

A third general difference can best be illustrated by a look at the character of legal scholarship in the two systems. In the civil law tradition, legal scholarship is pure and abstract, relatively unconcerned with the solution of concrete social problems or with the operation of legal institutions. The principal object of such scholarship is to build a theory or science of law. In its most extreme form such scholarship displays a detachment from society, people, and their problems that astonishes a common lawyer. On the common law side, we tend to think of the work of legal scholarship as another aspect of social engineering; it is our business as scholars to monitor the operating legal order, to criticize it, and to make recommendations for its improvement. Improvement, to us, means coping more adequately with concrete social problems. Our outlook is professional. These diverse attitudes, expressed in the form of legal scholarship, are also expressed in the content of legal education itself, since the scholars are, almost without exception, professors. In this way the minds of lawyers in the two systems are trained in ways that are fundamentally quite different.

---

10. Legal educators in the United States are accustomed to hearing from the practicing bar that law schools are too theoretical, too remote from practice. It all depends on the point of view. To a civil law professor our legal education looks much too pragmatic and professional, sadly weak on theory and "culture."

III. Professors

One can also sharply contrast the role played by the law professor. The law professor in the United States generally spends his working time at the law school, in the classroom and in his office. His office there is his study; that is where he does his writing, prepares for class, and meets with students and colleagues. His presence there makes him more available to students and encourages faculty-student contact outside of class. The number of faculty, when compared to the number of students, produces a ratio that encourages small classes and a more personal relationship between professor and student than in the civil law counterpart.

The contrast with law faculties in civil law nations is striking. In most of them (Germany is a major exception), the concept of a full-time professor is relatively unfamiliar. The professor comes to the law school to deliver his lecture and leaves when it is finished. Outside of his actual time in class he is seldom seen at the school and he is not expected to be there. Confronted by an enormous number of students, it is almost impossible for the professor to become familiar with them, even if he had the time and the inclination. At the end of the class, both he and the student leave the university.

The American professor's continual presence at the law school deeply affects collegial life. It is easy to find a colleague to talk to about an interesting problem or to get an authoritative reaction to an idea. The situation permits spontaneity and informality, encourages collaboration in teaching and research, and offers easy accessibility to a wide range of interests and expertise. The result is a natural tendency toward "horizontal" or collegial, scholarly, and personal relationships that is lacking in many civil law universities. There one more typically finds a hierarchical or vertical pattern. At the top is the professor who occupies the chair. Arrayed beneath him are junior colleagues, assistants, and researchers. Communication habitually runs vertically within the *cathedra.*

The full-time nature of law teaching in America tends to produce a substantial number of professors who maintain little, if any, direct contact with the practice of law. In most civil law jurisdictions, however, professors carry on law practice or engage in other careers; teaching is viewed as an accessory activity. Stipends reflect this difference: in the United States law professors are paid enough to support themselves without the necessity for additional income. But in Chile and Italy, for example, the pay for university law teaching is low because it is anticipated that the professor will devote a major portion of his time to law practice or some other remunerative career. Indeed, in some civil law nations the position of professor in the faculty of law is more important for the prestige (and the additional business) it provides than for the professorial stipend.

The organization of civil and common law law schools is another area of substantial difference. The typical civil law university is composed of a group of "faculties." Each faculty, in turn, is a collection of "chairs" or "*cathedra*" occupied by senior professors. Occupancy of a *cathedra* in a law faculty carries with it the direction of an institute, with its own budget, staff rooms and library, and the right to a certain number of younger assistants interested in academic careers. The assistants help the professor in his teaching and research. Where the professor maintains an active professional practice, his academic assistants are also likely to be his junior law associates. If he is engaged in a political career, his academic assistants will be part of his political staff. The professor is expected to promote the interests of his assistants, particularly to assist them in their academic careers. This system makes the senior professor lord of a substantial domain and gives him great power over the lives of his assistants and his staff. Indeed it is common to speak of the professor as a "baron" and to complain (if one is an impatient young scholar with unfulfilled academic aspirations) of the "baronial system."

American law schools are organized in a different way. Professors do not have their own institutes or retinues of assistants. Libraries, research funds, secretarial assistance, and the like are centrally administered by a strong dean. It is only in the case of a special grant from a foundation or a government agency for a substantial research project to be carried on by an identified professor that the tendency toward creation of an institute appears. On the whole, such tendencies have been resisted. Although institutes or their equivalents occasionally appear in American law schools, they are generally regarded with suspicion. The habit of central administration by a strong dean, a quite different tradition of recruitment of law professors, the emphasis on collegiality within the law schools, a different approach to teaching and to scholarship, all reinforce the resistance of American law schools to the establishment of institutes.

IV. CURRICULA AND TEACHING METHODS

The curricula of American law schools typically include a few prescribed courses and a large number of electives covering a broad range of subject matters. By comparison, the curricula at civil law universities tend to be much more limited, both in the number and in the scope of courses offered, and tend to include few electives. In part this difference may follow from the fact that the civil law faculty is less oriented toward professional training, and therefore less concerned with providing opportunities to study the nuances of various professional specializations. Another possible explanation is the greater freedom of American law schools to innovate and to experiment, unrestricted by an official policy of conformity or by the necessity for prior governmental approval of proposed reforms. Still another reason might be that the culture of the civil law takes a narrower, more restricted view of the nature of law and of the function of the lawyer in society, so that the conceptual limits on what seems appropriate for a law faculty curriculum are narrower.

There is yet another, more fundamental, basis for the difference. It is the belief, still widely held in the civil law world, that law is a science. From this it follows that the purpose of legal education is to instruct the students in the elements of the science. Such an approach tends to be dogmatic. The truth is known by the professor and is communicated to the students. There are, of course, disputes among scholars, and on some points one can find two or more theories that are sufficiently significant to deserve mention. But on the whole, the general structure, the broad outlines, are thought to be established. There are recognized categories. The law is divided into agreed subdivisions, which are taught as courses. The area of doubt is so narrow as to be imperceptible. Blessed with such certainty, the civil law feels less need for innovation and experimentation.

One could develop a surprising number of possible conclusions from this observation about the relative richness of the curriculum and the relative availability to students of options in the two systems. What does it tell us about the extent to which students are perceived as responsible individuals, capable of choosing intelligently among a variety of optional courses? Is this persuasive evidence that the development of new legal problems, as a consequence of social change, is only dimly perceived within the faculties of law in civil law universities? Or is it in part a matter, again, of chairs and institutes? To establish a new course may mean establishing a new *cathedra*—a new group of baronies; this is a grave step, and its accomplishment in the complex and slow-moving bureaucracy of nationally administered systems of higher education is risky and laborious.

Whatever the reasons, the tendency is for curricula in law faculties in civil law jurisdictions to be much more limited, more traditional, less responsive to social change, and less tentative and searching. The tentative nature of much of what is taught in the American law school deserves an additional comment.

American law schools have, over the last three decades, drastically reduced the proportion of the 3-year curriculum that is prescribed and have given the student an increasing opportunity (and obligation) to decide for himself which courses to take among a large body of available elective offerings during the remaining 2 years or so of law school. In one sense this movement reflects a loss of certainty among American legal educators about the substance of a proper legal education. It is not clear to us that all students should be required to take trusts and estates, or labor law, or international business transactions. As the area of doubt increases, the area of certainty—indicated by the required part of the curriculum—contracts.

In the civil law world, the educational focus is primarily on substance; method is deemphasized. In the United States, we are of course concerned about what we teach; but the emphasis is less on what is taught and more on how it is taught. We are concerned about developing certain qualities in the student: skill in legal analysis, the ability to distinguish the relevant from the irrelevant, the ability to deal with a large mass of facts in an authoritative way, the ability to put together careful and persuasive arguments on any side of a legal question, the ability to think usefully and constructively about social problems and their solution. Of course the student needs to be familiar with the existing law before he can responsibly discuss its application to concrete social questions, but we see that as the easy part. Rather than devote valuable class time to discussing what the law is, we expect the students to be familiar with it through prior reading. We focus, instead, on how it does or does not work, on its implications, on the social reality out of which it grew, and so on.

Our objectives accordingly raise important questions of method. How can we prepare students to deal thoughtfully, responsibly, and usefully with the kinds of social problems that will come before them as they assume public and private positions of leadership? The traditional system of education in civil law universities obviously assumes a different function: The professor lectures; the students listen. That system is clearly designed to convey information to the student. The information is substantive knowledge. There is little concern with method of the sort that preoccupies American law teachers.

There is a commonly held, but quite incorrect, notion that a case system or case method is the dominant method of instruction in American universities. This notion is particularly popular among foreigners who discuss our legal education, although it is also held by a surprisingly large number of Americans. In fact, there is no case method. It is true that we study cases, among other things, in law schools; but it is not true that we study all cases for the same reasons or in the same ways. Nor do we study only cases; we also study statutory and administrative materials and have an immense doctrinal literature that is heavily used in teaching.

Those in civil law nations who think that all American law schools teach by the case method share a number of incorrect assumptions. One of the most common of these is that we study cases because that is where the law is found. The common law, so the reasoning goes, is based on the principle of stare decisis. The law grows out of the decision of cases. Accordingly, in the common law country one studies cases, just as in the civil law nations one studies codes, because they are the prime sources of law. There is some truth in this, but only a small amount. Actually, to read a case is a very inefficient way to learn a rule of law. If all one is seeking is the rule, it is much easier to read it in a hornbook, and indeed our students frequently do this.

A second, somewhat more sophisticated view held by a number of civil lawyers is that we read cases for reasons analogous to the assumptions of traditional continental legal science: that one can abstract legal principles from specific legal rules, extract even broader principles from those derived by the first level of abstraction, and, by continuing the process, eventually produce a "general theory of law." Applying this notion to the common law world, one would study cases as the basic unit, draw from individual cases the broader principles of which they are specific manifestations, and so on up the scale, thus producing a general theory of law. In either tradition the data one works with are the naturally occurring materials of the law: in the civil law world, primarily statutes; in the common law world, primarily cases. Actually there was a period in American scholarship when such a view was prominent. Professor Langdell used such ideas to justify introducing the study of cases at Harvard in the 1870's. To a certain extent the great treatises of Williston and Wigmore and the *Restatement of the Law* are representations of this point of view. More recently the project undertaken by Professor Schlesinger of Cornell and colleagues on the "common core of legal systems" has sought to apply similar reasoning in the field of comparative law. (It has stayed alive in comparative law only because that field has a European, rather than American, center of gravity and is still dominated by European ideas.) This "scientific" rationale for the study of cases, however, was rather convincingly destroyed by the legal realists.[11] In any event, legal science never had a very large following in the United States, and it is doubtful that the writers of the great treatises or the drafters of the *Restatement of the Law* perceived themselves as en-

11. The attacks of the realists on the *Restatement* provide one of the few examples in American legal literature of the sort of academic mayhem that is relatively common in Europe (and in non-legal fields in the United States). *See, e.g.,* T. ARNOLD, THE SYMBOLS OF GOVERNMENT 25, 51 (1935); C. CLARK, REAL COVENANTS AND OTHER INTERESTS WHICH "RUN WITH THE LAND" (2d ed. 1947); Green, *The Torts Restatement,* 29 ILL. L. REV. 582 (1935); Lorenzen & Heilman, *The Restatement of the Conflict of Laws,* 83 U. PA. L. REV. 555 (1935); Patterson, *The Restatement of the Law of Contracts,* 33 COLUM. L. REV. 397 (1933); Radin, *Contract Obligation and the Human Will,* 43 COLUM. L. REV. 575 (1943); Sims, *The Law of Real Covenants: Exceptions to the Restatement of the Subject by the American Law Institute,* 30 CORNELL L.Q. 1 (1944); Yntema, *The Restatement of the Law of Conflict of Laws,* 36 COLUM. L. REV. 183 (1936). For more general expressions of antipathy toward the attitudes they saw represented in the *Restatement* and the great treatises, *see* J. FRANK, COURTS ON TRIAL (1949); L. GREEN, JUDGE AND JURY (1930); Llewellyn, *A Realistic Jurisprudence—The Next Step,* 30 COLUM. L. REV. 431 (1930); Llewellyn, *Some Realism about Realism—Responding to Dean Pound,* 44 HARV. L. REV. 1222 (1931).

gaged in what was essentially a 19th-century European scholarly movement. Accordingly, the "legal science" rationale for studying cases in American law schools does not today command much support. Even where something of the sort appears to exist, it is likely to go on totally without consciousness of its similarity to the much more sophisticated and articulated tradition of European legal science.

Why then do we study cases, if not to learn the rules of law or to build a general theory of law? There seem to be three important reasons. The first, and most important, is that the case is an example of the legal process at work. When one reads the case, as cases are reported in our tradition, one encounters the facts out of which the litigation arose, the way in which these facts were resolved into legal questions, the allegations and arguments of opposing counsel concerning their proper solution, and the way the court dealt with them to achieve a decision. One studies cases in order to become familiar with the process, to learn how the legal system operates. To refer to an earlier distinction, the emphasis is not on substance but on method.

It is true that cases reflect only part of the legal system at work.[12] That is why we also study legislative, administrative, and scholarly materials. Still, in the American system, the judge is the protagonist, the hero of our legal tradition. We perceive judicial activity to be central to the legal system, and accordingly we spend a great part of our effort in observing and learning from that process at work.

A second reason for studying cases in American law schools is that each case is a piece of social history. The study of judicial decisions for 3 years builds in the student a reservoir of familiarity with incidents in our social history, some great and far-reaching, some relatively modest. This gives the student a feeling of contact with the culture, of having seen the concrete social circumstances to which the law must respond. Frequently the parties are individuals with whom the student can identify and sympathize. It is easy to take a warm, personal interest in such cases, and to develop opinions as to the way the law operates. Was the result just? Should the legal system produce the kind of outcome that this case illustrates? What changes in the legal system should be made in order to prevent the recurrence of such results?

In many parts of the civil law world, that sort of case study is impossible or very difficult. Judicial decisions are published, if they are published at

---

12. It is also true that the cases are almost solely appellate cases in a system in which the parties are not entitled to review of the facts found in the trial. Accordingly, the facts stated in the opinion are those abstracted from real life by the parties, their counsel, and the trier of fact at the trial, further limited by the kind of trial record kept, the restrictions of the appellate process, the tactical decisions of the parties and their lawyers, and reduced further by the appellate judge in selecting the facts to be stated in his opinion. Still, despite these restrictions and distortions, the typical reported decision in the United States is much richer and fuller in facts than its civil law counterpart.

all, in a form that appears emasculated to an American lawyer: the facts are omitted or sharply reduced and the process of judgment is made to seem abstract, mechanical, and inhuman. The civil lawyer could respond that his system of reporting judicial decisions represents greater objectivity, provides less temptation to succumb to the human aspects of the case and to endanger the purity and objectivity of the law. (Whether such legal purity and objectivity are possible or desirable is another discourse that cannot be pursued here.) In response, the argument could be made that constant exposure to this sort of temptation as a law student may produce lawyers and judges who are less likely to succumb to its dangers and more likely to make intelligent use of the nuances and richness of social texture it provides in their professional careers.

We also study cases because they are difficult. They are difficult, first, because it takes a good deal of concentration to understand cases, to master them to the point at which informed discussion of them can begin. But there is another, more important kind of difficulty: it is the difficulty faced by the judge when the problem before him seems to provide no possibility of easy solution, when he is confronted by parties, both of whom can reasonably argue that justice is on their side. Often, in such cases, the law is unclear; there is no easy answer. Still, the judge must decide. It is good for students of the law to confront this difficulty early in their careers; they will have to live with it throughout their professional lives. At the extreme, a civil law legal education makes the student impatient with facts, unwilling to face disorder, unprepared for the encounter with the concrete. Ours immerses the student in such realities from the start.

The fundamental differences between the traditions of teaching can be reduced to two. First, American legal education assumes that the student has studied assigned material before the class. In the civil law world, it is assumed that the student has not studied in advance of class; indeed, the main purpose of the lecture is to instruct him, to transfer basic knowledge to him. Second, in the United States the student is expected to participate actively in class discussion. Again, the contrast with law schools in the civil law world is clear. There the student does not participate; he is a passive, receiving object. The professor talks; the student listens.

The two differences are obviously related; one cannot expect unprepared students to discuss complex legal materials with which they are unfamiliar. Accordingly, it is necessary that they have studied them in advance. Then, in the American classroom we ask questions to test their knowledge of the facts of the case, the content and purpose of the statute, or the argument made by the author of the article. Students are encouraged to take a critical view of what they have read; we ask them whether the outcome of a case would have changed if the facts were varied in certain ways; we ask them to discuss hypothetical cases, to suggest answers to hypothetical problems; we inquire whether the solution reached is a socially desirable one; and so on. The emphasis is on active participation in class by the students.

The reasons our methods differ so sharply relate to differences in university context and to divergences in attitude toward the objectives of legal education, the nature of legal scholarship, and the roles and functions of lawyers in the two systems. It bears repeating, however, that our objectives and methodology are not tied to judicial decisions. Our case law provides a rich, fascinating, and relevant body of study material, but equivalents or alternatives are certainly conceivable, and probably exist, in civil law nations. The active method does not necessarily presuppose the doctrine of stare decisis or the study of judicial decisions.

V. Students

I now turn to a range of less profound, but still significant, differences between the two systems of legal education. One is the fact that our student bodies are, on the whole, much smaller. At the Stanford Law School we have a total of approximately 450 students. The Harvard Law School, which is considered large by our standards, has approximately 1,500 students. In the civil law world one typically finds much larger student bodies. The University of Rome, with 12,000 or more, is not the most extreme example. At some point (or points) on a continuum between 450 and 12,000 students, the human dynamics of the process of legal education drastically change. There are important qualitative differences between large and small law schools flowing from the simple fact of different student body size.

Another significant point is that American law students are expected to be full-time students; they are expected to devote their full energies to their studies and not to engage in any other significant enterprise for the 3 years of law school.[13] In a number of civil law jurisdictions, attendance at the university faculty of law is very much a part-time undertaking. The difference can be exaggerated and is, in the end, one of degree, but the expectations of the two traditions are really quite different: in the United

---

13. This generalization must be qualified in two ways. First, there are part-time law schools in the United States. They normally offer courses in the evening, and the student normally must attend for 4 or 5 years in order to acquire the law degree after completing his university education. *See generally,* Association of American Law Schools, The AALS Study of Part-Time Legal Education (1972).

Second, even in the regular full-time law school it is not unusual for a number of ostensibly full-time students to hold part-time jobs. *See* Stevens, *supra* note 3, at 589–90.

States, our expectation that the students will be full time makes it reasonable for us to make greater demands on, and to maintain higher expectations of, their performance. Students' lives are expected to center around the law school. They are expected to be there not only to attend classes but to prepare for them, to work in the law library, and to involve themselves in law review or the other paracurricular organizations that seem to grow up around our law schools. In civil law universities, there is no such assumption and consequently no basis for such expectation. Frequently, if only because of inadequate classroom facilities, it is not even anticipated that the students will regularly attend classes.

A third unique feature of our system is that it places great responsibility on the student. One sign of this greater responsibility is the student-run law review, a phenomenon that exists at over a hundred law schools in the United States. This is a legal periodical, normally quarterly, which is entirely edited and published, and partly written, by law students. The tradition is for such reviews to be independent, free of faculty authority. It seems important that these students have power consistent with the responsibility they bear. We encourage them, we cooperate with them, we respond to their requests for advice and assistance, but they make the editorial decisions.

Law review experience is still the most prestigious component of what has become, at many law schools, an extremely rich extracurriculum. The student may choose from a variety of activities: trial and appellate moot court, legal aid and civil rights organizations, environmental law societies, international law journals. Such institutions are also student-initiated and student-run. Professors help (when they are asked) and activities are subsidized by law school funds or by gifts or grants solicited by the students themselves from foundations or private donors. The extracurriculum is an extremely important part of legal education for a substantial number of students in American law schools. There is nothing remotely comparable to it in European law faculties.

VI. CONCLUSION

The reader may have formed the impression by now that I consider legal education in the United States to be superior to that in most civil law universities.[14] That is a correct impression; ours is better. It is better because it has grander objectives; because it draws on the full time and energies of teacher and student; because it is concerned with human problems and their solution; because it engages students directly in the study and active discussion of such problems and of the process of their solution within the

---

14. Let me note that, as a comparative lawyer, I seldom make such judgments. On most qualitative comparisons between legal systems I would not even venture an opinion.

legal order; because it displays a higher opinion of the student and demands more of him; and because its conception of the work of the professional lawyer—and accordingly of the mission of legal education to prepare persons for that profession—is a much richer, more demanding, and more realistic one.

No one should infer from the preceding paragraph anything more than a judgment about a process and a tradition of legal education. It is not a judgment about people. The civil law world includes numbers of men and women of distinction and eminence who have somehow surmounted the barriers placed in their way by an inadequate and impoverished system of legal education. They are at least the equal, in every way, of the best of us. Conversely, many graduates of American law schools fail to justify the system. They lack scope, imagination, and the ability to deal productively with social problems. They are, and will always be, petty technicians. The wealth and the abundance of American legal education seem to have been wasted on them. No system of legal education can guarantee that the lawyers it produces will be great lawyers.

No one really knows how much effect education has on the student. One can always find instances of students who were apparently untouched by what would appear to be an enormously effective educational system. Others appear to surmount a weak legal education, to acquire in some mysterious way all those attributes that the system seemed to ignore or undervalue. Still, we must assume that education has some effect in a substantial number of cases. On that assumption, the common law education system seems to me to be more likely to produce the kind of lawyers society requires.

This does not mean, however, that American legal educators should be complacent. On the contrary, the real strength of the system in the past has rested on the fact that it was constantly under searching critical review by those responsible for it. The Carrington Report,[15] the Meyers Report,[16] and the Packer-Ehrlich Report[17] provide encouraging evidence that this tradition of critical self-examination is alive and well. The attitudes these studies express show no trace of complacency, no sense of superiority; the system is exposed as imperfect, in need of substantial reform. Since the authors are all law professors, they are in a position to do something: to change, to innovate, to abandon the field experiment, to take up the brilliant proposal. As law teachers they consciously bear the power and the responsi-

---

15. *Supra* note 3.
16. PROCEEDINGS, ASSN. OF AM. L. SCHOOLS, REPORT OF THE COMMITTEE ON CURRICULUM 7–38 (1968).
17. H. PACKER & T. EHRLICH, NEW DIRECTIONS IN LEGAL EDUCATION: A REPORT PREPARED FOR THE CARNEGIE COMMISSION ON HIGHER EDUCATION (1972).

bility to determine, and to re-determine, the form and substance of legal education. In civil law universities neither the power nor the responsibility is so consciously or conspicuously assumed by the law professors. On the contrary, most of them are unconcerned and uninterested. In the end, that may be the most significant difference of all.

The Covenant of Habitability and the American Law Institute

Charles J. Meyers*

At its May 1974 meeting, the American Law Institute approved in principle Tentative Draft No. 2 of the *Restatement of the Law, Second, Property*,[1] whose Reporter is the eminent scholar, Professor A. James Casner. That draft, which deals with a tenant's rights and remedies against the landlord, declares that a landlord has a general duty to provide habitable premises. It is the thesis of this Essay that the Institute's adoption of a warranty of habitability is unsound and should be reconsidered.

The duty of habitability is illustrated by the following hypothetical case:

> Landlord leases an apartment to Tenant on a month-to-month basis for $30 per month. The apartment is located in a slum and does not comply with the housing code in several important respects. Both Landlord and Tenant are aware of the violations but agree to enter into the lease anyway.[2]

Under the proposed *Restatement*, a court could hold that the landlord has breached a covenant of habitability, despite the agreement to the contrary, and the tenant would be entitled to any of five remedies: rescission, damages, rent abatement, application of the rent to eliminate the defects, or rent withholding. Moreover, the lease may not be subject to termination because of the defense of retaliatory eviction.

This Essay will begin with a description of the *Restatement*'s reasoning and will then present the case against the *Restatement*'s position.

I. The Restatement Rules

A. *The Duty of Habitability*

The substantive duty of the landlord is set forth in Chapter 5 of the *Restatement* draft. Section 5.1 states the black-letter rule for residential premises in substandard condition on the date the lease is made and at the time the tenant takes possession:

---

* B.A. 1949, Rice University; LL.B. 1949, University of Texas; LL.M. 1953, J.S.D. 1964, Columbia University. Charles A. Beardsley Professor of Law, Stanford University. Member of the American Law Institute.
    1. Restatement (Second) of Property, Landlord and Tenant (Tent. Draft No. 2, 1974) [hereinafter cited as Property Restatement].
    2. This hypothetical case parallels *id.* § 5.1, illustration 2, at 60.

Except to the extent the parties to a lease validly agree otherwise, there is a breach of the landlord's obligations if the parties contemplate that the leased property will be used for residential purposes and on the date the lease is made and on the date the tenant is entitled to possession, the leased property, through no fault of the tenant, is not suitable for residential use.[3]

The justification for the duty of habitability is stated in comment *b* on the section:[4] (1) Unlike the agrarian tenant for whom the common law rule was fashioned, the modern residential tenant "is seldom able to conduct an inspection of sufficient depth to discover even major defects."[5] Recognizing, however, the weaknesses of this rationale since most slum housing defects are open and obvious to the prospective tenant, the comment continues: (2) "In addition, when hidden defects become known, they are seldom within the ability of the tenant to repair."[6] This assertion is based on several empirically unvalidated assumptions. The language may mean to assert that the contemporary residential tenant lacks the financial ability to make repairs but that the landlord has that ability. Alternatively, the *Restatement* may be arguing that most needed repairs fall into one of two classes: (1) those which allow the landlord to take advantage of economies of scale or (2) those which only the landlord can perform (*e.g.*, defects in the heating system).[7] The housing shortage in urban areas is offered as a further justification for the habitability duty:

The harshness of the *caveat emptor* approach is magnified many times in the case of the urban residential tenant, who often finds himself with a severe shortage of adequate housing and therefore little or no bargaining power. To postulate that

---

3. The same duty applies to premises that are in satisfactory condition when the lease is made and thereafter deteriorate either before the tenant takes possession or while he is in possession. *Id.* §§ 5.2, 5.4. Since the concern of this Essay is with slum housing, the focus will be on § 5.1, the archetypal case of housing in bad condition at the outset of the landlord-tenant relationship.

4. *Id.* § 5.1, comment *b*, at 57.

5. *Id.*

6. *Id.*

7. No data are cited by the *Property Restatement* in support of the proposition that landlords personally have a greater ability to make repairs than tenants; neither has the author of this Essay been able to find any data in support or contradiction of the proposition. The only data apparently available merely deal with who makes repairs and even those data are scanty.

The most complete treatment of slum housing appears in G. STERNLIEB, THE TENEMENT LANDLORD (1966) and G. STERNLIEB & R. BURCHELL, RESIDENTIAL ABANDONMENT: THE TENEMENT LANDLORD REVISITED (1973) [hereinafter cited as RESIDENTIAL ABANDONMENT]. The latter book contains a comparison of practices and attitudes of owners of slum housing in Newark, New Jersey, over the time period 1964 to 1971. Data were obtained by in-depth interviews, which showed that in 1964, 8.8% of the respondents said they did practically all of the repairs themselves, while 62.6% said they rarely or never did repair work. In 1971, the number of respondents who said they rarely or never did repairs themselves barely changed (62.4%), while the number who did practically all their own repairs climbed to 23.1%. *Id.* at 85.

By strenuously stretching the *Property Restatement* language, one could construe it to assert that, in general, landlords in making repairs can achieve economies of scale that are unavailable to tenants, and hence the duty to repair should fall to the landlord. If the factual assertion were true, then it would be more efficient for landlords to make repairs than for tenants to do so. But again factual data are not available one way or the other. Moreover, allocating the duty to repair to landlord or tenant, depending on the availability of scale economies, assumes that repairs *should* be made and hence assumes the conclusion sought to be proved.

such a tenant has an opportunity to bargain with the landlord for repairs is un-realistic.[8]

Thus the comment seems to be saying: There is a housing shortage and tenants cannot through bargaining obtain "necessary" repairs from land-lords. Since poor tenants deserve better housing and since rich landlords can afford to provide it, the law should require it.

Two observations can be made about this rationale, both to be amplified in later sections of the Essay. On the basis of the limited empirical evidence available, one can question the portrayal of the owners of dilapidated prop-erty as rich and rapacious, the notorious slumlord so vital to the middle-class reformer's iconography of villainy.[9] But if it is true that rich slumlords are the typical owners of dilapidated rental property, it does not follow that placing the nonwaivable duty of repair upon them will improve urban housing conditions. The rich slumlord may be rich because as a profit-max-imizing man he does not invest his money in losing properties. If improv-ing slum property is uneconomical, the *Restatement* rule is hardly likely to change a landlord's behavior. Hence, though housing may be in short supply and though tenants may be poor and landlords rich, the duty of habitability may not change the bargaining position of tenants or improve the condition of rental housing. Whether or not it will do so depends on other considerations, primarily the rents that can be collected and the cost of repairs. In short, the *Restatement*'s rationale for the habitability duty is based on moral philosophy and distributive justice, but the objectives it seeks to achieve cannot be accomplished outside the narrow and perhaps selfish confines of economic behavior.[10]

B. *Waivability and Remedies*

Once the *Restatement* adopts the duty of habitability on moral grounds, the rules on the waivability of the duty, on remedies, and on lease termina-tion follow inexorably. Nonwaivability is accomplished by authorizing the court to declare "unconscionable" or "significantly against public pol-icy" a clause in the lease providing that the tenant takes the property as is.[11] The intent is to subject residential leases to close scrutiny with the expec-tation that waiver clauses will be held unenforceable in the case of slum

---

8. Property Restatement § 5.1, comment *b*, at 57.

9. Of the landlords questioned in Residential Abandonment, *supra* note 7, 47.2% stated that they had incomes of $11,000 a year or less and 31.1% reported incomes of $8,000 a year or less. *Id.* at 312.

10. And if the rationale depends on distributive justice, still another question arises: Why are landlords singled out as the class from whom wealth should be taken for redistribution to the poor? Even if landlords as a class are rich, so are entrepreneurs in other businesses, and they are not often the subject of wealth redistribution schemes. The nonwaivable duty of habitability would seem to be a welfare proposal that ought to be financed not by one class of citizens but by all taxpayers under a progressive income tax.

11. Property Restatement § 5.6.

housing. The inevitability of this conclusion flows from the moral rationale of the duty itself, as the comment itself states: "The mere elimination of the *caveat emptor* doctrine without appropriate curtailment of the freedom of the parties to agree to have it apply would accomplish little where the tenant has little or no bargaining power . . . . Consequently, the elimination of the doctrine as to residential leases is accompanied by some such curtailment (see § 5.6)."[12]

So it is with the remedies:

> Furthermore, little would be accomplished if the tenant's only remedy is to terminate the lease because in most cases the tenant would have no place to turn for other housing. Therefore, the elimination of the doctrine of *caveat emptor* is accompanied with the adoption of the doctrine of dependence of covenants, so that the tenant has options that enable him to go on with the lease, even though the landlord is in default as to the conditions of the leased premises, without being in default himself, when such options permit the tenant to refuse to perform his obligations under the lease.[13]

The invocation of the contract doctrine of dependency of covenants is mainly ornamental, for modern contract law does not support either the *Restatement*'s nonwaivable duty or its more extreme remedies. Contract law recognizes "as is" sales. Contract law does not recognize a sales-price abatement remedy comparable to the rent-abatement remedy of the *Restatement*. The moving force behind the *Restatement* is not contract law but the moral principle of redistribution of wealth from landlord to tenant.

A final, necessary step to implement the principle is to deny the landlord the power to terminate the lease when the tenant claims breach of duty and asserts his remedies. The entire structure collapses if, in the typical month-to-month lease of slum housing, the landlord can give a 30-day notice, terminate the tenancy, and evict the tenant. The present draft is not explicit on the subject, stating only, "His power to terminate the periodic lease of a rent-withholding tenant is, however, somewhat limited (see the section on Retaliatory Evictions § —)."[14] But the Reporter quite logically, and not surprisingly, affirmed at the May meeting that the doctrine of retaliatory eviction will protect the month-to-month tenant, for the rationale that sustains the imposition of the landlord's duty, denies to the parties the power to waive the duty, and allows the tenant to abate or withhold the rent also requires that the tenant be allowed to remain in possession after asserting the landlord's default.

A closer look at the remedies is now in order. Damages are provided

---

12. *Id.* § 5.1, comment *b*, at 57.
13. *Id.* at 58.
14. *Id.* § 10.3, comment *g*, at 277. The reference is forward to a section not yet submitted to the Institute.

for in Chapter 9, but as the *Restatement* implicitly recognizes, that remedy has little significance for the slum tenant. The important remedies, by which the tenant may remain in possession and reduce the rent, are contained in Chapter 10. Those remedies are threefold: abatement of the rent, application of the rent to repairs, and withholding rent.

The rent-abatement section (§ 10.1) must be quoted in full:

§ 10.1. Rent Abatement

When the tenant is entitled to an abatement in the rent, the amount of the abatement is to that proportion of the rent which the fair rental value after the event giving the right to abate bears to the fair rental value before such event. Such abatement is allowed until the default is eliminated or until the lease terminates, whichever first occurs.[15]

In response to a question, the Reporter explained this formula at the May meeting as follows:

Question: If the fair rental value of the premises in "suitable" condition (that is, in substantial compliance with the housing code) would be $100 a month, and if at the beginning of the tenancy the fair rental value of the premises in their existing, dilapidated condition is $20 a month, and if the contract rent is $30 a month, is the tenant entitled to reduce his rent by the amount of $24 a month to the sum of $6 a month? *Answer*: Yes.

Remarkable as this answer may seem, it is exactly what § 10.1 calls for. The section provides that

the amount of the abatement is to that proportion of the rent [$30] which the fair rental value after the event giving the right to abate [*read*: the fair rental value of deteriorated premises] bears to the fair rental value before such event [*read*: in "suitable" condition, or up to code].

Since that proportion on the figures assumed is $20 to $100 or 1:5, the contract rent is reduced to one-fifth of the agreed amount, or from $30 to $6 a month. If the tenant has paid more than $6 a month, he is entitled to recover the $24 excess; the section is not specific about the tenant's right to withhold all rent until the excess is recovered, but the point becomes moot under § 10.3, by which he can withhold all rent in any event. The rent-abatement remedy obtains as long as the defects remain uncorrected, or until the lease terminates, but as we have seen earlier, a slum tenancy (even from month-to-month) may not be terminable by the landlord because of the defense of retaliatory eviction.[16]

The second remedy is the application of the rent to repairs to make the

---

15. *Id.* § 10.1.

16. It is an open question under the *Restatement* whether a rent increase restoring the contract rent, followed by nonpayment, followed by an eviction proceeding, amounts to retaliatory eviction. If it does, then the *Restatement* is proposing rent control administered by courts, a substantial undertaking that ought to be made explicit. If, on the other hand, the rent increase is effective, then the abatement remedy is ineffective.

premises suitable for residential occupancy. The section (§ 10.2)[17] requires
notice to the landlord and makes the tenant's expenditures on repairs subject to judicial review on a standard of reasonableness.

The third remedy is rent withholding. Section 10.3 allows the tenant to
place the rent in escrow if the condition of the premises is unsuitable for
residential use.[18] Sections 10.1 and 10.3 are cumulative; the tenant may abate
the rent under the formula of § 10.1 and place the rent then due ($6 in the
example) in escrow until the defects are eliminated.[19] There is no provision
enabling the landlord to make withdrawals from the escrow to pay property taxes, insurance, mortgage charges, or maintenance expenses, and the
Reporter indicated at the May meeting that he did not favor such a privilege.[20]

The real thrust of the *Restatement* is most clearly and forthrightly stated
in comment *a* to § 10.3, which is quoted in full:

> *a. Rationale.* In the modern urban community, the indigent tenant may find
> himself forced to live in conditions dangerous to his life, health, or safety despite
> any covenants of repair, housing codes, or implied warranties of habitability which
> may exist for his benefit. The traditional remedy of constructive eviction which
> requires him to abandon the premises and look elsewhere for housing is often too
> costly for the indigent tenant and the available alternative housing is often sim-
> ilarly substandard. Chapters Five and Six give the tenant in various situations the
> right to stay where he is and to put pressure on his landlord by withholding the
> rent until the landlord eliminates the default that gives rise to the tenant's right
> to withhold the rent. The parties may agree that the remedy of rent withholding
> is not to be available and such agreement is valid unless it is unconscionable.[21]

The fudge factor of unconscionability applies to both the duty and the
remedies. While the courts may uphold waiver clauses, they are empowered
to set them aside, and the logic that drives both chapters 5 and 10 of the
Restatement would make the waivers unenforceable.

C. *Summary*

In summary, the *Restatement* declares that, regardless of the agreement
of the parties, a court may impose a new form of tenancy on landlords in
the following circumstances: A tenant leases a slum apartment at a market rent, fully aware of its defects, and moves in. Tenant may thereafter
abate part of the rental payments if there are serious housing code violations and deposit the remaining rent into escrow until the code violations
are remedied. Presumably the landlord cannot raise the rent, and the tenant,

17. PROPERTY RESTATEMENT § 10.2.
18. *Id.* § 10.3.
19. *Id.* § 10.1, comment *h*, at 254; *id.* § 10.2, comment *f*, at 267; *id.* § 10.3, comments *b–c*, at 275–76.
20. However, the landlord may use the money in escrow to cure the defect after giving proper assurances. *Id.* § 10.3, comment *g*, at 277.
21. *Id.* § 10.3, comment *a*, at 275.

making these payments, may remain in possession indefinitely if the land-lord does not correct the defects.

This result is said to be the consequence of abandoning the outmoded common law principle of the independence of covenants in leases and of adopting modern contract law. But the analogy to contract law is not close. A better characterization of the *Restatement* is a judicially imposed regulation of the residential rental business, with judges determining the suitability of housing for residential purposes and fixing rents (or no rent) in accordance with their determination of a property's fitness for occupation. The resulting legal interest in land may be described as a decisional (as opposed to statutory) tenancy for life, at the option of the tenant.[22]

This Essay takes the position that the *Restatement* position is unsound and should be reconsidered by the Institute. Two principal objections are raised against the *Restatement* position: (1) The legal system does not have the resources to administer the proposed new rules and (2) the new rules are more likely than not to make housing conditions worse, not better, as the Institute presumably expects.

Before turning to these objections, the state of the case authority should be discussed briefly. The Reporter has conscientiously and accurately collected the current case authority on the covenant of habitability, and the *Restatement* reflects the trend of the contemporary decisions on the question. While no reported decision known to the author has combined all of the rules to produce the case of a month-to-month tenant staying on indefinitely under the retaliatory eviction defense while paying no rent to the landlord under the withholding rule, a number of cases have imposed the nonwaivable duty of habitability on the landlord and have granted the remedy of rent abatement (with the possibility of the tenant paying no rent at all).[23] The objection to the *Restatement*, then, is not to the lack of some authority to support the black-letter rules but to the rules themselves. If the rules are unsound, if they produce bad social results, the Institute should reject them even if the emerging contemporary case law has embraced them. The Institute should not lend its authority to new rules just because they are new.

II. ADMINISTRATION OF THE RESTATEMENT RULES

Depending on the definition of habitability, there may be a minimum of 1.6 to 2.1 million substandard rental units in the United States.[24] What-

---

22. Even an optional tenancy for life may not be an accurate characterization: perhaps the tenant's family can stay on after his death. Just how long the retaliatory eviction defense operates, the *Restatement* has not yet revealed.

23. *See, e.g.,* Javins v. First Nat'l Realty, 428 F.2d 1071 (D.C. Cir. 1970).

24. There are no reliable statistics on the quality of housing in the United States. The 1940, 1950, and 1960 decennial censuses classified housing units as dilapidated, deteriorating, or sound, but gave

ever the number may be, as to most of them, the *Restatement* would impose on the courts the following responsibilities:

1) to determine, by some definition, whether or not those units are "suitable for residential use" if the tenants claim they are not;[25]

2) to determine, if the premises are found unsuitable, whether or not the condition arose "through no fault of the tenant";[26]

3) to determine, if the premises are found unsuitable through no fault of the tenant, what the fair rental value of the premises would be if they were suitable and what the fair rental value is in their present condition, if tenant seeks to abate rent under § 10.1;[27]

4) to determine whether or not the boilerplate waiver clauses that will appear in most leases are "unenforceable in whole or in part because they are unconscionable or significantly against public policy,"[28] concepts "not capable of precise definition,"[29] as the comment concedes;

5) to determine what are the reasonable costs of repairs, if the tenant chooses to eliminate the defects under § 10.2;[30] and

6) to determine whether or not repairs made by landlord or tenant have put the premises in a condition "suitable for residential use" so that tenant may no longer abate, apply, or withhold rent.[31]

In a typical eviction case, each of the first four issues of fact is likely to arise in the litigation. The fifth issue, the reasonableness of the tenant's

---

up the effort in the 1970 census because "of the gross shortcomings in statistics on dilapidated housing." H. AARON, SHELTER AND SUBSIDIES 26 (1972). The chief problems seemed to be (a) difficulty in stating meaningful standards of quality evaluation and (b) the inability of the census enumerators to follow whatever standards were given.

It may be, however, that some quantitative measurements will give the reader at least a rough estimate of the minimum number of "unsatisfactory" rental units in the United States. One definition of "unsatisfactory" is lack of "hot and cold piped water, as well as a flush toilet and bathtub or a shower inside the structure for exclusive use of the people in the unit." U.S. DEP'T OF COMMERCE, STATISTICAL ABSTRACT OF THE UNITED STATES 1973 [hereinafter cited as STATISTICAL ABSTRACT]. Nine percent of the renter-occupied housing units lacked one or more of these facilities in 1970. *Id.* at 162. In absolute numbers, this amounted to 2,124,000 units. (The total number of renter-occupied units in 1970 was 23,600,000. *Id.* at 689.)

Rental prices may also be some guide to housing quality. Of the 23,600,000 renter-occupied housing units, over half (12,100,000) rented for less than $100 a month in 1970, and over one-third (8,800,000) rented for less than $80 a month. *Id.* at 687.

25. PROPERTY RESTATEMENT §§ 5.1–5.4. The housing codes do not furnish a sure guide to the "suitability" of housing. The *Uniform Housing Code* (1973) promulgated by the International Conference of Building Officials, adopted by California among other states, *see* CAL. HEALTH AND SAFETY CODE § 17922 (West 1964), defines standards in vague, qualitative language: "improper water closet . . . [and] kitchen sink," "lack of adequate heating facilities," "improper operation of . . . ventilating equipment," "dampness," "general dilapidation" (all taken from UNIFORM HOUSING CODE § 1001 (1973)). THE AMERICAN PUBLIC HEALTH ASSOCIATION, PUBLIC HEALTH SERVICE RECOMMENDED HOUSING MAINTENANCE AND OCCUPANCY ORDINANCE (rev. 1971) is usually more precise, but it too refers to "premises . . . fit for human occupancy." *Id.* § 3.01.

26. PROPERTY RESTATEMENT §§ 5.1–5.2, 5.4–5.5.

27. *Id.* § 10.1.

28. *Id.* § 5.6.

29. *Id.*, comment *e*, at 115. Unconscionability is a defense to waivers of both the landlord's duty (in chapter 5), *see id.* § 5.6, and the tenant's remedies (in chapter 10), *see id.* at 273.

30. *Id.* § 10.2.

31. *Id.* §§ 10.1 & 10.3 expressly provide for the continuation of the remedy until "the default is eliminated."

expenditures for repairs, is not likely to arise often, for that remedy lacks appeal to a tenant who can both abate some rent and withhold the rest. A tenant would be ill-advised to risk the expense of repairs, even if he had the money, when a judge or jury can second-guess him on the reasonableness of his expenditures. The sixth issue will come up in the second round of litigation, when the landlord has made some repairs and claims the premises are now suitable for residential use. The evidentiary questions will be similar to those considered in the first suit: what is the quality of the residential unit? But it is worth noting that the *Restatement* necessarily contemplates two rounds of litigation on the question of the suitability for residential purposes of rental housing: the initial determination of fitness and a later determination of fitness after repairs have been made.

That a substantial amount of resources must be devoted to landlord-tenant litigation under the *Restatement* rules seems inescapable. In many states by statute, and in the District of Columbia under the seventh amendment of the Constitution, either side is entitled to a jury trial.[32] Evidence must be presented on the condition of the premises and the requirements of the housing code. A qualitative determination must be made as to how bad conditions are, for presumably not all violations of the code amount to breach of duty. There is apt to be in many cases a hotly contested issue of fact over who has the blame for the defects, for the landlord can escape liability if the tenant is at fault.[33]

So far, the issues can probably be resolved by testimony from ordinary witnesses who have observed the premises and can describe what they saw. But the third issue, the value of the premises in suitable condition and the value in their present, defective condition, must surely require the testimony of an expert, qualified as such and paid according to the fee schedule of the expert's association. There appears to be no way to standardize these proceedings. Perhaps in a large apartment house, a joint action by the tenants can reduce costs somewhat, but in general, each apartment building is different and rental values in suitable and unsuitable condition must be established on a case-by-case basis.

Lastly, the issue of unconscionability may present triable issues. The *Restatement* is somewhat vague about this. The pervading spirit is to strike down boilerplate clauses that eliminate the landlord's duty of habitability, for it is recognized that the duty is meaningless if these clauses are

---

32. Pernell v. Southall Realty, 94 S. Ct. 1723 (1974), requires a jury trial in eviction proceedings in the District of Columbia. Twelve states provide for jury trials by statute. *Id.* at 1734 n.34.

33. The literal wording of § 5.1 would excuse the landlord if the tenant is to any degree responsible for the defects, for the *Restatement* language makes the landlord's breach of duty depend on the fact of the premises being in unsuitable condition "through *no* fault of the tenant." PROPERTY RESTATEMENT § 5.1 (emphasis in original). But the probable intention of the draftsmen was less severe, and one can expect an apportionment of blame when both have contributed to the defects. That apportionment will present a nice issue in itself.

valid. Yet the draftsmen are reluctant to establish a flat rule prohibiting waiver clauses. The result, from the standpoint of litigation, is costly. Comment *e* of § 5.6 lists seven complex factors which a court may consider in determining the validity of a waiver clause.[34]

If courts actually follow the *Restatement* standards, every residential lease containing a waiver clause could be a field of battle over (a) the financial condition of the landlord and the tenant, (b) the income position of the premises under lease, and (c) the general economic condition of the rental housing market, including supply, demand, vacancy rates, operating expense levels, abandonment rates, and so on. The list seems as long as the imagination of counsel and his economic expert can make it.

What will be the result of the inherently complex nature of litigation under the *Restatement* rules?[35] If they are to have a wide and decisive impact, litigated cases will have to be numerous; the courts will become clogged with extremely complex trials with the attendant delay in obtaining a hearing, not only in landlord-tenant matters but in all the other cases on the calendar. With such congestion, tenants will be empowered to remain in possession of premises of suitable as well as unsuitable quality for protracted periods of time, while the landlord awaits a hearing on his eviction suit.[36] Moreover, tenants and their attorneys may use the *Restatement*

---

34. Those relevant to slum housing are the following (the original numbers are retained):

"(1) Whether and to what extent the agreement will be counter to . . ." public policy reflected in the housing codes and other public health and safety regulations;

". . . .

"(3) Whether and to what extent the agreement or provision serves a reasonable business purpose and appears to have been the result of conscious negotiations for the distribution of risks . . . .:

"(4) Whether the provision appears to be part of an unduly harsh and unreasonable standard, 'boilerplate' lease document;

"(5) Whether and to what extent the parties or either of them, habitually (or on a discriminatory basis) disregard and do not enforce the agreement or provision in actual operations under the lease or, in the case of a landlord, under similar leases;

"(6) Whether and to what extent the agreement or provision (especially if it relates to low or moderate income residential property) imposes unreasonable liabilities or burdens on persons who are financially ill-equipped to assume such burdens and who may have had significant inequality of bargaining power; and

"(7) Whether and to what extent the parties were each represented by counsel in the course of negotiating the lease."

Id. § 5.6, comment *e*, at 115–17.

35. The *Stanford Law Review* is now engaged in a study attempting to determine the consequences in California of the adoption of the habitability duty in Green v. Superior Court, 10 Cal. 3d 616, 517 P.2d 1168, 111 Cal. Rptr. 704 (1974).

36. It does not require an aberrant imagination to foresee poverty lawyers advising tenants of the practical possibilities in the *Restatement* rules:

"Write your landlord claiming breach of the duty of habitability, stop paying rent and sit tight; when the courts get around to trying the lawsuit against you, you may be evicted and you may not; if you are, at least you have had a rent-free dwelling for a while.

"P.S. If you have any assets, the landlord may try to collect a judgment from you, but don't worry —the most he can get is the rent you agreed to pay in the first place, plus costs and maybe attorney's fees."

The suggestion is not fanciful. On August 8, 1974, the radio station KCBS (San Francisco) broadcast a news item about a recent California Supreme Court decision on tenants' rights, Green v. Superior Court, 10 Cal. 3d 616, 517 P.2d 1168, 111 Cal. Rptr. 704 (1974). Over the air, tenants were invited by a tenants' association to bring their complaints about the condition of their premises to the association for possible legal action.

rules as a bargaining club. With the threat of a costly trial facing him, a landlord could be forced to bow to tenant demands that are wholly unrelated to the warranty of habitability, for example, by tolerating occupancy by deadbeats or even destructive tenants.

Certainly, the draftsmen of the *Restatement* never intended these consequences, but considering the number of cases that could arise, the individuality of the cases, and the complexity of the litigation, such consequences are not improbable.

III. Economic Consequences of the Restatement Rules

Let us consider next the probable economic consequences of the *Restatement* rules.

Four categories of rental housing may be identified, one of which is unaffected by the covenant of habitability and therefore need not be considered further. That category consists of dwellings that substantially comply with the housing code and are considered "suitable" for residential purposes.

The other three categories of housing will be affected by the covenant and consist of:

1) dwellings that do not comply with the housing code and are considered unsuitable for residential use, but that can be brought up to code standards by additional investment that can be recovered through higher rents.

2) dwellings that do not comply with the housing code and are considered unsuitable for residential use but that can be brought up to code standards by an expenditure that will reduce the landlord's rate of return (because rents cannot be raised sufficiently to cover repair costs) but will not eliminate a positive return on sunk capital.[37]

3) dwellings that do not comply with the housing code and are considered unsuitable for residential use, for which the costs of repair to meet code standards (together with other expenses) will result in a negative return on sunk capital.

No one knows how the nation's substandard housing stock is divided among these three categories, and the proportions are likely to vary from city to city. Whatever those proportions may be, some portion of the housing stock will fall into category (3) and will be withdrawn from the market because of the imposition of the duty of habitability. To the extent such withdrawal occurs, low-income tenants as a class are hurt, not helped, by

---

37. Sunk capital is the amount of money already invested by the landlord in the property. Sunk capital yields a positive return, in the terminology used here, when rents exceed out-of-pocket expenses, such as taxes, insurance, maintenance, utility bills, and interest on a mortgage (if any). The cost of *Restatement*-mandated repairs amortized over the life of the improvement is an additional cost which is assumed, for this category of housing, not to reduce the return to zero.

the *Restatement* rules. It is the further contention here that application of the *Restatement* rules to the other two categories of slum housing will also adversely affect the interests of low-income tenants, certainly in the long run.[38]

As to rental housing in category (1), housing that can be profitably improved, the *Restatement* says, in effect, that such housing cannot be rented in substandard condition. Therefore, the landlord will improve the property and charge higher rents. The class of tenants theretofore occupying the premises will either lose occupancy because they cannot afford the new rents or will remain in possession and have less disposable income for other goods and services. In the latter case, the *Restatement* makes a judgment for the tenant, that he should (must) spend more money on housing and less on clothes, food, recreation, and other items, even though left to his own devices he would and previously did make the opposite choice. Where courts derive the authority to make this choice for tenants and why it is a better choice than the tenants' own is not apparent.

Rental housing in category (2)—housing that can be improved by expenditures reducing, although not eliminating, the landlord's return—presents different considerations. Here low-income tenants as a class are initially benefited by the *Restatement* rules. As long as the landlord recovers from rents all of his out-of-pocket expenses, including the cost of repairs plus interest on the investment in repairs, he is likely to make the repairs in order to protect his equity in the property. Even if his equity is zero (because no one will buy the property), he may still invest in repairs if the rents cover all costs, including as costs the return the landlord would have received by investing the repair money in some other venture.

A simple example may illustrate the point: Landlord owns an apartment house on which he has a positive return of $1800 a year (*i.e.*, rents exceed out-of-pocket expenses by that amount). By hypothesis, rents (in terms of constant dollars) cannot be raised for this category of housing. If repairs cost $6400 and if their useful life is 10 years, landlord must recover $640 per year in order to amortize his investment. In addition he must recover interest on the $6400 in an amount equal to the interest he could obtain on an alternative investment. If such interest rate is 10 percent, he must recover an average of $320 in interest per year,[39] for a total

---

38. An economist friend, who is also a law skeptic, suggests that the *Restatement* rules would make no difference out in the real world because either (a) they would never be enforced owing to tenant ignorance of their existence or to lack of legal resources, or (b) tenants themselves, in all three categories of housing, knowing of the rules would not enforce them out of self-interest. The Institute, however, and the courts faced with deciding the issue, must assume the contrary, the Institute in order to make its endeavor worthwhile, and both the Institute and the courts because economists, too, can be wrong about predictions of human behavior. As indicated above, *see* note 36 *supra*, the news media took note of the California case within months of its publication.

39. For simplicity, interest was calculated on $3,200, the average amount of outstanding capital during the amortization period. Precise figures can be obtained from annuity tables.

annual recovery of $960. Since the property was yielding a positive annual return of $1800 before the repairs were made and would yield a positive annual return of $840 after the repairs are made, the landlord will make the repairs. If, however, the repairs must be amortized over a 4-year period, then return of capital must be $1600 a year, which when added to an average interest return of $320 a year aggregates to $1920 a year. Landlord will not make the repairs since he will suffer a negative return from the property if he does so.

The landlord might, however, be uncertain about the amortization period and calculate it as something between 4 and 5 years. If he picks the longer period, his return from the property will remain positive, but he may still be reluctant to make the repairs. Amortization will be $1280 per year and average interest $320, for a total of $1600, leaving a positive return of $200. Yet the margin may be too thin to justify the investment. Any number of events could convert the positive return to a loss—a tenant who skips out owing rent, a vacancy for a month or two, a small fire drastically increasing insurance rates, or a rise in taxes or other costs at a faster rate than a general rise in price levels.[40]

It is nevertheless true that as to some portion of the substandard housing supply, the *Restatement* rules will benefit the low-income tenant class in the short term, for the landlord can afford a reduced return on capital for a period of time. In the long run, however, unless rents fully reflect the costs of the additional repairs required by the *Restatement*, the quantity of category (2) property will decline. First, because of the lower profit position, the operating costs associated with increasing building age will take their toll faster than normal and the building will be prematurely forced into a deficit position and removed from the market.[41] Second, no new

---

40. While it was assumed in the text that rents cannot be raised in terms of constant dollars, it is also assumed that rents may be raised to keep up with inflation. The point in the text is not concerned with inflation, but with a rise in landlord costs relatively greater than the rise in general price levels. Two typical landlord expense items illustrate this point: real estate taxes and repairs tend to go up faster than the cost of living because goods and services purchased by tax and repair money are labor intensive rather than capital intensive, and labor-intensive services increase in price at a faster rate than capital-intensive goods and services.

Even if Landlord anticipates operating at a loss, he may make the required repairs to save the equity he has in the property, if it is large enough to cover the anticipated deficit. But note that there is not likely to be much equity in a property that operates at a loss over time, because the only purchasers will be those who calculate that they can operate the property more efficiently than the present landlord, thereby eliminating the deficit while at the same time obtaining the necessary return on their capital investment.

The purchaser must also recover what the economists call transaction costs, which would include information costs in investigating and acquiring title, legal and recording fees, and other expenses connected with real estate transfers.

41. This point is easily illustrated by an example. Buildings *A* and *B* are both 10-year-old apartment complexes. At the present time, they take in $20,000 a year in rent and have costs of $10,000 a year; however, because of increasing age, their costs are growing by $1,000 a year. A warranty of habitability is established in *A*'s jurisdiction and *A* is forced to make repairs that will increase its costs by $5,000 a year. While *A* will currently remain in operation, it will shift to a deficit position in 5 years and be removed from the housing market. Building *B*, which was not forced to make any repairs, will remain in business for another 10 years. Thus, the effect of adopting a warranty of habitability is to force category (2) housing off the market sooner than would otherwise occur.

category (2) property will be built; while present owners need only cover their operating costs, potential owners must be able to cover their initial capital expenses.

Category (3) consists of housing unsuitable for residential use (under the *Restatement* rules) for which the cost of repairs (when added to other operating expenses) exceeds the rental income that may be obtained from the property. This housing will be abandoned sooner or later, the timing depending on the landlord's perceptions and the financing arrangements for the property.

If the property is not mortgaged,[42] the property will be abandoned as soon as the landlord concludes that his deficit position is irreversible. Once the property starts to lose money, the only reason for holding onto it is the expectation that sometime in the near future, the situation will turn around, and by an amount in excess of the losses previously suffered. For this reversal to occur it is probably necessary for rents to rise, which by hypothesis cannot happen for property in category (3).

If the property is mortgaged, the mortgagor will default, leaving the lending institution to take over.[43] The lending institution will operate the property as long as rental income exceeds costs (including the cost of *Restatement*-mandated repairs plus interest), thereby reducing the bad-debt loss the lender would otherwise suffer. The lender can afford to operate the property when the mortgagor-landlord could not, because the lender obviously does not have to pay himself interest. All the lender requires is a positive return on irretrievably sunk capital so as to reduce the unpaid balance on principal.

When neither the landlord without a mortgage nor the foreclosing mortgagee can break even on the property, the residuary legatee is the state. The state can take over the property for taxes, remove it from the tax rolls, and in theory pay for the *Restatement* repairs out of rental income not reduced by taxes. The state's ability to continue operation of the property depends, of course, on its ability either to divert public funds from former objects of support or to increase taxes to subsidize low-rent housing. Em-

---

42. RESIDENTIAL ABANDONMENT, *supra* note 7, at 210, indicates that in the sample studied, about 20% of rental housing was not mortgaged.

43. There will be no other buyer at the foreclosure sale unless the property has been so badly mismanaged that another real estate operator can, by efficient management, recover the necessary return on capital and the transaction costs of title transfer.

The text assumes, for simplicity, that the mortgagor will not have to pay the outstanding loan. This will be true in some instances because of antideficiency judgment statutes, in other instances because the property is held by a dummy corporation with no other assets, and in still others because the landlord-mortgagor, though legally liable, has no other assets reachable by creditors.

Where none of these circumstances is applicable, the landlord-mortgagor may be slower to abandon the property. For example, if the outstanding principal is $10,000 payable in installments over 10 years and if the property is producing enough income after payment of other out-of-pocket expenses to reduce the debt by some amount each year, the landlord may not default even though his equity is zero. His decision whether to default will depend on what kind of settlement of the $10,000 claim he could make if he defaulted at once.

pirical evidence of what actually happens to slum housing after the state takes it over for taxes is lacking, but the prospects are probably poor that the properties will remain in the housing stock, for central city expenses are rising faster than tax revenues.[44] Moreover, as cities increase the tax rate more rental properties slip into a deficit position, with landlords refusing to invest in repairs and ultimately abandoning the property to the city for taxes.[45] Thus tax foreclosures tend to result in a vicious circle unless substandard structures are demolished after the city acquires them: city expenses rise, real estate taxes rise, and more structures are abandoned for taxes, to start the process all over again.

In summary, the economic consequences of the *Restatement* rules on habitability are likely to be the following:

1) Some proportion of the substandard rental housing stock would be upgraded and rents would be raised to cover the added costs. Tenants formerly occupying the housing would either be forced out or be required to pay a higher proportion of their income for rent. Those tenants who are unable or unwilling to pay for the upgraded housing will move out, creating an increased demand for lower-priced, lower-quality housing.

2) For some proportion of the substandard rental housing stock, rents could not be raised, but landlords could still upgrade the housing without incurring a deficit. In these cases the tenants would enjoy a short-term wealth transfer, for they would enjoy better housing at no increase in rent. But low-income tenants as a class would not benefit in the long run, for the covenant of habitability will retire this component of the housing stock sooner than would otherwise be the case and will discourage new investment in low-rent housing.

3) The third portion of the substandard housing stock will be abandoned as soon as the owner determines that income will not cover the expenses of *Restatement* repairs and concludes that this deficit is likely to persist.

IV. THE EMPIRICAL EVIDENCE

The conclusions reached above are based on theory; that is, on the assumption that landlords, along with the rest of mankind, are rational economic beings who seek to maximize profits and minimize losses. If landlords do in fact fit this model, then the prediction that some portion of the housing stock will be abandoned seems to be well-founded. Moreover, under this model, the *Restatement*'s assertions that there is a housing shortage and that landlords enjoy excessive bargaining power relative to tenants, even if true, are simply irrelevant to the consequences that can be

44. RESIDENTIAL ABANDONMENT, *supra* note 7, at 181–82.
45. *Id.* at 226.

expected from the adoption of the *Restatement* rules. A landlord owning
rental housing in category (1) will raise rents and will abandon housing
in category (3), unless he is altruistic, in which case the housing would
meet code standards in the first place.

Lawyers, however, are loath to base action on anyone's theories except
their own. A lawyer will confidently write an opinion letter predicting
what courts will do on the basis of legal theory, but will take the stance
of the man from Missouri when it comes to predictions of behavior based
on economic theory. This is a curious posture, for the behavioral assumptions of economic theory seem far better supported by everyday experience
than the assumptions of legal theory.

It is fortunate, therefore, that the case against the *Restatement* rules
need not rest on economic theory alone. In his pioneering studies of slum
tenements, George Sternlieb has gathered empirical data on landlord behavior in the slums. His two books, *The Tenement Landlord*[46] and *Residential Abandonment: The Tenement Landlord Revisited*[47] deserve to be
read in full by anyone concerned with low-rental housing. Sternlieb's principal conclusions relevant to our inquiry may be summarized:

1) "Actual abandonment of blighted neighborhoods by landlords has
reached shockingly high levels."[48]

2) The classic view of the rapacious slumlord waxing fat as he milks
the property is a myth.

> The reality is that the white owner in an urban core area increasingly is unable to
> rent his mortgage-free structures to poor blacks and still derive the necessary in-
> come to meet expenses (prime among them are taxes) and turn the necessary profit
> to remain solvent. . . .
>
> It . . . does *not* appear to hold that succeeding waves of tenement landlords
> were milking parcels and from this deriving substantial income.[49]

3) Code enforcement, even of the conventional sort resulting in modest
fines, is counterproductive.

> The pace of urban decay, exemplified by the secondary industrial cities, has
> outrun all the remedies that have been applied . . . [Assigning blame to malad-
> ministration and corruption tends] to hide rather than typify the underlying reality,
> providing a false feeling of assurance that, given a better administration, or more
> comprehending funding agencies, or some magic inspiration of imagination, all
> could be made well.[50]

. . . Code enforcement, for example, when private owners are fleeing the market,
becomes self-defeating.[51]

---

46. G. STERNLIEB, *supra* note 7.
47. RESIDENTIAL ABANDONMENT, *supra* note 7.
48. *Id.* at xiii.
49. *Id.* at xvi–xvii (emphasis in original).
50. *Id.* at xviii.
51. *Id.* at xix.

TABLE 1
CASH FLOW OF A TYPICAL RESIDENTIAL PROPERTY*
NEWARK (1972)

INCOME	
Two Apts. @ $140/mo.	
(assuming no vacancy)	$3,360/yr.
EXPENSES	
Amortization/interest	
(6 percent, thirty yrs. $13,500)	930
Maintenance	200
Heating	400
Insurance (risk pool)	300
Electricity	290
Water	40
	−$2,160/yr.
CASH FLOW (before taxes)	$1,200
Annual property tax	−$1,200
Net cash flow	0

* Two-and-one-half-story frame dwelling, two-family nonresident owner, parcel assessed value $15,000, market value $6,000, †, annual property tax $1,200.
† Sales/assessment ratio 0.40 (Noninsured Property Turnovers 1964–1972).
Demolition costs: $1,500.
Source: Newark Tax Department, spring 1972.

4) Landlords in slum areas do not believe that repairs can be economically justified by increased rentals or resale potential.

When owners were asked what it would cost to repair their parcels and whether they could get rent increases that would cover such repairs, only a quarter of the owners in Area 1 versus approximately a third of the owners in Areas 2 and 3 answered in the affirmative, *i.e.*, that the tenants could or would pay rents commensurate with the cost of improvement. The gaps, however, are substantial and the level of positive feeling in securing the additional rents is low at best. When, in addition, owners were asked if they were to make improvements could they get their money back on resale, the answers in all cases were terribly somber, with only 15.4 percent of the owners in Area 1 answering yes, definitely or probably, as compared with 20.4 percent of the owners in Area 2, and 24.8 percent of the owners in Area 3.[52]

The reason for these depressing conclusions is revealed in part by the cash-flow position of slum landlords. Sternlieb characterizes the data presented in Table 1[53] as depicting "the *typical* cash flow posture of a two-family parcel in Newark."[54]

52. *Id.* at 65. Areas 1–3 comprise the 40 census tracts making up the central core of the City of Newark. Based on 1960 observations, Area 1 contained less than 25% sound housing, Area 2 contained 25% to 50% sound housing, and Area 3 contained 50% to 67% sound housing. *Id.* at 6.
53. *Id.* at 232.
54. *Id.* at 231 (emphasis added).

It is not possible to summarize, much less present in detail, all of Sternlieb's data in support of his conclusions. Suffice it to adduce some of his
information on abandonment and some of his explanations of the causes.
Using first the Urban League's definition of abandonment—unoccupied
buildings (not scheduled for demolition to make the land available for
other productive uses) and occupied buildings for which the landlord provides no services and allows taxes and mortgages to go unpaid—Sternlieb
quotes abandonment rates of 2 percent for New York City, 6 to 10 percent
for Brooklyn (East New York section), 16 percent for the most afflicted
portion of St. Louis, and 20 percent for Chicago (Woodlawn and Lawn-
dale).[55] Reporting a study using a different definition of abandonment—
structures unoccupied and vandalized, boarded up, deteriorated, or un-
maintained—he stated that 4 percent of St. Louis' housing stock was abandoned as of January 1, 1971. The same study reported that in North Lawn-
dale, Chicago, 2.6 percent of the area's housing units were abandoned in a
2-month period between September and November 1970.[56]

Sternlieb then reports on his studies of Newark, defining abandonment
as applicable to a building "which has been removed from the housing
stock for no apparent alternative profitable reason and for which no succeeding use occurs on the land."[57] He found a gross abandonment rate of
2 percent per year of the combined residential, commercial, and industrial
stock.[58] Referring then to a study sample of 569 residential buildings first
studied in 1964, Sternlieb found that by late 1971, 84, or more than 15 percent, had been abandoned.[59]

In another Newark sample, composed of 286 parcels, 20 percent had been
abandoned between 1964 and 1971.[60] For the city as a whole, during the
more recent 4-year period of 1967–71, 2553 structures had been abandoned,
representing 8 percent of the housing stock of the city.[61]

Abandonment figures alone do not prove much, but when combined
with the reasons for abandonment, they forcefully support the argument
that increasing the repair costs of slum housing or, in the alternative, reducing rental income by allowing tenants to withhold rent, will raise the abandonment rate. Sternlieb reports that the combination of low rents, collection difficulties, high taxes, high maintenance costs (in part due to tenant

---

55. *Id.* at 276. These statistics were based on estimates by "informed persons." *Id.* at 274.
56. *Id.* at 276.
57. *Id.* at 277.
58. *Id.* at 283.
59. *Id.* at 284.
60. *Id.* at 318. Even for the buildings not abandoned by 1971, approximately 50% of their owners thought as early as 1964 that the market was not strong enough to make extensive improvement worth-while.
61. *Id.* at 278.

vandalism and in part to price levels), and the unavailability of insurance cause the abandonment of his sampled residential buildings. A typical case is reported as follows:

> Parcel number 89 is a four-story masonry building with three apartments on the upper floors and a store on the lower floor. It was part of an estate involving more than twenty parcels in Newark. Even in 1964, at the time of our earlier interview, it was vacant, the last tenant just having left at the time of the survey. The owner's responses to why he had abandoned the parcel, assessed at $9,200 including land, was: "I gave up because I couldn't maintain it. To tell the truth, I don't think I even own it anymore. A lot of the tenants owed rents and they just left. We [the receivers of the estate] weren't going to put our own money into it; if repairs had to be made they'd have to come from rents; we just couldn't handle it anymore. . . ."[62]

It is true that Sternlieb's data are limited, both in the questions he asks and the sample he draws upon. He does not provide an answer to an important question the economic analysis raises: what proportion of the substandard housing stock falls into category (2)? But he does provide convincing evidence that inner-city landlords face economic burdens that can only be exacerbated by imposing additional costs of repair, and that evidence supports the predictions based on economic theory. Moreover, there is, so far as research has been able to discover, little evidence to contradict economic theory. If the question is whether enforcement of the *Restatement* covenant of habitability will raise the quality of low-rental housing and improve the condition of the low-income tenant, both theory and the available evidence indicate a negative answer. In fact, conditions are likely to worsen.

V. Final Observations: The Sources of Authority for the Restatement Rules

The *Property Restatement* raises a final troublesome question: In a representative democracy, is the judiciary the appropriate branch of the government to promulgate the new rules? Whatever ultimate effect the *Restatement* rules would have on the supply of low-rental housing, it seems irrefutable that those rules would bar some tenants from voluntarily choosing to live in lower-quality, lower-priced housing and would compel a short-term wealth transfer from landlords to tenants in one subset of the housing market. That the legislature is empowered to adopt the *Restatement* rules in order to accomplish those objectives would not be disputed by many today. But whether courts should do so is a more difficult question.

---

62. *Id.* at 289 (brackets in original). Ironically, one class of owner who would be hurt by the *Restatement* rules is the lower middle-income, minority landlord caught by the profit squeeze. Sternlieb cites a number of cases, *id.* at 117–22.

A. *Deriving Authority from Legislative Enactments*

The distinguished Executive Director of the Institute, Herbert Wechsler, offered a justification for judicial action in his Foreword to the Tentative Draft:

> Those who are troubled by the fact that the Reporter's formulations move in some respects beyond the statutory mandates with respect to tenant's rights and remedies may find some comfort in the famous statement by Mr. Justice Stone at the Harvard Tercentenary in 1936: "I can find in the history and principles of the common law no adequate reason for our failure to treat a statute much more as we treat a judicial precedent, as both a declaration and a source of law, and as a premise for legal reasoning" (*The Common Law in the United States*, 50 HARV. L. REV. 4, 13). What is occurring at long last in this important field is that the total body of the statutory law, together with its underlying policy, has become "a premise for legal reasoning" in the judicial reappraisal of old rules and doctrines urged to be unsuitable for modern needs. The challenge of this draft is to discern the proper implications of this process in the areas presented for consideration.[63]

But one may wonder whether Mr. Justice Stone would have carried his reasoning to those lengths. He argued for judicial recognition and implementation of social policies and judgments expressed in legislation enacted "by the lawmaking agency which is supreme . . . ."[64] The *Restatement* seeks to persuade courts to follow *its* lead, although the legislature of the state has *not* expressed a policy judgment on the distribution of wealth between landlords and tenants or upon the right of the parties to enter into bargains on low-quality housing at low rents.

Take the case of Indiana as an example. The *Restatement* proposes itself as a guide to the Indiana courts in all particulars: the duty of habitability, the nonwaivable nature of the duty, the remedies of rent abatement and suspension, and the forthcoming defense of retaliatory eviction. Yet the Reporter cites not a single statute from Indiana expressing any legislative policy on the condition of rental premises. Mr. Justice Stone's prescription can hardly guide Indiana courts, unless policies adopted by New York or Pennsylvania legislatures somehow apply in Indiana. Just what principle of government makes out-of-state policies applicable locally is hard to discover.

Minnesota is another case in point. The Reporter cites a Minnesota statute[65] relieving the tenant of the obligation to pay rent if the premises are totally destroyed by fire or other disaster not the fault of the tenant. The parties are free under the statute to make agreements to the contrary. Surely no one would contend that the policy of that statute supplies

---

63. PROPERTY RESTATEMENT at vii–viii.
64. Stone, *The Common Law in the United States*, 50 HARV. L. REV. 4, 14 (1936).
65. MINN. STAT. ANN. § 504.05 (1947), *cited in* PROPERTY RESTATEMENT at 46.

the "premise for legal reasoning" that leads to the conclusion that a tenant in substandard housing may, contrary to a clause in the lease, abate some rent and put the rest in escrow while remaining on the premises indefinitely unless the landlord makes court-mandated repairs.

A third example, from Texas, demonstrates that if the *Restatement* draftsmen had taken Mr. Justice Stone's prescription seriously, they would have found statutory premises that lead judicial reasoning to conclusions opposite to those of the proposed rules. The Texas statute,[66] cited by the Reporter, provides:

> Should the landlord . . . fail to comply in any respect with his part of the contract, he shall be responsible to said tenant or lessee for whatever damages may be sustained thereby . . . . [The statute continues by giving a lien on rents and landlord's property to enforce the obligation.]

Reasoning from the underlying premise of this statute, the Texas courts could not embrace most of the *Restatement* rules. If the lease specified that the landlord should maintain the premises in habitable condition (or if such duty could be imposed by the court in the absence of a contractual provision), the remedy would be damages for the breach of contract. The remedies of abating rent under the *Restatement* formula and placing the rent into escrow until repairs are made go far beyond the statutory command. More important, a rental contract specifying that the tenant takes the premises "as is" and that the landlord has no duty to repair would be enforced as written. Rightly or wrongly, the Texas statute lays down the premise that the bargain of the parties is the starting point for judicial reasoning.

The three examples given above demonstrate that in some states existing legislation either provides no policy basis on which to rest the *Restatement* rules, or provides policy grounds for rejecting the *Restatement* rules. In those states, then, the appeal to Mr. Justice Stone's prescription is unavailing.

B. *Reliance on Judicial Precedents: The* Green *Case*

The weakness of relying on Mr. Justice Stone to support the *Property Restatement* is particularly evident if one considers some of the cases the *Restatement* cites as authority for its position. Instead of taking a statutory premise as the starting point for legal reasoning, those courts have announced decisions contrary to the policy of the statute in question by, in Mr. Justice Stone's words, "construing it narrowly and treating it as though it did not exist for any purpose other than that embraced within the strict construction of its words."[67]

---

66. Tex. Rev. Civ. Stat. art. 5236 (1962), *cited in* Property Restatement at 49.
67. Stone, *supra* note 64, at 14.

The California case of *Green v. Superior Court*,[68] cited as supporting authority by the *Restatement*, illustrates the point. In 1970, the California Legislature, after a considerable amount of political infighting, overhauled the state's landlord and tenant law.[69] Of crucial importance here, the legislature amended Civil Code section 1941.1 to specify the defects which render premises untenantable and amended Civil Code section 1942 to provide that the remedy of deducting 1 month's rent to make repairs could not be exercised more often than once a year. When deciding the *Green* case, the California Supreme Court brushed aside this legislative policy judgment, declaring:

> Although past cases have held that the Legislature intended the remedies afforded by section 1942 to be the sole procedure for enforcing the statutory duty on landlords imposed by section 1941 (see, e.g., *Van Every v. Ogg* (1881) 50 Cal. 563, 566; *Sieber v. Blanc* (1888) 76 Cal. 173, 174 [18 P. 260]), no decision has suggested that the Legislature designed these statutory provisions to displace the common law in fixing the respective rights of landlord and tenant. On the contrary, the statutory remedies of section 1942 have traditionally been viewed as additional to, and complementary of, the tenant's common law rights.[70]
>
> Furthermore, the limited nature of the "repair and deduct" remedy, in itself, suggests that it was not designed to serve as an exclusive remedy for tenants in this area. As noted above, section 1942 only permits a tenant to expend up to one month's rent in making repairs, and now also provides that this self-help remedy can be invoked only once in any 12-month period. These limitations demonstrate that the Legislature framed the section only to encompass relatively minor dilapidations in leased premises. (See *Nelson v. Myers* (1928) 94 Cal. App. 66, 75 [270 P. 719]; Loeb, *The Low-Income Tenant in California: A Study in Frustration* (1970) 21 Hastings L. J. 287, 292.) As the facts of the instant case reveal, in the most serious instances of deterioration, when the costs of repair are at all significant, section 1942 does not provide, and could not have been designed as, a viable solution.[71]

What the California court has done with the statute, it is respectfully suggested, is precisely the opposite of what Mr. Justice Stone was advocating.

It may well be true that when speaking in 1936 what Mr. Justice Stone had in mind was crabbed judicial treatment of statutes intended to enlarge on rights and expand on remedies, but the philosophy he expounds cuts both ways. Surely Justice Stone would argue, as would most traditionalists, that when a legislature has examined a controversial issue and through the political process of contention and compromise produced a statutory norm

---

68. Green v. Superior Court, 10 Cal. 3d 616, 517 P.2d 1168, 111 Cal. Rptr. 704 (1974), *cited in* PROPERTY RESTATEMENT at 64 (as Green v. Sumski).
69. [1970] Cal. Stats. ch. 1280, *codified in* CAL. CIV. CODE §§ 1941.1–.2, 1942(a)–(b), 1942.1, 1942.5 (West Supp. 1974).
70. Green v. Superior Court, 10 Cal. 3d 616, 629–30, 517 P.2d 1168, 1177, 111 Cal. Rptr. 704, 713 (1974) (brackets in original).
71. *Id.* at 630–31, 517 P.2d at 1177–78, 111 Cal. Rptr. at 713–14 (brackets in original).

for settling disputes, the courts are not free to ignore the legislative mandate and proceed with the development of the common law in directions contrary to the legislative policies. The California case did just that; yet the *Restatement* cites the case as support.

In summary, there are two objections to invoking Mr. Justice Stone's advice to "treat a statute much more as we treat a judicial precedent"[72] in support of the *Restatement*: (1) the statutes of one state hardly provide a legislative policy for another state and (2) the statutes of some states implicitly declare policies contrary to the *Restatement* rules, even though cases from those states—ignoring or overriding the legislative policy, and disregarding the advice of Justice Stone—may support the *Restatement* position.

C. *Deriving Support from Housing Codes*

The Reporter advances another argument in support of the *Restatement* rules; he contends that the housing codes establish a legislative policy which the judiciary merely implements when it applies the *Restatement* rules.[73] The argument is hard to sustain, however, if the housing code is taken as a whole and not artificially separated into two independent, unrelated parts consisting of (1) standards of housing quality and (2) enforcement. Viewed in its totality, the code prescribes housing standards which, if violated, may result in the penalty of a fine.[74] Enforcement of the code is committed to a building inspector who has the equivalent of prosecutorial discretion.[75] Further discretion is vested in courts with respect to the size of fines.[76] In short, the policy underlying the code is discretionary administration: if better housing can be obtained through enforcement of the code, citations may be issued. But if code enforcement will increase the abandonment rate or will price the poor out of the housing market, enforcement can be stayed.[77] Discretionary enforcement is delegated to public officials who know the housing market and who are expected to, and do, proceed with enforcement cautiously and prudently.[78] Unlike the *Property*

---

72. Stone, *supra* note 64, at 13.

73. PROPERTY RESTATEMENT § 5.1, Reporter's Note *e* at 66: "*Comment e* also accepts housing, health and safety codes as evidencing a legislatively established minimum standard for human habitation, and therefore where the lease involves human occupancy, a substantial violation of the code is a ground for invoking the rule of this section" (italics in original). *Accord, id.* § 5.3, Reporter's Note 3, at 86; *id.* § 5.5, Reporter's Note 2, at 107–08.

74. UNIFORM HOUSING CODE, ch. 2 (1973).

75. J. ROSENBLATT, DISCRETION AS A VARIABLE IN HOUSING CODE ENFORCEMENT 22–24 (Urban Institute, Working Paper 112–12, 1970).

76. M. TEITZ & S. ROSENTHAL, HOUSING CODE ENFORCEMENT IN NEW YORK CITY 42–43 (N.Y. City Rand Institute 1971).

77. *See generally*, S. PARRATT, HOUSING CODE ADMINISTRATION AND ENFORCEMENT (U.S. Dep't HEW 1970) (specifically Chapter 8). Chapter 5 contains a discussion of the economics of rental housing, which generally agrees with the economic analysis of Part III of this Essay and with the empirical data cited in Part IV of this Essay.

78. Though apparently being of the opinion that code enforcement helps low-income tenants rather than hurting them and therefore holding the view that code enforcement should be vigorous,

Restatement, the code does *not* provide for rent abatement and rent withholding, for those remedies frustrate the achievement of the code's objective,
which is the maintenance of the housing stock and its improvement where
economically feasible in the judgment of knowledgeable public officials.
The *Restatement* bifurcates the code, preserving the standards and discard-
ing the remedies, replacing discretionary code enforcement with remedies
that allow the tenant, at his option, to remain in possession indefinitely at a
drastically reduced rent that may never reach the landlord since it can be
paid into an escrow account. To pull out of the code only its standards
and then to cite the code as expressing a legislative policy in support of
the *Restatement*'s remedies is to misunderstand both the purpose of the
code and the means of achieving its ends.

VI. Conclusion

To persuade the reader that neither Mr. Justice Stone's prescription nor
the housing codes justify the *Restatement* rules does not persuade him that
no good reasons remain for courts to play an activist role in landlord-
tenant law. The concern about the proper role of judges in making wealth
transfers and restricting the bargaining area of parties is answered in part,
perhaps, by the fact that courts have done the same thing in other areas of
the law for some time. Yet the doubts persist, for the fact that judges have
behaved in a certain manner does not itself explain or justify the behavior.

The fundamental reason offered here against assigning judges the rulemaking power endorsed by the *Restatement* is that the rules are too closely
tied to basic social and economic policies to emanate from the judiciary.
The quality of housing that the poor can afford to rent or buy is the product of political decisions on income distribution on the purchasers' side and
the organization and operation of the market on the sellers' side. Raise the
income of the poor and they can afford better housing. Reduce such restrictions on housing output as labor monopoly and land-use controls and
the poor will have better housing. But each of those changes involves basic
political choices that must be made by the society in order to gain accep-

one writer concedes that most housing officials have a "go-slow" attitude toward code enforcement
and exercise a broad discretion in bringing complaints. Lieberman, *Administrative Provisions of Housing Codes,* in Housing Code Standards: Three Critical Studies (National Comm'n on Urban Problems, Research Report No. 19, 1969). *See also* Housing Urban America 499 (J. Pynoos, R. Schafer,
& C. Hartman eds. 1973).

Perhaps code enforcement should be viewed from a more realistic—or cynical—perspective than
that adopted in the text. It could be argued that housing codes are enacted to assuage the social guilt
that arises from the housing conditions of the poor, on the tacit understanding that enforcement will be
kept to a minimum out of practical considerations. Our society seems to have a penchant for passing
high-minded laws which either consciously are not enforced or become unenforceable because of
widespread disobedience of them. If this phenomenon explains the high-sounding, largely unenforced
housing codes, one may still question whether the "policy" of the codes supports the *Restatement*
rules, because policy is made up of enforcement as much as, or more than, the statement of norms.

tance. When courts intrude on a problem of such dimension, without the political base or the political tools, especially the spending power, to effect significant change, they have both in theory and in practice exceeded the powers confided in them by the people.

To sum up: the *Property Restatement* proposes landlord and tenant rules that are likely to involve courts in costly and time-consuming litigation; that are likely to injure the interests of many tenants by pricing them out of some housing and causing the abandonment of other housing; and that are likely to transfer wealth from some landlords to their tenants, although the landlords themselves may be as victimized by present housing policies as the tenants. While these arguments can also be brought to bear against legislative adoption of the *Restatement* rules, no one would doubt the legislature's authority to act. But for the judiciary to promulgate the *Restatement* rules raises serious doubts, for the judges have neither the political mandate nor the institutional tools to attempt to solve the housing problem.

Preclusion of Judicial Review in the Processing of Claims for Veterans' Benefits: A Preliminary Analysis

Robert L. Rabin*

Power tends to corrupt, and absolute power corrupts absolutely. Lord Acton's aphorism has more than stood the test of time. Read in the context of administrative action, his admonition underlies the popular tendency to consider access to court a fundamental aspect of due process of law. In a much-cited case, *Abbott Laboratories v. Gardner*, the Supreme Court spoke in terms of a "basic presumption of judicial review of administrative action."[1] Although rarely a point of contention, that pronouncement has been enthusiastically reaffirmed in later decisions.[2] Indeed, wholly apart from the judiciary, a broad consensus undoubtedly exists that access to court ought to be guaranteed to those complaining of arbitrary treatment by administrative officials. Using the federal statutes as a measuring stick, one would search long and hard for an explicit congressional exemption of administrative action from judicial review.[3]

A sufficiently diligent search, however, reveals one striking instance of unfettered administrative discretion. The Veterans Administration stands in splendid isolation as the single federal administrative agency whose major functions are explicitly insulated from judicial review.[4] And those functions are truly major, whether measured in dollar or caseload terms. In 1973, the agency expended $6.6 billion on almost 5 million active disability and pension cases, its two principal benefit-disbursing activities.[5] Moreover, the agency's activities are not limited to the rote performance of routine, nondiscretionary benefit determinations. In 1973, claimants filed over 50,000 appeals with the final arbiters in the administrative system.[6] Nor does the VA deal merely with a short-term spillover from our involvement in Viet-

---

* B.S. 1960, J.D. 1963, Ph.D. 1967, Northwestern University. Professor of Law, Stanford University.
1. 387 U.S. 136, 140 (1967).
2. *See, e.g.*, Citizens to Preserve Overton Park v. Volpe, 401 U.S. 402, 410 (1971).
3. *See* K. DAVIS, ADMINISTRATIVE LAW ch. 28 (3d ed. 1972); text accompanying notes 18–19 *infra*.
4. *See* 38 U.S.C. § 211(a) (1970).
5. ADMINISTRATOR OF VETERANS AFFAIRS, 1973 VETERANS ADMINISTRATION ANNUAL REPORT 63 (1974) [hereinafter cited as 1973 VA ANNUAL REPORT].
6. *See id.* at 177.

nam. The rather startling fact is that even if we never engage in another
war, the agency—if its present functions remain intact—will be engaged
in the distribution of benefits a century from now.[7]

Like other high-volume benefit-distribution systems, the Veterans Administration has largely avoided critical attention from reformers and academics.[8] The mainstream of interest in agency practices has focused primarily on the regulation of important commercial activities and the restriction of vital civil liberties. But in view of its significant impact on such a
substantial number of individuals, the Veterans Administration is simply
too important to be written off as an insignificant part of the administrative
system.[9]

The case for examining the operations of the VA is especially compelling in light of the agency's insulation from judicial review. Unreviewable
administrative discretion, as suggested at the outset, can serve as a corrupting influence. Moreover, the absence of a forum for review reinforces the
low level of visibility afforded any federal agency administering a massive
benefit-distribution system.

Our starting point is the preclusion statute itself, which provides that:

> [T]he decisions of the Administrator on any question of law or fact under
> any law administered by the Veterans Administration providing benefits for vet-
> erans and their dependents or survivors shall be final and conclusive and no other
> official or any court of the United States shall have power or jurisdiction to review
> any such decision by an action in the nature of mandamus or otherwise.[10]

This statute has proved to be a truly impressive barrier to judicial review,
withstanding periodic forays in the judicial forum and the halls of Congress attempting to reduce it to rubble.[11] Indeed, the most recent congressional amendment to the VA statute sealed an opening deftly secured by

---

7. At the end of 1973, there were still more than 500 widows and children of Civil War veterans
receiving compensation payments from the VA. *See id.* at 65. More importantly, past experience indi-
cates that claims for disability benefits peak a number of years after a war; for example, World War
II disability benefit claims reached a high point in 1952. *See* ADMINISTRATIVE CONFERENCE STAFF
REPORT, VA DISABILITY PROCEDURES 5 (1972) [hereinafter cited as VA DISABILITY PROCEDURES].
Hence, Vietnam War claims can be expected to increase steadily in the near future.

8. One benefit-distribution system that has been extensively studied, however, is the Aid to
Families with Dependent Children (AFDC) program of HEW. *See, e.g.,* J. HANDLER, THE "DESERV-
ING POOR": A STUDY OF WELFARE ADMINISTRATION (1971); Rabin, *Implementation of the Cost-of-
Living Adjustment for AFDC Recipients: A Case Study in Welfare Administration,* 118 U. PA. L.
REV. 1143 (1970).

9. This is particularly true as we move into an era where a wide variety of social insurance proposals will raise troublesome questions of administrative design. If we are to have the benefit of
experience in developing new systems for processing injury and accident claims, we should be evaluating existing schemes such as the VA.

10. 38 U.S.C. § 211(a) (1970).

11. For a discussion of the history of the provision, *see* Davis, *Veterans' Benefits, Judicial Review, and the Constitutional Problems of Positive Government,* 39 IND. L.J. 183 (1964); Note, *Judicial Review and the Governmental Recovery of Veterans' Benefits,* 118 U. PA. L. REV. 288 (1969).
Extensive hearings on the judicial review issue can be found in *Hearings on Judicial Review of Veterans' Claims Before a Special Subcomm. of the House Comm. on Veterans Affairs,* 86th Cong., 2d
Sess. (1960) & 87th Cong., 2d Sess. (1962).

the ingenuity of the Circuit Court of Appeals for the District of Columbia[12] and a 1974 Supreme Court opinion appears to provide additional fortification to the preclusion mandate.[13] Although the VA's isolation from judicial scrutiny may be anachronistic, it is hardly through political oversight.

The interesting question, of course, is whether explicit preclusion can be justified. The discussion that follows explores various aspects of that question, ranging from constitutional considerations to administrative practicalities. I would emphasize, however, that I view this Essay as exploratory in nature. While I state my conclusions on those issues that can be examined without exhaustive investigative data, my principle objective is to clarify the issues that require more detailed empirical work. At the same time I hope to achieve the broader goal of illustrating some of the tensions that exist between a high-volume benefit-distribution system and our politico-cultural notions of due process. But, this Essay should be read as a preliminary rather than a comprehensive analysis of the VA's claims-processing system.

I. CONSTITUTIONAL DISCOURSE ON PRECLUSION

Despite its longevity,[14] the VA no-review provision was not construed by the Supreme Court until the 1973 Term. The case that finally brought section 211(a) before the Court, *Johnson v. Robison*,[15] involved a claim by a conscientious objector for educational benefits under the Veterans Readjustment Act of 1966. Because Robison had performed alternative civilian service, he was denied benefits on the grounds that he failed to meet the statutory requirement of service on "active duty." Attacking the constitutionality of the active-duty requirement, Robison argued that the statute denied his right to free exercise of religion and equal protection of the laws under the first and fifth amendments, respectively.

The VA countered by seeking dismissal under section 211(a) as well as contesting his substantive constitutional claims. While the Supreme Court denied Robison's claim on the merits, it did grant him the right to judicial review, despite the language of section 211(a). The Court distinguished a

---

12. That court read the earlier statutory language precluding review of "a claim for benefits" as applying solely to *initial* claims. Hence, the court allowed review of termination cases. *See, e.g.,* Tracy v. Gleason, 379 F.2d 469 (D.C. Cir. 1967); Wellman v. Whittier, 259 F.2d 163 (D.C. Cir. 1958).

The present language, *see* text accompanying note 10 *supra*, precludes review of "any question of law or fact" instead of "a claim for benefits" under the VA statute. Thus, termination cases are included within the preclusion ambit. The amendment was adopted in 1970. *See* 38 U.S.C. § 211(a) (1970).

13. Johnson v. Robison, 415 U.S. 361 (1974), discussed in text accompanying notes 15–16 *infra*.

14. Congress initially provided a specific preclusion of judicial review in 1887 for pension cases arising under the Tucker Act. *See Hearings on Judicial Review of Veteran's Claims Before a Special Subcomm. of the House Comm. on Veteran's Affairs,* 86th Cong., 2d Sess., at 2595 (1960).

15. 415 U.S. 361 (1974).

constitutional attack on the statutory scheme from a contested individual benefit determination:

> [Section 211(a)] would appear to be aimed at review only of those decisions of law or fact that arise in the administration by the Veterans' Administration of a statute providing benefits for veterans. A decision of law or fact "under" a statute is made by the Administrator in the interpretation or application of a particular provision of the statute to a particular set of facts. Appellee's constitutional challenge is not to any such decision of the Administrator, but rather to a decision of Congress to create a statutory class entitled to benefits that does not include 1–o conscientious objectors who performed alternate civilian service. Thus, as the District Court stated, "the questions of law presented in these proceedings arise under the Constitution, not under the statute whose validity is challenged."[16]

Unfortunately, this conceptual distinction between cases involving individualized application of the benefit provisions and those arising under the Constitution is considerably more troublesome than the Court was willing to recognize. Consider, for example, a disability claim by a veteran of wartime military service, which the VA contests on the grounds that the claimant's injury does not have the required service connection.[17] The veteran, on the other hand, argues that the agency denied his claim because of his postdischarge antiwar activities as a leader of Vietnam Veterans Against the War.

Obviously, the VA would contend that his claim "arises under" the statute, and is insulated from judicial review within the meaning of *Robison*. Presumably, the veteran would similarly cite *Robison* in support of his claim that the case "arises under" the Constitution—specifically, the first amendment guarantee of free speech. The fact that the target of the veteran's attack is not the exclusionary provision of a statute enacted by Congress serves as a dubious basis for distinguishing *Robison*. In the absence of other salient factors, why should an aggrieved party's access to a judicial forum turn on whether his first amendment protections have been abridged by a legislative classification rather than an administrative decision?

Indeed, framing the question in first amendment terms is unduly restrictive. Consider a typical case where no "protected activity" is involved. The veteran's constitutional claim is that the administrator's refusal to recognize his injury as service connected is an arbitrary act, constituting a denial of due process of law. Again, one confronts the question whether a hierarchy of constitutional claims ought to be established—a hierarchy that, by denying the claimant access to the courts, would tolerate administrative arbitrariness based exclusively on individualized factfinding determinations.

---

16. *Id., citing & quoting* Robison v. Johnson, 352 F. Supp. 848, 853 (D. Mass. 1973).

17. Disability benefits are payable only in cases where the veteran establishes that the injury or disease either arose out of or was exacerbated by military service. *See* 38 U.S.C. § 331 (1970).

Having indicated how *Robison* fails to suggest a satisfying basis for distinguishing between statutory classifications and administrative benefit determinations, are we left with an unlimited access-to-court principle? First of all, asserting a constitutional compulsion to provide a judicial forum in benefit-distribution cases is not tantamount to proclaiming a generalized right to judicial review of administrative activity. Where administrative decisions are "committed to agency discretion" it may be that courts ought properly to leave administrative decisions unexamined.[18] But the search for analogues to the VA process does not lead in the direction of "political" decisions to close army bases or recognize foreign governments. Rather, the appropriate comparison is with other high-volume benefit-distribution systems such as AFDC and social security, where the right to judicial review has been largely unquestioned.[19]

Secondly, however, even when due process concerns are clearly raised by explicit preclusion, it is quite another matter to assert an unqualified right to judicial review. The possibility still exists that the case for preclusion can be salvaged by a strong showing of the unique costs of reviewability in this particular administrative system. And those costs must be assessed in the context of the distinctive risks of according finality to VA decisions if we are to make a meaningful determination of what process is due.[20] In the final analysis, then, I am suggesting that a full exploration of

18. The Administrative Procedure Act § 10, 5 U.S.C. § 701(a) (1970) provides: "This chapter [on judicial review] applies . . . except to the extent that—(1) statutes preclude judicial review; or (2) agency action is committed to agency discretion by law." The "committed to agency discretion" provision is discussed at length in Saferstein, *Nonreviewability: A Functional Analysis of "Committed to Agency Discretion,"* 82 Harv. L. Rev. 367 (1968). It is outside the scope of this Essay.

19. However, there has been no concrete opportunity to raise an analogous preclusion question with respect to other benefit-distribution schemes since judicial review has never been explicitly eliminated. For a detailed analysis of one such administrative system, *see* Dixon, *The Welfare State and Mass Justice: A Warning from the Social Security Disability Program,* 1972 Duke L.J. 681.

20. There is strong judicial support for the "flexible" concept of due process. *See* Goldberg v. Kelly, 397 U.S. 254 (1970). Perhaps the leading recent case on procedural due process, *Goldberg* held that a trial-type administrative hearing was required prior to termination of AFDC benefits. But the Court clearly stated that its conclusions were based on a balancing of the costs of such a hearing against the benefits. *Id.* at 256. In fact, in Arnett v. Kennedy, 94 S. Ct. 1633 (1974), six of the Justices split evenly on how the *Goldberg* balancing test should apply to the dismissal of a federal employee who alleged inadequate procedural protections; as a consequence, the employee's dismissal without a trial-type hearing was upheld (the three remaining Justices regarded *Goldberg* as inapplicable and consequently considered the asserted due process concerns as unwarranted).

Of course, these and similar administrative hearing cases do not involve the access-to-court principle, which could be regarded as a more fundamental aspect of due process. But the virtually infinite diversity of administrative systems makes it highly unlikely that the Court would be so bold as to announce an absolute due process bar to preclusion of judicial review. Most critically, one must be cognizant of the fact that there is no magic to the terms "court" and "agency." From a due process perspective, an "agency" process could be established that afforded most of the procedural safeguards that we traditionally associate with a "court." In other words, at some point the internal administrative procedural safeguards may be sufficient, when measured against the additional costs of compelling judicial review, to satisfy due process requirements without access to court. Because we strongly identify the Rule of Law with access to court, I would expect the Court to entertain a very strong presumption, on due process grounds, in favor of access; nevertheless, I would not foreclose the possibility that the presumption could be rebutted.

In the few instances where Congress has enacted somewhat weaker versions of a preclusion statute, the Court has strained to avoid a direct confrontation on the question whether judicial re-due process considerations requires an empirical analysis of the VA claims-processing system.[21]

In practical terms, however, the linedrawing effort in the *Robison* case indicates that the Supreme Court is unlikely to extend the access principle to veterans' benefit claims. Supporting evidence for this conclusion is offered by a Supreme Court decision in the previous Term. In *Ortwein v. Schwab*,[22] the Court by a 5–4 vote upheld Oregon's $25 appellate court filing fee in a case brought by a welfare recipient contesting the county agency's reduction of his old-age benefits. He argued that the filing fee denied him access in fact to judicial review. The Court disagreed, distinguishing the case from a contrary decision 2 years earlier involving divorce filing fees[23] on the grounds that no "fundamental interest" was at stake in *Ortwein*.[24]

Whether the majority would extend this reasoning to an absolute preclusion of review is uncertain, but the "fundamental interest" distinction is strongly reminiscent of the largely discredited rights-privileges dichotomy.[25] To heighten the uncertainty, the *Ortwein* majority went on to assert that the "Court has long recognized that, even in criminal cases, due process does not require a State to provide an appellate system."[26] The statement overlooks the fact that all the cases cited by the Court involved appeals from

view is constitutionally compelled. Thus, in Estep v. United States, 327 U.S. 114 (1946), the Court interpreted the language in the Selective Service and Training Act of 1940, making draft board determinations "final," to create only administrative finality. *See also* Shaughnessy v. Pedreno, 349 U.S. 48 (1955), affording similar treatment to the administrative finality provision in the Immigration and Nationality Act of 1952.

The most comprehensive examination of the constitutional right to judicial review is Hart, *The Power of Congress to Limit the Jurisdiction of Federal Courts: An Exercise in Dialectic*, 66 HARV. L. REV. 1362 (1953), discussing the circumstances in which article III, § 1, as well as the due process clause, might be taken to compel judicial review.

21. *See* note 20 *supra*. In the next Part, I attempt to identify with some precision the major questions that a comprehensive analysis of the VA would be obliged to consider.

22. 410 U.S. 656 (1973).

23. Boddie v. Connecticut, 401 U.S. 371 (1971).

24. *Id.* at 659. The Supreme Court's reluctance to extend procedural due process beyond its existing limits in welfare-type cases is demonstrated in a series of recent decisions involving the right to a pretermination agency hearing. The Court has carefully avoided extending the procedural safeguards granted to AFDC recipients in Goldberg v. Kelly, 397 U.S. 254 (1970), to either Social Security disability recipients or unemployment compensation recipients. *See* Torres v. New York Dep't of Labor, 410 U.S. 971 (1973); Indiana Employment Security Div. v. Birney, 409 U.S. 540 (1973); Richardson v. Wright, 405 U.S. 208 (1972). *See generally* Meyerhoff & Mishkin, *Application of* Goldberg v. Kelly *Hearing Requirements to Termination of Social Security Benefits*, 26 STAN. L. REV. 549 (1974).

25. In essence, the Court is saying that welfare payments are a gratuity, since its holding is predicated upon the notion that the recipient takes the benefits subject to limiting conditions attached by the state which do not attach to more "fundamental" types of interests. That distinction would be especially embarrassing in the veterans' benefits context, since the VA has made a sustained effort to educate its various constituencies to regard veterans' benefits as an entitlement rather than a form of charity—a "right" earned by service to the nation in a critical calling. *See, e.g.,* G. STEINER, THE STATE OF WELFARE 275 (1971).

For a discussion of the rights-privileges distinction and a systematic argument regarding the injustice it has fostered, *see* Reich, *The New Property*, 73 YALE L.J. 733 (1964).

26. 410 U.S. at 660 (citations omitted).

judicial decisions whereas Ortwein's basic argument was that he had been denied access to *any* court.[27]

The Court's hesitation to embrace a constitutional access principle must be read alongside an earlier view, Justice Brandeis' oft-repeated injunction in the *St. Joseph Stock Yards* case, that "the supremacy of law demands that there shall be opportunity to have some court decide whether an erroneous rule of law was applied; and whether the proceeding in which facts were adjudicated was conducted regularly."[28]

Perhaps the statement is inordinately broad, but in its simplicity it does state a common sense notion of elemental fairness. Indeed, it is the intrinsic appeal of the proposition that explains the lengths to which the Court has gone over the years to avoid explicitly holding that administrative bodies may be given final authority to determine important individual interests in liberty and property. On the other hand, an undoubtedly genuine concern for the ambiguities and complexities of the administrative system has restrained the Court from unreserved acceptance of the Brandeis principle.

Thus, the Court is unlikely to invalidate the VA statute by proclaiming an absolute due process right to judicial review. Indeed, if it holds to the dubious distinction enunciated in *Robison*, VA benefit claims may be insulated from judicial scrutiny in the foreseeable future. On the other hand, one may hope that the Court will decide to include the preclusion question within its prescription that particularized analysis of an administrative scheme is required to determine what process is due.[29] If so, an empirical analysis of the VA, focusing on the risks and benefits of administrative finality, seems essential. In fact, if such an analysis raises serious doubts about the wisdom of preclusion, it should be as relevant to Congress as to the Court.

II. PRECLUSION AND THE ADMINISTRATIVE PROCESS

A. *The System on Paper and the System in Action:*
An Overview

Disability and pension cases generate the bulk of the contested claims for benefits.[30] Since the major concern of this Essay is with the processing of contested claims, it will focus exclusively on those categories, particularly the more troublesome disability claims.[31] A veteran is eligible for compen-

---

27. The dissents are quick to make this point. *See id.* at 662 (Douglas, J., dissenting); *id.* at 665 (Marshall, J., dissenting).
28. St. Joseph Stock Yards Co. v. United States, 298 U.S. 38, 84 (1936) (concurring opinion).
29. *See* note 20 *supra*.
30. It is estimated that 80% of the cases appealed to the Board of Veterans Appeals fall into these two categories. *See* VA DISABILITY PROCEDURES, *supra* note 7, at 26. The VA also administers a variety of housing, educational, and insurance programs that provide assistance to veterans.
31. Steiner estimates that about one-sixth of the appeals to the Board of Veterans Appeals involve

388ROBERT L. RABIN

sation payments, even if only partially disabled, where he can establish a "disability resulting from personal injury suffered or disease contracted in line of duty . . . in the active military, naval, or air service . . . ."[32] Included within this category are preexisting injuries aggravated by activity while in the military service.[33] Moreover, the injury or disease need not be combat-related; it is sufficient for the injury to have occurred while serving in any capacity in wartime service.[34]

To qualify for compensation under the pension program, a veteran must establish total and permanent disability, as well as an income falling below a prescribed level.[35] While such disability is presumed at age 65, a younger veteran must actually establish the existence of his incapacity.[36] Similarly, dependents of a deceased veteran may qualify for coverage under the pension program if they meet the standard of economic need.[37]

The VA has a highly decentralized system for processing benefit claims.[38] Under both the disability and pension programs, eligibility determinations are made by local rating boards in the regional offices, applying statutory rating schedules that establish degrees of disability in 10-percent increments, ranging from 10 percent to 100 percent.[39] The rating boards are 3-member panels, consisting of a doctor and either two legal specialists or a legal and

pension claims. *See* G. STEINER, *supra* note 25, at 276. Another researcher has estimated that while 80–90% of the pension claims are granted, only 40% of the disability claims are honored. VA DISABILITY PROCEDURES, *supra* note 7, at 25.

32. 38 U.S.C. § 331 (1970).
33. *Id.* § 353.
34. Disabilities incurred during peacetime service are also compensable, but at 80% of the amount that would be awarded for wartime service. *Id.* §§ 331, 334.
35. *Id.* § 521.
36. *Id.* § 502.
37. *Id.* §§ 541–43.
38. The following description of the system is based on information gathered in interviews conducted with VA administrative personnel, and on data gathered by the staff of the Administrative Conference of the United States. I would like to express my appreciation to the Conference for making available to me two internal staff reports prepared for the Conference, VA DISABILITY PROCEDURES, *supra* note 7, and ADMINISTRATIVE CONFERENCE STAFF REPORT; JUDICIAL REVIEW OF BENEFIT DETERMINATIONS IN THE SOCIAL SECURITY AND VETERANS ADMINISTRATION (1970). The conclusions reached in this Essay are my own, and should not be attributed in any sense to the Administrative Conference of the United States.
39. The rating schedules provide a highly detailed breakdown of injuries and diseases, based on experiential data collected by the VA. Disability ratings are scheduled on an objective scale, *e.g.*, "average impairment in earning capacity," rather than by individualized subjective standards. *See* 38 C.F.R. ch. 1, pt. 4 (1972). To provide some idea of the complexity of the schedule, consider the following ratings breakdown of bronchial diseases, reported at *id.* § 4.97: "*Bronchitis, chronic.* Severe; with dyspnea at rest or on slight exertion and considerable emphysema, 60. Moderately severe; persistent cough at intervals throughout the day, considerable expectoration, considerable dyspnea on exercise, rales throughout chest, beginning emphysema, 30. Moderate; considerable night or morning cough, slight dyspnea on exercise, scattered bilateral rales, 10. Mild; slight cough, no dyspnea, few rales, 0. *Bronchiectasis.* Pronounced; symptoms in aggravated form, marked emphysema, dyspnea at rest or on slight exertion, cyanosis, marked loss of weight or other evidence of severe impairment of general health, 100. Severe; with considerable emphysema, impairment in general health manifested by loss of weight, anemia, or occasional pulmonary hemorrhages; occasional exacerbations of a few days duration, with fever, etc., are to be expected; demonstrated by lipiodol injection and layer sputum test, 60. Moderate; persistent paroxysmal cough at intervals throughout the day, abundant purulent and fetid expectoration, slight, if any, emphysema or loss of weight, 30. Mild; paroxysmal cough, mostly night or morning purulent expectoration, 10. *Asthma, bronchial.* Pronounced; marked emphysema, attacks very frequent, dyspnea on slight exertion, between attacks, marked loss of weight or

a vocational specialist. In determining the merits of a veteran's disability claim, the board generally must answer two questions: whether the claimed incapacity is based on a service-connected injury or disease, and what disability rating will be assigned to the incapacity.[40]

A unanimous decision by a rating board is final, and if no grounds for reconsideration exist, the veteran has a right of appeal to the Board of Veterans Appeals. A nonunanimous decision goes to the regional Chief Adjudication Officer. If he agrees with the majority, the decision, again, is final and appealable at the option of the claimant; but, if the officer sides with the dissent, the decision is automatically certified to the Board of Veterans Appeals.

The Board of Veterans Appeals, located at agency headquarters in Washington, D.C., also sits in 3-member panels. In deciding appeals from the rating boards, the B.V.A. panels have access to specialized assistance, when deemed necessary, from the Chief Medical Director of the VA, or from independent specialists at medical schools. Again, unanimous decisions of B.V.A. panels are final, but if a dissent is registered, the Chairman of the B.V.A. must review the case. If he sides with the majority, finality is achieved. Otherwise, he designates an additional panel to consider the case along with the original panel; the majority vote of the enlarged 6-member panel then decides the case, with the Chairman again voting in case of a deadlock.

The veteran is entitled to a hearing at both stages, before the rating board and before the B.V.A. In fact, the B.V.A. has traveling panels which hold hearings at many of the regional offices on an annual basis. Whether the veteran participates in a hearing or not, both the B.V.A. and the rating board are required to reopen the case if the veteran can establish that he has new evidence to present. And, if an appeal is taken, the rating board customarily reconsiders the record before certifying it to the B.V.A.

With this capsule view of the formal process in mind, some central characteristics of the system in action may be considered. The overwhelming majority of cases are decided without formal hearings. During 1973, for example, the B.V.A. disposed of 29,825 appeals while holding only 971 formal hearings.[41] More than two-thirds of these appeals were denied or

---

other evidence of severe impairment of general health, 100. Severe; moderate emphysema, frequent attacks (one or more weekly), marked dyspnea on exertion between attacks, impairment in general health manifested by malnutrition, etc., 60. Moderate; slight to moderate emphysema, attacks rather frequent (10–14 day intervals), moderate dyspnea on exertion between attacks, 30. Mild; without emphysema, and occurring at widely separate intervals, 10. *Emphysema*. No separate rating: covered by basic condition."

40. The issues in pension cases are somewhat different. In that category, service connection ordinarily need not be established. However, where the claimant is the survivor of a veteran, establishing service connection results in a higher pension, so the issue is sometimes critical. Pension cases involving survivors also can raise a variety of legal-survivor-status questions that do not arise in disability cases.

41. 1973 VA ANNUAL REPORT, *supra* note 5, at 99. Roughly one-third of the appeals were heard in the regional offices by traveling sections of the B.V.A.

dismissed.[42] While no official statistics are available, VA officials suggest that the vast majority of claims determined by local rating boards are similarly decided without a hearing.[43]

When requested, however, both the rating boards and the B.V.A. hold hearings. Nonadversarial in nature, with no advocate appearing in opposition to the claimant, the hearings basically are designed to let the ex-serviceman tell his story with the assistance of any witnesses he wishes to present. By regulation the administrators are instructed to grant the claim unless a reasonable doubt exists as to its validity.[44]

To make matters more concrete, let us take the case of a hypothetical claimant. Suppose a veteran of the Vietnam War, honorably discharged from active service in 1971, claims disability benefits on the basis of an ulcer initially diagnosed in 1974, but which he firmly believes originated during his period of military service. Accordingly, he fills out the appropriate forms and applies for disability benefits at his regional VA office. He encloses an examination report and supporting letter from his personal physician, suggesting somewhat equivocally that the ulcer may have originated during the period of military service.

By regulation, many chronic diseases, including peptic ulcers, are subject to a 1-year presumption; more specifically, the occurrence of a disease that is at least 10-percent disabling within a year of discharge from the military creates a rebuttable presumption that the ailment is service connected.[45] At the time the claim is filed, the rating board automatically sends for the claimant's armed services health record, which, let us assume, shows no evidence of treatment for a condition likely to result in an ulcer. He is also sent to a VA hospital for an examination, which similarly provides no positive evidence on the service-connection issue. Since the presumptive period has run, the board informs our hypothetical claimant that his claim is denied. If he has no additional evidence to offer, his next step is either to request a hearing or to trigger the appeals process by filing a Notice of Disagreement with the rating board.

By this time the claimant is almost certainly aware of the single most distinctive characteristic of the VA process: the availability of assistance from military service organizations. For many years, the major service organizations, including the American Legion, the Veterans of Foreign Wars, Amvets, and a number of other smaller veterans' associations have played an indispensable role in the administration of veterans' claims cases. By congressional charter, these service organizations provide free assistance,

---

42. *Id.*
43. VA Disability Procedures, *supra* note 7, at 99.
44. 38 C.F.R. § 3.102 (1972).
45. *Id.* § 3.307(a)(3).

through their certified service representatives, to claimants seeking benefits from the VA. Indeed, only a certified service representative, or an attorney, may represent a veteran before the rating board and the B.V.A. And, since the fee an attorney can collect in a claims case is limited by statute to $10, lawyers have been effectively frozen out of the process.[46] Hence, the disability claimant either represents himself or seeks assistance from a service representative.

However, there are real limitations on the claimant's capacity to represent himself. Most importantly, perhaps, he is denied access to his personal file, including his military service health record. Frequently, crucial aspects of the case turn on the veteran's military service record, which includes a complete rundown on every reported health problem experienced by the claimant while in the service. Obviously, such a record is vastly more precise than the claimant's dim recollections based on inexpert personal assessment. By contrast, when authorized by the veteran, a service representative is granted full access to these records.

Apart from the problem of access to the records, most claimants are wholly inexperienced at assembling and interpreting medical evidence or arguing a case; the service representative, on the other hand, is a professional. Moreover, the claimant may find it inconvenient to appear before the rating board, and he will almost certainly encounter difficulties in appearing before the B.V.A., particularly if he cannot be placed on its limited local hearing docket. In contrast, the service organizations maintain their offices in VA headquarters and, consequently, are available on a routine basis for any required formal appearance in a case. Most critically, the claimant deals with a faceless bureaucracy; the service representative, on the other hand, is linked into an established network of informal contacts with the administrators.

Let us return now to our serviceman with the peptic ulcer. Probably, either through word-of-mouth or close reading of the application form for compensation, he was aware of the service organizations when he filed his claim. In any event, he is virtually certain to become cognizant of their role prior to a personal appearance—if from no other source, then from the VA officials with whom he deals. Clearly, compelling reasons exist for requesting assistance from a service representative: representation is highly professional, free of charge, and imposes no obligations. The chances are that our claimant will forego the opportunity of handling his own case.

The service representative's first step is to exhaust all administrative remedies at the local level. These are predominantly informal. An expe-

---

46. Less than 2% of the claimants appealing to the B.V.A. in 1973 were represented by an attorney. 1973 VA ANNUAL REPORT, *supra* note 5, at 99.

rienced service representative will personally review a case with the rating board, pointing out why he thinks they are taking an unreasonably harsh view or suggesting why they ought to gather further information. Most cases are so resolved, through discussion rather than hearing.

If the case cannot be satisfactorily concluded, the representative will suggest that the claimant file a Notice of Disagreement, thereby triggering his appeal. The rating board will respond with a Statement of the Case, a largely conclusory statement of its reasons for denial. If the claimant remains unsatisfied, he files an appeal. The rating board then takes a last look at the case before certifying it to the B.V.A.

If the claimant is represented by a service organization with representatives at central VA headquarters, informal negotiations will resume in that forum. Indeed, even before a B.V.A. panel is assigned, the Washington service representative will receive the claimant's file. And, whether the service organization has a national office or not, it is given the opportunity to insert detailed comments in the file, in anticipation of B.V.A. consideration.

If the B.V.A. upholds the rating board, the appeals process is exhausted, and judicial review is unavailable. But perhaps the claimant has received a sufficient amount of attention; perhaps there is no need for further review. It is to that question that we now turn.

B. *The Troublesome Aspects of Preclusion*

For better or worse, the VA benefit-distribution system represents a significant departure from the prevailing norms of procedural justice incorporated in the common law, adversary model. In most cases, the claimant is confronted with two alternatives, both of which breach the due process model. On the one hand, he can represent himself in a decisionmaking process in which he has limited access to relevant information, insubstantial contact with the deciding officials, no discernible adverse party, and no opportunity for judicial review. Or, on the other hand, he can retain a service representative who has virtually unlimited access to data, and absolute freedom to initiate ex parte contacts with the decisionmakers.

Let us examine these two alternatives, with primary emphasis on the problem of precluding access to the courts. If a claimant decides to represent himself—a situation that occurs with surprising frequency[47]—one can easily imagine a scenario that makes the absence of judicial review problematic. Putting aside the classic function of review as a check on the possibility of arbitrary official behavior,[48] a real question exists whether the

---

47. Of the claimants who appealed to the B.V.A. in 1973, 22% represented themselves. *Id*. Almost certainly, an even higher percentage of cases dropped prior to appeal involve self-representation.

48. This function will be deemphasized only because the possibility of an arbitrary official deci-

claimant can effectively present his case for decision within the limits of the present system. Lacking access to his army file, with no skills of advocacy, without a clear sense of the value of obtaining additional evidence nor of the interpretation to be given existing, highly specialized information, the claimant may be hopelessly inept at presenting his case. Small comfort derives from the VA's assurances that it sees its mission as providing aid and assistance to veterans.[49] For the agency's favorable disposition may be largely irrelevant if the claimant who represents himself must overcome serious handicaps to the effective presentation of his case.

Moreover, we need to know considerably more about the entire range of constraints on the decisionmakers. Rating board and B.V.A. decisions, for example, are subject to a sophisticated internal quality-control review that provides both individualized feedback to operating personnel and information used in the agency's promotion and demotion system.[50] Such constraints can have the effect of limiting the extent to which officials will liberally construe an inadequate paper record.

It may be objected that the developing line of argument proves too much —that the only effective judicial safeguard against administrative inability to assess fairly the case of an unrepresented claimant is de novo judicial review—and that such a remedy would create an intolerable burden on the federal courts.[51] It is beyond the scope of this preliminary analysis to choose between limited and de novo review. Even assuming, however, that de novo review would create an intolerable burden on the judicial system,[52] limited appellate review for "arbitrariness" would arguably have a highly salutary effect, encouraging the agency to establish general procedures that would ensure the construction of a record capable of withstanding the threat of judicial review.

But what price judicial review? Would we be opening the door, as both the VA and the service organizations fear, to the requirement of trial-type

---

sion—*i.e.,* one not based on rational inferences drawn from the facts of the case—is common to all administrative systems. Rather than downplaying the role of judicial review generally as a safeguard against such arbitrariness, I seek to highlight specifically troublesome aspects of precluding review in the VA context.

49. Agencies making determinations of entitlement do not have a history, by and large, of playing the role of advocate for their client groups; witness the HEW welfare bureaucracy and the Selective Service System. For a discussion of these respective agencies, *see* Rabin, *Implementation of the Cost-of-Living Adjustment for AFDC Recipients: A Case Study in Welfare Administration,* 188 U. Pa. L. Rev. 1143 (1970); Rabin, *Do You Believe in a Supreme Being: The Administration of the Conscientious Objector Exemption,* 1967 Wis. L. Rev. 642. It has been forcefully argued, however, that the VA perceives its mission primarily as a service organization for veterans, including those seeking benefits. *See* G. Steiner, *supra* note 25, at 275–76.

50. For a description of the VA internal audit system, *see* Mashaw, *The Management Side of Due Process,* 59 Cornell L. Rev. 772 (1974).

51. Lay testimony might be relevant on issues of employability or overt pathological behavior, for example.

52. But it is questionable whether such an overload would in fact occur. *See* text accompanying notes 61–64 *infra.*

procedures in contested cases? This conclusion seems unwarranted. One must keep in mind that the critical issues in VA disability cases—service connection and degree of disability—do not rest to any important extent on determinations of credibility. Disputed claims generally involve conflicting inferences in medical reports or inconclusive evidence on occupational capabilities. Thus, a strong argument can be made that "hearings," in the sense of oral testimony or demeanor evidence, should not be woodenly regarded as essential elements of fundamental fairness.

If experience shows that the VA decisionmakers can provide an intelligible rationale for their decisions on the basis of largely written evidence—typically, army medical records, subsequent medical history, and relevant lay testimony—then the courts are highly unlikely to judicialize the agency's procedures.[53] A court would be likely, however, to demand that an equally intelligible and persuasive basis for denial of benefits exist, whether the claimant was represented by a service organization or not.

Now, consider the other alternative: the claimant decides to put his case in the hands of a service representative. Would the compulsion to require judicial review still exist in this situation? Again, let us put the ever-present possibility of arbitrary official behavior aside;[54] not on grounds of irrelevance, but to search for reasons specific to the VA system for favoring judicial review. To ascertain those reasons, we must take a closer look at the role of the service organization.

As indicated earlier, the service organizations are uniquely bound up in the administrative system. By signing the requisite power of attorney, a client provides his service representative with access to the claimant's army health records and any relevant supporting documents in the file. The established norms, emphasizing interchange, cooperation and mutual support, make it possible for the representative to probe informally the predispositions of the administrators assigned to a particular case, and to attempt to persuade agency officials to see the claimant's case in the most favorable light.

Service representatives rather quickly develop expertise in interpreting technical medical records and predicting the behavior of specific administrative officials. They are trained by experienced colleagues and introduced into the fraternity at an early date, where daily encounters with agency

---

53. Other mass disability and status determination systems have long operated with informal nonadversary decisionmaking processes, and have successfully withstood due process attacks in the courts. Examples include: Social Security disability determinations, Immigration and Naturalization Service change-of-status determinations, and Selective Service System classification changes. Indeed, the Supreme Court has reiterated in a number of recent decisions its intention to treat procedural due process as a flexible concept when measuring the adequacy of specific administrative hearing procedures. See, e.g., Richardson v. Wright, 405 U.S. 208 (1972); Richardson v. Perales, 402 U.S. 389 (1971).

54. See note 48 supra.

officials are the inevitable byproduct of the office-sharing arrangement. In fact, VA officials tend to regard the service representatives as partners in administering the system.[55]

Arguably, of course, experience, informality, and mutual trust are indispensable attributes of a system designed to handle mass claims in an expeditious manner. Unfortunately, it is just this atmosphere of mutual supportiveness that generates concern over the absence of judicial review. Experience with other decisionmaking systems teaches that where the "advocate" develops loyalty and a sense of obligation to the decisionmaker as well as to his client, role conflict is inevitable.[56] The best interests of the client do not necessarily jibe with the perceived interests of "the system."

While the VA appears to be a strongly client-oriented organization, the fact is that in 1973, the B.V.A. alone denied more than 20,000 benefit claims.[57] In other words, the VA is confronted with an impressive number of demands that it regards as unwarranted. And, judging from the reversal rate on appeal, a very substantial number of difficult cases occur that require careful scrutiny. In 1973 alone, rating board decisions were overturned by the B.V.A. in 4,143 cases and remanded for further consideration in an additional 4,928 situations.[58] In total, disagreement arose between the rating boards and the B.V.A. in almost one out of three cases disposed of on appeal during the year.[59]

The inevitable conclusion is that cases must arise fairly regularly in which the rating board and the service representative honestly disagree on the appropriate disposition. On a close question of the service-connected origin of a claim, does the veteran's interest sometimes take second place to the service representative's ongoing relationship with VA officials? After all, there will be other battles to fight in the future. Where the extent of disability is at issue, are disagreements compromised by splitting the difference in rating disputes? Where the service representative is satisfied with the proposed resolution of the dispute, how vigorous are his efforts to persuade his client that further contentiousness would be useless? And, do service representatives slacken their continuing efforts where claimants are regarded as overly persistent? These are questions that call for empirical

---

55. *See* G. STEINER, *supra* note 25, at 277–79.

56. The most frequently cited example is plea-bargaining practice in the criminal justice system. For a particularly harsh view of the practice from a sociological perspective, *see* Blumberg, *The Practice of Law as Confidence Game: Organization Cooptation of a Profession,* 1 LAW & Soc'Y REV. 15 (1967). On the prosecutor's role constraints, *see* Rabin, *Agency Criminal Referrals in the Federal System: An Empirical Study of Prosecutorial Discretion,* 24 STAN. L. REV. 1036 (1972).

57. *See* 1973 VA ANNUAL REPORT, *supra* note 5, at 99.

58. *Id.*

59. The B.V.A. disposed of a total caseload of 29,825 during 1973. A substantial number of appeals are closed by recommendation of the rating board prior to certification of the case to the B.V.A. In 1973, 9,803 cases were so decided. *Id.*

answers, rather than mere speculation. But in the absence of a careful study, they raise unsettling issues about the absence of judicial review.[60]

Let me reiterate that I am not arguing for de novo review, nor am I suggesting the omniscience of attorneys or courts in ferreting out every instance of potential injustice. It is the deterrent effect of judicial review— its tendency to counter decisionmaking through private accommodation by encouraging a certain degree of arms-length formality—that is the salient characteristic here. The mere existence of a forum for review may indirectly benefit claimants who in fact never proceed beyond the agency, as well as those sufficiently aggrieved to consult a lawyer after exhausting all administrative remedies.

The existence of the preclusion statute cannot be explained solely by reference to logical arguments generated by its proponents. The VA and service organizations have strenuously resisted judicial review; but, one suspects, not entirely for disinterested reasons. Like the rest of us, the VA undoubtedly harbors an instinctive distaste for the idea of formal supervision. Most administrators, one might guess, would prefer not to have their decisions reviewed, if that option were available. One would suspect that self-interest plays a role in the service organizations' resistance to judicial review, as well. Access to the courts is most likely perceived as the lawyers' entering wedge into the system, to be followed by formalization of the administrative process at the expense of the service organizations.

But it would be a mistake to dismiss the preclusion position as merely a product of effective lobbying by groups narrowly pursuing their own self-interest. Its proponents have formulated serious arguments, albeit in conclusory form, that demand refutation by advocates of judicial review. I have already discussed one such argument: that judicial review would inevitably lead to time-consuming and expensive trial-type administrative adjudication.[61] The other major arguments focus on the undesirable consequences reviewability would impose on the judicial system itself.

First, the VA has argued that judicial review would seriously overburden the courts. The B.V.A. has disposed of approximately 30,000 cases per

---

60. Moreover, I may be grossly oversimplifying the client-representative relationship by suggesting a twofold categorization of claimants, comprising those who seek representation and those who do not. In fact, it seems quite likely that substantial groups of veterans find the two alternatives almost equally disagreeable and almost randomly opt for one or the other. Intuitively, for example, one would suppose that a "new breed" of serviceman coming out of the Vietnam War would be less disposed than their fathers or older brothers to be represented by the traditional service organizations. While those organizations have no membership prerequisites—indeed some, like the American Red Cross, are not exclusively veterans organizations—they do possess a longstanding politico-cultural identification that creates a reluctant client-representative relationship, at best. Similarly, one wonders how frequently black and other minority veterans—who constitute an extremely small percentage of service organization membership—seek representation, and whether background and cultural variables affect the nature of the relationship in these cases.

61. See text accompanying notes 51–53 supra.

year over the last decade, a staggering caseload sufficient in the past to dampen congressional enthusiasm for judicial review. In fact, however, about 10,000 of those appeals are reversed or remanded during a typical year; hence, if we assume that judicial review would not increase the number of appeals to the B.V.A., the potential judicial caseload is reduced to 20,000 per year.[62]

While this decrease would not be likely to raise congressional enthusiasm to a high pitch, more refined analysis of the caseload may suggest a further reduction of the potential burden on the courts. It is possible, for example, that virtually all of these cases are appealed only because it is essentially costless to do so. If that is true, correspondingly frivolous judicial appeals would be far less likely to occur for economic reasons. A specialized bar does not exist, nor would the highly decentralized pattern of claims be likely to generate one. In general, disability cases would require attorneys who were able to understand and interpret highly technical medical chronologies. Furthermore, if review were to be de novo, judicial rules of evidence would require validation of complex medical records by expert witnesses. All of these factors add up to a high cost of litigation, with fees dependent upon the successful outcome of the case.[63] Hence, it is far from clear that frustrated litigants would overwhelm the courts.[64]

Nor is Congress helpless to determine how wide the floodgates are to be opened. As implied above, the choice between de novo review and limited appellate review would impose differential costs on litigants, and consequently influence the size of the appellate docket. In addition, it would be possible to circumscribe the caseload by limiting jurisdiction to specific issues—such as service connection in disability cases. In sum, once we have detailed data on the types of cases likely to be appealed, the floodgates can be controlled by careful system design.

A second argument made by the VA goes to the competence rather than the capacity of the courts. The suggestion is that since benefit controversies tend to involve highly technical issues, turning on conflicting medical interpretations of specific factual circumstances, judicial review would serve no useful purpose.

62. 1973 VA Annual Report, *supra* note 5, at 99.

63. The treatment of attorneys' fees raises distinctive issues. For an example of a statutory resolution of the problem, see 42 U.S.C. § 406(b)(2) (1970) (attorneys' fees in Social Security disability cases). Obviously, an alternative to statutory treatment would be to let the market work out its own resolution of the issue.

64. A further refinement in analysis would take into account the real possibility that systematic differences exist in the likelihood of appeal, depending on the issue in controversy. For example, degree-of-disability cases frequently tend to involve relatively slight differences of opinion—and correspondingly limited dollar amounts in controversy—over the proper interpretation of the ratings schedule. See note 39 *supra*. On the other hand, service connection is an all-or-nothing issue; if the claimant fails to establish the required nexus, he receives no benefits. Correspondingly, the differing inferences drawn by the parties are more sharply defined in the latter situation. Hence, even

Here the VA position appears to misconceive the role of judicial review. An argument can be made that the generalist federal district court judge would be severely hampered as a factfinder by lack of expertise. But the argument merely sets up a straw man; those who advocate de novo review anticipate a specialized court of veterans appeals. If jurisdiction were to be vested in the federal district courts, it would be true *appellate* jurisdiction—limited in scope, presumably, to reviewing for arbitrariness on the record. And, it is not unusual to provide for appellate review of technical findings of fact; indeed, judicial review of administrative action characteristically requires judges to review findings of highly specialized bodies.

Finally, one should not be overwhelmed by the notion of expertise in disability and pension determinations. Essentially, the service-connection issue involves establishing an activity-injury nexus similar to that classically encountered in statutory no-fault injury compensation schemes, as well as in common law tort cases where it appears under the rubric "cause in fact." While B.V.A. opinions are punctuated by highly technical language, the issue is basically whether the disease (or injury) either arose out of or was exacerbated by military service. Presented with somewhat more detailed elaboration of the typical medical reports and supporting findings of fact, as well as a discussion of related past precedents, courts would not face insurmountable obstacles in determining whether a given decision was arbitrary.[65]

III. A Tentative Appraisal

My bias in favor of judicial review is undoubtedly apparent. As a general proposition, the constraints and loyalties generated in a bureaucratic system create a potential problem of arbitrariness in the handling of individual cases. Moreover, bureaucratic specialization has its costs as well as its benefits; one who regularly decides hard cases of a certain kind can easily become case-hardened. Hence, my general presumption in favor of judicial review. In dealing specifically with the VA, I have focused on those aspects of its claims-processing system that seem to suggest distinctive reasons for concern about the preclusion of judicial review.

Safeguards, however, are costly, and judicial review is no exception. I have tried to indicate the inadequacies of the in terrorem arguments that

---

assuming nonfrivolous administrative appeals, service-connection cases may be more likely to reach the courts than degree-of-disability cases.

65. Neither rating boards nor the B.V.A. adheres to a system of precedent. Opinions are not published and they are not generally circulated. The VA takes the position that every case is unique and must be decided on its own facts. If judicial review were instituted, the VA practice would undoubtedly be attacked in court. Thus, we encounter another set of questions on the agenda for empirical research: to what extent do the agency files indicate that generalized types of cases arise, and to what extent are those cases, in fact, decided in a similar fashion?

either the VA or the courts would collapse if judicial review were allowed. But I have responded with a series of questions rather than a set of conclusions. On the existing information about the system, the case for access to court seems strong—sufficiently strong to cast a long shadow over the preclusion statute. The need for a detailed, systematic analysis of the VA claims-processing system is correspondingly apparent.

Moral Character

D. L. Rosenhan*

Gross violations of law and public trust generate strong opinions about the moral character of the violators. In the Watergate matters, for example, as one public figure after another was indicted and convicted, the public's response was not merely "What law was violated?," but much more vigorously, "How could these men have so violated their public trust?" These generalized moral concerns were expressed by the violators as well as the observers. Thus, Charles Colson remarked, "Try as I have, I cannot fully explain to myself how I could have strayed as I did from what I know to be right,"[1] while Jeb Magruder observed, "Somewhere between ambition and ideals, I lost my ethical compass."[2]

This Essay reviews our current understanding of moral character with a view to determining the extent to which "moral" behavior can be expected from people. Inspired by the grimness of Watergate, drafted before Richard Nixon resigned, and completed afterwards, this Essay has immediate relevancy, although its focus is not entirely contemporary. Watergate is only the most recent of history's litany of illegalities. In modern times alone Teapot Dome, Auschwitz, Eichmann and Hess, Mississippi, Vietnam, My Lai, and Cambodia raised similar questions about men's moral capacities and sensitivities, and such issues will undoubtedly arise again.

I. Is Moral Character Unitary?

The difficulties inherent in defining moral character seem not to prevent most of us from assuming that such character exists. Moral character is commonly thought of as unitary; it implies not only thought and behavior guided by ethical considerations but consistency in the application of these considerations to behaviors across situations.[3] Thus, we expect people to practice what they preach: people who insist on law and order should not cheat on their income taxes; those trusted with the implementation of justice should not seem to violate the canons of justice; one who speaks often about the dignity of the nation's highest office should not demean it. Dis-

---

* A.B. 1951, Yeshiva College; M.A. 1953, Ph.D. 1958, Columbia University. Professor of Law and Psychology, Stanford University.

1. Washington Post, June 22, 1974, at A8, col. 8.
2. N.Y. Times, May 22, 1974, at 28, col. 7.
3. *See* J. Aronfreed, Conduct and Conscience: The Socialization of Internalized Control over Behavior (1968).

crepancies between statement and deed, or from situation to situation, occasion public distress not only that the law has been violated, but also that
massive flaws have appeared in the moral character of those in high office.

In fact, moral character may be but a figment of our aspirations. This is
to say that we need to believe that moral character exists, but it may not.
Indeed, the disparity between our belief in moral character and the evidence that supports it constitutes a remarkable paradox.

Nearly 50 years ago, in their multivolume *Studies in the Nature of
Character*,[4] Hartshorne and May examined the relationship between diverse
measures of moral character such as honesty, integrity, helpfulness, coop-
erativeness, self-control, and persistence. These measures constitute the
behavioral core of what we commonly mean by moral character; given the
importance of consistency to traditional norms of moral character, one
would expect a high degree of relationship between these measures. To their
distress, Hartshorne and May found the relationship so weak that they concluded that these measures are groups of specific habits rather than generalized traits.[5]

These findings have been confirmed in a host of studies conducted during the last half century.[6] They contradict ordinary intuition and raise serious questions regarding our expectation of consistency in moral behavior.
They tell us that people can be as scrupulous in one situation as they are
unscrupulous in another—absolutely truthful in reporting their income tax,
and yet liars to their wives and children; or frank and open to their families while creating justifiable suspicion at the Internal Revenue Service.
People can be enormously loyal—surely a moral trait—while being devious
and deceptive, often in the name of loyalty. There may be occasional saints
and occasional sinners, people whose morality transcends particular situations and who would be viewed by all of us as having high or low character,
but in the main, few men are utterly moral or immoral.

---

4. H. HARTSHORNE & M. MAY, 1 STUDIES IN THE NATURE OF CHARACTER: STUDIES IN DECEIT
(1928); H. HARTSHORNE, M. MAY & J. MALLER, 2 STUDIES IN THE NATURE OF CHARACTER: STUDIES IN
SERVICE AND SELF-CONTROL (1929); H. HARTSHORNE, M. MAY & F. SHUTTLEWORTH, 3 STUDIES IN
THE NATURE OF CHARACTER: STUDIES IN THE ORGANIZATION OF CHARACTER (1930). Hartshorne, May,
and their co-workers found that the average intercorrelation among 23 tests of moral character (including tests of moral behavior and moral information) was +.30, associated with less than 10% of
the total variance. Individual correlations among the tests rarely exceeded +.45, leaving, at best, better
than 80% of the variance unaccounted for.
5. H. HARTSHORNE, M. MAY & F. SHUTTLEWORTH, *supra* note 4, at 372.
6. For a recent summary of these studies, *see* J. ARONFREED, *supra* note 3. Among the more
significant studies supporting Hartshorne and May's findings, *see* authorities cited in note 4 *supra*, are
R. SEARS, L. RAU & R. ALPERT, IDENTIFICATION AND CHILD REARING 199–240 (1965); Burton, Maccoby
& Allinsmith, *Antecedents of Resistance to Temptation in Four-Year-Old Children*, 32 CHILD DEVELOP.
689 (1961); Stein, *Imitation of Resistance to Temptation*, 38 CHILD DEVELOP. 157 (1967). Factor
analyses of the Hartshorne and May data have produced somewhat greater evidence of consistency in
moral character than the above studies would indicate. *Cf.*, *e.g.*, Burton, *The Generality of Honesty Reconsidered*, 70 PSYCHOL. REV. 481 (1963); Maller, *General and Specific Factors in Character*, 5 J. Soc.
PSYCHOL. 97 (1934). However, evidence from this analysis is not sufficiently powerful to contradict the
statements in the text.

The apparent absence of generalized moral character leaves us vulnerable, both as doers and as judges, precisely because morality in one domain is no guarantor of morality in the remaining ones. However, before remolding our expectations of moral conduct to fit the lack of consistency in moral character, we must distinguish moral behavior from both moral information and moral judgment.

Moral information consists of broad social rules such as: "Be loyal," "Thou shalt not steal," "Support socially constructive programs," and "Be a good samaritan." We are exposed to this kind of information early on and constantly. One's score on a test of moral information is likely to reflect such things as intelligence, socioeconomic station, desire to make a good impression, and the like. But because moral teachings do not come with assigned priorities, moral information has only weak implications for moral behavior. To be taught to be honest and loyal tells us nothing about what to do when honesty and loyalty conflict. Since most of life's critical situations allow the application of two or more conflicting moral rules, the outcome of that conflict is full of ambiguities and significances. For example, should a person kill in order to defend his country? One ought not kill, but neither ought one allow one's country to be overrun by enemies. Should one be loyal to a public servant who asks him to trim a bit off the Constitution? Loyalty is unquestionably a moral virtue, but the Constitution is not to be regarded lightly. Should one cause a "learner" extraordinary pain in the name of a scientific study? Scientists often contribute to the social weal, and knowledge is a virtue in its own right, but how does one disregard human suffering?

Moral judgment refers to the conclusions people reach when moral rules conflict or are ambiguous. But even more significantly, it includes the reasons people offer to support their judgments. These reasons and judgments appear to derive from the kinds of people they are and the ways they see the world, matters that seem to develop independently of moral information but often impinge on how that information is used. Consider the following example: Your employer, a high public servant, has violated a significant law. Should his action be reported or should you forget about it? One person's thinking might go as follows: "If I tell, I'll lose my job. If I don't tell and the matter becomes public, I'll be implicated." The horns of this dilemma are entirely personal, egocentric. For another person the conflict takes the conventional form: "If I tell, I'll violate my obligations of loyalty, of being a good team member, and undermine the programs that my employer espouses. And if I don't tell, I'm a criminal." The judgments here involve maintaining the social order and responding to the expectations of others, and they are quite different from judgments based primarily on egocentric concerns. One can also imagine judgments based on abstract principled considerations, such as contractual obligations to one's employer, his right to privacy and to the trust of his intimates, versus the legal rights of others, perhaps even the majority's welfare.[7]

Whether moral judgment is finally egocentric, conventional, or principled, it is only minimally related to moral behavior. First, moral judgments are much more easily applied to others than they are to one's self. Few people demand of themselves the kind of consistency that is implied in the notion of moral character.[8] Where consistency is not demanded, it is relatively easy for situational temptations to occur: though moral character has its rewards, moral lapses have theirs too. Second, the intention behind an action may not be readily apparent; seemingly moral actions may be motivated by immoral or amoral reasons. Honesty on one's income taxes is hardly a moral virtue when that honesty is predicated on fear or insufficient ingenuity. Conceivably, the lack of relationship between the separate behaviors that comprise moral character reflects differences in intention. Therefore moral behavior in situations where the actor's intention is irrelevant to moral character cannot be used to predict behaviors where moral intentions play a large role. This is not to say that moral judgments are trivial things. Men live in their minds and thoughts as well as in their acts, and what people think is significant and important in its own right. But moral judgments are by no means entirely descriptive or dispositive with regard to moral behavior.[9]

While it would be entirely surprising were there no relationship at all between moral judgment and moral behavior, the fact of the matter is that in study after study moral behavior—how we behave in situations involving moral issues and temptations—and moral judgment—how we view our own or others' behaviors in those situations—are only weakly related. Thus, there is some evidence that people who have achieved "higher" levels of moral thought will cheat less than those whose levels are "lower."[10] In the same study, however, nearly an equally strong relationship was found be-

---

7. The cognitive and philosophical basis for such judgments is elaborated in Kohlberg, *Stage and Sequence: The Cognitive-Developmental Approach to Socialization*, in HANDBOOK OF SOCIALIZATION THEORY AND RESEARCH 347 (D. Goslin ed. 1969). *See also* J. RAWLS, A THEORY OF JUSTICE (1971); Grey, *The First Virtue*, 25 STAN. L. REV. 286 (1973).

8. For a general discussion of this issue, and a provocative point of view, *see* Bem & Allen, *On Predicting Some of the People Some of the Time: The Search for Cross-Situational Consistencies in Behavior*, 81 PSYCHOL. REV. —— (forthcoming 1974).

9. For a fuller discussion of these issues, *see* Rosenhan & London, *Character*, in FOUNDATIONS OF ABNORMAL PSYCHOLOGY 251, 267–79 (P. London & D. Rosenhan eds. 1968); Rosenhan, Moore & Underwood, *The Social Psychology of Moral Behavior*, in MAN AND MORALITY (T. Lickona ed. forthcoming 1975). For a recent summary of the literature on the relationship between moral judgment and moral behavior, *see* W. MISCHEL, PERSONALITY AND ASSESSMENT (1968); Mischel, *A Cognitive Social Learning Approach to Morality and Self-Regulation*, in T. Lickona ed., *supra*.

10. Schwartz, Feldman, Brown & Heingartner, *Some Personality Correlates of Conduct in Two Situations of Moral Conflict*, 37 J. PERSONAL. 41 (1969).

tween people's need for achievement and their tendency to cheat; a much stronger relationship was found between their needs for affiliation and helpfulness and their tendency to cheat. Since needs for achievement, affiliation, and helpfulness coexist with levels of moral judgment, it can readily be seen that predicting behavior from moral judgment alone is bound to be a tenuous matter.

II. Determinants of Moral Behavior

Regardless of cause, consistency in moral behavior is rare indeed. Greater consistency will of course obtain in the presence of well-delineated external constraints, such as explicit rules and clearly defined punishments. But to expect moral consistency from those holding the public trust—be they elected officials or lawyers sworn to uphold the law—on the basis of internalized moral codes, is to be disappointed often. If we are to develop more realistic expectations with respect to moral conduct, we must begin by identifying and examining the factors that significantly affect moral behavior. Justification, situational conditions, and "addiction" are three of the factors that appear to produce inconsistencies in moral behavior.

A. *Justification*

Abandoning the notion of generalized moral character, it seems reasonable to ask: Are there behaviors that most civilized people will refuse to engage in? Violence? Murder? Robbery? Arson? Are there means which nearly all men will abjure, because the men are civilized and the means are immoral? The answer, as far as we understand it and in accord with our worst fears, is: No. There appears to be no limit to the barbarities in which nearly all people will engage, provided they have or have been given sufficient justification. Neither cardinal sins nor felonious acts are beyond the repertoire of most of us. It is clear that these observations, while perhaps consonant with our worst suspicions, are at marked variance with our perceptions and expectations of ourselves and of others. Ask Everyman whether he would murder, and the answer is an unequivocal "No." Most people view themselves as basically honest and upright, hardly prone to violence, and devoid of impulses to plunder. If such impulses are ever acknowledged, they are vigorously suppressed to guarantee that they will never appear in behavior. Or so it seems. Yet the evidence of history—illustrated by the Turkish massacre of nearly a million Armenians in 1915,[11] the brutalities of the Second World War, and My Lai—provides repeated evidence to the

---

11. P. MacKendrick, D. Geanakoplos, J. Hexter & R. Pipes, Western Civilization: The Struggle for Empire to Europe in the Modern World 608 n.* (W. Langer ed. 1968). Interestingly, this massacre is noted as a passing footnote in this leading textbook.

contrary. Those who did not participate directly in the massacres stood by while others did; insofar as moral behavior is concerned such passive acceptance is no better than active participation.

I have purposely taken murders during war as an example because we are all so accustomed to treating them as an exceptional category. This view of war has served to protect the notion that men are basically decent. An opposing view, for which there is growing evidence, holds that acts committed during extreme situations are merely instances of a more general rule that holds that a proper justification, an appropriate construction of reality, or the proper cognitive set can produce an apparently immoral act—often in the name of morality itself.

Justification plays such a large role in behavior that its openendedness creates serious difficulties for moral education. The mind takes its reasons from endless sources, most of them unpredictable by either the individual or those who would judge him. Thus we expect ourselves and others to behave morally because we cannot imagine the variety of justifications that might cause us to behave immorally. Behavioral experiments make the importance of justification clear. One scientist easily induced people to throw bubbling nitric acid into the face of his assistant,[12] the justification being that he was conducting an experiment. Many of his experimental subjects obeyed simply because they were told to do so. Others were certain that the assistant *had* to be protected, even though they couldn't know how. In another experiment, nurses willingly administered seemingly lethal doses of medicine to patients, simply because the doctor had prescribed the dosages.[13] His authority apparently provided the justification for acts clearly contrary to the patients' welfare. Perhaps the nurses felt that they were only executing orders—a defense that may seem acceptable until its similarity to Eichmann's in Jerusalem is recognized.[14]

The most compelling example comes from a series of brilliant experiments conducted by Stanley Milgram.[15] In the name of a scientific experiment ostensibly concerned with examining the effects of punishment on learning, people were asked to "teach" paired-associate words to learners. Each time the learner made an error, the teacher was required to give him a burst of electric shock in increasingly severe dosages. The shock levels ranged from 15 to 450 volts, in steps of 15 volts. The voltages were further designated by labels that read "slight shock," "strong shock," "extreme intensity shock," "danger: severe shock," "XXX." Despite heart-rending pleas

12. Orne & Evans, *Social Control in the Psychological Experiment: Antisocial Behavior and Hypnosis*, 1 J. PERSONAL. & SOC. PSYCHOL. 189 (1965).
13. Hofling, Brotzman, Dalrymple, Graves & Pierce, *An Experimental Study in Nurse-Physician Relationships*, 143 J. NERVOUS & MENTAL DISEASE 171 (1966).
14. *See* H. ARENDT, EICHMANN IN JERUSALEM: A REPORT ON THE BANALITY OF EVIL (1963).
15. S. MILGRAM, OBEDIENCE TO AUTHORITY: AN EXPERIMENTAL VIEW (1974).

from the learner and the evident implications of continuing to shock the learner, nearly 70 percent of the people in the basic experiment obeyed the experimenter's command to continue the experiment throughout the entire series of 450 volts. No person terminated the basic experiment prior to 300 volts.

From Milgram's description of the experiment, people clearly were not blasé about their performance. "Subjects were observed to sweat, tremble, stutter, bite their lips, groan, and dig their fingernails into their flesh. These were characteristic rather than exceptional responses to the experiment."[16]

Most of us would not have expected so many people to obey the experimenter and deliver such harsh, even apparently lethal, pain. Even sophisticated psychiatrists and psychologists had estimated that fewer than two percent (all allegedly psychopathic or otherwise crazy) would administer the full 450 volts.[17] These findings led Milgram to observe:

> With numbing regularity good people were seen to knuckle under to the demands of authority and perform actions that were callous and severe. Men who are in everyday life responsible and decent were seduced by the trappings of authority, by the control of their perceptions, and by the uncritical acceptance of the experimenter's definition of the situation, into performing harsh acts.
>
> . . . .
>
> The results . . . raise the possibility that human nature, or—more specifically—the kind of character produced in American democratic society, cannot be counted on to insulate its citizens from brutality and inhumane treatment at the direction of malevolent authority. A substantial proportion of people do what they are told to do, irrespective of the content of the act and without limitations of conscience, so long as they perceive that the command comes from a legitimate authority.[18]

One ought not generalize too much from these findings. But it does seem clear that ordinary people, many of them well educated, even morally educated, can easily be induced to engage in behaviors that they themselves view as immoral if one provides them with the proper justifications. Invoking God (in whose name nearly all wars have been fought), country, or science, will often serve as sufficient justification. Clearly, powerful moral justifications can motivate immoral behaviors.

Is it so surprising for Charles Colson to say of his activities in the White House: "I suppose on reflection I would have done almost anything I was asked to do without regard to the legal consequences if I believed it was justified as a part of an effort to end the war in Viet Nam. . . . It troubles me because I now realize how easy it is for even strong and well-dis-

---

16. Milgram, *Behavioral Study of Obedience*, 67 J. ABNORMAL & SOC. PSYCHOL. 371, 375 (1963).
17. S. MILGRAM, *supra* note 15, at 30–31.
18. Milgram, *Some Conditions of Obedience and Disobedience to Authority*, 18 HUMAN RELATIONS 57, 74–75 (1965).

ciplined men to lose their perspective under pressure. In my case, while I had studied constitutional law both in college and in law school, . . . I never once even remotely thought that my conduct might trespass upon the Constitution or anyone's rights under it. I had one rule—to get done that which the President wanted done."[19]

B. *Situational Conditions*

Moral behavior seems mainly influenced by situational conditions, conditions that often cannot be anticipated beforehand. The recent work of Darley and Batson provides an especially clear and edifying example.[20] They studied students at a theological seminary, people who certainly had a great deal of moral information and considerable experience in arriving at moral judgments. All of these people were asked to prepare a speech, half to speak on the parable of the Good Samaritan, and half on the vocational problems of ministers. The speeches were carefully rehearsed and were to be delivered at a nearby building. While in transit, however, each of the subjects passed a slumped "victim" planted in an alley way. The critical question for this research was whether these ministry students offered aid to the victim.

One might have expected that those students who had just prepared to speak on the parable of the Good Samaritan would be more sensitized to a victim's need for aid than those speaking on the vocational tribulations of the ministry. That, however, seems not to have been the case. Whether or not the student was going to give a speech on the Good Samaritan did not significantly affect his helping behavior. What did seem to have an effect, interestingly, was the degree to which the students were in a hurry to get to the other building. Some students had been told that they were late for the appointment, others that they were on time, and still others that they were slightly early. Sixty-three percent of the students who were early offered to aid the victim, while only ten percent of those who were late and in a hurry offered to help.[21] Thus, despite moral education and extensive practice in moral judgment, despite being sensitized to the needs of others by the parable of the Good Samaritan, the variable that really seemed to make a difference was the situational one: whether or not one was in a rush.

One may readily identify numerous situational variables that may make more of a difference for moral behavior than does moral information or judgment. Status of, and relationship to, the person who makes the request; opportunity to think about the issues; expectations regarding out-

19. Washington Post, June 22, 1974, at A8, col. 6.
20. Darley & Batson, *"From Jerusalem to Jericho": A Study of Situational and Dispositional Variables in Helping Behavior*, 27 J. PERSONAL. & SOC. PSYCHOL. 100 (1973).
21. *Id.* at 105.

comes; degree to which one is involved in other matters, such that this particular matter seems unimportant and less central to ongoing endeavors —these among a host of others are as likely to be powerful determinants of particular behaviors as moral judgment or information.

Significantly, many of the variables that impinge upon behavior cannot be anticipated beforehand. Nor are they commonly described in portrayals of the apparent moral transgression as powerful determinants. Consequently, it is easy to attribute to one's own or others' behavior intentions that were never present. The press, for example, in describing particularly egregious behavior may not observe that the actor was heavily involved in other issues at the time and thus unable to fully appreciate the consequences of his behavior. Indeed, since we are all so imbued with the notion that each individual is entirely responsible for his own behavior, the notion of situational inducements necessarily seems alien.[22]

C. *Addiction*

What makes it especially difficult to understand the participants in the Watergate crisis, and simultaneously easy to pass moral judgments, is that their addictions are not our addictions. We do not stand in their places; we are not captives of their goals. The notion of addiction is especially expressive of what is meant in this context. It describes the relentless and often passionate pursuit of specific goals. We know, for example, that narcotics are addictive and that men and animals can easily be captive to them. Woods and Shuster taught monkeys to give themselves a "fix" and shortly thereafter found that the monkeys preferred the fix over food, drink, and sex.[23] Since these monkeys did not suffer from unhappy childhoods or other emotional trauma, one does not need to assume that personal anguish or idiosyncrasy precedes this kind of addiction. Rather, monkeys, like people, tend to pursue the things that are available and that give them satisfaction.

If narcotics are addictive, so too are love, science, security, justice, power, personal gain, success, and status—not physiologically, but powerfully nonetheless. Often, a taste of any of them is sufficient to stimulate dreams, and an occasional meal sufficient to make these the dominant rewards in one's life.[24] All of us are potential addicts. And what distinguishes us from the Water-

---

22. For a fuller discussion of the difficulty of evaluating individual behavior without considering situational factors, *see* D. PETERSON, THE CLINICAL STUDY OF SOCIAL BEHAVIOR (1968); W. MISCHEL, *supra* note 9.

23. Shuster & Thompson, *Self-Administration of and Behavioral Dependence on Drugs*, 9 AN-NUAL REV. PHARMACOL. 483 (1969). *See also* Goldstein, *The Pharmacologic Basis of Methadone Treatment*, in PROCEEDINGS OF THE FOURTH NAT'L CONFERENCE ON METHADONE TREATMENT OF THE NAT'L ASS'N FOR THE PREVENTION OF ADDICTION TO NARCOTICS 27 (1972).

24. On the utility of the "addiction model" in understanding personality, *see* Tomkins, *The Psychology of Commitment, Part I: The Constructive Role of Violence and Suffering for the Individual and for his Society*, in AFFECT, COGNITION AND PERSONALITY 148 (S. Tomkins & C. Izard eds. 1965).

gate addicts is not the degree to which we are prone to addiction, but often the form or object of the addiction. Many of us have simply not tasted sufficiently of power to have it affect our dreams and behaviors. Many more of us have found that our addictions are in areas that conflict less, if at all, with law and morality. It is one thing to have been bitten by love and to marry it, and quite another to have been bitten by a love that is already married. One who is in love, of course, cannot make this distinction as easily as we do.

III. THE OUTLOOK FOR IMPROVING MORAL EDUCATION

These fragments from the behavioral science of morality give us some intimation of the nature of moral character: that it is not unitary, that it is subject to situational strains and stresses, that moral judgments are not themselves unitary and that, most important, they bear little relationship to moral behavior.

These studies give us a normative picture. They describe the status of moral character as it appears over the past 50 years. Can the picture be improved? Can one create a group of people, lawyers perhaps, and public servants in general, who have greater unity and strength of moral character?

The question is both good and reasonable, but answers are not readily forthcoming. As evidenced by Watergate, we spend infinitely more time and resources punishing moral infractions than we do examining the components of moral character or the creation of morally constructive roles and rules. It should not surprise us that ready answers to compelling social questions are not presently available.

Yet we know enough, even now, to say what should not be done, and to speculate on what might be done. With regard to the former, it is clear that leaders and potential leaders cannot be selected or eliminated on the basis of their performance on tests of moral character. Moral character is so fragmented that it does not lend itself readily to tests. The suggestion that candidates for admission to law school ought to be screened on the basis of a yet-to-be-constructed test of morality will not succeed on empirical grounds. Test performance would be based largely on moral information and moral judgment and therefore would be unreliable as a predictor of behavior in critical situations.

We can speculate that if moral training is to be at all useful, its major function will lie in anticipatory avoidance, in guiding us away from the full apple after the first bite stimulates desire. The "first bite" will have to be part of the training program, and that is not the typical manner in which moral training is conducted. Presently, moral training takes the form of adjuration, or preaching, or threat. Yet the evidence from a host of studies is that these are very weak methods for inducing moral behavior, because they embody no personal temptation, and little conflict, and therefore little useful resolution that might generalize to other situations.[25] Any program that is worth its name will not merely preach decency but will tempt students to violate ethical canons. And, at the same time, it will provide them examples or personal models of how to resist those temptations. For much as immoral behavior spreads by contagion from above—that is, after all, one of the lessons of Watergate—so too does moral behavior proceed best from moral example, and especially from those who are powerful and attractive.[26]

Problems of moral behavior have long been with us. Watergate is only the most recent of a long series of examples. Despite the prevalence of such problems and the social cost and unrest that is associated with them, very few reasonable solutions have presented themselves. Our current psychological understanding of the nature of moral character does not yet permit us a shred of optimism that these dilemmas will resolve themselves. The need, therefore, is great for applied and theoretical research into moral problems that are fundamental to law and to the fabric of society.

---

25. *See, e.g.,* J. Aronfreed, *supra* note 3; Bryan & Walbek, *Preaching and Practicing Generosity: Children's Actions and Reactions,* 41 Child Develop. 329 (1970); Rosenhan & White, *Observation and Rehearsal as Determinants of Prosocial Behavior,* 5 J. Personal. & Soc. Psychol. 424 (1967).

26. *Cf.* A. Bandura, Principles of Behavior Modification (1969).

Two Models of the Civil Process

Kenneth E. Scott*

The title of this Essay invokes the memory of one whose absence from this volume is much to be regretted and whose contributions to the stature of the Stanford Law School were multifarious, the late Professor Herbert L. Packer.[1] As did Professor Packer in the criminal area, I want to use the device of contrasting two conceptual models. However, in this instance the objective is to shed light on the design of civil procedure and the proper uses of the civil sanction. Specifically, what is the purpose of imposing civil liability on a person, and how should the rules governing civil actions be shaped toward achieving that end?

I

A. *The Conflict Resolution Model*

One possible view of the civil process is a Conflict Resolution Model that sees civil process primarily as a method of achieving peaceful settlement of private disputes. If *A* has acted in a way that injures or threatens to injure *B*, *B*'s resort to force in order to forestall the injury or obtain redress is undesirable, if for no other reason, because violence has a tendency to escalate and to injure innocent bystanders in the process. So in the interests of preserving the peace, society offers through the courts a mechanism for the impartial judgment of personal grievances, as an alternative to retaliation or forcible self-help. The services of the court system are furnished free or at nominal cost to the disputants in order to make the alternative of recourse to the courts more attractive.

This model has only weak implications for the precise content of the legal rules whereby judgment is rendered. To facilitate acceptance of the outcome and resort to the process, the rules should be seen as "fair" in terms of prevailing community values, but notions of what is fair may vary a great deal from one era or society to another. Such variations are of only secondary importance; it is more important for society that the dispute be settled peaceably than that it be settled in any particular way. Indeed, in such applications of the model as arbitration or grievance proceedings, the award may stand by itself, without any opinion undertaking to explain the outcome in terms of rules at all.

* A.B. 1949, William and Mary College; M.A. 1953, Princeton University; LL.B. 1956, Stanford University. Professor of Law, Stanford University.
    1. *See* H. PACKER, THE LIMITS OF THE CRIMINAL SANCTION 149–246 (1968); Packer, *Two Models of the Criminal Process*, 113 U. PA. L. REV. 1 (1964).

The Conflict Resolution Model quite naturally leads to emphasis, first, on the extent to which the plaintiff has been harmed, for that is correlated with the possibility that he may resort to means of redress leading to violence, and second, on compensating him if he is determined to be in the right. Conversely, if his grievance is less intense, concern with giving him a judicial remedy is much less; if he is content to grumble and let it pass, society feels no threat. Hence this model is strongly inclined to let sleeping dogs lie. It does not welcome anyone stirring up trouble or "fomenting litigation," and it takes a dim view of officious intermeddlers. Seeking out persons who are unaware that they have a cause of action or unlikely to litigate a claim or pursue any other remedy, and persuading them to file suit, burdens the courts with matters beyond their proper function and wastes the judicial subsidy on trivia. Champerty and maintenance are genuine abuses of their position by members of the bar, who should be forced to look elsewhere for their subsistence.

B. *The Behavior Modification Model*

A Behavior Modification Model, on the other hand, sees the courts and civil process as a way of altering behavior by imposing costs on a person. Not the resolution of the immediate dispute but its effect on the future conduct of others is the heart of the matter. Consistency and predictability of outcome, therefore, assume an importance that they do not possess in the Conflict Resolution Model.

The implications of the Behavior Modification Model are at their most powerful if coupled with a view of the substantive rules of civil liability as designed to contribute to economic efficiency. If a person negligently injures another, the law of torts requires him to pay for the damages he has caused; if he breaches his agreement, contract law requires him to make whole the person who has relied on it. As a result he is led to take appropriate precautions to avoid injury and to make appropriate judgments about honoring agreements; and consequently, the social loss from such conduct is minimized.[2] The imposition of legal liability is, in economists' jargon, a way of making a person "internalize" or take into account the costs of his actions, thereby inducing appropriate levels of care and performance toward others.[3] But this Essay is not principally concerned with the correctness or justification of the substantive rules of civil liability. Whatever their actual merits may be, if legal rules are seen as attempts to alter public behavior in ways that have been deemed desirable, the civil sanction

---

2. This assumes that social costs and the private damages to the plaintiff are the same, which is not always the case.

3. For a more adequate exposition, *see* R. POSNER, ECONOMIC ANALYSIS OF LAW (1973).

contributes toward that end by depriving one who violates them of his gains or by imposing on him the costs occasioned by his violation.

The Behavior Modification Model, then, focuses on the defendant, not on the plaintiff. The fact that the cost imposed on the defendant takes the form of a payment to the plaintiff is significant only in that it affords the needed incentive for the plaintiff to bring the action and activate the machinery. The real concern is to confront the defendant (and the rest of society) with the right set of costs for different behavioral choices rather than to compensate the plaintiff for his harm or effect a wealth redistribution in the name of equity.

Nonetheless, the incentive to the plaintiff is an aspect of the model's operation that may not be ignored. In particular, the plaintiff's incentive causes difficulty in the class of situations where the costs of the defendant's conduct, while large in the aggregate, are not concentrated on a few but are widely shared in amounts that are in general fairly small. Air pollution provides familiar examples, as does the field of consumer protection.[4] Despite subsidization of the court system (which this model would not generally call for), the private costs of litigation are still substantial. Especially in a system which does not charge the winner's attorneys' fees to the loser, few individuals will sue to recover modest amounts. And even if one person did sue, an award of merely his own damages would not impose the proper total amount of costs on the defendant.

If the Behavior Modification Model is not to prove ineffectual in cases where damages are widely spread, a way to surmount the incentive gap has to be found. The creation of an administrative agency charged with the duty of enforcing the legal rules in these situations is one solution that has been tried. But a statutory instruction is not the same as an incentive for efficient enforcement, as continuing dissatisfaction with the performance of administrative agencies has led a growing number to perceive. Furthermore, agency resources are limited by the political process; in an area in which by definition the stakes for the defendants are large while the theoretical plaintiffs are numerous and only moderately concerned, it is not difficult to predict what will be the balance of pressures exerted on the political process and the agency.

Another device that has evolved to meet this need is the private representative action. In the stockholder's derivative suit or the class action, one plaintiff may sue on behalf of, and seek a judgment in the amount of aggregated damages for, the entire group. This procedure in no way changes the size of the plaintiff's individual recovery, which is still inadequate. If

---

4. *See, e.g.,* Note, *Recent Developments in Truth in Lending Class Actions and Proposed Alternatives*, 27 STAN. L. REV. 101 (1974).

the device is to function effectively, therefore, the incentive must lie else-where, and of course in fact it does—in the recovery of sizeable fee awards by plaintiff's counsel if successful.

II

These two models, like all models, are abstractions from reality; they bring together and organize certain aspects of the civil process as it exists and of our attitudes toward it. They are not the only models which could be constructed and they do not purport to capture all of a complex world. In practice, judges and decisions may reflect a blend of both models, in varying proportions. Nonetheless, it may be enlightening to consider their separate implications for a number of actual problems and cases.

A. *Consumer Class Actions.*

In its most primitive form, the class action is justified on grounds of simple judicial economy. On occasion there exist a number of cases involv-ing common issues of law and fact and often a common defendant, for example, cases involving injuries resulting from a train wreck. Such actions might well be tried separately under either model, but if the commonality is sufficient, there is a saving of time and cost for everyone in trying them to-gether, through joinder or through a class suit where joinder is impractical.

The kind of class action for monetary damages previously discussed, however, is in a different category; it consists of cases that could not be maintained in any other form and it therefore has nothing to do with ju-dicial economy. Two recent leading cases, *Daar v. Yellow Cab Co.*[5] and *Eisen v. Carlisle & Jacquelin*,[6] illustrate the point. In *Daar*, the plaintiff alleged that the defendant Los Angeles cab company had stepped up all of its mileage meters in order to overcharge taxicab passengers, resulting in effective rates above those established by the city public utilities commis-sion. Plaintiff sued on behalf of the thousands of taxicab passengers over-charged during the 4-year period open under the statute of limitations. Under the Behavior Modification Model there is no question that this is a proper suit. Such a suit imposes on the defendant an amount of damages corresponding to his illegal overcharges (which plaintiff alleged could be calculated in the aggregate by applying the overcharge percentage to the trip and mileage information in defendant's records) and thereby removes the incentive to exceed legally established rates. Under the Conflict Resolu-tion Model, on the other hand, this is a quite artificial and unnecessary suit because the loss to the great majority of individual passengers would be so

---

5. 67 Cal. 2d 695, 433 P.2d 732, 63 Cal. Rptr. 724 (1967).
6. 479 F.2d 1005 (2d Cir. 1973), *vacated and remanded*, 417 U.S. 156 (1974).

trifling—a few cents on the dollar—that almost none would bother to pursue the matter for himself.[7]

The fact that there are a large number of class members, many with trifling damages, leads to the recurring question of what disposition should be made of that portion of the judgment that remains after awarding counsels' fees. The standard answer is that, for equitable compensatory reasons, it goes to the injured class. The costs of filing a claim and proving the amount of personal damage are, of course, a great deal less than the cost of conducting the entire litigation. Therefore, one would expect a great many more class members to appear as claimants than as litigants or intervenors at an earlier stage of the action. But the claimants who turn out will not necessarily amount to the whole class, and indeed there would be no way on earth to identify every person who paid for a Los Angeles taxicab ride between 1960 and 1964.

In a case like *Daar*, what follows from the fact that the total damages can be estimated and collected from the defendant without ever knowing or receiving claims from all of the persons injured, and perhaps without ever exhausting the recovery? Under the Behavior Modification Model, nothing follows—the primary objective of imposing the appropriate amount of liability on the rule-breaker has been achieved, there was a sufficient incentive for the plaintiff's attorney to bring the suit, and any surplus remaining after payment of readily identifiable claims might as well go to any designated worthy cause.[8] But under the Conflict Resolution Model, an unidentifiable class and a surplus recovery after claims constitute major embarrassments: why was the suit brought in the first place, if not to redress grievances that were not only identifiable but also large enough to be potentially troublesome? The answer is, of course, to enrich the attorney, which according to conventional wisdom is ethically shocking.

The choice in *Daar* was clear, and so was the decision. The California Supreme Court in a unanimous opinion held that there can be an ascertainable class, bound by the judgment, even though it is not possible to identify all of its individual members. And the court was evidently less troubled by the possibility of an unclaimed recovery than by the prospect that, "absent a class suit, defendant will retain the benefits from its alleged wrongs."[9]

But while California appears to have opted for the Behavior Modifica-

---

7. *Cf.* Berley v. Dreyfus Co., 43 F.R.D. 397, 398 (S.D.N.Y. 1967).

8. The State of California, as amicus curiae, suggested itself. 67 Cal. 2d at 715 n.15, 433 P.2d at 746 n.15, 63 Cal. Rptr. at 738 n.15. When the case was settled, however, the entire amount of $1.4 million (less $200,000 in attorneys' fees) was used to lower taxi rates in Los Angeles for a period of 8 years.

9. 67 Cal. 2d at 715, 433 P.2d at 746, 63 Cal. Rptr. at 738.

tion Model in its approach to class actions,[10] the federal courts seem to be
moving in the other direction. In *Eisen* the plaintiff sued the two New York
Stock Exchange member firms which executed all orders for less than 100
shares ("odd lots"), claiming that they had agreed in violation of the antitrust laws to fix the commission or "differential" which they charged for
this service. The class consisted of all those who had bought or sold odd
lots on the New York Stock Exchange over a 4-year period from 1962 to
1966; its size was estimated at approximately 6 million people, of whom
only about 2¼ million could be identified by name.

Essentially, *Eisen* was like *Daar*—a suit to recover illegal overcharges
collected in small amounts from a large group. While many in the group
could never be identified or expected to come forward to obtain a small
rebate, since the treble damages to which the average class member would
be entitled were estimated to $3.90,[11] it was alleged that the aggregate
damages could be calculated from the volume of transactions shown by
defendants' records and might amount to as much as $120 million.[12] If
there were a surplus in the judgment ultimately collected over attorneys'
fees awarded and claims actually filed, the district court indicated that it
would follow a "fluid recovery" approach in which the surplus would be
used until consumed to reduce the current odd-lot commission, thereby
benefiting odd-lot traders in general as the nearest practical approximation
for the injured class.[13]

But the attitude of the United States Court of Appeals for the Second
Circuit was very different from that of the California Supreme Court. To
quote from Judge Medina's opinion:

> [S]tatements about "disgorging" sums of money for which a defendant may be
> liable, or the "prophylactic" effect of making the wrongdoer suffer the pains of re-
> tribution and generally about providing a remedy for the ills of mankind, do little
> to solve specific legal problems. The result of this approach is almost always confu-

---

10. *See also* Vasquez v. Superior Court, 4 Cal. 3d 800, 484 P.2d 964, 94 Cal. Rptr. 796 (1971), upholding a consumer-fraud class action. The troublesome issue was the extent of common elements and issues necessary to constitute a class. But if damage is so individualized as not to permit reason-ably accurate estimation even in toto without each person's participation, then the class action de-vice would seem to lose one of its major potential advantages. *See* San Jose v. Superior Court, 12 Cal. 3d 447, 525 P.2d 701, 115 Cal. Rptr. 797 (1974).

11. 479 F.2d 1005, 1010 (2d Cir. 1973), *vacated and remanded*, 417 U.S. 156 (1974).

12. *Id.* at 1009. Whether treble damages are appropriate depends upon the probability of success-ful detection and suit for this type of violation. Where the existence of an infraction of the legal rule and the identity of the violator will almost always be known to the injured party, as in a breach of contract, imposing actual damages is a reasonably correct deterrent. But where the violation goes un-detected much of the time, as in a secret price-fixing agreement, the penalty when caught would have to be correspondingly increased to achieve the same expected value of the deterrent.

13. Eisen v. Carlisle & Jacquelin, 52 R.F.D. 253, 264–65 (S.D.N.Y. 1971), *rev'd*, 479 F.2d 1005 (2d Cir. 1973), *vacated and remanded*, 94 S. Ct. 2140 (1974). The court found support for a fluid recovery technique, which benefits the "class" in a general and prospective sense, in prior decisions authorizing use of a recovery to reduce subsequent bus fares, Bebchick v. Public Utilities Comm'n, 318 F.2d 187, 203–04 (D.C. Cir.), *cert. denied*, 373 U.S. 913 (1963), or to support public health services, West Virginia v. Charles Pfizer & Co., 314 F. Supp. 710, 728 (S.D.N.Y. 1970), *aff'd*, 440 F.2d 1079 (2d Cir.), *cert. denied*, 404 U.S. 871 (1971) (the *Drug Cases*).

sion of thought and irrational, emotional and unsound decisions. In cases involving claims of money damages all litigation presumes a desire on the part of the judicial establishment to make the wrongdoer pay for the wrongs he has committed, but to do this by applying settled or clearly stated principles of law, rather than by some process of divination.[14]

Having disposed of the claims of the Behavior Modification Model as an exercise in emotionalism, the opinion went on:

> As soon as the evidence on the remand disclosed the true extent of the membership of the class and the fact that Eisen would not pay for individual notice to the members of the class who could be identified, and the evidence further disclosed that the class membership was of such diversity and was so dispersed that no notice by publication could be devised by the ingenuity of man that could reasonably be expected to notify more than a relatively small proportion of the class, a ruling should have been made forthwith dismissing the case as a class action. . . . The fact that the cost of obtaining proofs of claim by individual members of the class and processing such claims was such as to make it clear that the amounts payable to individual claimants would be so low as to be negligible also should have been enough of itself to warrant dismissal as a class action.[15]

In other words, the only justification for a lawsuit is to compensate the injured party, and if that cannot be achieved the suit should be thrown out.

This plaintiff-compensation attitude toward the function of civil damage suits affected the way the court interpreted the requirement of rule 23(c)(2) of the Federal Rules of Civil Procedure that the members of the class be given "the best notice practicable under the circumstances, including individual notice to all members who can be identified through reasonable effort."[16] The Second Circuit held that all members of the class who could be identified, some 2¼ million people, had to be sent individual mail notice at the outset of the action, at a cost of $315,000.[17] This decision overturned the ruling of the trial judge that it would be sufficient to give individual mail notice to the larger potential claimants, such as institutions and persons with 10 or more transactions, and inform the rest of the class by a process of random selection and newspaper publication, at a total cost of $22,000.[18]

This reading of rule 23(c)(2) subordinates the rule's general standard of what is "practicable under the circumstances" to the subsequent reference to individual notice, although as a matter of language and grammar

---

14. 479 F.2d at 1013.
15. *Id.* at 1016–17.
16. The purpose of the notice is to enable the members of the class to protect their rights personally, if they prefer, by opting out of the class or participating in the suit directly. Under the circumstances of *Eisen*, neither would be likely.
17. 417 U.S. at 167 n.7.
18. *Id.* at 168, *citing* 52 F.R.D. at 263, 267–68. The district court also held a mini-hearing on the merits and then allocated the notification cost between defendants (90%) and plaintiff (10%), an innovation that both the Second Circuit and the Supreme Court held was unauthorized.

the word "including" could easily be read as subordinating individual notice to practicality. To support its adoption of a reading that is both somewhat unnatural and the source of insurmountable difficulties for class action plaintiffs, the Second Circuit opinion intimated without argument or authority that it was necessitated by due process.[19] It is a landmark in judicial sophistry to use the due process concept, in the name of protecting the interests of class members, to reject the only litigation procedure capable of doing so, but Judge Medina brushed the matter aside: "The problem is really one for solution by the Congress. Numerous administrative agencies protect consumers in various ways."[20]

After placing the most costly—and useless—obstacle of an individual notice requirement in the path of a very large class whose members are known, the Second Circuit also took care of the class that has many unidentifiable members. In a sweeping pronouncement it stated: "We hold the 'fluid recovery' concept and practice to be illegal, inadmissable as a solution of the manageability problems of class actions and wholly improper."[21]

It would be incorrect to see the Second Circuit's decision in *Eisen* as destroying the class action device, but in effect it cuts the device back to classes of moderate size whose members for the most part (1) can be personally identified and (2) have individual claims of a size sufficient to warrant putting together a claim and to survive the costs of claims administration. The larger potential of the class action for effective cost deterrence, so important to the Behavior Modification Model, is not merely unattained but is ringingly denounced along the lines of the Conflict Resolution Model.

The Supreme Court opinion in *Eisen* did not display the extreme hostility toward the consumer class action that marked Judge Medina's opinion, and it did not reach the issue of whether the fluid-recovery approach may be used to render a class action manageable. It did, however, uphold the Second Circuit on the crucial individual-notice requirement, founding its position on the "unambiguous requirement of Rule 23,"[22] which, as noted, is unambiguous only if the word "practicable" is ignored. The Supreme Court also held that the notification cost must be borne by the plaintiff rather than allocated between plaintiff and defendant as the district court had done.

---

19. *See, e.g.*, 479 F.2d at 1015, 1018.
20. *Id.* at 1019. The due process requirements for imposing liability on a class of defendants should be distinguished from the due process requirements for representing and binding a class of plaintiffs seeking recovery.
21. *Id.* at 1018. Despite the breadth of the statement, perhaps it should be limited to the context in which it was made—a statutory private antitrust action. *Cf. In re* Hotel Telephone Charges, 500 F.2d 86, 89–90 (9th Cir. 1974).
22. 417 U.S. at 175.

Viewed in terms of the Behavior Modification Model, the Supreme Court, by its *Eisen* construction of the federal notice requirement, has increased the costs of many class actions to no purpose, and has thereby made the deterrence of socially undesired behavior through private court actions less likely and efficient. Apart from the fact that the notice cost is excessive, its imposition on the plaintiff is not itself objectionable, provided it is treated as part of counsel's risky investment in the suit and appropriately compensated in the event plaintiff succeeds.[23] But consumer class actions will not have been completely crippled so long as the Supreme Court does not adopt the Second Circuit's position that fluid-recovery techniques may not be employed.[24]

B. *Appeals and Due Process*

Let me turn from an area of current controversy and unsettled doctrine to one of the most firmly established landmarks in the shifting sands of procedural due process—the proposition that a right of appeal from a trial court judgment is never constitutionally guaranteed. As stated by the Supreme Court in 1894 in *McKane v. Durston*, "[a] review by an appellate court of the final judgment in a criminal case, however grave the offense of which the accused is convicted, was not at common law and is not now a necessary element of due process of law."[25] This view of the requirements of the 14th amendment due process clause in a state criminal case has been regularly cited ever since with approval,[26] and applies with equal force to the federal government under the 5th amendment.[27] If an appeal is not essential in a criminal case, then a fortiori it is not necessary in a civil case.[28]

What is the basis for this firmly held position? One possible answer is historical: when the 14th amendment was adopted, and even today, many states do not by statute provide for appeals in minor criminal offenses or in civil suits below a certain amount; furthermore, there was no appeal of

---

23. The Court's opinion notes that a plaintiff with only $70 at stake would not pay even the more reasonable notice cost of $22,000, which is correct but continues to indulge the fiction that such actions are maintained by plaintiff rather than by counsel. *See id.* at 168.

24. Unfortunately, prior decisions of the Court have in effect confined class actions in the federal courts to situations covered by statutes which confer jurisdiction without the $10,000-amount-in-controversy limitation. Snyder v. Harris, 394 U.S. 332 (1969), held that the separate claims of individual class members could not be aggregated to satisfy the amount requirement, and Zahn v. International Paper Co., 414 U.S. 291 (1973), ruled that no plaintiff whose own claim was below $10,000 could be included in the class. The merit of these constructions of a requirement aimed at excluding minor litigation is a matter for another day.

25. 153 U.S. 684, 687 (1894).

26. *See, e.g.,* Ross v. Moffitt, 94 S. Ct. 2437, 2442, 2444 (1974); Douglas v. California, 372 U.S. 353, 365 (1963) (Harlan, J., dissenting); Griffin v. Illinois, 351 U.S. 12, 18 (1956); Rogers v. Peck, 199 U.S. 425, 435 (1905).

27. District of Columbia v. Clawans, 300 U.S. 617, 627 (1937).

28. Lindsey v. Normet, 405 U.S. 56, 77 (1972); Ohio v. Akron Park Dist., 281 U.S. 74, 80 (1930); Pittsburgh C. C. & St. L. Ry. Co. v. Backus, 154 U.S. 421, 427 (1894); *cf.* Standard Oil Co. v. Missouri, 224 U.S. 270, 286–87 (1912).

right before 1889 in federal criminal cases.[29] But that is not a completely dispositive answer, for as Mr. Justice Frankfurter once noted,[30]

> "Due process" is, perhaps, the least frozen concept of our law—the least confined to history and the most absorptive of powerful social standards of a progressive society.

The position that appeals are never essential draws intellectual support from the Conflict Resolution Model. In terms of a mechanism for settling disputes, one hearing is enough to do the job, and it is all that arbitration and grievance procedures customarily afford. No doubt the loser would like another chance, but that is endlessly true. Rather than the outcome, it is the existence of a form of impartial arbitrament that is essential. Indeed, it is not (so far as due process is concerned) vital that a court provide the one hearing—an administrative agency could serve the purpose just as well.[31]

When approached in terms of the Behavior Modification Model, however, the question is not so clear. Since this model centers on affecting behavior by correctly imposing costs, it necessarily must be quite concerned with the effects of error. There are two types of error—erroneous judgments for the plaintiff and erroneous judgments for the defendant—and each carries with it certain costs. Furthermore, many procedural rules aimed at reducing one type of error will have the effect of increasing the other. For example, if the burden of proof on the plaintiff is increased from a "preponderance of the evidence" standard to one of "clear and convincing evidence" or to proof "beyond a reasonable doubt," errors against the defendant fall but errors against the plaintiff rise. What the model must attempt, therefore, is to minimize the sum of the costs of the two kinds of error and of the operations of the procedural system itself.

How does a right of appeal fare in this framework? The costs of appeals as such are rather low in comparison to those of trials, but how much do appeals contribute to a reduction of error? The answer requires an appraisal of the institutional strengths of appellate courts as compared to trial courts, an endeavor rendered largely speculative by the absence of empirical investigations. Presumably, however, the trial court is usually in the better position to make findings of fact due to the direct and extended exposure of judge and jury to the witnesses and evidence. If the appellate courts substituted their own conclusions, there is no systemic reason to believe they would be more accurate. If anything, the opposite is true, and hence there are a number of rules which call for deference to the initial finder of fact.

---

29. *See* United States v. Sanges, 144 U.S. 310, 319–22 (1892).
30. Griffin v. Illinois, 351 U.S. 12, 20–21 (1956) (concurring opinion).
31. *Cf.* Ortwein v. Schwab, 410 U.S. 656, 659–60 (1973).

On occasion the more intimate involvement of the trial court with the parties and witnesses may activate its prejudices in a way that the more detached appellate court would be less likely to fall prey to, but it would be hard to express that possibility in terms of a defined category of cases. In short, it is difficult to argue that an appeal procedure is necessary in order to reduce the incidence of factfinding errors in initial proceedings.

On the other hand, it can be argued that an appeal procedure contributes to correction of errors of law for two reasons. First, there is the element of specialization. Just as trial courts spend most of their time pursuing disputed facts, appellate courts spend most of their time on questions of law, including matters of statutory interpretation and the reconciliation of conflicting enactments. They may, therefore, do a better job of ascertaining and effectuating the legislative purpose imperfectly expressed. Second, if legal rules are to be effective in exerting pressure on behavior, they must be interpreted consistently and applied in litigation in a predictable manner. A lack of uniformity undermines the Behavior Modification Model in a way that it does not undermine the Conflict Resolution Model, but it is inevitable if there are numerous courts of first instance to handle the volume of cases in a large community. The need for coordination can be met only by the addition of appellate courts, in which the function of making law to some extent has to be vested. When an appellate court announces a rule of law, therefore, a contrary decision by a trial court constitutes genuine error, in more than a circular sense. The combination in the same act of establishing the legal rule and reversing the error below does not make it any less the avoidance of an improper imposition of liability and misdirected cost deterrence.

This suggests that the role of appeal is primarily in reducing the incidence of legal errors, especially as they relate to the lawmaking function of appellate courts. This function may not loom so large as to support a constitutional due process requirement of access to appellate review in every case, and to that extent, there is agreement between the two models. But traditional due process doctrine goes on to conclude that it is entirely up to the state whether or not to afford *any* appellate review—a result that does not necessarily follow. The Behavior Modification Model supports an intermediate position—that a *discretionary* channel of review be open for cases where the costs of legal error are high. Such a position explicitly recognizes the lawmaking function of appellate courts and would require as a matter of due process that they be given the discretion to grant review in order to prevent the erroneous imposition of substantial costs or penalties (that is, in cases above a threshold level of severity).

C. *Standing*

In a number of contexts, courts have voiced concern with the "standing" of a plaintiff to bring suit. Though standing doctrine is tangled and often incoherent, it supposedly focuses on the plaintiff's "personal stake"[32] in the outcome of the controversy—whether that stake is sufficient to ensure "that the questions will be framed with the necessary specificity, that the issues will be contested with the necessary adverseness and that the litigation will be pursued with the necessary vigor to assure that the constitutional challenge will be made in a form traditionally thought to be capable of judicial resolution."[33] For his stake to be sufficient, the plaintiff must have suffered "injury in fact";[34] mere "abstract injury" is not enough.[35]

The content and use of standing doctrine have created numerous problems, which have been discussed elsewhere by the author.[36] Here, however, the doctrine is considered in terms of the two models of the civil litigation process. Under the Conflict Resolution Model, it is not unnatural to be concerned with whether the plaintiff really has enough at stake to warrant invoking the judicial process, particularly since court services are provided at almost no cost to the plaintiff. Does he have a personal grievance of the sort the judicial system was created to resolve, or does he merely have a general dissatisfaction with some aspect of public policy or administration? If the latter, he should talk to his fellow citizens and resort to the political process rather than trying to drag the courts into it. Hence, this model leads to an effort to distinguish between personal and general grievances, between direct injuries (actual or threatened) and abstract injuries, between wrongs that are individual and wrongs that are shared by all citizens. The line may be well-nigh invisible to the uninitiated,[37] but the need to find it is understandable.

The Behavior Modification Model, on the other hand, directs attention to the defendant's conduct rather than to the plaintiff's personal stake. Indeed, it finds more to be concerned about in actions that may never be brought because of inadequate incentives than in those that do make their way into the courts. Damage actions, save in the class context, do not present much of a problem, for they automatically provide an incentive if the proper amount of damages is correctly calculated. But the standing cases commonly involve injunctive or declaratory relief, not damages, and the defendant is usually a government official, not a private citizen. This latter

32. Baker v. Carr, 369 U.S. 186, 204 (1962).
33. Flast v. Cohen, 392 U.S. 83, 106 (1968).
34. Association of Data Processing Serv. Organizations v. Camp, 397 U.S. 150, 152 (1970).
35. O'Shea v. Littleton, 414 U.S. 488, 494 (1974).
36. Scott, *Standing in the Supreme Court—A Functional Analysis*, 86 Harv. L. Rev. 645 (1973).
37. Or even to the Supreme Court, as is demonstrated by the variety of opinions in United States v. Students Challenging Regulatory Agency Procedures (*SCRAP*), 412 U.S. 669 (1973).

is a different kind of civil litigation: judicial review of government action.

How does the Behavior Modification Model operate in this domain? In a way, this is the area where Judge Medina's solution for *Eisen* has been adopted: administrative agencies are making and enforcing legal rules. And, just as for lower courts, it is important that they do so correctly, in the sense discussed in connection with appeals. Under this model, the standing issue disappears and is replaced by the opposite concern—how to draw before the courts cases of official error where no damage judgment serves to induce the plaintiff. If someone is personally sufficiently concerned to bear the litigation expense, well and good;[38] if not, there is reason to consider supplying the incentive through the award of substantial fees to plaintiff's counsel, if successful, though determination of the proper amount (in proportion to benefits achieved) can be quite difficult.

The usual objection to such a position is that it would greatly enlarge the lawmaking role of the courts, a dubious achievement in view of their unelected and unrepresentative character.[39] The concern is legitimate, but it has very little to do with standing. For instance, a suit that calls for a sweeping assertion of judicial power under the 14th amendment may affect the plaintiff in the most direct and pocketbook sense, while a modest request for an application of a narrow and specific constitutional or statutory provision may seem to confer no more benefits on the plaintiff than on any other citizen. In other words, the breadth of the questions the plaintiff calls on the court to decide has no necessary relation to how directly the answer will affect him. By invoking an irrelevant objection on some occasions and finding ways around it on others, the Supreme Court has turned standing doctrine into an incomprehensible jumble and avoided articulating any set of concepts to define the limits of its law-creating role.[40] It certainly seems much more sensible for courts to go beyond the straw man of plaintiff's standing and give substantive reasons why they believe the issue is or is not a proper one to decide or provide a remedy for.

III

The major purpose of this Essay is to suggest two contrasting models of the civil process and to explore their implications, as a way of demonstrat-

38. It is not the artificial intricacies of standing rules but rather the fact that the plaintiff must feel strongly enough to pay the costly expense of litigation that gives assurance of adverseness and a personal stake in the outcome and provides vigor in conducting the litigation.

39. *See, e.g.,* the arguments of the Solicitor General set forth in an appendix to Justice Douglas' dissent in Sierra Club v. Morton, 405 U.S. 727, 753–55 (1972).

40. For example, why would it have been undesirable in terms of the judicial-policy role for the courts to become involved in enforcing the quite limited constitutional provisions at issue in Schlesinger v. Reservists Comm. to Stop the War, 94 S. Ct. 2925 (1974), and United States v. Richardson, 94 S. Ct. 2940 (1974)? If there are good reasons, no one will discern them from the opinions, which instead devote all their energies to manipulating standing arcana.

ing the value of this device in analyzing different sorts of procedural problems. But a secondary purpose is methodological—to contribute to an awareness of the different sorts of models which may be useful. The models developed here are not altogether analogous to those employed by Professor Packer in his work. He established procedural models (Crime Control and Due Process) and then derived substantive implications for the proper use of the criminal sanction. The two civil process models are functional to begin with, based on different ideas as to the purpose of civil litigation, and are then used to derive procedural implications.

Furthermore, his models were polar opposites. Although not described in those terms, they were each directed at one of the two types of error mentioned previously. The Due Process Model was concerned with minimizing erroneous verdicts for the prosecution, *i.e.*, convictions of the innocent; the Crime Control Model was aimed at minimizing erroneous verdicts for the defendant, *i.e.*, acquittals of the guilty.[41] Seen in these terms, the problem does not lie in choosing one model over the other, but in finding the right intermediate procedural mix that minimizes the sum of the costs created by both kinds of error. It is a trade-off problem, not a choice problem.

In this Essay, however, the models are not really in opposition as competing poles. The second model, behavior modification, subsumes the first, conflict resolution, as a special and limited case. Where the plaintiff has suffered a substantial and direct personal injury for which he seeks monetary compensation, the second model as well as the first would direct that it be paid to him by the defendant if the latter is found to be in the wrong. The two models conflict only if the first is taken as exclusive, as defining the outer bounds of the proper use of the civil process.

Presently, that seems too often to be the case. The Conflict Resolution Model is in the ascendant, and its implications seem to be carrying the day, at least in the federal courts.[42] An additional purpose of this Essay, therefore, is to urge a more careful consideration of the claims and implications of the Behavior Modification Model. It has a powerful and consistent underlying rationale, here developed in only the briefest fashion, and it warrants much more than the emotional or casual rejection afforded it by the courts in *Eisen*.

---

41. In statistician's terms, the first is a Type-I error in rejecting the null hypothesis of innocence, while the second is a Type-II error in rejecting the alternative hypothesis of guilt. *See* Friedman, *Trial by Jury*, 26 AM. STATISTICIAN, Apr. 1972, at 21.

42. *See, e.g., In re* Hotel Telephone Charges, 500 F.2d 86 (9th Cir. 1974).

Consumer Credit Law: Rates, Costs, and Benefits

William D. Warren*

Consumer credit legislation can be described as political regulation of an economic process guided by social concerns. According to Richard Posner: "Since the consumer movement and its legislative product do not make the consumer better off, an explanation of this phenomenon in terms of economic theory is rather difficult."[1] Without accepting Posner's conclusion that consumer protection legislation is ineffectual, one can readily agree that an explanation for the nature of much of consumer-oriented law cannot be found in microeconomic theory. Rather it derives from social considerations—largely as perceived by lawyers.

In general, consumer credit legislation represents a pragmatic, ad hoc legislative response to consumer demands for greater consideration and status. Though this growing body of law sometimes confounds economists and exasperates businessmen, a social psychologist might well view it as a relatively minor current of reform in relation to the strong flow of public sentiment toward recognition of an expanding number of asserted social claims, such as civil rights, ethnic identity, environmental protection, and campaign reform. Admittedly, consumers have urged a set of legislative priorities that in some instances may have little or no relation to the efficient allocation of credit resources. For example, a few years ago consumers were offended by the cheekiness of some creditors in showering them with unsolicited credit cards and demanded congressional action to curtail the practice. The resulting federal law prohibiting distribution of unsolicited credit cards has generated enough technical problems—Is a checkbook a credit card? Why not?—to keep many lawyers employed for years to come. The statute provides consumers with no more effective protection than they could achieve by using scissors on the offending cards and may have anticompetitive effects in inhibiting entry by new card issuers into the credit card field. Nonetheless, the unsolicited mailings touched "a particularly sensitive concern: most individuals regard their financial affairs as highly personal matters and are offended when an account is created for them

* A.B. 1948, J.D. 1950, University of Illinois; J.S.D. 1957, Yale University. William B. and Luna M. Scott Professor of Law, Stanford University. The author served as Co-Reporter–Draftsman of the Uniform Consumer Credit Code (U3C) from 1964 to 1974. It seems longer.
1. Adams, *Measuring the Worth of Consumerism*, Wall St. J., Nov. 24, 1972, at 6, col. 4.

without their consent . . . ."[2] Some form of legislative action was required
to dampen the public outcry, even if its effects were only cosmetic.

It is true that social appeal has been the touchstone of consumer legislation—a condition true of most kinds of legislation—with economic considerations too often ignored. This Essay will contend, however, that much
consumer legislation is beneficial and not as inconsistent with economic
principles as Professor Posner suggests.

Daniel Bell has observed: "[R]ationality, as an end, finds itself confronted by the cantankerousness of politics, the politics of interest and the
politics of passion."[3] Indeed, the major obstacle to the development of a
rational system of granting consumer credit is the political process, which
in recent decades has extended control over all aspects of the consumer
credit field. The issue this Essay treats is central to the problem of attaining
rationality in the regulation of consumer credit. The pricing of consumer
credit has been under government control since the inception of the consumer credit industry in this country, with the result that the consumer
credit market has major imperfections which have prevented its efficient
operation in allocating credit resources.[4] It is this writer's view that until a
consensus can be reached on a rational approach to rate regulation, attempts
at meaningful consumer credit reform cannot be fully successful.

I. EVOLUTION OF RATE REGULATION

A. *Usury Background*

George Stigler has described usury legislation as a "simple and almost
uncontroversial field."[5] It is characteristic of the violent differences of opinion that have always swirled around the subject that while most economists see usury laws as simply and uncontroversially evil, virtually all consumers, legislators, administrators—even many creditors—see them as simply and uncontroversially good.

The existence of usury laws in the United States has been the principal
factor shaping the structure of the consumer credit industry. The classic
economic theory of the effect of rate ceilings is that they tend to exclude
from the legitimate credit market those least likely to repay (those with
the fewest assets) and those most expensive to deal with (those who bor-

---

2. Weistart, *Consumer Protection in the Credit Card Industry: Federal Legislative Controls*, 70
MICH. L. REV. 1475, 1499 (1972). The impact on competition is discussed in *id.* at 1501–03.
3. D. BELL, THE COMING OF POST-INDUSTRIAL SOCIETY 366 (1973).
4. Market imperfections are discussed in NAT'L COMM. ON CONSUMER FINANCE, REPORT ON CON-
SUMER CREDIT IN THE UNITED STATES 110–14 (1972) [hereinafter cited as NCCF REPORT]. A market imperfection is "any restriction which tends to inhibit the free interactions of potential borrowers and suppliers of credit." *Id.* at 113.
5. Stigler, *The Law and Economics of Public Policy: A Plea to the Scholars*, 1 J. LEGAL STUDIES
1, 6 (1972).

row the smallest amounts), thus relegating these unsatisfied borrowers to illegal markets.[6] Nineteenth-century economic history confirms this analysis, for during that period the reluctance of creditors to serve consumer borrowers at legal interest rates (usually from 6 to 12 percent)[7] led to the growth of a flourishing illegal loan market.[8]

It is crucial to an understanding of the subsequent development of consumer credit law in this country to observe that the legislative response to the plight of the consumer borrower early in the 20th century was to deal with the problem as social rather than economic in nature. Instead of abandoning usury laws and allowing creditworthy consumers to obtain credit at prices determined by market forces, legislatures were induced to make exceptions to the usury laws for consumer loans by a social welfare movement in the early years of this century—a part of the "crusading progressivism" of that era[9]—that with the best of motives desired to save the "necessitous borrower" from the "loan sharks."

The problem of the day was how to legitimize consumer loans in a manner acceptable to legislatures at a time when "muckraking" was in vogue and popular journals featured articles on moneylenders with titles like "The Lures of the Loan Shark" and "Parasites of the Poor."[10] The solution adopted was to license a narrow class of lenders to charge higher rates for small loans. Licenses were obtainable only by those who could meet standards of character and fitness and who were willing to submit to a regime of heavy administrative supervision. Given the public attitudes of the time toward lenders, there is no reason to believe that any other legislative course lay open.

Subsequently, other exceptions to usury laws were carved out for industrial banks, installment lenders, credit unions, insurance premium financers, and others.[11] The pattern of regulation, however, was the same: access to the market was limited by licensing barriers; ceilings were set on rates; and heavy administrative controls were imposed. The business of granting credit to consumers came to be regulated virtually as a public utility.[12] Ironically, the residual usury laws, which probably owe their continued existence to a vague, inertial public belief that somehow they protect the

---

6. *See id.* The NCCF REPORT, *supra* note 4, at 113, adds: "In some instances a restrictive rate ceiling may also lead to an increase in market concentration."
7. *See* Benfield, *Money, Mortgages, and Migraine—The Usury Headache*, 19 CASE W. RES. L. REV. 819, 838 (1968).
8. *See id.* at 839; I. MICHELMAN, CONSUMER FINANCE: A CASE HISTORY IN AMERICAN BUSINESS 106–11 (1966).
9. *See id.* at 62.
10. *See id.* at 63.
11. A helpful survey of the legislation regulating lender credit is found in B. CURRAN, TRENDS IN CONSUMER CREDIT LEGISLATION, ch. III (1965).
12. Theoretical and practical difficulties in regulating consumer-credit granting as though it were a public utility are noted in NCCF REPORT, *supra* note 4, at 102–03.

needy, now have almost no application to consumer credit transactions except in home-mortgage lending, an activity characterized by high-balance, well-secured loans and good price information—in short, the very area where the case for rate regulation is weakest.[13]

B. *Popularity of Rate Regulation*

The die was cast. From the first draft of the Uniform Small Loan Law in 1916 until the present time, the pricing of consumer credit has been viewed by legislatures as the social problem of protecting the weak against the strong and not as the economic problem of allocating credit resources at prices determined by such factors as the consumer's creditworthiness, the value of the collateral, and the potential costs of collection. Given the current low state of public confidence in government's ability to solve anything by price controls, it is difficult to explain why pricefixing has always been popular with respect to consumer credit in this country. This phenomenon is particularly anomalous when we consider that it has not been repeated in other industrialized countries that are at least as solicitous of the welfare of their consumers as we are of ours.[14]

Perhaps a significant part of the explanation lies in the fact that in America the consumer loan industry, consumers, legislators, and credit administrators have never known a condition other than a regime of price control. The small loan industry or, as it is now called, the consumer finance industry, conceived as it was in the original sin of usury laws, has depended upon rate regulation *cum* licensing to legitimize its very existence.

---

13. *See* Benfield, *supra* note 7, at 843.

14. *Australia* and *New Zealand:* Both rely on the market to set rates in credit transactions and both allow their courts to police transactions on the basis of unconscionability. NCCF REPORT, *supra* note 4, at 95.

Germany: "[M]aximum rates for interest, as in the American usury laws, are unknown in Germany . . . . Section 138 [of the Civil Code] declares a contract void when one person, exploiting the difficulties, indiscretion or inexperience of another, causes to be promised or granted advantages that exceed the value of his consideration to such an extent that the disproportion is obvious." Marschall, *Recent Legislative and Judicial Trends in Consumer Credit in Germany,* in J. ZIEGEL & W. FOSTER, ASPECTS OF COMPARATIVE COMMERCIAL LAW 169 (1969). Section 138 has been applied to interest rate cases. See judgment of Sept. 28, 1965, 19 Neue Juristiche Wochenschrift 836 (Oberlandesgericht Munchen).

Great Britain: The Consumer Credit Act of 1974 does not fix rate ceilings. It provides that: "If a court finds a credit bargain extortionate it may reopen the credit agreement so as to do justice between the parties." Section 138(1). A credit bargain is extortionate if it requires payments that are "grossly exorbitant" or it "otherwise grossly contravenes ordinary principles of fair dealing." Section 139(1). Factors to be taken into consideration in determining whether a credit bargain is extortionate include: (1) interest rates prevailing at the time it was made; (2) the debtor's age, health, experience, and business capacity; (3) the degree to which the debtor was under financial pressure and the nature of that pressure; (4) the degree of risk accepted by the creditor, his relationship to the debtor, and "whether or not a colourable cash price was quoted for any goods or services included in the credit bargain." Section 139(2)–(4).

Sweden: Although Sweden has an elaborate and sophisticated system of consumer protection law, it has apparently never utilized rate ceilings. (Authority for this statement is Rolf Höök, a Swedish lawyer who has done research in consumer law.)

Reared in a habitat of governmental controls, the industry rapidly learned to manipulate these controls for what it perceived to be its own benefit. By the seventh draft of the Uniform Small Loan Law, the "convenience and advantage" standard had been added, allowing administrators to withhold licenses from otherwise qualified lenders on the vague basis that an additional loan office in a given area was not in the "public interest."[15] Thus, over time, the regulated industry has come to have great influence in its own regulation: access to the market is limited to those concerns already in operation; prices are administered by legislative bodies with which the industry has established close relations; and activities are supervised by administrators often friendly to creditors.

Rate regulation in the consumer credit industry is enormously popular with consumers—at least with those able to get credit. In 1968 the state of Washington enacted by popular initiative a 12 percent ceiling on all retail credit,[16] and in 1970 California voters resoundingly rejected by statewide referendum a modest proposal that would have removed the state's constitutional 10 percent interest limitation on loans of more than $100,000 made to corporations and partnerships.[17] Liberal groups have generally favored rate ceilings, and, although they sponsored the first high-rate loan legislation, it is probably a fair statement that liberals have usually wanted rate ceilings to be kept as low as possible.

At the legislative level, two strong incentives can be identified for preserving rate regulation in consumer credit. First, most voters are favorably disposed to it, and far more important politically, a few powerful voter groups—for example, labor unions—are passionate supporters of rate regulation. Second, rate-ceiling laws bestow upon legislators enormous leverage over a giant industry, with all the perquisites that power of this magnitude can bring to its wielders. Of course, rate regulation is the *raison d'être* for credit administrators. Without it there would be no audits, no examinations, no reports—no jobs.

II. Consumer Benefits

Although the past 40 years of consumer credit regulation have seen an enormous expansion in statutorily-created "benefits" for consumers, legislative attitudes toward rate regulation have not substantially changed. When one borrowed $100 in 1942 under the seventh draft of the Uniform Small Loan Law, he could be charged up to 36 percent interest per year,

---

15. *See* B. Curran, *supra* note 11, at 144–57 for the seventh draft of the Uniform Small Loan Law. The "convenience and advantage" standard is found in § 4(b). *Id.* at 147.
16. Wash. Rev. Code Ann. § 63:14:130 (Supp. 1973) (Initiative Measure No. 235, § 3).
17. Proposition 10 was defeated by a vote of 55% to 45%. L.A. Times, Nov. 5, 1970, at 28, col. 2.

and he received only minimal safeguards: confessions of judgment were barred; balloon payments were prohibited; wage assignments were limited; lenders were licensed; and forfeiture of principal and interest was prescribed as the penalty for a lender's violations.[18] By comparison, when one borrows $100 or buys goods on credit for that amount under the 1974 text of the Uniform Consumer Credit Code (U3C), the rate ceiling is still 36 percent per year, but the range of statutory benefits is vastly greater. The consumer has, in fact, brought himself within several extensive, protective legal systems. They include:

(1) A state-regulated system governing agreement-making, which requires: Truth in Lending disclosure of all credit aspects of the transaction;[19] limitations on credit charges;[20] limitations on credit life insurance, credit accident and health insurance, and insurance on collateral;[21] inclusion of cautionary legends on contract forms;[22] notice of changes of terms in open-end credit accounts;[23] furnishing receipts for cash payments;[24] furnishing periodic statements of accounts;[25] giving separate notice to co-signers;[26] limitations on advertising;[27] limitations on security interests a creditor can take;[28] prohibition of the use of multiple agreements for evasion of the act;[29] prohibition of assignments of earnings and confessions of judgment;[30] limitations on balloon payments;[31] outlawing of referral sales and leases;[32] limitations on provisions contracting for attorney's fees;[33] and notification of the right to rescind door-to-door sales.[34]

(2) A state-regulated system governing default, which requires: limitations on acts constituting default;[35] a right of cure on the part of a defaulting-consumer;[36] a right on the part of a consumer to raise sales claims or defenses against assignees of the seller,[37] certain lenders,[38] and, in some situ-

---

18. The Uniform Small Loan Law is set out in B. CURRAN, *supra* note 11, at 144–57.
19. UNIFORM CONSUMER CREDIT CODE § 3.201 [hereinafter cited as U3C]. All references to the U3C in this Article are to the 1974 Official Text.
20. *Id.* §§ 2.201, 2.202, 2.401.
21. *Id.* art. 4.
22. *Id.* § 3.203.
23. *Id.* § 3.205.
24. *Id.* § 3.206.
25. *Id.*
26. *Id.* § 3.208.
27. *Id.* § 3.209.
28. *Id.* § 3.301.
29. *Id.* § 3.304.
30. *Id.* §§ 3.305, 3.306.
31. *Id.* § 3.308.
32. *Id.* § 3.309.
33. *Id.* § 2.507.
34. *Id.* § 3.503.
35. *Id.* § 5.109.
36. *Id.* § 5.111.
37. *Id.* § 3.404.
38. *Id.* § 3.405.

ations, credit card issuers;[39] restrictions on deficiency judgments;[40] limitations on garnishment;[41] no discharge from employment for garnishment;[42] limitations on debt collection tactics;[43] limitations on deferral and delinquency charges;[44] limitations on a creditor's right to repossess;[45] and limitations on enforcement of security interests in exempt property.[46]

(3) A state-regulated system of enforcement and administration, which provides for: the right of a consumer to rescind unconscionable agreements or agreements unconscionably induced;[47] civil penalties recoverable by consumers for violations;[48] criminal sanctions;[49] attorney's fees for consumers;[50] limitations on venue in actions against consumers;[51] restrictions regarding default judgments;[52] administrative powers of investigation;[53] administrative enforcement by cease and desist orders or injunctions against violations;[54] administrative injunctions against unconscionable agreements;[55] administratively-imposed penalties;[56] and licensing of certain high-rate lenders.[57]

III. THE COST OF BENEFITS

One must ask how much these statutorily-mandated consumer benefits cost, who pays for them, and whether those who pay for them believe them to be worth the price. Certainly it is the consumer who pays for regulatory benefits, through finance and other charges. It is likely that legislators have not the foggiest notion of how much these benefits add to the costs of consumer transactions. No one, apparently, has been concerned whether the benefits are worth the cost on microeconomic bases in terms of maximizing individual value, for their desirability has always been determined on the basis of sociopolitical considerations of "fairness" and "justice."

It would, perhaps, be asking too much to expect legislatures to "cost

39. *Id.* § 3.403.
40. *Id.* § 5.103.
41. *Id.* § 5.105.
42. *Id.* § 5.106.
43. *Id.* § 5.108.
44. *Id.* §§ 2.502, 2.503.
45. *Id.* § 5.112.
46. *Id.* § 5.116.
47. *Id.* § 5.108.
48. *Id.* § 5.201.
49. *Id.* § 5.301.
50. *Id.* § 5.201.
51. *Id.* § 5.113.
52. *Id.* § 5.115.
53. *Id.* § 6.106.
54. *Id.* §§ 6.108, 6.111.
55. *Id.* § 6.111.
56. *Id.* § 6.113.
57. *Id.* art. 2, pt. 3.

out" the statutory systems they create to protect consumers, but rates should at least be regulated in a manner that would recognize that consumer protection measures do cost money and that would allow these costs to be passed through to those intended to be benefited. The post-usury system of rate regulation obtaining in most states, under which rate ceilings are set for various segments of the industry at levels very close to the market price of credit, conflicts with the movement to extend greater government protection to consumers, for it provides creditors with an incentive to oppose any protective legislation increasing their costs. Too often the consumer advocate who demands greater consumer protection is the very person who pushes for lower finance charge ceilings, as though regulating rates, on the one hand, and placing limits on creditor agreements and practices, on the other, were somehow independent and unrelated methods of protecting consumers.

The only person in a position to know what consumer protection costs—and he must know it in order to survive—is the creditor, who must adjust his prices to recoup the added costs. To the extent that social legislation, however desirable, increases the creditor's costs of doing business, it creates an incentive for him either to raise his price, which he cannot do if rate ceilings are at or below the market level, or lower his operating costs, which may mean entering into less expensive transactions (making high-balance rather than low-balance loans) with more creditworthy consumers. The small borrower of modest means tends to be excluded from the legal loan market and pushed toward either the legal creditor of last resort, the infamous "schlock" retailer who sells for grossly inflated prices, or the illegal loan market.[58]

The whipsaw effect on creditors of low, rigid rate ceilings and mounting costs for consumer protection has led some of them to conduct bitter and often effective rearguard actions against any reform in consumer credit, however meritorious it may be. It is the writer's personal conviction, based on many years of discussion with creditor representatives, that if consumer credit grantors were allowed to price their product in the same manner as in other businesses—that is, free of governmentally-imposed price restrictions—creditor attitudes toward reform measures would become more affirmative.

---

58. See NCCF REPORT, *supra* note 4, at 104: "It would be fallacious to assume that higher risk consumers thus denied legal cash loans would forego their desired credit-financed consumption. Some will turn to sales credit where some portion of the finance charge may be buried in the cash price of the goods or service. Others may turn to the illegal loan market." With respect to rate ceilings on sales credit, Professor Dunkelberg concludes that lower rate ceilings tend to reduce credit availability. "The incidence of this reduction in availability will not be random in the population of consumers, but will fall primarily on low income or otherwise disadvantaged consumers." *Id.* at 106, *quoting* Dunkelberg, *A Lower Rate Maximum for Retail Credit: The Impact on Consumers*, prepared for NCCF (1972).

IV. The Worth of Benefits

Is all this legislative protection worth what the consumer has to pay for it? Could consumers bargain out a satisfactory credit contract without government intervention? The major premise of consumer credit legislative theory has been that the consumer cannot fend for himself in the credit marketplace and needs help at both the agreement-making and default stages of a transaction. Posner challenges the assumption that there is a disparity of bargaining power in consumer transactions. He contends that contracts are not offered to consumers on a take-it-or-leave-it basis without negotiation over terms because the consumer has no choice but to accept, but rather because the seller wishes to avoid the costs involved in negotiating and drafting a separate agreement with each consumer. If he does not like the terms, the consumer can refuse to contract and enter into a more favorable agreement with another seller. If a consumer enters into an unfavorable agreement, it is because either there is an absence of competition and he cannot get better terms, or there is fraud and he does not understand what he is agreeing to.[59]

One can accept this assumption and still make a case for legislative intervention. Two points should be made. First, the consumer credit industry has been cursed by the presence of predatory operators who expect to deal with a consumer only once and who do so in a fraudulent manner. Laws curbing their activities unavoidably impose costs on legitimate transactions as well. Second, the credit aspects of even the simplest transaction are relatively complex, and the costs of furnishing the consumer enough information to bargain intelligently on these matters are so great that there is in fact an absence of any basis for meaningful negotiation. Posner believes that a housewife can buy food as well as a businessman can transact his business. That may be true, but how knowledgeable is any consumer concerning default and deferral charges, rebates for prepayment, refinancings, and the like?[60]

Professor Posner puts the simple case in which a seller sells defective furniture to a buyer and assigns the buyer's note for the price to a financer.[61] Under traditional negotiable instruments law, the buyer must pay the financer and seek his remedies, by suit if necessary, against a paid seller. Posner states:

> It would be incorrect, however, to draw from the correct observation that such a contractual provision operates in favor of the seller the conclusion that the pur-

---

59. *See* R. Posner, Economic Analysis of Law 53–54 (1973).
60. Some of the intricacies involved concerning rebates for prepaid finance charges are helpfully discussed in Bone v. Hibernia Bank, 493 F.2d 135 (9th Cir. 1974). It is the writer's personal observation that even experienced counsel have difficulties with these issues. So does he.
61. *See* R. Posner, *supra* note 59, at 54–55.

chaser must have been coerced into agreeing to it. The provision reduces the cost of financing installment purchases by making collection suits cheaper and more certain. In its absence the finance cost—a cost borne mainly by the consumer—would be higher. Is it obviously wiser for a consumer to decide to pay more for a product than to decide to surrender one of his legal remedies against the seller? Of course, if the purchaser does not understand the effect of such provisions, he does not have a meaningful choice. This may be a problem but again it is one of fraud rather than of inequality of bargaining power.[62]

It is an attractively simple alternative to the complex bulk of statutory and case law that has grown up around the holder-in-due-course concept in consumer transactions to hypothesize a "private" solution, in which the finance charge rate is adjusted according to the consumer's choice of whether he wants the right to raise sales defenses against the financer as well as against the seller.[63] However, the significant qualification in the paragraph quoted above is that the buyer cannot bargain meaningfully unless he understands the effect of the holder-in-due-course doctrine. What is the cost of making clear to the buyer the economic consequences of that doctrine? Of explaining to the buyer the difference between the value of the self-help remedy of refusal to make payments to an unpaid financer until settlement is reached, as against the value of the remedy of recovering his money from a paid seller? Of explaining the impact of making the financer subject to defenses on the symbiotic relationship between dealer and financer, with the resulting pressures that the financer can bring to bear on the dealer to encourage settlement of the buyer's claim?[64] No paragraph in a form contract can perform these tasks.

V. THE REALITIES OF REGULATION

The romantic, emotional period of consumer protection legislation is at an end. The time is past when those of us working with consumer legislation could regard ourselves as defending the oppressed consumers against the bloated lenders without having to understand much more about the consumer credit process than that a lot of fraud and overreaching was

---

62. *Id.* at 55.

63. This idea was considered by the U3C Committee during the interminable discussions on the holder-in-due-course complex of problems, but no drafting was done on the issue.

64. The two bases for abrogation of the holder-in-due-course doctrine in the U3C are: first, the buyer is afforded the self-help remedy of refusing to pay for the goods until his grievance is settled; second, subjecting the financer-assignee to sales defenses of the consumer provides an incentive for the financer-assignee, in the short run, to press the seller to satisfy the consumer's claim, and, in the long run, to provide financing only for sellers who sell good merchandise in a nonfraudulent manner. Allowing the consumer to assert sales defenses against the financer-assignee is a highly efficient manner of settling disputes regarding merchandise quality or fraudulent inducement. The relationship between a dealer and his financer is often such that the latter's pressure on the former to settle the dispute can be most effective, while, if the consumer had to pay the financer and retain counsel to sue the dealer, the cost to the consumer of asserting his defense could be prohibitively high. *See* A. Schwartz, *Optimality and the Cutoff of Defenses Against Financers of Consumer Sales*, 15 B.C. IND. & COM. L. REV. 499 (1974).

occurring and should be checked. It is time to usher in a new, realistic era of consumer protection in which we develop procedures for ascertaining whether our well-intended laws are helping consumers more than they are hurting them. In this regard, the growing group of lawyer-economists, like Richard Posner, perform an invaluable service by challenging lawmakers to take into consideration the economic implications of consumer-oriented legislation. But the task of securing sound, professional economic advice on proposed consumer legislation is difficult. It has become almost axiomatic that when a consumer problem rises to the level of identification, let alone definition, it is ready for legislative solution, not study. Study comes, if ever, later, when short-range legislative remedies have already been set in motion.[65] One difficulty with interim solutions is that they often benefit certain groups which then come to have a vested interest in opposing any final legislation that distributes benefits more generally. This "interest group liberalism" tends to freeze interim solutions.

To legislative draftsmen, principles of economics—like those of philosophy—seem to peter out at a level of generality well above that of the operational problems facing the draftsmen, leaving them to their own experience and sense of fairness in meeting the issues at hand.[66] Since they are usually lawyers, they feel comfortable making decisions which produce short-run solutions that seem equitable in the hypothetical cases the draftsmen anticipate arising. They act without much regard as to whether these solutions have any theoretical justification or empirically-established bases. The product of lawyers is justice,[67] and they resist cost-benefit analyses of the way they do justice.

A. *Fraud and Overreaching*

It is a tempting generalization to suggest that the lawyer-draftsmen who have written most consumer legislation have done their best work

---

65. State legislatures have often been guilty of "shooting from the hip" in consumer matters. Both the U3C project and the National Consumer Law Center model legislation were attempts to present state legislatures with carefully considered provisions. Three recent projects touching consumer credit concerns show how helpful prelegislative studies can be. They are the Brookings Institution study of bankruptcy, published in D. STANLEY & M. GIRTH, BANKRUPTCY: PROBLEM, PROCESS, REFORM (1971); the National Commission on Consumer Finance, whose REPORT ON CONSUMER CREDIT IN THE UNITED STATES, *supra* note 4, was published in 1972; and the Commission on the Bankruptcy Laws of the United States, whose report was published in 1973.

66. Groups like the National Conference of Commissioners on Uniform State Laws make a strong effort to bring a broad range of experience to bear on their acts. In their U3C project, the drafting committee included several members with a great deal of expertise in credit law. This group worked with a larger advisory committee whose members were chosen as representing consumer, creditor, and public viewpoints. Academics who were either lawyers or economists performed most of the staff work. The Commission utilized several consultants who were specialists in various technical areas of consumer credit. Behavioral scientists provided limited assistance. In short, given their limited budget, the Commissioners did about all that any group could do to produce a long-range program designed on the basis of accurate, up-to-date information on what was really happening in the field.

67. *See* Stigler, *supra* note 5, at 2.

in such justice-oriented fields as fraud and overreaching, while in such intensely economic areas as enhancement of competition and regulation of rates, their quest for justice has sometimes led them astray. The U3C has dealt with fraud and overreaching in two quite disparate ways. First, the entire spectrum of creditor activities, from inducement of contract to collection of debt, is subjected to judicial policing under the unconscionability standard.[68] This flexible standard relieves legislatures of the endless task of passing laws each session in order to keep up with the latest innovations in fraud; moreover, it helps to minimize the number of specific restrictions on credit practices, which, though aimed at the reprehensible creditor, must be borne by all creditors. Second, for those areas in which the consumer lacks sufficient information to protect himself against overreaching, the statute prescribes specific contract standards. Examples include regulations of delinquency charges, deferrals, refinancings, rebates on prepayment, security interests, referral sales, and holder-in-due-course status.[69]

B. *Disclosure*

In the early days of retail credit transactions, laws requiring disclosure of the terms of an agreement were badly needed as antifraud measures. Sometimes reprehensible sellers revealed little more than the amount of monthly payments. With the advent of the Truth in Lending Act (TIL),[70] however, disclosure legislation achieved a more exalted status as an aid to credit shopping. Former Senator Paul Douglas' simple and appealing idea was that if all creditors would quote their credit charges as an "annual percentage rate" (APR), consumers would compare credit rates before buying or borrowing and shop for the best deal.[71] Now, 6 years after passage of TIL legislation—with a body of statute, administrative, and case law rapidly approaching IRS proportions—it appears that the idea probably doesn't work. At least it doesn't work in the manner Senator Douglas intended—namely, providing accurate, point-of-transaction disclosures influencing credit-purchasing decisions.

The rate of compliance with the statute has been high. Consumers are more aware of credit costs, and legislators are pleased with the Act. But there is no convincing evidence that information about APR's has led

---

68. *See* U3C §§ 5.108, 6.111.
69. That is, the U3C provides that the credit agreement cannot violate certain standards regarding these issues. For example, U3C § 2.502 contains provisions intended to avoid abuses by creditors with regard to delinquency charges. It is quite unlikely that a consumer could anticipate all of the difficulties he might face upon making a single late payment. *See id.* § 2.502, Comment 2. The same is true of each of the areas enumerated.
70. 15 U.S.C. §§ 1601 *et seq.* (1970).
71. *See* Jordan & Warren, *Disclosure of Finance Charges: A Rationale*, 64 MICH. L. REV. 1285 (1966).

consumers to do any more comparative credit shopping than they did before TIL.[72] What is more, the method of granting consumer credit has shifted in many kinds of transactions from closed-end credit, for which TIL requires point-of-transaction disclosures accurate to the nearest one-quarter of 1 percent, to open-end credit (department store revolving charge accounts, bank credit cards, etc.), with respect to which no point-of-transaction disclosure need be made and only a rough estimate of an APR need be given.[73] The movement toward open-end credit seems to be accelerating.

From a sociopolitical standpoint, TIL has been a rousing success. We all enjoy making creditors "come clean" about their high credit charges. From an economic point of view, however, TIL must be characterized as a rather elaborate and expensive endeavor to promote long-term consumer education. It will be a long time before we know whether TIL is worth what consumers pay for it.

C. *Rate Regulation and Market Structure*

In a free market one would expect credit grantors to differentiate between customers on the basis of their creditworthiness. Creditors would compete for the business of consumers at all levels of creditworthiness, charging higher rates for higher-risk consumers and lower rates for lower-risk consumers. It is probably due in large measure to the existence of legislation setting ceilings on finance charges and limiting market entry that the consumer credit market in this country has exhibited major imperfec-

---

72. The studies are collected and evaluated in Whitford, *The Function of Disclosure Regulation in Consumer Transactions*, 1973 WIS. L. REV. 400, 405–20. *See also* NCCF REPORT, *supra* note 4, at 175–84 (1972). "The principal finding of this research is that awareness of APR's does *not* appear to inspire credit users to search actively for the best sources of credit by considering alternate types of sources." Deutscher, *Credit Legislation Two Years Out: Awareness Changes and Behavioral Effects of Differential Awareness Levels*, in 1 NCCF TECHNICAL STUDIES 43 (Supp. 1973) (emphasis in original). "[O]ur conclusion is that *after fifteen months* Truth in Lending disclosure has not significantly altered the shopping behavior of most consumers." Day & Brandt, *A Study of Consumer Credit Decisions: Implications for Present and Prospective Legislation*, in *id.* at 100 (emphasis in original).

73. Closed-end credit denotes a single credit extension in which the contract is written for a specified period of time and the total amount financed, number of scheduled payments, and due dates of payments are agreed upon in advance. Open-end credit denotes an arrangement drawn to facilitate successive credit extensions under which new balances are added to an open account, finance charges are computed periodically on unpaid balances, and payments are made periodically.

Open-end credit disclosure for the typical department store charge account merely requires the seller to disclose to the customer at the time of entering into the credit arrangement and on each monthly billing statement that the seller is charging 12 times the monthly rate: if the monthly rate is 1½%, the APR disclosed is 18%. Regulation Z, 12 C.F.R. § 226.7 (1974). This calculation does not take into account the variations in the consumer's purchase and payment practices which may have a great effect on the true APR. Nor does it reflect the different methods of calculating rates employed by different creditors, *e.g.*, the previous-balance method, the adjusted-balance method, and the average-daily-balance method. A recent study of finance charges in retail revolving credit shows that the true actuarial method of calculating rates would yield 115% of that yielded by the previous balance method while the adjusted-balance method yields only 86%. *See* Touche, Ross & Co., Economics of New York State Retail Store Revolving Credit Operations for the Fiscal Year Ended Jan. 31, 1973, at 10 (unpublished report). But the APR required to be disclosed to the customer by sellers using the adjusted-balance method is identical to that disclosed by those using the previous balance method. And neither is close to a true actuarial rate.

tions.[74] Owing in part to its usury legacy, the consumer credit market is highly segmented. In some states there are separate statutes setting different rate ceilings for consumer finance companies, industrial banks, commercial banks, credit unions, insurance premium financers, pawnbrokers, mortgage lenders, and so forth.[75] Some of these statutes limit the amounts and maturities of loans. In substance, creditors in each segment of the industry charge a single rate applicable to all customers dealing with them, whatever the customer's credit standing. Thus low-risk customers, for whom the rate is too high, subsidize high-risk customers, for whom the rate is too low. Low-risk customers find lower rates not by convincing a consumer finance company that they are entitled to them but by going to a bank or credit union.

If the credit market is to be shaped in the legislature and its prices fixed there rather than in the marketplace, it is predictable that competition will occur in legislative halls as well as in the marketplace. The consequences of intensive lobbying by various segments of the consumer credit industry have been wasteful and unseemly legislatives squabbles in which the consumer comes off the loser. Banks fight to limit loan amounts and maturities for consumer finance companies; competitors urge continuation of the restrictions limiting savings and loan associations to home mortgage loans; other creditors snipe at the tax subsidies enjoyed by credit unions; and each group looks with a jaundiced eye at attempts by others to obtain rate-ceiling increases.

This combination of factors has produced a consumer credit regime of market segmentation, barriers to entry, and rigid rate ceilings that has, in turn, led to monopolistic conditions, administered prices, and, probably, an undersupply of loan credit.[76] And all this has been done—with cynicism in knowledgeable quarters—in the name of protecting consumers![77]

VI. Rate Regulation Reform

In 1964 the National Conference of Commissioners on Uniform State Laws, fresh from its triumphs in obtaining general enactment of the Uniform Commercial Code, undertook to draft a Uniform Consumer Credit Code and to grapple with the anticompetitive nature of the consumer credit

74. See NCCF Report, supra note 4, at 113.
75. The NCCF Report provides a summary of the various consumer credit statutes in New York. Id. at 94.
76. See id. at 113: "Such market imperfections include legal restraints, regardless of intent, as well as noncompetitive behavior of suppliers. Legal factors of most potential significance are rate ceilings, restrictions on other credit terms such as loan size and maturity, limitations on creditors' remedies, and legal constraints on the entry of new firms."
77. One broad area of consumer legislation that this brief Essay makes no attempt to evaluate is that concerning limitations of creditors' remedies at the default stage. The problem has been well examined in Wallace, The Logic of Consumer Credit Reform, 82 Yale L.J. 461 (1973).

industry.[78] Utilizing professional economic assistance at each step of their project, they set out to do what no other group had done in this country—to develop a set of rate-ceiling provisions that were as rational from an economic viewpoint as possible within the constraints of the political process. Their approach was an attempt to reconcile the economizing mode, in which market forces set the price of credit, with the sociopolitical mode, in which rate ceilings would continue to fulfill some function in safeguarding consumers.

The mechanics of the U3C provisions on rates are simple. First, residual usury laws are repealed, and rate ceilings apply only to consumer transactions—in commercial transactions businessmen are free to contract for any rate of charge they desire.[79] Second, relatively high rate ceilings are placed on all consumer credit extensions.[80] A bifurcated rate system is employed. A graduated rate is first applied, permitting 36 percent on the first $300, 21 percent on the next $700, and 15 percent on that portion of the loan exceeding $1000. However, a superordinate basic rate is applied, assuming that the ceiling rate never drops below 18 percent. Third, artificial barriers to competition are removed. Any creditor can make a credit extension of any size to any consumer for any purpose, the only limitation being that lenders transacting business at rates above 18 percent must be licensed.[81] Sellers, their assignees, and seller credit card issuers need not be licensed. Convenience and advantage standards are abolished, and no minimum dollar amount is set for a showing of financial responsibility by licensees. Thus the Commissioners conceive the proper function of rate regulation to be to set ceilings which satisfy the sociopolitical interest in preventing "gouging" when competition is not effective to keep rates down, but which allow market forces to allocate credit free of anticompetitive barriers. This pattern of regulation has been substantially endorsed by the 1972 Report of the National Commission on Consumer Finance.[82]

During the late 1960's another group entered the field of consumer credit reform: the National Consumer Law Center (NCLC), an Office of Economic Opportunity research and drafting operation, which published its National Consumer Act in 1970 and its Model Consumer Credit Act in 1973. An important asset of the NCLC is the close communication it has maintained with legal services attorneys in the consumer credit field, and perhaps its major contributions have been in redefining areas of con-

---

78. *See generally* Jordan & Warren, *The Uniform Consumer Credit Code,* 68 COLUM. L. REV. 387 (1968).
79. *See* U3C § 2.601 and the Comment to that section.
80. *Id.* §§ 2.201, 2.202, 2.401.
81. *Id.* §§ 2.301 *et seq.*
82. NCCF REPORT, *supra* note 4, at 147–49. *See* the *Shay Memorandum* in *id.* at 243–58.

sumer abuse and proposing legal remedies for dealing with them.[83] The
two NCLC statutes can be looked upon as authoritative statements of what
the consumer establishment wants by way of a credit regulation statute.[84]

The NCLC, however, does not view consumer credit from an economic
perspective. Its model legislation takes no position on such a basic issue as
usury laws,[85] and its posture on barriers to market entry through restrictive
licensing seems equivocal.[86] One can only speculate about why the NCLC
has proposed model legislation dealing in such detail with the symptomatic
abuses in the consumer credit field, while largely ignoring the underlying
defect which has contributed so directly to the continuance of those abuses,
that is, the imperfection of the consumer credit market. The NCLC measures are peculiarly lawyers' statutes; their emphasis is on providing effective legal remedies for consumers represented by attorneys. There is no
evidence of any significant professional economic input with respect to the
drafting or consideration of these two acts, nor any reason to believe that
the NCLC saw need for such input.

The dismaying fact is that after decades of experience with rate regulation in the area of consumer credit, there is still no consensus among
interested parties on what approach to the problem is best. Moreover, the
dry pages of a law review article are completely inadequate to portray the
depths of distrust and bad feelings between consumer and creditor groups
on this issue. Their standoff on rate regulation reform leaves undisturbed
the present segmented, totally illogical patchwork of rate-ceiling laws in
most states.[87]

---

83. NCLC personnel shared their expertise in this field with representatives of the U3C Committee in a series of joint sessions at the early stages of the preparation of the 1974 version of the U3C.

84. The enumeration of groups represented on the NCLC's special committee of experts includes most of what one might describe as the "consumer establishment": Consumer Federation of
America, AFL–CIO, and Consumers Union. In contrast to the NCLC statutes, the U3C attempted a
middle-of-the-road approach in which both creditor and consumer groups were represented. A
familiar criticism of the U3C has been that creditor groups were overrepresented.

85. The provisions on rate ceilings in its model legislation read: "The finance charge, calculated
according to the actuarial method, may not exceed [   ] per cent per year on the unpaid balance of
the amount financed." NATIONAL CONSUMER ACT § 2–201 [hereinafter cited as NCA]; MODEL CON-
SUMER CREDIT ACT §§ 2–202, 2–203 [hereinafter cited as MCCA]. See NCA § 2–201, Comment 2:
"The draftsmen take no position on what the rate ceiling should be. It is probably not advisable to
become involved in lengthy arguments with industry over rate ceilings."

86. The most troublesome problem in interpreting the NCA and MCCA relates to the issue of
licensing. The NCA is silent on the issue of licensing and merely provides for a system of notification
and fees in §§ 6–201 and 6–202 similar to that afforded by U3C §§ 6.202 and 6.203. This may mean
that the intent of the NCA is to leave open to an enacting state the decision whether to continue
licensing for high-rate lenders. The writer is unable to find a recommendation on the subject in the
official comments to the NCA. However, the MCCA has an expanded Part on Registration and Fees.
MCCA, art. 9, pt. 2. Again, there is no explanatory comment on what a state is to do about its existing
licensing laws upon adoption of the MCCA, but Part 2 could be enacted either as an addition to
existing licensing laws for high-rate lenders or in place of them.

87. The U3C has now been enacted in Colorado, Idaho, Indiana, Iowa, Kansas, Maine, Oklahoma,
Utah, and Wyoming. In several of these states the rates provisions were amended to make them more
similar to prior law. Virtually all other states have variations of the rate regulation system described
in this Essay.

The dilemma facing lawmakers on the rate regulation issue today is similar to that a cartographer would confront were he to attend a meeting of the American Geographic Society only to find that one group in attendance believes the world to be flat (populist consumer groups who believe flat 10 to 12 percent across-the-board rate ceilings should be applied); another group sees the world as perfectly round and inexorably governed by the laws of the universe (economists who believe rates should be controlled only by market forces); still another group thinks the world is round in the middle and flat on both ends (U3C position that the market should be permitted to operate within high-rate ceilings); and, finally, yet another group, busily engaged in mapping the world, takes no interest in its shape (the NCLC which makes no proposals on rate ceilings). One would be tempted to call out for the coming of a consumer Galileo but for the inevitability of the heresy trial.

VII. CONCLUSION

What should legislatures be doing about rate regulation in consumer credit during the last quarter of this century? Some broad societal trends that may affect their decisions are already discernible. First, there is a strong trend toward more general risk allocation and abatement, represented by the imminent or already present national health care system, guaranteed annual income, no-fault compensation plans, disaster insurance, and portable pensions. These programs will enhance the creditworthiness of consumers by maintaining a steadier flow of income. Family patterns of fewer children and more women in the work force also contribute to this end. Second, information will become vastly more accessible,[88] as some form of centralized data bank seems inevitable. Though this development raises a new range of problems, it will make possible more individualized evaluations of creditworthiness. It should be more feasible to judge each credit applicant on his own performance rather than on generalized objective criteria like job status, marital status, income, assets, and the like.[89]

---

88. Daniel Bell describes our present industrial society as "the coordination of machines and men for the production of goods," and contrasts the emerging postindustrial society as "organized around knowledge, for the purpose of social control and the directing of innovation and change . . . ." D. BELL, *supra* note 3, at 20.

89. David Caplovitz suggests: "I would like to see the credit industry give up these harsh [collection] remedies, which often turn out to be self-defeating, as when the debtor loses his job because of the garnishment order. In return, I would be in favor of the credit industry functioning according to the principles of a free market economy. Thus I would allow free entry in the lending business and I would eliminate rate ceilings. I have confidence that in a truly free market, one in which lenders would not be ashamed to advertise their rates, the mechanism of competition would insure reasonable rates, and would sort debtors according to their ability to pay. In this market system, I would approve of creditors charging higher interest rates to the poor than to the rich. But, by the same token, I would demand that interest rates be determined by past performance rather than by

The consumer credit industry has long since outlived its reputation as a shady, backstairs operation, but in terms of rate regulation there has been little change in legislative attitudes over the past 60 years. The social trends outlined above promise increasing stability in consumer credit consumption. If lawmakers can abandon more than a half century of misguided rate regulation and concentrate on the considerable task of making the consumer credit market more competitive, they are likely to find that desirable results will follow. With only a moderate level of governmental intervention (largely in the fraud and overreaching areas), consumers will be able to shop for credit as wisely as they bargain for other services. Rate ceilings will become increasingly irrelevant, and our national paranoia about the price of credit will be relieved.

The National Commission on Consumer Finance Report recommendation should be followed: "The Commission recommends that policies designed to promote competition should be given the first priority, with adjustments of rate ceilings used as a complement to expand the availability of credit. As the development of workably competitive markets decreases the need for rate ceilings to combat market power in concentrated markets, such ceilings may be raised or removed."[90]

The U3C appears to offer the best interim solution to the rate regulation problem. It frees business transactions from the shackles of totally anachronistic usury laws and does so in the context of comprehensive credit reform, which is probably the only politically feasible way to bring about repeal of the usury statutes—a step Victorian England took in 1854 without shaking the Empire. It sets rate ceilings high enough to allow the competitive forces of the market to operate in most kinds of consumer transactions. It retains rate ceilings to perform their only legitimate social function, the prevention of gouging in cases in which competition is not effective. What is far more important, it moves strongly and, considering the political problems involved, courageously to rid the credit-granting market of the barriers to competition that have plagued it throughout its troubled exisence.

arbitrary criteria. Thus if a poor person has demonstrated that he is a good risk in that he pays promptly, he should be entitled to the same low interest rate as the more affluent debtor." Caplovitz, *Breakdowns in the Consumer Credit Marketplace*, 26 Bus. Law. 795, 799 (1971).

90. NCCF REPORT, *supra* note 4, at 149. *See id.* at 136–39 for the Commission's far-ranging recommendations for encouraging all creditors to compete across-the-board for consumers at all levels of creditworthiness.

Some Ingredients of a National
Oil and Gas Policy

Howard R. Williams*

Many Americans first became aware of what has come to be known as "the energy crisis" when shipments of oil from the Middle East were curtailed as one consequence of the Arab-Israeli War of 1973. Knowledgeable observers, however, had long been aware of the implications of increasing energy consumption without a corresponding increase in readily available domestic energy supplies. In fact, almost a quarter century ago the Paley Commission, appointed by President Truman to study and report on mineral resources and needs for the year 1975, found that the nation had an adequate supply of coal but that we could anticipate difficulties in providing an adequate supply of crude oil and natural gas to meet the national energy requirements in 1975.[1] Although expressing guarded optimism concerning the availability of energy from nuclear sources—an optimism subsequently proven to have been unjustified[2]—the Commission's Report called upon the nation to take drastic measures with regard to anticipated shortages of crude oil and natural gas.

Unfortunately, despite the report, little has been accomplished to meet the problems posed. The present energy shortage requires response on a number of levels. Of course, our first and foremost concern should be the curbing of wasteful practices.[3] Both public and private agencies should cooperate in a program of public education to develop an awareness of the

---

* A.B. 1937, Washington University; LL.B. 1940, Columbia University. Stella W. and Ira S. Lillick Professor of Law, Stanford University.

1. 3 PRESIDENT'S MATERIALS POLICY COMM'N, RESOURCES FOR FREEDOM 2–9, 15–21 (1952). The Commission underestimated 1975 requirements for oil and gas. The Commission projected the 1975 demand for petroleum products at 13.7 million barrels daily, *id.* at 4, a rate of consumption the United States exceeded some years ago. In 1973 the United States consumed about 18 million barrels of oil per day. W. PEACH, A STUDY PREPARED FOR THE USE OF THE SUBCOMM. ON ECONOMIC PROGRESS OF THE JOINT ECON. COMM., 93D CONG., 1ST SESS., THE ENERGY OUTLOOK FOR THE 1980's, at 11 (Jt. Econ. Comm. Print 1973).

2. *See* 1 PRESIDENT'S MATERIALS POLICY COMM'N, *supra* note 1, at 129. In fact, only about 0.6% of our present energy requirements are supplied from nuclear sources. Furthermore, because of lack of economies of scale and the nonperfected state of the art, the energy cost of those sources presently approximates the energy output. Wood provides roughly twice as much of our energy needs. *See* A. HAMMOND, W. METZ & T. MAUGH II, ENERGY AND THE FUTURE 5, 133 (1973). The Commission was also more optimistic than subsequent events have justified concerning the energy available in 1975 from shale. 1 PRESIDENT'S MATERIALS POLICY COMM'N, *supra* note 1, at 127.

3. The movement of petroleum products into distribution channels in May 1974, averaged 7.5% less than a year earlier. The major transportation fuels, gasoline and kerosene, accounted for half of the overall decline. Consumption of distillate and residual fuel oil declined 5.1% and 6.1%, respectively. "Those reductions provided additional evidence of conservation efforts, particularly in electric utility and industrial energy markets." Energy Economics Division of The Chase Manhattan Bank, The Petroleum Situation, June 24, 1974, at first page.

energy shortage and a willingness to conserve energy. But beyond such general palliatives, government action on more specific solutions is required, and the recommendations outlined in this Essay regarding oil and gas policy represent an attempt to steer a middle course between unacceptable dependence on foreign energy sources and prohibitively expensive complete self-sufficiency.

I. REGULATORY POLICIES

The failure of federal and state regulatory policies has led both to excessive costs of oil and gas and to diminished supplies. Clearly, a revamping of those regulatory policies is mandated, and this Part proffers various suggestions for improvement.

A. *Deregulation of Natural Gas*

The history and present consequence of natural gas regulation demonstrate that the Federal Power Commission (FPC) should deregulate natural gas as rapidly as is possible.

The Natural Gas Act of 1938[4] was designed to fill a "gap" in regulation. State governmental agencies in consuming states adequately regulated local distributing utilities, and state governmental agencies in producing states adequately regulated production activities. But neither the producing nor the consuming states had power to regulate interstate pipeline companies that were natural monopolies. To fill this "gap" the Natural Gas Act gave the FPC regulatory jurisdiction over these pipeline carriers.

The avowed purpose of the Act was to protect the consumer from high prices. While the FPC resisted efforts to require it to regulate wellhead sales, in *Phillips I*[5] in 1954 the Supreme Court, over strong dissents, charged the FPC with responsibility to regulate the rates charged by a natural gas producer and gatherer in the sale in interstate commerce of gas for resale.

FPC regulation since 1954 surely merits the label of unmitigated failure. In part, this failure has been due to insufficient funding of the Commission. Congressional representatives of the consuming states were in the position to prevent new legislation deregulating natural gas sales; representatives from producing states were in the position to prevent adequate funding of the Commission. The result was, in short order, a complete breakdown of regulation.

The Commission first embarked on a futile attempt to apply the cost-of-service method of regulating individual sales.[6] Next it attempted to set

4. Natural Gas Act, 15 U.S.C. § 717 (1970).
5. Phillips Petroleum Co. v. Wisconsin, 347 U.S. 672 (1954) (*Phillips I*).
6. Wisconsin v. Federal Power Comm'n, 373 U.S. 294 (1963) (*Phillips II*), signaled the end of this method.

rates through certificate conditions, a task also involving immense complexities and administrative difficulties.[7] The Commission then moved to the area-pricing method for regulating sales—a method based on the average cost of service for the industry in a producing area.[8] Insofar as this method succeeded in determining an area's "average costs," which could then be used in fixing prices, high-cost producers inevitably found continued production uneconomical; the result of regulation was, therefore, to reduce the supply of natural gas.

At the same time, the Commission continued to expand its jurisdiction,[9] a course of action made necessary by the increasing commitment of gas to uses previously beyond the Commission's jurisdiction. It became apparent that effective Commission authority over natural gas required elimination of the boundary between jurisdictional and nonjurisdictional sales—a policy that members of Congress from the producing states strongly resisted—coupled with a policy of end-use control[10] and, possibly, preemption of certain aspects of the regulatory systems of the producing states.[11] Subsequent attempts by the Commission to ease its administrative burdens were frequently frustrated by the courts,[12] and some members of the Commission understandably came to accept the view that regulation was a failure.

FPC price regulation has had the effect of increasing the demand for natural gas by holding the price to the consumer low in relation to the price of competing energy sources,[13] while at the same time decreasing the supply

7. A major landmark was Atlantic Refining Co. v. Public Service Comm'n, 360 U.S. 378 (1959), a case which has come to be known by the acronym *CATCO*.
8. The Court sustained the propriety of this method in Permian Basin Area Rate Cases, 390 U.S. 747 (1968).
9. *See, e.g.,* Federal Power Comm'n v. Transcontinental Gas Pipe Line Corp., 365 U.S. 1 (1961) (the *Transco* case), sustaining Commission jurisdiction over a direct sale to a consumer as distinguished from a sale for resale in interstate commerce.
10. The *Transco* case, in authorizing consideration of "end use" in certificate proceedings, *id.* at 18–19, offers no guidance—if any can be offered—on the criteria relevant to the determination of socially valuable end uses.
11. Northern Natural Gas Co. v. State Corp. Comm'n, 372 U.S. 84 (1963), established that state "ratable take" orders infringed upon the exclusive regulatory jurisdiction of the FPC and were therefore preempted under the Natural Gas Act.
12. *See, e.g.,* the attempt to exempt small producers from direct rate regulation under §§ 4–5 of the Natural Gas Act, invalidated in Texaco Inc. v. Federal Power Comm'n, 474 F.2d 416 (D.C. Cir. 1972), *vacated,* 94 S. Ct. 2315 (1974). *See also* Public Serv. Comm'n v. Federal Power Comm'n, 487 F.2d 1043 (D.C. Cir. 1973), remanding to the FPC for further consideration orders establishing "just and reasonable rates" under §§ 4–5 of the Natural Gas Act for sales of natural gas in interstate commerce from the Texas Gulf Coast producing area.
13. The increase in demand caused by FPC regulation is illustrated by a study of comparative costs per million Btu for competing conventional fuels purchased by United States electrical utilities for power generation. Utilities found that natural gas was cheaper than oil and often cheaper than coal for power generation. See Hearings Pursuant to S. Res. 45 Before the Senate Comm. on Interior and Insular Affairs on the Causes, Effects, and Implications of Current Trends in Exploration For Domestic Oil and Gas, 92d Cong., 2d Sess., ser. 92–33, pt. 2, at 993 (1972).
"In the third quarter of 1972, utilities reporting to the FPC paid 31¢ per MMBtu for natural gas, 38¢ for low sulphur coal, 68¢ for low sulphur residual fuel oil, and 82¢ for distillate fuel oil. Certainly these price relationships are indefensible." DiBona, *Administration Policies Affecting the Natural Gas*

available in the interstate market by making it advantageous for the producer to keep his gas in the unregulated nonjurisdictional local market.[14]

Clearly the Commission has reached the end of the road in its attempts
to regulate wellhead prices to protect the consumer under its present statutory authority. Two alternatives remain: it may either (a) deregulate and
let the market operate to establish an equilibrium between supply and
demand, or (b) increase regulation by enacting new legislation that will
eliminate the shelter of nonjurisdictional sales, give the Commission complete authority over end uses, and presumably control other competing
energy sources not now regulated, namely coal and oil.[15] Best estimates of
the economic consequences of complete deregulation of natural gas prices
indicate that such deregulation might increase the price of gas to consumers
by only about 10 percent.[16] That fact, together with the dismal history of
attempts to regulate natural gas, should dictate the choice of alternatives

---

Industry, 6 NAT. RES. LAW. 503, 508 (1973). Under such circumstances it was obviously appropriate for
the utilities to consume gas, though in short supply, rather than coal, which was in relatively abundant
supply.

14. The decrease in supply caused by FPC regulation is evidenced by the decrease in the quantity
of gas moving in interstate commerce and by the flight of industry to the producing states. Thus, while
the amount of gas produced in Texas increased during the 4 years ending in 1973, the amount ex-
ported decreased. *See* N.Y. Times, Sept. 3, 1973, at 24, col. 5: "In June, 1969, Texas marketed 592-
billion cubic feet of gas, sending 276-billion cubic feet into interstate channels. By June, 1973, . . .
the total value of gas marketed had risen to 634-billion cubic feet, but exports were down to 266-
billion cubic feet." Formerly the producing states had argued that FPC regulation was contrary to
their best interests; now we are witnessing a growing awareness that FPC regulation may be benefitting the producing rather than the consuming states, as it has caused a migration of industry and
jobs from the consuming to the producing states. The Governor of Texas has opined that it is to
Texas' advantage for the federal government to maintain a ceiling on the price of gas piped outside the
state, for such action increases the supply available for consumption within the state itself. *See* Address by Governor Dolph Briscoe to the Annual Meeting of the Interstate Oil Compact Comm'n, Dec.
1973, in 32 OIL & GAS COMPACT BULL., Dec. 1973, at 5, 6.

State after state has been enacting statutes authorizing the change of the royalty provisions of
state oil and gas leases so as to permit the state to require delivery of gas in kind. The purpose of such
statutes is to make available for local consumption the state's royalty share of gas.

It also has been reported that newly discovered gas in Louisiana bound for out-of-state customers
sells for $0.26 per MCF while natural gas staying in Louisiana is selling for $1.01 per MCF. *See*
N.Y. Times, Dec. 20, 1973, at 1, col. 6. "The result of these price differences is that virtually all
newly discovered natural gas in Louisiana, Texas and Oklahoma is being sold within the states." *Id.* at
30, col. 5.

15. *See, e.g.*, the bill proposed by Senator Adlai E. Stevenson III, of Illinois, to continue and extend FPC regulation of wellhead price of natural gas. N.Y. Times, Oct. 2, 1973, at 24, col. 1. Ingredients in the proposed legislation are (a) extension of FPC jurisdiction over sales currently classified as nonjurisdictional; (b) partial deregulation of "small producers" leaving only about 70 of the
largest of some 4,700 producers to be regulated; (c) power to allocate natural gas during periods of
shortages among all customers and regions, *viz.*, extensive end-use controls.

16. Precise data on the elasticity of supply of and demand for natural gas are not available.
However, the elasticity of supply has been estimated to be at least 0.5—suggesting that each 10%
increase in price should result in about a 5% increase in supply. DiBona, *supra* note 13, at 509. *But
see* STAFF OF SENATE COMM. ON INTERIOR AND INSULAR AFFAIRS, 93D CONG., 1ST SESS., NATURAL GAS
POLICY ISSUES AND OPTIONS 13 (Comm. Print 1973) (indicating a higher elasticity ratio). Inasmuch
as many gas consumers may substitute other fuels, *e.g.*, coal, for natural gas consumption, it is clear
that there is also a significant elasticity of demand. It is probable that a 100% increase in field prices
would be market clearing. *See id.* at 78. Since the price of natural gas at the wellhead constitutes only
about 10% of the cost to residential consumers of natural gas in markets distant from producing areas
(the balance representing pipeline and distribution costs), W. PEACH, *supra* note 1, at 17, such an
increase in wellhead prices would increase the price of gas to residential consumers by only about
10%.

and should be persuasive that those who suggest that the remedy for the failure of FPC regulation of natural gas is more regulation manifest what Dr. Samuel Johnson described in another connection as "the triumph of hope over experience"—a recurring phenomenon among regulators.

B. *Improved Regulation in the Oil Industry*

Public economic regulation of the oil industry has been no more success-ful than regulation of the natural gas industry. In many instances totally inconsistent policies have been pursued. For example, in certain of the pro-ducing states, particularly Texas, a variety of rules—some of legislative origin and others developed in the administrative agencies or in the courts —have encouraged the wasteful practices of excessively dense drilling[17] which have caused waste of reservoir energy, physical waste of recoverable hydrocarbons, and profligate waste of resources expended in the drilling of unnecessary wells.[18] Better rules must be established to encourage more efficient development of hydrocarbon resources; for example, compulsory unitization to stop the practice of overdrilling a field.

C. *Prices of Oil and Gas Should Be Set by Market*

Both demand for and supply of petroleum products are somewhat inelas-tic, but events of the past year have clearly demonstrated that neither is totally inelastic.[19] The increased price of oil has increased the supply from stripper wells and has caused a boom in the drilling of new wells. Undoubt-edly, the increased price has also reduced demand and encouraged con-

---

17. *See, e.g.,* the rules in Texas under which (a) the landowner of every tract, however small, having a separate existence prior to the application of the spacing rule to the area, was entitled to one well as a matter of right if necessary to prevent net uncompensated drainage, and (b) the permitted production given a well on a separate tract could not be cut down to the point where it would no longer produce, nor below the point where it could not be drilled and operated at a reasonable profit. *See* H. WILLIAMS, R. MAXWELL & C. MEYERS, CASES ON OIL AND GAS 612–47 (3d ed. 1974).

18. In 1972 Texas production averaged 20.6 barrels per day per well from 171,369 oil wells. 32 OIL & GAS COMPACT BULL., Dec. 1973, at 49. And daily production in the United States during the first 6 months of 1972 averaged 18 barrels per day per well from 525,885 wells. U.S. TARIFF COMM'N FOR THE SENATE COMM. ON FINANCE, 93D CONG., 1ST SESS., WORLD OIL DEVELOPMENTS AND U.S. OIL IMPORT POLICIES 20 (Comm. Print 1973). At the same time, Arab nations were producing a greater quantity of oil from a much smaller number of wells—an average of 10,117 barrels per day per well in Saudi Arabia, 12,616 barrels per day per well in Iraq, and 15,479 barrels per day per well in Iran. *Id.* at 21.

19. One must be cautious with estimates both of elasticity of demand and elasticity of supply of petroleum products. Certainly we saw in early 1974 that consumption of petroleum products could be reduced substantially. *See* Energy Economics Division of The Chase Manhattan Bank, The Petroleum Situation, Mar. 31, 1974, at first page, which reported that the combined demand for (surely the writer meant "consumption of") petroleum products in February averaged 17 million barrels a day—11.8% less than a year earlier. In large part this evidenced simple nonavailability of petroleum products to cer-tain consumers rather than the decline of demand with an increase in price, although some of the latter element was undoubtedly present. Shortrun elasticity of demand (up to 2 years) has been esti-mated as running between −.2 and −.4 and longrun estimates range from a −.4 to −.7 elasticity. *Id.* at third page. It does not appear unreasonable to accept as probable the lower of these figures for shortrun elasticity—that is, −.2. In other words, a price increase of 10% will reduce demand by 2%; a price increase of 50% will reduce demand by 10%. One must be more cautious about estimates of longrun elasticity but almost certainly it is higher than shortrun elasticity.

sumers to abandon gasoline-guzzling vehicles for smaller, more economical models. It is probable that a price of about 60 cents per gallon for gasoline will be market clearing.[20]

In light of the dismal failure of attempts to regulate the price of hydrocarbons and in view of the market elasticity of such products, the price of gasoline, fuel oil, and other petroleum products should be permitted to rise to the market-clearing level.

II. TAX POLICIES

A. *Abolition of Percentage Depletion*

The federal government has provided major tax benefits—particularly percentage depletion and the foreign tax credit—designed to encourage investment in oil exploration and development.[21] Then to avoid the otherwise inevitable consequences of encouraging investment through tax benefits, namely, increased supply and reduced prices, the producing states and the federal government adopted measures—market demand prorationing in the producing states and an oil import quota system on the federal level— designed to decrease supply and maintain the price of oil.[22]

It is here recommended that the primary link in this scheme—the tax subsidy of percentage depletion—be eliminated on the ground that the social cost of the subsidy far outweighs the relatively modest effect it may have on exploration and development of oil and gas. The tax-cost of this deduction is substantial: until the 1969 reduction in the percentage depletion allowance—from 27.5 percent to 22 percent—the deduction provided an annual tax subsidy of about $1.3 billion; the reduction to 22 percent reduced this subsidy by about one-third.[23] The subsequent substantial increase in the price of oil as a result of the Arab embargo in late 1973 undoubtedly greatly increased the tax-cost of this subsidy.

---

20. *Cf.* Wall St. J., May 13, 1974, at 12, col. 1, which noted that a consumer of 20 gallons per week would have to pay $3 a week more as a result of a rise in the price of gasoline from 45¢ to 60¢ per gallon. "If this really is an intolerable burden on some low-income families, surely there is a better way to get them $3 a week, or $6 if necessary. In such a plan, one could do a great deal with the $1.5 billion a year it would cost merely to operate the rationing system Senator Jackson's proposals would ultimately give us." *Id.*

21. INT. REV. CODE OF 1954, §§ 611–13.

22. Mead, *The System of Government Subsidies to the Oil Industry*, 10 NAT. RES. J. 113, 123 (1970), *reprinted in* H. WILLIAMS, R. MAXWELL & C. MEYERS, *supra* note 17, at 63, 72.

23. Dodyk, *The Tax Reform Act of 1969 and the Poor*, 71 COLUM. L. REV. 758, 777 (1971). The tax-cost of permitted expensing of exploration and development costs was put at $300 million, both before and after the Act. *Id.*

Representative Les Aspin of Wisconsin estimated the tax-cost of percentage depletion to be $1.5 billion and the tax cost of the expensing of intangibles at $325 million. N.Y. REV. BOOKS, Mar. 7, 1974, at 28. *See* U.S. NEWS & WORLD REP., Feb. 4, 1974, at 49, estimating the cost of the depletion deduction at $1.7 billion. *Cf.* N.Y. Times, Mar. 16, 1974, at 30, col. 1 (an editorial estimating that federal revenues would be increased by $9 billion by elimination of percentage depletion and the expensing of intangibles). This estimate seems unduly high even in the light of the substantial increase in the price of oil as a result of the actions of the Organization of Petroleum Exporting Companies cartel in 1973.

The fundamental fault, however, with this tax subsidy is that it is an inefficient method of encouraging exploration and development of oil and gas. The owner of an operating interest with a relatively high basis in the property derives no benefit from percentage depletion, for he will be taking cost depletion, an ordinary deduction not different in kind from deductions available to any business enterprise. But percentage depletion is available to nonoperating owners—primarily the landowner-lessor but also other owners of nonoperating interests not risking capital in exploration and development—and to the extent a tax subsidy is given to persons not risking capital, the subsidy fails to encourage exploration and development. Instead, it primarily serves merely to increase land values by freeing some of the income from land from tax burdens. Percentage depletion may have increased somewhat the drilling of development wells, but it is doubtful that it has materially increased exploration.

Although the oil industry has argued strenuously during the entire life of the percentage depletion deduction that it is required to assure the nation an adequate domestic supply of crude oil and natural gas, elements of the industry somewhat belatedly have come to recognize that the deduction has become an albatross, generating more harm by way of criticism of tax favoritism to the industry than the value of the benefits realized.[24] In any event, it now seems probable that the percentage depletion allowance for the oil industry will be phased out over a period of several years—a change eminently to be desired.

B. *Expensing Intangible Costs*

The option to expense intangible drilling and development costs[25] incurred in domestic oil and gas operations should be preserved. The tax-cost of this option for domestic operations is relatively modest, as the difference between expensing and capitalizing is merely the time when the tax deduction bcomes available to the taxpayer.[26] Unlike the percentage depletion deduction, which is available to nonoperating as well as to operating owners, the benefits of the expensing option go to the persons whose activities

---

24. Late in 1973 the Atlantic Richfield Company took a corporate position advocating repeal of the oil depletion allowance, urging that it be phased out simultaneously with price controls. *See* N.Y. Times, Dec. 27, 1973, at 57, cols. 1–2. More recently, Standard Oil Co. of California has announced that it would not be opposed to phasing out percentage depletion if prices were decontrolled concurrently. 51 BULL., Spring, 1974 (published by Standard Oil Co. of Cal.) (unpaged insert entitled "Updating the energy picture"). One proposal for the phasing out of the percentage depletion deduction calls for the elimination of the deduction on oil not subject to price controls. *See* Wall St. J., Mar. 13, 1974, at 4, col. 1. At that time, about 70% of domestically produced oil was subject to price controls. Another proposal called for phasing out the percentage depletion deduction over a 7-year period. *See id.*

25. The option permits the taxpayer to claim a deduction on his income tax return for the year in which such costs were incurred instead of capitalizing the costs. *See* INT. REV. CODE OF 1954, § 263(c); Treas. Reg. § 1.612–4 (1965).

26. *See* note 23 *supra* for estimates of the tax-cost of the expensing deduction.

contribute to an increase in the supply of oil and gas, namely those persons who expend money in exploration and development. As between the expensing option and the percentage depletion allowance, expensing is much cheaper and is also more efficient in encouraging expenditures of private moneys in exploration and development.[27]

C. *Changes in Foreign Profits Tax*

The effect which the Internal Revenue Code provisions relating to taxation of income from oil and gas operations in other countries exert upon domestic exploration for oil and gas and upon the availability of imports of oil and gas from other countries merits careful examination and rethinking.

Few if any other provisions of the Internal Revenue Code approach the high standard of opacity which characterizes the foreign tax credit provisions permitting the taxpayer to claim a credit against his United States tax on foreign income in the amount of the foreign tax paid on that income.[28] Although for some years domestic oil companies paid relatively modest United States taxes on income realized from foreign operations, we have now reached the stage where there is little if any tax revenue from this source. The structure of our tax law has encouraged the oil-producing nations to increase taxes to the extent necessary to exhaust the credit available under the Internal Revenue Code—much in the same manner as our own state governments were led to enact estate tax provisions designed to exhaust the credit made available under the federal estate tax law for state death taxes. And to the extent that the increase in the producing nation's share of the gross proceeds of sale of oil and gas provided a dollar-for-dollar credit against United States taxes, as long as the host country's "take" did not exceed the United States tax, no particular economic reason existed for the producing companies to resist the ever-increasing demands of the producing nations.

In effect, the producing nations are exacting excise taxes from the producing companies; these taxes are then used as a credit against United States

---

27. This argument does not justify the availability of the expensing option for foreign operations, however, insofar as the option may provide a tax shelter for the domestic income of companies operating both in the United States and abroad. *See* note 29 *infra* and accompanying text.

28. *See* INT. REV. CODE OF 1954, §§ 901–06. The most commonly voiced rationale for the foreign tax credit is couched in terms of our own national interest: if American companies are taxed abroad on their foreign income and then are taxed again in the United States on the same income, they will have been subjected to double taxation and will not be able to compete abroad with companies from other capital-exporting countries. *See, e.g., Hearings on S. 2806 Before the Subcomm. on Energy of the Senate Comm. on Finance*, 93d Cong., 1st Sess., pt. 1, at 103, 119–23 (1973) (testimony of Frederic M. Hickman, Assistant Secretary of the Treasury for Tax Policy).

A second rationale is founded on the needs of developing countries to obtain appropriate revenue from the exploitation of mineral resources. *See* Due, *The Developing Economies, Tax and Royalty Payments by the Petroleum Industry, and the United States Income Tax*, 10 NAT. RES. J. 10, 22–23 (1970).

income taxes, rather than as a deduction—the treatment given state production and severance taxes in the federal tax returns of companies engaged in domestic production of oil and gas. Arguably if a deduction rather than a credit had been available to the taxpayer on his United States tax return, he would have had a greater incentive to resist the increased "take" of the host country. A change now from credit to deduction would presumably do no good. It is too late to close the barn door—the horse has fled.[29]

There is substantial support in America for a liberal international trade policy.[30] Moreover, in view of the world energy situation, it is ultimately to our long-term interest to have energy supplies throughout the world explored and developed, even though from time to time we may witness expropriation in one country or another or the institution of an oil embargo for political or economic purposes. The greater the world supply of oil and gas, the less is the damage done to our national interest by expropriation or embargo. For that matter, the greater the world supply, the smaller the risk of expropriation or embargo. The investor who takes his capital abroad does so with full recognition of the risk of expropriation or other changes in the ground rules in the host country, and his requirements for an "adequate" return on the investment are based in part on his estimate of the probability of such conduct by the host country. Under such circumstances, the American investor should not be denied the opportunity to earn a return on his foreign investment that is appropriate to the risk the investor has assumed.

In light of the above, the United States not only should continue to permit the exportation of capital for foreign investment, it should allow the exporter of capital to earn a return on that capital commensurate with the risk involved. To that end, the United States should subject such investors to income tax liability only when foreign income is brought to the United States. Further, a company should not be permitted to employ its foreign operations as a shelter to avoid United States taxation of its domestic income. Such a measure would require that separate accounts be kept for for-

---

29. There was a time when the availability of the percentage depletion deduction for foreign oil was a matter of some controversy in the United States, but today that is a meaningless controversy inasmuch as the foreign tax credit is sufficient to enable domestic taxpayers engaged in foreign production to avoid any United States income tax on their income from foreign operations. In any event, percentage depletion makes no more sense in the case of foreign operations than it does in the case of domestic operations.

There remains, however, a situation in which the option to expense intangible drilling and development costs on federal income tax returns continues to have economic value to concerns engaged in foreign operations, despite the availability of the foreign tax credit for what are in effect excise taxes. This is due to the fact that the intangible deduction may be available during the early periods of foreign operations to shelter domestic income of the oil companies. Then, after the foreign operations begin to produce income, the taxes to the foreign government are credited against the United States tax, thus avoiding any liability to the United States despite the prior shelter of domestic income. *See Hearings on S. 2806, supra* note 28, at 121–22 (testimony of Assistant Secretary Hickman).

30. *See* L. KRAUSE & K. DAM, FEDERAL TAX TREATMENT OF FOREIGN INCOME 6 (1964).

eign and domestic operations—a requirement presenting difficult but manageable problems of allocation between domestic and foreign operations.

III. OIL POLICY

A. *Shale Oil*

Reasonable incentives are required to encourage private research and
development of new energy sources—such as extraction of oil from the oil
shale deposits—without excessive environmental damage. A minimum price
guarantee for a given quantity of oil extracted by such new methods—perhaps including a price escalator—should be sufficient to encourage private
industry to undertake research and development while minimizing the
contingent liability of the treasury.[31] An adequate minimum guaranteed
price per barrel of shale oil should be sufficient to encourage the industry
to invest in shale development free from concern that an influx of Middle
Eastern oil might cause oil prices to drop below the level at which shale oil
would be competitive. Such guaranteed price would be preferable to a
new quota system for oil imports or to variable import duties designed to
maintain oil prices, since, whereas a quota system establishes a minimum
price for all oil, a guarantee of purchase of shale oil at a specified price will
not prevent the price of oil from dropping to the level dictated by market
considerations.

B. *Changes in Bidding Policies*

The bidding for oil shale leases and for oil and gas leases on federal lands
should be converted from a bonus-competition to a competition based on
guarantee of performance[32] by the lessee and the reservation by the government of a sliding-scale net-profits interest or a carried interest.[33]

---

31. *See, e.g.*, the proposal made by Secretary of Commerce Frederick B. Dent to offer a
" 'guaranteed price' plan to induce private companies to produce oil and gas from such new sources
as liquefying coal." N.Y. Times, Mar. 18, 1974, at 45, col. 4.

Politics vs. Synthetics, FORBES MAGAZINE, Feb. 15, 1974, at 42, discusses estimates by Continental
Oil Company that "by 1985 the company could be getting 15 to 25% of its earnings from synthetic
oil and gas" obtained from tar sands and oil shale and by gasification of coal. "The problem is . . .
that in the long run, alternatives to natural crude oil and gas will cost the equivalent of $10.40 a
barrel, not excessive in the current market. But if the Saudis, say, dropped the price to well below that
level, where would you sell oil that needed a $10.40 price?" *Id.*

32. Parties can agree to performance obligations concerning the speed of exploration and development and concerning the volume of production after discovery. If, for example, the share of
the lessor is on a sliding scale and increases as the volume increases, the lease necessarily should contain
a provision authorizing an appropriate governmental official to require production at the maximum
efficient rate, lest the lessee produce at a lower level to minimize the lessor's share. A good faith, or
duty of fair dealing, standard could be adopted to prevent an abuse of this power.

33. Numerous bidding systems are available. Under the bonus-competition system, the variable
in the sealed bids for leases providing for a standard fixed royalty (*e.g.*, 1/8) is the amount of the
cash consideration (bonus) tendered for the lease. Under a royalty-competition system, the variable
in the sealed bids providing for a fixed sum as bonus is the share of the production (*e.g.*, 1/6, 1/5) to
be delivered to the lessor as royalty, free of costs of production. Under a net profits–competition sys-

Traditionally, federal leases have been granted on the basis of a bonus competition, and the bonus receipts by the government from competitive sale of leases have provided substantial government revenues. However, a landowner with holdings as extensive as the federal government (or as Alaska, California, or Texas) would certainly recover a greater return from its leases by taking a larger share of production in lieu of a bonus.[34] A system of competitive sales based on a share of profits or production rather than an advance bonus would also open the bidding to companies lacking the substantial assets required to make large bonus offers. Moreover, even the largest oil companies have limits on the cash available at any moment of time for expenditures, and the payment of a very large bonus reduces the funds available for exploration and development. Bonus is paid by the oil company at the outset and thus is a capital investment not contributing to production.

A sliding-scale net-profits interest or a carried interest may also be preferable to a royalty interest, inasmuch as the requirement of payment of a high royalty may lead to early abandonment of marginally productive leases.[35]

C. *Increased Refinery Capacity*

The nation requires a major increase in refinery capacity, for there has been virtually no expansion of such capacity in recent years. Doubtless some of the responsibility for failure to increase capacity must be borne by environmentalists who have resisted the building of new refineries in one part of the nation after another.

---

tem, all production will accrue to the lessee and the variable in the sealed bids is the share of the operator's net profits to be delivered to the lessor. Under a carried interest–competition system the variable in the sealed bids is the lessor's share of gross production from the lease (*e.g.*, 50%) which is subject to the right of the lessee to recover therefrom the lessor's proportionate share of expenses which are borne in the first instance by the lessee (thus "carrying" the lessor).

34. The Texas School Land Board voted in March 1974 to change lease policies to provide for a larger minimum royalty (1/5 rather than 1/6), to reduce the minimum cash-bonus payment from $25 per acre to $10 per acre, and to reduce the primary term of leases from 5 years to 3 years except on deep-trend areas. "The board also agreed to submit for bids development leases on high-royalty bidding, and to put some leases on a combination high-bonus and high-royalty bidding basis . . . ." N.Y. Times, Mar. 22, 1974, at 53, col. 4.

The first lease sale conducted on this basis produced 704 bids on 499 tracts totaling 336,038 acres. It was reported that there were more competitive bids on leases than in many of the earlier sales including a great number of bids from smaller operators who had not bid on state leases before. "Several leases were awarded on high-royalty bidding on development leases, adjoining production, ranging up to 43.125 per cent in the Gulf of Mexico and to 95.218 per cent in the Rio Grande near Laredo where 13 bidders competed for six small leases in a provant [*sic*] area." N.Y. Times, July 3, 1974, at 41, col. 4.

Knowledgeable lessors have long known that if they were willing to accept a smaller bonus and thus assume some of the risk of unsuccessful operations, the lessee, freed of the requirement of advancing bonus money, would pay as consideration for the lease a much more substantial part of production or net profits.

35. The Interior Department has reluctantly undertaken a "small-scale test" of leasing on the basis of a royalty bid rather than a bonus bid. N.Y. Times, May 7, 1974, at 63, col. 4. A spokesman for the Department declared that "experience indicates that a large cash bonus encourages rapid exploration and development . . . ," whereas, "[a] high royalty bid may result in abandonment of potential recoverable reserves." *Id.* at 69, cols. 5–6.

The oil companies themselves have had second thoughts about new investment in refineries in the light of uncertainty over the availability of crude oil and uncertainty over profitability if crude oil prices were to be rolled back by governmental action.[36] Moreover, a relationship apparently exists between the continued availability of the percentage depletion allowance and the availability of refinery capacity. Because of the availability of the depletion deduction, an oil company that is self-sufficient in crude oil production for its refineries has an incentive to report income in its production account rather than its refining account. An independent refiner not self-sufficient in crude oil production must, then, buy oil in the market at the higher price posted by the oil-sufficient integrated producer-refiner. And to the extent the two refineries compete in the same market, the independent refiner will be selling with no profit at a price which yields a profit to the integrated producer-refiner. Under such circumstances, it is indeed a hazardous venture for an independent company without crude oil of its own to embark upon the construction of a new refinery.[37]

The Federal Trade Commission, in a complaint filed against eight major oil companies in 1973, sought to have some refinery operations divested by the defendants.[38] Such action obviously would lead to some change in the practice of posting a high price by oil-sufficient producer-refiners. A different and more efficient method of accomplishing some of the same objectives would be the abolition of the percentage depletion deduction, thereby eliminating the incentive of the oil-sufficient integrated producer to post a high price for oil.

Another reason for the dearth of new refineries in recent years has been the increasing dependence of refineries on foreign oil and the abolition of

---

36. *See* N.Y. Times, Mar. 16, 1974, at 37, col. 8.

37. "The shifting of industry profit from refining to the crude-oil department has quite naturally had a devastating impact on independent refining operations. From 1938 to 1970 the share of refining capacity accounted for by the twenty largest refiners had increased from 79.5% to 85.7% while the share of smaller nonintegrated refiners has declined from 21.5% to 14.3%. Furthermore, most of the remaining 14.3% are now small integrated companies themselves. With the artificial inflation of crude-oil prices it became practically impossible to operate an independent refinery without the refinery producing a significant proportion of its own crude-oil requirements. The principal exceptions are those independent refineries operating in the northern tier of the country or on the West Coast that are able to reduce their crude-oil costs by processing a high proportion of low-price imported crude oil and a few refineries competing in relatively sheltered markets." *See* F. ALLVINE & J. PATTERSON, COMPETITION, LTD.: THE MARKETING OF GASOLINE 223 (1972) (footnote omitted).

See also Hearings Pursuant to S. Res. 45, supra note 13, at 1167 (statement by Robert E. Yancey, President of Ashland Oil Co.). He pointed to the enormous competitive advantages to integrated companies resulting from the depletion allowance and oil import quotas and he indicated that the bargaining position of the crude-deficient refiner is growing steadily weaker. *Id.* at 1181.

Substantial variation exists among the 10 major refinery companies in worldwide crude oil self-sufficiency—ranging from 193% for Standard (Calif.), to 28.9% for Sun. *See* J. BARTON, T. CONNOLLY, R. GILBERT, D. LEAVER, & J. SWEENEY, ENERGY AND SOCIETY 26 (1974).

38. The complaint, filed July 18, 1973, did not specify the relief sought but staff lawyers subsequently filed with the administrative law judge in the antitrust proceeding a recommendation that the eight companies be ordered to eliminate half of their oil-refining capacity in the East and Gulf Coast areas to increase competition in the oil industry. *See* N.Y. Times, Feb. 26, 1974, at 58, col. 7.

the oil import quota. While the oil import quota was in effect, allowable imports were divided among the different companies on the basis of refinery capacity. Thus a refinery not engaged in importing received a right to import, and this right (or import ticket) could be exchanged for domestic oil. The termination of quotas had the effect of increasing the difficulty experienced by small inland refineries in obtaining crude.[39] A way must be found to assure independent refiners access to crude oil, domestic as well as imported. The Federal Energy Office has made efforts to accomplish this and such efforts must continue.

IV. Gas Policy

Negotiations for the construction of a gas pipeline to deliver gas from the North Slope of Alaska to the lower 48 states should be prosecuted with diligence. Initially, much of the gas produced from the North Slope will probably be reinjected to maintain reservoir pressures and to permit the maximum recovery of oil from the formation, but after about 2 years of oil production, marketing of the gas will become expedient. El Paso Natural Gas Company has proposed a pipeline to Valdez paralleling the oil pipeline.[40] A gas pipeline through Canada might, however, be more economical.[41] A gas pipeline presents fewer environmental problems than an oil pipeline, as the gas in the pipeline can be chilled, unlike oil, which must be heated and thus poses the problem of thawing the tundra.

We must also encourage the conservation of natural gas in areas such as the Persian Gulf states where much gas is now wasted.[42] This conservation may require expenditures of American capital in the development of liquefield natural gas (LNG) plants in some countries and the development of methanol plants—designed to convert natural gas into wood alco-

39. See *Hearings Pursuant to S. Res. 45 Before the Senate Comm. on Interior and Insular Affairs*, 93d Cong., 1st Sess., ser. 93-4 (92-39), pt. 2, at 686-87 (1973) (statement of Robert E. Yancey).

40. N.Y. Times, Mar. 22, 1974, at 59, cols. 6-7. It would cost about $3.5 billion, including tanker ships and a regasification plant on the California coast between Los Angeles and San Francisco.

41. Among the factors to be considered in this calculus are the gas losses in liquefication and regasification if the trans-Alaska route is adopted, and the possibility of tapping gas reserves along or near the trans-Canada route which otherwise might be insufficient in quantity to finance the building of a pipeline.

There are serious problems of negotiation with Canada on the pipeline, because of environmental problems and because of possible Canadian insistence on a majority interest in the equity of the pipeline—problems that will present financing difficulties. Twenty-seven Canadian and United States corporations have made a joint-venture proposal (the Canadian Arctic Gas Pipeline, Ltd.) to Ottawa and Washington for permission to build a 2,625-mile pipeline at a cost of $5.7 billion, running through the Mackenzie River region of Canada to Calgary, whence gas would be delivered by other lines to the Chicago area, to the West Coast of the United States, and to eastern Canada. When completed, the proposed pipeline would have a daily capacity of 4.5 billion cubic feet of gas (about 7% of present United States consumption). See N.Y. Times, Mar. 22, 1974, at 55, col. 8.

42. It has been estimated that about 60% of the natural gas production in the Persian Gulf is flared. *Hearings Pursuant to S. Res. 45 Before the Senate Comm. on Interior and Insular Affairs on the President's Energy Message Concerning Energy Resources and S. 1570, the Emergency Fuels and Energy Allocation*, 93d Cong., 1st Sess., ser. 93-10 (92-45), at 246 (1973).

hol—in other gas-surplus areas so distant from the market that the additional transportation costs of LNG exceed the greater processing costs of methanol. Methanol projects will probably not be viable, however, until the present import duty of 7.6 cents per gallon of methanol ($3.19 per barrel) is lowered.[43]

V. Diplomatic Opportunities

Our dealing with the OPEC (Organization of Petroleum Exporting Countries) and the OAPEC (Organization of Arab Petroleum Exporting Countries) cartels will require diplomatic skill of the highest order.

It may appear to some that the best way to deal with a monopolistic cartel of producers is to form a monopsonistic cartel of consumers. However, the unsuccessful attempt by Secretary Kissinger to coordinate such a cartel with the European Common Market indicates the difficulty in obtaining agreement among the oil-consuming nations on a unified policy in dealing with the OPEC. In the first place, the degree of dependence on foreign oil varies greatly: we are less dependent than the other major consuming nations, and in time Britain may be substantially self-sufficient. France and Japan, on the other hand, are heavily dependent on Middle Eastern oil. Another difference is seen in historic relationships between particular nations—France with Iraq, on the one hand, the United States with Iran and Saudi Arabia, on the other.

Certainly the oil cartels have discovered that by turning the spigot down a bit the price of oil can be raised dramatically. And we cannot hold high hopes for a substantial easing of the OPEC or OAPEC control over available crude oil supplies in the near future. The Western reaction to the Arab group's muscle-flexing during the Arab-Israeli War of 1973 quickly established the producing cartel's great strength. Earlier attempts to affect supply and price in a major manner had been largely unsuccessful, but the 1973 effort came at just the proper moment for the Arab powers: there was no excess capacity in the non-Arab nations which could be called upon to meet the situation and, moreover, the Arabs had become the major supplier of oil and had the power to affect price by a relatively modest decrease in production.[44] We must anticipate that the Arab powers will continue to have substantial market control over crude oil.[45] And, although there are

---

43. *See* Energy Economics Division of The Chase Manhattan Bank, The Petroleum Situation, Mar. 31, 1974, at third to fourth pages.

44. At the end of 1972, 24.3% of the free-world reserves (20.7% of the world reserves) of crude oil were in Saudi Arabia. The OPEC nations accounted for 77.5% of the free-world reserves. U.S. Tariff Comm'n for the Senate Comm. on Finance, *supra* note 18, at 14, 16.

45. Substantial reserves have been discovered under the North Sea amounting to between 11 and 12 billion barrels with an estimated ultimate reserve potential of as much as 40 billion barrels. Warman, *The Significance and Future of North Sea Oil,* 11 S.W. Legal Found. Inst. on Exploration

some disagreements among the Arab states about ends and means,[46] it is obviously to the interest of those nations to agree on some production limits which will maximize current return while extending the life of their petroleum reserves. Moreover, at the present time they are enjoying an unprecedented surplus of incoming revenue. Under such circumstances, they may be wiser to keep the money in the ground in the form of oil: its value can only go up, and while in the ground it cannot be pilfered. The monopoly price exacted by the producers' cartel has created havoc for the economies of both underdeveloped and developed nations. In light of this, the consuming nations must join efforts to force a reduction in price.

VI. Unification of National Policy

One of the reasons for the failure of national oil and gas policies has been the multiplicity of jurisdictions that oversee decisions. This problem can be dealt with on several levels. The proposal for the reorganization of federal government activities concerned with energy into a single cabinet-level department—a need foreseen by the Paley Commission nearly a quarter century ago—merits continued study and early action by Congress.

We must engage in some serious thinking about the interrelationship of local, state, regional, and national interests. In what might have been summarized by a newspaper headline as "Aristotle Onassis Goes to a New England Town Meeting," a much needed new $600 million oil refinery was rejected through a demonstration of local democracy in Durham Point, New Hampshire, in March 1974.[47] Without attempting to pass on the question whether the particular location proposed by Onassis was appropriate in light of all relevant considerations, a new refinery in New England would appear to make sense in view of the heavy demands of that region for fuel oil.

Another issue posing the problem of local autonomy is the restriction on the use of "dirty" fuel for power generation. Local groups have sought to restrict the use of coal or high-sulphur crude oil for consumption as boiler fuel; these efforts have, obviously, increased the demand for natural gas and for low-sulphur crude. Thus, although Consolidated Edison was permitted

---

AND ECON. OF THE PETROLEUM INDUSTRY 63, 71–73 (1973). For purposes of comparison, the proven oil reserves in some of the OPEC nations are as follows (in units of billions of barrels): Saudi Arabia 145, Kuwait 66, Iran 55.5, Iraq 36, Libya 25, Abu Dhabi 18.9, and Qatar 6. N.Y. Times, Apr. 16, 1973, at 1, col. 3.

46. The interests of the members of the cartel do not coincide in all particulars. For example, Iran, though Muslim, is a non-Arab country and reportedly increased its production of oil during the Arab reduction of production in late 1973 and early 1974. *See id.*, Mar. 9, 1974, at 35, col. 6. Similarly, the interests of Nigeria, Indonesia, and Venezuela differ in some respects from the interests of certain participants in OPEC. The critical question may be whether Saudi Arabia, with its tremendous production, is willing to serve as the balance wheel for OPEC, just as Texas served as the balance wheel for states in the Interstate Oil Compact Commission for so many years.

47. *See id.*, Mar. 7, 1974, at 28, col. 7; *cf. id.* Mar. 16, 1974, at 11, col. 5.

to burn coal rather than oil for a brief period during the 1973 oil shortage, in late 1973 the new New York State Commissioner of Environmental Conservation argued that the energy crisis was "overblown and exaggerated" and suggested that the power company be prevented from continuing its use of coal.[48]

Such examples demonstrate that there must come a time when veto at the local level is subject to being overruled by reason of state, regional, or national interest, through the mechanism of preemption.

VII. CONCLUSION

In a 6-month period beginning in late 1973, the American people for the first time became aware that the United States was no longer self-sufficient in meeting its energy requirements. Public debate, not always rational or temperate, has begun on the steps that should be taken in the light of this situation. Some have urged that we must attain a position of energy self-sufficiency at an early date, but to this observer that objective appears attainable, if at all, only at an excessive cost. On the other hand, a do-nothing policy would render the United States vulnerable to new manifestations of economic and political extortion by the nations in the OPEC—an equally unacceptable alternative. This Essay has attempted to suggest some of the elements that might enter into a rational energy policy that seeks to reduce the risks of international extortion by oil-producing nations—increasing national self-sufficiency without incurring the astronomical costs of a crash program of complete self-sufficiency. One can only hope that rational discussion will yield a program of development and conservation competent to meet the needs of the nation in the decades immediately ahead.

48. *Id.*, Dec. 28, 1973, at 1, col. 5.

Index

Index

Abbott Laboratories v. Gardner, 381
Abrams v. United States, 196ff, 202, 209f, 217–26, 228
Acts: English Habeas Corpus, 8f, 11, 15; Civil Rights, 68, 79; Judiciary, 69; Voting Rights, 80–86 *passim*, 90, 96; Uniform Revised Sales, 102; World War I Espionage, 196–201 *passim*, 211, 218, 222, 226, 229; Sedition, 198, 219; Smith, 227ff; Harrison, 280–85 *passim; Clayton*, 317–34 *passim*; Sherman, 317–34 *passim*; Truth in Lending, 438f; Model Consumer Credit, 441; National Consumer, 441; Natural Gas, 446
Aid to Families with Dependent Children, 72
American antitrust laws, economic tests of legality, 317–34; ways to increase seller's profits, 318–20; P-MC test, 320–21; unit-output test, 322–23; seller-profit test, 323–24; buyer-welfare test, 324–26; Sherman & Clayton Act tests, 326–29; rival offer test, 329–34
American Law Institute, *see* Covenant of Habitability
American Legion, 390
Amvets, 390
Antiguest statutes, choice-of-law problems in Wisconsin and New York, 251–65; *Babcock v. Jackson*, 252–54; results of *Neumeier* rules, 254–63; future of *Neumeier* rules, 263–65
Antitrust laws, *see* American antitrust laws
Appellate court opinions, control of publication of, 267–75; proposals for reducing volume of, 268–70; criticism of selective reporting, 270–71; effects on judicial system, 271–72; efforts to limit, 272–74; suggested solutions, 274–75

Babcock v. Jackson, 252ff, 262, 265
Bailey v. Drexel Furniture Co., 67
Barker v. Wingo, 14, 15–17
Bell, Daniel, 428, 443
Bibb v. Navajo Freight Lines, 76f
Bickel, Alexander M., 188

Bill of Rights, 72, 79, 96, 187, 189
Bills: Jenner, 69; Omnibus Crime Control and Safe Streets, 69; Tuck, 69; of Rights, 72, 79, 96, 187, 189
Black, Charles, 182
Black, Hugo L., 86f, 93, 179ff, 185f, 191, 194
Bork, Robert H., 180f
Braden v. 30th Judicial Circuit Court, 17–19
Brandeis, Louis D., 227, 230, 387
Brandenburg v. Ohio, 198, 205, 230f
Branzburg v. Hayes, 95
Brennan, William J., Jr., "ratchet" theory, 82–85, 88–89, 91–92
Brown, John R., Chief Judge of 5th Circuit, 272
Brundage v. United States, 33
Burger, Warren E., 10, 12f, 21
Burleson, Albert, Postmaster General, 199, 216
Burlingham, Charles C., 207

Calder v. Bull, 184
California Civil Code, 376
California Supreme Court, 268–74 *passim*, 376, 417f
Caplovitz, David, 443
Cardozo, Benjamin N., 12
Casner, A. James, 355
Chafee, Zechariah, Jr., 195–249
Challenge for cause, 25–34
Chase, Salmon P., 70, 184
China, politics and health care, 303–16; problems since 1949, 303–4; health care progress, 304–10; paramedic training, 305–6; financing of, 307–10; professionalism and egalitarianism, 310–15; political review, 316
Choice-of-law problems, *see* Antiguest statutes
Cipolla v. Shaposka, 259f, 264
Civil law education, *see* Legal education
Civil process, two models of, 413–26; Conflict Resolution Model, 413–14; Behavior Modification Model, 414–16; Consumer class actions, 416–21; appeals and due

process, 421–23; standing doctrine, 424–25; Packer models, 426
Civil Rights Act, 68, 79
Civil Rights Cases, 92f
Clayton Act, 317–34 *passim*
Codes: Uniform Commercial, 97–111, 440; California Civil, 376; Uniform Housing, 377; Uniform Consumer Credit, 432, 438–44 *passim*; Internal Revenue, 450ff
Coke, Lord, 269
Common law education, *see* Legal education
Congressional interpretive power of due process and equal protection, 79–96; rationales of *Katzenbach v. Morgan*, 80–85; *Oregon v. Mitchell rationale*, 85–88; federalism vs. individual rights, 89–92; reconciliation of *Morgan* and *Mitchell*, 93–95
Conklin v. Horner, 255–59 *passim*, 264
Constitution, *see* United States Constitution
Constitutional interpretation, *see* United States Constitution
Consumer credit law: rates, costs, and benefits, 427–44; evolution of rate regulation, 428–31; consumer benefits, 431–33; cost of benefits, 433–34; worth of benefits, 435–36; realities of regulation, 436–40; rate regulation reform, 440–43
Covenant of Habitability and American Law Institute, 355–79; Restatement rules, 355–61; administration of rules, 361–65; economic consequences of rules, 365–69; empirical evidence, 369–73; sources of authority for rules, 373–78
Currie, Brainerd, 252ff, 264

Daar v. Yellow Cab Co., 416ff
Dandridge v. Williams, 72–75 *passim*
Debs, Eugene V., 214f
Debs v. United States, 211–16
Dennis v. United States, 227ff
Douglas v. California, 38f, 41
Dual federalism, 79f
Due process, 8, 23, 70f, 79–96, 186ff, 192f, 421–23

Eastman, Max, 199f
Eight Amendment, 189
Eisen v. Carlisle & Jacquelin, 416–20 *passim*, 425f
Ely, John, 180f, 186f
English Habeas Corpus Act, 8f, 11, 15
Equal protection, 71–75 *passim*, 79–96, 188
Ethos, development of, 54–58

Ex parte McCardle, 69

Federalism, 79f, 89–92
Federal Power Commission, 446–49 *passim*
Federal rules, *see* Rules
Federal Trade Commission, 456
Fifteenth Amendment, 84, 86, 93f, 96
Fifth Amendment, 186f, 383
First Amendment, 61ff, 72, 95, 189, 195–249, 383f
Fletcher v. Peck, 184
Foreign affairs, *see* Legal process
Fourteenth Amendment, 8, 23, 63, 68, 70ff, 73, 80–96 *passim*, 185–88 *passim*, 192f, 421
Fourth Amendment, 189
Frankfurter, Felix, 28f
Frohwerk v. United States, 211–15, 218

Gas, national policy, 445–60
George, Alexander, 118–19
Gitlow v. New York, 227
Godbold, John C., 1, 8f, 14f
Goldschmidt, Levin, 100
Green v. Superior Court, 376
Griffin v. Illinois, 38f, 41

Hague Convention of 1912, 280
Hammer v. Dagenhart, 67
Ham v. South Carolina, 22, 40f
Hand, Learned, and First Amendment doctrine, 195–249; review of correspondence exchange, 195–98; background of *Masses* decision, 198–200; Hand's contribution to *Masses*, 200–205; response to *Masses*, 205–11; *Schenck-Frohwerk-Debs* cases, 211–17; *Abrams* dissent, 217–26; vindication of Hand's *Masses* approach, 226–30; correspondence appendix, 231–49
Harlan, John M., 84, 87, 229ff
Harrison Act of 1914, 280–85 *passim*
Hart, H. M., 99–111
Heath v. Zellmer, 255–58 *passim*, 264
Heroin, 277–302; geography, pharmacology, and history, 277–82; use and effects, 282–89; solutions to addiction problems, 289–301; problems of legal reform, 302
Hickman v. Taylor, 154ff
Hoebel, E., 101
Holmes, Oliver Wendell, 100, 187, 195–249
Hough, Charles Merrill, 205f

Internal Revenue Code, 452
Interstate Agreement on Detainers, 8
Iredell, James, 184

Jackson, Robert H., 75
Jacobson v. Massachusetts, 210
Jenner Bill, 69
Johnson v. Robison, 383–87 *passim*
Jones v. Alfred H. Mayer Co., 92f
Judiciary Act of 1789, 69
Jury, examination of, 21–34; investigation services, 34–36; government investigation of, 37
Justices, Supreme Court, *see by name*

Katzenbach v. McClung, 68
Katzenbach v. Morgan, 80, 84–95 *passim*
Kurland, Phillip B., 274

Laski, Harold, 222
Legal education there and here, a comparison, 335–54; educational differences, 337–41; goals, 341–43; professorial differences, 344; differences in curricula and methods, 345–51; organizational differences, 345; student differences, 351–52
Legal explosion, 43–60; complexity hypothesis, 43–44; traditional explanations, 43–48; economic analysis, 44–48; individual's helplessness hypothesis, 44; cultural analysis, 48–54; development of common ethos, 54–58; new roles for legal academicians, 58–60
Legal process in foreign affairs, 113–28; suggested lines of approach, 118–22 (executive), 122–27 (legislative), legal profession, 128
Legal realism, 97–105 *passim*
Legislators, guide to, 61–77; obligations, 63–65; motives, 65–70
Lewis v. United States, 21, 32
Linde, Hans, 180f, 186
Llewellyn, Karl, 97–111
Lochner v. New York, 187, 190, 194
Lowell, Abbot Lawrence, 226f

McCulloch v. Maryland, 67
McKane v. Durston, 421
Marbury v. Madison, 63, 181–84 *passim*, 194
Marshall, Thurgood, 40, 63, 67, 73ff, 183–86 *passim*
Masses Publishing Co. v. Patten, 196f, 198–200, 201–30 *passim*
Medina, Harold R., 418, 420, 425
Methadone maintenance, 298–302 *passim*
Model Consumer Credit Act, 441
Models of civil process, *see* Civil process
Moral behavior, 401–11; determinants of,

405–10; justification for, 405–8; situational conditions, 408–9; addiction to, 409–10
Moral character, 401–11; moral information, 403; moral judgment, 403–5
Moral education, outlook for improvement in, 410–11
Morphine, 277–81 *passim*

Narcotic antagonists, 301
National Consumer Act, 441
National Consumer Law Center, 437, 441ff
National Environmental Protection Act, 55f
National oil and gas policy, some ingredients of, 445–60; regulatory policies, 446–50; tax policies, 450–54; oil policy, 454–57; gas policy, 457–58; diplomacy in, 458–59; unification, 459–60
Natural gas, deregulation, 446–49
Natural Gas Act of 1938, 446
Negotiable Instruments Law, 110
Neumeier v. Kuehner, 251–65 *passim*
New York Court of Appeals, 251–56 *passim*, 260–65 *passim*
New Zealand, *see* Personal injury accidents
Ninth Amendment, 185, 192f

OAPEC, 458ff
Oil, *see* National oil and gas policy
Omnibus Crime Control and Safe Streets Bill, 69
OPEC, 458ff
Opium, 277–81 *passim*, 293f
Oregon v. Mitchell, 79–84 *passim*, 85–88, 90–96 *passim*
Organization of Arab Petroleum Exporting Countries, 458ff
Organization of Petroleum Exporting Countries, 458ff
Ortwein v. Schwab, 386

Packer, Herbert L., 413, 426
Paley Commission, 445, 459
Palmer v. Thompson, 66
Patten, Thomas G., N.Y. Postmaster, 199
Patterson v. Colorado, 199f
People v. Davis, 36
Peremptory challenge, 25–34
Personal injury accidents, New Zealand and U.S. similarities, 129–48; statistical review, 129–34; death figures, 134–37; injury figures, 138–43; remedies and costs, 143–48
Peters v. Kiff, 27
Phillips Petroleum Co. v. Wisconsin, 446

Posner, Richard, 427f, 435, 437
Pound, Roscoe, 99, 104, 106
Powell, Lewis F., Jr., 73f
President's Materials Policy Commission, 445, 459
Property Restatement rules, 355–79

Realism, legal, 97–105 *passim*
Restatement of the Law, 348; Second Property, 355–79
Roberts, Owen J., 259f
Rogers, Henry Wade, 206
Rules: of Civil Procedure, 150, 153, 419; of Evidence, 151ff, 158–61, 419; Work Product, 153–58; Property Restatement, 355–79

Sacks, A., 99–111
St. Joseph Stock Yards Co. v. United States, 387
San Antonio School District v. Rodriguez, 73ff
San Benito County, 1890, legal snapshot, 163–77; judicial institutions, 166–72; criminality in, 169–72; court system, 172–74; local government control, 174; community attitudes, 175–76; legal role, 177
Scales v. United States, 228ff
Schenck v. United States, 196ff, 202, 208, 211–16, 218, 224–31 *passim*
Sedition Act of 1798, 198, 219
Selective Service amendment, 61f
Seventh Amendment, 27, 31f
Shapiro v. Thompson, 66
Sherman Act, 317–34 *passim*
Sixth Amendment, 1–19, 27, 31f, 37, 189
Smith Act, 227ff
Southern Pacific Co. v. Arizona, 76f
Speedy criminal trial, 1–19; controls on timing of prosecution in, 2–8; confusion of *Strunk v. U.S.,* 8–15; confounded confusion of *Barker v. Wingo,* 15–17; beginning of effective amendment, 17–19
Sternlieb, George, 370–73 *passim*
Stewart, Potter, 72, 84, 93
Stigler, George, 428
Stilson v. United States, 31f
Stone, Harlan Fisk, 374–78 *passim*
Story, Joseph, 268
Strunk v. United States, 8–15, 17
Supreme Court justices, *see by name*
Supreme Courts: California, 268–74 *passim,* 376, 417f; Wisconsin, 263f
Swain v. Alabama, 26–32 *passim*

Taylor v. McKeithen, 273
Tenth Amendment, 93f, 96
Thirteenth Amendment, 86, 92f
Truth in Lending Act, 438f
Tuck Bill, 69
Twenty-sixth Amendment, 95f

Uniform Commercial Code, 54f, 440
Uniform Commercial Code (Art. II), jurisprudence of, 97–111
Uniform Consumer Credit Code, 432, 438–44 *passim*
Uniform Housing Code, 377
Uniform Revised Sales Act, 102
Uniform Small Loan Law, 430f
United Nations, 116
United States antitrust laws, *see* American antitrust laws
United States Constitution, amendments, *see by number*
United States Constitution, legislator's guide to interpretation of, 61–77; obligations, 63–65; unconstitutional motives, 65–70; rationality standards, 70–75; interstate commerce regulation, 75–77
United States Constitution, unwritten?, 179–94; pure interpretative model, 179–82; beyond interpretation, 182–86; implications, 186–90; program of inquiry, 190–93
United States Court of Appeals, Second Circuit, 418, 420
United States Courts of Appeals, 267–75
United States military intervention, 113–28
United States Supreme Court, rulemaking power, 149–62; role of judges, 151–53; defects of Work Product rules, 153–58; results of inadequate judical supervision, 153–61; Rules of Evidence problems, 158–61
United States Supreme Court justices, *see by name*
United States v. Delliger, 40
United States v. O'Brien, 61–66 *passim*
United States v. Robinson, 40

Veterans' benefits claim processing, preclusion of judicial review in, 381–99; constitutional discourse on, 383–87; administrative process, 387–98; tentative appraisal, 398–99
Veterans of Foreign Wars, 390
Vinson, Frederick M., 227
Voir Dire, preservation of power, 21–41; limitations on, 22–25; functions of

challenges, 25–34; constitutional problems in limiting, 34–39; suggestions for control, 39–41
Voting Rights Act of 1965, 80f, 84ff, 90, 96

Warren, Earl, 61
Wechsler, Herbert, 89, 374
Whitney v. California, 227, 230
Wigmore, John, 41

Williamson v. Lee Optical Co., 71ff
Wisconsin, Supreme Court of, 263f
Wisconsin v. Federal Power Commission, 446
Work Product Rules, 153–58
World War I Espionage Act, 196–201 *passim*, 211, 218, 222, 226, 229

Yates v. United States, 228ff